# Lecture Notes of the Institute for Computer Sciences, Social Informatics and Telecommunications Engineering 711

The LNICST series publishes ICST's conferences, symposia and workshops.

LNICST reports state-of-the-art results in areas related to the scope of the Institute.

The type of material published includes

- Proceedings (published in time for the respective event)
- Other edited monographs (such as project reports or invited volumes)

LNICST topics span the following areas:

- General Computer Science
- E-Economy
- E-Medicine
- Knowledge Management
- Multimedia
- Operations, Management and Policy
- Social Informatics
- Systems

Yiliang Liu · Xin Yang · Li Li
Editors

# Communications and Networking

20th EAI International Conference, ChinaCom 2025
Xi'an, China, November 8–9, 2025
Proceedings

Springer

*Editors*
Yiliang Liu
Xi'an Jiaotong University
Xi'an, China

Xin Yang
Northwestern Polytechnical University
Xi'an, China

Li Li
Northwestern Polytechnical University
Xi'an, China

ISSN 1867-8211 ISSN 1867-822X (electronic)
Lecture Notes of the Institute for Computer Sciences, Social Informatics and Telecommunications Engineering
ISBN 978-3-032-33661-3 ISBN 978-3-032-33662-0 (eBook)
https://doi.org/10.1007/978-3-032-33662-0



This Springer imprint is published by the registered company Springer Nature Switzerland AG
The registered company address is: Gewerbestrasse 11, 6330 Cham, Switzerland

# Preface

We are delighted to introduce the proceedings of the 20th edition of the European Alliance for Innovation (EAI) International Conference on Communications and Networking in China (ChinaCom 2025). Hosted by Northwestern Polytechnical University, Xi'an, China, the conference was held on 8–9 November 2025. The conference focuses on the integration of cyberspace security, wireless communications and networks, and intelligent computing to address emerging challenges and opportunities in the rapidly evolving digital landscape. The conference aims to bring together researchers, industry professionals, and academics to discuss and exchange ideas on the latest advancements. The theme of ChinaCom 2025 was "Advancing the Frontier of Communication and Intelligent Services".

The technical program of ChinaCom 2025 consisted of 42 full papers. The conference tracks were: Track 1 - Wireless Communications; Track 2 - Networks and Intelligent Computing; Track 3 - Network Security; Track 4 - Communications Systems and Networks; and Track 5 - Nonlinear Photonics and Information & Communication Technologies. These papers were selected from 106 submissions. Each submission was reviewed following a single-blind process with a minimum of 3 reviews per paper. Aside from the high-quality technical paper presentations, the technical program also featured six keynote speeches and four invited talks. The keynote speeches were delivered by Rui Zhang from National University of Singapore, Singapore; Shiwen Mao from Auburn University, USA; Chengxiang Wang from Southeast University, China; Zhiyong Feng from Beijing University of Posts and Telecommunications, China; Haijun Zhang from University of Science and Technology Beijing, China; and Haochen Liu from Northwestern Polytechnical University, China. The invited talks were presented by Ju Wang from Northwest University, China; Nan Cheng from Xidian University, China; Yinghui Ye from Xi'an University of Posts and Telecommunications, China; and Zhisheng Yin from Xidian University, China.

We coordinated closely with the steering chairs, Victor C. M. Leung and Hsiao-Hwa Chen, whose support and guidance were essential to the success of the conference. It was also a great pleasure to work with such an excellent organizing committee team for their hard work in organizing and supporting the conference. In particular, we thank the Technical Program Committee, led by our TPC Chairs (Yiliang Liu, Xin Yang, and Li Li), for completing the peer-review process and assembling a high-quality technical program. We are also grateful to the Conference Manager, Natasha Onofrei, for her support and to all the authors who submitted their papers to the ChinaCom 2025 conference.

We strongly believe that ChinaCom provides a good forum for all researchers, developers, and practitioners to discuss all science and technology aspects that are relevant to communications and networking. We also expect that future ChinaCom conferences will be as successful and stimulating as evidenced by the contributions presented in this volume.

Yiliang Liu
Xin Yang
Li Li

# Organization

## Steering Committee

| | |
|---|---|
| Victor C.M. Leung | Shenzhen University, China |

## Organizing Committee

### General Chairs

| | |
|---|---|
| Ling Wang | Northwestern Polytechnical University, China |
| Hsiao-Hwa Chen | National Cheng Kung University, Taiwan |

### Program Chairs

| | |
|---|---|
| Yiliang Liu | Xi'an Jiaotong University, China |
| Xin Yang | Northwestern Polytechnical University, China |
| Li Li | Northwestern Polytechnical University, China |

### Workshops Chair

| | |
|---|---|
| Lili Chen | Northwestern Polytechnical University, China |

### Publicity and Social Media Chair

| | |
|---|---|
| Wenbin Sun | Northwestern Polytechnical University, China |

### Publications Chair

| | |
|---|---|
| Lim Wei Yang Bryan | Nanyang Technological University, Singapore |

### Web Chair

| | |
|---|---|
| Yanan Du | University of Sheffield, UK |

### Local Chairs

| | |
|---|---|
| Ke Cheng | Xidian University, China |
| Zhisheng Yin | Xidian University, China |
| Peihan Qi | Xidian University, China |

## Technical Program Committee

| | |
|---|---|
| Bin Qiu | Xidian University, China |
| Bodong Shang | Eastern Institute of Technology, China |
| Chao Liu | Xi Hang University, China |
| Chunpeng Liu | Harbin Engineering University, China |
| Cong Yang | Zhengzhou University, China |
| Deyue Zou | Dalian University of Technology, China |
| Fan Wu | Central South University, China |
| Geng Sun | Jilin University, China |
| Guodong Li | Harbin University of Science and Technology, China |
| Haichao Wang | Army Engineering University, China |
| Haiqin Wu | East China Normal University, China |
| Hang Wang | Nanjing University of Posts and Telecommunications, China |
| Hanyu Zhou | Northwestern Polytechnical University, China |
| Haochen Liu | Northwestern Polytechnical University, China |
| Haoran Peng | Chinese University of Hong Kong, China |
| Hongbin Pei | Xi'an Jiaotong University, China |
| Huimin Hu | Xi'an University of Posts & Telecommunications, China |
| Jichong Guo | Suzhou University of Science and Technology, China |
| Jie Feng | Xidian University, China |
| Jie Zhang | Xi'an University of Posts and Telecommunications, China |
| Jin Cui | Northwest University, China |
| Jincheng Shi | Northwestern Polytechnical University, China |
| Jinhua Cui | Huazhong University of Science and Technology, China |
| Jinyu Wang | Xi'an Jiaotong University, China |
| Jinyun Wu | Information Support Force Engineering University, China |
| Jun He | Shanxi University, China |
| Li You | Southeast University, China |

| | |
|---|---|
| Li Zhou | Beijing Jiaotong University, China |
| Lijun He | China University of Mining and Technology, China |
| Linkang Du | Xi'an Jiaotong University, China |
| Lixin Li | Northwestern Polytechnical University, China |
| Meng Shi | Chinese Academy of Science (CSU), China |
| Minghui Xu | Shandong University, China |
| Nan Cheng | Xidian University, China |
| Pan Cheng | Xi Hang University, China |
| Peng Yang | Beihang University, China |
| Qian Xu | Northwestern Polytechnical University, China |
| Qinghe Du | Xi'an Jiaotong University, China |
| Quoc-Viet Pham | Trinity College Dublin, Ireland |
| Ruofei Ma | Harbin Institute of Technology, China |
| Shunrong Jiang | China University of Mining and Technology, China |
| Shuyi Chen | Harbin Institute of Technology, China |
| Siying Niu | Northwest University, China |
| Tao Jiang | Xidian University, China |
| Tiantian Zhang | Xi'an Jiaotong University, China |
| Tianyu Zhao | Harbin Institute of Technology, China |
| Ting Liu | Northwestern Polytechnical University, China |
| Wei Wang | Nanjing University of Aeronautics and Astronautics, China |
| Wei Yang Bryan Lim | Nanyang Technological University, Singapore |
| Wen-bin Sun | Northwestern Polytechnical University, China |
| Wenchi Cheng | Xidian University, China |
| Wenting Wei | Xidian University, China |
| Xin Yang | Northwestern Polytechnical University, China |
| Xuewen Luo | Northeastern University, China |
| Yamun Gang | Northwestern Polytechnical University, China |
| Yanan Du | University of Sheffield, UK |
| Yang Li | Harbin Institute of Technology, China |
| Yang Qiu | Zhuhai College of Science and Technology, China |
| Yanyu Cheng | Hangzhou Dianzi University, China |
| Yaru Fu | Hong Kong Metropolitan University, China |
| Yimeng Ge | Xi'an University of Posts & Telecommunications, China |
| Ying Liu | Chang'an University, China |
| Yongjia Zhu | Chang'an University, China |
| Yongsheng Gao | Northwestern Polytechnical University, China |
| Youhang Feng | Anhui Normal University, China |

| | |
|---|---|
| Yu'e Jiang | Anqing Normal University, China |
| Yuanchen Wang | Xi'an Jiaotong University, China |
| Yuchao Zha | China Electronics Technology Group Corporation 54th Research Institute, China |
| Yuchuan Fu | Xidian University, China |
| Yunpeng Song | Xi'an Jiaotong University, China |
| Yuntao Wang | Xi'an Jiaotong University, China |
| Zheng Shi | Jinan University, China |
| Zhouzhou Liu | Xi Hang University, China |
| Ziye Jia | Nanjing University of Aeronautics and Astronautics, China |

# Contents

**Sensing and Localization**



**Internet of Things**

# Wireless Signal Processing, Modulation, and Receiver Design

# Implementation of an Interference Detection Algorithm Based on Wideband Digital Channelized Receivers

Tong Zhou, Mingqi Li, Jvfeng Fei, Mengfan Wang, and Jiajian Pan(✉)

Shanghai Radio Equipment Research Institute, Shanghai 201109, Shanghai, China
jiajianpan182@163.com

**Abstract.** Anti-jamming reconnaissance receivers are typically required to possess a wide instantaneous bandwidth for broad frequency coverage, high sensitivity and dynamic range, capability for detecting concurrent signals, as well as high precision in frequency measurement and resolution. To meet these demands, this paper presents a channelized receiver design incorporating a polyphase filter bank. The channelization technique partitions the full frequency spectrum into multiple sub-channels of equal bandwidth, facilitating the processing of simultaneously arriving signals and ensuring a probability of intercept approaching unity. The proposed receiver demonstrates robust efficacy in detecting various jamming signals within the operational band, including tone, comb-spectrum, and partial-band jamming, making it highly suitable for deployment in electronic warfare (EW) applications.

**Keywords:** Digital Channelization · Jamming Detection · Polyphase Filtering · Fourier Transform

## 1 Research Background

With the rapid advancement of modern science, technology, and radio monitoring capabilities, the field of military research has been profoundly transformed. In this era of information-based warfare, electronic warfare (EW) has become an indispensable component of military operations [1]. Within this domain, jamming and anti-jamming constitute a critical area of research. To address anti-jamming issues in communication systems, it is essential to first resolve the problem of jamming signal detection [2]. Only by acquiring relevant information about the jamming signals can effective countermeasures be developed for anti-jamming studies. In electronic warfare, jamming detection receivers are required to perform real-time analysis and processing of signals with wider bandwidth, higher frequency resolution, and shorter processing times [3].

Channelization technology, as a key method for processing wideband signals, employs a parallel processing approach to decompose a wideband signal into multiple adjacent sub-bands. By replacing traditional analog filter banks with digital filter banks, it enables digital sampling and signal processing, ultimately outputting sub-band


Y. Liu et al. (Eds.): ChinaCom 2025, LNICST 711, pp. 3–8, 2027.
https://doi.org/10.1007/978-3-032-33662-0_1

signals in segments [4]. This significantly reduces system pressure and enhances the efficiency of wideband signal processing. Digital channelization algorithms can adapt to the complex electromagnetic environment of modern electronic warfare, supporting real-time or near-real-time processing of large volumes of intercepted non-cooperative signals.

The processing results of digital channelization include both strong and weak signals [5, 6]. If a fixed threshold is used for signal detection, weak signals are likely to be missed at a high rate, leading to the loss of faint targets. This paper proposes an adaptive threshold detection algorithm based on digital channelization technology. It generates tailored adaptive detection thresholds for different sub-channel sets, enabling effective detection of both strong and weak signals [7]. The method achieves efficient separation of signals of varying strengths and facilitates accurate extraction of target signals.

## 2 Introduction to Algorithms

### 2.1 Derivation from a Lowpass Prototype Filter Bank to an Efficient Polyphase Filtering Structure

The channelized receiver investigated in this paper employs a polyphase filter bank structure [8], which features a common input and multiple output ports. This architecture enables the uniform division of an input wideband signal into several sub-band signals that are output in parallel [9]. A key advantage of this receiver is its capability to simultaneously detect, process, and demodulate signals across the entire instantaneous processing bandwidth [10], thereby achieving a full probability of intercept for wideband signals. Such channelized receivers are not only widely used in electronic warfare systems but also demonstrate promising potential for applications in mobile communications and other related fields [11, 12]. In particular, within cognitive radio systems, this receiver architecture is regarded as an ideal solution for detecting "spectrum holes."

For a complex signal s(n), it can be partitioned into D channels with a channel spacing of $2\pi$ /D, as illustrated in Fig. 1.

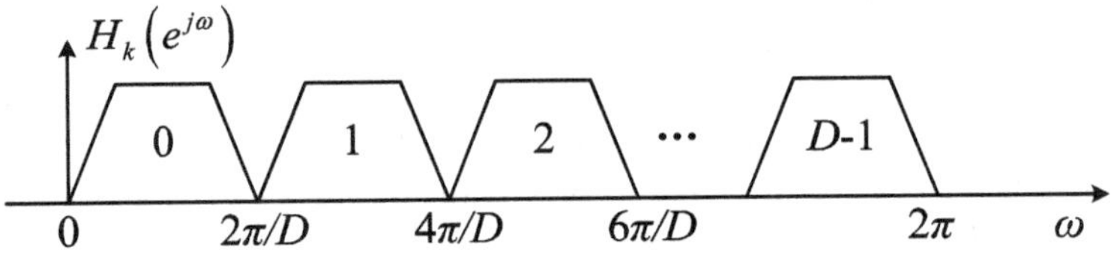


**Fig. 1.** Channelization of complex signals

Under the current research framework, various methodologies exist for implementing filter banks, such as structures employing post-decimators or those based on lowpass prototype filters [13]. This study adopts the lowpass prototype implementation approach, as illustrated in Fig. 2, and utilizes this architecture as the basis for deriving a subsequent efficient polyphase filtering-based channelized receiver. In this system, $h_{LP}(n)$ denotes the prototype lowpass filter, with a local oscillator angular frequency of $\omega_k$ (k =,1,2,...,D-1).

$$\omega_k = \left(k + \frac{1}{2}\right) \cdot \frac{2\pi}{D}$$

Its function is to downconvert the k-th sub-band (channel) in Fig. 2 to baseband (zero intermediate frequency), and then extract the corresponding sub-band signal through a subsequent lowpass filter. Since the filtered signal bandwidth is 2π/D, it can be decimated by a factor of D to achieve a reduced sampling rate.

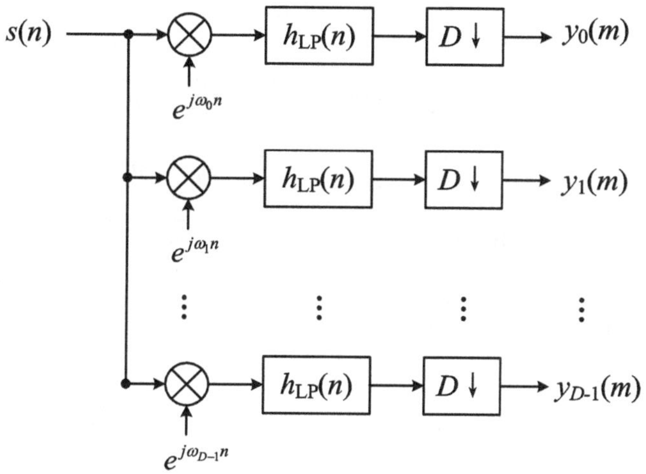


**Fig. 2.** Lowpass implementation of complex signal filter banks

However, the practical implementation of such filter bank-based channelized receivers presents significant challenges, particularly when the number of channels is large and the value of D is high. In such cases, the required order of the lowpass filters in each branch may become exceedingly high, resulting in complex filter designs. Moreover, each channel requires such a high-order filter, leading to low computational efficiency and substantial consumption of hardware resources, which makes engineering implementation difficult. To address these issues, this paper derives a channelized receiver structure based on polyphase filtering techniques within the same theoretical framework [14]. The proposed approach significantly reduces computational complexity and hardware resource requirements on FPGA platforms, thereby enabling real-time signal processing capabilities.

### 2.2 Polyphase Filter Bank Channelized Receiver

Based on the original channelized structure shown in Fig. 3, the output of the k-th channel can be expressed as:

$$y_k(m) = \left\{ \left[ s(n)e^{j\omega_k n} \right] \cdot h(n) \right\} \Big|_{n=mD}$$

$$= \sum_{p=0}^{D-1} \sum_{i=-\infty}^{\infty} s(mD - iD + p)e^{j\omega_k(mD-iD-p)}$$

Define the transfer function $s_p(m) = s(mD - p)$ and $h_p(m) = h(mD + p)$, then the output

$$y_k(m) = \sum_{p=0}^{D-1} \left[ \sum_{i=-\infty}^{\infty} \left( s_p(m-i)e^{j\omega_k(m-i)D} \right) \cdot h_p(i) \right] e^{-j\omega_k p}$$

Assumption:

$$x_p(m) = \sum_{i=-\infty}^{\infty} \left[ s_p(m-i)e^{j\omega_k(m-i)D} \right] \cdot h_p(i)$$

$$= \left[ s_p(m)e^{j\omega_k mD} \right] \cdot h_p(m)$$

Hence, it can be concluded that:

$$y_k(m) = \sum_{p=0}^{D-1} x_p(m)e^{-j\omega_k p}$$

Based on the equation $\omega_k = \left(k + \frac{1}{2}\right)\frac{2\pi}{D}$, the final result can be obtained as follows:

$$x_p(m) = \left[ s_p(m)(-1)^m \right] \cdot h_p(m)$$

$$y_k\ (m) = \sum_{p=0}^{D-1} \left[ x_p(m) \cdot e^{-j\frac{\pi}{D}p} \right] e^{-j\frac{2\pi}{D}kp}$$

$$= \sum_{p=0}^{D-1} x'_p(m)e^{-j\frac{2\pi}{D}kp} = DFT\left[ x'_p(m) \right]$$

# 3 FPGA Implementation

## 3.1 FPGA Implementation of Polyphase Filter Bank Channelized Receivers

This paper presents the FPGA implementation of the aforementioned polyphase digital channelized receiver based on the Xilinx Virtex-4 series XC4VSX160-UFF1148 platform. The design was developed using the Vivado 2024.2 integrated design environment and implemented in Verilog HDL.

The actual interference signals received by the final implemented receiver are shown in Fig. 3.

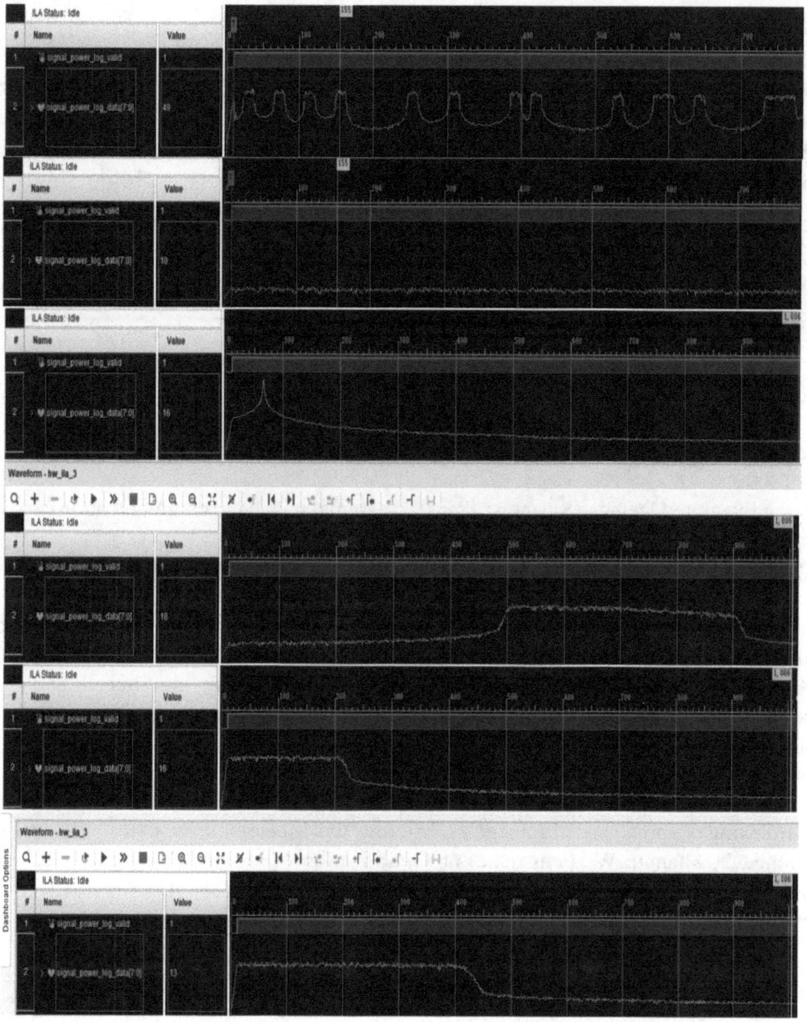


**Fig. 3.** Time-domain waveform of the interference signal

The channelized receiver effectively divides a wideband interference signal with a bandwidth of 500 MHz into 16 subchannels, enabling simultaneous detection, reception, and processing of multiple signals. In practical engineering applications, this architecture significantly enhances the system's subsequent anti-jamming capabilities while substantially improving the speed and efficiency of signal processing. It provides a robust technical foundation for reliable signal analysis in complex electromagnetic environments.

## 4 Conclusion

This paper addressed the challenges of interference signal detection in complex electromagnetic environments by designing and implementing a wideband digital channelized receiver based on a polyphase filter bank. This receiver architecture effectively divides the entire frequency band into numerous narrowband subchannels, enabling a high probability of intercept and high-accuracy frequency measurement of multiple simultaneously arriving signals.

## References


1. Zangi, K.C., Koilpillai, R.D.: Software radio issues in cellular base stations. IEEE J. Sel. Areas Commun. **17**(4), 561–573 (1999)
2. Spezio, A.E.: Electronic warfare systems. IEEE Trans. Microwave Theory Tech. **50**(3), 633–644 (2002)
3. Boeing Integrated Defense Systems: Transformational wideband communication capabilities for the warfighter (2009)
4. Mitola, J.: Software radio architecture: a mathematical perspective. IEEE J. Sel. Areas Commun. **17**(4), 514–538 (1999)
5. Radchenko, S.D., et al.: Detection of the frequency hopping spread spectrum signal sources and estimation of their number by direction finding data. Eng. Lett. **30**(2) (2022)
6. Zahirniak, D.R., Sharpin, D.L., Fields, T.W.: A hardware-efficient, multirate, digital channelized receiver architecture. IEEE Trans. Aerosp. Electron. Syst. **34**(1) (1998)
7. Vaidyanathan, P.P.: Multirate digital filters, filter banks, polyphase networks, and applications: a tutorial. Proc. IEEE. **78**(1), 56–93 (1990)
8. Jiebing, Z., Wenquan, F., Yong, X.: Interferometer direction-finding system with time-division multiplexing of spread spectrum signals. Microw. Opt. Technol. Lett. **64**(6), 983–991 (2022)
9. Junfeng, Z., Zhenyu, W., Pengzhan, Y.: Optimization of channelized digital receiver. Fire Control Command Control. **36**(7), 68–71 (2011)
10. Bose V, Ismert M, Welborn M, et al.: Virtual radios. IEEE J. Sel. Areas Commun. **17**(4):591–602 (1999)
11. Xiaojing, W., Meijun, Y., Jinzhong, Z.: Design and implementation of real number channelization engineering based on FPGA. Shipboard Electron. Countermeasure. **42**(6), 99–102 (2019)
12. Fateev, A.A., Tokarev, A.B., Chernoyarov, O.V., Salnikova, A.V.: Influence of the radiation pattern errors for the correlation interferometer. J. Phys. Conf. Ser. **2094**(2) (2021)
13. Alekseev E A., Zakharenko V V.: Direct digital synthesizer as a reference source of a millimeter-wave frequency synthesizer. Fifth International Kharkov Symposium on Physics and Engineering of Microwaves, Millimeter, and Submillimeter Waves (2004), 782–783
14. Qiang, D.: Design and FPGA implementation of high-efficient structure of digital channelization. Meas. Control Technol. **41**(7), 93–97 (2022)

# Chirp Optimization for Affine Frequency Division Multiplexing PAPR Reduction

Liang Sun, Xin Yang(✉), Wen-Bin Sun, Qian Xu, Lili Chen, Yanyun Gong, and Jia Su

Northwestern Polytechnical University, 127 Youyi West Road, Xi'an 710072, China
xinyang@nwpu.edu.cn

**Abstract.** As a state-of-the-art modulation waveform, Affine Frequency Division Multiplexing (AFDM) demonstrates significant potential and application prospects in high-mobility communication scenarios compared to Orthogonal Frequency Division Multiplexing (OFDM). AFDM is a multicarrier modulation based on chirp signals, distinguished primarily by two tunable parameters: the pre-chirp parameter and the post-chirp parameter. These adjustable parameters enable the waveform to better adapt to Doppler spread in doubly dispersive channels. However, due to the randomness of modulated symbols, AFDM suffers from a critical drawback: the high peak-to-average power ratio (PAPR), which imposes stringent linearity and power requirements on transmitters in practical applications. To address this issue, we leverage the tunable pre-chirp parameter. We first prove that this parameter has no effect on the average power of modulated symbols. Subsequently, we optimize its frame-wise parameter values using a hybrid particle swarm optimization approach. Finally, we present a comparative analysis of the optimized system bit error rate (BER) and the complementary cumulative distribution function (CCDF) of PAPR with other modulation waveforms and other two PAPR reduction methods.

**Keywords:** Affine frequency division multiplexing (AFDM) · Orthogonal Frequency Division Multiplexing (OFDM) · peak-to-average power ratio (PAPR) · complementary cumulative distribution function (CCDF)

## 1 Introduction

The evolution toward next-generation wireless communication, represented by 6G and beyond (B5G) systems, is widely regarded as a key enabler of future intelligent and ubiquitous connectivity. These systems are expected to support a wide range of emerging application scenarios, such as unmanned aerial vehicle (UAV) networks, vehicle-to-everything (V2X) communications, low Earth orbit (LEO)


Y. Liu et al. (Eds.): ChinaCom 2025, LNICST 711, pp. 9–20, 2027.
https://doi.org/10.1007/978-3-032-33662-0_2

satellite systems, and high-speed railway communications. Moreover, they aim to provide users with dependable and real-time communications and extremely high data rates, meeting the stringent requirements of future networked environments [1]. The orthogonal frequency division multiplexing (OFDM) waveforms, widely deployed in 4G and 5G systems, face significant challenges in high-mobility scenarios: severe Doppler shifts break subcarrier orthogonality, which makes OFDM no longer suitabe for next-generation wireless communications. Consequently, the development and implementation of novel waveforms constitute a critical research priority for advancing future wireless systems.

Following this, a modulation waveform named OTFS (Orthogonal Time Frequency Space) is proposed [2]. It utilizes a two-dimensional transformation to transmit information in the delay-Doppler domain, enabling better resistance against multipath effects and Doppler shifts. OCDM (Orthogonal Chirp Division Multiplexing) [3], using linear orthogonal chirp symbols, exhibits enhanced performance over OFDM in double-dispersive channels. The AFDM (Affine Frequency Division Multiplexing) employed in this paper, based on the Discrete Affine Fourier Transform (DAFT), achieves its advantages by adjusting the pre-chirping parameter and the post-chirping parameter [4], and the information symbols are multiplexed in the DAFT domain such that the propagation paths are mutually separated, while each symbol experiences all path coefficients. This property results in a sparse equivalent channel matrix, allowing AFDM to exploit full diversity gain over double-dispersive channels. Moreover, compared to OTFS, AFDM requires nearly half the pilot overhead, significantly improving spectral efficiency [5]. Besides, the presence of CFO (carrier frequency offset) induces a loss of orthogonality in OCDM [6]. After AFDM is first proposed, its advantages and compatibility in high-mobility communication soon catches the attention of a wide range of scholars.

There are lots of work done here, such as channel estimation, equalization, and combinations with Index modulation (IM) [10, 11]and Integrated sensing and communications (ISAC) [12,13]. In [7], diagonally-reconstruction of effective channel matrix is verified, according to which a channel estimation algorithm with low complexity is proposed. While literature [8] superimposed pilot symbols in DAFT domain, sufficiently reducing the channel estimation error. As reported in [9] a kind of Turbo equalizer based on LMMSE (Linear Minimum Mean Squared Error) equalization and BP (Belief Propagation) decoding is introduced to increase BER (bit error rate) performance. Collectively, literatures [10, 11] show that AFDM over IM exhibits higher robustness than original AFDM. Turn to ISAC, [12,13] reveal the compatibilities for AFDM with sensing and communication in ISAC.

Despite its numerous advantages, AFDM suffers from the same drawback as traditional OFDM: a high peak-to-average power ratio (PAPR), which poses significant challenges for practical hardware implementation. For OFDM, there are many ways to reduce PAPR, such as coding [14], SLM (selective mapping) [15], TR (Tone Reservation) [16]. And inspired by [10], where the post-chirp parameter is modified for lowing BER using intelligent optimization algorithm. PAPR reduction can also be achieved through the optimization of post-chirp parameter. In this letter, Particle Swarm Optimization (PSO) algorithm is employed to derive optimal values with two scenarios: one parameter for whole subcarriers, or one parameter for one subcarrier [17].

## 2 First Proposed AFDM

The classical AFDM is showed in Fig. 1. After M-ary modulation, the bit stream is first mapped onto the DAFT domain. At the transmitter, inverse DAFT (IDAFT) is performed on $x[m]$ to create time-domain symbols. With $N$ representing the number of chirp subcarriers, the IDAFT operation can be defined as

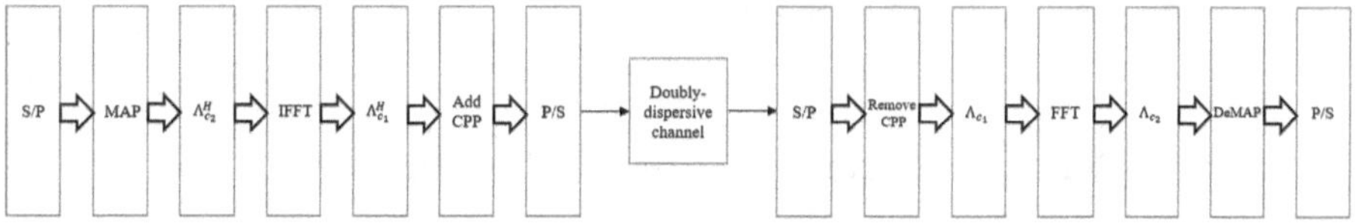


**Fig. 1.** AFDM system model

$$X[p] = \frac{1}{\sqrt{N}} \sum_{q=0}^{N-1} x[q] \cdot e^{j2\pi\left(c_1 p^2 + c_2 q^2 + pq/N\right)}, \tag{1}$$

where $x[q]$ denotes the signal in time domain, and $q, p \in 0, 1, ..., N-1$, while $c_1$ and $c_2$ are post-chirp and pre-chirp parameters. Like OFDM, AFDM also needs a prefix to combat multi-path effects. AFDM's Chirp-Periodic Prefix (CPP), derived from DAFT's natural periodicity, plays an equivalent role to OFDM's Cyclic Prefix (CP), with its mathematical formulation given by

$$X[p] = X[N+p]e^{-\mathrm{j}2\pi c_1(N^2+2Np)}, p = -C_{\mathrm{cp}}, \dots, -1, \tag{2}$$

where $C_{\mathrm{cp}}$ is the length of CPP. In high-dynamic scenarios, time-domain signals pass through doubly-selective channel, whose impulse response is

$$h[d] = \sum_{p=1}^{P} h_p e^{-j2\pi f_p p} \delta(d - d_p), \tag{3}$$

Let $P \geq 1$ denote the number of propagation paths, and $\delta(\cdot)$ is the Dirac delta function. The parameters $h_p, f_p$ and $d_p$ correspond to the complex gain, Doppler shift (in digital frequencies), and integer delay of the $i$-th path, respectively.

After receiving, time-domain symbols are given by

$$R[p] = \sum_{p=1}^{P} h_p X[p - d_p] e^{-\mathrm{j}2\pi f_p p} + w[p], \tag{4}$$

where $w[p] \sim \mathcal{CN}(0, N_0)$ is the additive white Gaussian noise (AWGN). The DAFT/IDAFT operations and the effect of the channel can both be rewrited into matrix, which can be formulated as

$$\mathbf{y} = \mathbf{A_N}\mathbf{H}\mathbf{A_N}^{-1}\mathbf{x} + \widetilde{\mathbf{w}}, \tag{5}$$

where $\widetilde{\mathbf{w}} \sim \mathcal{CN}(\mathbf{0}, N_0\mathbf{I}_N)$, $\mathbf{H} = \sum_{i=1}^{P} h_i \boldsymbol{\Gamma}_{\mathrm{CPP}_i} \boldsymbol{\Delta}_{f_i} \boldsymbol{\Pi}^{l_i}$and $\boldsymbol{\Pi}$ is the permutation matrix. $\Delta_{f_i} \triangleq \mathrm{diag}(e^{-i2\pi f_i n}, p = 0, 1, \ldots, N-1)$ and $\boldsymbol{\Gamma}_{\mathrm{CPP}_i}$ is a $N \times N$ diagonal matrix

$$\boldsymbol{\Gamma}_{\mathrm{CPP}_i} = \mathrm{diag}\begin{cases} e^{-j2\pi c_1 (N^2 - 2N(l_i - p))} & p < l_i \\ 1 & p \geq l_i \end{cases} \tag{6}$$
$$p = 0, \ldots, N-1.$$

The DAFT matrix ‘ in Fig. 1 is expressed as

$$\mathbf{A_N} = \boldsymbol{\Lambda}_{c_2}\mathbf{F}\boldsymbol{\Lambda}_{c_1}, \tag{7}$$

where $\mathbf{F} \in \mathbb{C}^{N \times N}$ is the normalized N-point DFT matrix and

$$\boldsymbol{\Lambda}_{c_i} = \mathrm{diag}\left(e^{-j2\pi c_i p^2}, p = 0, 1, \ldots, N-1, i = 1, 2\right). \tag{8}$$

The IDAFT matrix can be easily expressed since $A$ is unitary

$$\mathbf{A_N}^{-1} = \mathbf{A_N}^{H} = \boldsymbol{\Lambda}_{c_1}^{H}\mathbf{F}^{H}\boldsymbol{\Lambda}_{c_2}^{H}. \tag{9}$$

With respect to two chirp parameters, according to [5], post-chirp $c_1$ satisfies

$$c_1 \geq \frac{2\alpha_{\max} + 1}{2N} \tag{10}$$

where, $\alpha_{\max}$ is defined as the maximum Doppler shift normalized to the subcarrier spacing. Achieving full diversity in AFDM critically depends on the value of $c_1$. In contrast, the constraint on $c_2$ is less stringent, offering sufficient design freedom to optimize $c_2$ specifically for reducing PAPR.

Two detection methods can be utilized for data. One is ML (Maximum Likelihood) Detector [19], which considers all possible signal realizations by searching all the signal constellation points. We can get the expression according to (5) by

$$\tilde{\mathbf{x}} = \arg\min_{\forall \mathbf{x}} \|\mathbf{y} - \mathbf{H_{eff}}\mathbf{x}\|_F^2, \tag{11}$$

where $\mathbf{H_{eff}} = \mathbf{A_N}\mathbf{H}\mathbf{A_N}^{-1}$, its computational complexity scales as $\mathcal{O}(M_{mod}^N)$, increasing exponentially with the number of AFDM subcarriers.

Following simulation will use another one:minimum mean square error (MMSE) equalization, which is given by

$$\hat{\mathbf{x}}_{\mathrm{MMSE}} = \mathbf{H_{eff}}^H(\mathbf{H_{eff}}\mathbf{H_{eff}}^H + \frac{1}{\gamma}\mathbf{I}_N)^{-1}\mathbf{y}, \tag{12}$$

where $\gamma$ represents the average SNR, and its computational complexity scales as $\mathcal{O}(N^3)$.

## 3 Pre-chirp Parameter Optimization Scheme

In AFDM, each data symbol is modulated onto a chirp waveform via the Inverse Discrete Affine Fourier Transform (IDAFT), producing a time-domain signal with a distinctive structure. However, when the pre-chirp parameters are not properly selected, the coherent addition of certain chirped components can still lead to high peak power in specific time samples, especially when data sequences contain high correlation or similar patterns. This phenomenon is more pronounced when phase rotations are applied.

Thus, while AFDM offers high Delay-Doppler robustness, its PAPR is still influenced by the modulation structure and parameter design. So in this section, we first prove that the value of pre-chirp parameter have no effect on average power, then two intelligent algorithms are used to minimize PAPR by selecting suitable $c_2$.

The PAPR is defined as

$$\text{PAPR} = \frac{\max_{0\leq p\leq N-1} |X[p]|^2}{E\left[|X[p]|^2\right]} \tag{13}$$

where $X[p]$ is the time-domain signals, $E\left[|X[p]|^2\right]$ represents the average power of signals. While PAPR is defined in the context of continuous-time bandpass signals, with at least 4 times oversampling, $X[p]$ and the continuous-time bandpass signals have almost the same PAPR [19]. The complementary cumulative distribution function (CCDF) is introduced to quantitatively characterize the PAPR metric, which is defined as

$$\text{CCDF}_{\text{PAPR}}(\gamma) = Pr(\text{PAPR} > \gamma), \tag{14}$$

where $\gamma$ is a specific threshold value of the PAPR, and $Pr(\cdot)$ denotes the probability function.

### 3.1 Analysis of AFDM PAPR

*Remark 1.* The average power of AFDM signals remain unchanged, then PAPR only depends on the maximum power of signals.

We first prove that the average power of AFDM signals remain unchanged, then PAPR only depends on the maximum power of signals

*Proof.* First, the average power is defined as

$$E\left[|X[p]|^2\right] = \frac{1}{N}\sum_{p=0}^{N-1} |X[p]|^2. \tag{15}$$

$X[p]$ can be expressed as

$$\begin{aligned} |X[p]|^2 &= \left(\frac{1}{\sqrt{N}}\sum_{q=0}^{N-1} x[q]g_{p,q}\right)\left(\frac{1}{\sqrt{N}}\sum_{k=0}^{N-1} x^*[k]g_{p,k}^*\right) \\ &= \frac{1}{N}\sum_{q=0}^{N-1}\sum_{k=0}^{N-1} x[q]x^*[k]\cdot g_{p,q}g_{p,k}^*, \end{aligned} \tag{16}$$

where $g_p = e^{j2\pi(c_1p^2+c_2q^2+pq/N)}$, then we simplify the expression like

$$g_{p,q}g_{p,k}^* = e^{j2\pi(c_2q^2-c_2k^2)}\cdot e^{j2\pi\frac{(q-k)n}{N}}, \tag{17}$$

$$\begin{aligned} \sum_{p=0}^{N-1}|X[p]|^2 &= \frac{1}{N}\sum_{q=0}^{N-1}\sum_{k=0}^{N-1} x[q]x^*[k]e^{j2\pi(c_2q^2-c_2k^2)}\cdot N\cdot(\delta_{q,k}) \\ &= \frac{1}{N}\sum_{q=0}^{N-1} x[q]x^*[q]\cdot N\cdot 1 = \sum_{q=0}^{N-1}|x[q]|^2 \end{aligned} \tag{18}$$

We can see that the average power of signal after IDAFT is the same as before and have no relationship with $c_1$ and $c_2$, so the optimization focuses on the maximum value of signal power.

Demonstrations above can be also achieved by the property of unitary matrix since DAFT matrix $\mathbf{A_N}$ is a unitary matrix.

### 3.2 Pre-chirp Selection

In classical AFDM systems, a fixed pre-chirp parameter $c_2$ is applied across all subcarriers. However, as demonstrated in [11,18], they consider a generalized formulation where each subcarrier is allowed to have its own pre-chirp parameter $c_2$. By carefully designing the $c_2$ vectors, it is possible to improve the robustness (Fig. 2).

Therefore, we also explored different subcarriers corresponding to different $c_2$, and the resulting performance is examined in next sections. Corresponding expression is expressed as

$$X[p] = \frac{1}{\sqrt{N}}\sum_{q=0}^{N-1} x[q]\cdot e^{j2\pi\left(c_1n^2+c_{2,k}q^2+pq/N\right)}, k = 0,\ldots,N-1. \tag{19}$$

*Remark 2.* Different $c_2$ don't break the orthogonality of AFDM subcarriers.

*Proof.* We can derive the cross-correlation function of subcarriers with same $c_1$ but different $c_2$ in (17) as $\Phi_l(q)$. First, subcarrier is represent by

$$\begin{aligned} \Phi_p(q) &= \frac{1}{N}g_n \\ &= \frac{1}{N}e^{j2\pi(c_1p^2+c_2q^2+pq/N)} \end{aligned} \tag{20}$$

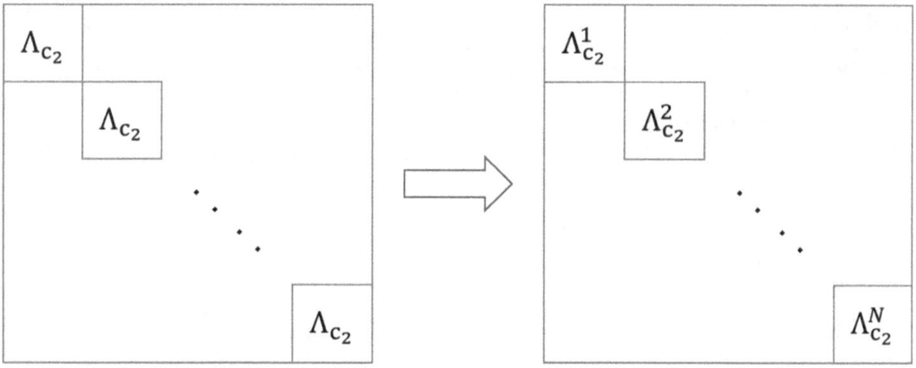


**Fig. 2.** Pre-chirp matirx

Then the Cross-Correlation function is formulated as

$$\begin{aligned}
&\sum_{p=0}^{N-1} \Phi_p^{c_1,c_{2,q}}(q_1)\Phi_n^{c_1,c_{2,p}*}(q_2) \\
&= \frac{1}{N} e^{-i2\pi(c_{2,q}q_1^2 - c_{2,p}q_2^2)} \sum_{p=0}^{N-1} e^{-i\frac{2\pi}{N}(q_1-q_2)l} \\
&= \frac{1}{N} e^{-i2\pi(c_{2,q}q_1^2 - c_{2,p}q_2^2)} \frac{1 - e^{-i2\pi N\left(\frac{q_1-q_2}{N}\right)}}{1 - e^{-i2\pi\left(\frac{q_1-q_2}{N}\right)}} \\
&= 0\,(q_1 \neq q_2).
\end{aligned} \tag{21}$$

The above calculations indicate that changes in $c_2$ do not affect the orthogonality of AFDM subcarriers.

### 3.3 Parameter Optimization

According to what we investigate above, the following problem is formulated to decrease PAPR

$$\min \max |X[p]|^2, \tag{22a}$$

$$\text{s.t. } c_2 \in [0, 1], \tag{22b}$$

The optimization problem above is inherently non-convex, rendering the attainment of a globally optimal solution computationally intractable. Consequently, a Particle Swarm Optimization is employed to derive a near-optimal solution. This approach is deliberately chosen due to its rapid convergence characteristics and demonstrably robust global exploration capabilities within complex, high-dimensional solution spaces.

**Algorithm 1:** Particle Swarm Optimization for Optimizing $\mathbf{c}_2$ Vector

**Input**: Number of particles $P$, maximum iterations $T$, dimension $N$, inertia weight $w$, acceleration coefficients $c_1$, $c_2$, search range $[0, 1]$
**Output**: Optimal solution $\mathbf{c}_2^*$

Initialize particles $\mathbf{X}_i \in \mathbb{R}^N$, velocities $\mathbf{V}_i$, personal best $\mathbf{P}_i$, and global best $\mathbf{g}$;
**for** $t \leftarrow 1$ **to** $T$ **do**
  **for** $i \leftarrow 1$ **to** $P$ **do**
    Evaluate fitness $F(\mathbf{X}_i)$;
    **if** $F(\mathbf{X}_i) < F(\mathbf{P}_i)$ **then**
      $\mathbf{P}_i \leftarrow \mathbf{X}_i$;
    **if** $F(\mathbf{P}_i) < F(\mathbf{G})$ **then**
      $\mathbf{G} \leftarrow \mathbf{P}_i$;
  **for** $i \leftarrow 1$ **to** $P$ **do**
    Update velocity:
      $\mathbf{V}_i \leftarrow w\mathbf{V}_i + c_1 r_1(\mathbf{P}_i - \mathbf{X}_i) + c_2 r_2(\mathbf{G} - \mathbf{X}_i)$;
    Update position:
      $\mathbf{X}_i \leftarrow \mathbf{X}_i + \mathbf{V}_i$;
    Enforce bounds: clip $\mathbf{X}_i \in [0, 1]^N$;
**return G** *as* $\mathbf{c}_2^*$

## 4 Simulation Results

In this section, we consider an AFDM system employing QPSK over a doubly-dispersive channel, with $N$ set to 64. At the receiver, perfect channel state information (CSI) is assumed, and minimum mean square error (MMSE) equalization is applied.

Figure 3 illustrates the comparison of simulated PAPR performance among AFDM, OTFS, OFDM, and two optimized AFDM variants. The figure indicates that both the original AFDM and OFDM exhibit high PAPR levels, while OTFS shows a slightly reduced value. This situation could lead to significant challenges in practical implementations, particularly concerning power consumption in small terminals like UAVs and the linearity of amplifiers. The two PSO optimizations result in considerable improvements, and variations in c2 optimization produce fewer performance gains compared to using the same $c_2$ optimization.

We evaluate BER under a more practical setup: QPSK modulation, $N = 64$ for the DAFT-based schemes, and $N_{OTFS} = M_{OTFS} = 8$ for OTFS. A three-tap channel is assumed, with the maximum Doppler and delay indices set to $\alpha_{\max} = l_{\max} = 2$. In this configuration, AFDM attains lower BER than OFDM and performs on par with OTFS. When channel estimation is accounted for, OTFS requires nearly twice the pilot resources of AFDM due to its two-dimensional transform. Both PSO variants incur a slight loss relative to the original AFDM.

Inspite of small BER performance decreasion, two methods after PSO optimization show lower PAPR than original one. Moreover, the optimization with N $c_2$ may have better application prospects. Literature [10] has investigated Index modulation with N $c_2$ to improve BER (Fig. 4).

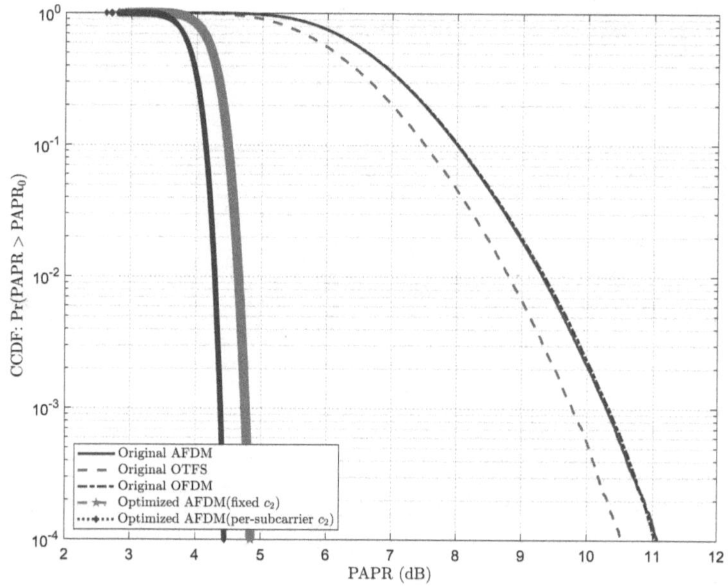


**Fig. 3.** PAPR performance comparison between AFDM, OTFS, OFDM and two PSO-based algorithms

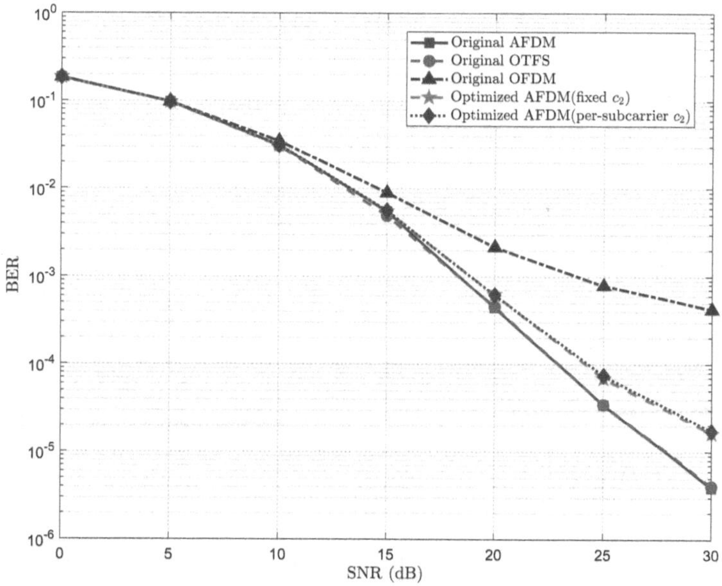


**Fig. 4.** BER performance comparison between AFDM, OTFS, OFDM and two PSO-based algorithms

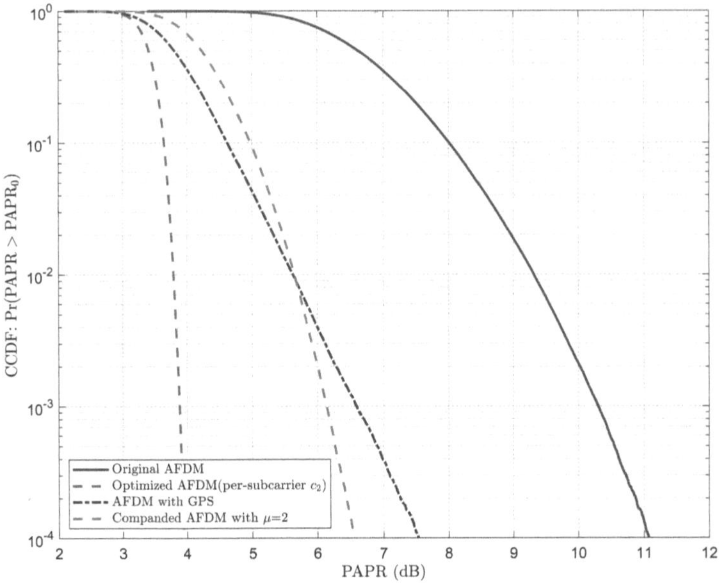


**Fig. 5.** PAPR performance comparison between AFDM, Optimal AFMD with N $c_2$, AFDM with GPS and Companded AFDM

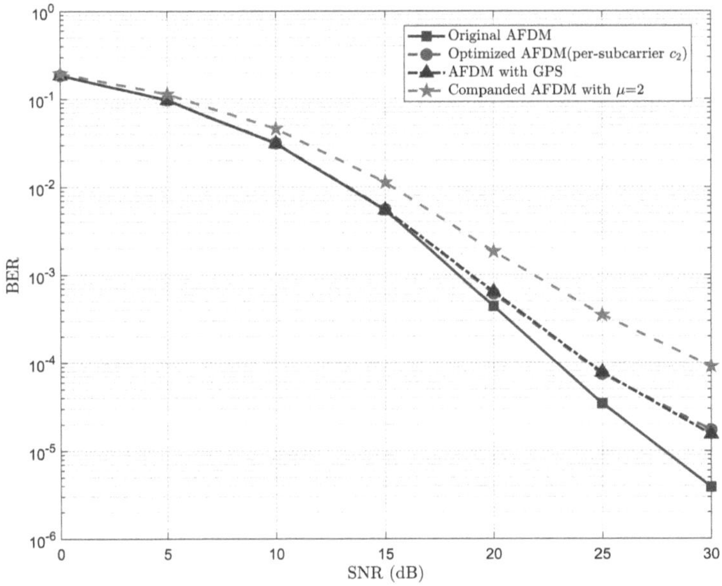


**Fig. 6.** BER performance comparison between AFDM, Optimal AFMD with N $c_2$, AFDM with GPS and Companded AFDM

Also, other two PAPR reduction schemes are compared. As shown in Fig. 5 and Fig. 6, AFDM with GPS (grouped pre-chirp selection) [17] and Companded AFDM [18] both have advantages in PAPR reduction while companded AFDM inevitably sacrifices some BER performance. However, optimizations in this letter show greater potential in PAPR reduction and keep the same communication performance.

## 5 Conclusion

In this letter, we discuss the possibility for AFDM to reduce PAPR. First charactristics of AFDM PAPR is analyzed, finding out the optimization problem. Then we try another realization: one $c_2$ for one subcarriers. Finally, PSO algorithm is applied for both AFDM. And the simulation results show that with an acceptable degradation in BER performance, PSO algorithm achieves a lower PAPR than OTFS and the original AFDM.

## References


1. Liu, R., Lin, H., Lee, H., Chaves, F., Lim, H., Sköld, J.: Beginning of the journey toward 6G: vision and framework. IEEE Commun. Mag. **61**(10), 8–9 (2023)
2. Hadani, R., et al.: Orthogonal time frequency space modulation. In: Proc. IEEE Wireless Commun. Netw. Conf. (WCNC), pp. 1–6 (2017)
3. Ouyang, X., Zhao, J.: Orthogonal chirp division multiplexing. IEEE Trans. Commun. **64**(9), 3946–3957 (2016)
4. Bemani, A., Ksairi, N., Kountouris, M.: Affine frequency division multiplexing for next generation wireless communications. IEEE Trans. Wireless Commun. **22**(11), 8214–8229 (2023)
5. Rou, H.S., et al.: From Orthogonal Time-Frequency Space to Affine Frequency-Division Multiplexing: a comparative study of next-generation waveforms for integrated sensing and communications in doubly dispersive channels. IEEE Signal Process. Mag. **41**(5), 71–86 (2024)
6. Omar, M.S., Ma, X.: Performance analysis of OCDM for wireless communications. IEEE Trans. Wireless Commun. **20**(7), 4032–4043 (2021)
7. Yin, H., Wei, X., Tang, Y., Yang, K.: Diagonally reconstructed channel estimation for MIMO-AFDM with inter-doppler interference in doubly selective channels. IEEE Trans. Wireless Commun. **23**(10), 14066–14079 (2024)
8. Zheng, K., Wen, M., Mao, T., Xiao, L., Wang, Z.: Channel estimation for AFDM with superimposed pilots. IEEE Trans. Veh. Technol. **74**(2), 3389–3394 (2025)
9. Qu, X., Shen, X., Wang, H., Li, X.: Turbo equalization scheme for polar-AFDM system. In: 2024 16th International Conference on Communication Software and Networks (ICCSN), pp. 278–282, Ningbo, China (2024)
10. Liu, G., et al.: Pre-chirp-domain index modulation for full-diversity affine frequency division multiplexing towards 6G. IEEE Trans. Wirel. Commun.
11. Liu, G., Mao, T., Liu, R., Xiao, Z.: Pre-chirp-domain index modulation for affine frequency division multiplexing. In: 2024 International Wireless Communications and Mobile Computing (IWCMC), Ayia Napa, Cyprus, pp. 0473–0478 (2024)

12. Ni, Y., Yuan, P., Huang, Q., Liu, F., Wang, Z.: An integrated sensing and communications system based on affine frequency division multiplexing. IEEE Trans. Wireless Commun. **24**(5), 3763–3779 (2025)
13. Ranasinghe, K.R.R., Seok Rou, H., Thadeu Freitas de Abreu, G., Takahashi, T., Ito, K.: Joint channel, data, and radar parameter estimation for AFDM systems in doubly-dispersive channels. IEEE Trans. Wireless Commun. **24**(2), 1602–1619 (2025)
14. Hua, L., Wang, Y., Lian, Z., Su, Y., Xie, Z.: LADMM-based PAPR-aware precoding for massive MIMO-OFDM downlink systems. IEEE Trans. Veh. Technol. **72**(1), 735–746 (2023). https://doi.org/10.1109/TVT.2022.3203859
15. Gopi, S., Kalyani, S.: An optimized SLM for PAPR reduction in non-coherent OFDM-IM. IEEE Wirel. Commun. Lett. **9**(7), 967–971 (2020)
16. Li, H., et al.: On the PAPR of the LTE-based 5G terrestrial broadcast system. In: Proc. IEEE Int. Symp. Broadband Multimedia Syst. Broadcast. (BMSB), pp. 1–6 (2023)
17. Yuan, H., et al.: PAPR reduction with pre-chirp selection for affine frequency division multiplexing. IEEE Wirel. Commun. Lett. **14**(3), 736–740 (2025)
18. Reddy, V.M., Bitra, H.: PAPR in AFDM: upper bound and reduction with normalized $\mu$ -law companding. IEEE Access **13**, 86553–86561 (2025)
19. Kim, K.-H.: Low-complexity suboptimal ML detection for OFDM-IM systems. IEEE Wirel. Commun. Lett. **12**(3), 416–420 (2023)

# Non-Orthogonal HARQ-CC Over SDR: A GNU Radio-Based Implementation

Hongling Huang[1], Jintao Wang[1(✉)], Zheng Shi[1(✉)], Xu Wang[1], Guanghua Yang[1], Shaodan Ma[2], and Haichuan Ding[3]

[1] School of Intelligent Systems Science and Engineering, Jinan University, Zhuhai, China
curryhhl@stu.jnu.edu.cn, wang.jintao@connect.um.edu.mo, {zhengshi,xuwang,ghyang}@jnu.edu.cn

[2] State Key Laboratory of Internet of Things for Smart City, University of Macau, Macau, China
shaodanma@um.edu.mo

[3] School of Cyberspace Science and Technology, Beijing Institute of Technology, Beijing, China
hcding@bit.edu.cn

**Abstract.** Hybrid Automatic Repeat Request (HARQ) schemes typically allocate all available resources to retransmit failed packets to ensure reliability. However, under stringent delay constraints, these schemes often exhibit low spectral efficiency and increased transmission latency. To address these challenges, this paper proposes an efficient Non-Orthogonal HARQ with Chase Combining (N-HARQ-CC) transmission strategy. Specifically, the proposed approach allocates a larger portion of retransmission resources to new data packets, reserving only a small fraction for retransmitting previously erroneous packets. This is based on the observation that only a small number of information bits are typically incorrect, enabling surplus communication resources to be utilized for transmitting new messages. The N-HARQ-CC scheme retransmits the same redundant version of a failed packet and employs Maximum Ratio Combining (MRC) for decoding. To minimize complex packet scheduling and decoding complexity, the proposed scheme limits superposition to at most two messages per transmission round. At the receiver, Successive Interference Cancellation (SIC) is used to decouple the superimposed messages. The proposed N-HARQ-CC system was implemented using GNU Radio and USRP platforms for validation. Compared to conventional Type-I HARQ and HARQ-CC schemes, the proposed scheme achieves a significant improvement in spectral efficiency of approximately 0.5 bps/Hz, aligning with the low-latency requirements of 6G networks.

---

Supported in part by National Natural Science Foundation of China under Grants 62171200, 62171201, and 92367201, in part by Guangdong Basic and Applied Basic Research Foundation under Grant 2023A1515010900, in part by Fundamental Research Funds for the Central Universities under Grant 21625361, in part by the Science and Technology Development Fund, Macau SAR under Grant 0020/2025/RIB1.


Y. Liu et al. (Eds.): ChinaCom 2025, LNICST 711, pp. 21–34, 2027.
https://doi.org/10.1007/978-3-032-33662-0_3

**Keywords:** GNU Radio · hybrid automatic repeat request · non-orthogonal multiple access · software-defined radio · USRP

## 1 Introduction

Compared with the fifth-generation (5G) mobile communication system, which primarily focuses on three typical scenarios—enhanced mobile broadband (eMBB), ultra-reliable low-latency communication (URLLC), and massive machine-type communication (mMTC)—the sixth-generation (6G) mobile communication technology not only inherits the core capabilities of 5G but also introduces several key enhancements. Specifically, 6G incorporates further enhanced mobile broadband (FeMBB) to support terabit-per-second (Tbps) data rates; extremely reliable low-latency communication (ERLLC) to meet the stringent demands of critical applications; and ultra-massive machine-type communication (umMTC) to achieve significantly higher global device connectivity [1].

As 6G imposes more stringent requirements on latency and reliability, conventional hybrid automatic repeat request (HARQ) mechanisms are expected to face unprecedented challenges. HARQ, a key reliability enhancement mechanism in 5G, improves robustness by combining forward error correction and retransmission strategies. However, in the context of 6G URLLC scenarios, conventional HARQ schemes suffer from excessive feedback and queuing delays, limiting their suitability for latency-critical applications such as industrial automation, vehicular communications, and holographic services.

To address these limitations, various advanced HARQ schemes have been proposed. For multicast channels and delay-sensitive services, fixed-rate HARQ schemes based on superposition coding (SC), as well as multiplexed HARQ (M-HARQ), were shown to enhance throughput and spectral efficiency via power allocation and iterative interference cancellation [2,3]. Furthermore, multi-packet HARQ (MP-HARQ) was proposed to allow multiple packets to share the same radio resource. Through dynamic coding strategies guided by Markov decision processes (MDPs), MP-HARQ achieves significant performance gains in high spectral efficiency scenarios [4,5].

On the other hand, hybrid non-orthogonal multiple access (NOMA) systems enable energy-efficient user scheduling through joint optimization of power allocation and block length [6]. Grant-free NOMA (GF-NOMA) and power-domain NOMA (PD-NOMA) are also considered as key enablers for 6G [7,8]. These approaches facilitate the integration of multi-packet transmission with HARQ schemes, improving both system capacity and reliability [9,10].

Non-orthogonal HARQ (N-HARQ) mechanism enables simultaneous transmission of new and retransmitted packets within the same time slot via power-domain superposition. This significantly reduces queuing delays, thereby enhancing delay performance [11,12]. Moreover, dynamic adjustment of the maximum number of retransmissions allows a flexible trade-off between latency and reliability, resulting in improved overall system throughput. In terms of practical implementation, numerous downlink NOMA systems have been experimentally validated on software-defined radio (SDR) platforms using GNU Radio and universal software radio peripheral (USRP) [13–15]. However, most HARQ and N-HARQ schemes remain in the theoretical or simulation stage with limited real-world deployment or system-level validation, highlighting the need for further experimental research.

In this work, we propose a practical N-HARQ with Chase Combining (N-HARQ-CC) scheme that integrates non-orthogonal SC with HARQ mechanisms. The N-HARQ-CC scheme retransmits the same redundant version of a failed packet and employs Maximum Ratio Combining (MRC) for decoding. By superimposing user packets in the power domain, the proposed scheme achieves enhanced throughput while supporting low-latency retransmissions. Furthermore, we implement and validate the proposed mechanism using a combination of GNU Radio and USRP hardware, demonstrating its practical feasibility and performance advantages.

## 2 System Model

This section introduces the proposed N-HARQ-CC scheme first, with which the procedure of signal reconstruction and the analysis of signal-to-interference-plus-noise (SINR) are presented.

### 2.1 N-HARQ-CC Scheme

This paper investigates an N-HARQ-aided downlink communication system with one transmitter and one receiver. Unlike traditional HARQ schemes, which retransmit only the redundancy information of a failed message, the N-HARQ scheme incorporates a new information message during retransmissions. This approach leverages the fact that only a small portion of the information bits are typically erroneous, allowing surplus communication resources to be utilized for transmitting the next message. Consequently, the N-HARQ scheme enhances spectral efficiency and reduces transmission delay, albeit with a slight increase in computational complexity. In this paper, we propose a practical N-HARQ scheme, termed as N-HARQ-CC, which capitalizes on both chase combining and superposition coding. In particular, similar to the HARQ-CC scheme, our proposed scheme assumes that the same redundant information of failed messages is retransmitted and MRC is used at the receiver. Moreover, to avoid a complex packet scheduling mechanism and high decoding complexity, at most two messages are allowed to be superimposed at each transmission round. At the receiver, the technique of successive interference cancellation (SIC) is applied to separate the two superimposed messages. Moreover, to avoid network congestion, the maximum number of HARQ rounds for each message is limited to $M$. According to whether a positive or negative acknowledgement (ACK/NACK) message is fed back to the transmitter, the following two transmission modes are triggered by the proposed N-HARQ-CC scheme.

**Initial Transmission Mode.** If there is no NACK feedback or the maximum number of HARQ rounds for each message is reached, a new HARQ cycle begins. Accordingly, a new message will be delivered in the first HARQ round, i.e., initial transmission mode (ITM). The received packet in the initial HARQ round can be written as

$$\mathbf{y}_1 = h_1\sqrt{P}\mathbf{x}_1 + \mathbf{n}_1, \tag{1}$$

where $\mathbf{x}_1$ refers to the encoded message with normalized average power, $P$ denotes the transmission power, $h_1$ refers to the channel coefficient, and $n_l$ represents the complex additive white Gaussian noise (AWGN) with zero mean and unity variance. The decoding is performed at the receiver according to the observation $\mathbf{y}_1$. If the receiver successfully recovers $\mathbf{x}_1$, an ACK message will be sent back and a new HARQ cycle will be started. Otherwise, if an NACK is returned, a retransmission mode will be triggered subsequently, that is, a new message will be superimposed with the failed message in the power domain in a retransmission HARQ round.

**Retransmission Mode.** A retransmission mode (RM) is initiated if at least one NACK message is received, unless the maximum number of HARQ rounds for each message has been reached. In the retransmission mode, two messages are superimposed at the transmitter. Without loss of generality, we denote by the two messages $\mathbf{x}_{k_1}$ and $\mathbf{x}_{k_2}$ with $k_1 < k_2$. For expositional simplicity, we refer to $\mathbf{x}_{k_1}$ and $\mathbf{x}_{k_2}$ as the old and new packets, respectively. Hence, the received signal in the $l$-th HARQ round can be written as

$$\mathbf{y}_l = h_l\left(\alpha\sqrt{P}\mathbf{x}_{k_1} + \sqrt{(1-\alpha^2)P}\mathbf{x}_{k_2}\right) + \mathbf{n}_l, \tag{2}$$

where $h_l$ corresponds to the channel coefficient, $\alpha$ represents the power allocation coefficient of the old packet, and $\mathbf{n}_l$ denotes the complex AWGN. Since there is a small amount of erroneous information bits, more power can be allocated to the new packet. According to the principle of NOMA, the new packet $\mathbf{x}_{k_2}$ is decoded first. After successfully reconstructing $\mathbf{x}_{k_2}$, the SIC is applied to decode the old packet $\mathbf{x}_{k_1}$ by subtracting $\mathbf{x}_{k_2}$ from $\mathbf{y}_l$. If the receiver successfully decodes both messages, a new cycle will start in the next HARQ round. Otherwise, the retransmission mode continues and the delivered messages (old message $\mathbf{x}_{\text{old}}$ and new message $\mathbf{x}_{\text{new}}$) in the next HARQ round are given by

$$[\mathbf{x}_{\text{old}}, \mathbf{x}_{\text{new}}] = \begin{cases} [\mathbf{x}_{k_1}, \mathbf{x}_{k_2}], & \mathcal{F}_O^{\text{NACK}} \wedge \mathcal{F}_N^{\text{NACK}} \\ [\mathbf{x}_{k_2}, \mathbf{x}_{k_2+1}], & \mathcal{F}_O^{\text{ACK}} \wedge \mathcal{F}_N^{\text{NACK}} \\ [\mathbf{x}_{k_1}, \mathbf{x}_{k_2+1}], & \mathcal{F}_O^{\text{NACK}} \wedge \mathcal{F}_N^{\text{ACK}} \end{cases}, \tag{3}$$

where $\mathcal{F}_O^{\text{ACK}}$ and $\mathcal{F}_O^{\text{NACK}}$ denote the success and the failure of recovering the old message, respectively, and the similar definitions are also applicable to $\mathcal{F}_N^{\text{ACK}}$ and $\mathcal{F}_N^{\text{NACK}}$ for the new message.

According to the transmission mechanism of the N-HARQ-CC scheme, the previously received packets and the currently received packet can be jointly decoded through MRC. Furthermore, the new message is decoded first due to its higher power allocation coefficient and the old message is then decoded by leveraging the operation of SIC. Hence, the signal reconstruction and SINR analysis for these two messages are discussed separately.

### 2.2 Signal Reconstruction and SINR Analysis

**Decoding of the New Message.** To proceed, we assume that the new message has been transmitted for $m_2$ HARQ rounds. In the $l$-th HARQ round, the receiver attempts to recover the new message $\mathbf{x}_{k_2}$ by combining the received signals from the latest $m_2$ HARQ rounds, i.e., $\mathbf{y}_{l-m_2+1}, \cdots, \mathbf{y}_l$. By employing MRC, the combined signal is written as

$$\mathbf{y}_{m_2}^{\mathrm{MRC}} = \frac{1}{\left\|\mathbf{h}_{l-m_2+1:l}\right\|^2} \sum_{i=l-m_2+1}^{l} h_i^* \mathbf{y}_i, \tag{4}$$

where $\mathbf{h}_{l-m_2+1:l} = (h_{l-m_2+1}, \cdots, h_l)^{\mathrm{T}}$. Substituting (2) into (4) leads to

$$\begin{aligned}\mathbf{y}_{m_2}^{\mathrm{MRC}} =& \sqrt{(1-\alpha^2)P}\mathbf{x}_{k_2} + \alpha\sqrt{P}\mathbf{x}_{k_1} \\ &+ \frac{1}{\left\|\mathbf{h}_{l-m_2+1:l}\right\|^2} \sum_{i=l-m_2+1}^{l} h_i^* \mathbf{n}_i,\end{aligned} \tag{5}$$

Since the old message is directly treated as noise, the received SINR for the new message can be derived as

$$\gamma_{m_2}^{\mathrm{new}} = \frac{(1-\alpha^2)P\left\|\mathbf{h}_{l-m_2+1:l}\right\|^2}{\alpha^2 P\left\|\mathbf{h}_{l-m_2+1:l}\right\|^2 + 1}. \tag{6}$$

**Decoding of the Old Message.** After recovering the new message $\mathbf{x}_{k_2}$, the old message $\mathbf{x}_{k_1}$ is decoded by using SIC. For notational simplicity, we assume that the old message $\mathbf{x}_{k_1}$ has been delivered for $m_1$ times. Since messages that fail after the maximum number of transmissions cannot be canceled, they will interfere with the decoding of the old message $\mathbf{x}_{k_1}$. Clearly, at most one such failure event presents due to the restriction on the number of HARQ rounds, i.e., $M$. Depending on whether a single failed SIC operation occurs, we categorize the subsequent discussion into two cases, i.e., no SIC failure and one SIC failure.

*No SIC Failure.* This case indicates that all the messages from $\mathbf{x}_{k_1+1}$ to $\mathbf{x}_{k_2}$ can be cancelled out. Hence, subtracting the interfered signals $\mathbf{x}_{k_1+1}, \cdots, \mathbf{x}_{k_2}$ from $\mathbf{y}_{l-m_1+1}, \cdots, \mathbf{y}_l$ yields $\tilde{\mathbf{y}}_{l-m_1+1}, \cdots, \tilde{\mathbf{y}}_l$ that only contain the desired signal $\mathbf{x}_{k_1}$. Therefore, $\tilde{\mathbf{y}}_i$ can be written as

$$\tilde{\mathbf{y}}_i = h_i \alpha\sqrt{P}\mathbf{x}_{k_1} + \mathbf{n}_i,\ i \in [l-m_1+1, l]. \tag{7}$$

By applying MRC for $\tilde{\mathbf{y}}_{l-m_1+1}, \cdots, \tilde{\mathbf{y}}_l$, the combined signal can be written as

$$\tilde{\mathbf{y}}_{m_1}^{\text{MRC}} = \frac{1}{\|\mathbf{h}_{l-m_1+1:l}\|^2} \sum_{i=l-m_1+1}^{l} h_i^* \tilde{\mathbf{y}}_i. \tag{8}$$

Accordingly, the received SNR for decoding the old message $\mathbf{x}_{k_1}$ can be calculated as

$$\gamma_{m_1}^{\text{old}} = \alpha^2 P \|\mathbf{h}_{l-m_1+1:l}\|^2. \tag{9}$$

*One SIC Failure.* When an SIC failure occurs for a given message, the transmission round count of the other message in the superimposed signal is necessarily smaller, since the new packet is only superimposed on the previous message that requires retransmission, and there exists only one such message at a time. Therefore, it can be concluded that during the entire HARQ process for a given message, at most one message may experience SIC failure. For simplicity, we assume that the SIC failure occurs at the $l_1$-th HARQ round, and the message $\mathbf{x}_{k_0}$ is discarded after $M$ HARQ rounds. Clearly, all the messages from $\mathbf{x}_{k_1+1}$ to $\mathbf{x}_{k_2}$ have been successfully recovered and can be subtracted from $\mathbf{y}_{l_1+1}$ to $\mathbf{y}_l$. Whereas, the message $\mathbf{x}_{k_0}$ cannnot be cancelled out from $\mathbf{y}_{l-m_1+1}$ to $\mathbf{y}_{l_1}$ and interferes the recovery of the old signal $\mathbf{x}_{k_1}$. Accordingly, the combined signal can be written as

$$\begin{aligned}\tilde{\mathbf{y}}_{m_1}^{\text{MRC}} =& \frac{1}{\|\mathbf{h}_{l-m_1+1:l}\|^2} \left( \sum_{i=l-m_1+1}^{l_1} h_i^* \mathbf{y}_i + \sum_{i=l_1+1}^{l} h_i^* \tilde{\mathbf{y}}_i \right) \\ =& \alpha\sqrt{P}\mathbf{x}_{k_1} + \frac{\|\mathbf{h}_{l-m_1+1:l_1}\|^2}{\|\mathbf{h}_{l-m_1+1:l}\|^2} \sqrt{(1-\alpha^2)P}\mathbf{x}_{k_2} \\ &+ \frac{1}{\|\mathbf{h}_{l-m_1+1:l}\|^2} \sum_{i=l-m_1+1}^{l} h_i^* \mathbf{n}_i. \end{aligned} \tag{10}$$

As a consequence, the received SINR for the old message is given by

$$\gamma_{m_1}^{\text{old}} = \frac{\alpha^2 P \|\mathbf{h}_{l-m_1+1:l}\|^4}{(1-\alpha^2)P\|\mathbf{h}_{l-m_1+1:l_1}\|^4 + \|\mathbf{h}_{l-m_1+1:l}\|^2}. \tag{11}$$

The illustration of one SIC failure in decoding the old message with $M = 3$ is presented in Fig. 1.

## 3 SDR-Based Implementation of N-HARQ-CC

GNU Radio is an open-source software development toolkit that offers a wide range of signal processing modules. It enables flexible construction and implementation of SDR systems. When integrated with hardware platforms such as the USRP, GNU Radio serves as an ideal tool for rapid prototyping, experimental validation, and cognitive radio research [16].

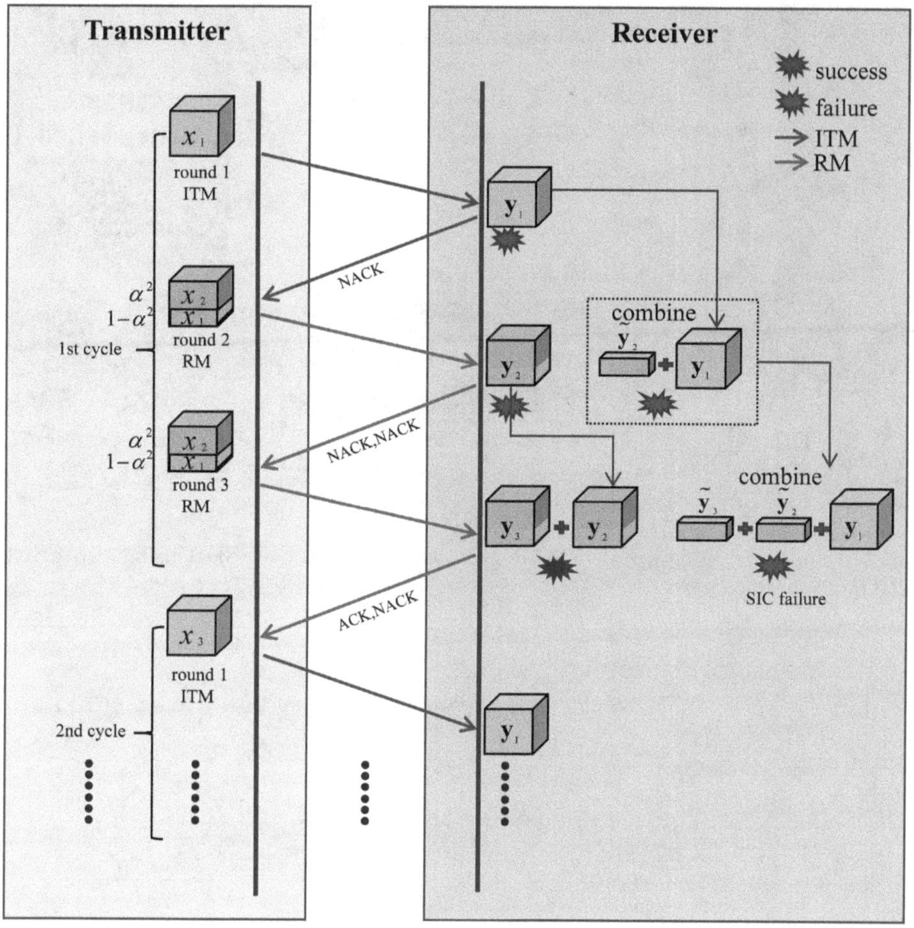


**Fig. 1.** The example of one SIC failure in decoding the old message with $M = 3$.

In this study, we develop a SC transmission framework to support two data packets, which is implemented on the GNU Radio platform using two USRP B210 devices. As illustrated in Fig. 2, one USRP B210 serves as the BS and the other as the UE. Both USRPs are configured with two channels to construct the downlink transmission and uplink feedback paths. The system architecture of the proposed N-HARQ-CC scheme is shown in Fig. 3 and the GNU Radio flowgraph of the transmitter and receiver is presented in Fig. 4.

### 3.1 Transmitter

On the transmitter side, the core module is a custom Python Embedded Block, referred to as the *Transmitter Block*, which is responsible for data packet construction and automatic repeat request (ARQ) control. The input file is first seg-

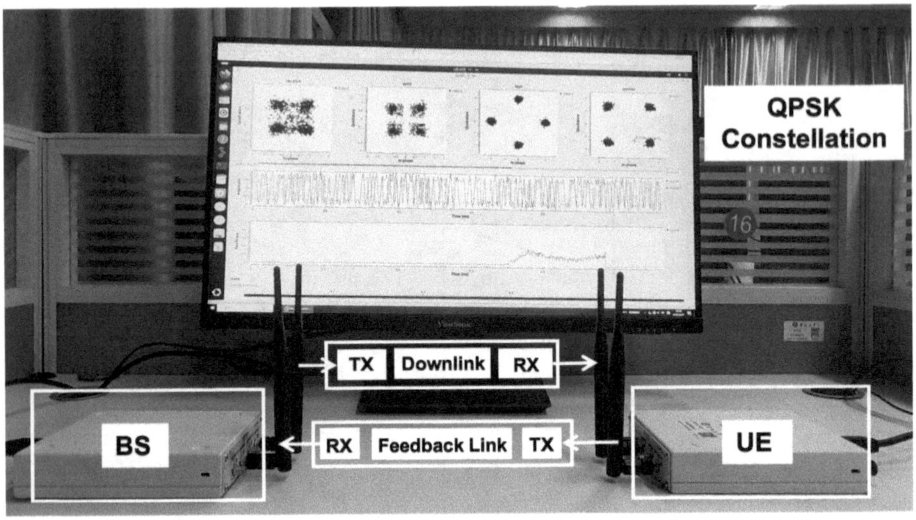


**Fig. 2.** Experimental setup of N-HARQ-CC transmission over SDR using two USRP B210 devices.

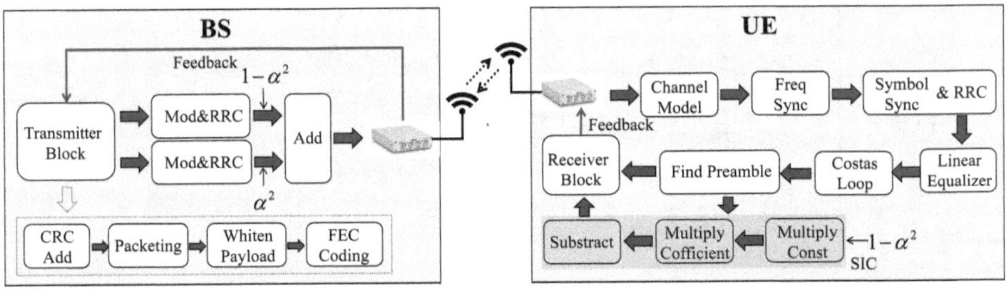


**Fig. 3.** System architecture of the proposed N-HARQ-CC scheme based on GNU Radio.

mented into multiple packets with fixed byte lengths. Each packet is appended with a cyclic redundancy check (CRC) checksum for error detection, followed by the insertion of fixed-format headers and tails to complete the packetization. To enhance the randomness and ensure uniform bit distribution, whitening is applied to the CRC, header, and tail bits. The whitened packet is then encoded using forward error correction (FEC) to improve error resilience.

In the ARQ control module, packets are selectively transmitted based on feedback results and predefined retransmission strategies. The selected packets are modulated into quadrature phase shift keying (QPSK) symbols and processed with a root-raised cosine (RRC) filter. The resulting superimposed signal is transmitted via the USRP B210 to the receiver. And the CRC code has a length of 32 bits, the FEC employs a Reed–Solomon (RS) code with a coding rate of approximately 0.6, and the roll-off factor of the RRC filter is set to 0.35.

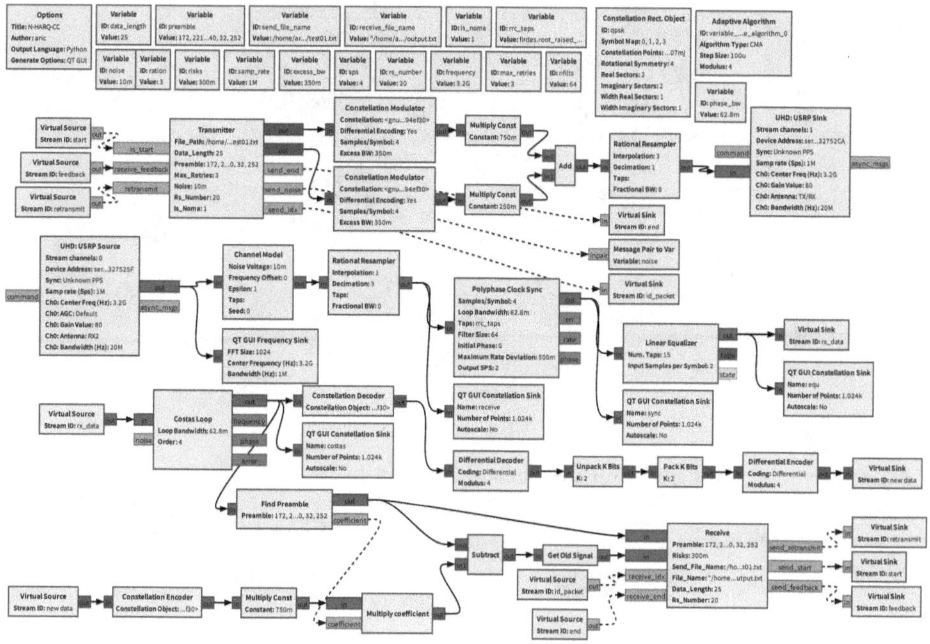


**Fig. 4.** GNU Radio flowgraph of the proposed N-HARQ-CC through 2 USRPs.

## 3.2 Receiver

On the receiver side, the wireless signal is captured using the USRP B210. To facilitate performance evaluation under various SNR conditions, a Channel Model block is used to introduce AWGN. The received signal then undergoes a series of preprocessing steps, including frequency synchronization, symbol synchronization, and RRC filtering. To mitigate channel distortion, a linear equalizer based on the Constant Modulus Algorithm (CMA) is employed for channel equalization. Subsequently, a Costas loop is applied to achieve carrier phase synchronization, thereby improving demodulation accuracy. Finally, SIC is performed to separate the superimposed signals.

The demodulated signals are passed to the custom *Receiver Block*, which serves as the core processing module at the receiver. It is responsible for data packet parsing and HARQ feedback generation. During packet parsing, the signal is first decoded using FEC to recover the original bit stream, followed by dewhitening. The packet header is then checked for integrity. If the header is invalid, the packet is discarded; otherwise, a CRC check is performed to verify data integrity. Based on the CRC result, the system determines whether retransmission is required and generates the corresponding HARQ feedback message.

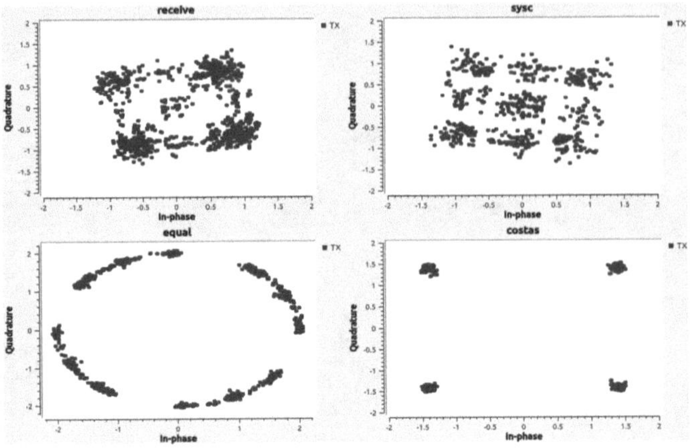


**Fig. 5.** QPSK constellation in ITM mode.

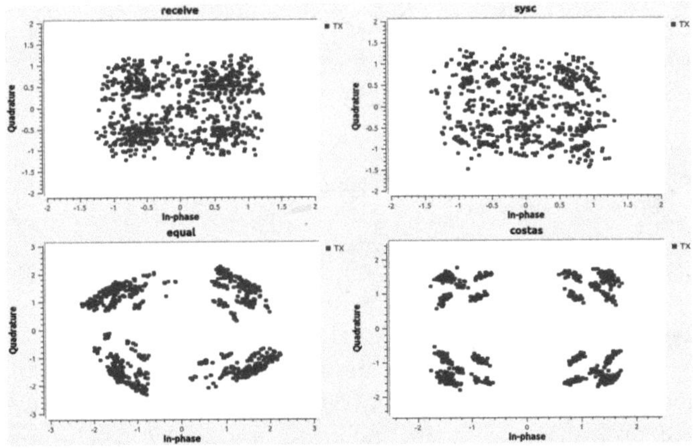


**Fig. 6.** QPSK constellation in RM mode.

## 4 Experimental Results

In this experiment, the SDR platform is employed for both transmission and reception to evaluate system performance under varying channel conditions. To ensure stable operation within a band-limited channel, the experimental setup is configured with a 3.2 GHz carrier frequency, 1 MHz sampling rate, and 20 MHz channel bandwidth. Each transmitted frame contains 200 information bits. A total of 1757 packets are transmitted to ensure statistically meaningful results for performance evaluation. To investigate the impact of different SNR levels on system performance, AWGN is introduced through the channel block to enable controlled variation of the SNR. For each SNR level, the BER and the normalized average throughput per frame are measured, providing a comprehensive performance profile of the system across different channel qualities.

Figure 5 and Fig. 6 depict the QPSK constellation diagrams for the ITM and RM transmission modes, respectively. Each figure presents four constellation diagrams that capture the signal at successive stages of the receiver processing chain: (i) the received signal at the user, (ii) the signal after synchronization and RRC filtering, (iii) the output after CMA equalization, and (iv) the result after phase and frequency correction using the Costas loop.

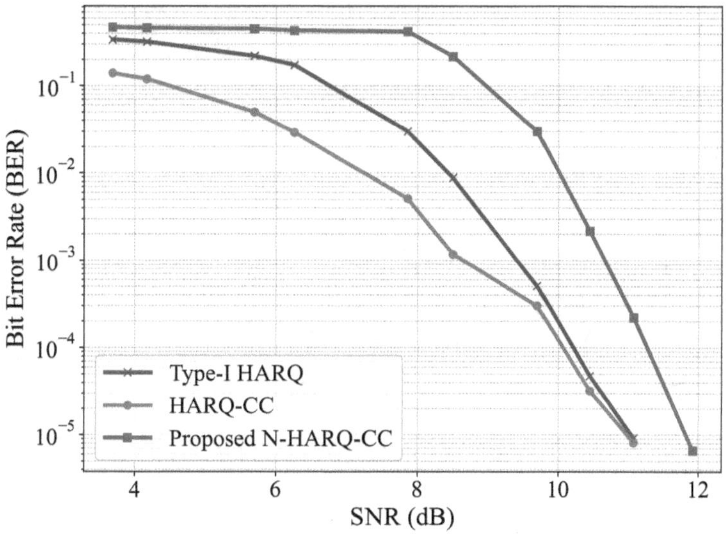


**Fig. 7.** BER analysis of conventional and proposed transmission schemes.

Figure 7 presents the BER performance of three transmission schemes under varying SNR conditions. Generally, the BER of all schemes decreases as the SNR increases, which is consistent with the theoretical expectation. Among the compared schemes, the Type-I HARQ exhibits significantly inferior BER performance relative to the HARQ-CC scheme in the low-to-moderate SNR range (approximately 4–10 dB). This is attributed to the fact that Type-I HARQ only performs simple retransmissions upon initial decoding failure, thereby failing to exploit the decoding gain provided by soft combining. In contrast, the MRC achieves better BER performance by leveraging soft combining of multiple received copies. As the SNR increases, the BER performance of both schemes converges in the high-SNR regime, ultimately approaching zero. This indicates that under favorable channel conditions, the relative benefits of retransmission strategies and coding gains diminish, as error-free transmission becomes more readily achievable.

In comparison, the proposed scheme experiences notable BER degradation in the low-to-moderate SNR region. This is primarily attributed to inter-packet interference and resource allocation dilution inherent in parallel packet transmission, which effectively reduces the received SNR. A significant improvement in BER is observed only when the SNR exceeds approximately 10 dB. This behavior indicates that while the RM can enhance system throughput.

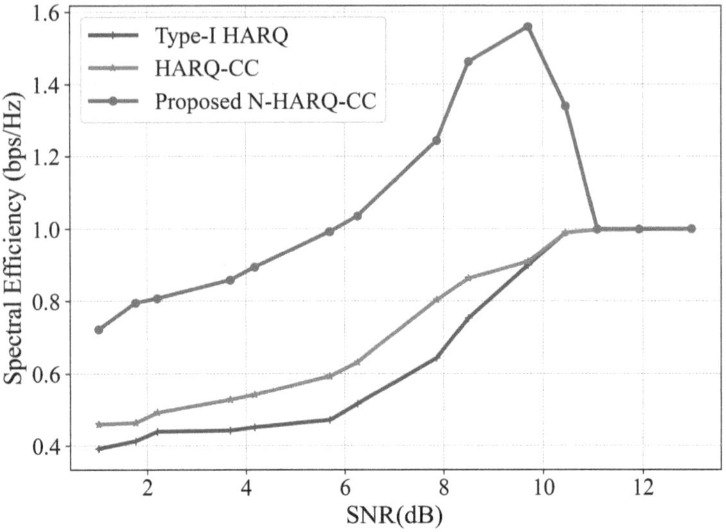


**Fig. 8.** Spectral efficiency analysis of conventional and proposed transmission schemes.

Figure 8 illustrates the spectral efficiency (SE) of three representative transmission schemes under varying SNR conditions. This metric reflects how efficiently data bits are transmitted relative to the theoretical maximum. At low SNR levels, all three schemes exhibit poor SE performance due to high error rates. As the SNR increases, the SE of both the HARQ-CC and Type-I HARQ schemes gradually improves, saturating around 11 dB and approaching the theoretical limit. This saturation indicates that most packets are successfully decoded on the first attempt. However, the SE of Type-I HARQ remains slightly lower than that of HARQ-CC, as it does not exploit soft combining gains. The proposed N-HARQ-CC scheme reaches its peak SE at moderate SNRs (around 10 dB), but the SE then declines and stabilizes at higher SNRs. This behavior is attributed to that improved channel conditions reduce the retransmission frequency, thereby causing the system to revert to RM and thus diminishing the throughput benefit of parallel ITM operation. Overall, the proposed N-HARQ-CC scheme improves spectral efficiency by around 0.5 bps/Hz over the conventional HARQ-CC scheme. Its dynamic adaptability makes it particularly suitable for low latency in 6G networks.

## 5 Conclusion

This paper proposed an efficient N-HARQ-CC transmission strategy to address the limitations of traditional HARQ schemes, namely, low spectral efficiency and increased transmission latency under stringent delay constraints. The N-HARQ-CC scheme retransmitted the same redundant version of a failed packet with a superimposed new packet and the SIC technique was used to decouple the superimposed messages. Furthermore, we implemented the proposed N-HARQ-CC system using GNU Radio and USRP platforms for validation. The experimental results demonstrated that the proposed N-HARQ-CC achieves significantly higher throughput compared to Type-I HARQ and HARQ-CC schemes.

Furthermore, this study reveals a robustness challenge under poor channel conditions, where fixed power allocation can lead to the SIC failure and sustained multi-packet superposition, thereby limiting throughput. This observation underscores the necessity for joint optimization of dynamic power allocation and adaptive transmission mode switching (e.g., fallback to ITM), potentially leveraging reinforcement learning frameworks, which is a primary direction for our subsequent investigation.

## References


1. Zhang, Z., et al.: 6G wireless networks: vision, requirements, architecture, and key technologies. IEEE Veh. Technol. Mag. **14**(3), 28–41 (2019)
2. Takahashi, F., Higuchi, K.: HARQ for predetermined-rate multicast channel. In: Proc. IEEE Veh. Technol. Conf. (VTC), Taipei, Taiwan, pp. 1–5 (2010)
3. Zhang, R., Hanzo, L.: Superposition-coding-aided multiplexed hybrid ARQ scheme for improved end-to-end transmission efficiency. IEEE Trans. Veh. Technol. **58**(8), 4681–4686 (2009)
4. Jabi, M., Hamss, A.E., Szczecinski, L., Piantanida, P.: Multipacket hybrid ARQ: closing gap to the ergodic capacity. IEEE Trans. Commun. **63**(12), 5191–5205 (2015)
5. Hamss, A.E., Szczecinski, L., Piantanida, P.: Increasing the throughput of HARQ via multi-packet transmission. In: Proc. IEEE Global Commun. Conf. (GLOBECOM), Austin, TX, USA, pp. 1485–1491 (2014)
6. Xu, Y., Shen, C., Cai, D., Zhu, G.: Latency constrained non-orthogonal packets scheduling with finite blocklength codes. IEEE Trans. Veh. Technol. **69**(10), 12312–12316 (2020)
7. Shahab, M.B., Abbas, R., Shirvanimoghaddam, M., Johnson, S.J.: Grant-free non-orthogonal multiple access for IoT: a survey. IEEE Commun. Surv. Tutorials **22**(3), 1805–1838 (2020). Thirdquarter
8. Liu, Y., Qin, Z., Elkashlan, M., Ding, Z., Nallanathan, A., Hanzo, L.: Nonorthogonal multiple access for 5G and beyond. Proc. IEEE **105**(12), 2347–2381 (2017)
9. Kotaba, R., Manchón, C.N., Balercia, T., Popovski, P.: How URLLC can benefit from NOMA-based retransmissions. IEEE Trans. Wireless Commun. **20**(3), 1684–1699 (2021)
10. Ghanami, F., Hodtani, G.A., Vucetic, B., Shirvanimoghaddam, M.: Performance analysis and optimization of NOMA With HARQ for short packet communications in massive IoT. IEEE Internet Things J. **8**(6), 4736–4748 (2021)
11. Nadeem, F., Shirvanimoghaddam, M., Li, Y., Vucetic, B.: Non-orthogonal HARQ for delay sensitive applications. In: Proc. IEEE Int. Conf. Commun. (ICC), Dublin, Ireland, pp. 1–6 (2020)

12. Nadeem, F., Shirvanimoghaddam, M., Li, Y., Vucetic, B.: Nonorthogonal HARQ for URLLC: design and analysis. IEEE Internet Things J. **8**(24), 17596–17610 (2021)
13. Bhatia, V., Bisen, S.: Implementation and performance analysis of NOMA on software defined radio. In: Proc. IEEE Int. Conf. Adv. Netw. Telecommun. Syst. (ANTS), Jaipur, India, pp. 485–490 (2023)
14. Garnier, J.-R., Fabre, A., Farès, H., Bonnefoi, R.: On the performance of QPSK modulation over downlink NOMA: from error probability derivation to SDR-based validation. IEEE Access **8**, 66495–66507 (2020)
15. Champi Castro, M.A., Luis Arizaca Cusicuna, J.: Implementation of a NOMA Downlink with SIC receiver for 2 users over SDR and GNU Radio. In: Proc. IEEE Colomb. Conf. Commun. Comput. (COLCOM), Barranquilla, Colombia, pp. 1–4 (2024)
16. Sokolowski, C., Petrova, M., de Baynast, A., Mahonen, P.: Cognitive radio testbed: exploiting limited feedback in tomorrow's wireless communication networks. In: Proc. IEEE Int. Conf. Commun. (ICC), Beijing, China, pp. 493–498 (2008)

# Energy-Efficient Multi-path Routing Scheme for Space-Ground Integrated Networks

Lijun He[1(✉)], Yutong Li[2], Ziye Jia[3], Lei Liu[4], Yanting Wang[2], and Shiyin Li[1]

[1] School of Information and Control Engineering, China University of Mining and Technology, Xuzhou, China
{lijunhe,lishiyin}@cumt.edu.cn
[2] School of Software, Northwestern Polytechnical University, Xi'an, China
yantingwang@nwpu.edu.cn
[3] Ministry of Industry and Information Technology, Nanjing University of Aeronautics and Astronautics, Nanjing, China
jiaziye@nuaa.edu.cn
[4] School of Electronic and Communication Engineering, Xi'an University of Posts and Telecommunications, Xi'an, China
leiliu@xupt.ecu.cn

**Abstract.** In the context of Space-Ground Integrated Networks (SGINs), conventional multi-path routing schemes face a significant challenge: the reduction of energy consumption. To tackle this issue, we have developed a comprehensive optimization framework integrating network resource scheduling with network routing for designing an energy-efficient multi-path routing over dynamic network topologies. A Dual-Scale Time-Varying Graph (DSTVG) model of SGINs is first presented, which models both the time-evolving network topology over large timescales and mission data transmission over small timescales. Based on the DSTVG model, the optimization problem is formulated as a Mixed-Integer Non-Linear Program (MINLP) aiming to minimize the total energy consumption of SGINs. Employing relaxation techniques, we reformulate the MINLP into a convex optimization problem, thereby obtaining an optimal solution in low computation cost. Simulation results verify the correctness and effectiveness of the proposed approach, which can significantly enhance the energy efficiency of multi-path routing in SGINs.

**Keywords:** Space-air-ground integrated network · Two-scale time-expanded graph · Routing strategy · Power allocation

## 1 Introduction

The sixth generation (6G) communication networks are mainly characterized with high transmission rate, low transmission delay, and wide communication

This work was supported in part by the National Natural Science Foundation of China under Grant 62201463.


Y. Liu et al. (Eds.): ChinaCom 2025, LNICST 711, pp. 35–47, 2027.
https://doi.org/10.1007/978-3-032-33662-0_4

coverage [1]. Industry and academia have reached to a consensus that low-latency Terrestrial Networks (TNs) alone can not achieve the vision of 6G, due to their high operation costs and limited geographical locations. Non-Terrestrial Networks (NTNs), consisting of both space and air networks, provide broad coverage and high throughput. NTNs and TNs together form Space-Ground Integrated Networks (SGINs) that achieve service continuity, ubiquity, and scalability required in 6G networks [5]. As such, SGINs have been recognized as a cornerstone to establish a global mobile communication network to enhance user experience in both densely populated areas and rural zones.

The SGIN constitutes a sophisticated three-layer 3-D network architecture composed of various heterogeneous network nodes in Terrestrial Layer (TL) and non-TL including Space Layer (SL) [6], as shown in Fig. 1. In the TL, heterogeneous TNs are strategically deployed to achieve wireless communication service coverage in densely populated urban areas. In the SL, LEO satellites, MEO satellites, and GEO satellites provide global-scale coverage with high-speed data transmission services, especially for remote, rural, and maritime areas. By seamlessly integrating these heterogeneous nodes and communication links including Inter-Satellite Links (ISLs) and Satellite-Ground Links (SGLs) across both TL and non-TL, the SGIN facilitates global connectivity for data exchange, sharing, and transmission among user terminals [3]. Effective management of heterogeneous network nodes and communication links within SGINs, while challenging, is of paramount importance to guarantee superior end-to-end transmission services. Consequently, the design of efficient routing strategies for SGINs has increasingly become a focal point in academic research [11].

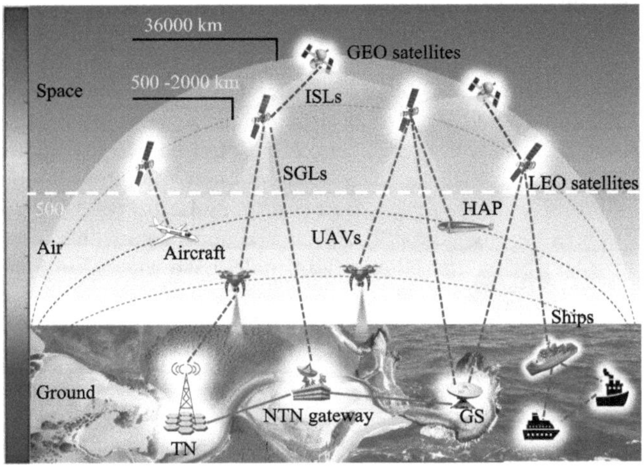


**Fig. 1.** SGIN.

In contrast to single-path routing schemes, multi-path routing schemes allocate several paths for each mission to fully exploit the availability of ISLs and

SGLs in SGINs. To approach the multi-path routing issues, the existing works resort to some efficient mathematical tools, such as graph theory [12], swarm intelligence [7], and Deep Reinforcement Learning (DRL) [9]. Specifically, Zhang *et al.* [12] explored the storage time aggregated graph to transform multi-path routing problem for maximizing the mission number in satellite networks into single-source-single sink multi-commodity flow problem. Ouyang *et al.* [7] proposed an Particle Swarm Optimization (PSO)-based algorithm to address the adaptive multi-path selection issue, aiming to balance the overhead and reliability of the SDN-based integrated satellite-terrestrial networks. The proposed PSO-based algorithm is tailored to the mesh network topology of satellite networks and is suitable for that all the paths has the same destination. Tsai *et al.* [9] proposed a DRL-based algorithm to address the multi-path total network latency minimization problem for LEO satellite networks, achieving multiple source-destination pair matching.

Furthermore, Tang *et al.* [8] combined with traditional network coding and multi-path routing protocols to achieve the coordination among multiple paths, aiming at the network throughput improvement of LEO satellite networks. Liu *et al.* [4] jointly optimized the Quality-of-Service and the load-balancing to guarantee the network stability of the LEO satellite networks. However, these multi-path routing schemes do not take energy consumption into account, thereby interrupting routing paths and deteriorating the routing performance. In this regard, Wang *et al.* [10] developed a computing-dependent multi-path transmission strategy by combining with communication and computation resources to minimize the total energy consumption of Satellite and Terrestrial Integrated Networks (STINs). In particular, the proposed scheme used the STIN time-expanded graph (STITEG) to discretize the dynamic topology of STIN, which is actually an adjacency matrix Graph. However the matrix would be so large when the number of time slots and satellites increase. To address the above issues, we jointly optimize link assignment, storage allocation, power control, and network routing to achieve low-cost energy-saving SGINs. Specifically, we investigate multi-path routing strategies that reduce energy consumption while considering both link capacity and node storage restrictions.

## 2 DSTVG Model

We consider a SGIN consisting of a set $\mathcal{U} = \{1, 2, ..., U\}$ of data collectors and a set $\mathcal{D} = \{1, 2, ..., D\}$ of data sinks. Data collectors incorporate space nodes consisting of Low Earth Orbit (LEO) satellites and Data Relay Satellites (DRSs), as well as terrestrial nodes including gateway nodes and Ground Stations (GSs). In the SGIN, data collectors forward their captured data on the ISLs and low signal-noise-ratio SGLs to a set of data sinks involving a set $\mathcal{R} = \{1, 2, ..., R\}$ of DRSs, a set $\mathcal{G} = \{1, 2, ..., G\}$ of GSs, and a set $\mathcal{L} = \{1, 2, ..., L\}$ of LEO satellites, i.e., $\mathcal{D} = \mathcal{R} \cup \mathcal{G} \cup \mathcal{L}$. Each network node is equipped with one transmit and receiver antenna.

Compared to TNs, Space-Ground Integrated Networks (SGINs) involving space nodes typify line-of-sight communication systems. This implies that two

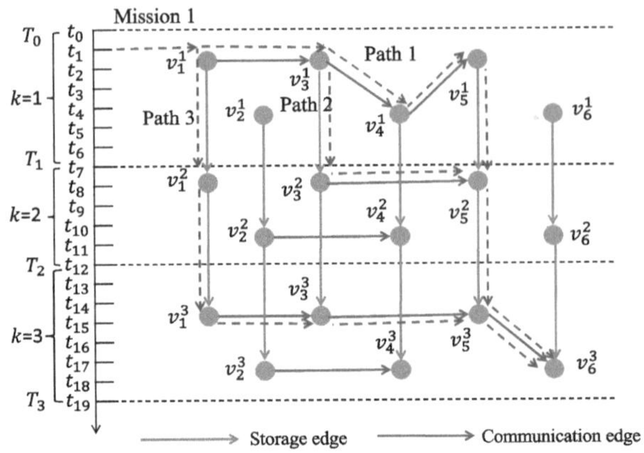


**Fig. 2.** An illustration of the proposed DSTVG model.

network nodes within SGINs can only exchange mission data when they come within each other's coverage range. We represent these coverage ranges using time windows, each characterized by a 2-tuple of start and end times. These windows subdivide the time axis into distinct intervals. We employ a large-timescale slot $k$ to denote the interval $[T_{k-1}, T_k)$, as illustrated in Fig. 2. To minimize the count of large-timescale slots, we amalgamate identical network topologies within any two consecutive slots. Let $\mathcal{K}$ signify the set of large-timescale slots. Moreover, we consistently discretize each large-timescale slot $k \in \mathcal{K}$ into a set of equally sized small-timescale slots, represented as $\mathcal{T}_k$.

Based on the set of dual-scale slots, we construct a Dual-Scale Time-varying Graph (DSTVG) $G_{\mathcal{T}}(\mathcal{V}, \mathcal{E}, \mathcal{W})$ to represent the network resources of SGINs, where $\mathcal{V}$ denotes the set of vertices, $\mathcal{E}$ represents the set of edges, and $\mathcal{W}$ indicates the set of weights. As shown in Fig. 2, a DSTVG $G_{\mathcal{T}}(\mathcal{V}, \mathcal{E}, \mathcal{W})$ is a weighted direction graph of $T$ layers, each corresponding to the network topology in a large-timescale slot. In particular, we let $\mathcal{V} = \{v_i^k, i \in \mathcal{U} \cup \mathcal{G}, k \in \mathcal{K}\}$, where vertex $v_i^k$ represents the network node $i$ in large-timescale slot $k$.

The set of edges $\mathcal{E}$ is composed of the set of communication edges $\mathcal{E}_{\text{Com}}$ and the set of storage edges $\mathcal{E}_{\text{Stor}}$, i.e., $\mathcal{E} = \mathcal{E}_{\text{Com}} \cup \mathcal{E}_{\text{Stor}}$. We let $\mathcal{E}_{\text{Com}} = \{(v_i^k, v_j^k) | i \neq j \in \mathcal{U} \cup \mathcal{D}, k \in \mathcal{K}\}$, where $(v_i^k, v_j^k)$ denotes the available communication link between vertexes $v_i^k$ and $v_j^k$. According to the types of communication links, we further divide $\mathcal{E}_{\text{Com}}$ into $\mathcal{E}_{\text{Com}}^{\text{ISL}}$ and $\mathcal{E}_{\text{Com}}^{\text{SGL}}$, i.e., $\mathcal{E}_{\text{Com}} = \mathcal{E}_{\text{Com}}^{\text{ISL}} \cup \mathcal{E}_{\text{Com}}^{\text{SGL}}$, such that $\mathcal{E}_{\text{Com}}^{\text{ISL}} = \{(v_i^k, v_j^k) | i \neq j \in \mathcal{R} \cup \mathcal{L}, k \in \mathcal{K}\}$ and $\mathcal{E}_{\text{Com}}^{\text{SGL}} = \{(v_i^k, v_j^k) | i \in \mathcal{R} \cup \mathcal{L}, j \in \mathcal{G}, k \in \mathcal{K}\} \cup \{(v_i^k, v_j^k) | j \in \mathcal{R} \cup \mathcal{L}, i \in \mathcal{G}, k \in \mathcal{K}\}$ respectively denote the edge set of ISLs and the edge set of SGLs. Let $\mathcal{E}_{\text{Stor}} = \{(v_j^k, v_j^{k+1}) | j \in \mathcal{U} \cup \mathcal{D}, k \in \mathcal{K}\}$ with $(v_j^k, v_j^{k+1})$ representing the storage edge of vertex $v_j^k$. Correspondingly, we have $\mathcal{W} = \mathcal{C} \cup \mathcal{B}$ with $\mathcal{C} = \{C_{v_i^k, v_j^k}(t)\}$ and $\mathcal{B} = \{B_{v_i^k}^{\max}\}$ respectively representing the set of weights on the communication links and the storage links. In particular, $C_{v_i^k, v_j^k}(t)$ represents the channel capacity of communication edge $(v_i^k, v_j^k)$ in small-timescale slot $t$ and $B^{\max}_{v_i^k}$ denotes the maximum storage space of vertex $v_i^k$.

# 3 System Model and Problem Formulation

## 3.1 System Model

We denote by $\mathcal{M} = \{1, 2, ..., M\}$ a set of missions. Each mission $m \in \mathcal{M}$ is modeled as a 5-tuple $(u_m, D_m, t_m, d_m, g_m)$, where $u_m$ indexes the data collector for producing mission $m$, $D_m$ denotes the data amount of mission $m$, $t_m$ represents the arrival time of mission $m$, $d_m$ is the deadline of mission $m$, and $g_m$ indicates the destination data sink for collecting the data of mission $m$. As such, any successful mission $m$ means that it is modeled as a flow $f_m$ first produced by data collector $u_m$ in arrival time $t_m$ and then delivered to a data sink before deadline $d_m$ via network route. Let $\mathcal{F} = \{f_m\}$ denote the set of all the flows.

In view of the diversity of network nodes of SGINs, we introduce two types of channel models to calculate the channel capacity for various communication links. The channel capacity of the ISL $(v_i^k, v_j^k) \in \mathcal{E}^{\mathrm{ISL}}_{\mathrm{Com}}$ in small-timescale slot $t \in \mathcal{T}_k$ is expressed as

$$C_{v_i^k, v_j^k}(t) = g^{\mathrm{ISL}}_{v_i^k, v_j^k}(t) P_{v_i^k, v_j^k}(t), \forall k, \tag{1}$$

where $P_{v_i^k, v_j^k}(t)$ is the transmit power of vertex $v_i^k$ in small-timescale slot $t$ and $g^{\mathrm{ISL}}_{v_i^k, v_j^k}(t)$ is the channel gain of the ISL $(v_i^k, v_j^k)$ in small-timescale slot $t$, given by

$$g^{\mathrm{ISL}}_{v_i^k, v_j^k}(t) = \frac{G^{\mathrm{tran}}_{v_i^k}(t) G^{\mathrm{rec}}_{v_j^k}(t) L_f(t) L_l(t)}{\kappa T_s (E_b/N_0)_{\mathrm{req}} M}, \forall t \in \mathcal{T}_k, k. \tag{2}$$

In (2), $G^{\mathrm{tran}}_{v_i^k}(t)$ denotes the transmit antenna gain of vertex $v_i^k$ in small-timescale slot $t$, $G^{\mathrm{rec}}_{v_j^k}(t)$ represents the data receiver antenna gain of vertex $v_j^k$ in small-timescale slot $t$, $L_f(t)$ is the free space loss in small-timescale slot $t$, $L_l(t)$ is the total line loss in small-timescale slot $t$, $\kappa$ is the Boltzmann's constant (in $JK^{-1}$), $T_s$ is the total system noise temperature (in $K$), $(E_b/N_0)_{\mathrm{req}}$ is the required ratio of received energy-per-bit to noise-density, and $M$ is the link margin [2].

The channel capacity of the SGL $(v_i^k, v_j^k) \in \mathcal{E}^{\mathrm{SGL}}_{\mathrm{Com}}$ in small-timescale slot $t$ can be computed by the Shannon formula:

$$C_{v_i^k, v_j^k}(t) = B_c \log_2 \left(1 + \gamma_{v_i^k, v_j^k}(t)\right), \forall t \in \mathcal{T}_k, k, \tag{3}$$

where $B_c$ is the link bandwidth and $\gamma_{v_i^k, v_j^k}(t)$ is the signal-to-noise ratio of edge $(v_i^k, v_j^k)$ in small-timescale $t$, given by

$$\gamma_{v_i^k, v_j^k}(t) = g^{\mathrm{SGL}}_{v_i^k, v_j^k}(t) P_{v_i^k, v_j^k}(t), \quad \forall t \in \mathcal{T}_k, k. \tag{4}$$

In (4), $g^{\mathrm{SGL}}_{v_i^k,v_j^k}(t)$ is the channel gain of the SGL $(v_i^k, v_j^k)$ in small-timescale slot $t$, calculated by

$$g^{\mathrm{SGL}}_{v_i^k,v_j^k}(t) = \frac{G^{\mathrm{tran}}_{v_i^k}(t)G^{\mathrm{rec}}_{v_j^k}(t)L_f(t)L_l(t)}{N_0}, \forall t \in \mathcal{T}_k, k, \tag{5}$$

where $N_0$ is the noise power [13].

We further define a variable $x_{v_i^k,v_j^k}(t) \in \{0,1\}$ to denote the link assignment strategy. Here, $x_{v_i^k,v_j^k}(t) = 1$ signifies that the link $(v_i^k, v_j^k) \in \mathcal{E}$ is chosen in the small-timescale slot $t \in \mathcal{T}_k$, while $x_{v_i^k,v_j^k}(t) = 0$ indicates the opposite. As such, the total energy consumption of SGINs is evaluated by

$$E^{\mathrm{total}} = \sum_{\substack{k\in\mathcal{K}\\ t\in\mathcal{T}_k}} \sum_{(v_i^k,v_j^k)\in\mathcal{E}} x_{v_i^k,v_j^k}(t)E^{\mathrm{dyn}}_{v_i^k,v_j^k}(t). \tag{6}$$

In (6), $E^{\mathrm{dyn}}_{v_i^k,v_j^k}(t)$ is the dynamic energy consumption of the mission data transmission from $v_i^k$ to $v_j^k$ in any small-timescale slot $t \in \mathcal{T}_k$, expressed by

$$E^{\mathrm{dyn}}_{v_i^k,v_j^k}(t) = P_{v_i^k,v_j^k}(t)\tau, \quad \forall (v_i^k, v_j^k), t \in \mathcal{T}_k. \tag{7}$$

### 3.2 Problem Formulation

We introduce the following constraint to ensure that for any data sending vertex $v_i^k$ within any small-timescale $t$, at most one data receiving vertex is selected for receiving its data:

$$\sum_{v_j^k:(v_i^k,v_j^k)\in\mathcal{E}} x_{v_i^k,v_j^k}(t) \le 1, \quad \forall v_i^k, t \in \mathcal{T}_k, k. \tag{8}$$

Similarly, constraint (9) is used to guarantee that for any data receiving vertex $v_j^k$ within any small-timescale $t$, at most one data sending vertex is selected for sending its data:

$$\sum_{v_i^k:(v_i^k,v_j^k)\in\mathcal{E}} x_{v_i^k,v_j^k}(t) \le 1, \quad \forall v_j^k, t \in \mathcal{T}_k, k. \tag{9}$$

Moreover, we introduce constraint (10) to indicate that any vertex in DSTVG cannot send and receive data at the same time, i.e., for any $v_i^k, t \in \mathcal{T}_k, k$,

$$\sum_{v_j^k:(v_i^k,v_j^k)\in\mathcal{E}} x_{v_i^k,v_j^k}(t) + \sum_{v_j^k:(v_j^k,v_i^k)\in\mathcal{E}} x_{v_j^k,v_i^k}(t) \le 1. \tag{10}$$

We further introduce route variable $\lambda^{f_m}_{v_i^k,v_j^k}(t) \ge 0$ to indicate the fraction of data amount $D_m$ of flow $f_m$ on edge $(v_i^k, v_j^k)$ in small-timescale slot $t$. The following constraint reveals that the amount of the flows allocated to any edge $(v_i^k, v_j^k)$ in any small-timescale slot is constrained by the communication capacity, i.e.,

$$\sum_{f_m \in \mathcal{F}} \lambda^{f_m}_{v_i^k, v_j^k}(t) D_m \le x_{v_i^k, v_j^k}(t) C_{v_i^k, v_j^k}(t)\tau, \forall t \in \mathcal{T}_k, k. \tag{11}$$

We introduce the storage strategy variable $b^t_{v_i^k}(f_m) \ge 0$ to represent the fraction of storage data amount of vertex $v_i^k$ in small-timescale $t$. The following constraint indicates that all the data amount of any flow $f_m$ should be fully collected by collector $u_m$ at $t_m$:

$$b^t_{v_i^k}(f_m) = 1, \forall f_m, v_i^k = u_m, t = t_m. \tag{12}$$

Similarly, the following constraint reflects that all the data amount of any flow $f_m$ should be delivered to the destination $g_m$ before deadline $d_m$, i.e.,

$$b^t_{v_i^k}(f_m) = 1, \forall f_m, v_i^k = g_m, t \le d_m. \tag{13}$$

Furthermore, constraint (14) is used to enforce the flow conservation for any network node:

$$\sum_{v_j^k : (v_j^k, v_i^k) \in \mathcal{E}} \lambda^{f_m}_{v_j^k, v_i^k}(t) - \sum_{v_j^k : (v_i^k, v_j^k) \in \mathcal{E}} \lambda^{f_m}_{v_i^k, v_j^k}(t)$$
$$= b^t_{v_i^k}(f_m) - b^{t-1}_{v_i^k}(f_m), \forall v_i^k, f_m, t \in \Gamma_k(f_m), \tag{14}$$

where $\Gamma_k(f_m) = [t_m + 1, d_m] \bigcap \mathcal{T}_k$. In addition, the storage data amount $b^t_{v_i^k}$ of any vertex $v_i^k$ in any small-time slot does not exceed its buffer size $B^{\max}_{v_i^k}$, i.e.,

$$0 \le \sum_{f_m \in \mathcal{F}} b^t_{v_i^k}(f_m) D_m \le B^{\max}_{v_i^k}, \quad \forall v_i^k, t \in \mathcal{T}_k, k. \tag{15}$$

Constraint (16) dictates that the quantity of storage and release of $v_i^k$ must not exceed its inflow and outflow amounts, i.e.,

$$- \sum_{v_j^k : (v_i^k, v_j^k) \in \mathcal{E}_{\text{Com}}} x_{v_i^k, v_j^k}(t) \le b^t_{v_i^k}(f_m) - b^{t-1}_{v_i^k}(f_m)$$
$$\le \sum_{v_j^k : (v_j^k, v_i^k) \in \mathcal{E}_{\text{Com}}} x_{v_j^k, v_i^k}(t), \quad \forall v_i^k, f_m, t \in \mathcal{T}_k, k. \tag{16}$$

Constraint (17) represents the transmit power control range:

$$P_{\min} \le P_{v_i^k, v_j^k}(t) \le P_{\max}, \forall t \in \mathcal{T}_k, k, \tag{17}$$

where $P_{\min}$ and $P_{\max}$ denote the minimum transmit power and the maximum transmit power, respectively. We use constraint (18) to represent that the data amount of any mission remains unchanged for any small-timescale slot:

$$\sum_{v_i^k \in \mathcal{V}} b^t_{v_i^k}(f_m) = 1, \quad \forall f_m, k, t \in [t_m + 1, \mathcal{T}_k], k. \tag{18}$$

To minimize the total energy consumption of SGINs, we utilize the DSTVG model to formulate the multi-path routing problem into the following MINLP:

$$\begin{aligned} \textbf{P0}: \quad & \min_{\boldsymbol{x},\boldsymbol{b},\boldsymbol{P},\boldsymbol{\lambda}} \quad E^{\text{total}} \\ & \text{s.t. } (8) - (18), \\ & x_{v_i^k,v_j^k}(t) \in \{0,1\}, \forall v_i^k \neq v_j^k, t \in \mathcal{T}_k, k, && (19) \\ & 0 \leq \lambda_{v_i^k,v_j^k}^{f_m}(t) \leq 1, \forall v_i^k \neq v_j^k, f_m, t \in \mathcal{T}_k, k, && (20) \\ & 0 \leq b_{v_i^k}^t(f_m) \leq 1, \forall v_i^k, f_m, t \in \mathcal{T}_k, k, && (21) \end{aligned}$$

where $\boldsymbol{x} = \{x_{v_i^k,v_j^k}(t)\}$, $\boldsymbol{b} = \{b_{v_i^k}^t(f_m)\}$, $\boldsymbol{P} = \{P_{v_i^k,v_j^k}(t)\}$, and $\boldsymbol{\lambda} = \{\lambda_{v_i^k,v_j^k}^{f_m}(t)\}$.

## 4 DSTVG-Aided Reformulation and Solution

In **P0**, the decision variables $(\boldsymbol{x}, \boldsymbol{b}, \boldsymbol{P}, \boldsymbol{\lambda})$ can be classified into two distinct categories: $(\boldsymbol{x}, \boldsymbol{b}, \boldsymbol{\lambda})$ and $\boldsymbol{P}$. Moreover, the variables $(\boldsymbol{x}, \boldsymbol{b}, \boldsymbol{\lambda})$ can be further divided into path selection $(\boldsymbol{x}, \boldsymbol{b})$ and traffic allocation $\boldsymbol{\lambda}$. To simplify the problem-solving process for **P0**, we introduce a new continuous variable that simultaneously represents both path selection and traffic allocation. This is followed by an introduction to path construction, after which we present the reformulation and solution of **P0**.

### 4.1 Path Construction

We define $\mathcal{F}(v_i^k, v_j^{k'}) = \{\rho_\sigma(v_i^k, v_j^{k'})\}$ as the set of all possible paths, corresponding to large-timescale slots, originating from vertex $v_i^k$ and terminating at vertex $v_j^{k'}$ within a DSTVG $G_\mathcal{T}(\mathcal{V}, \mathcal{E}, \mathcal{W})$, where $\rho_\sigma(v_i^k, v_j^{k'})$ signifies the $\sigma$-th candidate path within set $\mathcal{F}(v_i^k, v_j^{k'})$. For instance, as shown in Fig. 2, $\mathcal{F}(v_1^1, v_6^3)$ is consist of three candidate paths $\rho_1(v_1^1, v_6^3)$, $\rho_2(v_1^1, v_6^3)$, and $\rho_3(v_1^1, v_6^3)$, i.e., $\mathcal{F}(v_1^1, v_6^3) = \{\rho_1(v_1^1, v_6^3), \rho_2(v_1^1, v_6^3), \rho_3(v_1^1, v_6^3)\}$, where $\rho_1(v_1^1, v_6^3) = (v_1^1, v_3^1, v_4^1, v_5^1, v_5^2, v_5^3, v_6^3)$, $\rho_2(v_1^1, v_6^3) = (v_1^1, v_3^1, v_3^2, v_5^2, v_5^3, v_6^3)$, and $\rho_3(v_1^1, v_6^3) = (v_1^1, v_1^2, v_1^3, v_3^3, v_5^3, v_6^3)$.

In the DSTVG $G_\mathcal{T}(\mathcal{V}, \mathcal{E}, \mathcal{W})$, it is observed that for any given vertex and its adjacent vertex, there must be a storage edge spanning two successive large-timescale slots. Additionally, a communication edge may exist within the same large-timescale slot. Therefore, it is crucial to determine whether a vertex $v_i^k$ stores or transmits any mission $m$ in a small-timescale $t = t_m$, when the mission arrives at the vertex within the large-timescale slot $k$ of the DSTVG $G_\mathcal{T}(\mathcal{V}, \mathcal{E}, \mathcal{W})$. If a communication edge exists, then vertex $v_i^k$ has the option to either immediately transmit the data of mission $m$ to an adjacent vertex in the small-timescale $t_m$ or to store the data across several small-timescale slots before initiating transmission. Conversely, if no communication edge is present, vertex $v_i^k$ stores the data of mission $m$ until the end of the current large-timescale slot, after which it determines whether to continue storing the data or proceed with its transmission in the subsequent large-timescale slot. It is imperative to ensure that mission $m$ reaches its target vertex $g_m$ before the deadline $d_m$. The path selection process described above necessitates integration with small-timescale slots.

Building on the definition of $F(v_i^k, v_j^{k'})$, we further define $\Gamma(v_i^k(t), v_j^{k'}(t')) = \{\varrho_\sigma(v_i^k(t), v_j^{k'}(t'))\}$ as the set of paths corresponding to small-timescale slots, where $\varrho_\sigma(v_i^k(t), v_j^{k'}(t))$ indicates the $\sigma$-th candidate small-timescale time slot path within set $\Gamma(v_i^k(t), v_j^{k'}(t'))$. These paths originate from vertex $v_i^k(t)$ in small-timescale time slot $t$ and terminate at vertex $v_j^{k'}(t')$ in small-timescale time slot $t'$. Compared to $\rho_\sigma(v_i^k, v_j^{k'}) \in F(v_i^k, v_j^{k'})$, $\varrho_\sigma(v_i^k(t), v_j^{k'}(t)) \in \Gamma(v_i^k(t), v_j^{k'}(t'))$ includes small-timescale time slots. Therefore, multiple paths of small-timescale time slots are derived from a single path of $\rho_\sigma(v_i^k, v_j^{k'}) \in F(v_i^k, v_j^{k'})$. For example, as shown in Fig. 2, $\rho_1(v_1^1, v_6^3) = (v_1^1, v_3^1, v_4^1, v_5^1, v_5^2, v_5^3, v_6^3)$ can generate multiple paths of small-timescale time slots, such as $\varrho_1(v_1^1(t_1), v_6^3(t_{14})) = (v_1^1(t_1), v_3^1(t_2), v_4^1(t_3), v_5^1(t_7), v_5^2(t_{11}), v_5^3(t_{13}), v_6^3(t_{14}))$, $\varrho_2(v_1^1(t_2), v_6^3(t_{14})) = (v_1^1(t_2), v_3^1(t_3), v_4^1(t_4), v_5^1(t_7), v_5^2(t_9), v_5^3(t_{13}), v_6^3(t_{14}))$, and $\varrho_3(v_1^1(t_3), v_6^3(t_{14})) = (v_1^1(t_3), v_3^1(t_4), v_4^1(t_5), v_5^1(t_7), v_5^2(t_9), v_5^3(t_{13}), v_6^3(t_{14}))$. That is, we can use the set of $F(v_i^k, v_j^{k'}) = \{\rho_\sigma(v_i^k, v_j^{k'})\}$ to obtain the set of $\Gamma(v_i^k(t), v_j^{k'}(t')) = \{\varrho_\sigma(v_i^k(t), v_j^{k'}(t'))\}$ within a DSTVG $G_\mathcal{T}(\mathcal{V}, \mathcal{E}, \mathcal{W})$.

Furthermore, we denote $\Psi_{f_m}$ by the set of feasible paths for any mission $m$, constructed using the set of $\Gamma(v_i^k(t), v_j^{k'}(t'))$. Specifically, any path $\varrho_\sigma(v_i^k(t), v_j^{k'}(t')) \in \Gamma(v_i^k(t), v_j^{k'}(t'))$ is incorporated into $\Psi_{f_m}$, if its originating vertex, $v_i^k(t)$, corresponds to the data collector $u_m$ in small-timescale $t$ that is equal to the arrival time $t_m$. Moreover, its terminating vertex, $v_j^{k'}(t')$, should be the destination data sink $g_m$ in small-timescale $t'$ that is before the deadline $d_m$ and thus satisfies $t' \leq d_m$. Therefore, $\Psi_{f_m}$ can be expressed as follows:

$$\begin{aligned}\Psi_{f_m} = \{\psi_{f_m} | \psi_{f_m} = \varrho_\sigma(v_i^k(t), v_j^{k'}(t')) \in \Gamma(v_i^k(t), v_j^{k'}(t')),\\ v_i^k(t) = u_m, t = t_m, v_j^{k'}(t') = g_m, t' \leq d_m\}.\end{aligned}$$

Finally, we define $\Omega^m_{v_i^k(t), v_j^k(t)}$ as the subset of paths in $\Psi_{f_m}$ that incorporate communication link $(v_i^k(t), v_j^k(t))$.

### 4.2 Reformulation and Problem Solution

We introduce continuous variable $\pi_{\psi_{f_m}} \in [0, 1]$ to indicate the traffic of flow $f_m$ allocated to the path $\psi_{f_m} \in \Psi_{f_m}$, which satisfies the following constraint:

$$0 \leq \pi_{\psi_{f_m}} \leq 1, \forall f_m, \psi_{f_m}. \tag{22}$$

For each flow $f_m$, its all the traffic amount should be allocated to the set of feasible paths $\Psi_m$, i.e.,

$$\sum_{\psi_{f_m} \in \Psi_{f_m}} \pi_{\psi_{f_m}} = 1, \forall f_m. \tag{23}$$

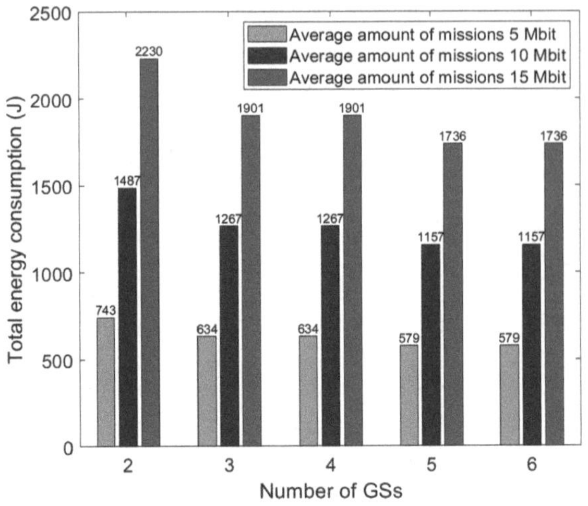


**Fig. 3.** Total energy consumption versus the number of GSs.

The communication capacity constraint for each communication link $(v_i^k(t), v_j^k(t))$ in any small-timescale slot $t$ should be satisfied:

$$\sum_{m \in \mathcal{M}} \sum_{\psi_{fm} \in \Omega^m_{v_i^k(t), v_j^k(t)}} \pi_{\psi_{fm}} D_m \leq C_{v_i^k, v_j^k}(t), \tag{24}$$

which indicates that all traffic amount allocated to the paths incorporating the each communication link $(v_i^k(t), v_j^k(t))$ should not exceed its capacity in any small-timescale slot.

The storage capacity constraint for each storage link $(v_i^k(t), v_i^k(t+1))$ within the same large-timescale slot $k$ reveals that the storage data amount of vertex $v_i^k(t+1)$ must be less than the buffer size $B^{\max}_{v_i^k}$, i.e.,

$$\sum_{m \in \mathcal{M}} \sum_{v_i^k(t) \in \mathcal{V}} \sum_{\psi_{fm} \in \Omega^m_{v_i^k(t), v_i^k(t)}} \pi_{\psi_{fm}} D_m \leq B^{\max}_{v_i^k}, \forall t, k. \tag{25}$$

Similarly, the storage capacity constraint for each storage link $(v_i^k(t), v_i^{k+1}(t+1))$ within the adjacent large-timescale slots $k$ and $k+1$ is given by

$$\sum_{m \in \mathcal{M}} \sum_{v_i^k(t) \in \mathcal{V}} \sum_{\psi_{fm} \in \Omega^m_{v_i^k(t), v_i^{k+1}(t)}} \pi_{\psi_{fm}} D_m \leq B^{\max}_{v_i^{k+1}}, \forall t, k. \tag{26}$$

Based on the above constraints, we reformulate **P0** into the following optimization problem:

$$\mathbf{P1}: \min_{\boldsymbol{\pi}, \boldsymbol{P}} \sum_{\substack{k \in \mathcal{K} \\ t \in \mathcal{T}_k}} \sum_{(v_i^k, v_j^k) \in \mathcal{E}} P_{v_i^k, v_j^k}(t)\tau$$
$$\text{s.t. } (17), (22) - (26),$$

where $\boldsymbol{\pi} = \{\pi_{\psi_{fm}}\}$. Compared with **P0, P1** is more tractable since it is a convex problem with respect to the continuous variables $(\boldsymbol{\pi}, \boldsymbol{P})$. As such, we can use some convex optimization solvers (e.g., Gurobi, SDPT3, SeDuMi) to solve **P1** to obtain an optimal solution in polynomial time.

## 5 Simulation Evaluation

The scheduling horizon spans from 20 March 2025 14:40:00.00 to 20 March 2025 16:20:00.00. We employ the software tools from Anaconda and the Satellite Tool Kit (STK) to develop two co-simulation platforms. Scenario 1 features a Walker constellation of four LEO satellites, six GSs, and one DRS, designed using STK. These LEO satellites are evenly distributed across four orbital planes, each with an altitude of 550 Km and a phase factor of 1. This results in a Walker constellation configuration code of 4/1/1. In this scenario, the number of GSs is systematically increased from two to six. The coordinates for these stations are as follows: (39.61°N, 115.89°E), (29.66°N, 91.1°E), (52.2°N, 106.4°W),(42.81°S, 147.44°E),(47.6°N, 52.68°W), and (49.6°N, 34.5°E).

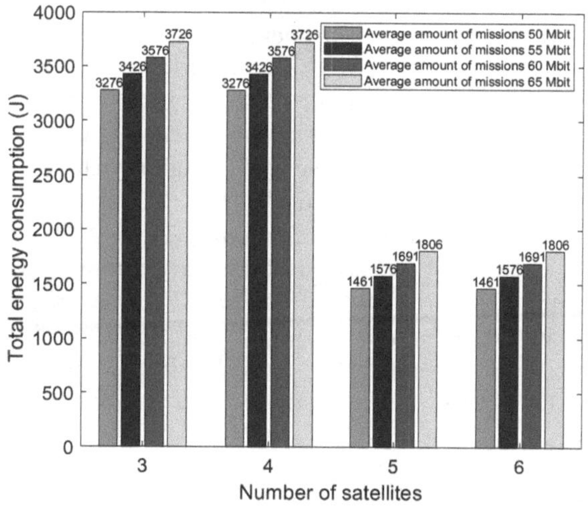


**Fig. 4.** Total energy consumption versus the number of satellites.

Scenario 2, also designed using STK, comprises two Walker constellations, two GSs, and one DRS. The first constellation contains three LEO satellites spread across three orbital planes, each at an altitude of 550 Km with a phase factor of 1, leading to a configuration code of 3/1/1. The second constellation similarly consists of three LEO satellites on three distinct orbital planes, but at an altitude of 1,100 km, resulting in a configuration code of 3/1/1. In this simulation, the number of LEO satellites is augmented from 3 to 6 by sequentially adding satellites from the second Walker constellation based on their individual satellite numbers to the first constellation. The coordinates for the two GSs are: (39.61°N, 115.89°E) and (47.60°N, 52.68°W). The DRS is located at a longitude of 0°E.

We set the small-timescale slot length to 1 s and define a total of 100 small-scale time slots. We randomly generate tasks from LEO satellites within these small-timescale slots. The data volume sizes are established as 5 Mbit, 10 Mbit, and 15 Mbit respectively for Scenario 1, and 50 Mbit, 55 Mbit, 60 Mbit, and 65 Mbit respectively for Scenario 2. The maximum storage capacity of each is designated as 1000 Mbit. We allocate $G^{\text{tran}}_{v_i^{T_k}}(t) = 37\,\text{dB}$, $G^{\text{rec}}_{v_i^{T_k}}(t) = 37\,\text{dB}$, $L_f(t) = 10^{-23}$, $L_l(t) = 1$, $\kappa = 1.38054 * 10^{23}\,\text{JK}^{-1}$, $T_s = 316.2278\,\text{K}$, $(E_b/N_0)_{\text{req}} = 9.6\,\text{dB}$, $B_c = 4 * 10^{10}\,\text{Hz}$, and $M = 1.4125\,\text{dB}$. To address **P1**, we employ Anaconda software to activate the Gurobi 11.0 solver.

Figure 3 plots the total energy consumption versus the number of GSs for different average amount of mission. In Fig. 3, it is observed that as the number of GSs increases, the total energy consumption for SGIN decreases correspondingly, until it eventually stabilizes. This can be attributed to the creation of more, yet shorter, transmission paths as the number of GSs rises. The SGIN then prioritizes these shorter paths for transmission, thereby reducing the overall energy consumption. However, upon reaching the minimum path length, further reduction becomes challenging. At this stage, each task selects the shortest possible path, resulting in an unchanged total energy consumption. Additionally, from Fig. 3, it is evident that an increase in the average task volume also escalates the total energy consumption. This is due to the heightened data volume of tasks, necessitating the selection of additional paths for task transmission.

Figure 4 shows the total energy consumption against the number of satellites for varying average mission amount. In Fig. 4, it is observed that an increase in the number of satellites leads to a corresponding decrease in the energy consumption of SGIN, until it eventually stabilizes. This trend can be attributed to the incorporation of LEO satellites as relay satellites. As the number of these relay satellites grows, more numerous yet shorter transmission paths are created. Consequently, the SGIN tends to select the shortest path for transmission, thereby reducing the overall energy consumption. However, beyond a certain point, further additions of satellites do not significantly alter the path lengths, having already reached their minimum. Hence, each task begins to utilize the shortest available path, resulting in no further changes in the total energy consumption. Additionally, it is evident from Fig. 4 that a rise in the average data volume of missions corresponds to an increase in the total energy consumption of SGIN. This because the higher volume of data requiring the selection of more extensive transmission paths.

## References


1. Chen, X., Tan, J., Kang, L., Tang, F., Zhao, M., Kato, N.: Frequency selective surface toward 6G communication systems: a contemporary survey. IEEE Commun. Surveys Tuts. **26**(3), 1635–1675 (2024). 3rd Quart
2. Golkar, A., i Cruz, I.L.: The federated satellite systems paradigm: concept and business case evaluation. Acta Astronaut. **111**, 230–248 (2015)
3. He, L., Jia, Z., Guo, K., Gan, H., Han, Z., Yuen, C.: Online joint data offloading and power control for space-air-ground integrated networks. IEEE Trans. Wireless Commun. **23**(12), 18126–18141 (2024)
4. Liu, Q., Li, X., Ji, H., Zhang, H.: Multi-path routing algorithm with joint optimization of load-balancing for cluster-based LEO satellite networks. In: Proc. IEEE IC-NIDC, pp. 264–268, Beijing, China (2023). https://doi.org/10.1109/IC-NIDC59918.2023.10390619
5. Mahboob, S., Liu, L.: Revolutionizing future connectivity: a contemporary survey on AI-empowered satellite-based non-terrestrial networks in 6G. IEEE Commun. Surveys Tuts **26**(2), 1279–1321 (2024). 2nd Quart
6. Mao, S., Liu, L., Hou, X., Atiquzzaman, M., Yang, K.: Multi-domain resource management for space-air-ground integrated sensing, communication, and computation networks. IEEE J. Sel. Areas Commun. **42**(12), 3380–3394 (2024). https://doi.org/10.1109/JSAC.2024.3459026
7. Ouyang, M., et al.: Flow granularity multi-path transmission optimization design for satellite networks. In: Proc. IEEE WCNC, Glasgow, United Kingdom, pp. 1–6 (2023). https://doi.org/10.1109/WCNC55385.2023.10118901
8. Tang, F., Zhang, H., Yang, L.T.: Multipath cooperative routing with efficient acknowledgement for LEO satellite networks. IEEE Trans. Mobile Comput. **18**(1), 179–192 (2019)
9. Tsai, K.C., Fan, L., Wang, L.C., Lent, R., Han, Z.: Multi-commodity flow routing for large-scale LEO satellite networks using deep reinforcement learning. In: IEEE WCNC, Austin, TX, USA, pp. 626–631 (2022). https://doi.org/10.1109/WCNC51071.2022.9771734
10. Wang, C., Ren, Z., Cheng, W., Zhang, H.: CDMR: effective computing-dependent multi-path routing strategies in satellite and terrestrial integrated networks. IEEE Trans. Netw. Sci. Eng. **9**(5), 3715–3730 (2022)
11. Zhang, J., Wang, K., Li, R., Chang, Z., Zhang, X., Wang, W.: MaCro: mega-constellations routing systems with multi-edge cross-domain features. IEEE Wireless Commun. **30**(6), 69–76 (2023)
12. Zhang, T., Li, H., Zhang, S., Li, J., Shen, H.: STAG-based QoS support routing strategy for multiple missions over the satellite networks. IEEE Trans. Commun. **67**(10), 6912–6924 (2019). https://doi.org/10.1109/TCOMM.2019.2929757
13. Zhou, D., Sheng, M., Wang, Y., Li, J., Han, Z.: Machine learning-based resource allocation in satellite networks supporting internet of remote things. IEEE Trans. Wireless Commun. **20**(10), 6606–6621 (2021)

# Improved RT-DETR Model for Blind Parameter Estimation of FH Signals Under VLF Interference

Qinghua Ying[1,2], Tiantian Zhang[1,2], and Dongyang Xu[1,2](✉)

[1] Information and Communications Engineering, Xi'an Jiaotong University, Xi'an 710049, China
{2213611676,tiantianzhang}@stu.xjtu.edu.cn, xudongyang@xjtu.edu.cn
[2] State Key Laboratory of Integrated Services Networks, Xidian University, Xi'an, China

**Abstract.** In pervasive Very-Low Frequency (VLF) communication environment, significant challenges arise in the reliable detection and blind parameter estimation of frequency hopping (FH) signals. In this paper, we proposed an improved RT-DETR for blind parameter estimation of FH signals. By deeply identifying the unique characteristics of FH signals in time–frequency (TF) grid and matching it with RMT backbone, we are able to generate a powerful model, named improved RT-DETR to better detect FH signals. To begin, we employ S Transform to generate the TF diagram of the FH signals. Second, based on the diagram, we formulate an improved RT-DETR model which is then utilized for precise parameter estimation of the FH hops. Finally, simulation results show that under the improved RT-DETR model, S Transform is superior to STFT under low signal-to-noise ratios (SNR). Moreover, the improved RT-DETR surpasses YoloV8, YoloV9, and RT-DETR across various SNR, under both S Transform and STFT, indicating the effectiveness of proposed scheme for FH signals and robustness under low SNR and VLF interference.

**Keywords:** VLF Communication · Frequency Hopping · S Transform · Deep Learning · RT-DETR

## 1 Introduction

Very-Low Frequency (VLF) signals exhibit resistance to significant signal loss, multipath interference, and challenges associated with underwater environments,

This work was supported in part by the Open Research Fund of State Key Laboratory of Integrated Services Networks, Xidian University, under Grant ISN25-19, in part by the National Key Research and Development Program of China under Grant 2022YFB2902203.


Y. Liu et al. (Eds.): ChinaCom 2025, LNICST 711, pp. 48–59, 2027.
https://doi.org/10.1007/978-3-032-33662-0_6

including poor visibility and high levels of oceanic noise. This facilitates information exchange among miniature bionic robots and supports underwater wireless communication [1–3]. However, electromagnetic interference within this frequency band poses a significant challenge due to nonlinear interactions among emissions, complicating prediction and mitigation efforts.

Frequency-Hopping Spread Spectrum (FHSS) is a technique that is extensively utilized in both commercial and military applications. The primary rationale for its widespread adoption is its inherent characteristic of being difficult to detect and intercepted, agility, and resilience against jamming [4]. In FHSS, the carrier frequency of the signal is rapidly changed in a pseudo-random pattern, spreading the base-band signal across the frequency hopping (FH) range [5]. The properties of FHSS, such as resistance to jamming and a reduced likelihood of interception, while advantageous, also introduce a significant security concern. This is particularly relevant in scenarios where unauthorized entities might manipulate these characteristics to engage in illicit operations within licensed frequency ranges.

Beyond anti-jamming performance, secure and low-latency device authentication is critical in modern IIoT deployments over 5G, where initial access optimizations can introduce new attack surfaces; cross-layer, privacy-preserving approaches have been proposed to mitigate these risks [6].

In the area of spectrum sensing, blind parameter estimation of frequency hopping signals involves determining key characteristics including hopping frequency, hopping time and so forth [7]. Blind parameter estimation is transitionally done by using advanced signal processing techniques while being enhanced by exploring deep learning (DL) [8–14]. The challenges in this area encompass three aspects. First, it is challenging to accurately extract and separate the features of non-noise signals under low signal-to-noise ratios (SNR) conditions in VLF communications. Second, it is hard to distinguish FH signals from interference and therefore exhaustive when estimating signal parameters. Third, how to develop a unified and stable DL model to deal with signal data under various SNR levels is crucial.

Strategies utilizing time–frequency analysis (TFA) facilitate the representation of signal attributes within the TF domain, offering a viable approach to address the initial challenge. Short-time Fourier Transform (STFT) is a extensively applied method in this field [8–12]. However, this technique suffers from its fixed time–frequency (TF) resolution trade-off, susceptibility to windowing effects, spectral leakage and the added complexity of handling overlapping windows. The S Transform (ST) [15] offers variable resolution analysis, directly linked to Fourier spectrum, providing improved time–frequency localization and reduced cross-term interference, which enhances the analysis and interpretation of complex signals. In this research, the ST is applied to analyze the time–frequency attributes of FH signals.

Many researchers employed DL in detecting or blind parameter estimating of FH signals. The work in [11] employed a hybrid CNN/RNN-based scheme leveraging multiple spectrograms, demonstrating superior performance over conventional methods and the CNN-only model, showcasing robustness in blind detection scenarios. A semantic segmentation network, Deeplabv3+, was employed in [12], demonstrating superior performance compared to constant false alarm rate detection methods. Authors of [13] proposed an adaptive detection method that used compressive sensing theory and designed an adaptive measurement matrix by optimizing it for task-specific information and incorporating ANN. In [14], the researchers proposed an optimized generalized S Transform combined with a ResNet for FH signal detection, demonstrating improved detection performance and reduced computational complexity.

However, these schemes have not effectively addressed the challenges posed by low SNR and interference. Recently, the Real-Time Detection Transformer (RT-DETR) model [16] has been introduced, presenting a novel approach to object detection technology. Its uncertainty-minimal query selection and efficient hybrid encoder, which employs self-attention mechanisms on high-level features that possess a more profound semantic depth, enhance the connectivity among conceptual entities, thereby improving object localization and recognition in subsequent modules. Additionally, this Transformer-based detector eliminates the need for Non-Maximum Suppression and obviates the requirement to specify post-processing thresholds due to its end-to-end architecture, enhancing its adaptability under different SNR conditions [17], tackling the third challenge aforementioned. We find that RT-DETR model can accommodate above challenges well, and in this paper, we verify its effectiveness through simulations.

Moreover, to better address the challenges and enhance the applicability of the RT-DETR model for detection and blind parameter estimation, after thoroughly recognizing the unique features of FH signals in the TF grid, we found that the RMT [18] backbone, which incorporates a spatial decay matrix based on Manhattan distance to improve Self-Attention, forming the Manhattan Self-Attention (MaSA) mechanism with a explicit spatial prior, can significantly enhance the efficacy of the RT-DETR model.

Therefore, we propose a scheme of FH signal detection and blind parameter estimation for VHF interference environment, leveraging ST and improved RT-DETR model with the RMT backbone. The contribution of this work is summarized as follows:

- To cope with low SNR conditions and VLF interference, we employ ST to obtain the TF diagram for the detection and blind parameter estimation of FH signals, thus reducing the effect of intense noise and providing more valuable information for model.
- We find that utilizing RMT as the backbone can incorporate more spatial prior information of TF diagram into the sub-process of RT-DETR model and enlarge the receptive field while more focusing on information around the center of frequency hop in TF diagram, thus improving the performance of RT-DETR model.
- Simulation results show that our propose architecture can outperforms several typical DL architectures, such as RT-DETR, YOLOv8, YOLOv9, under various SNR levels in VLF FH signal dataset. Especially when SNR is higher

than -12 dB, our scheme maintains the $AP_{50-95}$ value over 0.73, while achieving the $AP_{50}$ value approach 1. This demonstrates the superior ability of our proposed architecture in detecting FH signals and its robustness in VLF communication conditions.

The rest of this paper is organized as follows: The VLF environment is modeled in Sect. 2. The scheme we proposed is presented in Sect. 3. Section 4 details the comparative performance analysis among the schemes we employ. Finally, Sect. 5 concludes this paper.

## 2 VLF Environment Modeling

VLF interference arises from the simultaneous emissions of electromagnetic waves from various sources in a specific environment, significantly complicating the electromagnetic landscape. This interference spans a broad spectrum of frequencies, characterized by nonlinear interactions among different electromagnetic emissions, making prediction and mitigation efforts particularly challenging. Typically, the FH signal experiences interference from fixed-frequency signals, linear-frequency modulation (LFM) signals, and burst signals [19]. After channel equalization, the modeling of VLF environment $c(t)$, which includes FH signals $s_{fh}(t)$, M LFM signals $l_m(t)$, N fixed frequency signals $f_n(t)$, K burst signals $b_k(t)$ and Additional Gaussian White Noise (AWGN) $n_0(t)$ characterized by a mean of zero and a variance of $\sigma^2$, is formulated as

$$c(t) = s_{fh}(t) + \sum_{m=1}^{M} l_m(t) + \sum_{n=1}^{N} f_n(t) + \sum_{k=1}^{K} b_k(t) + n_0(t). \tag{1}$$

Considering the FH signal has a hopping time of $T_m$, we can observe $G$ hops during the observation period $T_0$. The carrier frequency of the $g$th hop is represented by $f_g$. Given the first hop in the observation time may not be complete, the duration can be denoted as $t_0$. Then the $s_{fh}(t)$ can be stated as

$$s_{fh}(t) = a_g \sum_{g=1}^{G} e^{j(2\pi f_g t_g + \phi_g)} \text{rect}\left(\frac{t_g}{T_m}\right), \tag{2}$$

where $a_g$ is the amplitude of the FH signal, $\phi_g$ is the phase of the $g$th hop, $t_g = t - (g-1)T_m - t_0$, and rect(•) represents a unit rectangular pulse.

The LFM signals can be expressed as

$$l_m(t) = a_m \, \text{rect}\left(\frac{t}{T_m}\right) e^{j\left(2\pi\left(f_m t + \frac{K}{2}t^2\right) + \phi_m\right)}, \tag{3}$$

where $T_m$ stands for the last time of $l_m(t)$, $f_m$ is the carrier frequency, $K$ is the chirp rate of $l_m(t)$, the amplitude of $l_m(t)$ is denoted by $a_m$ while its initial phase is represented by $\phi_m$.

The fixed frequency signal can be denoted as

$$f_n(t) = a_n \operatorname{rect}\left(\frac{t}{T_n}\right) \sin(2\pi f_n t + \phi_n), \tag{4}$$

where $T_n$ stands for the last time of $f_n(t)$, $f_n$ is the carrier frequency, the amplitude of $f_n(t)$ is denoted by $a_n$ while its initial phase is represented by $\phi_n$.

The burst signal has the same math expression as fixed frequency signal while its last time is quiet shorter compared to other signals.

Based on (1), it is clear that the FH signals exhibit no statistical correlation with the remaining signals. Therefore, signals excluding FH signal can be collectively considered as additive interference $n(t)$. Then, we can reformulate (1) as

$$c(t) = s_{fh}(t) + n(t). \tag{5}$$

## 3 Proposed Scheme

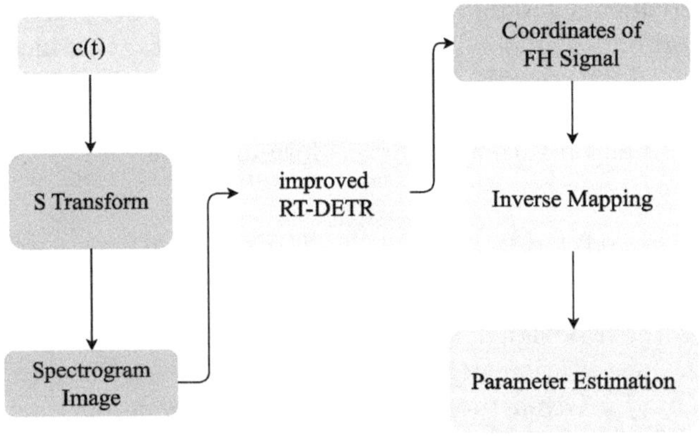


**Fig. 1.** Workflow of proposed scheme.

The workflow of the our scheme is depicted in Fig. 1. First, the time-domain input signal is transformed into a TF grid via ST. Subsequently, this grid is processed by the improved RT-DETR, which treats it as an image for detection and locates the bounding boxes (Bboxes) corresponding to the FH signals. In the final stage, the hopping frequency and hopping time of the FH signals are inferred by reverse mapping the coordinates extracted from the TF grid.

### 3.1 S Transform Based Time–Frequency Analysis

The TFA technique reveals the constituent frequencies of a signal and illustrates how they vary over time. The ST is a significant tool for time–frequency analysis, merging the properties of the STFT and the continuous Wavelet Transform. The ST employs a Gaussian window whose width is inversely related to the frequency. Given a observation signal, the ST is defined as follows:

$$C(t,f) = \int_{-\infty}^{+\infty} c(\tau)w(\tau - t)e^{-j2\pi f\tau}d\tau, \tag{6}$$

where $\tau$ represents the time shift factor and $f$ denotes as the frequency, $w(t)$ is the window function, which can be stated as:

$$w(t) = \frac{1}{\sigma\sqrt{2\pi}}e^{-\frac{t^2}{2\sigma^2}}, \tag{7}$$

the scale factor function is defined as

$$\sigma(f) = \frac{1}{|f|}. \tag{8}$$

Carrying out the ST on both sides of (8) concurrently results in

$$\begin{aligned} C(t,f) &= \int_{-\infty}^{+\infty} \left(s_{fh}(t) + n(t)\right) w(\tau - t)e^{-j2\pi f\tau}d\tau \\ &= \int_{-\infty}^{+\infty} s_{fh}(t)w(\tau - t)e^{-j2\pi f\tau}d\tau \\ &+ \int_{-\infty}^{+\infty} n(t)w(\tau - t)e^{-j2\pi f\tau}d\tau \\ &= S_{fh}(t,f) + N(t,f), \end{aligned} \tag{9}$$

where $C(t,f)$, $S_{fh}(t,f)$ and $N(t,f)$ is the ST of $c(t)$, $s_{fh}(t)$ and $n(t)$, respectively.

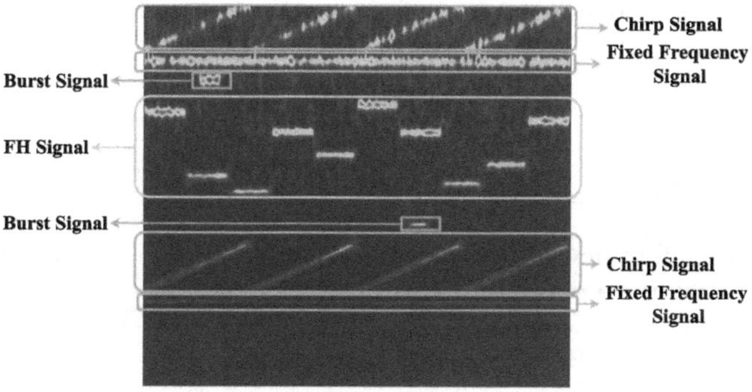


**Fig. 2.** Spectrogram of the FH signal under VLF interferences in ST (SNR = 6 dB).

As illustrated in Fig. 2, the spectrogram characterizes FH signals as brief, extended horizontal streaks. In contrast, fixed frequency signals are manifested as continuous, prolonged horizontal bands. The LFM signal are discernible by their diagonal patterns with uniform slopes, consistent frequency ranges, and regular intervals. Burst signals, on the other hand, are composed of brief horizontal lines that vary in length. AWGN is distributed throughout the spectrogram as irregularly scattered points, which become increasingly prominent and brighter as the SNR decreases. Consequently, the identification of FH signals within a spectrogram can be conceptualized as an object recognition challenge, entailing the differentiation of these distinctive short horizontal features from the array of patterns present in the spectrogram.

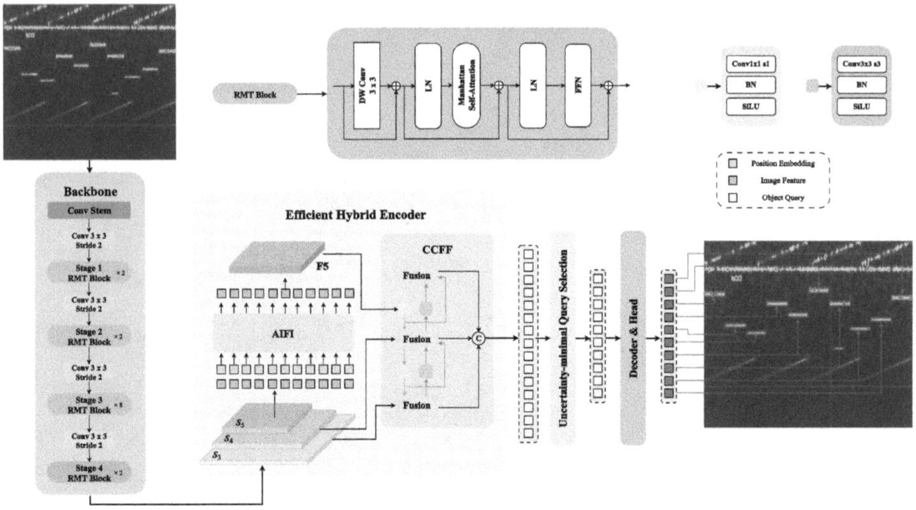


**Fig. 3.** Architecture of improved RT-DETR. The backbone consists of four stages, the initial three stages employ the decomposed MaSA while the last employs the original MaSA. AIFI: Attention-based Intra-scale Feature Interaction. CCFF: CNN-based Cross-scale Feature Fusion.

## 3.2 Improved RT-DETR

To cope with the aforementioned challenges, we propose an improved RT-DETR model for FH signal detection. In this approach, we substitute the ResNet-50 backbone utilized in the original RT-DETR with the RMT backbone. The architecture of the enhanced detection model is depicted in Fig. 3. While ResNet [20] employs residual connections to alleviate vanishing gradients and enhance training depth, RMT incorporates MaSA, which utilizes a spatial decay matrix based on the Manhattan distance. This introduces a two-dimensional spatial prior that greatly enhances the model's ability to concentrate on pertinent local features while maintaining global context. The MaSA mechanism enables RMT to model global information with linear complexity, expanding the receptive field while placing greater focus on the information around the center of the FH signal in the TF diagram. These features collectively enable RMT to achieve superior performance in various vision tasks, such as object detection and segmentation, outperforming traditional architectures in accuracy. Simulation results validate that our proposed model demonstrates superior performance and increased detection accuracy.

The backbone initially extracts features from the image using a Convolution Stem, which enhances local information and thereby improves the model's performance across various tasks. To reduce the resolution of the feature map, $3 \times 3$ convolutions with a stride of 2 are used between stages. Each stage employs the RMT block, as illustrated in Fig. 3, to capture global information and explicit spatial priors through the MaSA mechanism.

The outputs of the final three stages of RMT $\{\mathcal{S}_3, \mathcal{S}_4, \mathcal{S}_5\}$ are extracted and used as input for the hybrid encoder. The efficient hybrid encoder, converts the multi-scale features into a series of object queries by employing AIFI and CCFF modules. Subsequently, the uncertainty-minimal query selection scheme is employed to statically identify a predetermined number of encoder features to act as the initial object queries for the decoder. Ultimately, the decoder, augmented with additional prediction modules, successively refines these object queries to produce final classifications and Bbox predictions.

### 3.3 Parameter Estimation of the FH Signal

For a single FH hop, its predicted Bbox is defined by the coordinates $(x_a, y_a, x_b, y_b)$, where $x_a$ and $y_a$ represent the of the center of the Bbox, $x_b$ and $y_b$ specifying its dimensions of width and height. Also the coordinate of the spectrogram can be stated as $(x_c, y_c, x_w, y_h)$. Then, the predicted frequency $f_p$ is given by

$$f_p = f_M(\frac{1}{2} + \frac{y_c - y_a}{y_h}), \tag{10}$$

where $f_M$ represents the max frequency of the spectrum. The predicted hopping period $T_p$ can be stated as

$$T_p = T_M \frac{x_b}{x_w}, \tag{11}$$

where $T_M$ represents the hopping time of the FH signal.

## 4 Simulation and Performance

### 4.1 Experiment Design

We generated the datasets for the experiment using Matlab R2021b, observed for 0.08 s in ST. The frequencies of the FH signals varied randomly within the VLF band, with a hopping period of 0.008 s. The SNR of the AWGN varied from −14 dB to 10 dB, in 2 dB increments. During the observation time, the interference described in Sect. 2 occurs randomly, consisting of 2 fixed frequency signal, 8 LFM signals with a duration of 0.02 s, and 2–3 burst signals, each with a duration of 0.004 s.

To ensure statistical accuracy and robustness of the algorithm, we generated 512 spectrograms for each SNR value. To further enhance the model's precision in detection, we also created 50 background spectrograms incorporating AWGN and the interference signals described in Sect. 2. This process resulted in a comprehensive dataset of 7,306 spectrograms.

In order to conduct the comparison experiment between ST and STFT, we also generate the same datasets with a 128-point Hamming window in STFT.

The data we generated was allocated into training and validation subsets, comprising 466 and 96 spectrograms for each dB step, respectively. To assess the efficacy of the improved algorithm, we conduct a series of comparative experimental analyses using YOLOv8 [21], YOLOv9 [22], and RT-DETR. The size of the images for experiment is 640 × 640. The batchsize is 8, and training concludes after 150 epochs. We employ AdamW as the optimizer with the learning rate of 1E-3.

## 4.2 Performance Analysis

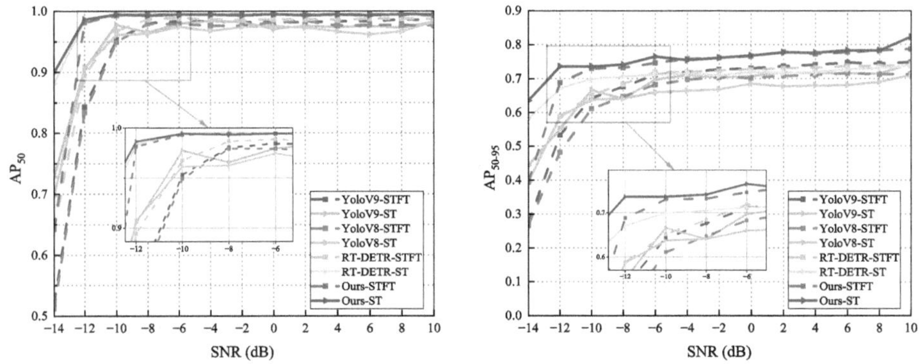


(a) (b)

**Fig. 4.** Performance comparison of the DL architectures by SNR. (a) $AP_{50}$ of the DL architectures. (b) $AP_{50-95}$ of the DL architectures.

**Performance Comparison of ST and STFT.** Figure 4 delineates the $AP_{50}$ and $AP_{50-95}$ of the schemes across various SNR. Overall, all models demonstrate an increasing trend in performance with rising SNR, stabilizing around 0 dB. At lower SNR values (below −10 dB), models utilizing STFT experience a sharp decline in performance, showing significant drops in both $AP_{50}$ and $AP_{50-95}$. Conversely, models employing ST exhibit better robustness under these conditions. As SNR increases, all models exhibit improved performance. In high SNR environments (0 dB and above), models utilizing STFT either outperform or match their ST counterparts, achieving high accuracy. Specifically, the STFT-based models demonstrate a stabilization in performance metrics, reaching near-perfect accuracy in both $AP_{50}$ and $AP_{50\text{–}95}$ metrics (all models achieve an $AP_{50}$ of over 0.95 for SNR values above −10 dB). Overall, while STFT models excel under high SNR conditions, ST models are more effective and robust across a broader range of noise conditions, especially under complex VLF interference.

**Performance Comparison of The DL Architectures.** A comparative analysis of four models—Our model, RT-DETR, YOLOv8, and YOLOv9—reveals a general improvement in performance across all models as the SNR increases. Our model demonstrates superior capabilities, particularly under low SNR conditions. As illustrated in the $AP_{50\text{–}95}$ graph, all models exhibit high $AP_{50}$ values in high SNR regions, indicating robust signal detection. However, Our model consistently outperforms the others in precise localization, as evidenced by its higher $AP_{50\text{–}95}$ values.

In low SNR regions, where signal degradation poses significant challenges, the performance disparity becomes more pronounced. Both YOLOv8 and YOLOv9 show a significant performance decline starting at −6 dB SNR. In contrast, Our model maintains high accuracy, with a sharp performance decline only beginning at −12 dB SNR, maintaining an $AP_{50\text{–}95}$ value over 0.73 at −12 dB and above. This decline is less pronounced than in other models, which demonstrates remarkable robustness and reliability under adverse conditions. This highlights Our model's exceptional ability to handle noise and maintain high accuracy in signal detection and localization.

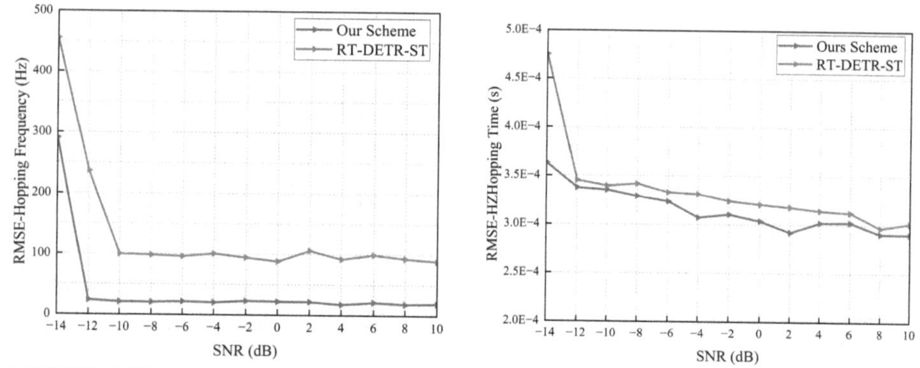


(a) RMSE of FH signal hopping frequency by SNR.

(b) RMSE of FH signal hopping time by SNR.

**Fig. 5.** Performance of Our scheme and RT-DETR-ST in estimating parameters of FH signal.

**Performance Evaluation on Parameter Estimation.** Further, we assess the performance of our proposed scheme and RT-DETR-ST under varying SNR for estimating FH signal parameters. Figure 5 illustrates the RMSE of the estimated hopping frequency and hopping time of the FH signal. Figure 5a shows that both schemes have high RMSE at −14 dB, with Our Scheme sharply dropping and stabilizing below 30 Hz, while RT-DETR-ST stabilizes at a higher RMSE of approximately 100 Hz. Figure 5b shows both schemes improve RMSE-hopping time with increasing SNR, with Our Scheme consistently achieving lower RMSE values across all SNR levels compared to RT-DETR-ST. These results align with the AP metrics in Fig. 4, validating that Our Scheme demonstrates excellent performance in both hopping frequency and hopping time estimation, offering greater accuracy and robustness under complex VLF interference.

## 5 Conclusion

In this paper, we proposed a novel scheme for the detection of FH signals and blind parameter estimation under VLF interference. Our scheme was based on ST and the improved RT-DETR model with the RMT backbone. We compared TFA techniques and DL models through simulations. Results revealed that ST eased the difficulty of recognition under low SNR conditions compared to the STFT. Additionally, RT-DETR demonstrated superior detection performance under VLF interference, with the introduction of explicit spatial priors further enhancing recognition accuracy. In future research, we aim to concentrate on refining the model's capability for information extraction by improving the hybrid efficient encoder, extending for detection and parameter estimation under lower SNR and interfered conditions.

## References

1. Bickford, J.A., Duwel, A.E., Weinberg, M.S., McNabb, R.S., Freeman, D.K., Ward, P.A.: Performance of electrically small conventional and mechanical antennas. IEEE Trans. Antennas Propag. **67**(4), 2209–2223 (2019)
2. Liu, Y., Gong, S., Liu, Q., Hou, M.: A mechanical transmitter for undersea magnetic induction communication. IEEE Trans. Antennas Propag. **69**(10), 6391–6400 (2021)
3. Wang, W., Liu, J., Xie, G., Wen, L., Zhang, J.: A bio-inspired electrocommunication system for small underwater robots. Bioinspiration Biomimetics **12**(3), 036002 (2017)
4. Khan, M.T.: A modified convolutional neural network with rectangular filters for frequency-hopping spread spectrum signals. Appl. Soft Comput. **150**, 111036 (2024)
5. Pickholtz, R., Schilling, D., Milstein, L.: Theory of spread-spectrum communications - a tutorial. IEEE Trans. Commun. **30**(5), 855–884 (1982)
6. Xu, D., Yu, K., Ritcey, J.A.: Cross-layer device authentication with quantum encryption for 5G enabled IIoT in industry 4.0. IEEE Trans. Industr. Inf. **18**(9), 6368–6378 (2021)

7. Hasan, M.Z., Couto, D.J., Abdel-Malek, M.A., Reed, J.H.: Frequency hopping signal detection in low signal-to-noise ratio regimes. In: Proceedings of the IEEE International Symposium on Personal, Indoor Mobile Radio Communications (PIMRC), pp. 1–7. IEEE, Toronto, ON, Canada (2023)
8. Chen, Z., Shi, Y., Wang, Y., Li, X., Yu, X., Shi, Y.: Unlocking signal processing with image detection: a frequency hopping detection scheme for complex EMI environments using STFT and CenterNet. IEEE Access **11**, 46004–46014 (2023)
9. Chen, Z., Shi, Y., Wang, Y., Jiang, L., Yu, X., Li, X.: A small-object detection based scheme for multiplexed frequency hopping recognition in complex electromagnetic interference. IEEE Commun. Lett. **28**(4), 902–906 (2024)
10. Ye, J., et al.: A new frequency hopping signal detection of civil UAV based on improved K-means clustering algorithm. IEEE Access **9**, 53190–53204 (2021)
11. Lee, K.-G., Oh, S.-J.: Detection of frequency-hopping signals with deep learning. IEEE Commun. Lett. **24**(5), 1042–1046 (2020)
12. Deng, Z., Lei, J.: Spectrogram-based frequency hopping signal detection in a complex electromagnetic environment. In: Proceedings of the International Conference on Signal Image Processing (ICSIP), pp. 6–10. IEEE, Suzhou, China (2022)
13. Huang, Y., Meng, X., Zhang, S., Liu, F.: Adaptive detection of frequency-hopping spread spectrum signals based on compressed measurements and artificial neural networks. In: Proceedings of the Advanced Information Technology, Electronic and Automation Control Conference (IAEAC), pp. 271–277. IEEE, Chongqing, China (2021)
14. Li, C., Chen, Y., Zhao, Z.: Frequency hopping signal detection based on optimized generalized S transform and ResNet. Math. Biosci. Eng. **20**(7), 12843–12863 (2023)
15. Stockwell, R.G., Mansinha, L., Lowe, R.P.: Localization of the complex spectrum: the S transform. IEEE Trans. Signal Process. **44**(4), 998–1001 (1996)
16. Zhao, Y.: DETRs beat YOLOs on real-time object detection. In: Proceedings of the IEEE Conference on Computer Vision and Pattern Recognition (CVPR), pp. 16965–16974. IEEE, Seattle, WA, USA (2024)
17. Hosang, J., Benenson, R., Schiele, B.: Learning non-maximum suppression. In: Proceedings of the IEEE Conference on Computer Vision and Pattern Recognition (CVPR), pp. 6469–6477. IEEE, Honolulu, HI, USA (2017)
18. Fan, Q., Huang, H., Chen, M., Liu, H., He, R.: RMT: retentive networks meet vision transformers. In: Proceedings of the IEEE Conference on Computer Vision and Pattern Recognition (CVPR), pp. 5641–5651. IEEE, Seattle, WA, USA (2024)
19. Zhang, Y.-J., Liu, R.-Y., Song, H.-J.: A method of the detection of frequency-hopping signal based on channelized receiver in the complicated electromagnetic environment. In: Proceedings of the International Conference on Intelligent Information Hiding and Multimedia Signal Processing (IIH-MSP), pp. 294–297. IEEE, Adelaide, SA, Australia (2015)
20. He, K., Zhang, X., Ren, S., Sun, J.: Deep residual learning for image recognition. In: Proceedings of the IEEE Conference on Computer Vision and Pattern Recognition (CVPR), pp. 770–778. IEEE, Las Vegas, NV, USA (2016)
21. Jocher, G., Chaurasia, A., Qiu, J.: Ultralytics YOLO. https://github.com/ultralytics/ultralytics. Accessed 5 Sep 2024
22. Wang, C.-Y., Yeh, I.-H., Liao, H.-Y.M.: YOLOv9: learning what you want to learn using programmable gradient information. arXiv preprint arXiv:2402.13616 (2024)

# Efficient Simultaneous Energy and Information Transfer Across Heterogeneous-Sized Devices

Wenjie Guo, Lili Chen(✉), Wenbin Sun, Haochen Liu, and Ling Wang

Northwestern Polytechnical University, Xi'an, China
guowji@mail.nwpu.edu.cn,
{lilichen,sunwenbin,haochenliu,lingwang}@nwpu.edu.cn

**Abstract.** This paper presents a surface-assisted dual-frequency antenna architecture for simultaneous wireless information and power transfer (SWIPT) system designed for heterogeneous-sized devices. The system consists of a large transmitting antenna and a small receiving antenna, operating in dual resonance across 13.56 MHz and 300 MHz frequency bands. The low-frequency band enables efficient energy transfer, while the high-frequency band facilitates information transmission. To enhance transmission efficiency and link isolation, an intelligent metasurface (MTS) is introduced between the transmitting and receiving antennas. This design enables energy focusing and beam direction enhancement for signals across both frequency bands, thereby optimizing performance in both energy and information transmission. Simulation results demonstrate that this architecture achieves stable and efficient operation in both low-frequency energy transfer and high-frequency information transmission while significantly reducing mutual interference. The proposed dual-frequency SWIPT design not only resolves the applicability issues of traditional dual-frequency antennas in mismatched device configurations but also provides an efficient integrated energy and information transmission solution for IoT systems, smart city infrastructure, and medical implantable devices.

**Keywords:** SWIPT · Dual-Frequency Antenna · Metasurface · Energy Harvesting · Heterogeneous Devices

## 1 Introduction

With the rapid development of the Internet of Things (IoT), smart cities, and healthcare monitoring systems, a growing number of low-power sensors and intelligent devices are being integrated into daily life and industrial applications [1]. These devices require both energy supply and communication capabilities. However, traditional battery-powered solutions face challenges such as limited lifespan, high maintenance costs, and environmental burdens. Consequently, SWIPT


Y. Liu et al. (Eds.): ChinaCom 2025, LNICST 711, pp. 60–73, 2027.
https://doi.org/10.1007/978-3-032-33662-0_7

has emerged as a key research focus in recent years, recognized as an effective approach to integrate device power supply with communication functions [2].

Existing SWIPT research primarily focuses on the following implementation approaches: a) Time-division multiplexing (TDM): Alternating energy and information transmission, simple but inefficient [3]; b) Power allocation: Allocating power within a single signal, requiring algorithmic optimization to balance efficiency and rate [4]; c) Spatial/polarization multiplexing: Relying on multi-antenna or polarization isolation, but with high hardware complexity [5]; d) Dual-band architecture: Using different frequency bands to carry energy and information separately, an effective method to enhance isolation and overall efficiency [6].

Although the dual-band architecture is promising, prior attempts have mainly focused on transmit–receive antennas of identical size [7,8]. In practice, however, communication devices often differ significantly in their physical dimensions, making conventional dual-band antenna designs no longer work.

In this paper, we explore a new dual-frequency SWIPT architecture that enables two antennas of vastly different sizes to operate simultaneously in the same two frequency bands, thereby supporting concurrent energy and information transfer across devices of different sizes. Despite this, the uneven size of transmitter (Tx) and receiver (Rx) antennas inherently restricts the transmission efficiency, both in dual bands. To address this, we involve a smart metasurface [9–11] between the Tx and Rx antennas to direct the transmission beam more effectively from Tx to Rx. We also carefully design the MTS to make it resonate at those desired disparate frequencies and optimize its structure for high-freedom control and low transmission loss.

The contributions of this paper can be summarized as followings:

- To our knowledge, this is the first dual-band SWIPT architecture capable of operating efficiently between devices with vastly different sizes.
- We introduce a dual-band antenna design that facilitate SWIPT across disparate frequency bands, as well as an MTS to enhance focusing and isolation in both energy and information links.
- We conduct extensive simulations to demonstrate the proposed architecture's effectiveness in both low-frequency energy transfer and high-frequency communication, showcasing its potential applications in smart city infrastructure, medical implants, and industrial IoT scenarios.

## 2 System Architecture and Principles

### 2.1 Overall Architecture

The proposed system consists of three components: a large antenna transmitter, a small antenna receiver, and a dual-band MTS auxiliary layer.

- The low-frequency energy link (13.56 MHz) achieves stable power transmission through magnetic coupling between the antennas.

- The high-frequency information link (300 MHz) utilizes the same antenna pair for communication transmission.
- The MTS operates across both frequency bands, serving dual functions of electromagnetic wave focusing and signal isolation.

Figure 1 shows the basic concept of SWIPT, and also shows the corresponding relationship between the overall framework of the system and SWIPT.

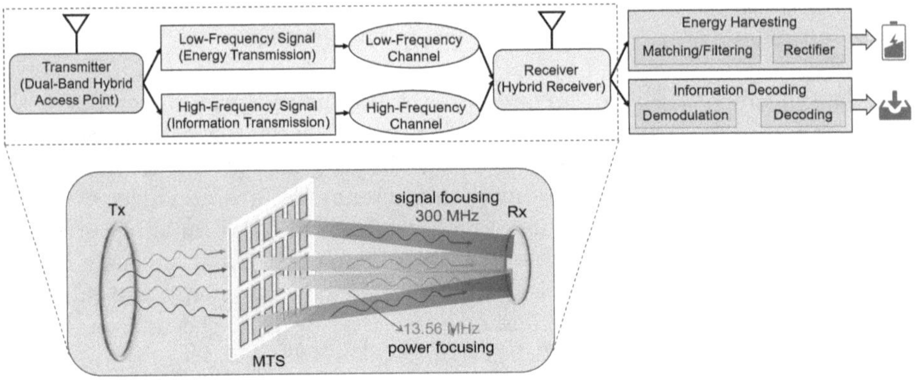


**Fig. 1.** System architecture diagram. Energy and information are emitted from the transmitting antenna and transmitted to the receiving antenna via MTS focusing.

## 2.2 Multi-mode Principle

In general, the multi-mode characteristic of the MTS-assisted SWIPT system is achieved by the capacitors connected to the Tx, Rx, and MTS units. Figure 2 (left) illustrates the equivalent circuit of the Tx, Rx, and MTS units, including self-inductance ($L_T$), ohmic losses ($R_{ohm}$), resistance ($R_c$) caused by the connected capacitor ($C_c$), parasitic self-capacitance ($C_{par}$), and dielectric losses ($R_d$). This equivalent circuit can be simplified as an RLC circuit model, as shown in Fig. 2 (right). In this work, we utilize the characteristic of impedance in radio frequency (RF) circuits. The capacitance value of the connected capacitor ($C_c$) is relatively higher compared to the parasitic self-capacitance ($C_{par}$). The differences in the capacitance values enable the MTS-assisted SWIPT system to exhibit a multi-mode property. We can obtain the capacitive reactance of the equivalent circuit and the connected capacitor using the subsequent equations:

$$\begin{cases} \frac{1}{X_C} = \frac{1}{X_{C_{\text{par}}}} + \frac{1}{X_{C_c}} \\ X_{C_c} = \frac{1}{2\pi f C_c}, \quad X_{C_{\text{par}}} = \frac{1}{2\pi f C_{\text{par}}} \end{cases} \tag{1}$$

where $X_C$, $X_{C_{par}}$, and $X_{C_c}$ represents the capacitive reactance of the equivalent circuit, $C_{par}$, and $C_c$ respectively, and $f$ denotes the operating frequency.

According to Eq. 1, $X_{C_c}$ is determined based on its operating frequency and the value of the connected capacitor. If the operating frequency is relatively high, such as hundreds of megahertz, $X_{C_c}$ becomes extremely small due to the significant values of both $f$ and $C_c$ terms. This implies that the connected capacitor is effectively short-circuited. This observation reflects that at a high operating frequency, the resonant frequencies of the Tx, Rx, and MTS unit cells remain unchanged due to the presence of connected capacitors. Instead, these resonant frequencies are determined by the intrinsic antenna/MTS structures, dimensions, and configurations ($L_T$, $R_T$, and $C_{par}$) in the circuit.

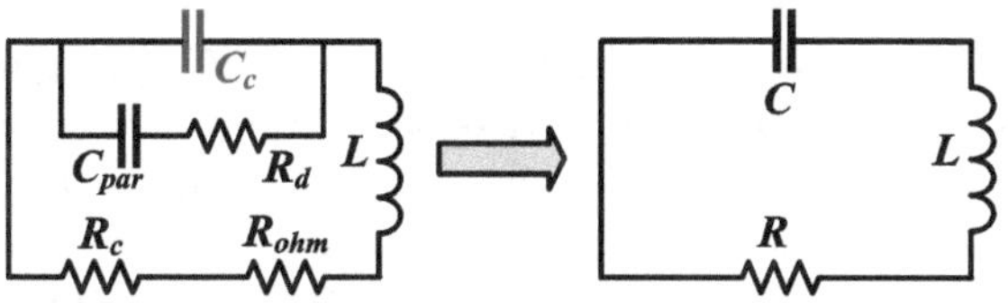


**Fig. 2.** Equivalent (left) and simplified (right) circuits of the Tx, Rx, and MTS unit cell.

Meanwhile, at relatively lower frequency bands like tens of megahertz, $X_{C_c}$ cannot be ignored as the value of $f$ is small. Consequently, by adjusting the value of the connected capacitor, the resonant frequencies of the MTS and the Tx, Rx antennas can be modified. This distinctive capacitive reactance property at different frequency bands is harnessed for the operation of the multi-frequency based mode-selective MTS-assisted SWIPT. After determining the geometries of the Tx, Rx, and MTS unit cells for the far-field mode, the values of the connected capacitors are carefully chosen for magnetic resonant coupling (MRC) operation in the near-field mode. Exploiting this property, we can design an MTS-assisted SWIPT system that exhibits multi-mode SWIPT functions for both low and high frequency band.

**Frequency Selection.** In this work, we choose the two resonant frequency bands of 13.56 MHz and 300 MHz as example to validate the multi-mode characteristics of the proposed SWIPT system. These frequencies can be adapted to other bands like depending on needs. Our choice of these frequencies in this work considers the small size of receiving devices, adheres to licensed frequency bands for wireless charging, and aims to minimize path loss and interference issue [12,13].

### 2.3 Transceiver Antennas Design

**Design Goals.** To achieve multi-mode wireless charging and communication for small mobile devices, the transceiver antennas must fulfill two essential: (i) transceiver antennas are resonant at two disparate frequency bands; (ii) the receiver antenna needs to be compact enough to be easily integrated into the small mobile devices.

For more efficient power transfer, we choose four-antenna structure to conduct power transfer in this work. The four-antenna SWIPT system includes the source antenna, transmitter antenna, receiver antenna, and load antenna. Consider practical use cases for charging small mobile devices, the Tx antenna (source and transmitter antennas) can be larger (like a mural that is easily hung on the wall) to provide a higher efficiency benchmark, while to facilitate the integration of the Rx antenna (receiver and load antennas) into small mobile devices, it is essential to design it in a compact size. So we need to design a large-Tx and small-Rx system.

***Challenge of Designing Two Antennas with Very Different Sizes to Operate in the Same Two Disparate Frequency Bands.*** It is intuitive for a single antenna structure to achieve the resonance of the above two frequency bands, but it is not easy to achieve such a function with two antennas of drastically different sizes due to the wavelength constraints.

We first design the Tx antenna structure in accordance with the design principles outlined in [14,15], to make it operate at higher frequency band of 300 MHz. Then we adjust the value of capacitance integrated on the antenna to make it also resonant at lower frequency band of 13.56 MHz, while keeping the dimension of antenna. The Tx antenna is designed with the diameter of 334 mm.

While the Rx antenna is expected to be small as a few centimeters. If we directly shrink the Tx antennas structure to the required size, it would result in both resonance frequencies shifting towards higher frequencies. Therefore, the challenge lies in how to maintain the original resonance frequencies when reducing the size of the antenna. To address this, first, we shrink the overall antenna size to meet the small size requirement for the outer diameter. Then, while ensuring that the outer diameter remains unchanged, we independently optimize the inner diameter, wire diameter, spacing between adjacent turns, and capacitance value. Eventually, the diameters of Tx and Rx antennas is designed to be 334 mm and 6 mm, respectively. These dimensions can be adjusted to other sizes as needed to meet specific requirements. The parameters and structures of the transceiver antennas are shown in Fig. 3.

The simulated return losses by high frequency structure simulator (HFSS) of the designed antennas are depicted in Fig. 4. The results show that the resonant frequencies of both the large and small antennas remained consistent across various capacitor values in the high-frequency band (300 MHz). Because the connected capacitor acts liken short circuit, the resonant frequencies of the large and small antennas are not affected by the connected capacitor. However, in the low-frequency band (13.56 MHz), we observe that the resonant frequency of the large and small antennas could be tuned by adjusting the value of the connected capacitor. The return loss of the small antenna is higher than that of the large antenna, this is expected due to its size limitation in given operating bands, Nevertheless, these results demonstrate that the 4-antenna SWIIPT system constructed with the designed antennas exhibits the multi-mode property.

| Antennas | Parameters | Values |
|---|---|---|
| Drive | Diameter of coil | 334mm |
| | Diameter of conductor wire | 4.3mm |
| Transmitter | Outer diameter of coil | 334mm |
| | Turn-to-turn pitch | 14.5mm |
| | Diameter of conductor wire | 4.3mm |
| | Number of turns | 6 |
| Receiver | Outer diameter of coil | 60mm |
| | Turn-to-turn pitch | 2.5mm |
| | Diameter of conductor wire | 2mm |
| | Number of turns | 5 |
| Load | Diameter of coil | 60mm |
| | Diameter of conductor wire | 2mm |

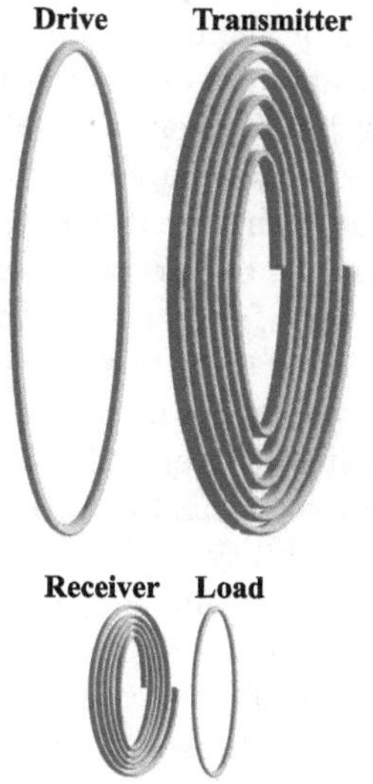


**Fig. 3.** Parameters and structures of the transceiver antennas.

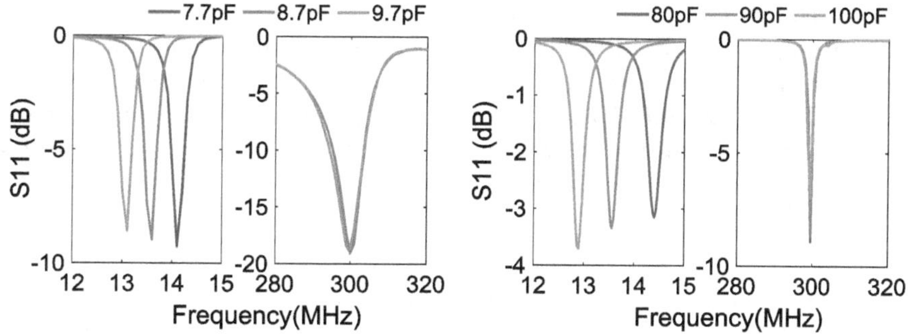


(a) Large antenna (167mm radius). (b) Small antenna (30mm radius).

**Fig. 4.** Return loss (S11) of designed large and small antennas.

Based on the parametric simulation results, we configure the values of capacitance values connected to the large and small antennas to 8.7 pF and 100 pF, respectively.

## 2.4 MTS Design

**Design Goals.** To effectively enhance the PTE of the dual-frequency SWIPT system at low frequency energy link (13.56 MHz) and high frequency information link (300 MHz) by using a MTS, the MTS must fulfill two primary objectives: (i) operate at the same two frequency bands as the transceiver antennas; (ii) achieve high-freedom control and with low loss.

Guided by the multi-mode principle introduced in §2.2, one can scale the geometric parameters of an existing MTS structure to make it operate at 300 MHz frequency band, then manipulate the capacitance value to make it resonant at second frequency band of 13.56 MHz. However, such direct operation cannot satisfy the second goal above.

In order to realize the dual function of low frequency band energy transmission and high frequency band information transmission, it is crucial to design the MTS with both positive and negative permeability. As the absolute permeability of the MTS increases, the deflection angle produced when the incident magnetic field traverses it also enlarges. However, a problem arises with this: as the absolute permeability rises, the imaginary component of the complex magnetic permeability also surges, leading to increased attenuation and consequently diminishing the efficiency of power transfer. To solve this problem, we choose a spiral-shaped resonator meta-atom structure, as it has been reported to exhibit a higher quality-factor compared to the split ring resonator unit. Additionally, we opt for a thin-thickness and low-loss material (F4B) as the substrate for meta-atom. The thicknesses of the substrate and metal (copper) pattern are 0.5 mm and 0.036 mm, respectively. This strategic selection of materials and dimensions allows us to reach our second objective, and then the multi-band resonance of meta-atom can be achieved based on the multi-mode principle detailed in §2.2. In our approach, we initially scale the dimensions of the meta-atom to attain near-zero refraction index for a frequency of 300 MHz. Subsequently, we vary the value of the connected capacitor to induce a permeability change around 13.56 MHz. This enables the MTS to exhibit beam focusing capabilities in both frequency bands. Finally, the MTS is composed of an array of meta-atoms with an equal number of rows and columns.

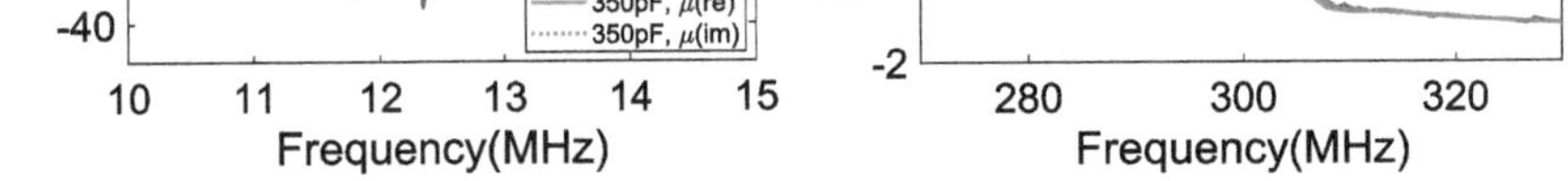


(a) Permeability of MTS at low frequency band.

(b) Refraction index of MTS at high frequency band.

**Fig. 5.** Dual-band property verification of the designed MTS.

Figure 5 presents the simulation results of the permeability and refraction index of the meta-atom. From Fig. 5 (left), it can be seen that when the real part of the permeability of the meta-atom is negative, its imaginary part of the permeability is as low as 0.15, which ensures low attenuation when adjusting over a wide range of angles. Moreover, the resonance frequency of the meta-atom can be changed by varying the capacitance integrated on the meta-atom, thereby changing the permeability at a given frequency. Figure 5 (right) shows that the real part of refractive index of meta-atom at high frequency band exhibits near zero values, which indicates that the MTS has the beam-focusing property. To validate this, we construct the MTS with $4 \times 4$ meta-atoms, and simulate the magnetic and electric field distribution effects in the low-frequency and high-frequency links. Figure 6 demonstrates that MTS can successfully steer the magnetic field (left) and focus the electric field (right), enhancing power transmission efficiency at low frequencies and improving channel directionality and isolation at high frequencies.

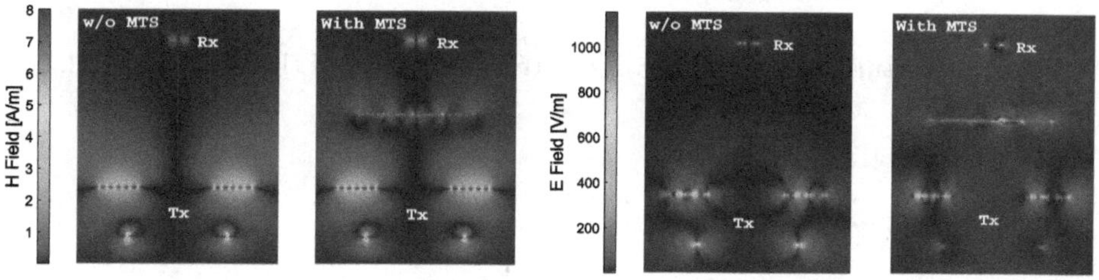


(a) Low frequency. (b) High frequency.

**Fig. 6.** Magnetic (a) and electric (b) field distribution of the SWIPT without MTS and with MTS.

The structural schematic and geometric parameters of the MTS unit cell are depicted in Fig. 7.

# 3 Evaluation

## 3.1 Multimode Characteristic Verification

To validate the system's multimode characteristics, we conducted a series of performance simulation tests using HFSS, measuring transmission coefficients ($S_{21}$) at different transmitter-receiver distances. The simulation results demonstrated successful energy and information transfer across both designed frequency bands. As shown in Fig. 8, the transmission efficiency of low frequency band is significantly better than that of high frequency band, especially in the short distance range, low frequency band can transmit energy efficiently. However, with the increase of transmitter-receiver distance, the efficiency of low frequency band decreases rapidly. The transmission efficiency of high frequency band decreases relatively slowly, and it can still maintain high efficiency with the increase of distance. After a certain distance, the transmission efficiency of high frequency

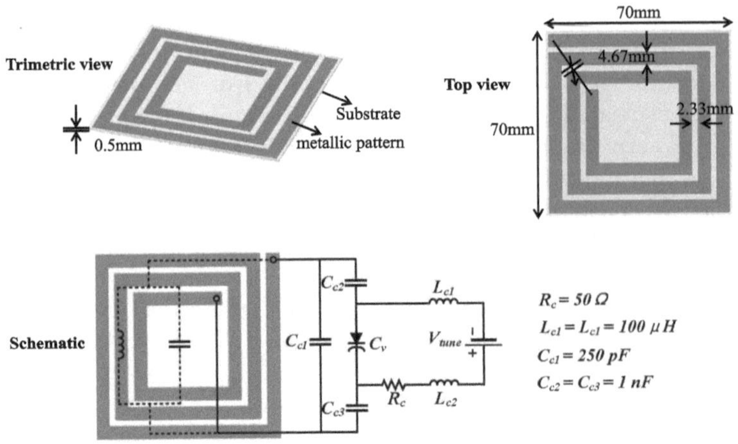


**Fig. 7.** Structural schematic and geometric parameters of the MTS unit cell.

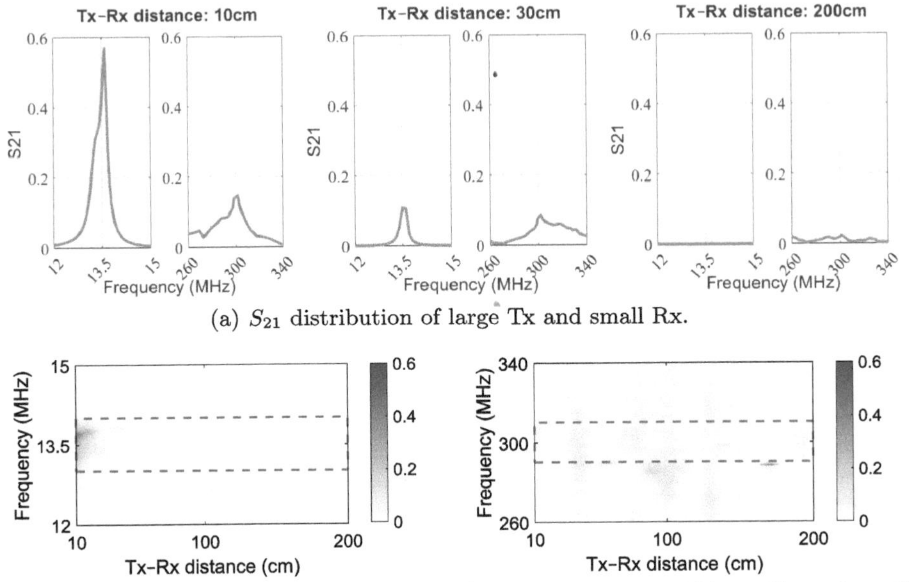


(a) $S_{21}$ distribution of large Tx and small Rx.

(b) $S_{21}$ distribution of large Tx and small Rx at low frequency.

(c) $S_{21}$ distribution of large Tx and small Rx at high frequency.

**Fig. 8.** Multi-mode verification – $S_{21}$ measurements without MTS. Low frequency is used for energy transmission, and high frequency is used for information transmission. It can be seen that low frequency has higher efficiency in short distance energy transmission, while high frequency maintains good efficiency in long distance information transmission.

band is more than that of low frequency band, showing its advantage in information transmission.

The simulation results conclusively validate the system's multimodal characteristics. Specifically, the low-frequency band is primarily employed for energy transmission with high efficiency, while the high-frequency band demonstrates superior information transmission performance over longer distances. Notably, although the high-frequency band achieves higher transmission efficiency at greater distances, the low-frequency band still outperforms it within a 2–3 meter range. This indicates that beam focusing using MTS in SWIPT systems is crucial for enhancing overall transmission efficiency.

### 3.2 PTE Improvements Brought by MTS

**PTE at Varying Transfer Distance.** To further evaluate the performance improvement of MTS on Power Transfer Efficiency (PTE) across varying transmission distances, we conducted simulations using HFSS for small receiver. The results demonstrate that MTS-equipped SWIPT systems exhibit significant PTE enhancements across dual frequency bands and transmitter-receiver distances.

Figure 9 (a), demonstrate the PTE under different transmitter-receiver distances. Calculations using the $S_{21}$ parameter reveal that when MTS is not employed, the PTE value drops significantly. However, the introduction of MTS notably slows down the decline rate of PTE, indicating that MTS can effectively assist in beam focusing, thereby improving both PTE and effective transmission distance. Through the comparison between low frequency band and high frequency band, it can be found that the low frequency band performs better in short distance transmission, while the high frequency band achieves higher PTE in long distance transmission. This further verifies the importance of introducing adaptive multi-mode transfer function to achieve efficient wireless charging technology in long distance.

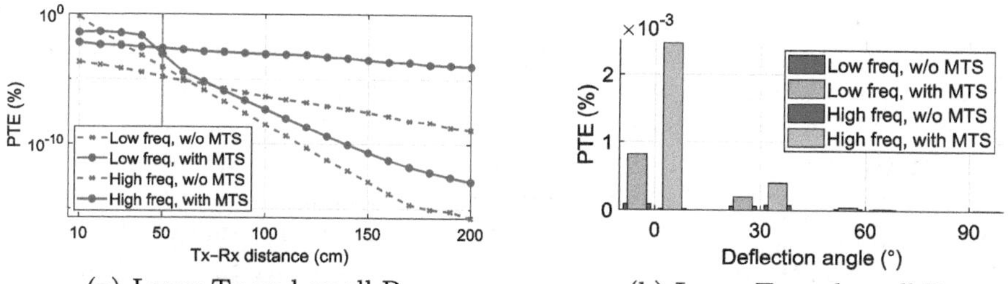


(a) Large Tx and small Rx.

(b) Large Tx and small Rx.

**Fig. 9.** PTE under varying Tx-Rx distance (a) and orientation (b), with both large Tx and small Rx.

**PTE at Varying Rx Orientation.** We investigated the impact of Rx rotation angles on PTE. In simulations, the distance between the transmitting and receiving antennas was fixed at 50 cm. The Rx was rotated around its central point to four distinct angles (0°,30°,60°,90°), where 0° represents ideal alignment and 90° indicates perpendicular orientation.

As shown in Fig. 9 (b), in the case of no MTS, PTE decreases significantly as the rotation Angle of the receiving antenna increases, especially when the receiving antenna is perpendicular to the transmitting antenna, where effective energy transfer is almost impossible. However, after implementing MTS, the decline rate of PTE significantly slowed down even when receiving antennas were deflected. This demonstrates that small antennas can maintain relatively stable energy reception capabilities despite deflection, validating the effectiveness of MTS in compensating angular mismatch.

# 4 Application Scenarios and Discussions

## 4.1 Application Scenarios

**Smart City Sensor Networks:** In smart city applications such as environmental monitoring, traffic detection, and public safety systems, numerous distributed sensor nodes commonly face challenges including difficult cabling and energy consumption sensitivity. The proposed system utilizes a 13.56 MHz low-frequency link to continuously power nodes, eliminating the need for frequent battery replacements, while simultaneously enabling data transmission through a 300 MHz high-frequency link. This configuration supports city-scale distributed sensor networks. Compared with traditional "single-frequency power supply + independent communication links" approaches, this system demonstrates superior advantages in energy efficiency, reduced maintenance requirements, and enhanced reliability [16].

**Medical Implantable and Wearable Devices:** Such as implantable cardiac pacemakers, neurostimulators, and wearable health monitoring devices require long-term stable operation with stringent communication power consumption requirements. Traditional battery or single-frequency wireless power supply methods face efficiency and safety issues. The 13.56 MHz low-frequency link designed in this paper meets human body safety standards while providing stable power supply, whereas the 300 MHz high-frequency link enables high-speed data transmission, supporting real-time vital sign acquisition and telemedicine applications [17].

**Drone and Robot Systems:** The limited endurance of drones and mobile robots often restricts mission execution. The dual-frequency antenna design enables wireless charging via the 13.56 MHz energy link or remote recharging during missions, while the 300 MHz information link ensures low-latency communication and control. With metamaterial surface assistance, communication directionality is enhanced, facilitating channel maintenance in complex environments and preventing interference between energy and information links [18].

**Industrial Internet of Things:** In smart factories or automated environments, numerous sensors and actuators require stable operation under high temperatures or strong electromagnetic interference. Traditional wired power supply proves difficult to deploy, while single-frequency wireless power solutions are susceptible to interference. This system utilizes the 13.56 MHz low-frequency band to deliver robust energy supply, while simultaneously employing the 300 MHz high-frequency band for equipment status monitoring and edge control. This dual approach significantly enhances the automation level and reliability of industrial production [19].

### 4.2 Discussion

**Band Selection:** Low frequency link should be selected to meet the safety standard of ISM band (such as 13.56 MHz), and high frequency link can be 300 MHz, so as to balance the communication rate and hardware implementation complexity.

**Linkage Isolation:** Simulation results show that the metamaterial can significantly reduce $S_{21}$ coupling and improve dual-frequency independence in high frequency band, but the geometric parameters still need to be optimized to adapt to different environments in practical applications.

**Scalability:** Power scheduling and spectrum management are key issues to be addressed in multi-node networks. In the future, adaptive beamforming and multi-user isolation can be achieved by combining reconfigurable intelligent surface (RIS) technology.

**Application Value:** Compared with the traditional SWIPT method, this scheme has advantages in hardware integration, near-field transmission efficiency and application flexibility, especially suitable for low power consumption and low maintenance requirements.

## 5 Conclusion

This paper proposes and validates a SWIPT architecture utilizing dual-frequency antennas and metasurfaces. The system establishes a dual-resonance link between a large transmitting antenna and a small receiving antenna at 13.56 MHz and 300 MHz, respectively, while enabling simultaneous near-field energy supply and medium-band information communication through MTS dual-frequency assistance. Simulation results demonstrate that the low-frequency link maintains high PTE, while the high-frequency link exhibits directional characteristics and isolation performance. Performance degradation remains minimal when operating with dual frequencies. This research provides innovative implementation solutions for smart city applications, medical implant devices, and industrial IoT systems.

**Acknowledgement.** This work is supported by National Natural Science Foundation of China under Grant No. 62472355 and No. 62301433.

## References

1. Makhetha, M.J., Markus, E.D., Abu-Mahfouz, A.M.: Integration of wireless power transfer and low power wide area networks in IoT applications—a review. Sens. Int. **5** (2024)
2. Zaino, R., Chuah, T.C., Hassan, M.S.: SWIPT-enabled relaying networks for next-generation wireless systems: a review of achievable rates and future challenges. IEEE Access **13**, 131234–131256 (2025)
3. Jaiswal, A., Kumar, S., Kaiwartya, O., Prasad, M., Kumar, N., Song, H.: Green computing in IoT: time slotted simultaneous wireless information and power transfer. Comput. Commun. **168**, 155–169 (2021)
4. Perera, T.D., Jayakody, D.N., Sharma, S.K., Chatzinotas, S., Li, J.: Simultaneous wireless information and power transfer (SWIPT): recent advances and future challenges. IEEE Commun. Surv. Tutorials **20**(1), 264–302 (2018)
5. Zhang, Z., Liu, Y., Wang, Z., Mu, X., Chen, J.: Simultaneous wireless information and power transfer in near-field communications. IEEE Internet Things J. **11**(16), 27760–27774 (2024)
6. Li, Y., Chang, M., Xue, H., Liu, H., Li, L.: Simultaneous wireless information and power transmission system based on a dual-frequency metasurface design. Front. Inform. Technol. Electron. Eng. **25**, 1732–1741 (2024)
7. Lee, W., Yoon, Y.-K.: High efficiency multiscale wireless power transfer system using metasurface slabs. IEEE Access **10**, 46214–46223 (2022)
8. Zheng, Z., Fang, X., Zheng, Y., Feng, H.: A wireless power transfer system based on dual-band metamaterials. IEEE Microwave Wirel. Compon. Lett. **32**(6), 615–618 (2022)
9. Wang, Y., et al.: GPMS: enabling indoor GNSS positioning using passive metasurfaces. In: Proceedings of the 30th Annual International Conference on Mobile Computing and Networking (ACM MobiCom '24), pp. 1424–1438. Association for Computing Machinery, New York, NY, USA (2024)
10. Lili, C., Wenjun, H., Kyle, J., Xiaojiang, C., Dingyi, F., Jeremy, G.: In: 18th USENIX Symposium on Networked Systems Design and Implementation (NSDI 21), pp. 425–438 (2021)
11. Song, Y., Pan, H., Ge, L., Qiu, L., Kumar, S., Chen, Y.-C.: MicroSurf: guiding energy distribution inside microwave oven with metasurfaces. In: Proceedings of the 30th Annual International Conference on Mobile Computing and Networking (ACM MobiCom '24), pp. 1346–1360. Association for Computing Machinery, New York, NY, USA (2024)
12. Lu, X., Wang, P., Niyato, D., Kim, D.I., Han, Z.: Wireless charging technologies: fundamentals, standards, and network applications. IEEE Commun. Surv. Tutorials **18**(2), 1413–1452 (2016)

13. ECC report 333 (2022). https://docdb.cept.org/download/4769
14. Cao, Y., Dang, Z., Abu Qahouq, J.A., Phillips, E.: Dynamic efficiency tracking controller for reconfigurable four-coil wireless power transfer system. In: 2016 IEEE Applied Power Electronics Conference and Exposition (APEC), pp. 3684–3689. Long Beach, CA, USA (2016)
15. Clark, D.: Considerations when designing a wireless charging system. Abracon, Spicewood (2018)
16. Syed, A.S., Sierra-Sosa, D., Kumar, A., Elmaghraby, A.: IoT in smart cities: a survey of technologies, practices and challenges. Smart Cities **4**, 429–475 (2021)
17. Essa, A., Almajali, E., Mahmoud, S., Amaya, R.E., Alja'Afreh, S.S., Ikram, M.: Wireless power transfer for implantable medical devices: impact of implantable antennas on energy harvesting. IEEE Open J. Antennas Propag. **5**(3), 739–758 (2024)
18. Triviño, A., Casaucao, I., Quirós, J.C., Pérez, P., Rojas, A.: Novel sustainable magnetic material to improve the wireless charging of a lightweight drone. RSC Adv. **13**(16), 10556–10563 (2023)
19. Lu, P., et al.: Power-efficient simultaneous wireless information and power transfer (SWIPT) for batteryless IoT devices using a co-designed rectifying metantenna. IEEE J. Microwaves **5**(1), 34–47 (2025)

# VPAO-SIM: Vision-Based Perception and Alternating Optimization for SIM Beamforming in Vehicular Networks

Shuyi Chen[1], Jiaye Wang[1], Lin Ma[1], Liang Ye[1(✉)], Yu'e Jiang[2], Yao Xu[3], and Weixiao Meng[1]

[1] School of Electronics and Information Engineering, Harbin Institute of Technology, Harbin, China
[2] Anqing Normal University, Anqing, China
[3] Nanjing University of Information Science and Technology, Nanjing, China

**Abstract.** Next-generation vehicular networks require high-throughput, low-latency, and adaptive beamforming to support intelligent transportation systems. Stacked Intelligent Metasurfaces (SIM), as a transmissive alternative to Reconfigurable Intelligent Surfaces (RIS), offer passive beamforming with enhanced spatial control. However, challenges such as the difficulty of acquiring accurate Channel State Information (CSI) in dynamic environments and the limitations of low-resolution phase control hinder their practical deployment. To address these issues, we propose VPAO-SIM—a vision-based perception and alternating optimization framework for SIM beamforming. VPAO-SIM employs monocular 3D vision to estimate real-time angles of arrival, which guide a quantization-aware alternating optimization algorithm to configure SIM layers for hardware-constrained Linearly Constrained Minimum Variance (LCMV) beamforming. Simulation results show that VPAO-SIM achieves near-optimal target gain and interference suppression with few-bit quantization. The method is robust to vision errors and scales to multi-user scenarios, offering a practical solution for perception-driven beamforming in dynamic vehicular networks.

**Keywords:** Stacked intelligent metasurface (SIM) · vision-based beamforming · alternating optimization · vehicular networks · interference suppression

This work was supported in part by the National Science Fund for Young Scholars under Grant No. 62201176, in part by the National Natural Science Foundation of China under Grant Nos. 62431009 and 62271168, in part by the Natural Science Foundation of Heilongjiang Province, China (Grant No. YQ2023005), in part by the Basic Research Support Program for Excellent Young Teachers of Heilongjiang Province (Grant No. YQJH2023281), and in part by the Key Laboratory of Intelligent Aerospace Measurement and Control (Grant No. CYK2025-01-08).


Y. Liu et al. (Eds.): ChinaCom 2025, LNICST 711, pp. 74–87, 2027.
https://doi.org/10.1007/978-3-032-33662-0_8

# 1 Introduction

The proliferation of connected and autonomous vehicles has accelerated the demand for high-capacity, reliable, and directionally adaptive wireless communication systems. Reconfigurable Intelligent Surfaces (RIS) have emerged as a promising solution for their ability to manipulate signal propagation environments in a passive, low-cost, and energy-efficient manner. By adjusting the phase shifts of individual elements, RIS can enhance desired signals and suppress interference without relying on active radio chains, making them highly attractive for vehicular networks where hardware cost and power consumption are critical.

However, practical RIS-assisted vehicular communication faces two major challenges: acquiring accurate real-time directional information in highly dynamic environments, and overcoming hardware limitations due to quantized phase shifters typically used in practical RIS implementations. Traditional beamforming methods, such as the linearly constrained minimum variance (LCMV) [6] and minimum variance distortionless response (MVDR), achieve optimal spatial filtering under ideal conditions with continuous-phase control and full channel state information (CSI). Unfortunately, acquiring reliable CSI in vehicular scenarios is costly and often infeasible due to fast channel variations [2].

To address this limitation, recent efforts have incorporated computer vision for wireless beam alignment, using external imagery to infer angle information without CSI. For instance, Xu *et al.* [10] and Jiang *et al.* [5] demonstrated that camera-based angle estimation can effectively reduce beam training overhead, while He *et al.* [4] proposed vision-assisted adaptive beamforming for joint localization and communication. In particular, the lightweight monocular 3D detector FCOS3D [7] enables real-time estimation of object depth and orientation, making it well-suited for vehicular beam prediction.

On the RIS design side, recent studies have explored discrete phase control to address hardware quantization constraints. Xu *et al.* [9] showed that even few-bit quantization can preserve high beamforming gains, while Xu *et al.* [8] and Zhao *et al.* [12] investigated optimization and learning-based approaches to improve discrete RIS performance. Beyond single-layer architectures, stacked intelligent metasurface (SIM) structures have been proposed to increase wave control flexibility. An *et al.* [1] introduced SIM for wave-domain multiuser beamforming, and Chen *et al.* [3] extended SIM to edge-powered communication and energy transfer systems. Moreover, recent electromagnetic modeling work [11] has demonstrated that SIM can significantly benefit from diffraction-aware design, especially under near-field and multi-layer configurations, providing a solid physical foundation for SIM-based beamforming systems. Despite these advances, the integration of vision-based angle estimation, SIM architectures, and quantization-aware beamforming remains underexplored. To bridge this gap, we propose **VPAO-SIM** (Vision-based Layered Optimization for SIM in vehicular networks)—a unified framework that leverages monocular vision for direction estimation and employs an alternating optimization (AO) algorithm to configure SIM, effectively approximating ideal LCMV beamforming. The proposed framework eliminates the need for explicit CSI in vehicular scenarios, supports multi-layer phase control to address hardware quantization constraints, and achieves robust and efficient beamforming through perception-driven optimization. Extensive simulations show that VPAO-SIM delivers near-optimal target gain and strong interference suppression with only few-bit phase resolution, while maintaining robustness to visual estimation errors and scalability to multi-user vehicular scenarios.

## 2 System Model

We consider a vehicular wireless communication scenario where SIM is deployed to perform passive beamforming between infrastructure nodes (e.g., base stations or RSUs) and moving vehicles in urban environments, as illustrated in Fig. 1. In such environments, signal propagation is complicated by dynamic interference from surrounding vehicles and severe multipath reflections caused by buildings and road structures. These factors result in a highly non-stationary channel, posing challenges to maintaining reliable directional communication.

To ensure robust wireless performance under these conditions, the beamforming objective of the proposed system is two-fold: (1) to enhance signal strength toward the target vehicle, ensuring strong and stable connectivity, and (2) to suppress interference arriving from undesired directions, including nearby vehicles or reflections that could degrade link quality.

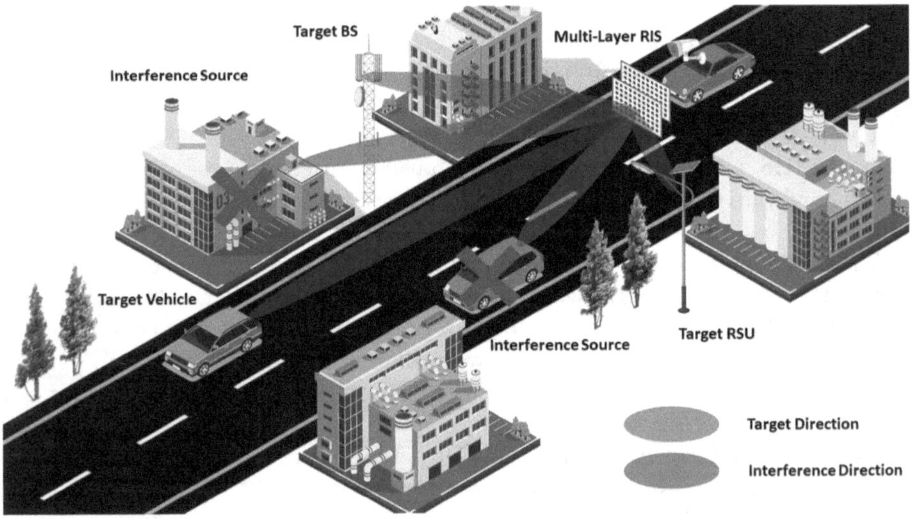


**Fig. 1.** Vehicular beamforming scenario with SIM and vision-based direction estimation. Camera-equipped vehicles provide visual angle estimation, enabling the SIM to steer beams toward the target vehicle while suppressing interference.

To realize this dual-objective beamforming in a dynamic vehicular context, we introduce the proposed **VPAO-SIM** framework. The following subsections elaborate on the signal model, the SIM architecture, and the vision-based angle acquisition pipeline using FCOS3D. We also present the beamforming formulation under practical quantized phase constraints, which serves as the basis for our quantization-aware optimization strategy.

### SIM Architecture

The SIM consists of $L$ passive transmitting layers, each containing $N = N_x \times N_y$ elements arranged on a uniform rectangular grid, where $N_x$ and $N_y$ are the numbers of elements along the horizontal and vertical axes, respectively. All elements within a layer are evenly spaced, and each transmitting element imposes a quantized phase shift selected from a $2^b$-level codebook, where $b$ is the phase resolution in bits. The total number of transmitting elements is $N_{\text{tot}} = L \times N$. Compared with single-layer RIS, SIM provides additional degrees of freedom for wavefront control under practical hardware constraints.

### Angle Estimation via Vision Sensing

Instead of relying on CSI, the directions of arrival (AoAs) for desired signals and interference sources are predicted using vision sensors. A monocular camera captures raw images $I$, which are processed by FCOS3D to extract 3D object positions, orientations, and bounding boxes. These results are then projected into the communication coordinate system to obtain the azimuth and elevation angle sets $\Theta = \{(\theta_m, \phi_m)\}_{m=1}^{M}$ for targets and $\Psi = \{(\theta_n, \phi_n)\}_{n=1}^{K}$ for interference sources, where $M$ and $K$ denote the numbers of target and interference sources, respectively. This approach avoids frequent CSI acquisition and provides low-latency directional information suitable for high-mobility vehicular scenarios.

### Beamforming Objective

The beamforming objective is to enhance signal power in all target directions while suppressing interference. Let $\mathbf{a}(\theta)$ denote the steering vector of a uniform planar array. Given the angle sets $\Theta$ and $\Phi$, an ideal fully-digital array can achieve these objectives using the LCMV beamformer. However, the SIM is a passive device with quantized phase control, making direct implementation of the continuous LCMV solution impossible. We therefore design a discrete-phase configuration for the SIM that emulates the LCMV beam pattern as closely as possible, subject to practical hardware constraints.

### Inter-Layer Coupling Model

Signal propagation between adjacent SIM layers is modeled using a Rayleigh–Sommerfeld diffraction formulation [1]. The inter-layer transfer matrix $\mathbf{W} \in \mathbb{C}^{N \times N}$ describes how the wavefront emitted by one layer propagates to the next:

$$[\mathbf{W}]_{mn} = \frac{\Delta x \Delta y \cos \chi_{mn}}{d_{mn}} \left( \frac{1}{2\pi d_{mn}} - \frac{j}{\lambda} \right) e^{j \frac{2\pi}{\lambda} d_{mn}}, \tag{1}$$

where $d_{mn}$ is the distance between element $m$ of one layer and element $n$ of the adjacent layer, $\chi_{mn}$ is the angle between the propagation vector and the surface normal, $\Delta x$ and $\Delta y$ are the element spacings, $j=\sqrt{-1}$ denotes the imaginary unit, and $\lambda$ is the carrier wavelength.

This coupling matrix is used in the proposed optimization algorithm to compute the overall response of the SIM.

The above system model defines all necessary parameters, including the number of SIM layers $L$, phase resolution $b$, element dimensions $(N_x, N_y)$, target and interference angle sets $(\Theta, \Phi)$, and operating wavelength $\lambda$, all of which are consistent with the simulation settings.

#### Discussion on Occlusion and NLOS Interference

Although the current simulations focus on line-of-sight (LOS) conditions with visually detectable targets and interferers, practical vehicular environments often involve partial occlusion and non-line-of-sight (NLOS) propagation. For example, visual sensing may fail under temporary blockages, night scenes, or adverse weather, where some interfering vehicles or reflectors are invisible to the onboard camera. While such scenarios are beyond the present simulation scope, the proposed VPAO-SIM framework can be extended to handle them through several engineering strategies.

First, a prior spatial masking scheme could reserve conservative null regions in typical interference directions (e.g., lateral lanes or roadside reflections), ensuring a baseline level of interference suppression even without visual input. Second, a lightweight energy-detection or spectrum-sensing module could provide coarse angular cues that guide subsequent AO iterations once vision becomes available again. Third, confidence-aware control of target and null gains can be implemented, where the weighting between enhancement and suppression dynamically adapts to the confidence of the visual detector.

These mechanisms are not yet simulated in this work but represent feasible extensions for real-world deployment. They enable the system to maintain stable performance when perception is incomplete or temporarily unreliable, ensuring graceful degradation without explicit CSI estimation.

## 3 VPAO-SIM Algorithm

We propose a unified beamforming framework, named **VPAO-SIM**, which integrates vision-based direction estimation, classical LCMV beamforming theory, and a quantization-aware AO algorithm tailored for SIM. The key idea is to replace CSI with computer vision, generate an ideal reference beamforming solution using the LCMV formulation, and then iteratively configure SIM layers with low-resolution phase shifters to approximate this reference.

### 3.1 Vision-Based Angle Estimation with FCOS3D

Instead of relying on wireless CSI, we adopt the monocular 3D object detector **FCOS3D** to estimate the spatial positions and orientations of surrounding objects directly from camera images. FCOS3D is a one-stage, anchor-free network that directly regresses the 3D bounding box parameters for each detected object:

$$\mathcal{B} = \{(u_c, v_c, d, w, h, l, \alpha)\}, \tag{2}$$

where $(u_c, v_c)$ denotes the 2D image center of the object, $d$ is the predicted depth from the camera center, $(w, h, l)$ are the object dimensions, and $\alpha$ is the yaw angle of the object in the camera frame.

*Camera to 3D Coordinate Transformation.* Given the camera intrinsic matrix:

$$\mathbf{K}_c = \begin{bmatrix} f_x & 0 & c_x \\ 0 & f_y & c_y \\ 0 & 0 & 1 \end{bmatrix}, \tag{3}$$

the 3D position of an object center in the camera coordinate system is computed as:

$$\mathbf{p}_c = \begin{bmatrix} x_c \\ y_c \\ z_c \end{bmatrix} = d \cdot \mathbf{K}_c^{-1} \begin{bmatrix} u_c \\ v_c \\ 1 \end{bmatrix}, \tag{4}$$

To align the camera frame with the wireless communication coordinate system, we apply an extrinsic transformation defined by rotation $\mathbf{R}_{cw} \in \mathbb{R}^{3\times3}$ and translation $\mathbf{t}_{cw} \in \mathbb{R}^3$:

$$\mathbf{p}_w = \mathbf{R}_{cw}\, \mathbf{p}_c + \mathbf{t}_{cw}, \tag{5}$$

where $\mathbf{p}_w = [x_w, y_w, z_w]^T$ is the position of the object in the communication (world) coordinate system.

*Angle Extraction for Beamforming.* These predictions are projected into the communication coordinate system to compute the azimuth and elevation angles of arrival (AoA) for each object. For a uniform planar array, the AoAs of object $i$ are given by

$$\theta_i = \arctan 2(y_{w,i}, x_{w,i}), \qquad \phi_i = \arctan 2(z_{w,i}, \sqrt{x_{w,i}^2 + y_{w,i}^2}), \tag{6}$$

By collecting all targets and interference sources, we define two angle sets for beamforming:

$$\Theta = \{(\theta_m, \phi_m)\}_{m=1}^{M} \qquad \Psi = \{(\theta_n, \phi_n)\}_{n=1}^{K}. \tag{7}$$

where $M$ and $K$ are the numbers of target and interference objects, respectively.

### 3.2 Vision-Aware Beamforming Formulation

The **VPAO-SIM** algorithm aims to approximate the ideal LCMV beamforming solution using vision-estimated angles and low-resolution SIM hardware. The angle sets $\Theta = \{(\theta_m, \phi_m)\}_{m=1}^{M}$ and $\Psi = \{(\theta_n, \phi_n)\}_{n=1}^{K}$ are used to construct the beamforming constraints.

We define the steering matrix as:

$$\mathbf{C} = [\mathbf{a}(\theta_1, \phi_1), \ldots, \mathbf{a}(\theta_M, \phi_M), \mathbf{a}(\theta_1, \phi_1), \ldots, \mathbf{a}(\theta_K, \phi_K)], \tag{8}$$

where $\mathbf{a}(\theta, \phi) \in \mathbb{C}^N$ is the steering vector of a uniform planar array (UPA) with half-wavelength spacing:

$$\mathbf{a}(\theta, \phi) = \mathbf{a}_x(\theta, \phi) \otimes \mathbf{a}_y(\theta, \phi), \tag{9}$$

$$\mathbf{a}_x(\theta, \phi) = \left[1, e^{j\pi \sin\phi \cos\theta}, \ldots, e^{j\pi(N_x-1)\sin\phi\cos\theta}\right]^T, \tag{10a}$$

$$\mathbf{a}_y(\theta, \phi) = \left[1, e^{j\pi \sin\phi \sin\theta}, \ldots, e^{j\pi(N_y-1)\sin\phi\sin\theta}\right]^T, \tag{10b}$$

The desired array response vector is given by:

$$\mathbf{f} = [1, \ldots, 1, 0, \ldots, 0]^T, \tag{11}$$

which enforces unit gain in target directions and nulls for interferers.

The optimal continuous-phase weight vector is obtained by solving the linearly constrained minimum variance (LCMV) problem:

$$\begin{aligned} \min_{\mathbf{w}} \quad & \mathbf{w}^H \mathbf{R}_x \mathbf{w} \\ \text{s.t.} \quad & \mathbf{C}^H \mathbf{w} = \mathbf{f}, \end{aligned} \tag{12}$$

with closed-form solution:

$$\mathbf{w}_{\text{LCMV}} = \mathbf{R}_x^{-1}\mathbf{C}\left(\mathbf{C}^H\mathbf{R}_x^{-1}\mathbf{C}\right)^{-1}\mathbf{f}, \tag{13}$$

where

$$\mathbf{R}_x = \mathbb{E}[\mathbf{x}\mathbf{x}^H], \tag{14}$$

is the spatial covariance matrix of the received baseband signal $\mathbf{x} \in \mathbb{C}^N$.

To emulate $\mathbf{w}_{\text{LCMV}}$ using SIM with quantized phase shifters, we define a $b$-bit phase codebook:

$$\mathcal{Q}_b = \{0, \Delta_\phi, 2\Delta_\phi, \ldots, 2\pi - \Delta_\phi\}, \quad \Delta_\phi = \frac{2\pi}{2^b}, \tag{15}$$

The SIM has $L$ layers, each with $N$ passive elements. The total RIS response is:

$$\mathbf{w}_{\text{RIS}} = \boldsymbol{\Phi}_L \mathbf{W}^{(L-1)} \cdots \boldsymbol{\Phi}_2 \mathbf{W}^{(1)} \boldsymbol{\Phi}_1 \mathbf{v}_{\text{in}}, \tag{16}$$

where each $\boldsymbol{\Phi}_\ell = \mathrm{diag}(e^{j\phi_\ell})$ and $\mathbf{v}_{\mathrm{in}} = \mathbf{1}_N$ is a spatially uniform incident wave. The inter-layer coupling matrices $\mathbf{W}^{(\ell)}$ are constructed using Rayleigh–Sommerfeld diffraction:

$$\mathbf{W}^{(\ell)} = \left([\mathbf{W}^{(\ell)}]_{mn}\right)_{m,n=1}^{N}, \quad \forall \ell = 1, \ldots, L-1, \tag{17}$$

We optimize $\mathbf{w}_{\mathrm{RIS}}$ to align with $\mathbf{w}_{\mathrm{LCMV}}$ by maximizing cosine similarity:

$$\begin{aligned} \max_{\{\boldsymbol{\Phi}_\ell\}} \quad & \Re\left\{\frac{\mathbf{w}_{\mathrm{RIS}}^H \mathbf{w}_{\mathrm{LCMV}}}{\|\mathbf{w}_{\mathrm{RIS}}\|}\right\} \\ \text{s.t.} \quad & \phi_\ell(i) \in \mathcal{Q}_b, \quad |\phi_\ell(i)| = 1, \\ & \left|\mathbf{a}^H(\theta_{\mathrm{intf}})\mathbf{w}_{\mathrm{RIS}}\right|^2 \leq \gamma, \\ & \|\boldsymbol{\Phi}_\ell - \boldsymbol{\Phi}_{\ell+1}\|_F^2 \leq \epsilon, \end{aligned} \tag{18}$$

These constraints reflect hardware limitations: phase quantization, passive (unimodular) operation, interference suppression, and inter-layer phase smoothness.

To initialize optimization, we apply a greedy strategy: each phase $\phi_\ell(i)$ is selected from $\mathcal{Q}_b$ to maximize the alignment objective, with other values fixed. Then, an alternating optimization (AO) loop updates each layer iteratively.

In each iteration, local perturbations (e.g., $\pm\Delta_\phi$) are applied to a subset of elements. Only updates that improve the objective and satisfy constraints are accepted.

We now state a lemma that explains the optimality of the cosine similarity metric:

**Lemma 1.** *Let* $\mathbf{w}_{\mathrm{LCMV}} \in \mathbb{C}^N$ *with* $\|\mathbf{w}_{\mathrm{LCMV}}\| = 1$. *Then, for any non-zero* $\mathbf{w}_{\mathrm{RIS}}$, *the cosine similarity objective*

$$J(\mathbf{w}_{\mathrm{RIS}}) := \Re\left\{\frac{\mathbf{w}_{\mathrm{RIS}}^H \mathbf{w}_{\mathrm{LCMV}}}{\|\mathbf{w}_{\mathrm{RIS}}\|}\right\}, \tag{19}$$

*achieves its maximum if and only if* $\mathbf{w}_{\mathrm{RIS}} = \alpha \mathbf{w}_{\mathrm{LCMV}}$ *for some scalar* $\alpha > 0$.

*Proof.* By the Cauchy–Schwarz inequality:

$$\left|\mathbf{w}_{\mathrm{RIS}}^H \mathbf{w}_{\mathrm{LCMV}}\right| \leq \|\mathbf{w}_{\mathrm{RIS}}\| \cdot \|\mathbf{w}_{\mathrm{LCMV}}\| = \|\mathbf{w}_{\mathrm{RIS}}\|. \tag{20}$$

Equality holds if and only if $\mathbf{w}_{\mathrm{RIS}} = \alpha \mathbf{w}_{\mathrm{LCMV}}$ for some $\alpha \in \mathbb{C}$. Since we maximize the real part of the inner product, the optimal alignment occurs when $\alpha > 0$.

The VPAO-SIM algorithm solves the optimization problem in Eq. (18) through layer-wise AO, initialized greedily, refined iteratively, and post-processed via local perturbation. The final quantized phases $\{\phi_\ell\}$ yield an RIS response $\mathbf{w}_{\mathrm{RIS}}$ that approximates $\mathbf{w}_{\mathrm{LCMV}}$ under vision-derived direction estimates. The overall algorithm is summarized in Algorithm 1.

**Algorithm 1.** VPAO-SIM: Vision-Based Perception and Alternating Optimization for SIM

**Require:** Image $I$, SIM config $(L, N_x, N_y, b, \lambda)$, constraints $(\gamma, \epsilon)$
**Ensure:** Optimized SIM phase configuration $\{\Phi_\ell\}_{\ell=1}^{L}$

**Initialize** quantization codebook $\mathcal{Q}_b = \{0, \Delta\phi, \ldots, 2\pi - \Delta\phi\}$, where $\Delta\phi = \frac{2\pi}{2^b}$
Predict angle sets $\Theta$ (targets), $\Psi$ (interferers) using vision model (e.g., FCOS3D)
Construct steering matrix $C = [a(\theta, \phi) \mid (\theta, \phi) \in \Theta \cup \Psi]$
Define response vector $f = [1, \ldots, 1, 0, \ldots, 0]^T$ (gain for targets, nulls for interferers)
Compute LCMV reference: $w_{\text{LCMV}} = R_x^{-1} C (C^H R_x^{-1} C)^{-1} f$
**Initialize** each layer $\Phi_\ell$ greedily from $\mathcal{Q}_b$ to align with $w_{\text{LCMV}}$
Compute inter-layer coupling matrices $W^{(\ell)}$ using diffraction model
**repeat**
  **for** $\ell = 1$ to $L$ **do**
    **for** each element $i$ in layer $\ell$ **do**
      **for** each $\phi_q \in \mathcal{Q}_b$ **do**
        Set $\phi_i^{(\ell)} \leftarrow \phi_q$
        Compute SIM response $w_{\text{RIS}}$
        **if** constraints satisfied: interference $\leq \gamma$, smoothness $\leq \epsilon$ **then**
          Evaluate similarity $\mathcal{J} = \Re\left(\frac{w_{\text{RIS}}^H w_{\text{LCMV}}}{\|w_{\text{RIS}}\|}\right)$
          Accept $\phi_q$ if it improves $\mathcal{J}$
        **end if**
      **end for**
    **end for**
  **end for**
**until** convergence or max iterations
**return** $\{\Phi_\ell\}_{\ell=1}^{L}$

In the next section, we evaluate the performance of the proposed algorithm via simulations under realistic vehicular settings.

## 4 Simulation Results

This section evaluates the performance of the proposed VPAO-SIM algorithm under various system parameters. Unless otherwise specified, the default settings are: two RIS layers, an array size of $5 \times 5$ ($N_x \times N_y = 25$ elements), 3-bit phase quantization, one target, two interferers, 30 dBm transmit power, and an operating frequency of 5.8 GHz. Both inter-element and inter-layer spacing are set to half the wavelength. We consider both actual and vision-predicted angles from FCOS3D, denoted as *Actual* and *Pred* in the figure legends. If not explicitly labeled as Actual or Pred, the results are assumed to be based on vision-predicted (Pred) angles. For fair comparison, the LCMV and DFT baselines are computed using a single-layer uniform planar array (UPA) with the same array dimensions ($N_x \times N_y$) as each layer in VPAO-SIM. These baseline methods assume ideal continuous-phase control without hardware quantization constraints. LCMV and DFT are chosen as representative baselines since they respectively define the upper and lower performance bounds. Other beamforming schemes were not further considered because they reduce to these two cases under the same hardware and constraint settings.

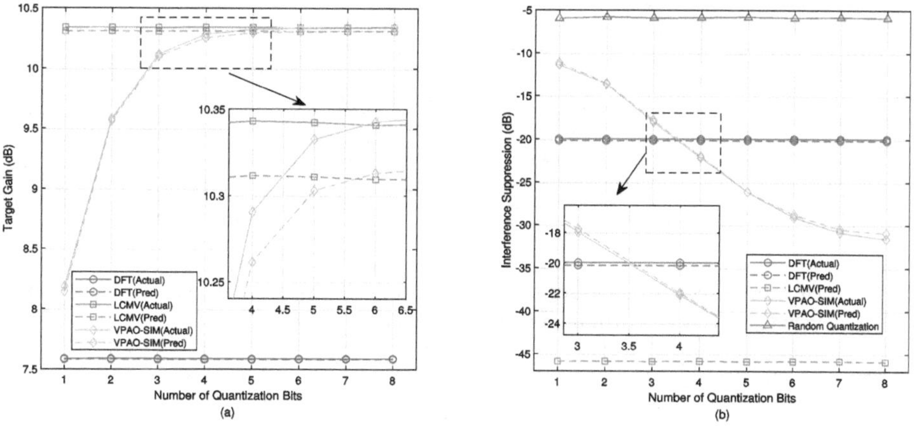


**Fig. 2.** Beamforming performance under varying quantization bit numbers: (a) target gain; (b) interference suppression.

Figure 2 compares DFT, LCMV, and VPAO-SIM across quantization resolutions from 1 to 8 bits, using both actual and vision-based angles. In the target direction, VPAO-SIM improves steadily with increased resolution, surpassing 10 dB at 5 bits and approaching the LCMV benchmark. DFT remains nearly flat at around 7.5 dB due to its fixed structure, while the random quantization baseline stays below $-6$ dB. In the interference direction, VPAO-SIM reaches roughly $-30$ dB suppression at 8 bits, outperforming DFT at around $-20$ dB. The actual LCMV null exceeds $-200$ dB and is omitted for clarity. These results show that VPAO-SIM converges toward LCMV behavior even under low-resolution control.

Figure 3 illustrates performance under varying transmit powers from $-10$ dBm to 30 dBm. All methods show increasing target gain with power. LCMV remains best, followed closely by VPAO-SIM with only minor deviation. DFT performs worst due to fixed steering. Although the interference power naturally varies with transmit power, the relative null depth of VPAO-SIM remains stable, indicating effective suppression regardless of power scaling.

Figure 4 examines RIS sizes from $3 \times 3$ to $15 \times 15$. Larger arrays enhance spatial resolution, leading to improved gain across all methods. VPAO-SIM with 3-bit quantization approaches LCMV performance at larger scales and consistently outperforms DFT, even under 2-bit control. In the interference direction, VPAO-SIM exhibits increasing suppression performance as the RIS array size grows, benefiting from enhanced spatial resolution even with coarse quantization. Although DFT achieves deeper nulls, this method lacks directional flexibility—its beam pattern is fixed and does not adapt to specific interference directions. In

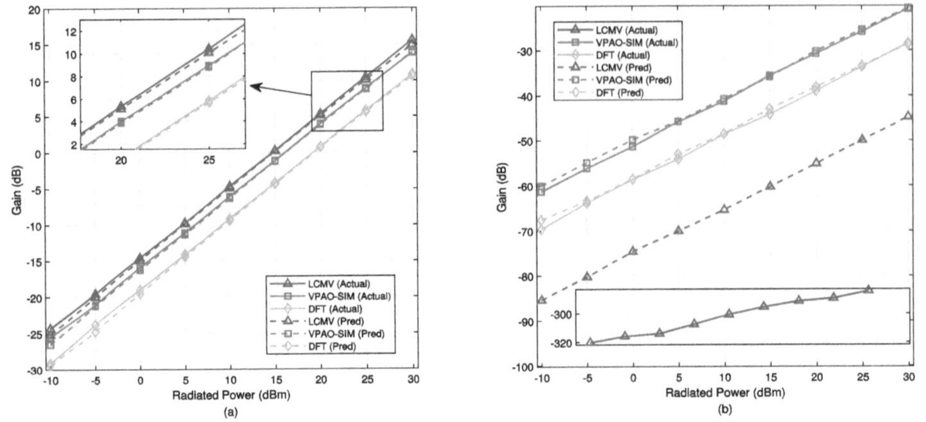


**Fig. 3.** Performance comparison under different radiated power levels: (a) performance in target direction; (b) performance in interference direction.

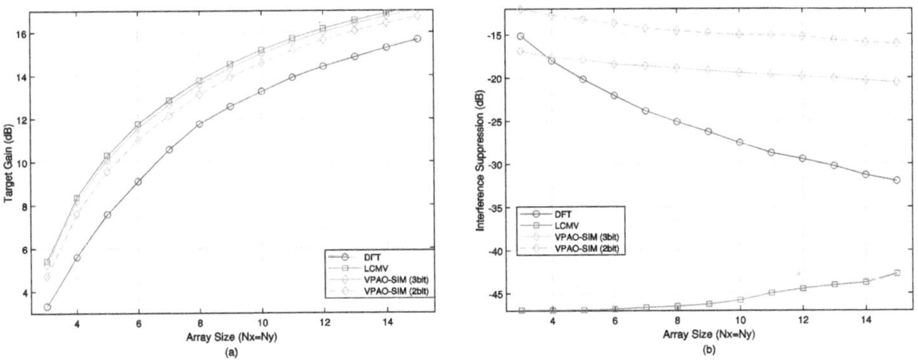


**Fig. 4.** Performance comparison under varying RIS array size ($N_x = N_y$) using predicted directions: (a) performance in target direction; (b) performance in interference direction.

contrast, VPAO-SIM dynamically steers nulls based on vision-estimated angles, enabling targeted suppression despite slightly shallower nulls.

Figure 5 evaluates the impact of RIS layer configurations under a fixed total number of 60 elements, with $L$ varying from 1 to 6 and corresponding $N = 60/L$. In the target direction, both 3-bit and 6-bit VPAO-SIM exhibit a gradual decrease in gain as the number of layers increases. This trend mirrors the degradation in the ideal LCMV performance, which serves as an upper bound and also declines with increasing $L$ due to reduced aperture per layer and lower spatial resolution. Notably, the 6-bit VPAO-SIM closely tracks the LCMV curve across all layer configurations, demonstrating that the proposed algorithm can accurately emulate the ideal beam pattern even under multi-layer RIS settings. While the 3-bit version shows a slightly larger gap, it still maintains a consistent

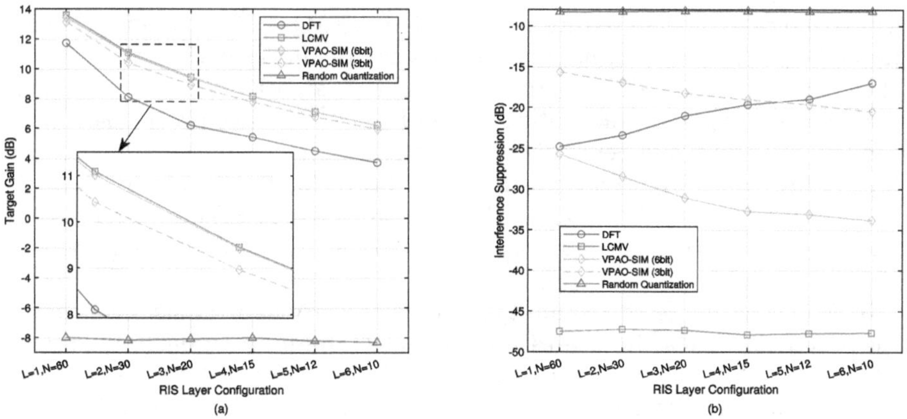


**Fig. 5.** Performance comparison with a fixed total number of RIS elements but varying layer configurations: (a) performance in the target direction; (b) performance in the interference direction.

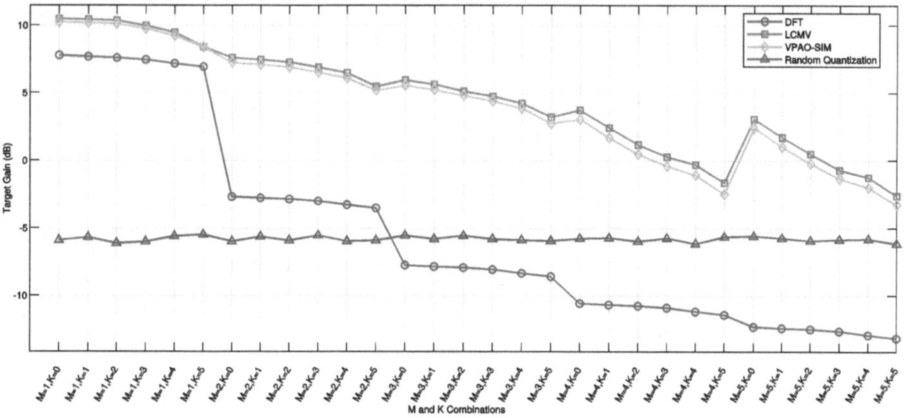


**Fig. 6.** Performance comparison under different numbers of targets and interferences.

shape and outperforms DFT. This highlights the algorithm's robustness: even under coarse quantization, it effectively leverages limited phase resolution to control beamforming behavior across stacked layers. In the interference direction, suppression performance also decreases with more layers for both VPAO-SIM and LCMV. Meanwhile, DFT performance weakens significantly as $L$ increases, since each layer contains fewer elements and its fixed beam pattern becomes less effective.

Figure 6 assesses beamforming under increasing numbers of targets ($M$) and interferers ($K$). All methods degrade with greater spatial complexity, but VPAO-SIM and LCMV retain relatively stable gain for moderate $M$. DFT drops sharply as it only adapts to the first target. Random quantization performs consistently poorly, underscoring the need for optimization. VPAO-SIM demonstrates scalability and resilience, validating its effectiveness in multi-user scenarios.

In summary, VPAO-SIM effectively bridges the gap between ideal continuous-phase beamforming and practical quantized RIS control. Even with coarse resolution (e.g., 2–3 bits) and perception-based angle estimates, it closely approaches LCMV performance while outperforming fixed-codebook baselines such as DFT. The algorithm scales well with array size, adapts to power variation, and remains reliable across multi-user conditions—highlighting its suitability for dynamic vehicular networks.

We further evaluate the computational complexity and timing performance of the proposed VPAO-SIM algorithm. For one AO outer iteration, evaluating all $2^b$ phase candidates across $L$ layers and $N = N_x N_y$ elements leads to an overall computational order of $\mathcal{O}(L\,N\,2^b)$ updates. Each update involves propagating through $(L-1)$ inter-layer coupling matrices $\mathbf{W}^{(\ell)}$ and recomputing the SIM response $\mathbf{w}_{\mathrm{RIS}}$ (Eq. (16)), resulting in $\mathcal{O}((L-1)N)$ operations per evaluation. Hence, the worst-case per-iteration complexity is $\mathcal{O}(L(L-1)N^2 2^b)$, while early-accept heuristics substantially reduce the actual cost in practice.

In timing tests conducted over 200 independent trials under the default configuration ($L$=2, $N_x$=$N_y$=5, $b$=3, SNR=INR=10 dB), the average total runtime of a full beamforming process was approximately 0.0398 s with a standard deviation of 0.0048 s. Among the major modules, signal generation and alternating optimization (AO) consumed the largest portions of time, accounting for roughly 28.4% and 22.8% of the total, respectively. The AO module converged within about 5.17 iterations on average, confirming the algorithm's fast convergence property. LCMV computation, quantization, and DFT baseline operations each required less than 1% of the total time. These results demonstrate that the proposed VPAO-SIM framework achieves efficient execution and meets the real-time requirements of vehicular beamforming systems.

## 5 Conclusion

We presented VPAO-SIM, a vision-based beamforming framework for vehicular networks that leverages monocular camera-based angle estimation and a quantization-aware alternating optimization algorithm for SIM control. VPAO-SIM achieves near-continuous LCMV performance using only vision-predicted angles and coarse phase quantization, outperforming conventional fixed-codebook designs such as DFT. Simulations confirmed its robustness under different power levels, SIM configurations, and multi-user scenarios, demonstrating its potential for practical, low-complexity beamforming in dynamic vehicular environments. Future work will focus on real-time deployment and prototype validation in live road conditions.

**Acknowledgment.** The work presented in this paper was supported by the National Science Fund for Young Scholars under Grant No. 62201176, partly by the National Natural Science Foundation of China under Grant No. 62271168, and in part by the National Natural Science Foundation of China under Grant No. 62431009.

## References

1. An, J., Di Renzo, M., Debbah, M., Vincent Poor, H., Yuen, C.: Stacked intelligent metasurfaces for multiuser downlink beamforming in the wave domain. IEEE Trans. Wireless Commun. **24**(7), 5525–5538 (2025). https://doi.org/10.1109/TWC.2025.3547779
2. Bjornson, E., Van der Perre, L., Buzzi, S., Larsson, E.G.: Massive mimo in sub-6 ghz and mmwave: physical, practical, and use-case differences. IEEE Wirel. Commun. **26**(2), 100–108 (2019). https://doi.org/10.1109/MWC.2018.1800140
3. Chen, S., et al.: Multi-layer ris on edge: communication, computation and wireless power transfer. IEEE Internet of Things Mag. **8**(3), 100–108 (2025). https://doi.org/10.1109/IOTM.001.2400191
4. He, J., Wymeersch, H., Sanguanpuak, T., Silven, O., Juntti, M.: Adaptive beamforming design for mmwave ris-aided joint localization and communication. In: 2020 IEEE Wireless Communications and Networking Conference Workshops (WCNCW), pp. 1–6 (2020). https://doi.org/10.1109/WCNCW48565.2020.9124848
5. Jiang, S., Hindy, A., Alkhateeb, A.: Camera aided reconfigurable intelligent surfaces: computer vision based fast beam selection. In: ICC 2023 - IEEE International Conference on Communications, pp. 2921–2926 (2023). https://doi.org/10.1109/ICC45041.2023.10279112
6. Van Veen, B., Buckley, K.: Beamforming: a versatile approach to spatial filtering. IEEE ASSP Mag. **5**(2), 4–24 (1988). https://doi.org/10.1109/53.665
7. Wang, T., Zhu, X., Pang, J., Lin, D.: Fcos3d: fully convolutional one-stage monocular 3d object detection. In: 2021 IEEE/CVF International Conference on Computer Vision Workshops (ICCVW), pp. 913–922 (2021). https://doi.org/10.1109/ICCVW54120.2021.00107
8. Xu, J., Xu, W., Swindlehurst, A.L.: Discrete phase shift design for practical large intelligent surface communication. In: 2019 IEEE Pacific Rim Conference on Communications, Computers and Signal Processing (PACRIM), pp. 1–5 (2019). https://doi.org/10.1109/PACRIM47961.2019.8985103
9. Xu, P., Chen, G., Yang, Z., Renzo, M.D.: Reconfigurable intelligent surfaces-assisted communications with discrete phase shifts: How many quantization levels are required to achieve full diversity? IEEE Wireless Commun. Lett. **10**(2), 358–362 (2021). https://doi.org/10.1109/LWC.2020.3031084
10. Xu, W., Gao, F., Tao, X., Zhang, J., Alkhateeb, A.: Computer vision aided mmwave beam alignment in v2x communications. IEEE Trans. Wireless Commun. **22**(4), 2699–2714 (2023). https://doi.org/10.1109/TWC.2022.3213541
11. Zhang, Q., Chen, S., Meng, W.: Eit-based modeling and performance analysis of spherical and plane wave diffraction propagation for sim-mimo system. In: IEEE International Conference on Communications (ICC) (2025). to be published
12. Zhao, B., Yang, C.: Learning beamforming for ris-aided systems with permutation equivariant graph neural networks. In: 2023 IEEE 97th Vehicular Technology Conference (VTC2023-Spring), pp. 1–5 (2023). https://doi.org/10.1109/VTC2023-Spring57618.2023.10200544

# Joint Receive Beamforming and Backscatter Device Grouping Design for Multi-source Ambient Backscatter Communication

Diancheng Cheng(✉), Xiang Li, Haoyue Zheng, Yu Feng, Lianyuan Li, Bo Wu, and Xin Ge

China Mobile Research Institute, Beijing, China
chengdiancheng@chinamobile.com

**Abstract.** Ambient backscatter communication (AmBC) is a cutting-edge technology for massive connection and ubiquitous communication in the six-generation (6G) network, where massive ultra-low power backscatter devices (BDs) can power themselves with radio frequency energy harvesting (RF-EH) and transmit their collected data with backscatter communication. However, massive connection with AmBC suffers from efficiency barrier because of its inherent direct-link interference (DLI) from ambient RF source (AS) and multiple BD access competition. In this paper, a joint receive beamforming and BD grouping design scheme is proposed to improve the sum-rate efficiency of massive BDs under multi-source AmBC networks. By utilizing beamforming management, the inter-AS DLI can be significantly suppressed while the grouped BDs can benefit from specific receive beamforming avoiding random access competition. Simulation results show the outstanding sum-rate performance of our proposed design strategy compared with traditional AmBC systems without careful beamforming management and/or BD grouping.

**Keywords:** 6g · ambient backscatter communication · receive beamforming management · backscatter device grouping

## 1 Introduction

To realize the vision of massive connection and ubiquitous communication for the six-generation (6G) network in the near future, low-power massive Internet of Things (IoT) technology, i.e., ambient backscatter communication (AmBC) has been highlighted for providing ultra low-power backscatter communication for massive terminal devices, especially for those passive devices [1,2]. The advantages of AmBC lie in its power self-maintenance and spectrum sharing. The backscatter devices (BDs) in an AmBC system power themselves with radio frequency energy harvesting (RF-EH) and piggyback their collected data on the


Y. Liu et al. (Eds.): ChinaCom 2025, LNICST 711, pp. 88–98, 2027.
https://doi.org/10.1007/978-3-032-33662-0_9

existing RF carrier signals from ambient RF sources (AS). The IoT networks closely bound up with AmBC, i.e., ambient Internet of Things (AIoT) has been standardized by the third generation partnership project (3GPP) since Release 19 (R19) specifications [3,4], because of the energy and spectrum efficiency of AmBC in massive connection.

However, AmBC suffers from severe inherent direct-link interference (DLI) and lacks efficient multi-BD access protocol on its way to achieve practical 6G massive connection. Due to sharing spectrum with AS, the interested backscatter signals from the BDs, which experiences double fading [2], will be heavily deteriorated by the RF carrier signals directly from the AS. This structural bottleneck has caused limited signal detection performance since AmBC was proposed in 2013 [1,5]. Besides, random access of multiple BDs lead to competition and conflict frequently with number expansion. Efficient multi-BD access control strategies are urgently needed [6].

Receive beamforming is widely utilized by multi-antenna AmBC systems to improve signal detection performance [7] and suppress DLI [8]. By carefully designing combining vector using zero-forcing (ZF) or other beamforming methods [7], the backscatter signals can be significantly enhanced while the DLI is suppressed via spatial filtering. BD grouping [9] can be used to reduce access competition and conflict among massive BDs by scheduling access order of grouped BDs rather than each-BD random access. However, receive beamforming generally requires perfect channel state information (CSI) which cannot be fully estimated in AmBC systems [10] mainly because of power- and hardware-constraints on passive BDs.

In this paper, a joint receive beamforming and BD grouping strategy is proposed for multi-AS and massive-BD AmBC systems to combat with DLI and improve access efficiency of the grouped BDs. The combining vectors are built to suppress inter-AS DLI using only partial direct-link channel estimation by solving a generalized eigenvalue problem. This introduces a spatial filter for the DLI signals from different AS according to their locations. Meanwhile, the activated BDs are naturally located surrounding the AS for harvesting sufficient energy. Thus, grouping the massive BDs referring to the designed combining vectors can assist the BDs suppressing severe inter-AS DLIs. Besides, the combining vectors are orthogonal to each other, which can ensure BDs from different groups access simultaneously. In this way, both intra-BD DLI suppression and inter-BD access conflict issues are jointly solved, which can significantly improve the sum rate of the multi-AS and massive-BD AmBC system and builds practical massive connection to 6G data uploading.

## 2 System Model

Consider a multi-AS and massive-BD AmBC system as illustrated in Fig. 1, which consists of $K$ ambient RF sources, $J$ passive BDs (e.g., Class A Tags in Ambient IoT [3]) and a backscatter receiver (BR) equipped with $M$ antennas. The BDs are assumed powered themselves only with RF-EH with a common RF-to-dc power conversion efficiency $\eta = 70\%$ [11] and their "wake-up" threshold is $p_{th} = -19\text{dBm}$ [4]. The ambient RF sources are surrounding RF infrastructures (e.g., base station) or devices (e.g., access point, smart phone) working in the same frequency band in a same AmBC system. As most work [7,8,12], the normalized sample signal of the $k$-th ambient RF source (AS) is distributed as $s_k(n) \sim \mathcal{CN}(0,1)$ since it is unknown to the BDs, where $n = 1, 2, ..., N$ and $N$ is the length of a backscatter symbol. Moreover, the block flat-fading channel is considered [8,12] since the BDs are widely deployed in quasi-static scenarios with slow movement. The direct-link from the $k$-th AS to the $m$-th receive antenna at the BR is denoted $g_{k,m}$. The forward-link from the $k$-th AS to the $j$-th BD is denoted by $f_{k,j}$, and the backward-link from the $j$-th BD to the $m$-th receive antenna is $h_{j,m}$. Due to dense objective deployed in massive IoT scenarios, the above channel coefficients can be assumed obey Rayleigh distribution as existing studies [8,13]. Thus, the channel coefficients can be modeled as Rayleigh random various, i.e., $g_{k,m} \sim \mathcal{CN}(0, \sigma^2_{g_{k,m}})$, $f_{k,j} \sim \mathcal{CN}(0, \sigma^2_{f_{k,j}})$, and $h_{j,m} \sim \mathcal{CN}(0, \sigma^2_{h_{j,m}})$. Generally, the channel coefficients keep constant during at least one backscatter symbol, i.e., $N$ samples [12].

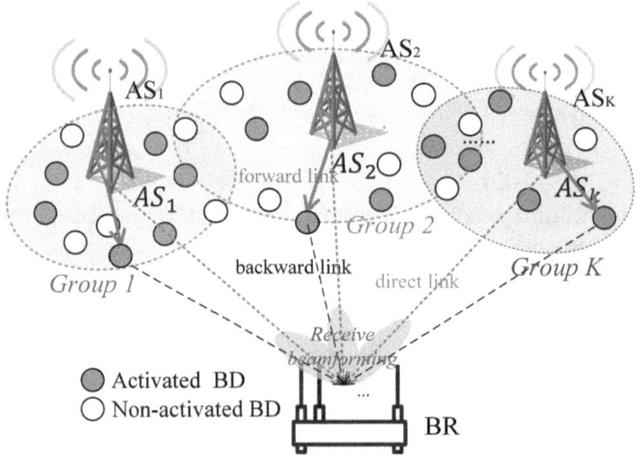


**Fig. 1.** The architecture of multi-AS and massive-BD system.

## 2.1 Signal Model

The BDs are illuminated by $K$ RF sources, harvesting energy while backscattering. Assume the transmit power of the $k$-th AS is $P_k$, the received signal at the $j$-th BD in $n$-th sample from the forward link can be expressed as

$$y^f_{k,j}(n) = \sum_{k=1}^{K} \sqrt{P_k} f_{k,j} s_k(n), \tag{1}$$

where the receive noise is ignored since the BDs are passive devices [2].

The received power in (1) is partially harvested while the remaining is backscattered. The backscatter power coefficient is assumed $\alpha \in (0, 1)$, so $(1-\alpha)$ received power is used for power supply. When the harvested power exceeds $p_{th}$, the BD is activated and then it can access to the BR for data uploading. The power constraint of the $j$-th BD can be given by

$$\eta(1-\alpha)\mathbb{E}[|y_{k,j}^f(n)|^2] = \eta(1-\alpha)\sum_{k=1}^{K} P_k|f_{k,j}|^2 \geq p_{th}. \tag{2}$$

Thus, the backscattered signal of the $j$-th BD from the backward link at the $m$-th receive antenna of the BR can be written by

$$y_{j,m}^b = \sqrt{\alpha}\sum_{k=1}^{K} y_{k,j}^f(n)h_{j,m}c_j, \tag{3}$$

where the BDs are assumed adopting BPSK modulation [2,8]. $c_j \in \{\pm 1\}$ is the backscatter symbol of the $j$-th BD during $N$ samples.

The BR will receive DLIs from $K$ RF sources at the same time, which severely deteriorates the backscattered signal in (3) since the DLI is generally 3–4 orders of magnitude higher [2,14]. The DLI signal received from direct link of the $k$-th AS at the $m$-th receive antenna is expressed as

$$y_{k,m}^d(n) = \sum_{k=1}^{K} \sqrt{P_k}g_{k,m}s_k(n), \tag{4}$$

Finally, the overall received signal at the $m$-th receive antenna from the $j$-th BD under $K$ RF sources is written by

$$\begin{aligned} y_{j,m}(n) = & \underbrace{\sum_{k=1}^{K} \sqrt{P_k}g_{k,m}s_k(n)}_{DLI} \\ & + \underbrace{\sum_{k=1}^{K} \sqrt{\alpha P_k}f_{k,j}h_{j,m}s_k(n)c_j + u_m(n)}_{\text{backscatter signal}}, \end{aligned} \tag{5}$$

where $u_m(n) \sim \mathcal{CN}(0, \sigma_m^2)$ is the additive white Gaussian noise (AWGN) with noise power $\sigma_m^2$ at the $m$-th receive antenna.

### 2.2 Receive Beamforming

The BR uses combining vector $\mathbf{w} \in \mathbb{C}^{M\times 1}$ to combine the received signal at each antenna to combat with DLI and obtain diversity gain. Rewriting (5) in vector form substituting $m = 1, 2, ..., M$, the combined signal is then given by

$$\hat{y}_j(n) = \mathbf{w}^H\mathbf{y}_j(n) \in \mathbb{C}, \tag{6}$$

where $\mathbf{y}_j(n) = [y_{j,1}(n), y_{j,2}(n), ..., y_{j,M}(n)]^T \in \mathbb{C}^{M\times 1}$ is the receive signal vector of the $j$-th BD at $n$-th sample, and $\|\mathbf{w}\|^2 = 1$.

Calculating signal power with the expectation of the square of the signal amplitude, e.g., $\mathbb{E}(|s_k(n)|^2)$ according to (6), the receive signal-to-interference-plus-noise ratio (SINR) of the $j$-th BD is expressed as

$$\gamma_j = \frac{\left(\sum\limits_{k=1}^{K} \alpha P_k |f_{k,j}|^2\right) |\mathbf{w}^H \mathbf{h}_j|^2}{\sum\limits_{k=1}^{K} P_k |\mathbf{w}^H \mathbf{g}_k|^2 + \sigma_m^2}, \tag{7}$$

where $\mathbb{E}[|s_k(n)|^2] = 1$ since $s_k(n) \sim \mathcal{CN}(0,1)$, and $\mathbb{E}[|c_j|]^2 = 1$ because $c_j \in \{\pm 1\}$. $\mathbf{h}_j = [h_{j,1}, h_{j,2}, ..., h_{j,M}]^T \in \mathbb{C}^{M\times 1}$ is the backward-link channel coefficient vector of the $j$-th BD. $\mathbf{g}_k = [g_{k,1}, g_{k,2}, ..., g_{k,M}]^T \in \mathbb{C}^{M\times 1}$ is the direct-link channel coefficient vector of $k$-th AS. The AWGN noise power is unchanged due to $\|\mathbf{w}\|^2 = 1$.

### 2.3 BD Grouping

Consider total $J$ activated BDs require accessing to the BR in a transmit period. For the sake of fairness, each BD has same $T$ access time and can only be divided into one group. If the $j$-th BD is divided into group $\mathcal{G}_i$, where $i = 1, 2, ..., G$, its group index $\xi_{j,i} = 1$. Otherwise, $\xi_{j,l} = 0, (l \neq i)$. Thus, the group index constraint can be given by

$$\sum_{i=1}^{G} \xi_{j,i} = 1. \tag{8}$$

Therefore, the sum rate of $J$ activated BDs is expressed as

$$R = \sum_{i=1}^{G} \sum_{j=1}^{J} \xi_{j,i} \log(1 + \gamma_j). \tag{9}$$

## 3 Joint Beamforming and BD Grouping Design

To maximize the sum rate of total $J$ activated BDs in (13) under $K$ RF sources, a two-step joint receive beamforming and BD grouping design is proposed in this section. In the first step, $K$ combining vectors (i.e., $\mathbf{w}_k, k = 1, 2, ..., K$) are generated based on only direct-link CSI by calculating generalized eigenvector, which can guarantee the inter-AS DLIs are eliminated and provide $K$ BD groups. Then, in the second step, the activated BDs are divided into the $K$ groups by searching maximum combined receive signal power (CRSP) among different combining vectors. In this way, the SINR can be significantly improved since severe DLIs are spatially filtered. Furthermore, due to combining vectors are orthogonal to each other, i.e., $\mathbf{w}_k^H \mathbf{w}_l = 0, (k \neq l)$, a more efficient BD grouping strategy is introduced by allowing BDs in different groups to access simultaneously.

### 3.1 Receive Beamforming Design (Step 1)

Although perfect full channel estimation is hard in AmBC systems [2,10] because of lack of pilot signals, the partial CSI of only direct-link (i.e., $\mathbf{g}_k$) can be estimated in an AIoT system [3] since BR can generally keep connection to the AS.

Using $\mathbf{g}_k, k = 1, 2, ..., K$, the inter-AS DLI can be eliminated via spatial filtering for every BD group based on the following optimal problem:

$$\mathbf{w}_k^{\dagger} = \arg\max_{\mathbf{w}_k} \frac{\mathbf{w}_k^H \mathbf{g}_k \mathbf{g}_k^H \mathbf{w}_k}{\sum_{i=1, i\neq k}^{K} \mathbf{w}_i^H \mathbf{g}_i^H \mathbf{g}_i \mathbf{w}_i} \tag{10}$$

$$\text{s.t.} \quad \|\mathbf{w}_i\|^2 = 1, i = 1, 2, ..., K \tag{10a}$$

The problem (10) can be transferred to a generalized eigenvalue maximization problem [15]. The original problem is in form of $\mathcal{L} = \frac{\mathbf{w}^H A \mathbf{w}}{\mathbf{w}^H B \mathbf{w}}$. By setting $\frac{\partial \mathcal{L}}{\partial \mathbf{w}} = 0$, we have $A\mathbf{w} = \lambda B\mathbf{w}$, which is a generalized eigenvalue problem. The maximization problem in (10) is equivalent to calculate maximum eigenvector of the generalized eigenvalue problem.

### 3.2 BD Grouping Design (Step 2)

**Direct Grouping Based on CRSP.** The forward-link and backward-link CSI (i.e., $f_{k,j}$ and $\mathbf{h}_j$) is absent in AmBC systems. To divide activated BDs into their groups with proper combining vector, the BR searches within $\{\mathbf{w}_k^{\dagger}\}_{k=1,2,..,K}$ and finds the max CRSP of a specific BD's received backscatter signal vector. The grouping rule of finding group index $\xi_{j,i}$ of the $j$-th BD can be given by

$$\xi_{j,i} = 1, \quad \text{if} \quad i = \arg \max_{i \in \{1,2,...,K\}} \underbrace{\mathbb{E}[\mathbf{w}_i^{\dagger} \mathbf{y}_j(n)]}_{\text{CRSP}}, \tag{11}$$

otherwise, $\xi_{j,i} = 0$.

**Simultaneous Access Grouping.** Since combining vectors are orthogonal to each other, there are BDs in different groups can access to the BR simultaneous. To find these BDs, the direct grouping rule is supposed to be refined. Considering the $j$-th BD in group $\mathcal{G}_i$, if there are some BDs from other groups respectively that can reduce its SINR (i.e., $\gamma_j$ in (12)) within an allowed range, e.g., the tolerance $\epsilon = 10\%$, these BDs in other groups are allowed to access with the $j$-th BD simultaneously. If a club of BDs are SINR-tolerant to each other, they will access to the BR simultaneously. Note that, in this paper, we only consider a linear-time inter-group simultaneous access for the sake of practicality, i.e., a BD will access to the BR alone if it cannot wait a mate within a time window, e.g., $KT$. In massive IoT scenario, the global optimum might be impractical for a large number of devices.

As for simultaneous-access BDs in a club $\mathcal{C}$, the SINR should consider inter-BD interference, which can be given by

$$\gamma_j' = \frac{\left(\sum_{k=1}^{K} \alpha P_k |f_{k,j}|^2\right) |\mathbf{w}^H \mathbf{h}_j|^2}{\sum_{k=1}^{K} P_k |\mathbf{w}^H \mathbf{g}_k|^2 + \underbrace{\left(\sum_{l\in\mathcal{C}, l\neq j} \alpha P_k |f_{k,l}|^2\right) |\mathbf{w}^H \mathbf{h}_l|^2}_{\text{inter-BD interference}, \quad \leq \epsilon} + \sigma_m^2}. \tag{12}$$

Therefore, the sum rate of simultaneous-access BDs in a club $\mathcal{C}$ can be calculated by

$$R_{\mathcal{C}}' = |\mathcal{C}| \sum_{i=1}^{G} \sum_{j=1}^{|\mathcal{C}|} \xi_{j,i} \log(1 + \gamma_j'), \tag{13}$$

where $|\cdot|$ is the cardinality of a set.

## 4 Simulation Results

Consider a multi-AS and massive-BD AmBC system in indoor IoT scenarios, where the number of AS is $K$=3, the number of BDs is $J$=100 and the BR is equipped with $M$=4 receive antennas. The RF sources are assumed access points (APs) for IoT devices with frequency $f_c$=915 MHz and transmit power $P_1$=$P_2$=$P_3$=20 dBm. As aforementioned, the power conversion efficiency and "wake-up" threshold of the BDs are $\eta$=70% [11] and $p_{th}$=−19 dBm [4], respectively. The backscatter power coefficient is set as $\alpha$=0.6 [13]. The variance of channel coefficients in Sect. 2 is determined by the path loss [2,4,12], which can be calculated via Friis formula [2]. The antenna gains at the AS, the BD and the BR are set as 4 dBi, 1.2 dBi, and 4 dBi, respectively [16,17], and the path loss exponents of the forward link, direct link and backward link are set as $\nu_f$=2, $\nu_d$=$\nu_b$= 3, respectively, since the BDs are close to the ASs for RF-EH. The distance between the ASs and the BR are 10 m. The BDs are settled about 1 m away from the ASs. As for the simultaneous access grouping, the tolerance is $\epsilon$=10%.

In Fig. 2, a random configuration of multi-AS and massive-BD AmBC system are illustrated. In (a), $J$=100 passive BDs are randomly distributed within a fan-shaped area centered on BR, with radius ranging from 9 m to 11 m around $K$=3 ASs. The following simulations are all conducted based on this system configuration. In (b), the activated BDs are highlighted in green. It shows that the activated BDs are naturally grouped together around the ASs, since the passive BDs close to source can harvest more RF energy. The proposed receive beamforming design in Section III-A can provide receive beamforming toward each natural BD groups to eliminate inter-AS DLIs by solving problem (10). However, the next Fig. 3 will shows that the BDs are actually not gathered in natural groups according to $\mathbf{w}_k^\dagger$ because the CRSP is affected by $\mathbf{h}_j$ as well.

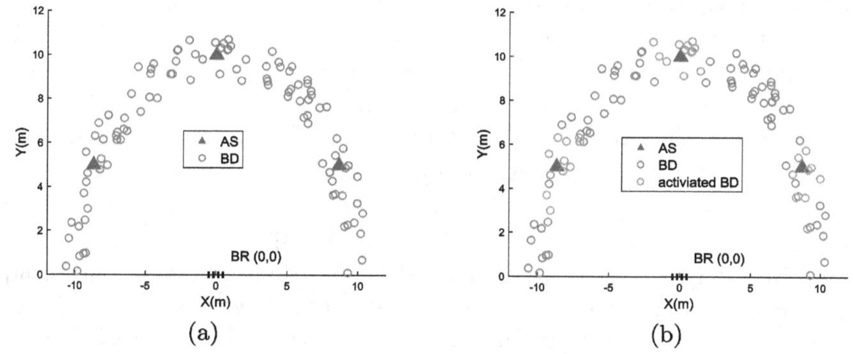


**Fig. 2.** The illustration of randomly distributed BDs and natural groups of activated BDs in a multi-AS and massive-BD AmBC system. (a) Original BDs. (b) Naturally grouped BDs.

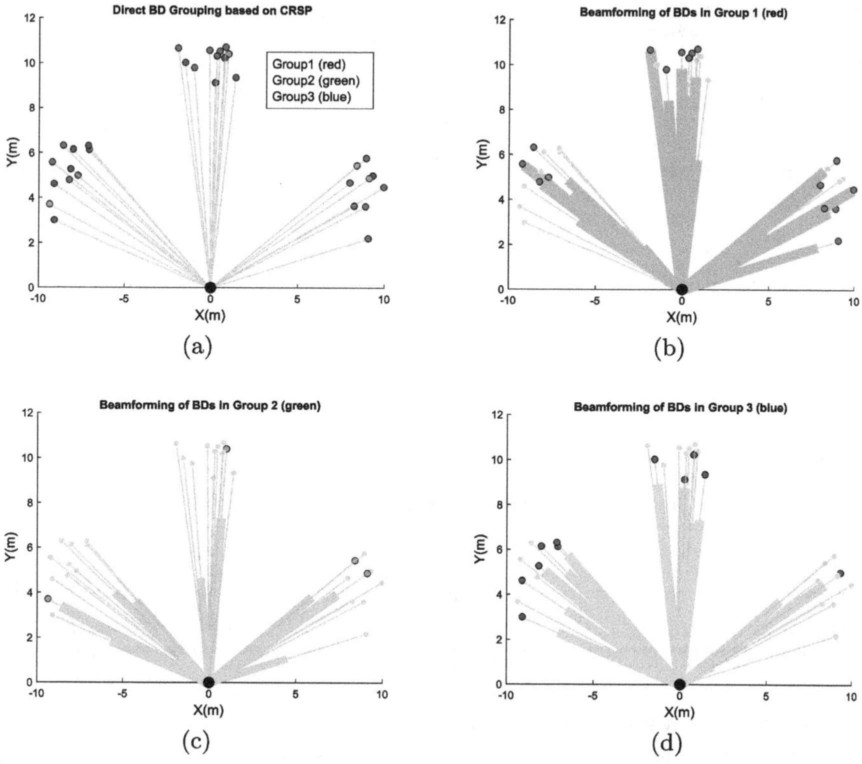


**Fig. 3.** The SINR distributions of the BDs using receive beamforming and BD grouping. (a) The grouped BDs. (b) BDs in group 1 (red) with their beamforming strength. (c) BDs in group 2 (green) with their beamforming strength. (d) BDs in group 3 (blue) with their beamforming strength. (Color figure online)

Figure 3 shows the actual BD groups and the receive beamforming of each group with respective $\mathbf{w}_k^\dagger$. The receive beamforming strength is calculated by the normalized SINR $\gamma_j$ with $\mathbf{w}_k^\dagger$, where $k = 1, 2, ..., K$. (a) illustrates the BD distribution using direct BD grouping based on CRSP in Section III-B 1), which is different from their natural grouping. In (b), the BDs in group 1 (red) can be scattered across all the natural activated BD groups. They utilize $\mathbf{w}_1^\dagger$ to suppress DLIs from $AS_2$ and $AS_3$. Meanwhile, their locations can guarantee $|\mathbf{w}_1^\dagger \mathbf{h}_j|^2$ is larger than $|\mathbf{w}_2^\dagger \mathbf{h}_j|^2$ and $|\mathbf{w}_3^\dagger \mathbf{h}_j|^2$. In this way, the SINR of BDs in group 1 is maximal. Similarly, (c) and (d) show the BDs in group 2 (green) and group 3 (blue), respectively. According to the comparison of receive beamforming of each group in (b), (c) and (d), we can find that some BDs can obtain close SINR using different $\mathbf{w}_k^\dagger$, e.g., the BDs in group 1 and group 3, which means that these BDs can be coordinated between these two groups to conduct simultaneous access at a tolerant SINR performance decrease. This observation inspires us to propose the simultaneous access grouping in Section III-B 2).

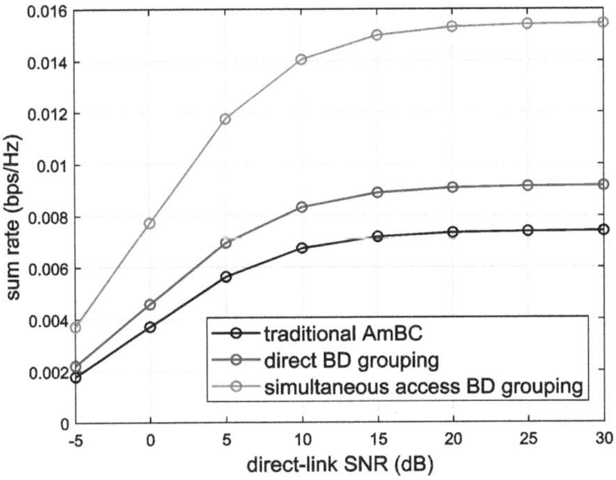


**Fig. 4.** The sum rate performances of different AmBC systems.

Figure 4 shows the sum rate performance comparisons vs. direct-link SNR of traditional multi-antenna AmBC system without BD grouping [7], our proposed joint receive beamforming and direct BD grouping based on CRSP and simultaneous access BD grouping. Since the backscatter signal is generally very weak, the total sum rate is much lower than the active RF transmit systems, e.g., cellular systems, mobile systems. Fortunately, the BD backscatters broadband RF signals, which guarantees the data rate is sufficient for IoT data uploading. The results show that using carefully beamforming design and proper BD grouping can significantly improve the SINR of each BD and finally promote the sum rate of all these BDs. Therefore, our proposed joint design achieves better performance than the traditional AmBC system. Besides, simultaneous access BD grouping boosts higher sum rate performance than direct BD grouping. When the SNR increases higher than 20 dB, the sum rate reaches its upper floor.

## 5 Conclusion

In this paper, we have investigated a joint receive beamforming and backscatter device grouping strategy to eliminate multi-source DLI and enhance massive access efficiency in ambient backscatter communication systems. We have developed a coordinated framework that employs receive beamforming optimization to suppress inter-AS DLIs while enabling efficient BD grouping that eliminates access conflicts. Extensive simulation results have demonstrated that the proposed scheme significantly improves the sum rate performance compared to conventional AmBC systems without beamforming and BD grouping design, particularly in dense IoT scenarios, thereby greatly promoting the application of massive AmBC in future 6G-enabled IoT networks. In the future, a more efficient receive beamforming design based on real BD groups rather than inter-AS DLI elimination will be studied which can provide higher sum rate performance. Besides, the BD grouping strategies that consider access priority in simultaneous access grouping will be further studied.

## References


1. Liu, V., Parks, A., Talla, V., Gollakota, S., Wetherall, D., Smith, J.R.: Ambient backscatter: wireless communication out of thin air. ACM SIGCOMM Comput. Commun. Rev. **43**(4), 39–50 (2013)
2. Van Huynh, N., Hoang, D.T., Lu, X., Niyato, D., Wang, P., Kim, D.I.: Ambient backscatter communications: a contemporary survey. IEEE Commun. Surv. Tutorials **20**(4), 2889–2922 (2018)
3. 3GPP. Ambient IoT: Redefining wireless communication for industry 4.0 (Accessed Jan- 22 2025). https://www.3gpp.org/technologies/anbient-iot-tsdsi
4. Butt, M.M., et al.: Ambient iot: a missing link in 3g pp iot devices landscape. IEEE Internet of Things Magazine **7**(2), 85–92 (2024)
5. Bowen, G., Li, D., Liu, Y., Yongjun, X.: Exploiting constructive interference for backscatter communication systems. IEEE Trans. Commun. **71**(7), 4344–4359 (2023)
6. Zhang, L., Feng, G., Qin, S., Sun, Y., Cao, B.: Access control for ambient backscatter enhanced wireless internet of things. IEEE Trans. Wireless Commun. **21**(7), 5614–5628 (2022)
7. Guo, H., Zhang, Q., Xiao, S., Liang, Y.-C.: Exploiting multiple antennas for cognitive ambient backscatter communication. IEEE Internet Things J. **6**(1), 765–775 (2019)
8. Liu, W., Shen, S., Tsang, D.H.K., Mallik, R.K., Murch, R.: An efficient ratio detector for ambient backscatter communication. IEEE Trans. Wireless Commun. **23**(6), 5908–5921 (2023)
9. Liu, J., Chen, M., Xiao, B., Zhu, F., Chen, S., Chen, L.: Efficient RFID grouping protocols. IEEE/ACM Trans. Netw. **24**(5), 3177–3190 (2016)

10. Ma, S., Wang, G., Fan, R., Tellambura, C.: Blind channel estimation for ambient backscatter communication systems. IEEE Commun. Lett. **22**(6), 1296–1299 (2018)
11. Moloudian, G., et al.: RF energy harvesting techniques for battery-less wireless sensing, industry 4.0, and internet of things: a review. IEEE Sens. J. **24**(5), 5732–5745 (2024)
12. Wang, G., Gao, F., Fan, R., Tellambura, C.: Ambient backscatter communication systems: detection and performance analysis. IEEE Trans. Commun. **64**(11), 4836–4846 (2016)
13. Wang, X., Yiğitler, H., Jäntti, R.: Gaining from multiple ambient sources: signaling matrix for multi-antenna backscatter devices. IEEE Wireless Commun. Lett. **12**(3), 491–495 (2022)
14. Liu, W., Shen, S., Danny, H.K., Tsang, R., Murch: MIMO ambient backscatter communications: capacity maximization and beamforming optimization. IEEE Trans. Veh. Technol. **72**(12), 15829–15843 (2023)
15. Ghojogh, B., Karray, F., Crowley, M.: Eigenvalue and generalized eigenvalue problems: Tutorial. arXiv preprint arXiv:1903.11240 (2019)
16. Nguyen Van Huynh, D.T., Hoang, D., Niyato, P., Wang, D.I.: Kim: optimal time scheduling for wireless-powered backscatter communication networks. IEEE Wireless Commun. Lett. **7**(5), 820–823 (2018)
17. Kapucu, K., Dehollain, C.: A passive UHF RFID system with a low-power capacitive sensor interface. In: 2014 IEEE RFID Technology and Applications Conference (RFID-TA), pp. 301–305. IEEE (2014)

# Polarization State Modulation Technology Based on Regular Polyhedral Constellation Points

Chenpeng Shi, Wen-Bin Sun(✉), Xin Yang, Qian Xu, Lili Chen, Yanyun Gong, and Jia Su

Northwestern Polytechnical University, 127 Youyi West Road, Xi'an 710072, China
shichp@mail.nwpu.edu.cn,
{sunwenbin,xinyang,qianxu,lilichen,yanyun_gong,jiasu1011}@nwpu.edu.cn

**Abstract.** With the continuous rapid growth of wireless communication services, the constraint of spectrum resource scarcity on the wireless communication industry will become increasingly prominent. This paper proposes a polarization state modulation technology based on the Poincaré sphere, which enhances the information-carrying capacity of individual polarization states by optimizing the distribution of constellation points on the Poincaré sphere. This technology breaks through the spectral efficiency bottleneck of traditional modulation techniques and provides an innovative modulation paradigm for high-capacity wireless communication systems. Simulation experiments demonstrate that the proposed method is consistent with theoretical predictions in performance metrics such as bit error rate and spectral efficiency, validating its effectiveness in improving spectrum utilization and transmission capacity, and providing new insights for the design of future wireless communication systems.

**Keywords:** Polarization state modulation · Spectrum multiplexing · Wireless communication systems · Spectral efficiency

## 1 Introduction

With the growing demand for Internet of Everything and the rapid development of wireless communication services, the need for information capacity and high-speed transmission has become increasingly urgent. However, the scarcity of spectrum resources poses significant constraints on the wireless communication industry [1]. Despite the increasingly tight wireless frequency band resources, there is still room for improvement in the utilization efficiency of these frequency bands. Current mainstream wireless communication technologies transmit data

Supported by National Natural Science Foundation of China under Grant No. 62201462 and 62301433.


Y. Liu et al. (Eds.): ChinaCom 2025, LNICST 711, pp. 99–117, 2027.
https://doi.org/10.1007/978-3-032-33662-0_10

by modulating carrier parameters such as amplitude, phase, and frequency, primarily utilizing the scalar characteristics of electromagnetic waves. In this context, utilizing the vector characteristic of electromagnetic wave polarization for wireless communication has become a highly promising solution.

As one of the fundamental properties of electromagnetic waves, polarization state is independent of traditional amplitude, phase, and frequency characteristics, characterizing the spatial variation pattern of the electric field vector in the propagation cross-section. Polarization, as another important information dimension following time-domain, frequency-domain, and spatial-domain information, is mutually independent of other parameters—changing polarization does not affect other parameters, and vice versa. This independent vector characteristic provides new possibilities for information transmission [2]. Adding polarization dimension modulation to existing modulation techniques can significantly improve the spectral utilization efficiency of wireless communications.

The application of polarization technology has precedents. Radar systems have long employed polarization methods to enhance their operational effectiveness in complex environments, extracting target polarization characteristics by analyzing scattering matrices to improve target identification and detection capabilities [3]. The optical communication field employs Polarization Shift Keying (PolSK) technology, leveraging the polarization characteristics of light waves to transmit data, significantly improving optical fiber communication rates [4,5]. However, compared to the stable environment of optical fiber transmission, wireless channels are affected by rich scattering due to multipath effects, causing distortion in signal polarization characteristics during propagation—a phenomenon known as depolarization [6]. This effect causes inconsistency in polarization states between transmitter and receiver, affecting the reliability of polarization modulation and becoming the main obstacle to its widespread application in wireless communications.

In response to the unique characteristics of wireless communication environments, electromagnetic wave polarization modulation communication technology has been developed. First are polarization multiplexing [7] and polarization diversity techniques [8]. In terrestrial wireless communication scenarios, although theoretically multiple orthogonal polarizations are possible, existing systems are typically limited to supporting only two orthogonal polarizations due to technical constraints. Polarization multiplexing utilizes polarization orthogonality to enhance channel capacity by simultaneously transmitting two orthogonal polarization data streams, but depolarization caused by multipath effects destroys the independence between data streams. Polarization diversity utilizes channel depolarization characteristics, employing multi-polarization antennas to obtain diversity gain, achieving advantages such as capacity enhancement and antenna spacing reduction. Literature [9] based on spatial electromagnetic field mathematical models, integrating amplitude modulation with polarization modulation, innovatively proposed a three-dimensional modulation framework utilizing signal amplitude, auxiliary polarization angle, and polarization phase difference angle. Other research from the perspective of RF power amplifier energy efficiency optimization developed joint modulation schemes combining polarization modulation with traditional amplitude-phase modulation [10]. Wei et al. combined polarization modulation with traditional modulation techniques, laying theoretical foundations for multi-dimensional modulation technology [11]. Due to the spatial directionality of polarization states and their changing characteristics during propagation, even if eavesdroppers intercept signals, it is difficult to accurately obtain complete polarization information. Literature [12–16] explored applications of polarization modulation in physical layer security. Yang et al. proposed integrated polarization and spatial modulation technology, combining polarization modulation and spatial modulation to transmit information through activated antenna indices and polarization modulation symbols, and proposed low-complexity near-optimal detection algorithms based on compressed sensing [17]. Li et al. further developed generalized polarization-spatial modulation technology, achieving higher spectral efficiency through multi-mode transmission [18]. Shang et al. proposed RIS-assisted polarization modulation schemes for vehicular communication, innovatively encoding information in three dimensions: dual-polarization antenna indices, polarization modulation symbols, and RIS reflection surface indices, employing deep neural network methods to analyze channel state information [19]. Buvarp et al. proposed RIS-assisted polarization-spatial modulation technology based on quaternion neural networks, achieving robust signal detection and estimation [20]. Li et al. designed polarized RIS-assisted polarized spatial scattering modulation technology, further expanding application scenarios of polarization technology [21]. In special environment applications, Liu et al. proposed rotational misalignment compensation schemes for underwater optical wireless communication, employing quaternary polarization shift keying modulation to address rotational misalignment problems in underwater environments [22]. Meng et al. studied sea surface ultraviolet communication performance based on circular polarization modulation [23]. Additionally, research on polarization modulation applications in satellite communications has been conducted [24,25].

Although existing research has proposed various polarization modulation schemes, little consideration has been given to the optimal distribution problem of polarization constellation points on the Poincaré sphere, particularly for high-order modulation cases. Traditional PolSK technology mainly includes the following forms: Binary PolSK uses two orthogonal polarization states, such as left-hand circular polarization and right-hand circular polarization, with each symbol carrying 1 bit of information; Quaternary PolSK uses four polarization states, typically distributed on the equator of the Poincaré sphere or at mutually orthogonal positions, with each symbol carrying 2 bits of information; Multi-state PolSK uses more polarization states, but traditional designs lack systematic methods for determining optimal constellation point distributions.

Based on the above background, this paper proposes a polarization state modulation technology based on the Poincaré sphere, improving the information-carrying capacity of individual polarization states through optimized design of polarization constellation point distribution on the Poincaré sphere. Increasing the number of constellation points enables each polarization state to carry more communication information, thereby further enhancing the efficiency and performance of polarization multiplexing. Compared to existing research, this paper has the following innovations:

1. Proposes a polarization constellation design method based on Poincaré sphere geometric characteristics, fully utilizing the high symmetry of regular polyhedra to maximize the minimum distance between adjacent polarization constellation points, improving the anti-noise performance of the modulation system;
2. Addressing the characteristic that polarization modulation occurs on the three-dimensional Poincaré sphere, establishes a noise model based on the Von Mises-Fisher distribution and derives theoretical expressions for symbol error rate under spherical geometric conditions;
3. Through theoretical analysis and simulation experiments, evaluates the proposed technology's performance metrics such as bit error rate and spectral efficiency, validating its characteristics compared to random constellations and traditional modulation techniques.

This research not only expands new dimensions of modulation technology in wireless communications but also provides new insights for designing future high-capacity, high-efficiency communication systems, having significance for alleviating spectrum resource constraints.

## 2 System Model and Modulation Technology

This section describes the system architecture using the Poincaré sphere as the foundation for polarization modulation. As shown in Fig. 1, the transmitter first performs source coding and channel coding on the bit stream, then divides the encoded binary sequence bit stream through a data rate allocation unit into two parts, where one part is used for traditional modulation and another part is used for polarization state modulation. The allocation ratio depends on system parameters; in this paper, the number of symbols transmitted by traditional modulation per unit time is set equal to the number of symbols transmitted by polarization state modulation. Each polarization state is associated with a traditional modulation constellation, achieving constellation dimension expansion. Let the order of traditional modulation be $M_T$ and the order of polarization modulation be $M_P$, then the total order of joint modulation is $M = M_T \times M_P$, with each symbol capable of carrying $\log_2 M = \log_2 M_T + \log_2 M_P$ bits of information. Specifically, if the input bit sequence is represented as $[b_1, b_2, ..., b_{\log_2 M}]$, the first $\log_2 M_T$ bits map to traditional modulation symbols, and the last $\log_2 M_P$ bits map to polarization state vectors. The traditional modulation part can employ PSK or QAM modulation methods to generate complex signal symbols, converting bits to complex symbols; the polarization modulation part maps bits to polarization constellation points, generating weighting factors for horizontal and vertical polarization branches. These two parts of information are combined through a polarization weighting unit to form complete high-dimensional modulation signals, finally transmitted through orthogonal dual-polarization antennas.

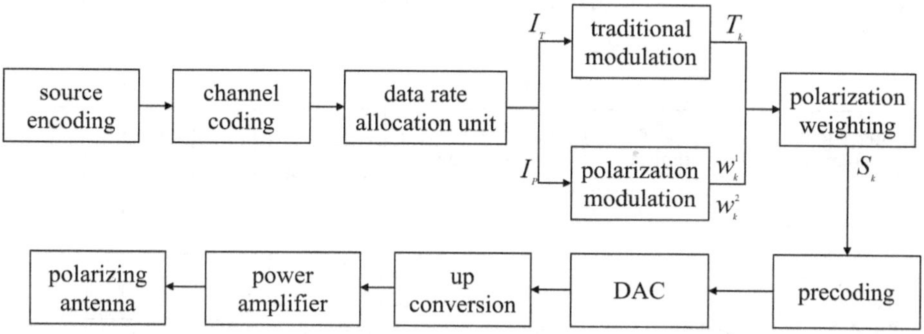


**Fig. 1.** Block diagram of the polarization modulation transmitter architecture

If $A_k$ and $\phi_k$ represent the amplitude and phase of traditional modulation symbols respectively, with $\Delta\phi_k$ as additional phase, the traditional modulation symbol is expressed as:

$$T_k = A_k e^{j(\phi_k + \Delta\phi_k)}. \tag{1}$$

The polarization weighting factors are expressed as:

$$\begin{bmatrix} w_k^1 \\ w_k^2 \end{bmatrix} = \begin{bmatrix} \cos\delta_k \\ \sin\delta_k \bullet e^{j\gamma_k} \end{bmatrix}, \tag{2}$$

where $\delta_k$ represents the auxiliary polarization angle ($0 \le \delta_k \le \pi/2$), $\gamma_k$ represents the polarization phase difference angle ($0 \le \gamma_k < 2\pi$), and $(\delta_k, \gamma_k)$ are polarization state description parameters that completely describe the polarization characteristics of electromagnetic waves. The key to system design lies in converting traditional modulation symbols $T_k$ through polarization weighting factors $w_k^1$ and $w_k^2$ into dual-path high-dimensional modulation symbols $S_k$ to be transmitted:

$$S_k = \begin{bmatrix} S_{kH} \\ S_{kV} \end{bmatrix} = \begin{bmatrix} w_k^1 \cdot T_k \\ w_k^2 \cdot T_k \end{bmatrix} = \begin{bmatrix} A_k e^{j(\phi_k + \Delta\phi_k)} \cos\delta_k \\ A_k e^{j(\phi_k + \gamma_k + \Delta\phi_k)} \sin\delta_k \end{bmatrix}, \tag{3}$$

where $S_{kH}$ is transmitted through horizontal polarization antenna and $S_{kV}$ through vertical polarization antenna. In the far field, these couple to form specific polarization states that correspond one-to-one with information $I_P$.

The polarization modulation receiver needs to recover original data bits from received waveforms. Its structure is shown in the figure. First, signals are received through polarization antennas, and after RF front-end processing such as down-conversion and analog-to-digital conversion, baseband signals of horizontal and vertical polarization components are obtained. The receiving system mainly consists of two processing units: polarization state identification unit and traditional demodulation unit. The polarization state identification unit recovers polarization state information by calculating Stokes parameters, while the traditional demodulation unit extracts signal amplitude and phase information. After combining both, maximum likelihood decision recovers original bit information (Fig. 2).

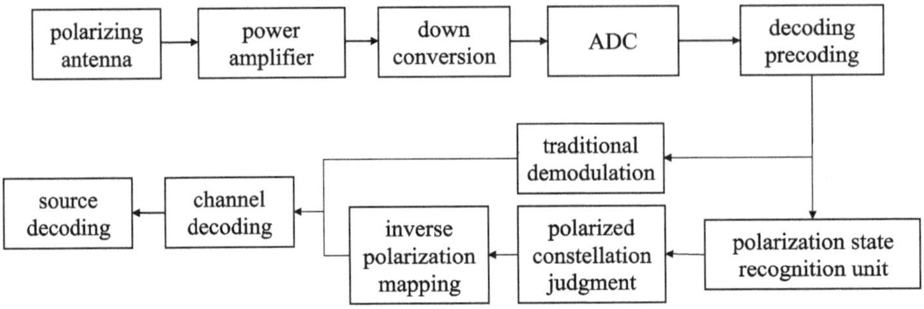


**Fig. 2.** Block diagram of the polarization modulation receiver architecture

The Jones vector of the received signal can be expressed as:

$$\begin{bmatrix} E_{rH} \\ E_{rV} \end{bmatrix} = A_k \begin{bmatrix} \cos \delta_k e^{j(\phi_k + \Delta\phi_k)} \\ \sin \delta_k e^{j(\phi_k + \gamma_k + \Delta\phi_k)} \end{bmatrix} + \begin{bmatrix} n_{rH} \\ n_{rV} \end{bmatrix}, \tag{4}$$

where $n_{rH}$ and $n_{rV}$ are additive white Gaussian noise. The receiver first recovers the polarization state through Stokes parameter analysis:

$$\begin{aligned} S_0 &= |E_{rH}|^2 + |E_{rV}|^2, \\ S_1 &= |E_{rH}|^2 - |E_{rV}|^2, \\ S_2 &= 2\,|E_{rH}|\,|E_{rV}|\cos\gamma_k, \\ S_3 &= 2\,|E_{rH}|\,|E_{rV}|\sin\gamma_k. \end{aligned} \tag{5}$$

Based on these parameters, polarization state parameters can be restored:

$$\begin{aligned} \delta_k &= \arctan\left(\frac{|E_{rV}|}{|E_{rH}|}\right) = \frac{1}{2}\arccos\left(\frac{S_1}{S_0}\right), \\ \gamma_k &= \arctan\left(\frac{S_3}{S_2}\right). \end{aligned} \tag{6}$$

Then, based on demodulated polarization parameters and traditional modulation parameters, combined with maximum likelihood decision, original information is recovered. The entire demodulation process fully utilizes joint information from polarization domain and traditional domain, effectively improving system performance.

# 3 Optimized Constellation Design Based on Poincaré Sphere

## 3.1 Physical Significance and Mathematical Representation of Polarization States

Polarization is an intrinsic characteristic of electromagnetic waves, describing the trajectory shape and rotation direction of the electric field vector over time in the plane perpendicular to the spatial propagation direction. From a physical perspective, the polarization state of electromagnetic waves characterizes the spatial orientation and phase relationships of electric field vector oscillations, which can be linear, circular, or elliptical. Polarization state, as a vector characteristic of electromagnetic waves, is completely independent of scalar characteristics such as amplitude, phase, and frequency utilized by traditional modulation techniques, providing an entirely new dimension for information modulation.

The polarization state of electromagnetic waves can be described through two orthogonal components of the electric field vector. For electromagnetic waves propagating along the z-axis, the instantaneous electric field can be expressed as:

$$\boldsymbol{E}(z,t) = E_x(z,t)\hat{x} + E_y(z,t)\hat{y}, \tag{7}$$

where $\hat{x}$ and $\hat{y}$ are unit vectors in horizontal and vertical directions respectively, and $E_x(z,t)$ and $E_y(z,t)$ are electric field components in corresponding directions.

The Jones vector is a commonly used tool for describing completely polarized waves, containing amplitude and phase information of two orthogonal electric field components. For monochromatic plane waves with frequency $\omega$, the Jones vector is expressed as:

$$J = \begin{bmatrix} E_x e^{j\phi_x} \\ E_y e^{j\phi_y} \end{bmatrix} = \begin{bmatrix} \cos\delta \\ \sin\delta e^{j\gamma} \end{bmatrix}, \tag{8}$$

where $E_x$ and $E_y$ are amplitudes of horizontal and vertical components respectively, and $\phi_x$ and $\phi_y$ are corresponding phases. Through parameter transformation, the Jones vector can be expressed using auxiliary polarization angle $\delta \in [0, \pi/2]$ and polarization phase difference $\gamma = \phi_y - \phi_x \in [0, 2\pi)$.

Stokes parameters provide another description method for polarization states. For completely polarized waves, the Stokes parameters can be expressed as:

$$\begin{aligned} S_0 &= |E_x|^2 + |E_y|^2, \\ S_1 &= |E_x|^2 - |E_y|^2, \\ S_2 &= 2|E_x||E_y|\cos\gamma, \\ S_3 &= 2|E_x||E_y|\sin\gamma. \end{aligned} \tag{9}$$

where $S_0$ represents the total intensity of the wave, and $S_1$, $S_2$ and $S_3$ jointly describe the polarization state. Through normalized Stokes parameters, a one-to-one correspondence between polarization states and points on the Poincaré sphere can be established.

### 3.2 Distribution Optimization Criteria for Polarization Constellation Points on Poincaré Sphere

To quantitatively evaluate the performance of different constellation designs, the geodesic distance between points on the Poincaré sphere is introduced as a metric standard. For two points $P_i$ and $P_j$ on a unit sphere, their geodesic distance is:

$$d(P_i, P_j) = \arccos(P_i \cdot P_j), \tag{10}$$

where $P_i \cdot P_j$represents the inner product of the two point coordinates. For constellation design, the key metric is minimum distance:

$$d_{min} = \min_{i \neq j} d(P_i, P_j). \tag{11}$$

For example, for a 4-point constellation, the minimum distance between regular tetrahedron vertices is $\arccos(-\frac{1}{3}) \approx 109.5°$, superior to any other 4-point distribution. Addressing the inadequacies of traditional polarization modulation techniques in constellation design, this paper proposes an optimized constellation design method based on regular polyhedra. When designing polarization state constellations, the following optimization criteria are followed:

1. Minimum distance maximization principle: The distance between adjacent constellation points should be as large as possible to improve system anti-noise performance;
2. Symmetry principle: The constellation structure should have good symmetry for convenient encoding and decoding implementation;
3. Mathematical processing convenience: Vertex coordinates have precise analytical expressions without requiring numerical optimization;
4. Standardized design: Based on clear geometric structures, convenient for engineering standardization implementation.

Based on these principles, this paper proposes a design method using vertices of regular polyhedra embedded in the Poincaré sphere as polarization constellation points. Regular polyhedra are geometric bodies in three-dimensional space with high symmetry, where all faces are congruent regular polygons and all vertices are equidistant from the center. According to Euclidean geometry, five regular polyhedra exist in three-dimensional space: regular tetrahedron, regular hexahedron (cube), regular octahedron, regular dodecahedron, and regular icosahedron. Mapping the vertices of these 5 regular polyhedra onto the Poincaré sphere constructs different-order polarization constellation point sets:
**Regular Tetrahedron ($M_P = 4$):** It has 4 vertices, corresponding to 4 polarization states, with each symbol carrying $\log_2 4 = 2$ bits of information. The distribution of regular tetrahedron structure on the Poincaré sphere is shown in

Fig. 3a, with vertex coordinates expressible as:

$$\begin{aligned} P_1 &= (1,0,0),\\ P_2 &= (-\frac{1}{3},\frac{2\sqrt{2}}{3},0),\\ P_3 &= (-\frac{1}{3},-\frac{\sqrt{2}}{3},\frac{\sqrt{6}}{3}),\\ P_4 &= (-\frac{1}{3},-\frac{\sqrt{2}}{3},-\frac{\sqrt{6}}{3}). \end{aligned} \tag{12}$$

These points are uniformly distributed on the Poincaré sphere, with minimum geodesic distance between any two points:

$$d_{\min} = \arccos\left(-\frac{1}{3}\right) \approx 109.47°. \tag{13}$$

The regular tetrahedron structure achieves theoretically optimal minimum distance for 4-point configurations, making it an ideal choice for low-complexity polarization modulation.

**Regular Octahedron ($M_P = 6$):** It has 6 vertices, corresponding to 6 polarization states, with each symbol carrying $\log_2 6 \approx 2.58$ bits of information. The distribution of regular octahedron structure on the Poincaré sphere is shown in Fig. 3b, with vertex coordinates expressible as:

$$\begin{aligned} P_1 &= (1,0,0), P_2 = (-1,0,0),\\ P_3 &= (0,1,0), P_4 = (0,-1,0),\\ P_5 &= (0,0,1), P_6 = (0,0,-1). \end{aligned} \tag{14}$$

These points are uniformly distributed on the Poincaré sphere, corresponding to three pairs of orthogonal polarization states.

**Regular Hexahedron/Cube ($M_P = 8$):** It has 8 vertices, corresponding to 8 polarization states, with each symbol carrying $\log_2 8 = 3$ bits of information. The distribution of cube structure on the Poincaré sphere is shown in Fig. 3c, with vertex coordinates expressible as:

$$P_i = (\pm\frac{1}{\sqrt{3}},\pm\frac{1}{\sqrt{3}},\pm\frac{1}{\sqrt{3}}), i = 1,2,...,8. \tag{15}$$

The cube provides intuitive and easily implementable polarization modulation technology, with each symbol encoding an integer number of bits.

**Regular Icosahedron ($M_P = 12$):** It has 12 vertices, corresponding to 12 polarization states, with each symbol carrying $\log_2 12 \approx 3.58$ bits of information. The distribution of regular icosahedron structure on the Poincaré sphere is shown in Fig. 3d. The vertex coordinates are more complex, involving the golden ratio

$\varphi = \frac{1+\sqrt{5}}{2} \approx 1.618$, expressible as:

$$P_i = \frac{(0, \pm 1, \pm \phi)}{\sqrt{1+\phi^2}}, i = 1, 2, 3, 4,$$
$$P_{i+4} = \frac{(\pm 1, \pm \phi, 0)}{\sqrt{1+\phi^2}}, i = 1, 2, 3, 4, \tag{16}$$
$$P_{i+8} = \frac{(\pm \phi, 0, \pm 1)}{\sqrt{1+\phi^2}}, i = 1, 2, 3, 4.$$

These coordinates are then normalized to unit vectors to ensure all points lie on the Poincaré sphere.

**Regular Dodecahedron ($M_P = 20$):** It has 20 vertices, corresponding to 20 polarization states, with each symbol carrying $\log_2 20 \approx 4.32$ bits of information. Regular dodecahedron provides extremely high spectral efficiency but also requires higher channel conditions.

The distribution of regular dodecahedron structure on the Poincaré sphere is shown in Fig. 3e, with vertex coordinates expressible through golden ratio $\varphi = \frac{1+\sqrt{5}}{2}$ as:

$$P_i = (\pm 1, \pm 1, \pm 1), i = 1, 2, ..., 8,$$
$$P_{i+8} = (0, \pm \varphi, \pm \frac{1}{\varphi}), i = 1, 2, 3, 4,$$
$$P_{i+12} = (\pm \frac{1}{\varphi}, 0, \pm \varphi), i = 1, 2, 3, 4, \tag{17}$$
$$P_{i+16} = (\pm \varphi, \pm \frac{1}{\varphi}, 0), i = 1, 2, 3, 4.$$

These coordinates need to be normalized to unit vectors.

Table 1 provides parameters for different regular polyhedron polarization constellations.

**Table 1.** Parameters of Different Regular Polyhedron Polarization Constellations

| Regular Polyhedron | Vertices | Adjacent Points | Min Angular Distance | Information Bits |
|---|---|---|---|---|
| Tetrahedron | 4 | 3 | 109.47° | 2 |
| Octahedron | 6 | 4 | 90° | 2.58 |
| Hexahedron | 8 | 3 | 70.53° | 3 |
| Icosahedron | 12 | 5 | 63.43° | 3.58 |
| Dodecahedron | 20 | 3 | 41.81° | 4.32 |

### 3.3 Performance Analysis of Polarization Modulation Based on Regular Polyhedron Constellation Points

Unlike traditional PSK or QAM modulation, polarization modulation occurs on the three-dimensional Poincaré sphere, where signal points are distributed on

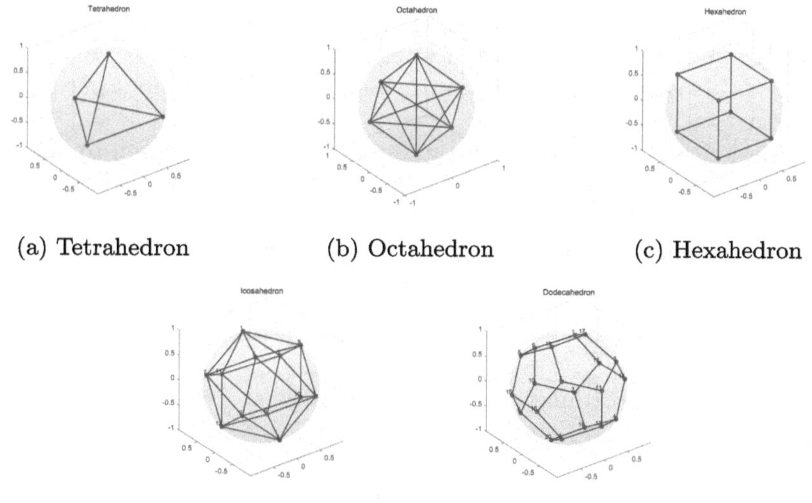


(a) Tetrahedron (b) Octahedron (c) Hexahedron

(d) Icosahedron (e) Dodecahedron

**Fig. 3.** Polarized constellation structure based on regular polyhedra

the unit Poincaré sphere $S^2 = \{P \in \mathbb{R}^3 : \|P\| = 1\}$. Let the constellation point set be $\mathcal{P} = P_1, P_2, \ldots, P_M$, where each point $P_i \in S^2, i = 1, 2, \ldots, M$ satisfies $\|P_i\| = 1$. Therefore, bit error rate analysis needs to consider spherical geometric characteristics.

When noise affects received signals, points on the sphere deviate from their original positions. In AWGN channels, the bit error rate is mainly determined by the minimum distance (geodesic distance) between constellation points. In spherical coordinate systems, assuming that noise affects the distribution of received points on the sphere as the Von Mises-Fisher distribution, which is a Gaussian distribution simulation on spheres:

$$f(\mathbf{P}|\mathbf{P}_0, \kappa) = \frac{\kappa}{4\pi \sinh \kappa} \mathrm{e}^{\kappa \mathbf{P}_0{}^T \mathbf{P}}, \tag{18}$$

where $\mathbf{P}_0$ is the transmitted polarization constellation point, $\kappa > 0$ is the concentration parameter proportional to signal-to-noise ratio, and $\mathbf{P}$ is the received polarization constellation point.

For constellation point $\mathbf{P}_i$, its decision region is defined as:

$$\Omega_i = \mathbf{P} \in S^2 : d(\mathbf{P}, \mathbf{P}_i) \leq d(\mathbf{P}, \mathbf{P}_j), \forall j \neq i. \tag{19}$$

When transmitting constellation point $\mathbf{P}_i$, demodulation error occurs when the received point falls in incorrect decision regions. The symbol error rate is

$$P_{e|i} = 1 - \iint_{\Omega_i} f(\mathbf{P}|\mathbf{P}_i, \kappa) ds = 1 - \iint_{\Omega_i} \frac{\kappa}{4\pi \sinh \kappa} \mathrm{e}^{\kappa \mathbf{P}_i^T \mathbf{P}} ds, \tag{20}$$

where $ds = \sin\theta d\theta d\phi$ is the area element on the sphere.

In spherical modulation systems, after matched filtering and symbol rate sampling, the noise variance on each Cartesian coordinate is: $\sigma^2 = \frac{N_0}{2T}$, where $N_0$ is single-sided noise power spectral density and $T$ is symbol period. After normalizing $T = 1$, $\sigma^2 = \frac{N_0}{2}$.

The relationship between concentration parameter $\kappa$ and signal-to-noise ratio SNR is: $\kappa = \frac{E_s}{\sigma^2} = \frac{E_s T}{N_0/2} = 2SNR$ , where $SNR = E_s/(N_0 T)$ is the symbol signal-to-noise ratio definition.

Due to complete symmetry of regular polyhedra, conditional symbol error rates for all constellation points are equal:

$$P_{\mathrm{e}|1} = P_{\mathrm{e}|2} = \cdots = P_{\mathrm{e}|M-1} = P_{\mathrm{e}|M}. \tag{21}$$

Considering a coordinate system centered at $P_i$, under symmetry assumptions:

$$P_{\mathrm{e}|i} = 1 - \frac{\kappa}{4\pi \sinh \kappa} \int_0^{2\pi} \int_0^{\theta_b} \mathrm{e}^{\kappa \cos \theta} \sin \theta d\theta d\phi, \tag{22}$$

where $\theta_b$ is the geodesic distance corresponding to decision boundary angle, satisfying: $\cos \theta_b = \frac{\mathbf{P}_i^T \mathbf{P}_j}{|\mathbf{P}_i||\mathbf{P}_j|}$.

This simplifies to:

$$P_{\mathrm{e}|i} = 1 - \frac{1}{2 \sinh \kappa} (\mathrm{e}^{\kappa} - \mathrm{e}^{\kappa \cos \theta_b}). \tag{23}$$

When $\kappa \gg 1$, with $\sinh \kappa \approx \frac{\mathrm{e}^{\kappa}}{2}$, it follows that:

$$P_{\mathrm{e}|i} \approx \mathrm{e}^{\kappa(\cos \theta_b - 1)}. \tag{24}$$

In polarization modulation technology with regular polyhedron constellation points, assuming all constellation points are transmitted with equal probability:

$$P(\mathbf{P}_i) = \frac{1}{M}, i = 1, 2, \ldots, M. \tag{25}$$

The average symbol error rate is:

$$P_s = \sum_{i=1}^{M} P(\mathbf{P}_i) P_{\mathrm{e}|i} = \frac{1}{M} \sum_{i=1}^{M} P_{\mathrm{e}|i}. \tag{26}$$

Due to regular polyhedron symmetry:

$$P_s = \frac{1}{M} \times M \times P_{\mathrm{e}|i} = P_{\mathrm{e}|i}, \quad \forall i. \tag{27}$$

The final average symbol error rate is:

$$P_s \approx \mathrm{e}^{\kappa(\cos \theta_b - 1)}. \tag{28}$$

For $M$-point constellations, each symbol carries $\log_2 M$ bits. Under independent error and uniform distribution assumptions, bit error rate is: $P_b \approx \frac{P_s}{\log_2 M}$.

Theoretically, the spectral efficiency of $M$-point constellations is:

$$\eta_{theory} = \log_2 M \quad [\text{bits/symbol}]. \tag{29}$$

Considering bit error rate effects, actual spectral efficiency is:

$$\eta_{actual} = \log_2 M \cdot (1 - P_b) \quad [\text{bits/symbol}]. \tag{30}$$

In polarization state modulation systems, different orders of modulation methods exhibit distinct performance trade-off characteristics. Low-order modulation such as regular tetrahedron configuration, while having lower spectral efficiency, possesses excellent reliability, particularly suitable for SNR-limited applications and scenarios with strict transmission reliability requirements. Medium-order modulation employs regular hexahedron or octahedron constellation configurations, achieving good balance between spectral efficiency and reliability, providing compromise solutions for most medium-complexity communication systems. High-order modulation employs complex geometric structures such as regular icosahedron or dodecahedron, capable of achieving very high spectral efficiency but requiring more stringent channel quality, only demonstrating rate advantages in high-SNR environments, suitable for high-quality channel applications with extremely high transmission rate requirements.

## 4 Simulation Results

To verify the effectiveness of the proposed polarization state modulation technology based on Poincaré sphere, this section provides comprehensive performance evaluation through Monte Carlo simulation experiments. Simulations employ MATLAB platform with additive white Gaussian noise (AWGN) channel model to eliminate effects of factors such as channel fading and focus on evaluating performance characteristics of the modulation technology itself.

Polarization modulation is respectively implemented through constellation configurations based on the regular tetrahedron, octahedron, hexahedron, icosahedron, and dodecahedron. The receiver recovers polarization states through Stokes parameter estimation and performs joint decision combined with traditional demodulation. To ensure fair comparison, all modulation technologies are tested under identical SNR conditions, with SNR range set from 0 dB to 25 dB.

Figure 4 shows the comparison between simulation results and theoretical analysis for symbol error rates of the proposed regular polyhedron-based polarization modulation technology. Simulation results agree with theoretical formulas derived in Sect. 2.3, verifying the accuracy of theoretical analysis. From the figure, it can be observed that as SNR increases, symbol error rates for various regular polyhedron constellations all decrease exponentially. Among them, regular tetrahedron constellation demonstrates optimal anti-noise performance due to having the largest minimum geodesic distance (109.47°); while regular dodecahedron constellation, although having the highest spectral efficiency, shows relatively high symbol error rates under low SNR conditions due to smaller minimum geodesic distance. Additionally, higher SNR further reduces deviation between simulation curves and theoretical curves, indicating that Von Mises-Fisher distribution can well approximate noise effects under high SNR conditions.

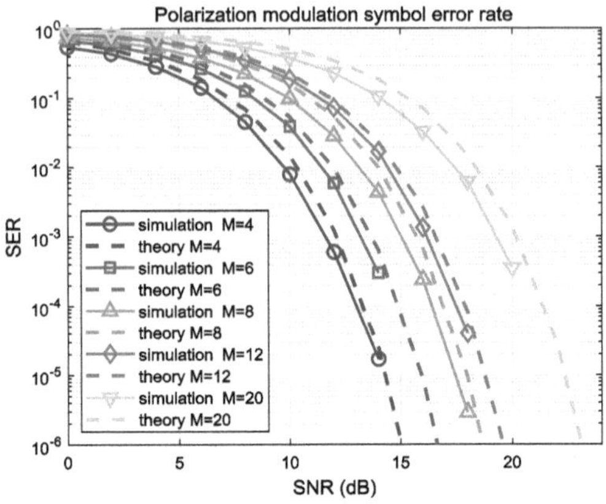


**Fig. 4.** Polarization modulation symbol error rate

Figure 5 provides bit error rate performance comparison for various regular polyhedron polarization modulation technologies. Considering different constellations carry different numbers of bits, bit error rate can more intuitively reflect information transmission quality of each method. Simulation results show that regular tetrahedron modulation maintains the lowest bit error rate throughout the entire SNR range, mainly attributed to its superior geometric characteristics and fewer constellation points. Regular octahedron and hexahedron modulation demonstrate good performance balance under medium SNR conditions, while high-order modulation technologies (regular icosahedron and dodecahedron), although showing relatively poor performance under low SNR, can achieve higher spectral efficiency under high SNR conditions.

To verify advantages of regular polyhedron-based constellation design compared to random constellation point distributions, Fig. 6 compares bit error rate performance between regular polyhedron constellations and random constellations under the same number of constellation points. Random constellations are constructed by randomly generating corresponding numbers of points on the Poincaré sphere, with each random constellation experiment repeated 3 times and averaged.

Simulation results show that regular polyhedron-based constellation designs significantly outperform random constellations for all tested constellation point numbers. Taking 8-point constellations as an example, regular hexahedron constellation achieves approximately 8dB performance gain compared to random

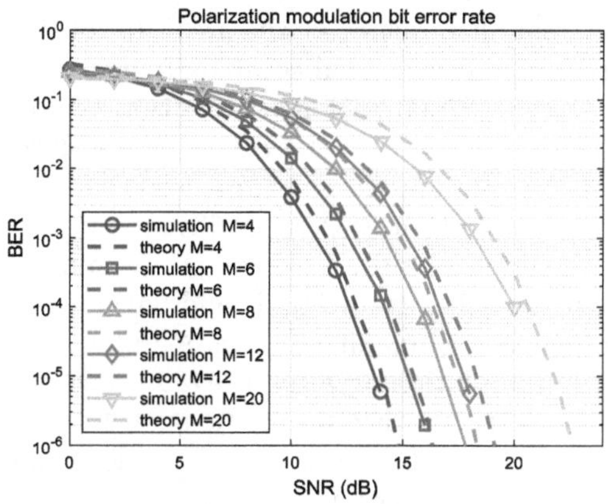


**Fig. 5.** Polarization modulation bit error rate

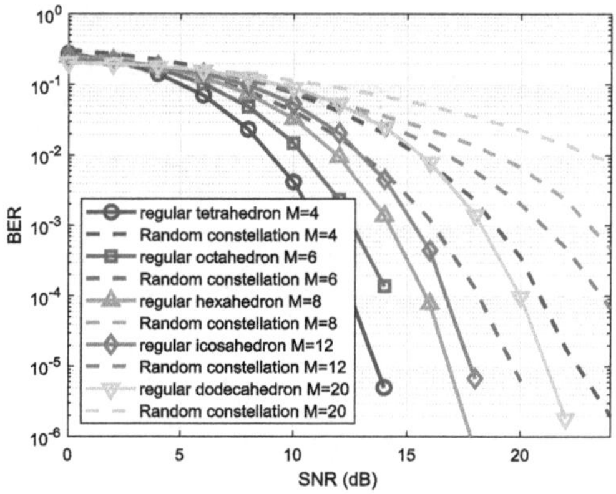


**Fig. 6.** BER of regular and random constellations

8-point constellation at $10^{-4}$ bit error rate. This significant advantage verifies the effectiveness of the proposed constellation optimization design based on regular polyhedron geometric structures. The high symmetry of regular polyhedra ensures maximization of minimum distances between constellation points, thereby maximally improving system anti-noise capability.

To objectively evaluate characteristics of the proposed technology, Fig. 7 compares bit error rate performance between regular polyhedron-based polarization modulation and traditional PSK, QAM modulation technologies. Compared traditional technologies include QPSK, 8PSK, 4QAM, and 32QAM, chosen to cover similar spectral efficiency ranges. Simulation results show that under identical order (same number of constellation points) conditions, polarization modulation technology's bit error rate performance is slightly lower than traditional technologies. This performance difference stems from fundamental differences in modulation mechanisms. Traditional PSK/QAM modulation, after decades of optimization development, has achieved theoretically optimal or near-optimal constellation designs in two-dimensional complex planes, with signal power concentrated on single carriers. Polarization modulation requires distributing signal power between horizontal and vertical orthogonal polarization components, and this power dispersion characteristic reduces effective SNR for each polarization component under identical total SNR conditions, thereby increasing system sensitivity to noise and interference. However, the main value of polarization modulation lies not in replacing traditional modulation but in providing additional modulation dimensions, opening up three-dimensional Poincaré sphere design space. The joint modulation architecture described in Sect. 1 can combine polarization modulation with traditional modulation to achieve higher spectral efficiency through dimension expansion. For example, combining QPSK with regular tetrahedron polarization modulation can achieve 4×4=16 total constellation points, carrying 4 bits/symbol information—a dimension expansion effect unachievable by using traditional modulation or polarization modulation alone.

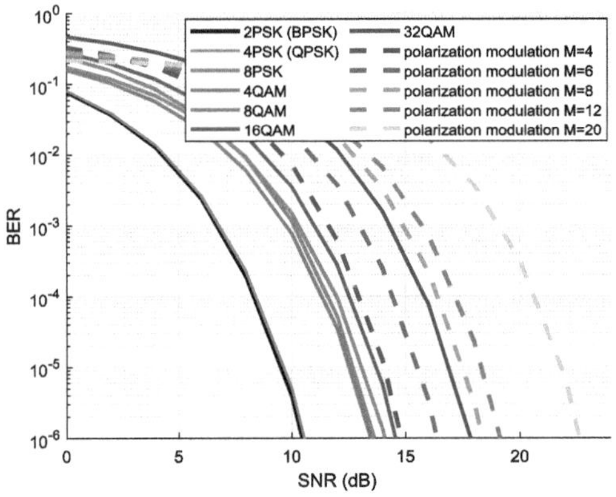


**Fig. 7.** BER of polarization and traditional modulation

Figure 8 shows effective spectral efficiency comparison for different modulation technologies under various SNR conditions. Effective spectral efficiency is defined as actual information transmission rate considering bit error rate effects. From the figure, it can be seen that as SNR increases, advantages of high-order modulation technologies gradually become apparent. When SNR reaches 20 dB, effective spectral efficiency of regular dodecahedron polarization modulation reaches 4.3 bits/symbol.

## 5 Conclusion

Regular polyhedron-based polarization constellation design provides not only large minimum constellation distances but also perfect symmetry, ensuring all

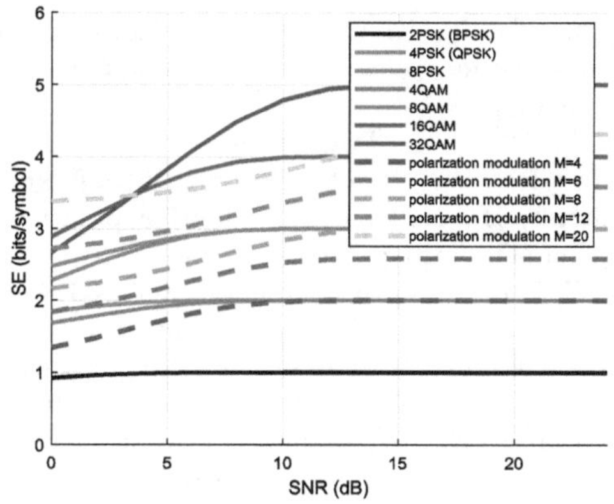


**Fig. 8.** Spectral efficiency of polarization and traditional modulation

constellation points have identical bit error rate performance. This balance has important value in practical system design, especially in adaptive modulation technologies, offering choices from low-order to high-order for different application requirements. By combining with traditional modulation technologies, higher information transmission rates can be achieved while maintaining good bit error rate performance. This high-dimensional modulation technology is particularly suitable for high SNR, high-capacity demand communication scenarios, providing new possibilities for future high-capacity wireless communication systems. However, challenges remain in terms of optimizing the constellation design for varying channel conditions, ensuring robustness in practical environments, and addressing computational complexity. Future research could focus on exploring these challenges and developing hybrid approaches that integrate polarization constellation design with existing physical layer technologies, such as MIMO and OFDM, to further enhance system performance and adaptability.

## References

1. Jiang, C., Zhang, H., Ren, Y., et al.: Energy-efficient non-cooperative cognitive radio networks: micro, meso, and macro views. IEEE Commun. Mag. **52**(7), 14–20 (2014)
2. Guo, C., Liu, F., Chen, S., et al.: Advances on exploiting polarization in wireless communications: channels, technologies, and applications. IEEE Commun. Surv. Tutorials **19**(1), 125–166 (2016)
3. Zhao, C., Wang, Y., Yang, Y., et al.: Research review on radar polarization information acquisition and polarization signal processing technology. J. Radars **5**(06), 620–638 (2016)

4. Tang, X., Xu, Z., Ghassemlooy, Z.: Coherent polarization modulated transmission through MIMO atmospheric optical turbulence channel. J. Lightwave Technol. **31**(20), 3221–3228 (2013)
5. Zhao, J., Zhou, F., Li, H., et al.: A novel high-precision polarization modulation technology. Spacecraft Recovery Remote Sensing **35**(02), 39–45 (2014)
6. Pratt, T., Walkenhorst, B., Nguyen, S.: Adaptive polarization transmission of OFDM signals in channels with polarization mode dispersion and polarization-dependent loss. IEEE Trans. Wireless Commun. **8**(7), 3354–3359 (2009)
7. Zhang, X., Zhang, B., Guo, D.: Performance of poly-polarization multiplexing in narrow-band wireless communication aided by pre-compensation and multi-notch OPPFs. IEEE Wireless Commun. Lett. **6**(4), 478–481 (2017)
8. Kalle, R.K.: Reliable and prioritized communication using polarization diversity for industrial Internet of Things. In: 2016 IEEE Conference on Wireless Sensors (ICWiSE), pp. 89–94. IEEE (2016)
9. Song, H.: Theoretical research on three-dimensional modulation demodulator. Ph.D. thesis, Fudan University (2012)
10. Wei, D., Feng, C., Guo, C.: An optimal pre-compensation based joint polarization-amplitude-phase modulation scheme for the power amplifier energy efficiency improvement. In: 2013 IEEE International Conference on Communications (ICC), pp. 4137–4142. IEEE (2013)
11. Wei, D., Kong, B., Qiao, R., et al.: High-efficiency wireless transmission scheme based on polarization state-amplitude-phase modulation. Scientia Sinica Informationis **45**(10), 1263–1279 (2015)
12. Wei, D., Liang, L., Zhang, M., et al.: A polarization state modulation based physical layer security scheme for wireless communications. In: MILCOM 2016-2016 IEEE Military Communications Conference, pp. 1195–1201. IEEE (2016)
13. Shah, S.N.H., Ansari, O., Sadiq, U.: Offset circular polarization modulation scheme. In: 2021 IEEE Global Communications Conference (GLOBECOM), pp. 1–6. IEEE (2021)
14. Qi, S., Zhang, B., Guo, D., et al.: Research on secure and reliable transmission technology based on directional polarization modulation. Inform. Technol. Netw. Sec. **37**(07), 27–32 (2018)
15. Liu, Z., Zhang, Q., Cheng, M.: OFDM physical layer security communication mechanism based on polarization multi-dimensional constellation modulation. J. Beijing Univ. Posts Telecommun. **41**(04), 9–15 (2018)
16. Li, M., Liang, L., Wei, D.: Wireless communication physical layer security transmission technology based on polarization state modulation. J. Inf. Secur. **3**(05), 105–117 (2018)
17. Yang, S., Xiao, Y., Chen, J., et al.: Integrated polarization and spatial modulation. IEEE Trans. Commun. **71**(1), 527–539 (2022)
18. Li, J., Li, S., Dang, S., et al.: Generalized polarization-spatial modulation with multi-mode transmission. IEEE Internet of Things J. (2025)
19. Shang, P., Xie, L., Li, J.: Polarized modulation for RIS-aided vehicular communication networks. IEEE Internet Things J. (2025)
20. Buvarp, A.M., Mili, L., Mishra, K.V.: Polarization-space modulation with reconfigurable intelligent surfaces, robust estimation and quaternion neural networks. IEEE Trans. Antennas Propag. (2025)
21. Li, Q., Peng, Y., Fawaz, A.L.H.: Polarized RIS-assisted polarized spatial scattering modulation. IEEE Internet Things J. (2025)

22. Liu, W., Ye, Z., Huang, N.: Rotational misalignment compensation for underwater optical wireless communication employing quaternary polarization shift keying modulation. In: 2023 International Conference on Wireless Communications and Signal Processing (WCSP), pp. 569–574. IEEE (2023)
23. Meng, X., Tang, Q.: Performance study of sea surface ultraviolet communication based on circular polarization modulation. In: 2024 4th International Conference on Artificial Intelligence, Robotics, and Communication (ICAIRC), pp. 670–673. IEEE (2024)
24. Zhang, X., Zhang, B., Guo, D., et al.: Application of polarization modulation in satellite communication. In: 2017 First International Conference on Electronics Instrumentation & Information Systems (EIIS), pp. 1–5. IEEE (2017)
25. Luo, Z., Wang, H., Lü, W.: Satellite MIMO secure transmission method based on direction-polarization state modulation. Syst. Eng. Electr. **39**(04), 888–892 (2017)

# Security, Privacy, and Trust

# 1-Bit Time-Modulated Array-Based UAV-Assisted Secure SDMA Communication

Dayong Zhao, Zhengkang Wang(✉), and Yong Xie

R&D Beijing Institute of Communication and Navigation, Beijing Institute of Communication and Navigation, Beijing, China
864125399@qq.com

**Abstract.** Unmanned aerial vehicle (UAV)-assisted communication systems, characterized by low cost, high mobility, and on-demand deployment, are suited for establishing communication links in adversarial environments. However, the broadcast of wireless channels makes these signals susceptible to eavesdropping. Considering the limited payload of UAV and the need to improve system throughput while ensuring security, this paper proposes UAV-assisted physical layer security communication scheme based on a 1-bit time-modulated array (TMA), where the signal transmitted from the UAV-mounted transmitter undergoes space-time modulation through the TMA, forming both fundamental and harmonic components and achieving harmonic beamforming. When the UAV transmitter sends multi-user signals at intervals defined by the 1-bit TMA modulation timing frequency, the signals of different users on various harmonics are remapped to the same frequency, enabling the system to achieve space-division multiple access (SDMA) using only a single RF chain. While multiple users communicate using various harmonic beams, aliasing is introduced in the direction of eavesdroppers, reducing their achievable rate and thereby enhancing system security. This paper analyzes the secrecy rate of the proposed system and employs particle swarm optimization (PSO) to jointly optimize the UAV deployment position, power allocation, and TMA modulation sequence, with the aim of maximizing the secrecy rate. Simulation results demonstrate that the proposed scheme maintains communication performance for legitimate users while significantly reducing the achievable rate for eavesdroppers, thereby improving physical layer security.

**Keywords:** Unmanned aerial vehicle · time-modulated array · physical layer secure · space-time modulation

## 1 Introduction

Unmanned aerial vehicle (UAV)-assisted communication technology has attracted increasing attention due to its high mobility, flexible deployment, and

Supported by organization x.


Y. Liu et al. (Eds.): ChinaCom 2025, LNICST 711, pp. 121–136, 2027.
https://doi.org/10.1007/978-3-032-33662-0_11

low operating cost [1]. As an unmanned aerial platforms, UAVs offer unparalleled advantages over traditional base stations, including the ability to take off and land at any time, flexible site deployment, and resilience to geographical limitations. They achieve the elimination of communication blind spots, the establishment of emergency links and high-quality mobile communications at low cost, achieving high economic efficiency. Consequently, UAVs can realize wider coverage of communication services to provide networking services for vessels, aircraft, wide-area IoT networks, and mobile terminals. However, in adversarial environments, due to the broadcast nature of wireless channels, air-to-ground communications are easily observed and UAV-assisted systems are vulnerable to eavesdropping attacks. As the computational power of eavesdroppers increases, conventional cryptography-based communication techniques are at risk of eavesdropping. In this context, physical layer security (PLS) provides a complementary mechanism to conventional cryptographic protocols, enhancing the security of wireless communication systems. Wyner in [2] analyzed the wiretap channel model and demonstrated that if the channel is a degenerate channel with respect to the legitimate user, then perfect secure communication can be achieved at a nonzero rate by the legitimate user. By employing a random coding scheme, it becomes feasible to ensure that legitimate users receive messages correctly while no information is leaked to eavesdroppers. Thus, PLS can effectively safeguard information security and prevent eavesdropping attacks.

The PLS techniques in UAV-assisted communications mainly include artificial noise (AN) techniques [3–5] and beamforming techniques [6,7]. In [4], a PLS scheme based on dual-UAV cooperation is proposed, where one UAV transmits information to ground users while an additional UAV generates interference signals to disrupt the eavesdropping link, thereby achieving secure transmission. By utilizing the mobility of UAVs, the channel states of communication UAVs and jamming UAVs for legitimate users and eavesdroppers can be effectively adjusted to create a disparity in the achievable rates of legitimate links and eavesdropping links, thereby enhancing security. The study employs alternating optimization and successive convex approximation algorithms to jointly optimize UAV trajectories and power allocation for maximizing the average secrecy rate. However, this approach only relies on UAV deployment to manipulate channel conditions, which limits its adaptability. Further, in [5], reconfigurable intelligent surfaces (RIS) is introduced into this scenario, leveraging their ability to reshape channels to further improve secure communications performance. With RIS-assisted passive beamforming, an information UAV transmits signals while a multi-antenna jamming UAV sends interference to eavesdroppers, ensuring secure communication between the information UAV and legitimate users. By jointly optimizing the UAV transmit power, trajectory, and RIS phase shifts, the average secrecy rate of system is maximized. In addition, [6] utilizes a UAV equipped with RIS (UAV-RIS) to maximize secrecy rates and enhance the secure communication performance of legitimate link while ensuring that legitimate users meet quality of service (QoS) requirements under eavesdropping and malicious jamming attacks. The minimum secrecy rate can be maximized through joint optimization of transmit beamforming, AN, UAV-RIS positioning, and RIS passive beamforming. Additionally, [7] considers a multi-UAV virtual antenna array, where coordinated beamforming is utilized to enhance secure communication. The study formulates a multi-objective optimization problem to maximize the minimum secrecy rate. The aforementioned works primarily focus on single-user scenarios. In contrast, [8] explores UAV-assisted integrated sensing and communication (ISAC) in a multi-user setting, where time-division multiple access (TDMA) is used for multi-user connectivity. A jamming UAV is deployed to improve system security, and each time slot is divided into ISAC and communication phases. During the ISAC phase, the source UAV detects multiple eavesdroppers and transmits their location information to the jamming UAV. By optimizing user scheduling, transmit power, and UAV trajectories, the system's physical layer secrecy rate is maximized. However, these techniques often require multiple RF chains on UAVs or the deployment of additional jamming UAVs, increasing system complexity. Given the constraints on UAV onboard equipment, there is a need to reduce system complexity and power consumption. Moreover, these works allow only a single user per time slot, which limits system throughput.

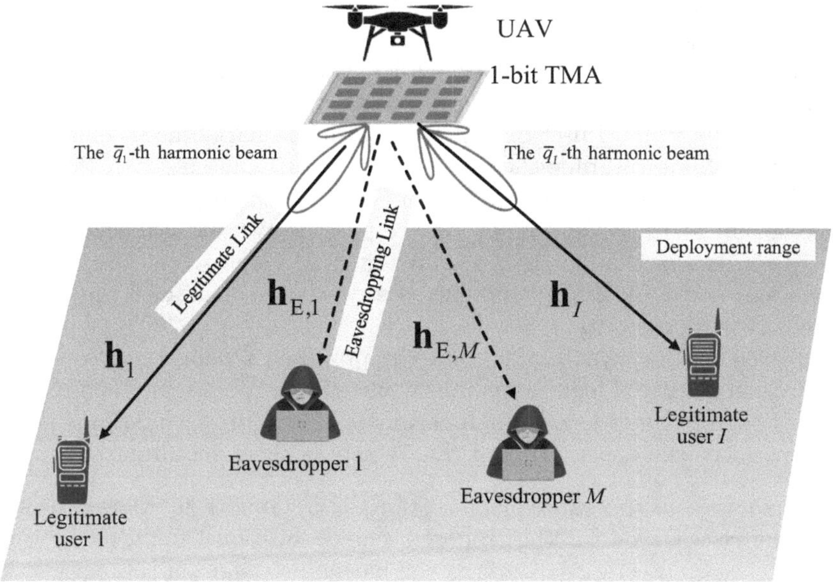


**Fig. 1.** Schematic representation of the UAV-assisted SDMA secure communication scenario based on 1-bit TMA.

Introducing space-division multiple access (SDMA) into UAV-assisted communication systems can effectively enhance system throughput, thereby improving the performance of UAV-assisted communication system [9]. In [10], a multi-user multiple-input single-output (MISO) UAV-assisted downlink communication system is studied, where a uniform planar antenna array (UPA) is used for digital beamforming to achieve multi-user SDMA. By optimizing the beamforming vectors and UAV trajectory, the UAV energy consumption is minimized while satisfying signal quality constraints. To further reduce the number of RF chains, [9] employs hybrid beamforming for multi-user SDMA. However, traditional hybrid beamforming requires the number of RF chains to be greater than the number of users to enable multi-user SDMA [11]. To further reduce the number of RF chains, [12] proposes using a single-pole single-throw time-modulated array (SPST-TMA) for multi-user SDMA communication. By leveraging the multi-harmonic beam characteristics of SPST-TMA, the multi-user signals at different frequencies from the UAV transmitter are remapped to the same frequency for transmission. In this scheme, a UAV can achieve multi-user SDMA using only a single RF chain, offering a low-complexity advantage. However, [12] only considers a uniform linear SPST-TMA, which cannot achieve 3D beamforming, and the system's secrecy rate performance remains unexplored. Additionally, SPST-based TMA suffers from low energy efficiency. In light of this, this paper proposes a multi-user secure SDMA communication based on a 1-bit TMA. The main contributions of this paper are as follows

- For the secure communication requirements in multi-user and multi-eavesdropper UAV-assisted scenarios, this paper proposes a UAV-assisted secure communication based on a 1-bit TMA. In this scheme, a UAV equipped with a 1-bit TMA leverages the multi-harmonic beam characteristics of the TMA to achieve multi-user SDMA while utilizing harmonic beamforming to interfere with and degrade the quality of eavesdropping links.
- This paper analyzes the secrecy rate of the system and proposes a joint iterative optimization method based on the particle swarm optimization (PSO) algorithm. The method jointly optimizes the UAV deployment position, power allocation, and 1-bit TMA modulation sequence to maximize the minimum secrecy rate of users.
- Simulation results demonstrate that the proposed scheme ensures the communication quality of legitimate links while effectively suppressing the achievable rate of eavesdroppers through harmonic beamforming and signal aliasing. Consequently, the secrecy rate of this system is effectively improved.

The structure of the subsequent sections is organized as follows. Section 2 presents the system model of the proposed scheme. Section 3 analyzes the secrecy rate of the system. Section 4 examines the harmonic radiation characteristics of the 1-bit TMA and verifies the secrecy rate of the proposed scheme. Section 5 presents numerical results, which not only verify the convergence and effectiveness of the proposed algorithm but also quantify the performance of the proposed scheme. Finally, Sect. 6 concludes this paper.

## 2 System Model

The schematic diagram of the UAV-assisted SDMA secure communication system based on a 1-bit TMA is shown in Fig. 1. In this system, the UAV transmits signals to $I$ ground terminals using a 1-bit TMA with $N$ array elements. The multi-harmonic beam characteristics of the 1-bit TMA enable multi-user SDMA communication. Meanwhile, $M$ eavesdroppers independently receive the signals transmitted by the UAV and attempt to intercept the communication of each user (Fig. 2).

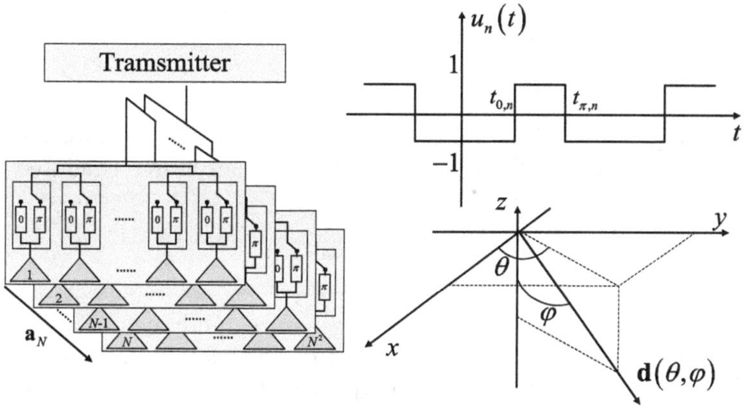


**Fig. 2.** Schematic diagram of the 1-bit TMA structure.

### 2.1 1-Bit-TMA Model

Let $x_i(t)$ denote the baseband signal transmitted by the UAV to user $i$, where $x_i(t)$ represents the $i^{\text{th}}$ channel's baseband signal, and $f_{\text{C},i}$ denotes the center frequency. After passing through an $N$-way power divider, the signal is transmitted to a 1-bit TMA for spatial-temporal modulation, where different array elements exhibit distinct modulation sequence. The modulated signal after the $n^{\text{th}}$ element of the 1-bit TMA can be expressed as

$$s_{i,n}(t) = x_i(t)\, u_n(t)\, \mathrm{e}^{\mathrm{j}2\pi f_c t}, \tag{1}$$

where $u_n(t)$ represents the modulation sequence of the $n^{\text{th}}$ antenna element in a 1-bit TMA. Due to the utilization of a 1-bit TMA for spatial-temporal modulation, the modulated waveform $u_n(t)$ can be expressed as

$$u_n(t) = \begin{cases} 1, & t_{0,n} + mT_{\text{M}} \leqslant t < t_{\pi,n} + mT_{\text{M}}; \\ -1, & \text{others}. \end{cases} \tag{2}$$

where $m \in \mathbb{Z}$, $\tau_{0,n}$ and $\tau_{\pi,n}$ are defined as the moments when the $n^{\text{th}}$ phase shifter switches to 0 and $\pi$ phase shift states, respectively. Since $u_n(t)$ is a square wave with a period of $T_{\text{M}}$, it can be expressed through Fourier series expansion as

$$u_n(t) = \sum_{-\infty}^{\infty} \beta_{n,q} e^{j2\pi q f_{\text{M}} t}, \tag{3}$$

where $\beta_{n,q}$ is the Fourier coefficient of the $q^{\text{th}}$ order frequency component and can be calculated as

$$\begin{aligned} \beta_{n,q} &= \frac{1}{T_{\text{M}}} \int_0^{T_{\text{M}}} u_n(t) e^{-j2\pi q f_{\text{M}} t} dt \\ &= \begin{cases} 2\tau_n - 1 \\ 2\tau_n \text{sinc}(\pi q \tau_n) e^{-j2\pi q \bar{\tau}_n} \end{cases} \end{aligned} \tag{4}$$

where $\tau_n = (t_{\pi,n} - t_{0,n})/T_{\text{M}}$ and $\bar{\tau}_n = (t_{\pi,n} + t_{0,n})/(2T_{\text{M}})$. Consequently, the transmitted signal on the $n^{\text{th}}$ array element in (1) can be reformulated as

$$s_{i,n}(t) = \sum_{q=-\infty}^{\infty} x_i(t) \beta_{n,q} e^{j2\pi(f_{\text{C},i} + q f_{\text{M}})t}. \tag{5}$$

As shown in (5), time-modulated signals generate fundamental and harmonic components. The complex-valued weights of the harmonic components for each array element are denoted by $\beta_{n,q}$. Consequently, harmonic beamforming can be achieved by adjusting the modulation sequence of the 1-bit TMA.

Considering UAVs mainly communicate with ground users, the UAV-borne array's normal is assumed perpendicular to the ground. Let the propagation direction vector of the far-field plane wave be denoted as $\mathbf{d}(\theta, \varphi)$. The angle between $\mathbf{d}(\theta, \varphi)$ and the z-axis is $\varphi$, and the angle between the projection of $\mathbf{d}(\theta, \varphi)$ onto the x-y plane and the x-axis is $\theta$. The normalized direction vector $\mathbf{d}(\theta, \varphi)$ can be expressed as

$$\mathbf{d}(\theta, \varphi) = [\sin(\varphi)\cos(\theta), \sin(\varphi)\sin(\theta), \cos(\varphi)]^{\text{T}}, \tag{6}$$

Consequently, the directional response of $n^{\text{th}}$ antenna element can be expressed as

$$\alpha_n(\theta, \varphi) = e^{j2\pi \mathbf{d}(\theta,\varphi)\mathbf{p}_n/\lambda}, \tag{7}$$

where $\mathbf{p}_n$ is the relative position coordinates of $i^{\text{th}}$ compared to the first element. Given that this study considers a uniform planar array with $N = \bar{N} \times \bar{N}$ elements and assumes an inter-element spacing of half a wavelength, $\mathbf{p}_n$ can be expressed as

$$\mathbf{p}_n = \left[\tfrac{\lambda}{2}\left((n-1)\%\bar{N}\right), \tfrac{\lambda}{2}\left\lfloor \tfrac{n-1}{\bar{N}} \right\rfloor, 0\right]^{\text{T}}. \tag{8}$$

By denoting $\mathbf{a}(\theta, \varphi) = [\alpha_1(\theta, \varphi), \alpha_2(\theta, \varphi), \ldots, \alpha_N(\theta, \varphi)]^{\text{T}}$ as the array steering vector, the radiation pattern of the $q^{\text{th}}$ harmonic can be expressed as

$$E(\theta, \varphi) = \xi(\theta, \varphi)\, \mathbf{a}^{\text{T}}(\theta, \varphi)\, \mathbf{b}_q. \tag{9}$$

where $\mathbf{b}_q \triangleq [\beta_{1,q}, \beta_{2,q}, \ldots, \beta_{N,q}]^{\mathrm{T}}$, $\xi(\theta, \varphi)$ represents the far-field radiation pattern of an individual array element. To simplify analysis, given that UAVs mainly serve ground users, the main lobe of $u(\theta, \varphi)$ is assumed to have equal 3dBi gain in all directions. From (9), it is evident that the modulation sequence $u_n(t)$ can influence the amplitude and phase weighting $\mathbf{b}_q$ of the array across various harmonics, thereby allowing for the adjustment of the radiation patterns of each harmonic. Due to the distinct directional characteristics of different harmonics, multi-user SDMA communication can be achieved through the utilization of various harmonic beams.

### 2.2 Received Signal Model

Considering $I$ users receiving downlink signals transmitted by the UAV at a center frequency of $f_{\mathrm{C}}$, to enable UAV-assisted SDMA communication, different users can be served using different harmonic beams. Assuming that user $i$ is transmitted through the $\bar{q}_i{}^{\mathrm{th}}$ harmonic, the center frequency of user $i$'s signal can be adjusted to the frequency point $f_{\mathrm{C}} - \bar{q}_i f_{\mathrm{M}}$. After space-time modulation by the 1-bit TMA, the frequency of user $i$ signal in the $\bar{q}_i{}^{\mathrm{th}}$ harmonic beam is precisely aligned with $f_{\mathrm{C}}$. Assuming the RF signal transmitted by the UAV for user $i$ is expressed as

$$s_i(t) = \sqrt{P_i}\bar{s}_i(t)\, e^{\mathrm{j}2\pi(f_{\mathrm{C}} - \bar{q}_i f_{\mathrm{M}})t}. \tag{10}$$

After time modulation, the received signal of user $i$ in the frequency $f_{\mathrm{C}}$ is given by

$$\bar{y}_i(t) = \underbrace{\sqrt{P_i}\bar{s}_i(t)\,\mathbf{h}_i^{\mathrm{T}}\mathbf{b}_{\bar{q}_i}}_{(\mathrm{a})} + \underbrace{\sum_{k=1,k\neq i}^{I} \sqrt{P_k}\bar{s}_k(t)\,\mathbf{h}_i^{\mathrm{T}}\mathbf{b}_{\bar{q}_k} + n(t)}_{(\mathrm{b})}, \tag{11}$$

where $n_i(t) \sim \mathcal{CN}(0, \sigma_i^2)$ is denoted as the local noise for user $i$. In (11), (a) represents the desired signal received by user $i$, while (b) corresponds to the interference signal. By adjusting the position of the UAV and modulation sequence, the channel state and harmonic beamforming vector can be optimized to enhance the signal reception quality for legitimate users while reducing the signal quality for eavesdroppers.

### 2.3 Air-to-Ground Channel Model

According to the measurement results in [13], when the UAV is deployed at a certain altitude, the energy of the line-of-sight (LoS) component becomes dominant, allowing the air-to-ground communication channel to be modeled as a LoS channel [14–16]. Let the three-dimensional coordinates of the deployed UAV be denoted as $\mathbf{l}_{\mathrm{U}} = [x_{\mathrm{U}}, y_{\mathrm{U}}, h_{\mathrm{U}}]^{\mathrm{T}}$, where $x_{\mathrm{U}}$ and $y_{\mathrm{U}}$ represent the horizontal coordinates of UAV, and $h_{\mathrm{U}}$ represents the flight altitude of UAV. Similarly, let the three-dimensional spatial coordinates of the ground user $i$ be denoted as

$\mathbf{l}_{\mathrm{G},i} = [x_{\mathrm{G},i}, y_{\mathrm{G},i}, 0]^{\mathrm{T}}$, thereby the channel state from the UAV to the ground user $i$ can be expressed as

$$[\mathbf{h}_i]_n = \sqrt{g_0/d_{\mathrm{UG},i}^{\eta}}e^{\mathrm{j}2\pi\left(\mathbf{d}_{\mathrm{UG},i}^{\mathrm{T}}\mathbf{p}_n - d_{\mathrm{UG},i}\right)/\lambda} \tag{12}$$

where $n \in \{1, 2, \ldots, N\}$, $[\cdot]_n$ represents the $n^{\mathrm{th}}$ element of the vector, $\lambda$ is denoted as the carrier wavelength, $g_0 = (\lambda/4\pi)^2$ represents the signal power gain at the reference distance $d_0 = 1\mathrm{m}$, and $\beta$ is the fading coefficient. For simplicity, this paper assumes that $\eta = 1$, $d_{\mathrm{UG},i} = \|\mathbf{l}_{\mathrm{G},i} - \mathbf{l}_{\mathrm{U}}\|_2$ is is the distance from the ground user to the UAV, and $\mathbf{d}_{\mathrm{UG},i} = (\mathbf{l}_{\mathrm{G},i} - \mathbf{l}_{\mathrm{U}})/d_{\mathrm{UG},i}$ represents the normalized direction vector from the UAV to user $i$.

## 3 Performance of Secrecy Rate

In an adversarial environment, as UAV transmit signals to ground stations, the transmissions from various users become vulnerable to eavesdropping by potential adversaries. Consequently, it is necessary to analyze the secrecy rate in the presence of eavesdroppers, while simultaneously formulating an optimization problem aimed at refining the system and strengthening the security of the communication system.

According to (12), upon receiving the desired signal, the user concurrently experiences interference from other users and the effects of local ambient noise. The user's signal-to-interference-plus-noise ratio (SINR) can be expressed as

$$\mathrm{SINR}_{\mathrm{U},i} = P_i\left|\mathbf{h}_i^{\mathrm{T}}\mathbf{b}_{\bar{q}_i}\right|^2 \Big/ \left(\sigma_0^2 + \sum_{k=1,k\neq i}^{I} P_k\left|\mathbf{h}_i^{\mathrm{T}}\mathbf{b}_{\bar{q}_k}\right|^2\right). \tag{13}$$

Assuming that the transmitted signals among users are independent and adhere to a Gaussian distribution, the achievable rate for the user can be articulated as

$$R_i = \log_2\left(1 + \mathrm{SINR}_{\mathrm{U},i}\right). \tag{14}$$

Similarly, the achievable rate for the eavesdropper while intercepting the user's signal can be articulated as

$$R_{\mathrm{E},m,i} = \log_2\left(1 + \frac{P_i\left|\mathbf{h}_{\mathrm{E},m}^{\mathrm{T}}\mathbf{b}_{\bar{q}_i}\right|^2}{\sigma_0^2 + \sum\limits_{k=1,k\neq i}^{I} P_k\left|\mathbf{h}_{\mathrm{E},m}^{\mathrm{T}}\mathbf{b}_{\bar{q}_k}\right|^2}\right) \tag{15}$$

where $\mathbf{h}_{\mathrm{E},m}$ represents the channel state of the $m^{\mathrm{th}}$ eavesdropper. Assuming that eavesdroppers independently eavesdrop on multiple users, the secrecy rate for the user can be given as

$$R_{\mathrm{S},i} = \max\left\{0, R_i - \hat{R}_{\mathrm{E},i}\right\}. \tag{16}$$

where $\hat{R}_{\mathrm{E},i} = \max_{\forall m \in [1,M]} \{R_{\mathrm{E},m,i}\}$ denotes the maximum achievable rate for the eavesdroppers when monitoring user $i$. Thus, the secrecy rate of the system can be calculated as

$$\bar{R}_{\mathrm{S}} = \sum_{i=1}^{I} R_{\mathrm{S},i}. \tag{17}$$

# 4 Optimization of Modulation Sequence, Power Allocation, and Deployment Locations

As shown in the previous analysis, the UAV's placement, power allocation, and the modulation sequence of 1-bit TMA can affect the system's secrecy rate. Consequently, this section formulates an optimization problem and introduces a joint optimization scheme based on PSO.

## 4.1 Formulation of the Optimization Problem

To enhance the security performance of the system while simultaneously maximizing fairness, the optimization of the lower bound of secrecy rate is considered in this paper. Consequently, the optimization problem can be formulated as

$$\begin{aligned} \mathbf{P1}: \quad & \underset{\mathbf{l}_{\mathrm{U}}, P_i, \tau_n, \bar{\tau}_n, \forall n, \forall i}{\arg\max} \quad \min_{\forall i \in \{1,\ldots,I\}} \{R_{\mathrm{S}}, i\} \\ & \text{s.t.} \quad \mathrm{C1}: 0 \leqslant \bar{\tau}_n \leqslant 1 \\ & \qquad \mathrm{C2}: 0 \leqslant \tau_n \leqslant 1 \\ & \qquad \mathrm{C3}: \mathbf{l}_{\mathrm{Min}} \preccurlyeq \mathbf{l}_{\mathrm{U}} \preccurlyeq \mathbf{l}_{\mathrm{Max}} \\ & \qquad \mathrm{C4}: 0 \leqslant \sum_{i=1}^{I} P_i \leqslant P_{\mathrm{Max}} \end{aligned} \tag{18}$$

where $P_{\mathrm{Max}}$ represents the maximum transmission power of the UAV, while $\mathbf{l}_{\mathrm{Min}}$ and $\mathbf{l}_{\mathrm{Max}}$ denote the lower and upper bounds of the UAV's deployment position, respectively.

## 4.2 PSO-Based Joint Optimization of UAV Deployment, Power Allocation, and Modulation Sequence

As shown in equation (1), the optimization problem has multi-dimensional coupled variables, making it difficult to directly solve for the optimal solution. Consequently, an optimization scheme based on PSO is designed in this paper. In the boundary condition C4 of (18), variables representing the signal power of each user are included. To simplify C4, the following mapping is introduced

$$P_i = \prod_{k=1}^{i-1} (1 - \rho_k) \rho_i P_{\mathrm{Max}}, \tag{19}$$

where $\rho_i$ must satisfy $0 \leqslant \rho_i \leqslant 1, \forall i \in \{1, \ldots, I\}$. Additionally, let $\boldsymbol{\eta}_{\mathrm{U}} \triangleq [\eta_{\mathrm{X}}, \eta_{\mathrm{Y}}, \eta_{\mathrm{Z}}]^{\mathrm{T}}$, where $\mathbf{0} \preccurlyeq \boldsymbol{\eta}_{\mathrm{U}} \preccurlyeq \mathbf{1}$, and define

$$\mathbf{l}_{\mathrm{U}} = \mathbf{l}_{\mathrm{Min}} + (\mathbf{l}_{\mathrm{Max}} - \mathbf{l}_{\mathrm{Min}}) \odot \boldsymbol{\eta}_{\mathrm{U}}, \tag{20}$$

where $\odot$ denotes the Hadamard product. Consequently, **P1** can be trans-

---

**Algorithm 1:** PSO-based joint optimization of power allocation, UAV deployment, and modulation sequence

---

**Input:** $\mathbf{l}_{\mathrm{E},m}$, $\mathbf{l}_{\mathrm{G},i}$, $P_{\mathrm{Max}}$,$\sigma^2$, $\mathbf{l}_{\mathrm{Min}}$, $\mathbf{l}_{\mathrm{Max}}$, $\bar{q}_i$
**Output:** $\mathbf{p}_{\mathrm{gbest}}$,
1: Initialize particle $\mathbf{p}_i^{(0)} \sim U(\mathbf{0}, \mathbf{1})$, initialize particle velocity $\mathbf{v}_i^{(0)} \sim U(-\mathbf{1}, \mathbf{1})$; $\mathbf{p}_{\mathrm{pbest},i}^{(0)} = \mathbf{p}_i^{(0)}$, initialize $\mathbf{p}_{\mathrm{gbest}}^{(0)}$, $k = 1$.
2: **repeat**
3: **for** $i \leftarrow 1$ to $D$ **do**
4: Pick random numbers $r_{1,i}^{(k-1)}, r_{2,i}^{(k-1)} \sim U(0, 1)$;
Determine the velocity vector $\bar{\mathbf{v}}_i^{(k)}$ according to (23), Correct $\bar{\mathbf{v}}_i^{(k)}$ to obtain $\mathbf{v}_i^{(k)}$ according to equation (24);
Determine the velocity vector $\bar{\mathbf{p}}_i^{(k)}$ according to (25), Correct $\bar{\mathbf{p}}_i^{(k)}$ to obtain $\mathbf{p}_i^{(k)}$ according to equation (26);
If $f\left(\mathbf{p}_{\bar{I}(k)}^{(k)}\right) > f\left(\mathbf{p}_{\mathrm{gbest}}^{(k-1)}\right)$, then $\mathbf{p}_{\mathrm{gbest}}^{(k)} = \mathbf{p}_{\bar{I}(k)}^{(k)}$,
else $\mathbf{p}_{\mathrm{gbest}}^{(k)} = \mathbf{p}_{\mathrm{gbest}}^{(k-1)}$;
5: **end for**
6: If $f\left(\mathbf{p}_{\bar{I}(k)}^{(k)}\right) > f\left(\mathbf{p}_{\mathrm{gbest}}^{(k-1)}\right)$, then $\mathbf{p}_{\mathrm{gbest}}^{(k)} = \mathbf{p}_{\bar{I}(k)}^{(k)}$,
else $\mathbf{p}_{\mathrm{gbest}}^{(k)} = \mathbf{p}_{\mathrm{gbest}}^{(k-1)}$;
$k = k + 1$.
7: **until** $k > K$ or $\max\limits_{\forall i \neq \bar{I}(k)} \left\| \mathbf{p}_i^{(k)} - \mathbf{p}_{\mathrm{gbest}}^{(k)} \right\| \leqslant \xi$

---

formed into

$$\begin{aligned} \mathbf{P2} \quad & \underset{\boldsymbol{\eta}_{\mathrm{U}}, \rho_i, \tau_n, \bar{\tau}_n, \forall n, \forall i}{\arg\max} \; \min_{\forall i \in \{1, \ldots, I\}} \{R_{\mathrm{S},i}\} \\ & \text{s.t.} \quad \mathrm{C1}, \mathrm{C2}, \\ & \quad \mathrm{C5}\text{: } \mathbf{0} \preccurlyeq \boldsymbol{\eta}_{\mathrm{U}} \preccurlyeq \mathbf{1}, \\ & \quad \mathrm{C6}\text{: } 0 \leqslant \rho_i \leqslant 1. \end{aligned} \tag{21}$$

Given the periodic nature of the modulation sequence, $\bar{\tau}_1 = 0$ is introduced in the optimization process to eliminate solutions with identical objective function values in the solution space and to reduce the search dimensionality. Hence, particles in PSO can be defined as

$$\mathbf{p} \triangleq [\bar{\tau}_2, \ldots, \bar{\tau}_N, \tau_1, \ldots, \tau_N, \rho_1, \ldots \rho_I, \eta_{\mathrm{x}}, \eta_{\mathrm{y}}, \eta_{\mathrm{h}}]^{\mathrm{T}}. \tag{22}$$

Assuming that the particle size is denoted by $D$, and let $\bar{\mathbf{v}}_i^{(k)}$ signify the displacement vector of the particles at the $k^{\mathrm{th}}$ iteration. Therefore, $\bar{\mathbf{v}}_i^{(k)}$ can be calculated as

$$\begin{aligned}\bar{\mathbf{v}}_i^{(k)} &= \omega \mathbf{v}_i^{(k-1)} + \alpha_1 r_{1,i}^{(k-1)} \left(\mathbf{p}_{\mathrm{Pbest},i}^{(k-1)} - \mathbf{p}_i^{(k-1)}\right) \\ &+ \alpha_2 r_{2,i}^{(k-1)} \left(\mathbf{p}_{\mathrm{gbest}}^{(k-1)} - \mathbf{p}_i^{(k-1)}\right),\end{aligned} \tag{23}$$

where $\omega$ represents the inertia weight, $\alpha_1$ and $\alpha_2$ is denoted as the acceleration coefficient, $r_{1,i}^{(k-1)}, r_{2,i}^{(k-1)} \sim U(0,1)$. $\mathbf{p}_{\mathrm{Pbest},i}^{(k-1)}$ represents the most favorable position that the $i^{\mathrm{th}}$ particle has encountered after the $k-1^{\mathrm{th}}$ iteration. $\mathbf{p}_{\mathrm{gbest}}^{(k-1)}$ is defined as the globally optimal position encountered after the $k-1^{\mathrm{th}}$ iteration, while $\mathbf{v}_i^{(k-1)} = \mathbf{p}_i^{(k-1)} - \mathbf{p}_i^{(k-2)}$ signifies the actual displacement of the $i^{\mathrm{th}}$ particle during the $k-1^{\mathrm{th}}$ iteration.

To constrain the maximum velocity of the particles in the $k^{\mathrm{th}}$ iteration, $\bar{\mathbf{v}}_i^{(k)}$ must be subjected to the following restrictions

$$\left[\mathbf{v}_i^{(k)}\right]_j = \begin{cases} -v_{\mathrm{Max}}, & \left[\bar{\mathbf{v}}_i^{(k)}\right]_j < -v_{\mathrm{Max}}; \\ \left[\bar{\mathbf{v}}_i^{(k)}\right]_j, & -v_{\mathrm{Max}} \leqslant \left[\bar{\mathbf{v}}_i^{(k)}\right]_j \leqslant v_{\mathrm{Max}}; \\ v_{\mathrm{Max}}, & v_{\mathrm{Max}} < \left[\bar{\mathbf{v}}_i^{(k)}\right]_j; \end{cases} \tag{24}$$

where $[\cdot]_j$ represents the $j^{\mathrm{th}}$ element of the vector, and $v_{\mathrm{Max}}$ is the maximum speed of the particle. Following the imposition of constraints on the maximum displacement, the position of the particle in the $k^{\mathrm{th}}$ iteration can be updated as

$$\bar{\mathbf{p}}_i^{(k)} = \mathbf{p}_i^{(k-1)} + \mathbf{v}_i^{(k)}, \tag{25}$$

where $\bar{\mathbf{p}}_i^{(k)}$ represents the position of particle $i$ after the $k^{\mathrm{th}}$ iteration. Given that $\bar{\mathbf{p}}_i^{(k)}$ may exceed the constraints, it necessitates a subsequent adjustment. Specifically, due to the periodic nature of $u_n(t)$, where $\bar{\tau}_n = \tau$ and $\bar{\tau}_n = \tau - 1$ represent identical modulation sequences, $\bar{\mathbf{p}}_i^{(k)}$ can be revised to

$$\left[\mathbf{p}_i^{(k)}\right]_j = \begin{cases} \left[\bar{\mathbf{p}}_i^{(k)}\right]_j \%1, & 1 \leqslant j \leqslant N-1; \\ 0, & \left[\bar{\mathbf{p}}_i^{(k)}\right]_j < 0, j \geqslant N; \\ 1, & \left[\bar{\mathbf{p}}_i^{(k)}\right]_j > 1, j \geqslant N; \end{cases} \tag{26}$$

where % denotes the remainder operation. Let $f(\mathbf{p})$ represent the objective function, and $\bar{I}^{(k)}$ be the index of the particle with the maximum objective function value after the $k^{\mathrm{th}}$ iteration. The PSO-based optimization algorithm is summarized in algorithm 1.

**Table 1.** default settings

| Parameter | Notation | Value |
|---|---|---|
| Lower bound of UAV deployment position | $\mathbf{l}_{\mathrm{Min}}$ | $[0, 0, 300]^{\mathrm{T}}\mathrm{m}$ |
| Upper bound of UAV deployment position | $\mathbf{l}_{\mathrm{Max}}$ | $[2000, 2000, 2000]^{\mathrm{T}}\mathrm{m}$ |
| Array size | $\mathbf{l}_{\mathrm{G},i}$ | $4 \times 4$ |
| Legitimate user coordinates | $\mathbf{l}_{\mathrm{G},i}$ | $\mathbf{l}_{\mathrm{G},1} = [200, 800, 0]^{\mathrm{T}}\mathrm{m}$<br>$\mathbf{l}_{\mathrm{G},2} = [1200, 1600, 0]^{\mathrm{T}}\mathrm{m}$<br>$\mathbf{l}_{\mathrm{G},3} = [1600, 800, 0]^{\mathrm{T}}\mathrm{m}$ |
| Eavesdropper coordinates | $\mathbf{l}_{\mathrm{E},m}$ | $\mathbf{l}_{\mathrm{E},1} = [300, 1000, 0]^{\mathrm{T}}\mathrm{m}$<br>$\mathbf{l}_{\mathrm{E},2} = [1300, 1800, 0]^{\mathrm{T}}\mathrm{m}$<br>$\mathbf{l}_{\mathrm{E},3} = [1400, 1000, 0]^{\mathrm{T}}\mathrm{m}$ |
| Harmonic allocation | $\bar{q}_i$ | $\bar{q}_1 = -1, \bar{q}_2 = 0, \bar{q}_3 = 1$ |
| Center frequency | $f_{\mathrm{C}}$ | 2.4 GHz |

## 5 Numerical Simulation

This section simulates and verifies the security performance of the proposed scheme. Initially, the simulation results of harmonic radiation characteristics are presented and compared with unsecure transmission. Subsequently, the system's achievable rate and secrecy rate performance are analyzed. Unless specified otherwise, the default parameters for the simulations in this study are outlined in Table 1.

### 5.1 Harmonic Radiation Characteristics

Due to the transmission of signals from different users utilizing distinct harmonics, the optimization algorithm will adjust the radiation characteristics of each harmonic in accordance with the objective function, thereby enabling the realization of varied radiation properties. Consequently, Fig. 3a plots the radiation intensity of each harmonic in the target area after maximizing the lower bound of the secure rate. To comprehensively explain the radiation characteristics' impact on system security performance, Fig. 3b shows the radiation intensity of each harmonic in the target area after maximizing the lower bound of the user's achievable rate in unsecure transmission, as a comparative experiment. As demonstrated in Fig. 3a, after the optimization of power allocation, UAV positioning, and modulation sequence, the maximum gain directions of each harmonic order approach the legitimate users, while the energy received by eavesdroppers is minimized. This effectively guarantees that the system achieves a high performance in terms of secure rate. In non-secure transmission as shown in Fig. 3b, though the maximum gain directions of harmonics are closer to legitimate users, eavesdroppers receive higher signal gains, increasing the eavesdropping risk.

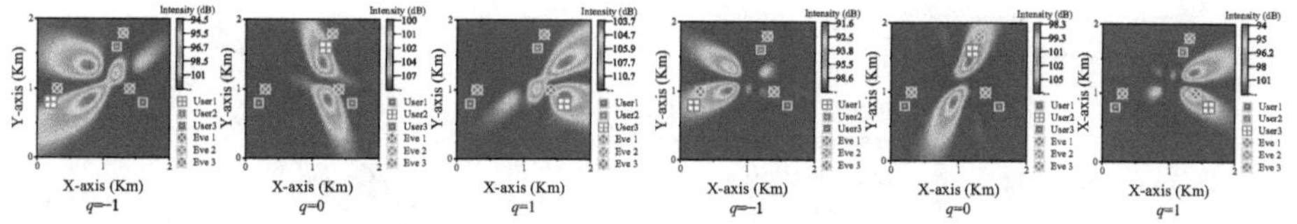


(a) Secure transmission. (b) Unsecure transmission.

**Fig. 3.** Harmonic radiation intensity of secure and unsecure transmission, where $P_{\mathrm{Max}} = 30\mathrm{dBm}$.

## 5.2 Performance Analysis of Secrecy Rate

Figure 4 illustrates the achievable rates for legitimate users and eavesdroppers. Specifically, it compares the maximized lower bound of the achievable rate in non-secure transmission and the achievable rate performance under the proposed scheme. The following conclusions can be drawn from the Fig. 4 .

- The proposed scheme can effectively suppress the achievable rate of eavesdroppers. As shown in Fig. 4, compared with the scheme of maximizing the lower bound of the achievable rate, the users' achievable rate decreases slightly, while the eavesdroppers' achievable rate is effectively suppressed.
- An increase in UAV power can significantly enhance the achievable rate of users. The rate of users monotonically increases with $P_{\mathrm{Max}}$, indicating the proposed algorithm effectively optimizes the harmonic beam and significantly suppresses harmonic mutual interference in the received signal.
- Leveraging the interference among harmonics can effectively suppress the achievable rates of eavesdroppers. In contrast to the achievable rates of users, the achievable rates of eavesdroppers approach a fixed value as $P_{\mathrm{Max}}$ increases. As evidenced by (13), in the low-power range, the achievable rate is mainly affected by the local noise. As the power increases, the mutual interference between harmonics becomes more significant, limiting the further increase of the eavesdropper's achievable rate.

Figure 5. Illustrates the secrecy rate performance of each user. The simulation results depicted in the figure lead to the following conclusions.

- The proposed scheme effectively enhances the secure rate performance of the system. Compared with non-secure transmission, the simulation results show that the proposed scheme achieves much higher physical layer secrecy rates for all users.
- The proposed scheme effectively ensures fairness within the system. As depicted in Fig. 5, the optimization algorithm's objective function is defined by the lower bound of the secrecy rate. Consequently, the secrecy rate performance among the users in the system is nearly uniform, thereby ensuring a high level of fairness.

Figure 6 presents the sum secure rate $\bar{R}_{\mathrm{S}}$ performance of multi-user systems based on SPST-TMA and 1-bit TMA. It is evident that both 1-bit TMA

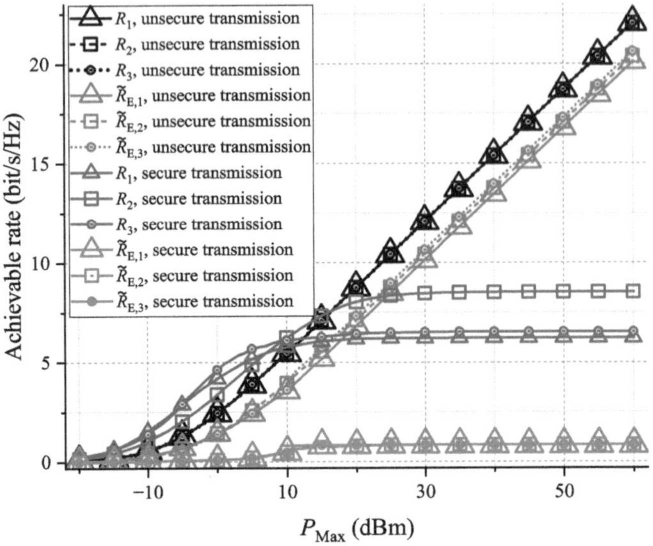


**Fig. 4.** Achievable rates for legitimate users and eavesdroppers.

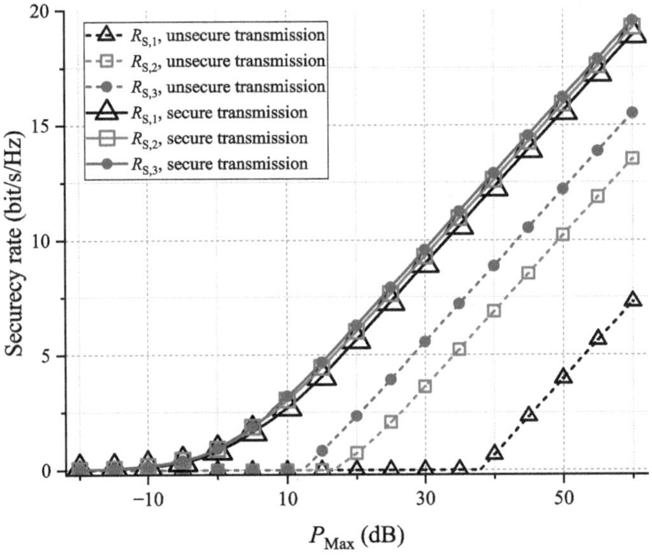


**Fig. 5.** Secrecy rate in secure and unsecure transmission scenarios.

and SPST-TMA significantly enhance the system's secrecy rate compared to non-secure transmission. Furthermore, in comparison to the secure transmission scheme employing SPST-TMA, the secure transmission based on 1-bit TMA is capable of achieving the same secrecy rate with a reduction of approximately 4

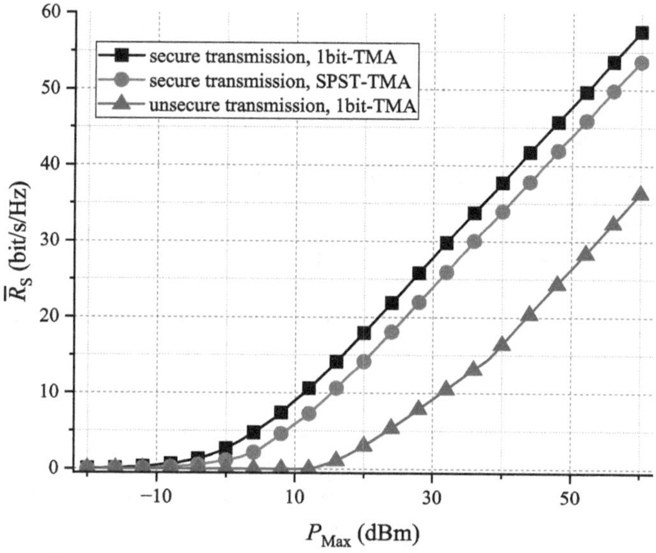


**Fig. 6.** Comparison of sum secrecy rate between 1-bit TMA-Based and SPST-TMA-Based systems.

dB in transmit power. Consequently, compared with SPST-TMA, the 1-bit TMA can effectively reduce the system's transmit power demand without significantly increasing its complexity.

## 6 Conclusion

This paper presents a UAV-assisted SDMA secure communication technology that employs 1-bit TMA for spatial-temporal modulation of signals, thereby generating fundamental and harmonic beams. As the UAV transmits multi-user signals at a modulation sequence period characterized by the frequency interval, the signals are subjected to spatial-temporal modulation through 1-bit TMA and are then remapped to the same frequency band for transmission, thereby achieve multi-user SDMA. This paper employs PSO to optimize the deployment location of the UAV, modulation sequence, and power allocation, with the aim of maximizing the lower bound of multi-user secure rates. Simulation experiments show that the proposed scheme can significantly degrade the eavesdropper's link quality while ensuring the legitimate user's link quality, thus achieving good secure rate performance. Notably, the proposed scheme utilizes a single RF chain for transmission and does not require additional artificial noise, thereby offering the advantage of low complexity.

## References


1. Zhang, S., Zhang, H., He, Q., Bian, K., Song, L.: Joint trajectory and power optimization for UAV relay networks. IEEE Commun. Lett. **22**(1), 161–164 (2018)
2. Wyner, A.D.: The wire-tap channel. Bell Syst. Tech. J. **54**(8), 1355–1387 (1975)
3. Li, A., Zhang, W.: Mobile jammer-aided secure UAV communications via trajectory design and power control. China Commun. **15**(8), 141–151 (2018)
4. Zhong, C., Yao, J., Xu, J.: Secure UAV communication with cooperative jamming and trajectory control. IEEE Commun. Lett. **23**(2), 286–289 (2019)
5. Ye, R., Peng, Y., Al-Hazemi, F., Boutaba, R.: A robust cooperative jamming scheme for secure UAV communication via intelligent reflecting surface. IEEE Trans. Commun. **72**(2), 1005–1019 (2024)
6. Yang, H., Liu, S., Xiao, L., Zhang, Y., Xiong, Z., Zhuang, W.: Learning-based reliable and secure transmission for UAV-RIS-assisted communication systems. IEEE Trans. Wireless Commun. **23**(7), 6954–6967 (2024)
7. Sun, G., et al.: UAV-enabled secure communications via collaborative beamforming with imperfect eavesdropper information. IEEE Trans. Mob. Comput. **23**(4), 3291–3308 (2024)
8. Liu, Y., et al.: Secure rate maximization for ISAC-UAV assisted communication amidst multiple eavesdroppers. IEEE Trans. Veh. Technol. **73**(10), 15843–15847 (2024)
9. Xiao, Z., Xia, P., Xia, X.-g.: Enabling UAV cellular with millimeter-wave communication: potentials and approaches. IEEE Commun. Mag. **54**(5), 66–73 (2016)
10. Xu, D., Sun, Y., Ng, D.W.K., Schober, R.: Multiuser MISO UAV communications in uncertain environments with no-fly zones: robust trajectory and resource allocation design. IEEE Trans. Commun. **68**(5), 3153–3172 (2020)
11. Xiao, Z., Zhu, L., Xia, X.-G.: UAV communications with millimeter-wave beamforming: potentials, acenarios, and challenges. China Commun. **17**(9), 147–166 (2020)
12. Chen, Q., He, C., Bai, L., Zhang, X.: A novel SDMA uplink method based on time-modulated array for UAV communications. In: 2018 IEEE International Conference on Communication Systems (ICCS), Chengdu, China, pp. 19–24 (2018)
13. Lin, X., et al.: The sky is not the limit: LTE for unmanned aerial vehicles. IEEE Commun. Mag. **56**(4), 204–210 (2018)
14. Wu, Q., Zhang, R.: Common throughput maximization in UAV-enabled OFDMA systems with delay consideration. IEEE Trans. Commun. **66**(12), 6614–6627 (2018)
15. Yang, Z., et al.: Joint altitude, beamwidth, location, and bandwidth optimization for UAV-enabled communications. IEEE Commun. Lett. **22**(8), 1716–1719 (2018)
16. Liu, L., Zhang, S., Zhang, R.: CoMP in the sky: UAV placement and movement optimization for multi-user communications. IEEE Trans. Commun. **67**(8), 5645–5658 (2019)

# Blockchain-Enabled Trustworthy Digital Twin Management System

Zhe Jiang[1], Xiuying Chen[1], Cai Guo[2], Yaru Fu[1], and Bishenghui Tao[1](✉)

[1] School of Science and Technology, Hong Kong Metropolitan University, Hong Kong, China
{s1366525,s1355634}@live.hkmu.edu.hk, {yfu,btao}@hkmu.edu.hk

[2] School of Computer and Information Engineering, Hanshan Normal University, Chaozhou, China
c.guo@hstc.edu.cn

**Abstract.** Digital twin (DT) technology exhibits significant potential across various industries, particularly within smart city mobile vehicular networks. However, its broader application and deeper exploration in this domain are hindered by persistent challenges concerning data integrity, system vulnerability, and centralized architectures. Blockchain technology, functioning as a distributed ledger, offers inherent properties of trustworthiness, decentralization, and tamper resistance, positioning it as a promising solution for overcoming these limitations. Nevertheless, existing blockchain-based approaches often inadequately address critical requirements such as computational load balancing, robust data verification, and deep scenario-specific integration, leaving substantial room for improvement in system efficiency, reliability, and usability. To overcome these inherent constraints, this paper proposes a blockchain-based trusted digital twin management system. Firstly, we develop a three-layer architecture for mobile vehicular digital twins, comprising the Digital Twin Layer, the Data Interaction Layer, and the Blockchain Layer, to manage every stage of DT data, from generation to processing and storage. Secondly, we introduce a fairness-oriented consensus mechanism, enhanced by a sigmoid-based smoothing function, to mitigate oligopoly risks and ensure computational load balance. Furthermore, we demonstrate that an isolation forest-based rollback verification method effectively facilitates anomaly detection and guarantees the consistency of historical digital twin data. Theoretical analysis and experimental results substantiate that the proposed system significantly enhances the reliability and robustness of digital twin management.

**Keywords:** Blockchain · Digital Twin · Vehicular Networks · Data Integrity · Trustworthy Systems

The work described in this paper was supported by the Katie Shu Sui Pui Charitable Trust-Research Training Fellowship (KSRTF/2024/06).


Y. Liu et al. (Eds.): ChinaCom 2025, LNICST 711, pp. 137–155, 2027.
https://doi.org/10.1007/978-3-032-33662-0_12

## 1 Introduction

Digital Twin (DT) technology has transformed cyber-physical system management through real-time synchronization and predictive simulation in critical domains such as autonomous vehicles [22] and smart city infrastructure [35]. The core value proposition of DTs lies in their bidirectional mapping between physical entities and virtual counterparts [37], a capability critically dependent on trustworthy heterogeneous data streams. However, centralized DT architectures exhibit fundamental vulnerabilities evidenced by recent failures in vehicular networks [18] and industrial systems [38]: monolithic control structures create single-point failure risks, multi-stakeholder environments lack transparent data provenance mechanisms, and quadratic scaling complexity impedes management of exponentially growing edge devices.

While blockchain-based solutions have emerged to address these concerns through decentralized ledgers [16,40,43], three persistent limitations undermine their effectiveness in DT contexts. Firstly, consensus centralization in conventional Delegated Proof-of-Stake (DPoS) mechanisms leads to oligopolistic control whereby nodes that hold a large number of tokens dominate block production and create systemic collusion risks. Secondly, validation ambiguity leaves systems vulnerable to delayed false-data injection attacks due to inadequate backward-compatible verification. Thirdly, the cross-layer consistency gap manifests itself as a misalignment between the physical sensor states and their digital representations, which compromises end-to-end traceability [47]. These limitations collectively constrain computational load balancing, data verification robustness, and scenario-specific integration depth.

To overcome these barriers, we propose a blockchain-enabled trustworthy digital twin management system with three foundational contributions:

- A *three-layer architecture* integrating Digital Twin, Data Interaction, and Blockchain layers that ensures reliable vehicle data management from generation through processing to immutable storage, eliminating single-point failures through distributed ledgering.
- An *improved DPoS consensus mechanism* incorporating a sigmoid-based smoothing function for fairer block selection and dynamic workload balancing, effectively mitigating oligopoly risks while maintaining high-throughput synchronization.
- An *Isolation Forest-based rollback validation* mechanism that enhances anomaly detection in historical DT data through adaptive feature combination analysis, ensuring contextual integrity and effective data validation.

The remainder of this paper is structured as follows: Section 2 reviews related work; Sect. 3 details the proposed three-layer architecture and modeling construction; Sect. 4 presents experimental validation using real vehicular datasets; finally, Sect. 5 summarizes key findings and future research directions.

## 2 Related Work

Building on the aforementioned trustworthiness challenges, particularly data security, multi-stakeholder transparency, and traceability limitations, DTs serve as virtual replicas enabling real-time simulation through IoT integration [38]. While empowering applications across manufacturing, energy systems, and urban infrastructure [35], persistent vulnerabilities identified by [35] and [12] directly motivate blockchain integration. Specifically, the tension between the requirement for end-to-end data trustworthiness in DT and the limitations of existing centralized architectures in scalable automation creates critical research gaps. The blockchain consensus mechanisms (Sect. 2.1) and the integration frameworks (Sect. 2.2) aim to address these gaps.

### 2.1 Blockchain Consensus Mechanisms

Given the stringent requirements for decentralized trust in vehicular DT systems identified, consensus mechanisms play a pivotal role in balancing the fundamental trade-offs between security, efficiency, and decentralization. Traditional approaches exhibit critical limitations in DT contexts: Proof of Work (PoW) [26] provides robust security but introduces prohibitive latency for real-time synchronization, while Proof of Authority (PoA) [2] sacrifices decentralization for speed—contradicting the multi-stakeholder transparency imperative. Practical Byzantine Fault Tolerance (PBFT) [5] offers strong fault tolerance at the cost of quadratic complexity incompatible with vehicular edge networks, and Proof of Stake (PoS) [30] risks wealth concentration that exacerbates power imbalances.

Delegated Proof of Stake (DPoS) [41] initially appears suitable for DT scenarios through its balance of scalability and decentralization, but persistent centralization trends—where power accumulates among a few nodes [17,21]—directly undermine the participation of the validator [14] and distort network dynamics [6]. This structural flaw manifests acutely in vehicular DT environments as it recreates the very oligopolistic risks that blockchain integration aims to resolve. Although architectural [1], protocol [29], and dynamic adjustments [41] have been proposed, these solutions fail to address the root cause of power consolidation in large-scale dynamic networks [21].

Our contribution directly bridges this gap by augmenting DPoS with a novel smoothing strategy that simultaneously prevents centralized oligopoly and ensures computational load balance—precisely aligning with the needs of vehicular DTs for distributed trust and real-time responsiveness.

### 2.2 Blockchain-Digital Twin Integration

Building upon the consensus mechanism requirements established in Sect. 2.1, blockchain integration with digital twins offers transformative potential through decentralized immutability and transparent audit trails [43]. However, critical gaps persist in achieving the *end-to-end data trustworthiness* essential for vehicular networks—directly undermining three core requirements. First, while frameworks like [16] ensure basic traceability, they lack backward-compatible validation mechanisms against delayed false-data injections, compromising data completeness. Second, solutions such as [28] decentralize component management but neglect the critical alignment between physical sensor states and their digital representations, creating cross-layer consistency vulnerabilities. Third, despite advances in IoT security [24] and simulation validation [8], existing approaches fail to quantify the trustworthiness of data, such as its reliability as determined by real-time spatiotemporal, source-state, and environmental factors, which is fundamental for dynamic vehicular environments [36].

Even industrial implementations that successfully ensure real-time integrity [10,31] cannot resolve persistent temporal-spatial misalignments during high-velocity vehicle maneuvers. These collective limitations necessitate an integrated approach that simultaneously addresses data completeness, cross-layer consistency, and contextual trust quantification. Our work bridges these gaps through a novel rollback verification mechanism (Sect. 3) embedded within a unified architecture, directly extending the fairness-enhanced consensus foundation established in Sect. 2.1 to deliver comprehensive trustworthiness across vehicular DT lifecycles.

To bridge these gaps, we propose a blockchain-based DT management framework. This multi-layer framework ensures the traceability and robustness of DT trusted data through different layers of data collection, processing, storage, and verification processes.

## 3 System Design

This section presents a blockchain-based trusted digital twin management system that ensures the high reliability and integrity of vehicle data. Specifically, we propose a three-layer network architecture that models the digital twin data process from generation to processing, storage, and verification. This design ensures that DT data is tamper-proof, loss-proof, and verifiable throughout the entire process. Secondly, we enhance the traditional Delegated Proof of Stake (DPoS) consensus mechanism by adopting a fairer election strategy to determine the proposer of new blocks. This approach effectively mitigates the risk of monopolization while ensuring a balanced computational load. Furthermore, the system employs an isolation forest-based rollback verification mechanism that promptly detects anomalies in historical data, thereby ensuring data integrity and reliability.

### 3.1 Architecture Overview

The system architecture is illustrated in Fig. 1, comprising three logically integrated layers: the Digital Twin Layer, Data Interaction Layer, and Blockchain Layer. In the Digital Twin Layer, the constructed real-time digital twin data is

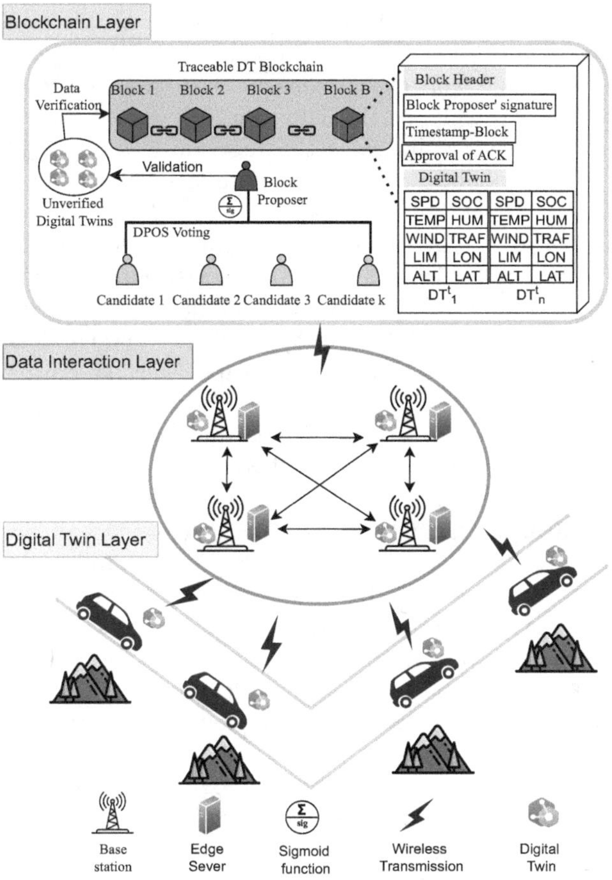


**Fig. 1.** Architecture overview

transmitted to the Data Interaction Layer. Subsequently, in the Data Interaction Layer, the processed digital twin information is relayed to the Blockchain Layer, where the data flow culminates in secure and immutable storage. Each layer is designed to operate synergistically, ensuring secure, efficient, and real-time data management and modeling.

**Digital Twin Layer** dynamically constructs and maintains high-fidelity virtual replicas of physical vehicular entities through continuous bidirectional synchronization of heterogeneous sensory data streams. This layer ingests real-time telemetry encompassing geospatial attributes (altitude, longitude, latitude), kinematic states (speed, GPS-derived velocity), energy metrics (state of charge), and environmental conditions (temperature, humidity, traffic density, speed limit, wind speed). Formally, let $\mathcal{V} = \{1, 2, \ldots, V\}$ denote the set of physical vehicles and $\mathcal{T} = \{1, 2, \ldots, T\}$ represent the discrete temporal horizon partitioned into synchronized operational intervals. At each epoch $t \in \mathcal{T}$, sensor data acquired via wireless networks undergoes dual concurrent processes: wireless transmission of multi-modal sensory readings and dynamic reconstruction of virtual representations, collectively generating a contextualized digital twin instance $\mathrm{DT}_v^t$ for each vehicle $v \in \mathcal{V}$. The resulting digital twins $\mathrm{DT}_v^t$ establish semantically consistent virtualizations that accurately mirror physical entities across spatiotemporal domains, providing foundational inputs for subsequent Data Interaction and Blockchain Layers.

**Data Interaction Layer** orchestrates secure and efficient data exchange between the Blockchain Layer and Digital Twin Layer, functioning as a critical middleware component. This layer ingests raw digital twin streams from distributed edge servers and cellular base stations via wireless transmission channels, subsequently transforming unstructured sensory data into standardized blockchain-compatible packets. During this transformation process, essential vehicular metadata—including geospatial coordinates (altitude, longitude, latitude), temporal markers, and transactional context—is preserved while schema consistency is enforced through predefined data contracts. To optimize system performance, the layer implements edge-based caching mechanisms that accelerate data retrieval through distributed memory stores, complemented by geospatial persistence utilizing the standardized GeoJSON format [4] for structured storage of location-aware datasets. Through parallel processing pipelines, this architectural design achieves significant latency reduction while simultaneously enhancing interoperability via schema normalization. Furthermore, the implementation ensures seamless integration with external analytics frameworks, collectively establishing a high-throughput conduit capable of sustaining rigorous real-time synchronization demands across the digital twin ecosystem.

**Blockchain Layer** establishes a decentralized trust framework through an optimized Delegated Proof-of-Stake (DPoS) consensus mechanism, where participants elect block proposers $\mathcal{P} = \{p_1, p_2, \ldots, p_M\}$ from a candidate pool $\mathcal{C} = \{c_1, c_2, \ldots, c_k\}$. Each elected proposer $p \in \mathcal{P}$ validates transactions and generates cryptographically signed blocks $B_b$ for $b \in \{1, 2, \ldots, B\}$, with each block containing header metadata $\langle \tau_b, \sigma_p, \Gamma_{\mathrm{ACK}} \rangle$ indicating the time stamp, proposer's signature and approval of ACK. A payload comprising digital twin states $\bigcup_{v=1}^{V} \mathrm{DT}_v^t$ aggregated at operational interval $t$. The resulting blockchain $\mathcal{B} = \{B_1, B_2, \ldots, B_B\}$ provides immutable storage for all validated blocks, where each digital twin state $\mathrm{DT}_v^t$ encapsulates essential vehicular parameters: altitude (ALT), longitude (LON), latitude (LAT), speed (SPD), GPS speed (GPSPD), state of charge (SOC), temperature (TEMP), humidity (HUM), traffic density (TRAF), speed limit (LIM), and wind speed (WIND). Block validation requires simultaneous satisfaction of cryptographic integrity through signature verification $\mathtt{Verify}(\sigma_p, \mathtt{PK}_p)$ [11], consensus acknowledgment evidenced by $|\Gamma_{\mathrm{ACK}}| > \lfloor 2|\mathcal{N}|/3 \rfloor$ from participating nodes $\mathcal{N}$, and data conformance to predefined validation rules $\Phi$. This integrated verification mechanism ensures Byzantine fault tolerance while preserving computing load balance. It establishes trustworthy, tamper-evident records through cryptographic chaining and distributed consensus as well.

In conclusion, the proposed three-layer architecture delivers a secure and efficient framework for vehicular digital twins. Its core purpose is to ensure data integrity from sensing to storage: the Digital Twin Layer creates accurate virtual models, the Data Interaction Layer optimizes and prepares data, and the Blockchain Layer guarantees tamper-proof record-keeping. This integrated design provides key improvements over traditional systems, including enhanced security through decentralization, guaranteed data authenticity, and robust, real-time performance for dynamic vehicular ecosystems.

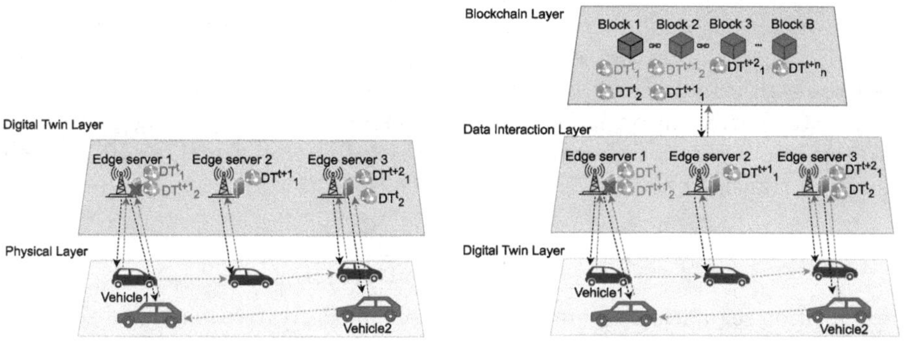


(a) Conventional architecture (b) Blockchain-enabled architecture

**Fig. 2.** Comparison on Single Point of Failures (SPOFs) Scenario

This multi-layered architecture demonstrates significant improvements in decentralization and data trustworthiness compared to conventional DT integration architectures. As illustrated in Fig. 2, providing a comparative reliability analysis, the system eliminates single points of failures (SPOFs). Consider two vehicles $\mathcal{V} = \{1, 2\}$ with dynamically updated digital twins $\mathrm{DT}_v^t$ migrating across edge servers $\mathcal{E} = \{1, 2, 3\}$ over time slots $t \in \{t, t+1, t+2\}$:

$$\begin{cases} \mathrm{DT}_1^t \mapsto \mathcal{E}_1, & \mathrm{DT}_2^t \mapsto \mathcal{E}_3 \\ \mathrm{DT}_1^{t+1} \mapsto \mathcal{E}_2, & \mathrm{DT}_2^{t+1} \mapsto \mathcal{E}_1 \\ \mathrm{DT}_1^{t+2} \mapsto \mathcal{E}_3. \end{cases}$$

In conventional architecture (Fig. 2a), the absence of blockchain centralizes control, making the system vulnerable to SPOFs. When $\mathcal{E}_1$ fails, twins $\mathrm{DT}_1^t$ and $\mathrm{DT}_2^{t+1}$ become incomplete, causing irreversible data loss and layer de-synchronization that compromises consistency [48], ultimately undermining system integrity [9]. Conversely, our blockchain-enhanced architecture (Fig. 2b) employs appropriate consensus to create tamper-proof records. Despite $\mathcal{E}_1$ failure, twins $\mathrm{DT}_1^t$ and $\mathrm{DT}_2^{t+1}$ remain accessible through blockchain synchronization.

The distributed ledger blockchain $\mathcal{B} = \{B_1, B_2, \ldots, B_B\}$ immutably stores:

$$B_1 \ni \{\mathrm{DT}_1^t, \mathrm{DT}_2^t\}, \quad B_2 \ni \{\mathrm{DT}_2^{t+1}, \mathrm{DT}_1^{t+1}\}, \quad B_3 \ni \{\mathrm{DT}_1^{t+1}\}.$$

By eliminating reliance on single authorities, this design ensures continuous data completeness, uniform cross-layer state transitions, and enduring trustworthiness. These properties collectively sustain reliability and auditability under adversarial conditions.

### 3.2 Delegated Proof-of-Stake with Smoothing Mechanism

The proposed consensus mechanism extends the classical DPoS framework by introducing a nonlinear voting weight adaptation scheme. Let $\mathcal{A} = \{a_1, a_2, \ldots, a_n\}$ denote the set of participating accounts, where each account $a_i$ possesses an initial voting weight $v_i \in \mathbb{R}^+$ proportional to its token holdings. To mitigate centralization risks caused by disproportionate voting power concentration, we design a differentiable smoothing function $f : \mathbb{R}^+ \to (0, 1)$ based on sigmoid transformation [15]:

$$f(v_i) = \frac{1}{1 + \exp\left(-\alpha(v_i - \beta)\right)}. \tag{1}$$

The transition regulation parameter $\alpha$ controls the derivative magnitude of $f(v_i)$, determining voting power transition sharpness between stakeholders, enabling continuous tuning from near-linear proportionality ($\alpha \to 0^+$) to quasi-binary thresholding ($\alpha \to \infty$). Whereas the threshold $\beta$ defines the inflection point where accounts transition between attenuated ($v_i < \beta$, sublinear growth) and amplified ($v_i > \beta$, superlinear scaling) influence regimes. Besides, the effective voting weight $\hat{v}_i$ for account $a_i$ is computed as:

$$\hat{v}_i = f(v_i) \cdot v_i. \tag{2}$$

Let $\mathcal{C} = \{c_1, c_2, \ldots, c_k\}$ represent candidate nodes. The block producer set $\mathcal{S}$ is determined through rank-based selection:

$$\mathcal{S} = \left\{ c_j \,\middle|\, \sum_{a_i \in \mathcal{V}_j} \hat{v}_i \in \mathrm{Top}_m \left( \left\{ \sum_{a_i \in \mathcal{V}_j} \hat{v}_i \right\}_{j=1}^{k} \right) \right\}, \tag{3}$$

where $\mathcal{V}_j \subseteq \mathcal{A}$ denotes accounts voting for candidate $c_j$, and $m$ specifies the committee size. This formulation ensures progressive decentralization by smoothing, preventing sudden dominance shifts through continuous weight adjustment. Moreover, its Sybil resistance through non-linear scaling discourages token splitting attacks. And its parameterized fairness through tunable $\alpha, \beta$ allows for governance-oriented consensus properties. The stability of the mechanism against voting power fluctuations is formally analyzed.

Additionally, we evaluated the impact of sigmoid-based smoothing in the delegate selection process under a DPoS consensus framework. The simulation

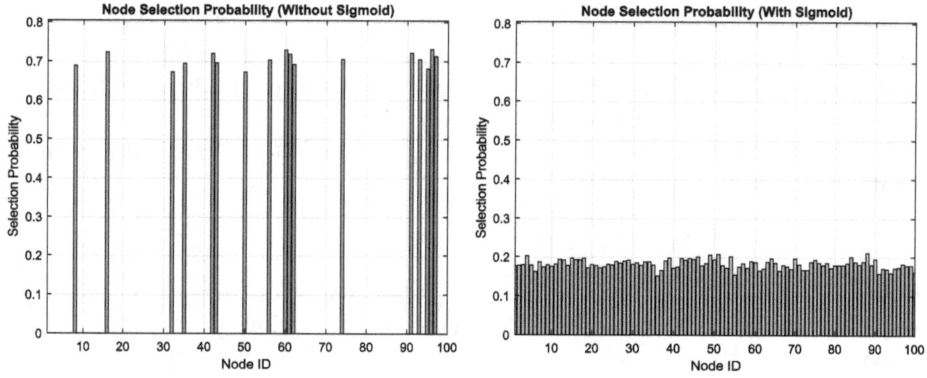


(a) Original DPoS (b) Smoothed DPoS

**Fig. 3.** Node selection probabilities under original and sigmoid-smoothed DPoS configurations.

models a scenario in which block producers are elected based on accumulated voting weights, and smoothing is applied to reduce the concentration of selection probabilities among high-voting-power nodes while considering load balancing across the network. Two configurations are under consideration: the original DPoS and the enhanced DPoS with sigmoid smoothing. The frequency with which each node is selected as a block producer over multiple election rounds is recorded, providing a direct view of the distribution of selection probabilities and the resulting load distribution across participating nodes.

Figure 3 shows the node selection probabilities under both configurations. Without smoothing, a small set of nodes consistently dominate the election process, leading to uneven computational and networking loads, while most nodes have near-zero chances of being selected. After applying sigmoid smoothing, the selection probabilities become more evenly distributed across all nodes while maintaining the relative order based on voting weights, resulting in a more balanced load distribution across the network.

The findings demonstrate the effectiveness of sigmoid-based smoothing in reducing selection concentration, promoting fairness in the election process, and enhancing load balancing among block producers. This adjustment supports broader participation in block production, enhances system robustness, and improves resource utilization in DPoS-based blockchain systems deployed for digital twin management.

### 3.3 Isolation Forest-Based Rollback Validation

To validate data integrity within blockchain-enabled digital twin systems, we adopt an Isolation Forest-based rollback mechanism that performs *post-hoc anomaly detection* on blockchain-committed digital twin records. This method identifies contextual inconsistencies retrospectively, while accommodating natural variations in vehicle dynamics and environmental conditions. Rather than detecting marginal outliers, our approach emphasizes the *interdependencies among features*, enabling identification of subtle deviations that violate the internal coherence of the contextual state.

At each discrete time step $t$, the contextual state of the vehicle is represented as a multivariate feature vector:

$$\mathbf{x}_t = [\pi_t, \nu_t, \sigma_t, \theta_t, \eta_t, \omega_t, \varphi_t, \lambda_t, \ldots]^\top, \tag{4}$$

where $\pi_t$ denotes the geographic position (typically comprising longitude, latitude, and altitude), $\nu_t$ represents the instantaneous velocity, $\sigma_t$ indicates the battery state of charge (SoC), $\theta_t$ and $\eta_t$ correspond to ambient temperature and relative humidity respectively, $\omega_t$ quantifies wind speed, $\varphi_t$ measures traffic density, and $\lambda_t$ specifies the regulatory speed limit of the current road segment.

To assess the integrity of a new data point, we denote the incoming sample as $x := \mathbf{x}_t$ and evaluate its contextual consistency against a reference set of historical data already committed to the blockchain. This reference set, constructed from the preceding $N$ time steps retrieved from the blockchain ledger, forms the *rollback window*. Its size is defined by the *data interception quantity* (DIQ), which determines the number of past contextual states used for offline model training.

In our experimental settings, the data interception quantity (DIQ) is set to 1000, 2000, or 4000, each exceeding the default subsampling threshold of the Isolation Forest. As a result, the per-tree subsampling size $\psi$ (corresponding to `max_samples`) follows the default rule:

$$\psi = \min(256, \text{DIQ}), \tag{5}$$

and since all DIQ values considered are greater than 256, we have $\psi = 256$ consistently throughout the experiments. To maintain alignment with standard practice and avoid overfitting, we retain this default subsampling policy across all experiments. Although DIQ governs the total number of historical records available for model training, only a fixed-size subset is drawn for each tree, as originally designed in the Isolation Forest framework [19]. Additionally, to mitigate the stochastic nature introduced by subsampling, we average performance metrics over multiple independent runs.

In short, all digital twin data is uploaded to the blockchain in its raw form. The rollback validation mechanism operates retrospectively by applying anomaly detection to on-chain records and tagging entries that deviate from historical patterns as suspicious. This process preserves data completeness while enabling contextual integrity assessments on immutable records.

As for the Isolation Forest algorithm, introduced by Liu et al. [19,20], constructs an ensemble of $n$ binary trees $\{T_i\}_{i=1}^n$ from the rollback data. Each tree $T_i$ recursively partitions the data space using randomly selected features and split values until individual samples are isolated. To evaluate the new data point $x$, it is passed through each tree $T_i$ in the ensemble. The *path length* $h_i(x)$ is defined as the number of edges from the root node to the external node at which

$x$ is isolated. This path length reflects how easily $x$ can be separated from the distribution of prior contextual data. The expected path length over all trees is given by:

$$E[H(x)] = \frac{1}{n}\sum_{i=1}^{n} h_i(x), \tag{6}$$

where $E[H(x)]$ is the average path length of $x$ across all trees, which measures the average score of splits needed to isolate $x$. A shorter expected path length indicates higher separability, suggesting a greater degree of anomaly. Furthermore, the normalized anomaly score is computed as:

$$s(x, \psi) = 2^{-\frac{E[H(x)]}{c(\psi)}}, \tag{7}$$

where $c(\psi)$ denotes the expected path length in a random binary tree of size $\psi$. This normalization ensures that anomaly scores remain comparable across different training set sizes and subsampling configurations.

Meanwhile, the function $c(\psi)$ is approximated by:

$$c(\psi) = 2\sum_{j=1}^{\psi-1} \frac{1}{j} - \frac{2(\psi - 1)}{\psi}, \tag{8}$$

which corresponds to the average path length of unsuccessful searches in a random binary search tree [19]. As $\psi$ increases, the harmonic sum grows logarithmically, reflecting the increased depth required to isolate a sample. The normalization term $c(\psi)$ thus compensates for this growth, enabling meaningful and consistent interpretation of the anomaly score $s(x)$ across different rollback window sizes. The anomaly score $s(x)$ is bounded in $(0, 1)$, with values close to 1 indicating that $x$ is highly anomalous, that is, it can be separated from past data with few cuts. In contrast, scores near 0 suggest that $x$ corresponds to the contextual distribution.

To systematically evaluate the rollback mechanism, we vary the data interception quantity (DIQ) and observe its influence on anomaly detection sensitivity. Since DIQ controls the size of the contextual reference set and indirectly impacts the anomaly score through the sample distribution and normalization term $c(\psi)$, it plays a key role in shaping the decision boundary. Additionally, the impact of feature dimensionality is examined in conjunction with the computed scores, offering insights into optimal parameter selection for robust and context-aware validation. By operating on immutable blockchain records, the proposed mechanism enhances traceability and supports reliable post-hoc integrity audits across digital twin deployments. The details of the experimental setup and analysis of the results will be presented in Sect. 4.

## 4 Experiments and Evaluation

This section presents an experimental evaluation of the proposed rollback validation framework, employing Isolation Forest for contextual anomaly detection in blockchain-immutable digital twin records. The investigation quantifies the impact of two critical parameters on detection performance: historical context depth and feature dimensionality. Subsequent subsections detail the dataset composition, experimental configuration, and rigorous analysis of results.

### 4.1 Dataset Description

All experiments leverage the **HELECAR-D dataset** [25], which provides comprehensive vehicular trajectory and environmental data collected from electric vehicles operating in the Rabat-Salé-Kénitra region, Morocco. This dataset captures both *urban* and *ring road* traffic environments and is particularly well-suited for studying urban mobility patterns and electric vehicle behaviors under realistic traffic conditions. The experiments extract continuous trajectory segments corresponding to individual vehicles. The dataset includes both vehicle dynamic states and environmental context, enabling robust analysis of anomaly detection mechanisms under diverse traffic scenarios.

**Table 1.** Feature Abbreviations and Descriptions in HELECAR-D Dataset

| Original Name | Abbreviation | Description |
|---|---|---|
| SPEED | **SPD** | Vehicle speed measured by onboard sensors (km/h) |
| GPSSPEED | **GPSPD** | Speed estimated from GPS positional data (km/h) |
| SOC | **SOC** | Battery state-of-charge indicating remaining capacity (%) |
| TEMPERATURE | **TEMP** | Ambient environmental temperature (°C) |
| HUMIDITY | **HUM** | Air relative humidity (%) |
| WINDSPEEDAV | **WIND** | Average wind speed over the sampling period (m/s) |
| TRAFFIC | **TRAF** | Traffic density indicator (normalized index) |
| SPEEDLIMIT | **LIM** | Speed limit of the current road segment (km/h) |
| ALT | **ALT** | Altitude above sea level (meters) |
| LAT | **LAT** | Latitude coordinates in WGS84 reference system |
| LON | **LON** | Longitude coordinates in WGS84 reference system |

The selected features and their abbreviations are summarized in Table 1. These features jointly capture the vehicle operational state, environmental factors, and traffic context. This rich feature set facilitates comprehensive validation of the proposed rollback mechanism by exposing it to a combination of vehicular dynamics, environmental variability, and geographic diversity.

Beyond their individual meanings, these features exhibit strong contextual interdependence across spatial, temporal, and physical dimensions. For instance, vehicle speed and GPS-derived speed are expected to exhibit a consistent relationship under normal operating conditions. Deviations from this pattern—such as unexpected divergences or unstable offsets—may indicate localization drift, sensor lag, or signal interference. Similarly, the relationship between speed, altitude, and speed limit often reflects driving behavior in varying terrain and regulatory zones. The presence of environmental variables such as temperature, humidity, and wind speed adds further contextual layering, enabling the model to differentiate between operational anomalies and natural variations.

This multi-dimensional correlation structure forms the foundation for detecting contextual anomalies, as the rollback mechanism evaluates not just individual values but their collective coherence across time and modality. The dataset's time-aligned sampling and geographic diversity allow consistent application of sliding-window validation across different road types and environmental scenarios.

*Synthetic Anomaly Injection.* To rigorously evaluate rollback validation performance, we inject synthetic anomalies into the HELECAR-D dataset. Specifically, Gaussian noise is added to valid data points to create subtle yet abrupt fluctuations in the trajectories. These anomalies are designed to mimic realistic deviations while still diverging from the expected distribution. The noise is carefully scaled to match the magnitude and units of each feature, ensuring that the injected anomalies remain within reasonable and interpretable bounds for variables such as speed, state-of-charge, and geolocation. The proportion of injected anomalies accounts for approximately 5% of the total dataset.

*Communication and Storage Overheads.* The data acquisition pipeline imposes notable operational overheads. Vehicles transmit GNSS measurements, vehicle dynamics, and environmental indicators at sampling rates of 1–10 Hz (Hz), generating roughly 10–50 megabytes (MB) of data per hour per vehicle. At fleet scale, multi-day deployments accumulate several hundred gigabytes (GB) of data. Continuous cellular uplink produces recurring bandwidth consumption and is susceptible to congestion and coverage variability. Long-term retention of raw and derived information further requires scalable storage back-ends with strict privacy and archival guarantees. These resource constraints highlight the necessity for rollback validation mechanisms that maintain anomaly discrimination while remaining compatible with bandwidth-limited and storage-constrained vehicular systems.

## 4.2 Experimental Setup

The purpose of this experiment is to evaluate the effectiveness of unsupervised anomaly detection models for blockchain-based rollback validation, with a particular emphasis on the role of feature composition and model selection. Each data sample corresponds to a contextual snapshot of a vehicle's operational and environmental state, encoded as a multivariate feature vector. The goal is to determine whether this new data point remains consistent with a recent historical window of on-chain records, thereby supporting post-hoc integrity validation.

To this end, we construct multiple feature combinations with dimensionality $d \in \{3, 5, 7\}$, drawn from a fixed candidate set of 11 vehicular and environmental variables. These combinations represent varying levels of contextual complexity and are designed to reflect diverse semantic categories such as dynamics, positioning, and external conditions. Each configuration is evaluated across several fixed-length historical windows (DIQ = 1000, 2000, 4000).

The central comparative axis of the experiment lies in benchmarking model performance. We adopt **One-Class SVM (OCSVM)** [32,33] as the baseline method, due to its widespread use in unsupervised anomaly detection and its geometric decision boundary formulation. Against this baseline, we assess the performance of **Isolation Forest (IF)**, which relies on random partitioning and is expected to capture context-dependent irregularities in multivariate time-series data.

For both models, we compute the F1-score and standard deviation over multiple runs under consistent anomaly injection settings. This allows us to compare not only average detection performance but also model stability across different feature combinations. By contrasting Isolation Forest with OCSVM under identical experimental conditions, we aim to demonstrate the relative advantage of IF in capturing complex contextual deviations that traditional boundary-based methods may miss. This design isolates the effect of feature selection and model structure on rollback validation effectiveness, providing evidence for selecting lightweight, robust validators in digital twin scenarios deployed over blockchain infrastructures.

### 4.3 Model Performance Under Varying Rollback and Feature Settings

To evaluate the effectiveness of Isolation Forest (IF) versus One-Class SVM (OC-SVM) in detecting contextual anomalies under different rollback window sizes (DIQ), we visualize their average F1-scores in three representative DIQ settings: 1000, 2000 and 4000, as presented in Fig. 4.

IF consistently outperforms OC-SVM across all DIQ values. Although the absolute F1-scores are moderate (0.5621, 0.4336, and 0.4343), IF demonstrates more reliable performance compared to OC-SVM, especially as the rollback window grows. These findings confirm that IF is better suited for time-dependent anomaly detection tasks on structured mobility datasets. Moreover, DIQ = 1000 offers the most favorable trade-off between detection accuracy and historical context size, and is therefore adopted as the default for subsequent analysis on feature dimensions.

With DIQ fixed at 1000, we further investigate how the number and composition of contextual features (Size of Features, SoF) affect model performance. As shown in Fig. 5, Isolation Forest achieves consistently strong performance across the examined feature dimensionalities (SoF = 3, 5, and 7), with F1 scores bounded within the narrow interval of **0.5492 to 0.5757**. This small variation reflects a notable degree of robustness, indicating that IF can effectively accommodate potential redundancy or noise within the contextual feature set. In contrast, OC SVM demonstrates a markedly stronger dependence on feature dimensionality. Its F1 score increases from **0.1818** at SoF = 3 to a peak of **0.5503** at SoF = 7.

A direct comparison under the same feature dimensions further reveals the superior stability of IF. At SoF = 3, IF outperforms OC SVM by **0.3939**. At SoF = 5, IF maintains an advantage of **0.1706**. Even at SoF = 7, where OC SVM attains its best performance, the two methods exhibit nearly consistent detection capability, indicating that OC SVM can only approach the reliability of IF when sufficiently informative contextual features are incorporated. These consistent positive gaps confirm that IF offers reliable detection capability regardless of dimensionality, while OC SVM requires significantly more informative features to remain competitive due to its reliance on precise boundary construction in higher-dimensional representation spaces.

Moreover, deeper analysis reveals that the effectiveness of IF can still vary substantially depending on the specific feature set used. While its overall sensitivity to feature dimensionality is low, the choice of features within each dimension remains critical. For instance, the best-performing 5-feature combination—**HUM**, **LIM**, **TEMP**, **TRAF**, and **WIND**—yields F1-scores of 0.6405 (DIQ = 1000) and maintains strong performance even as DIQ increases. In contrast, 7-feature combinations often introduce redundancy and lead to degraded robustness, while 3-feature sets show high variance under different DIQs.

Overall, these results demonstrate that Isolation Forest not only offers more stable detection across varying DIQs and feature dimensionalities *at a global level*, but also benefits most from carefully selected mid-sized feature sets. In contrast, OC-SVM performs well only when sufficient contextual dimensions are provided, highlighting its sensitivity to feature design. For production deployment, a 5-feature configuration centered on environmental and traffic-related context—as represented by **HUM**, **LIM**, **TEMP**, **TRAF**, and **WIND**—offers the best balance between accuracy and resilience.

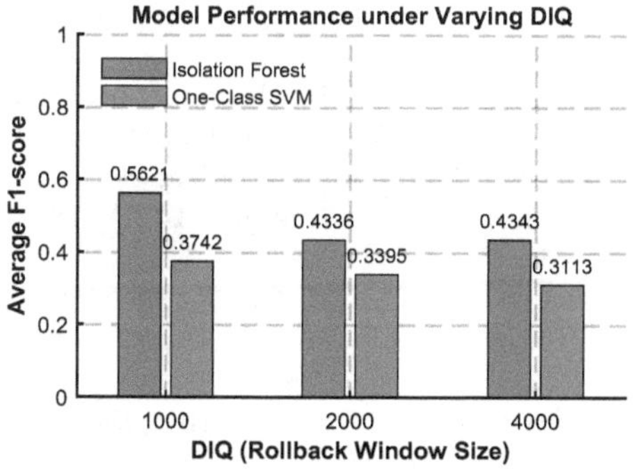


**Fig. 4.** Model performance comparison under varying DIQ values.

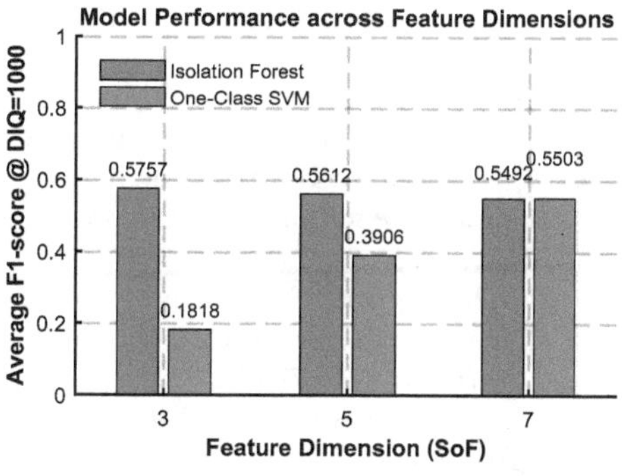


**Fig. 5.** Model performance across varying feature dimensions (SoF) at DIQ = 1000.

## 5 Conclusion

In this paper, we propose a blockchain-enabled trustworthy digital twin management system for mobile vehicular networks, addressing the limitations of traditional centralized architectures in terms of reliability, computing load balance, and traceability. The system is built upon a modular three-layer architecture consisting of the Digital Twin Layer, the Data Interaction Layer, and the Blockchain Layer. This design enables seamless integration between real-world vehicle data and its virtual representation while ensuring robust and traceable data management. Additionally, to enhance fairness and system decentralization, we introduce a smoothed DPoS consensus mechanism incorporating a sigmoid-based weighting function, which alleviates the dominance of high-power nodes and facilitates more balanced block producer selection. Furthermore, we have integrated a rollback verification component based on the Isolation Forest algorithm, which enables effective, context-aware anomaly detection. This achieves an increase in the F1 score of over 0.18 at the default rollback window size of 1000, and generally outperforms the One Class SVM baseline across representative configurations.

The proposed system provides a trustworthy foundation for digital twin deployment in dynamic and distributed vehicular environments by combining modular architecture, fairness-aware consensus, and traceable historical validation. Our experimental evaluation demonstrates improved detection reliability and robustness against anomalous data, strengthening the trustworthiness of digital twin-driven services in mobile vehicular networks. Future work will explore interoperability with cross-chain infrastructures, adaptive trust models, and large-scale implementation in realistic vehicular scenarios.

## References


1. Bachani, V., Bhattacharjya, A.: Preferential delegated proof of stake (PDPoS)–modified DPoS with two layers towards scalability and higher TPS. Symmetry **15**(1), 4 (2022)
2. Bamakan, S.M.H., Motavali, A., Bondarti, A.B.: A survey of blockchain consensus algorithms performance evaluation criteria. Expert Syst. Appl. **154**, 113385 (2020)
3. Borowski, P.F.: Digitization, digital twins, blockchain, and industry 4.0 as elements of management process in enterprises in the energy sector. Energies **14**(7), 1885 (2021)
4. Butler, H., Daly, M., Doyle, A., Gillies, S., Schaub, T., Schmidt, C.: The GeoJSON format. RFC 7946, Internet Engineering Task Force (IETF) (2016). https://tools.ietf.org/html/rfc7946
5. Castro, M., Liskov, B.: Practical byzantine fault tolerance and proactive recovery. ACM Trans. Comput. Syst. (TOCS) **20**(4), 398–461 (2002)
6. Chen, Y., Liu, F.: Research on improvement of DPoS consensus mechanism in collaborative governance of network public opinion. Peer-to-peer Netw. Appl. **15**(4), 1849–1861 (2022)
7. Colyar, J., Halkias, J.: NGSIM: US-101 dataset, Federal Highway Administration, U.S. Department of Transportation (2007). Tech. rep

8. Friederich, J., Francis, D.P., Lazarova-Molnar, S., Mohamed, N.: A framework for data-driven digital twins of smart manufacturing systems. Comput. Ind. **136**, 103586 (2022)
9. Fuller, A., Fan, Z., Day, C., Barlow, C.: Digital twin: enabling technologies, challenges and open research. IEEE Access **8**, 108952–108971 (2020)
10. Huang, S., Wang, G., Yan, Y., Fang, X.: Blockchain-based data management for digital twin of product. J. Manuf. Syst. **54**, 361–371 (2020)
11. Johnson, D., Menezes, A., Vanstone, S.: The elliptic curve digital signature algorithm (ECDSA). Int. J. Inf. Secur. **1**(1), 36–63 (2001)
12. Jones, D., Snider, C., Nassehi, A., Yon, J., Hicks, B.: Characterising the digital twin: a systematic literature review. CIRP J. Manuf. Sci. Technol. **29**, 36–52 (2020)
13. Krajewski, R., Bock, J., Kloeker, L., Eckstein, L.: The HighD dataset: a drone dataset of naturalistic vehicle trajectories on German highways for validation of highly automated driving systems. In: 21st International Conference on Intelligent Transportation Systems (ITSC), pp. 2118–2125. IEEE (2018)
14. Kwon, Y., Liu, J., Kim, M., Song, D., Kim, Y.: Impossibility of full decentralization in permissionless blockchains. In: Proceedings of the 1st ACM Conference on Advances in Financial Technologies, pp. 110–123 (2019)
15. Kyurkchiev, N., Markov, S.: Sigmoid functions: some approximation and modelling aspects. LAP LAMBERT Academic Publishing, Saarbrucken **4**, 34 (2015)
16. Lee, D., Lee, S.H., Masoud, N., Krishnan, M., Li, V.C.: Integrated digital twin and blockchain framework to support accountable information sharing in construction projects. Autom. Constr. **127**, 103688 (2021)
17. Li, C., Palanisamy, B.: Comparison of decentralization in DPoS and pow blockchains. In: Blockchain–ICBC 2020: Third International Conference, Held as Part of the Services Conference Federation, SCF 2020, Honolulu, HI, USA, September 18-20, 2020, Proceedings 3, pp. 18–32. Springer (2020)
18. Liu, C., Chau, K., Wu, D., Gao, S.: Opportunities and challenges of vehicle-to-home, vehicle-to-vehicle, and vehicle-to-grid technologies. Proc. IEEE **101**(11), 2409–2427 (2013)
19. Liu, F.T., Ting, K.M., Zhou, Z.H.: Isolation forest. In: Eighth IEEE International Conference on Data Mining, pp. 413–422. IEEE (2008)
20. Liu, F.T., Ting, K.M., Zhou, Z.H.: Isolation-based anomaly detection. ACM Trans. Knowl. Discov. Data (TKDD) **6**(1), 1–39 (2012)
21. Liu, J., Zheng, W., Lu, D., Wu, J., Zheng, Z.: Understanding the decentralization of DPoS: Perspectives from data-driven analysis on EOSIO. arXiv preprint arXiv:2201.06187 (2022)
22. Liu, T., et al.: Resource allocation in dt-assisted internet of vehicles via edge intelligent cooperation. IEEE Internet Things J. **9**(18), 17608–17626 (2022)
23. Mishra, A.K., Wazid, M., Singh, D.P., Das, A.K., Roy, S., Shetty, S.: ACKS-IA: an access control and key agreement scheme for securing industry 4.0 applications. IEEE Transactions on Network Science and Engineering **11**(1), 254–269 (2023)
24. Mohanty, S.N., et al.: An efficient lightweight integrated blockchain (ELIB) model for IoT security and privacy. Futur. Gener. Comput. Syst. **102**, 1027–1037 (2020)
25. Nait Malek, Y., Najib, M., Bakhouya, M., Gaber, J.: HELECAR-D: a dataset for urban electro mobility in Moroccan context. Data Brief **48**, 109080 (2023). https://doi.org/10.1016/j.dib.2023.109080
26. Nakamoto, S.: Bitcoin: A peer-to-peer electronic cash system. https://bitcoin.org/bitcoin.pdf (2008)
27. Piromalis, D., Kantaros, A.: Digital twins in the automotive industry: the road toward physical-digital convergence. Appl. Syst. Innovation **5**(4), 65 (2022)

28. Putz, B., Dietz, M., Empl, P., Pernul, G.: EtherTwin: blockchain-based secure digital twin information management. Inf. Process. Manag. **58**(1), 102425 (2021)
29. Rebello, G.A.F., Camilo, G.F., Guimarães, L.C., de Souza, L.A.C., Duarte, O.C.M.: Security and performance analysis of quorum-based blockchain consensus protocols. In: 2022 6th Cyber Security in Networking Conference (CSNet), pp. 1–7. IEEE (2022)
30. Saleh, F.: Blockchain without waste: proof-of-stake. Rev. Financ. Stud. **34**(3), 1156–1190 (2021)
31. Sasikumar, A., et al.: Blockchain-based trust mechanism for digital twin empowered industrial Internet of Things. Futur. Gener. Comput. Syst. **141**, 16–27 (2023)
32. Schölkopf, B., Platt, J.C., Shawe-Taylor, J., Smola, A.J., Williamson, R.C.: Estimating the support of a high-dimensional distribution. Neural Comput. **13**(7), 1443–1471 (2001)
33. Schölkopf, B., Williamson, R.C., Smola, A., Shawe-Taylor, J., Platt, J.: Support vector method for novelty detection. Adv. Neural. Inf. Process. Syst. **12** (1999)
34. Schwarz, C., Wang, Z.: The role of digital twins in connected and automated vehicles. IEEE Intell. Transp. Syst. Mag. **14**(6), 41–51 (2022)
35. Semeraro, C., Lezoche, M., Panetto, H., Dassisti, M.: Digital twin paradigm: a systematic literature review. Comput. Ind. **130**, 103469 (2021)
36. Sheraz, M., Chuah, T.C., Lee, Y.L., Alam, M.M., Al-Habashna, A., Han, Z.: A comprehensive survey on revolutionizing connectivity through artificial intelligence-enabled digital twin network in 6G. IEEE Access **12**, 49184–49215 (2024)
37. Singh, M., Fuenmayor, E., Hinchy, E.P., Qiao, Y., Murray, N., Devine, D.: Digital twin: origin to future. Appl. Syst. Innovation **4**(2), 36 (2021)
38. Tao, F., Xiao, B., Qi, Q., Cheng, J., Ji, P.: Digital twin modeling. J. Manuf. Syst. **64**, 372–389 (2022)
39. Tao, F., Zhang, H., Liu, A., Nee, A.Y.: Digital twin in industry: state-of-the-art. IEEE Trans. Industr. Inf. **15**(4), 2405–2415 (2018)
40. Xu, G., Liu, Y., Khan, P.W.: Improvement of the DPoS consensus mechanism in blockchain based on vague sets. IEEE Trans. Industr. Inf. **16**(6), 4252–4259 (2019)
41. Yang, F., Zhou, W., Wu, Q., Long, R., Xiong, N.N., Zhou, M.: Delegated proof of stake with downgrade: a secure and efficient blockchain consensus algorithm with downgrade mechanism. IEEE Access **7**, 118541–118555 (2019)
42. Yang, J., Wen, J., Jiang, B., Wang, H.: Blockchain-based sharing and tamper-proof framework of big data networking. IEEE Netw. **34**(4), 62–67 (2020)
43. Yaqoob, I., Salah, K., Uddin, M., Jayaraman, R., Omar, M., Imran, M.: Blockchain for digital twins: recent advances and future research challenges. IEEE Netw. **34**(5), 290–298 (2020)
44. Yuan, J., Zheng, Y., Xie, X., Sun, G.: Driving with knowledge from the physical world. In: Proceedings of the 17th ACM SIGKDD International Conference on Knowledge Discovery and Data Mining (KDD), ACM, New York, NY, USA (2011)
45. Yuan, J., et al.: T-Drive: driving directions based on taxi trajectories. In: Proceedings of the 18th SIGSPATIAL International Conference on Advances in Geographic Information Systems (GIS), pp. 99–108. ACM, New York, NY, USA (2010)

46. Yuan, J., Zheng, Y., Zhang, C., Xie, X., Sun, G., Huang, Y.: Driving with knowledge from the physical world. In: Proceedings of the 17th ACM SIGKDD International Conference on Knowledge Discovery and Data Mining, pp. 316–324. (2011)
47. Zhang, C., et al.: Hybrid mechanism and data-driven digital twin model for assembly quality traceability and optimization of complex products. Adv. Eng. Inform. **62**, 102707 (2024)
48. Zhang, H., Qi, Q., Tao, F.: A consistency evaluation method for digital twin models. J. Manuf. Syst. **65**, 158–168 (2022)

# Anomaly Detection and Attack Type Identification Based on IoT Traffic Characteristics

Ming Dai[1], Hongwei Xing[1], Jian Du[1], Jie Luo[2], Bingjie Wang[2], Linjia He[1(✉)], and Yicong Li[1]

[1] Transport Information Security Center Co., Ltd., Beijing 100011, China
qqyutou@126.com
[2] School of Information and Communication Engineering, Xi'an Jiaotong University, Xi'an 710049, Shaanxi, China

**Abstract.** With the rapid development of internet of things (IoT) technology, its applications in smart transportation and other scenarios are becoming increasingly widespread. Traditional anomaly detection algorithms have not deeply explored IoT traffic information and have certain limitations. Therefore, this paper proposes an anomaly detection and attack type identification algorithm based on traffic characteristics for IoT. The algorithm first analyzes traffic patterns on real IoT data and extracts key information for feature construction. In the anomaly detection phase, four features are constructed, utilizing the density-based spatial clustering of applications with noise (DBSCAN) clustering algorithm with Manhattan distance as a metric. Finally, in the attack type identification phase, multiple features are generated based on the key information, employing a joint algorithm of Principal Component Analysis and the C4.5 decision tree. Experimental results indicate that the features extracted from both phases have a certain degree of accuracy in the designed algorithm, providing practical technical support for anomaly detection and attack identification, and possessing theoretical significance and reference value.

**Keywords:** Internet of Things · Anomaly Detection · Traffic Characteristics · Machine Learning

## 1 Introduction

In recent years, the development of communication technologies such as the Internet of Things (IoT) has greatly surpassed traditional methods of perceiving the surrounding environment [1–3]. IoT technology can modernize and enhance the quality of life, as it has the capability to collect, quantify, and understand the environment. This simplification of communication between people and objects enables the realization of smart cities [4]. IoT is one of the fastest-growing fields


Y. Liu et al. (Eds.): ChinaCom 2025, LNICST 711, pp. 156–175, 2027.
https://doi.org/10.1007/978-3-032-33662-0_13

in computing history, with an estimated 50 billion devices by the end of 2020 [5]. On one hand, IoT technology plays a crucial role in intelligent applications that enhance everyday life, such as smart healthcare, smart homes, smart transportation, and smart education. On the other hand, the cross-cutting and large-scale nature of IoT systems, along with the various components involved in deploying these systems, presents new security challenges [6].

In the context of smart transportation systems, the application of IoT technology is particularly prominent. By connecting various transportation devices, such as smart traffic lights, vehicle sensors, and surveillance cameras, smart transportation systems can monitor and manage traffic flow in real-time, optimizing road usage efficiency and reducing traffic congestion and accident rates [7]. The traffic characteristic data collected by these devices provides valuable information for traffic management and planning. However, with the widespread deployment of IoT devices, associated security challenges have become increasingly apparent [8].

The complexity and large-scale nature of IoT systems make it extremely challenging to maintain security requirements. Particularly in smart transportation scenarios, most devices operate in unattended environments, making them susceptible to physical intrusion and cyberattacks. Attackers can eavesdrop on wireless communications to obtain sensitive information or even control transportation devices, leading to severe security incidents. Moreover, the IoT environment introduces new attack surfaces, resulting from the interdependent and interconnected nature of IoT systems. Consequently, the security risks for IoT systems are higher than those for other computing systems, and traditional solutions may be ineffective for such systems [9].

IoT systems can be accessed globally and are primarily composed of resource-constrained devices connected through lossy links [10]. Therefore, significant modifications to existing information and wireless network security concepts are necessary to provide effective security measures for IoT. Implementing existing defense mechanisms, such as encryption, authentication, access control, network security, and application security, is a challenging task [11]. IoT systems are comprised of many interconnected devices, each of which has inherent vulnerabilities. For instance, Mirai, a particular type of botnet, has recently leveraged IoT devices to launch large-scale DDoS attacks. As a result of the vulnerabilities in IoT systems, attacks that are more complex and destructive than Mirai may emerge. Additionally, due to the wide variety of IoT applications and scenarios, understanding which methods are suitable for protecting IoT systems is a challenge [12–14].

Therefore, the development of effective IoT security methods should be a research priority. This paper focuses on improving the security of IoT systems, specifically targeting anomaly detection and attack identification while considering their applicability. The paper first analyzes the traffic patterns in IoT. Next, it proposes incorporating attack type recognition based on the unique traffic patterns of IoT, along with attack information alerts. Features are established based on traffic size and clustering analysis is conducted. In the attack type recognition section, PCA is applied for dimensionality reduction, followed by the implementation of a decision tree algorithm. Finally, experiments validate the effectiveness of the selected features in the application of machine learning algorithms.

## 2 IoT Traffic Patterns

From the user's perspective, IoT traffic mainly consists of two types: one is the traffic generated autonomously by devices, such as DNS queries and NTP time queries, which are stable functions of IoT devices. This traffic is typically small and short-lived. The other type is the traffic generated from user interactions with devices, such as command messages sent to devices or data uploaded and downloaded from the server based on user instructions. This traffic varies in size and generally lasts longer.

From the perspective of traffic characteristics, traffic can be classified into several categories: (a) unicast, multicast, or broadcast; (b) sent to local hosts (LAN) or Internet servers (WAN); (c) the protocols involved (TCP, UDP, ICMP, or ARP); and (d) IP address and port information of the traffic. Among these, (a) reflects the local communication characteristics of devices, while (b) indicates the network type of the device's traffic. If an attack occurs, these two pieces of information can reveal whether the attack source is local or from the network. (c) presents protocol information, and (d) displays IP address and port information; if an attack occurs, this information can be used to infer the attack type and trace the attack source, which can guide the shutdown of vulnerable services on the devices.

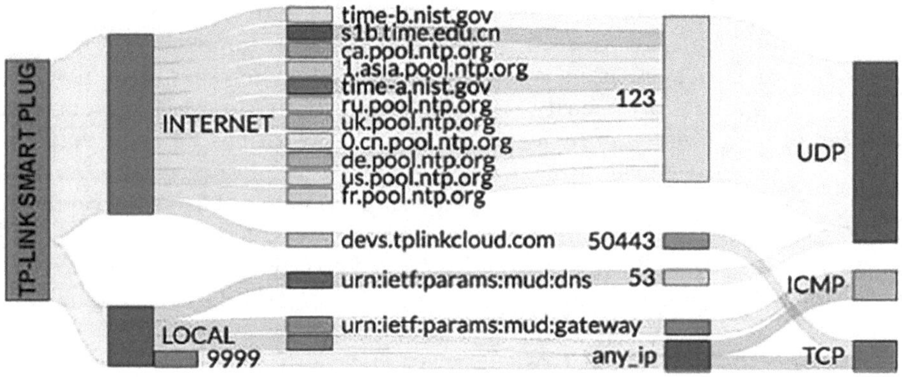


**Fig. 1.** Sankey Diagram of TP-Link Traffic.

This paper utilizes the Sankey diagram in Fig. 1 to illustrate the traffic flow of the TP-Link smart plug. It is evident that this IoT device exchanges DNS query and response information with the local DNS server, communicates with a range of NTP services (UDP port 123), and connects with its manufacturer's server (TCP port 50443). Additionally, the TP-Link smart plug exposes TCP port 9999 on the local network to its mobile application, enabling user interaction with the device. We also observe that the smart plug and its mobile application periodically send ping signals to the gateway and the plug itself for connectivity checks.

Assuming a statistical time window of T, the number of IP packets during time T is denoted as Packets, and the total byte count of the IP packets is referred to as Bytes. Therefore, packet_bytes represents the average number of bytes per packet over the time period T.

$$\text{packet\_bytes} = \frac{\text{Bytes}}{\text{Packets}}. \tag{1}$$

Figure 2 shows a bar chart where the x-axis represents 1-minute time intervals and the y-axis indicates the number of packets flowing through the TP-Link Plug per minute over a total duration of one hour. In this chart, the red bars represent anomalous attack traffic, while the green bars indicate normal traffic. It can be observed that, regardless of the type of traffic, the number of normal packets flowing through the device is generally low within each minute interval, with occasional spikes lasting only for short durations. In contrast, the anomalous

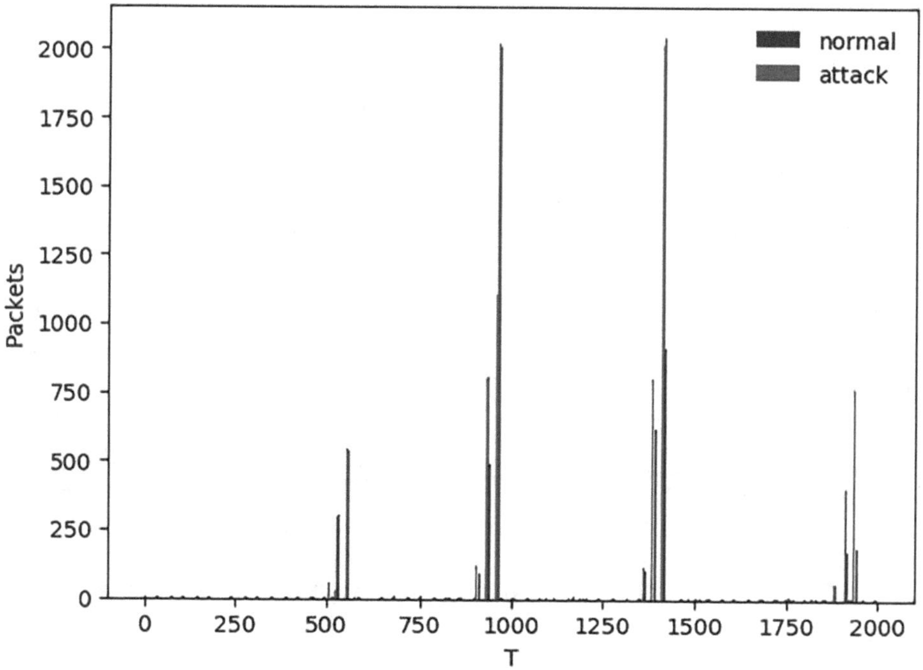


**Fig. 2.** Bar Chart Comparing Normal and Anomalous Traffic Packet Counts per Minute for TP-Link Plug.

traffic displays significantly higher packet counts, often persisting for several minutes.

Figure 3 presents a bar chart where the x-axis again represents 1-minute time intervals, and the y-axis indicates the average number of bytes per packet flowing through the TP-Link Plug per minute. The chart illustrates a clear distinction between the average bytes per packet for normal traffic and that for anomalous traffic. Typically, the average bytes per packet for anomalous traffic is lower, as the packets do not carry substantial communication data but rather consist of simple header control information.

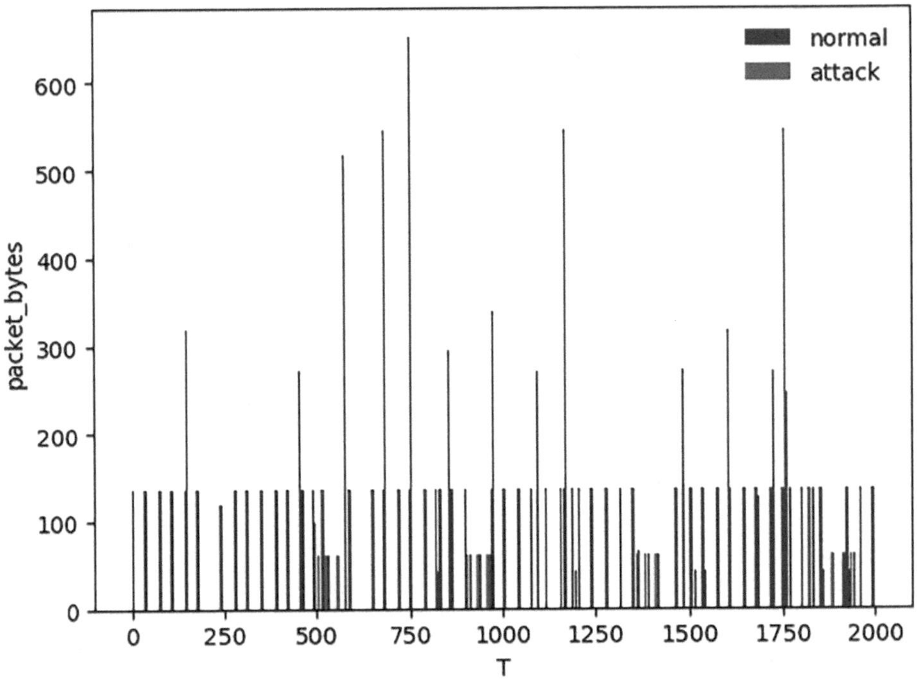


**Fig. 3.** Bar Chart Comparing Normal and Anomalous Traffic Bytes per Packet per Minute for TP-Link Plug.

Based on the above analysis, we have identified several key pieces of information regarding the traffic flowing through an IoT device: traffic direction, traffic source, protocol type, IP address, and port information.

## 3 IoT Anomaly Traffic Detection and Attack Type Identification Scheme

The proposed attack detection scheme consists of four parts: network traffic processing, anomaly traffic detection, attack type identification, and attack information alerting. Network traffic processing serves as the input part of the overall scheme, while anomaly traffic detection and attack type identification constitute the algorithm research segment, and attack information alerting forms the output part.

### 3.1 Network Traffic Processing

Network traffic processing is the first step in the entire scheme. The scenario of our scheme involves monitoring the network status of IoT devices at the edge node. As analyzed earlier, different IoT devices exhibit varying network traffic patterns, and during the sample construction process discussed later in this paper, different IoT devices will generate distinct features. This module adopts different processing methods at various stages. In the training phase, traffic is first grouped based on the destination MAC address into different sets, and then the traffic from the same device is divided into different flows based on a time window of T. Subsequently, the entropy of the IP information is calculated, the total packet count is tallied, and samples are generated based on the traffic patterns. In the traffic prediction phase, various feature information for different devices within the time window T is computed, and the corresponding information is sent to either the anomaly detection module or the attack type identification module.

### 3.2 Anomaly Traffic Detection Algorithm

The anomaly detection module primarily utilizes statistical analysis to determine whether traffic anomalies have occurred in the network. This paper selects two statistical metrics for the anomaly detection module: the total number of bytes in packets within the time window and the total number of packets within the time window. DDoS attacks involve attackers using a large number of network packets to occupy the target service, causing a significant number of service connections that disrupt the target's functionality. In the IoT environment, the device traffic generally remains at normal levels, but during a DDoS flood attack, a noticeable increase in traffic occurs within a short period. This increase can be represented by the total number of packets per unit time or by the total number of bytes per unit time. Since packet sizes can vary across different network protocols, we use the total number of packets received and sent by the device and the total bytes of these packets per unit time as features for clustering analysis.

**Traffic Data Processing.** This section focuses on preprocessing the traffic data to facilitate subsequent feature extraction. Anomaly traffic detection primarily assesses traffic conditions based on the number of packets and total bytes flowing through the device in a given unit of time. Thus, it is crucial to extract timestamps and packet sizes as the two key pieces of information.

**Feature Extraction.** Considering that incoming and outgoing traffic for devices generally differs, we use “From” to represent traffic received by the device and "To" to indicate traffic sent by the device. The number of packets received and the total bytes of incoming traffic, as well as the number of packets sent and the total bytes of outgoing traffic, are calculated based on timestamps measured in minutes, resulting in four features. There are two sample labels: normal or abnormal, represented as "good" and "bad," respectively, as shown in Table 1.

**Table 1.** Sample Example

| FromPacket | FromByte | ToPacket | ToByte | Label |
|---|---|---|---|---|
| 1 | 135 | 2 | 238 | good |
| 56 | 3431 | 3 | 164 | bad |

**Data Preprocessing.** The feature values obtained in Table 1 are numerical features. To analyze the anomaly traffic, clustering methods are employed. To mitigate the impact of different feature value ranges, normalization of the sample data is necessary.

**Algorithm Model Training.** In a network traffic environment, it is often challenging to obtain accurate label information. Unsupervised algorithms provide a solution to this issue. A portion of the sample set obtained during feature extraction is used as training samples. After training, another portion can be used for testing, with the label information serving as a metric for classification accuracy, though it is not included in the algorithm. The K-means clustering and density-based spatial clustering of applications with noise (DBSCAN) algorithms are utilized here; the steps for the K-means clustering algorithm are detailed in Algorithm 1, while the steps for the common distance metrics used in K-means include Euclidean distance and Manhattan distance, and the choice of values can also affect clustering outcomes.

**Sample Testing.** This paper trains on one portion of sample data and predicts with another portion, ultimately evaluating the effectiveness of our classification algorithm using metrics such as accuracy. It is important to note that clustering algorithms are unsupervised, meaning labels do not participate in training and are used only for comparison with prediction results. There are generally two testing approaches: one is percentage training, commonly using 66% for training and 34% for testing. The other is cross-validation, typically ten-fold cross-validation, where the sample is divided into ten parts, nine parts are used for training, and one part for testing, with accuracy averaged to estimate the algorithm's performance.

**Algorithm 1.** DBSCAN Algorithm.

**Input**: Sample set $D = \{x_1, x_2, \cdots x_m\}$; neighborhood parameter: $\epsilon, MinPts$.
Initialize the core object set: $\Omega = \varnothing$;
  for $j = 1, 2, \cdots, m$ do
    Determine the neighborhood $N_\epsilon(\mathbf{x}_j)$ of sample $\mathbf{x}_j$;
    if $|N_\epsilon(\mathbf{x}_j)| \geq MinPts$ then
      Add sample $\mathbf{x}_j$ to the core object set $\Omega = \Omega \cup \{x_j\}$;
    end if
  end for
Initialize the number of clusters: $k = 0$;
Initialize the unvisited sample set: $\Gamma = D$;
while $\Omega \neq \varnothing$ do
  Record the current unvisited sample set: $\Gamma_{old} = \Gamma$;
  Randomly select a core object $o \in \Omega$, and initialize a queue $Q = < o >$;
  $\Gamma = \Gamma \setminus \{o\}$;
  while $Q \neq \varnothing$ do
    Remove the first sample $q$ from the queue $Q$;
    if $|N_\epsilon(q)| \geq MinPts$ then
      let $\Delta = N_\epsilon(q) \cap \Gamma$;
      Add samples in the $\Delta$ to the queue $Q$;
      $\Gamma = \Gamma \setminus \Delta$;
    end if
  end while
  $k = k + 1$, get $C_k = \Gamma_{old} \setminus \Gamma$;
  $\Omega = \Omega \setminus C_k$;
end while
**Output**: Cluster partition $C = \{C_1, C_2, \cdots, C_k\}$

### 3.3 Attack Type Identification Algorithm

Anomaly traffic detection can partially identify abnormal traffic situations in the IoT environment, but it cannot specify the exact type of attack, and low-rate attacks may also be missed. The function of the attack type identification module is to address these shortcomings, and it includes dimensionality reduction to reduce complexity. This module comprises the following parts:

**Traffic Data Processing.** This section primarily involves preprocessing the traffic data to facilitate subsequent feature extraction. It is essential to extract key information from the traffic, including timestamps, packet types, protocol types, port information, traffic direction, and packet sizes. The calculation of the number of packets and total traffic size within the time window is based on timestamps, which are in Unix timestamp format. Different types of DDoS attacks, such as TCP SYN flood, UDP flood, ICMP flood, and ARP flood, exhibit significant differences in various flow statistics, which forms the basis for attack classification. For DDoS attacks, the target is a specific service on a machine, making port information an important reference. Reflection attacks are a new variant of DDoS attacks; in such cases, traffic direction can serve as an additional reference. The total number of packets and total byte sizes per unit time are used to construct feature values, facilitating subsequent analysis of attack intensity.

**Feature Extraction.** This part focuses on calculating and extracting features based on the information obtained in the previous section. Features consist of various types of flows from the devices; the number of flow types determines the number of features. Each feature is composed of five key pieces of information. The first is the traffic direction, which indicates whether the current traffic is received by or sent from the device; "From" indicates received traffic, and "To" indicates sent traffic. The second is the traffic source, indicating whether the traffic comes from a local device or an internet device; "Local" signifies local devices, while "Internet" signifies internet devices. The third is the protocol type, representing the type of protocol to which the traffic belongs, categorized as "ARP," "ICMP," "TCP," or "UDP." The fourth is port and IP information; different devices exhibit significant differences in their ports and IPs, resulting in varying feature counts. The fifth is the type of feature value, with "Packet" and "Byte" as options; "Packet" indicates the count of packets flowing through the device per unit time, while "Byte" indicates the total number of bytes of packets flowing through the device per unit time. Table 2 shows the key feature information.

**Table 2.** Key Feature Information

| Feature Information | Value |
|---|---|
| Flow direction | "From"; "to" |
| Source of traffic | "Local"; "Internet" |
| Protocol type | "ARP"; "ICMP"; "TCP"; "UDP" |
| Port and IP information | Unfixed |
| Types of eigenvalues | "Packet"; "Byte" |

Combining the key feature information from Table 1 generates different features, calculating corresponding feature values based on a one-minute unit according to the feature descriptions. The traffic dataset labels the start and end times of attacks, and scripts are written to add labels to the samples based on this information.

The sample labels consist of two parts: one indicates the type of attack, with values such as ArpSpoof, PingOfDeath, TcpSyn, Smurf, etc.; the other indicates the source of the attack, where "W" means the attack originates from the internet and "L" means it comes from a local area network. Note that some attack types do not include the source. When there is no attack, the label information is "good." Table 3 provides examples of three sample records, listing only two features, although there are many more in reality.

**Table 3.** Sample Examples

| FromLocal-IcmpPortAllPacket | ToInternet-TcpPort50443Byte | Label |
|---|---|---|
| 0 | 1484 | good |
| 0 | 2262 | PingOfDeath |
| 38 | 238 | Smurf |

**Data Preprocessing.** The samples established in this paper have feature values that are all numerical variables. First, missing values are filled, and duplicate samples—defined as data where feature values and sample labels are identical—are removed. Due to different dimensions among various features, normalization is necessary to avoid affecting the results under certain algorithms. For instance, the samples from the Tplink plug generated 70,000 samples, with normal samples accounting for over 90%. The distribution of different sample types can significantly impact the results, so random sampling and sampling with replacement methods are employed to maintain a balanced distribution between normal and attack samples.

**Dimensionality Reduction.** In general, good features are highly correlated with classification and exhibit low correlation among themselves. Features and classifications can be viewed as vectors, and the linear correlation between vectors can be measured using the linear correlation coefficient. Given the large number of sample features generated, it is necessary to analyze the correlations among them using a correlation matrix to represent the degree of correlation between features.

Let $(X_1, X_2, X_3, ..., X_n)$ denote an n-dimensional random variable, corresponding to n features. The correlation coefficient $\rho_{ij}(i, j = 1, 2, ..., n)$ exists between any two vectors $X_i$ and $X_j$; a matrix with elements $\rho_{ij}$ is termed the correlation matrix of the n-dimensional random vector, denoted as R:

$$\mathrm{R} = \begin{bmatrix} \rho_{11} & \rho_{12} & \cdots & \rho_{1n} \\ \rho_{21} & \rho_{22} & \cdots & \rho_{2n} \\ \vdots & \vdots & \vdots & \vdots \\ \rho_{n1} & \rho_{n2} & \cdots & \rho_{nn} \end{bmatrix} \tag{2}$$

For any two random variables $X_i$ and $X_j$;, if each has m values, here m corresponds to the actual number of samples. The formula for the correlation coefficient is as follows:

$$\rho_{ij} = \frac{\sum_{l=1}^{m}(X_{il} - \overline{X}_i)(X_{jl} - \overline{X}_j)}{\sqrt{\sum_{l=1}^{m}(X_{il} - \overline{X}_i)^2}\sqrt{\sum_{l=1}^{m}(X_{jl} - \overline{X}_j)^2}} \tag{3}$$

It should be noted that when $i = j$, it represents the autocorrelation coefficient, which is 1. When $i \neq j$ represents the correlation coefficient that we need to pay attention to. When considering $\rho$, we need to be mindful of its values. The range of the correlation coefficient $\rho$ is from -1 to 1; the closer the absolute value of $\rho$ is to 1, the more correlated the two variables are. Generally, an absolute value of $\rho$ greater than 0.8 is considered strong correlation, while values greater than 0.5 but less than 0.8 indicate moderate correlation, values greater than 0.2 but less than 0.5 indicate weak correlation, and values less than 0.2 indicate strong non-correlation.

Using the correlation matrix allows for an initial analysis of the correlation between features; however, for a 20×20 correlation matrix, the pairwise relationships become too complex for visual selection of necessary features. Therefore, Principal Component Analysis (PCA) can be employed. PCA can project high-dimensional data into a low-dimensional space based on correlation, achieving dimensionality reduction. Assuming the sample set is $X = \{x_1, x_2, \cdots x_m\}$, the general steps for PCA calculation are:

1. Standardize all samples.
2. Compute the covariance matrix $XX^T$ of the samples.
3. Perform eigenvalue decomposition on the covariance matrix $XX^T$.
4. Take the largest d eigenvalues and their corresponding eigenvectors $w_1, ..., w_d$.
5. The new projection is given by: $Y = W^T X$.

The variance of sample variables greatly affects PCA's effectiveness. If different variables have different ranges, those with larger ranges will disproportionately affect the principal components, leading to bias. Thus, standardization in Step 1 is essential. After standardization, the covariance matrix equals the correlation matrix. The most crucial aspect of PCA is selecting the dimension d to be reduced, which can be based on the error rate.

$$\mu_1 = \frac{1}{m}\sum_{i=1}^{m}\left\|X^{(i)} - X_{approx}^{(i)}\right\| \tag{4}$$

where $\mu_1$ represents the projection error, $X$ represents the vector before projection, $X_{approx}$ represents the vector after projection, and m denotes the temporarily selected number of vectors.

$$\mu_2 = \frac{1}{m}\sum_{i=1}^{m}\left\|X^{(i)}\right\| \tag{5}$$

where $\eta$ represents the total variance, $X$ represents the vector before projection, and $m$ represents the temporarily selected number of vectors.

$$\eta = \frac{\mu_1}{\mu_2} = \frac{\frac{1}{m}\sum_{i=1}^{m}\left\|X^{(i)} - X_{approx}^{(i)}\right\|^2}{\frac{1}{m}\sum_{i=1}^{m}\left\|X^{(i)}\right\|^2} \leq 0.01 \tag{6}$$

where $\eta$ represents the error rate, $\eta \leq 0.01$ represents error rate less than 0.01, meaning 99% of the variability is retained. Common error rates are set at 1%, 5%, and 10%.

**Algorithm Model Training.** After obtaining the sample data, further identification of attack types can be considered a multi-class classification problem. A portion of the sample set obtained in the feature extraction module is used as training samples. Once training is complete, a secondary identification of the attack type can be performed. Here, the C4.5 decision tree algorithm is employed. The steps are as follows:

Assuming the set of all samples mentioned earlier is D, the decision tree is constructed based on D.

1. The classification types are normal, TCP_SYN flood, UDP flood, ICMP flood, and ARP flood. The information entropy of the categories is calculated:

$$\mathrm{Info}(D) = -\sum_{i=1}^{n}\left(\frac{|C_i|}{|C|} \times \log_2 \frac{|C_i|}{|C|}\right) \tag{7}$$

   where n is the number of categories, $|C|$ is the total number of samples, and $|C_i|$ is the number of samples in the i-th category.
2. Next, calculate the conditional entropy for different attributes:

$$\mathrm{Info}(A) = -\sum_{i=1}^{m}\left(\frac{|D_i|}{|D|} \times \mathrm{Info}(D_i)\right) \tag{8}$$

   where A represents a certain attribute, m is the number of subsets partitioned by attribute A, $D_i$ is one of those subsets, $|D_i|$ is the number of samples in that subset, $|D|$ is the total number of samples, and $Info(D_i)$ is the information entropy for each subset.
3. Calculate the information gain:

$$\mathrm{Gain}(A) = \mathrm{Info}(D) - \mathrm{Info}(A) \tag{9}$$

4. Calculate the information entropy for each attribute as a measure of split information:

$$H(A) = -\sum_{i=1}^{n}\left(\frac{|D_i|}{|D|} \times \log_2 \frac{|D_i|}{|D|}\right) \tag{10}$$

5. Calculate the information gain ratio for each attribute:

$$\mathrm{ICR}(A) = \mathrm{Gain}(A)/\mathrm{H}(A) \tag{11}$$

   The information gain ratio penalizes attributes with more split information in addition to the information gain, making decision tree branching decisions more reliable.
6. Select the attribute with the highest information gain ratio as the root node of the decision tree. Among the remaining attributes, choose the one with the largest information gain ratio as a branching node, repeating previous steps until further branching is no longer possible, thus forming the decision tree.

Finally, for new traffic to be predicted, establish the sample format, and then classify according to the rules of the trained decision tree to detect the type of attack.

**Sample Testing.** This paper uses a portion of sample data for training the identification of attack types, while another portion is used for recognition, ultimately evaluating the effectiveness of our classification algorithm using metrics such as accuracy. There are generally two testing methods: one is percentage training, commonly using 66% of samples for training and 34% for testing. The other is cross-validation, commonly employing ten-fold cross-validation, where the sample is divided into ten parts, with nine parts used for training and one for testing, and the accuracy is averaged to estimate the algorithm's performance.

### 3.4 Attack Information Alerting

In normal IoT network environment, traffic typically follows expected activity patterns. When anomalies occur in the network, our anomaly detection and attack type identification scheme activates, informing us whether an attack is underway.

However, real networks are complex and variable; factors such as misoperations of IoT devices or malfunctions can also trigger attack alerts. The anomaly detection in our scheme aims to identify potential flood attacks on devices, while the attack type identification is particularly effective for low-rate attacks. No algorithm is completely accurate; therefore, the recognition results only provide the probability of an attack occurring. For devices facing anomalous attacks, defense measures are also crucial. This paper includes supplementary alert information, which is essential for future defensive strategies.

In our identification scheme, all traffic undergoes both anomaly detection and attack type identification, with different alert levels issued based on the specific outcomes of these processes.

**Table 4.** Joint Alert Levels for Initial and Secondary Checks

| Abnormal detection | Attack type identification | Alarm level |
|---|---|---|
| abnormal | abnormal | 3 |
| abnormal | normal | 2 |
| normal | abnormal | 1 |
| normal | normal | 0 |

In Table 4, alert levels are categorized into four tiers, ranked from high to low risk as 3, 2, 1, and 0. Anomaly detection serves as the initial perception of abnormal traffic. A notable characteristic of DDoS attacks is the increased access to specific services on targeted devices, which manifests as a significant rise in the number of packets per unit time and an unusually high number of bytes per unit time within the local network environment. Attack type identification analyzes current network anomalies from the perspective of traffic flows. This approach offers two benefits: it enhances the detection of low-rate attacks and allows for feature tracing of complex attack types to identify patterns. The detection results from attack type identification reveal the type of attack; during the training phase, to ensure reliability, normal samples were also included, introducing a new label, "normal," alongside attack types. When the predicted attack category for a sample is "normal," it corresponds to the normal category in the table; when it is a specific attack type, it corresponds to the abnormal category. The comprehensive results from the initial and secondary checks correspond to the alert levels.

In addition to alert levels, providing more detailed alert information is beneficial for administrators. For samples with issues in attack type identification, supplementary attack information can include the type of attack, packet rate, and byte rate. The main attack types include TCP_SYN flood, UDP flood, ICMP flood, and ARP flood.

The attack packet rate (packets per second, pps) is calculated as follows:

$$pps = \frac{\text{packets}}{T} \tag{12}$$

where $T$ is the calculated window time, typically measured in minutes in this paper, and packets represent the count of data packets within that window.

The Bytes per second, Bps is calculated as follows:

$$\text{Bps} = \frac{\text{Bytes}}{T} \tag{13}$$

where $T$ is the window time as defined above, and Bytes represent the count of bytes of the data packets within that window.

## 4 Experimental and Simulation Results

### 4.1 Experimental Objectives

This paper analyzes the traffic of IoT devices and proposes an attack type identification scheme tailored for these devices. The core of this scheme is to establish a security baseline feature for IoT device traffic, utilizing clustering algorithms for anomaly detection and decision tree algorithms for attack type identification. The combination of these two approaches allows for a determination of whether a device is under attack, with different levels of information alerts based on the severity of the attack. This section first introduces the experimental environment and data processing, compares the impact of key parameters in the algorithms on the results, and finally validates that the selected algorithms are currently optimal, providing an overall assessment of the algorithm's effectiveness.

### 4.2 Experimental Environment and Data Set Processing

All experiments in this paper were conducted on a desktop computer equipped with an Intel(R) Core(TM) i7-7700 CPU running at 3.60 GHz, featuring four cores and 8 GB of RAM. Key information extraction from network protocols was accomplished using Wireshark, which allows for the extraction and conversion of necessary information from raw pcap format traffic files into formats such as CSV or TXT for further analysis. Python has become a widely used programming environment for data analysis; in this experiment, Python was primarily used for feature value calculations and sample generation, along with data preprocessing steps, including data cleaning, missing value imputation, and sample labeling. Weka, a mature data mining and analysis tool, was utilized for comparative analysis of algorithms. Table 5 presents information about the devices and attacks.

**Table 5.** Device and Attack Information

| MAC Address | Device Name | Attack Information |
|---|---|---|
| ec:1a:59:83:28:11 | WEMO Motion Sensor | ICMP;TCP;ARP;UDP;SSDP Attack |
| ec:1a:59:79:f4:89 | WEMO Power Switch | ICMP;TCP;ARP Attack |
| 50:c7:bf:00:56:39 | TP Link Plug | ICMP;TCP;ARP Attack |
| 70:ee:50:18:34:43 | Netatmo Camera | TCP;ARP Attack |
| 00:17:88:2B:9A:25 | Huebulb | ICMP;TCP;ARP;SSDP Attack |
| 44:65:0D:56:CC:D3 | AmazonEcho | ARP;UDP Attack |
| F4:F5:D8:8F:0A:3C | chromecast | TCP;ARP;SSDP Attack |
| 74:C6:3B:29:D7:1D | ihome | ARP Attack |
| D0:73:D5:01:83:08 | lifx | ICMP;ARP;UDP Attack |

We obtained raw pcap format traffic files, which required extraction and preprocessing into samples for further analysis using Wireshark and custom Python scripts. The specific steps are as follows:

Step 1: Since this paper's scheme establishes a security baseline for each IoT device and identifies different IoT devices, traffic from all types of devices needs to be acquired. Besides the IoT devices listed in Table 5, other devices do not generate abnormal traffic. Therefore, the goal of Step 1 is to filter out devices not involved in modeling while categorizing traffic based on device MAC addresses. We generated traffic files for nine IoT devices, which include both normal and attack traffic.

Step 2: Next, key information extraction must be completed. In Wireshark, we will extract relevant packet information such as timestamps, packet types, protocol types, port information, traffic direction, and packet sizes, exporting this data as columns in a CSV file.

Step 3: Using the CSV files generated in Step 2, we will calculate the total number of packets, total bytes, and average packet size for each minute interval. Timestamps will serve as the time reference, and since they are in Unix time format, conversion will be necessary. This data will be utilized for anomaly traffic detection.

Step 4: Building upon the CSV files from Step 2, we will again calculate packet counts and total traffic size based on the combination of key information as features, focusing on minute intervals. Timestamps will be used as a time reference, requiring conversion from Unix time format. This data will be used for attack type identification.

Step 5: Steps 3 and 4 will generate nine CSV files: one set for anomaly traffic samples and another for attack type identification samples. In the former, features include packet count, total bytes, and average packet size. In the latter, the initial samples and feature counts differ across devices, as shown in Table 3. Additionally, both sets will have the same number of samples.

Step 6: Using the attack sample information from the dataset, labels will be added to the samples. The timestamp in the traffic statistics is in milliseconds, while the timestamp in annotations is in seconds. For example, an attack annotation such as "1527838552,1527839153, Localfeatures — Allfeatures — Arpfeatures, ArpSpoof100L2D" indicates that the attack began at 1527838552 and ended at 1527839153. "Localfeatures — Allfeatures — Arpfeatures" refers to the key information used to initiate the attack. "ArpSpoof100L2D" specifies that the attack is an ARP spoof, with a maximum limit of 100 packets per second sent locally to the device. To label the anomaly traffic samples, we use the following criteria: "If (flowtime $\geq$ startTime * 1000 and endTime * 1000 $\geq$ flowtime), then Attack=True." For labeling the attack type samples, the condition is: "If (flowtime $\geq$ startTime * 1000 and endTime * 1000 $\geq$ flowtime), then Label = ArpspoofL." As shown in Table 6, there are significant differences in feature and sample counts among different devices. Although the first four device samples total approximately 70,000, the subsequent five have around 40,000, they are trained and predicted separately, without influencing each other.

**Table 6.** Statistics of Samples and Features for Different Devices

| MAC address | Device name | Number of features | Number of Samples |
|---|---|---|---|
| ec:1a:59:83:28:11 | WEMO Motion Sensor | 74 | 70297 |
| ec:1a:59:79:f4:89 | WEMO Power Switch | 80 | 70299 |
| 50:c7:bf:00:56:39 | TP Link Plug | 34 | 70311 |
| 70:ee:50:18:34:43 | NetatmoCamera | 50 | 70358 |
| 00:17:88:2B:9A:25 | Huebulb | 40 | 43728 |
| 44:65:0D:56:CC:D3 | AmazonEcho | 50 | 43728 |
| F4:F5:D8:8F:0A:3C | chromecast | 78 | 43729 |
| 74:C6:3B:29:D7:1D | ihome | 34 | 43735 |
| D0:73:D5:01:83:08 | lifx | 40 | 43730 |

### 4.3 Experimental Analysis

**Anomaly Traffic Detection.** After processing the dataset, we obtained sample data. K-means, a commonly used clustering algorithm, requires parameter tuning for different datasets. In contrast, DBSCAN is a density-based clustering algorithm that performs well with density-concentrated data. Common distance metrics for clustering include Euclidean distance and Manhattan distance. Here, we compare both distance metrics and clustering algorithm performance. Using data from the TpLink plug device as an example, the comparison results when k is fixed at 2 are shown in Table 7.

**Table 7.** Clustering Performance Comparison of TpLink Plug Using Different Metrics and Algorithms

| Algorithm | Distance measurement | Accuracy rate | True case rate | False positive rate |
|---|---|---|---|---|
| K-means | Euclidean distance | 99.81% | 38.94% | 0.01% |
| | Manhattandistance | 98.35% | 68.25% | 1.56% |
| DBSCAN | Euclidean distance | 98.89% | 84.13% | 1.07% |
| | Manhattan distance | 97.84% | 89.42% | 2.18% |

From Table 7, although the K-means algorithm using Euclidean distance achieves the highest clustering accuracy, it incurs a very low true positive rate (detection probability). Using Manhattan distance shows some improvement. Additionally, the DBSCAN algorithm has a higher true positive rate compared to K-means, but it also increases the false positive rate, meaning that while detection rates rise, the false alarm rates do too. In an anomaly detection system, detection rate is quite significant, followed by the false alarm rate. Therefore, for the TpLink plug, using the density-based clustering algorithm DBSCAN with Manhattan distance achieves a detection rate of 89.42% and a false positive rate of 2.18%.

By averaging the accuracy, true positive rate, and false positive rate for all devices in Table 8, we find that for the proposed anomaly traffic detection problem, the overall performance is an accuracy of 77.61%, a true positive rate of 79.57%, and a false positive rate of 24.83%.

**Attack Type Recognition.** Taking the TP Link Plug as an example, the samples exhibit a severe imbalance between attack and non-attack samples. To balance the sample sizes, we employed sampling with replacement, keeping the total sample size unchanged. Table 9 shows the statistics of TP Link Plug samples before and after balancing.

**Feature Selection and Dimensionality Reduction.** As seen in Table 6, the number of features for IoT devices is over 30, with several exceeding 70. An

**Table 8.** Anomaly Traffic Detection Performance of Various Devices

| MAC address | Equipment name | Accuracy rate | True caserate | False positiverate |
|---|---|---|---|---|
| ec:1a:59:83:28:11 | WEMO MotionSensor | 78.91% | 86.96% | 21.13% |
| ec:1a:59:79:f4:89 | WEMO PowerSwitch | 88.50% | 87.74% | 15.13% |
| 50:c7:bf:00:56:39 | TP Link Plug | 97.84% | 89.42% | 2.18% |
| 70:ee:50:18:34:43 | Netatmo Camera | 92.14% | 77.78% | 7.82% |
| 00:17:88:2B:9A:25 | Huebulb | 64.65% | 81.48% | 35.47% |
| 44:65:0D:56:CC:D3 | AmazonEcho | 75.09% | 66.29% | 24.89% |
| F4:F5:D8:8F:0A:3C | chromecast | 60.63% | 40.48% | 29.20% |
| 74:C6:3B:29:D7:1D | ihome | 59.13% | 100% | 69.21% |
| D0:73:D5:01:83:08 | lifx | 81.58% | 86.00% | 18.43% |

**Table 9.** Statistics of TP Link Plug Sample Counts Before and After Balancing by Label

| Sample label | Number of original samples | Sample size after balancing |
|---|---|---|
| good | 70103 | 11718 |
| ArpSpoofL | 30 | 11718 |
| TcpSynL | 59 | 11718 |
| PingOfDeathL | 30 | 11718 |
| Smurf | 30 | 11718 |
| TcpSynW | 59 | 11718 |

excessive number of features can increase computational complexity. There are two approaches to reduce the number of features: one is to use various feature selection evaluation functions to assess each feature, followed by manual selection. The other is to use Principal Component Analysis (PCA) for dimensionality reduction, projecting high-dimensional features into a lower-dimensional space. PCA is primarily suitable for numerical features, as its core focuses on numerical correlation calculations.

First, we calculated the correlation coefficient matrix for each device sample. Due to the large size of the feature matrix, we present the correlation coefficient matrix for the first six features of the TpLink Plug:

$$\begin{bmatrix} 1 & 1 & 0.06 & 0.07 & -0.1 & -0.1 \\ 1 & 1 & 0.06 & 0.07 & -0.1 & -0.1 \\ 0.06 & 0.06 & 1 & 0.94 & -0.05 & -0.05 \\ 0.07 & 0.07 & 0.94 & 1 & -0.05 & -0.05 \\ -0.1 & -0.1 & -0.05 & -0.05 & 1 & 1 \\ -0.1 & -0.1 & -0.05 & -0.05 & 1 & 1 \end{bmatrix} \tag{14}$$

From the correlation coefficient matrix, we can see that the correlation coefficients between adjacent features are above 90%, indicating a strong correlation.

Why is this the case? Looking back at our feature generation process, the adjacent features refer to the number of packets and total byte count of the same key information stream. Generally, while individual packet sizes may vary due to differences in the information carried, these two variables tend to show a positive correlation. Thus, we can consider retaining only one of the adjacent features. This paper retains only the packet count feature, effectively reducing all features by half.

We also observed that some non-adjacent features exhibited strong correlations. However, cross-correlation situations can arise, making manual selection of certain features unrealistic. PCA provides an algorithmic approach to achieve dimensionality reduction. In this experiment, we selected a 5% error rate, ensuring that the reduced samples retain 95% of the original sample's information. Note that the feature counts in Table 10 refer to the number of features remaining after halving the initial set.

**Table 10.** Statistics of Feature Counts Before and After PCA Dimensionality Reduction for Each Device

| MAC address | device name | Number of features | Number of dimensionality reduction features after non-standardization | Number of dimensionality reduction features after standardization |
|---|---|---|---|---|
| ec:1a:59:83:28:11 | WEMOMotion Sensor | 37 | 4 | 17 |
| ec:1a:59:79:f4:89 | WEMOPower Switch | 40 | 3 | 14 |
| 50:c7:bf:00:56:39 | TP Link Plug | 17 | 3 | 10 |
| 70:ee:50:18:34:43 | Netatmo Camera | 25 | 3 | 11 |
| 00:17:88:2B:9A:25 | Huebulb | 20 | 5 | 12 |
| 44:65:0D:56:CC:D3 | AmazonEcho | 25 | 5 | 15 |
| F4:F5:D8:8F:0A:3C | chromecast | 39 | 2 | 19 |
| 74:C6:3B:29:D7:1D | ihome | 17 | 2 | 8 |
| D0:73:D5:01:83:08 | lifx | 20 | 4 | 10 |

From Table 10, we can see that with the same error rate, non-standardized PCA removes more features, while standardized PCA retains more features. As mentioned earlier, standardization allows each dimension to have the same weight, while non-standardization may impact the results. To compare the effects of non-standardization and standardization on classification outcomes, we used the simplest KNN algorithm, dividing each device's samples into 66% for training and 34% for prediction.

## 5 Conclusion

With the rapid development of IoT technology, security issues within IoT systems are becoming increasingly prominent, and this paper focuses on the network security challenges in IoT environments. We detail the research on anomaly detection and attack type recognition algorithms, outline the problems to be addressed, and propose a solution for IoT anomaly traffic detection and attack type recognition. Then, we provide a thorough description of each component, particularly the anomaly detection and attack recognition algorithms. Finally, experimental analysis demonstrate that the features constructed in this paper are the most effective for the selected algorithms.

## References


1. Li, C., Wang, J., Wang, S., Zhang, Y.: A review of IoT applications in healthcare. Neurocomputing **565**, 127017 (2024)
2. Chamara, N., Islam, M.D., Bai, G.F., Shi, Y., Ge, Y.: Ag-IoT for crop and environment monitoring: past, present, and future. Agric. Syst. **203**, 103497 (2022)
3. Dastjerdi, A.V., Buyya, R.: Fog computing: helping the Internet of Things realize its potential. Computer **49**(8), 112–116 (2016)
4. Babun, L., Denney, K., Celik, Z.B., McDaniel, P., Uluagac, A.S.: A survey on IoT platforms: communication, security, and privacy perspectives. Comput. Netw. **192**, 108040 (2021)
5. Ray, S., Jin, Y., Raychowdhury, A.: The changing computing paradigm with Internet of Things: a tutorial introduction. IEEE Design Test **33**(2), 76–96 (2016)
6. Sasi, T., Lashkari, A.H., Lu, R., Xiong, P., Iqbal, S.: A comprehensive survey on IoT attacks: taxonomy, detection mechanisms and challenges. J. Inf. Intell. **2**(6), 455–513 (2024)
7. Ul Hassan, M., Rehmani, M.H., Chen, J.: Anomaly detection in blockchain networks: a comprehensive survey. IEEE Commun. Surv. Tutorials **25**(1), 289–318 (2023)
8. Duo, R., Nie, X., Yang, N., Yue, C., Wang, Y.: Anomaly detection and attack classification for train real-time ethernet. IEEE Access **9**, 22:528–22:541 (2021)
9. Bertino, E., Islam, N.: Botnets and Internet of Things security. Computer **50**(2), 76–79 (2017)
10. Liu, Y., Wang, J., Li, J., Niu, S., Song, H.: Machine learning for the detection and identification of Internet of Things devices: a survey. IEEE Internet Things J. **9**(1), 298–320 (2022)
11. Kolias, C., Kambourakis, G., Stavrou, A., Voas, J.: DDoS in the IoT: Mirai and other botnets. Computer **50**(7), 80–84 (2017)
12. Liu, C., Raghuramu, A., Chuah, C.-N., Krishnamurthy, B.: Piggybacking network functions on SDN reactive routing: a feasibility study. In: Proceedings of the Symposium on SDN Research, pp. 34–40 (2017)
13. Altulaihan, E., Almaiah, M.A., Aljughaiman, A.: Anomaly detection IDS for detecting DoS attacks in IoT networks based on machine learning algorithms. Sensors **24**(2) (2024)
14. A comparative analysis of various machine learning methods for anomaly detection in cyber attacks on IoT networks. Internet Things **26**, 101162 (2024)

# CAP-GAN: Channel-Aware Perturbation for Secure Wireless Transmission

Menghao Chen[1], Zhisheng Yin[2(✉)], Nan Cheng[2], Zhijie Zhang[2], and Yusi Zhang[3]

[1] Guangzhou Institute of Technology, Xidian University, Xi'an, China
mhchen_@stu.xidian.edu.cn
[2] School of Telecommunications Engineering, Xidian University, Xi'an, China
zsyin@xidian.edu.cn, dr.nan.cheng@ieee.org, 24011211001@stu.xidian.edu.cn
[3] 63rd Institute, National University of Defense Technology, Nanjing, China

**Abstract.** This paper proposes a novel channel-aware adversarial perturbation generation framework, called CAP-GAN (Channel-Aware Perturbation GAN). The framework enables active defense in wireless communication systems with potential eavesdroppers. Unlike traditional receiver-side defenses that passively remove perturbations, CAP-GAN actively injects them into the original transmitted signal. Using the original signal and the channel responses of both Bob and Eve as inputs, the framework generates channel-aware perturbations that preserve reception quality of Bob while deceiving Eve. Based on the GAN framework, CAP-GAN is trained by jointly optimizing a multi-objective loss function. Simulation results verify the effectiveness of the proposed CAP-GAN framework, which provides an efficient active defense strategy for secure wireless transmission.

**Keywords:** channel-aware · adversarial perturbation · Automatic Modulation Recognition · GAN

## 1 Introduction

Automatic modulation recognition (AMR) is widely applied in wireless signal transmission and processing. However, AMR models are highly vulnerable to adversarial attacks, and small perturbations often cause significant degradation in modulation recognition performance [14]. Most studies on adversarial examples focus on the Eve's perspective, with perturbations generated by Eve to mislead Bob's AMR system and compromise communication security [8]. In contrast, research on defense mechanisms remains limited, and most strategies employ passive receiver-side techniques such as perturbation detection and removal [9]. Although some studies explore active defense at the transmitter

This work was supported in part by the National Natural Science Foundation of China under Grant 62201432.


Y. Liu et al. (Eds.): ChinaCom 2025, LNICST 711, pp. 176–188, 2027.
https://doi.org/10.1007/978-3-032-33662-0_14

to mislead Eve, they generally neglect the impact of channel characteristics. In summary, research on active defense methods that account for channel characteristics is still at an early stage.

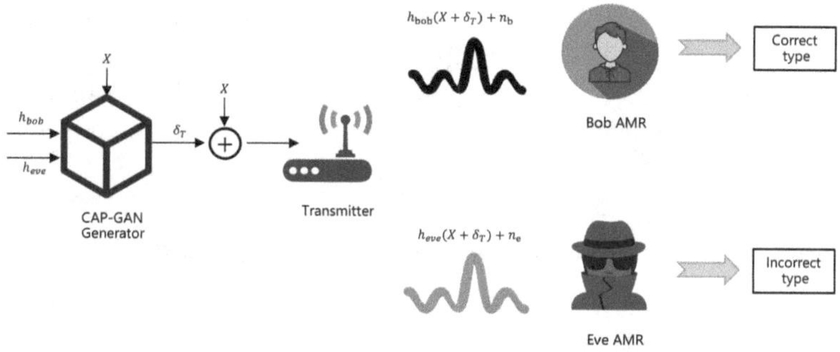


**Fig. 1.** CAP-GAN Scenario Schematic

To address these challenges, a novel channel-aware adversarial perturbation generation framework is proposed. As shown in Fig. 1, the framework is deployed at the transmitter. The original signal and the channel responses of both Bob and Eve are used as conditional inputs to generate adversarial perturbations, which are superimposed onto the signal before transmission. When transmitted through Bob's channel, the perturbations are effectively canceled, preserving Bob's modulation recognition performance. In contrast, when propagated through Eve's channel, the perturbations remain effective and significantly reduce the recognition accuracy of Eve's AMR model. CAP-GAN accounts for channel uncertainty and leverages channel information to optimize both communication reliability and defense effectiveness, realizing a truly active defense mechanism.

The CAP-GAN network is based on the GAN framework with targeted modifications [2]. A multi-objective loss function is incorporated during training for joint optimization [1]. The loss function simultaneously optimizes multiple objectives: constraining the perturbation magnitude, preserving the fidelity of Bob's received signal, and inducing deception of Eve. In summary, this work proposes an active defense mechanism that combines channel awareness with adversarial example generation. It provides a scalable solution for ensuring reliable and secure communication.

## 2 Related Work

### 2.1 Research on Automatic Modulation Recognition

AMR is a core technology in wireless signal processing and spectrum monitoring. Its objective is to automatically determine the modulation type of a received signal based on its characteristics. Traditional AMR methods mainly rely on feature extraction, including Higher-Order Cumulants (HOC) and instantaneous amplitude or phase features [3]. With the rise of deep learning models such as Convolutional Neural Networks (CNN), Recurrent Neural Networks (RNN), and hybrid architectures (e.g., CNN+LSTM) [15], AMR research enters a new phase. High-level and abstract features are automatically learned from raw signals (e.g., I/Q data), significantly reducing dependence on manual feature design. Deep learning-based AMR models achieve remarkable recognition accuracy and demonstrate superior performance in complex channel environments. Although recognition performance improves, AMR remains vulnerable to malicious attacks.

### 2.2 Research on Attacks Based on Adversarial Samples

Recent studies show that AMR models are highly sensitive to adversarial examples. Small perturbations can be introduced into transmitted or received signals, significantly degrading the recognition accuracy of Bob's AMR model [10]. Existing studies primarily focus on the Eve's perspective, aiming to generate perturbations that compromise Bob's AMR system. Existing methods include gradient-based attacks, optimization-based attacks, and generative model-based attacks [5]. Although these approaches can successfully mislead AMR models, the effects of channel fading and transmission uncertainties are often neglected, substantially reducing the practical effectiveness of perturbations. Consequently, some studies incorporate the channel responses between the Eve and Bob. For example, Paper [12] incorporates both channel information and noise between the Eve and Bob when generating perturbations, embedding adversarial examples within the channel. Similarly, Paper [6] designs a universal adversarial perturbation based on the channels between the attacker and multiple legitimate receivers, enabling simultaneous impact on multiple users. Nonetheless, the aforementioned attack techniques are unsuitable for transmitter-side active defense.

### 2.3 Research on Defenses Based on Adversarial Samples

Compared with research on adversarial attacks, studies on active defense using adversarial examples remain limited. Most existing defense methods focus on passive receiver-side protection [11] [7]. The core concept of active defense is to generate perturbations at the transmitter that induce recognition errors in Eve's AMR models while allowing Bob to correctly identify the modulation scheme. This strategy achieves active deception while safeguarding legitimate communication [13]. In [4], adversarial examples are generated using the Projected Gradient Descent (PGD) method in scenarios where Bob and Eve coexist. By taking the bit error rate into account, perturbations targeting Eve are incorporated into the original signals at the transmitter for active defense. Nevertheless, these perturbations do not fully consider the impact of channel conditions.

Building on these studies, the CAP-GAN proposed in this paper explicitly considers the differences between Bob's and Eve's channels and actively deceives

Eve while preserving legitimate communication. Once trained, the generator can operate across varying channel conditions, significantly reducing the computational cost of generating perturbations for each transmission.

The remainder of this paper is organized as follows:

Section 3 introduces the system model. It details the channel-aware perturbation generation mechanism and the design of the multi-objective loss function.

Section 4 presents the network training procedure and performance evaluation. It verifies the effect of the proposed framework on misleading Eve while preserving legitimate communication. Additional simulations are conducted using a CNN-based AMR model to evaluate generalization. The robustness of the proposed scheme is also evaluated under channel estimation errors.

Section 5 concludes the paper and summarizes its main contributions.

## 3 System Model

In a communication interference scenario, adversarial examples are used to induce misclassification at the receiver. A perturbation $\delta_T$ is constructed and added to the original signal $X$, producing the adversarial signal $X_{adv} = X + \delta_T$. After transmission through the wireless channel, the adversarial signal is processed by the receiver's modulation classifier $f$. The perturbation is designed so that $f(X_{adv}) \neq f(X)$, causing the original signal to be misclassified and the communication process to be disrupted.

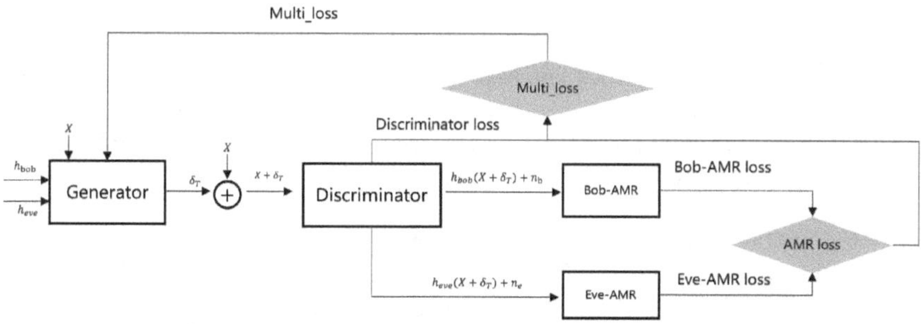


**Fig. 2.** CAP-GAN Training Overall Flow Chart

Based on the fundamental principle of adversarial examples, CAP-GAN is proposed to achieve proactive defense by considering the channel responses of both Bob and Eve. As shown in Fig. 2, the CAP-GAN system model consists of four core modules: a generator, a perturbation addition module, a discriminator, and AMR modules. These modules collaboratively generate channel-aware adversarial examples. The system input includes the original signal $X$ and the channel response information of Bob and Eve, denoted as $h_{bob}$ and $h_{eve}$, respectively. The generator receives the original signal and the current channel responses as conditional inputs to generate the adversarial perturbation $\delta_T$.

This perturbation is superimposed onto the original signal through the addition module to form the adversarial signal $X + \delta_T$. The adversarial signal is subsequently propagated through both Bob's and Eve's channels. The channel-aware perturbation is largely mitigated by Bob's channel but remains significant in Eve's channel. In this way, proactive defense is achieved. The functions of each module and the design of the multi-objective loss function are detailed as follows:

- Generator: The Generator is the core module. It is responsible for generating a small, carefully crafted perturbation $\delta_T$ for the original signal $X$. It takes the signal $X$ and the channel responses $h_{bob}$ and $h_{eve}$ as inputs and applies a multi-objective loss function to generate adversarial examples that specifically target Eve.
- Discriminator: The Discriminator is trained to assess the stealthiness of the adversarial samples. It takes the adversarial signal $X + \delta_T$ as input and attempts to distinguish it from the original signal. Through Discriminator training, the adversarial signal is made closer to the original signal, reducing the risk of detection.
- Bob-AMR Module: The Bob-AMR module represents the modulation recognition system of Bob. It employs an Adaptive Wavelet Network (AWN), which enables fast training and high recognition accuracy. To evaluate the generalization capability of the proposed method, additional simulations are conducted using a CNN-based AMR model. The module receives the signal transmitted through Bob's channel, expressed as $h_{bob}(X + \delta_T) + n_b$. It aims to correctly identify the modulation type and ensure reliable communication performance.
- Eve-AMR Module: The Eve-AMR module represents the modulation recognition system of Eve. It adopts the same network architecture as the Bob-AMR module. It receives the signal transmitted through Eve's channel, expressed as $h_{eve}(X + \delta_T) + n_e$. During training, the loss functions of both AMR modules are jointly backpropagated to the Generator.

To balance the quality of legitimate communication and the effectiveness of adversarial deception, CAP-GAN employs a multi-objective optimization strategy that jointly minimizes the following loss function:

$$L_{multi} = \lambda_1 \cdot loss_{bob}^{mse} + \lambda_2 \cdot (\alpha \cdot loss_{bob}^{ce} + \beta \cdot loss_{eve}^{ce}) + \lambda_3 \cdot loss_{discriminator} \quad (1)$$

As shown in Eq. (1), $loss_{bob}^{mse}$ is defined as the mean squared error between the original and adversarial signals received by Bob. This loss is designed to ensure that the signal received by Bob remains close to the signal originally transmitted without perturbation, thereby reducing the impact of perturbations on Bob's reception. $loss_{discriminator}$ denotes the GAN discriminator loss. This loss constrains the perturbation magnitude and enhances the stealthiness of the adversarial examples. $loss_{bob}^{ce}$ denotes the cross-entropy loss between Bob's predicted outputs and the true labels. $loss_{eve}^{ce}$ denotes the cross-entropy loss between Eve's predicted outputs and the target incorrect labels. Proper weighting of these losses improves the deceptive effectiveness against Eve while preserving legitimate communication.

# 4 Evaluation

## 4.1 Dataset

Most existing AMR studies rely on the RadioML 2016.10A dataset. The dataset contains signals transmitted through a simulated channel, which are often regarded as received signals. The channel conditions in this dataset are relatively complex, making it difficult to directly extract the specific channel responses corresponding to the transmitted signals. In most prior studies, the signals in RadioML 2016.10A are typically used to investigate adversarial attack techniques. However, the proposed active defense scheme requires the generator to take the original signal and the channel responses of both Bob and Eve as inputs. It then generates adversarial perturbations specifically targeting Eve. Therefore, the RadioML 2016.10A dataset cannot be directly applied to the proposed transmitter-side active defense scheme. To address this limitation, the dataset is modified and reconstructed. The original channel effects in RadioML 2016.10A are removed, retaining only basic signal processing operations such as filtering. After the perturbation is superimposed onto the original signal, a Rayleigh fading channel is reintroduced to simulate signal propagation through the channel. The AMR models are trained separately on our reconstructed dataset and on the RadioML 2016.10A dataset. The results show similar performance, demonstrating the effectiveness of our dataset. The RadioML 2016.10A dataset contains a large number of samples and diverse modulation types. To accelerate training, the dataset is further simplified and modified as follows. (1) The number of modulation types is reduced to six: BPSK, QPSK, 8PSK, QAM16, QAM64, and PAM4. (2) The signal-to-noise ratio (SNR) range is kept between –20 dB and 18 dB with a step size of 2 dB. (3) For each modulation type, 2,500 samples are included at each SNR level, resulting in 50,000 samples per modulation type. (4) The dataset is fully shuffled, and 80% of the samples are used for training while 20% are reserved for testing. The signal propagates through a Rayleigh fading channel, where the noise power is calculated based on the SNR and added before it is received.

## 4.2 Channel Parameter Settings

A Rayleigh fading channel model is used in the simulation to emulate the wireless environment, and different parameters are assigned to Bob and Eve to reflect channel disparities. As shown in Table 1, Bob's channel uses a path loss exponent of 1.5, a shadowing deviation of 2.0 dB, and a distance range of 1–10 m. This configuration represents a stable and low-loss link. Eve's channel uses a path loss exponent of 3.0, a shadowing deviation of 6.0 dB, and a distance range of 10–20 m. This setting represents a more obstructed and distant eavesdropping condition. Additionally, to simulate potential close-proximity eavesdroppers, a 10%

probability is assigned to generate near eavesdroppers with distances between 1 and 5 m.

**Table 1.** Parameter settings of the Bob and Eve channels

| Parameter | Bob channel | Eve channel |
|---|---|---|
| Path loss exponent $\alpha$ | 1.5 | 3.0 |
| Shadowing $\sigma_{\text{shadow}}$ (dB) | 2.0 | 6.0 |
| Distance range $d$ (m) | (1.0, 10.0) | (10.0, 20.0) |
| Near-eavesdropper probability $P_{\text{near}}$ | – | 0.1 |
| Near-eavesdropper distance range (m) | – | (1.0, 5.0) |

### 4.3 AMR Network

Bob and Eve employ the same network architecture in the simulation, where two AMR models, AWN and CNN, are used. Initially, the modulation recognition capability of the AWN network at Bob and Eve is assessed under clean and adversarial signal conditions. Subsequently, a CNN-based AMR model is employed at both Bob and Eve to validate the general applicability of the proposed scheme. The AWN network efficiently extracts features from input signals with low computational complexity, improving both training and inference efficiency. The CNN network is widely used in modulation recognition and provides strong classification performance. Evaluating both networks verifies the effectiveness and generality of the proposed scheme. Figure 3 shows the modulation recognition accuracies of Bob and Eve employing the AWN network under clean signal conditions. This simulation provides a baseline for subsequent AMR performance comparisons under adversarial signal conditions.

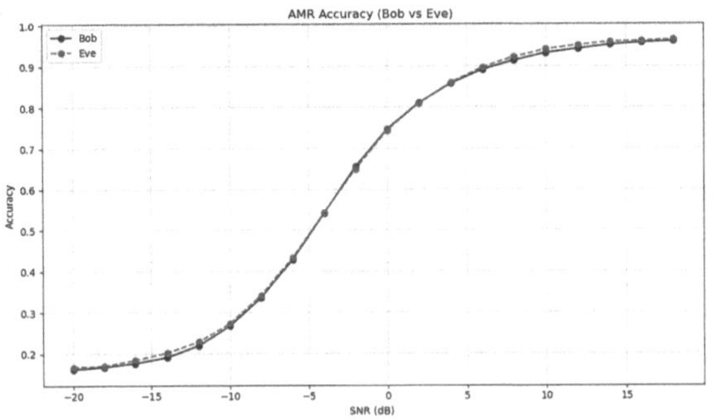


**Fig. 3.** Baseline Modulation Recognition Accuracy vs. SNR for AWN

### 4.4 CAP-GAN Training Network

In this work, the GAN framework is further modified to enable multi-objective joint optimization among the generator, discriminator, and AMR models. During training, perturbations are generated by the generator based on channel information and original data. These perturbations are then superimposed onto the original signal. The adversarial signal is transmitted through distinct channels for Bob and Eve with the aim of reducing recognition accuracy at Eve while maintaining recognition performance at Bob. The discriminator constrains the perturbation amplitude and enhances its stealthiness by distinguishing adversarial signals from original signals. The generator loss function comprises multiple components, and adversarial examples targeting Eve are generated by adjusting the hyperparameters in Eq. (1). In the implementation, both the generator and discriminator are optimized using the Adam algorithm. The detailed training parameters are summarized in Table 2.

**Table 2.** Training parameters of CAP-GAN model

| Parameter | Symbol | Value |
|---|---|---|
| Number of classes | $N_{\text{cls}}$ | 6 |
| Batch size | $B$ | 512 |
| Epochs | $E$ | 25 |
| Learning rate (Generator) | $lr_G$ | $1 \times 10^{-4}$ |
| Learning rate (Discriminator) | $lr_D$ | $1 \times 10^{-4}$ |
| Weight coefficient 1 | $\lambda_1$ | 10 |
| Weight coefficient 2 | $\lambda_2$ | 1 |
| Weight coefficient 3 | $\lambda_3$ | 0.5 |
| Weight coefficient 4 | $\alpha$ | 10 |
| Weight coefficient 5 | $\beta$ | 2 |
| Channel type | – | Rayleigh fading |
| Computation device | – | NVIDIA A40 GPU |

### 4.5 Training Results

During training, the changes in average recognition accuracy for both Bob and Eve are recorded under clean and adversarial signal scenarios. As shown in Fig. 4, with increasing training epochs, Bob's average recognition accuracy approaches the level under clean signals, while Eve's average accuracy decreases significantly.

### 4.6 Evaluation Results

**Trend of Accuracy with SNR Variation:** The trained model is evaluated on the test dataset. As shown in Fig. 5a, "Bob Clean" and "Bob Adv" denote the

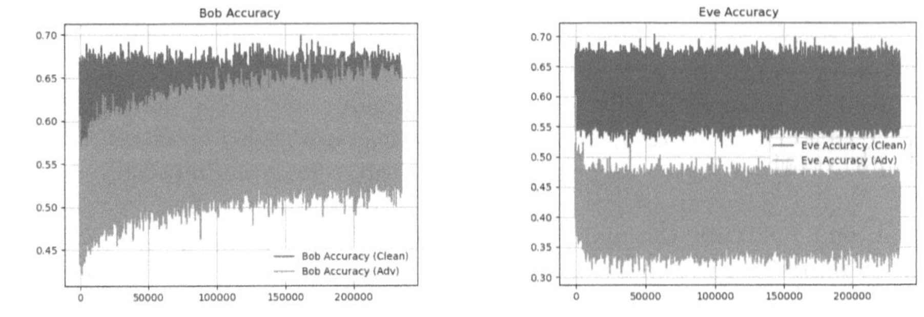


(a) Bob average accuracy

(b) Eve average accuracy

**Fig. 4.** Comparison of Average Accuracies between Bob and Eve During Training

recognition accuracy of Bob under clean and adversarial signals across different SNR values. It is observed that without perturbations, the recognition accuracies of Bob and Eve are close to the baseline shown in Fig. 3. After the signals are perturbed and propagated through the channels of Bob and Eve, the recognition accuracy of Bob remains almost unchanged, whereas the accuracy of Eve declines significantly. This decline becomes more pronounced at higher SNR levels.

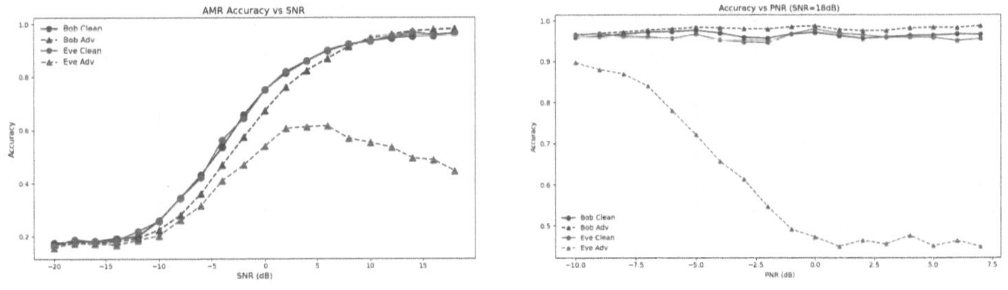


(a) Accuracy vs. SNR

(b) Accuracy vs. PNR

**Fig. 5.** AWN Model Recognition Accuracy for Bob and Eve vs. SNR and PNR(under clean and adversarial signals)

**Trend of Accuracy with PNR Variation:** Recognition accuracy is also recorded under varying Perturbation-to-Noise Ratio (PNR), a metric widely used in adversarial attack studies. Figure 5b shows the recognition accuracy of the test dataset at a fixed SNR of 18 dB as PNR varies. It is observed that the impact of the perturbations on Eve is pronounced and further increases as the PNR rises.

**Confusion Matrix of Recognition Accuracy under Clean and Adversarial Signals:** To further validate the deception effect of the perturbations, confusion matrices of modulation recognition accuracy for the test dataset are plotted under SNR = 18 dB. The matrices include results for both clean

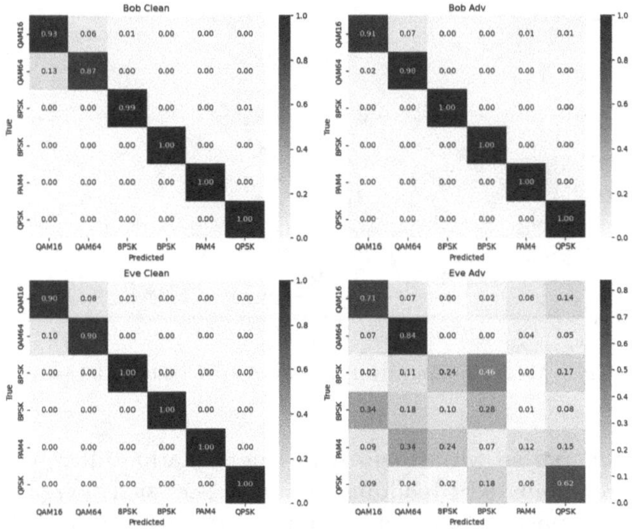


**Fig. 6.** AWN Model Recognition Accuracy Confusion Matrix (SNR=18dB, under clean and adversarial signals)

and adversarial signals, as shown in Fig. 6. It is observed that the recognition performance of Bob is almost unaffected, whereas the accuracy of Eve drops significantly across all modulation schemes.

**Validation for CNN-based AMR Model:** To validate the generality of the proposed framework, the commonly used CNN network in AMR is also employed for testing. CNN networks are deployed at both Bob and Eve. Figure 7 presents the recognition accuracy of Bob and Eve under clean and adversarial signals across different SNR values. The results show that the generated perturbations are also effective against CNN networks, although the deception effect is weaker than that for the AWN network. Analysis of the CNN confusion matrix indicates that the CNN model tends to confuse QAM16 and QAM64 modulation schemes, making it harder for CAP-GAN to generate highly targeted adversarial perturbations for these types. Nevertheless, for other modulation schemes, the generated perturbations still mislead Eve while preserving correct recognition at Bob.

**Verification under Channel Estimation Errors:** In practical communications, channel state information (CSI) is obtained through estimation and may be affected by delay or noise. To evaluate the robustness of CAP-GAN under channel estimation errors, two simulations are conducted using the test dataset at a fixed SNR of 18: one simulation introduces additive estimation noise, and the other uses a delayed channel model. In both simulations, perturbations are generated from imperfect channel estimates and added to the original signals. Recognition performance is then evaluated for Bob and Eve.

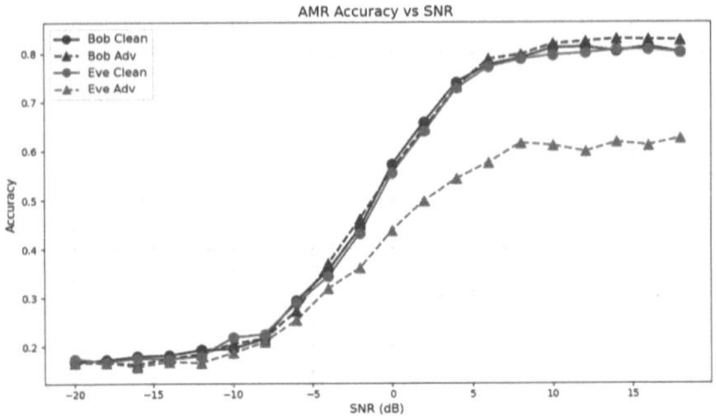


**Fig. 7.** CNN Model Recognition Accuracy for Bob and Eve vs. SNR

**(1) Additive Noise Simulation.** In this scenario, different levels of estimation error are simulated by adding complex Gaussian noise to the original channels. For each noise variance $\sigma^2 \in \{0.01, 0.02, 0.04, 0.06, 0.08, 0.1\}$, additive noise is applied to the original channels $h_{bob}$ and $h_{eve}$ to obtain the estimated channels $\hat{h}_{bob}$ and $\hat{h}_{eve}$. The estimated channels are then used as inputs to the generator to produce perturbations, which are added to the original signals. Subsequently, the adversarial signals are transmitted through the channels and recognized by the AMR networks.

**(2) Channel Estimation Delay Simulation.** In this scenario, a delayed CSI estimation model is employed: $\hat{h} = \rho h_{\text{true}} + \sqrt{1-\rho^2}n$, where $\rho$ denotes the temporal correlation coefficient. Delayed channel estimates are generated for $\rho \in \{1, 0.95, 0.9, 0.8, 0.7, 0.6\}$ and then used as inputs to the generator to produce perturbations.

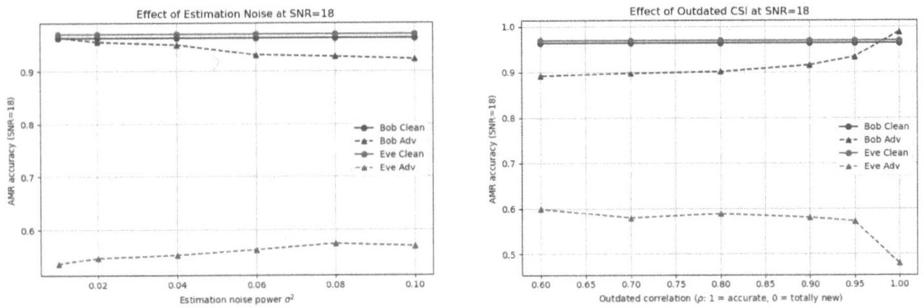


(a) Additive Channel Noise Error Simulation under SNR = 18 dB

(b) Channel Estimation Delay Error Simulation under SNR = 18 dB

**Fig. 8.** Verification under Channel Estimation Errors

By comparing the recognition accuracies of Bob and Eve under clean and adversarial signals for different $\sigma^2$ and $\rho$ values, the impact of channel estimation noise and delay on CAP-GAN performance is quantified. As shown in Fig. 8a, increasing channel estimation noise weakens the targeting effectiveness of the generated perturbations on Eve, causing a decrease for Bob and an increase for Eve. Figure 8b shows that when $\rho \to 1$, the channel is nearly error-free. In this case, perturbations are generated to strongly mislead Eve while leaving Bob largely unaffected. However, when $\rho < 1$, CSI delay effects emerge. As $\rho$ decreases, the targeting effectiveness of the perturbations declines, and the recognition accuracy of Eve increases. Overall, these simulations demonstrate that CAP-GAN exhibits strong robustness and can still achieve targeted deception and active defense under imperfect CSI conditions.

## 5 Conclusion

This paper investigates the vulnerability of AMR systems under adversarial attacks and proposes a novel CAP-GAN framework for active defense during wireless transmission. Unlike conventional passive defenses deployed at the receiver, CAP-GAN is implemented at the transmitter. It exploits the CSI differences between Bob and Eve to generate perturbations that mislead Eve while ensuring reliable reception at Bob.

Simulation results show that the proposed framework effectively misleads Eve while preserving legitimate communication under different SNR and PNR conditions. Its performance improves further at high SNR and PNR levels. Subsequently, the framework is evaluated on a CNN-based AMR model, confirming its generality across different AMR architectures. Finally, additive channel estimation noise and delayed channel models are introduced to simulate scenarios with channel estimation errors, demonstrating that the framework maintains its effectiveness under imperfect CSI conditions.

In summary, CAP-GAN overcomes the limitations of existing passive defense strategies. It achieves reliable communication while misleading Eve through active defense. This work provides a new perspective and a practical approach for the study of adversarial examples in secure wireless communications.

## References


1. Freitas de Araujo-Filho, P., Kaddoum, G., Naili, M., Fapi, E.T., Zhu, Z.: Multi-objective GAN-based adversarial attack technique for modulation classifiers. IEEE Commun. Lett. **26**(7), 1583–1587 (2022). https://doi.org/10.1109/LCOMM.2022.3167368
2. Creswell, A., White, T., Dumoulin, V., Arulkumaran, K., Sengupta, B., Bharath, A.A.: Generative adversarial networks: an overview. IEEE Signal Process. Mag. **35**(1), 53–65 (2018). https://doi.org/10.1109/MSP.2017.2765202
3. Dobre, O., Bar-Ness, Y., Su, W.: Higher-order cyclic cumulants for high order modulation classification. In: IEEE Military Communications Conference, 2003. MILCOM 2003, vol. 1, pp. 112–117 (2003). https://doi.org/10.1109/MILCOM.2003.1290087

4. Hameed, M.Z., György, A., Gündüz, D.: The best defense is a good offense: adversarial attacks to avoid modulation detection. IEEE Trans. Inf. Forensics Secur. **16**, 1074–1087 (2021). https://doi.org/10.1109/TIFS.2020.3025441
5. Ke, D., Huang, Z., Wang, X., Sun, L.: Application of adversarial examples in communication modulation classification. In: 2019 International Conference on Data Mining Workshops (ICDMW), pp. 877–882 (2019). https://doi.org/10.1109/ICDMW.2019.00128
6. Kim, B., Sagduyu, Y.E., Davaslioglu, K., Erpek, T., Ulukus, S.: Channel-aware adversarial attacks against deep learning-based wireless signal classifiers. IEEE Trans. Wireless Commun. **21**(6), 3868–3880 (2022). https://doi.org/10.1109/TWC.2021.3124855
7. Li, J., Zhang, S., Cao, J., Tan, M.: Learning defense transformations for counterattacking adversarial examples. Neural Netw. **164**, 177–185 (2023). https://doi.org/10.1016/j.neunet.2023.03.008
8. Lin, Y., Zhao, H., Ma, X., Tu, Y., Wang, M.: Adversarial attacks in modulation recognition with convolutional neural networks. IEEE Trans. Reliab. **70**(1), 389–401 (2021). https://doi.org/10.1109/TR.2020.3032744
9. Qiu, S., Liu, Q., Zhou, S., Wu, C.: Review of artificial intelligence adversarial attack and defense technologies. Appl. Sci. **9**(5) (2019). https://www.mdpi.com/2076-3417/9/5/909
10. Sadeghi, M., Larsson, E.G.: Adversarial attacks on deep-learning based radio signal classification. IEEE Wirel. Commun. Lett. **8**(1), 213–216 (2019). https://doi.org/10.1109/LWC.2018.2867459
11. Sahay, R., Love, D.J., Brinton, C.G.: Robust automatic modulation classification in the presence of adversarial attacks. In: 2021 55th Annual Conference on Information Sciences and Systems (CISS), pp. 1–6 (2021). https://doi.org/10.1109/CISS50987.2021.9400326
12. Sinha, S., Soysal, A.: Adversarial attacks and defenses for wireless signal classifiers using CDI-aware GANs. In: ICC 2024 - IEEE International Conference on Communications, pp. 2095–2100 (2024). https://doi.org/10.1109/ICC51166.2024.10622612
13. Yin, Z., Cheng, N., Wang, M., Li, C., Xiang, W.: Conceal truth while show fake: T/f frequency multiplexing-based anti-intercepting transmission. IEEE Trans. Inf. Forensics Secur. **20**, 6884–6894 (2025). https://doi.org/10.1109/TIFS.2025.3586489
14. Zhang, F., et al.: Deep learning based automatic modulation recognition: models, datasets, and challenges. Digital Sig. Process. **129**, 103650 (2022). https://doi.org/10.1016/j.dsp.2022.103650
15. Zhang, Z., Luo, H., Wang, C., Gan, C., Xiang, Y.: Automatic modulation classification using CNN-LSTM based dual-stream structure. IEEE Trans. Veh. Technol. **69**(11), 13521–13531 (2020). https://doi.org/10.1109/TVT.2020.3030018

# UAV-IRS-Assisted D2D Covert Communications With Multiple Eavesdroppers

Jimin Jiang[1], Yu'e Jiang[1(✉)], Yue Hong[1], Zhiqi Wu[1], and Muhammad Sohail[2]

[1] University Key Laboratory of Intelligent Perception and Computing of Anhui Province, Anqing Normal University, Anqing, China
jiang2012118@163.com

[2] Department of Computer Science Software Engineering, National University of Science and Technology, Islamabad, Pakistan
Muhammad.sohail@mcs.nust.edu.pk

**Abstract.** Unmanned aerial vehicle and intelligent reflecting surface (UAV-IRS)-assisted device-to-device (D2D) communication enhances coverage and improves channel reconfigurability, but it still faces significant challenges in maintaining covert transmission in the presence of multiple randomly distributed eavesdroppers. This paper studies covert communication in spectrum-sharing D2D networks assisted by UAV-IRS. Unlike existing works that focus on single or location-known eavesdroppers, this paper addresses practical scenarios with multiple spatially random eavesdroppers. We propose a novel system model, where the UAV-IRS dynamically reconfigures the wireless environment and a full-duplex base station generates artificial noise to enhance covertness. The minimum detection error probability at the eavesdroppers is adopted as the covertness metric, and a comprehensive joint optimization problem is formulated to maximize the covert transmission rate while ensuring the reliability of the cellular link. To tackle the non-convexity, a hierarchical alternating optimization (AO) algorithm is developed to obtain closed-form solutions for IRS phase shifts and UAV positioning, and to efficiently allocate power under covertness and outage constraints. Numerous analyses demonstrate that the proposed scheme outperforms baseline methods, validating the effectiveness of joint UAV and IRS optimization in enhancing both covertness and covert rate under multiple eavesdroppers environments.

**Keywords:** Covert communications · UAV-IRS · Multiple eavesdroppers

This work was supported in part by the National Natural Science Foundation of China (No. 62402007), the Anhui Provincial Natural Science Foundation (No. 2308085MF223), the Key Project on Anhui Provincial Natural Science Study by Colleges and Universities (No. 2024AH051096), the Special Project for the Construction of the Anqing New Energy Vehicle Industry Cluster(H20250091), the Horizontal Research Project (H20250090).


Y. Liu et al. (Eds.): ChinaCom 2025, LNICST 711, pp. 189–207, 2027.
https://doi.org/10.1007/978-3-032-33662-0_15

# 1 Introduction

## 1.1 Background

Device-to-device (D2D) communication enables direct information exchange between user devices, bypassing the cellular core network [4]. Due to the broadcast and open nature of wireless channels [12], D2D networks are exposed to significant security and privacy challenges, especially in the presence of multiple eavesdroppers [18]. However, the traditional secure communication techniques, such as physical layer security [14] and cryptography [10], cannot fully guarantee covertness. Therefore, covert communication hides the existence of transmission from eavesdroppers, thereby offering an enhanced level of security for transmitters, and is applied in D2D communication [2,5].

To further improve covert performance, the unmanned aerial vehicles (UAVs) can provide reliable and cost-efficient wireless communication services [16], and the intelligent reflecting surface (IRS) can adjust its amplitudes and phase shifts to dynamically reconfigure the wireless environment [17]. The incorporation of UAV-IRS improves mobility and dynamic beam coverage, thereby significantly enhancing the reliability and secrecy of wireless communication systems, serving as a solution to improve the performance of D2D covert communications [13].

However, many existing works often rely on simplified assumptions, such as the presence of a single eavesdropper [13] or known eavesdropper locations [3]. Furthermore, legitimate nodes are frequently assumed to be static, i.e., the UAV is considered to be in a hovering state at a fixed location in [3], neglecting the potential of trajectory optimization. More importantly, in D2D underlay networks, a substantial body of research on covert communication focuses solely on the D2D link performance, while overlooking the interference imposed on the primary cellular network and the resulting degradation in cellular link quality [15]. Therefore, we propose a comprehensive joint optimization framework for UAV-IRS-assisted covert D2D communication, and accounts for multiple randomly distributed eavesdroppers with unknown locations.

## 1.2 Related Work

Physical layer covert communication, also known as low probability of detection (LPD) communication, aims to hide the very existence of wireless transmission from a vigilant adversary [1,6]. The feasibility of covert communication is fundamentally rooted in the inherent uncertainty present in wireless environments, such as noise uncertainty at the unintended receiver [11], which prevents them from making a perfectly accurate detection eavesdropper. To exploit this, common techniques include transmit power control to keep the signal power below the noise floor [3], and the use of artificial noise (AN) [2,8] or friendly jamming generated by a cooperative node to increase the eavesdropper's uncertainty intentionally [7].

Recent advancements have explored the integration of emerging technologies like UAV-IRS to dynamically reconfigure the wireless propagation environment, thereby creating more favorable conditions for masking the covert signal and significantly enhancing the system's covert performance. Chen et al. in [3] proposed a covert communication scheme for non-D2D static scenarios with a single fixed eavesdropper. This scheme employs uncertainty introduced by random phase shifts via UAV-IRS and interference generated by a full-duplex receiver, optimizing the transmit-to-interference power ratio to maximize the covert rate. In [13], Wang et al. addressed non-D2D scenarios involving a single non-stationary eavesdropper, i.e., there is an estimation error in eavesdropper's location. Qian et al. in [9] proposed a method for jointly optimizing UAV trajectories and IRS phase offsets in non-D2D dynamic scenarios with a single fixed eavesdropper, aiming to maximize the average rate of legitimate users while satisfying covertness constraints. [15] investigated a dynamic scenario involving a single fixed eavesdropper, where a UAV-IRS is employed to assist in overlay D2D covert communication. Zuo et al. in [18] investigated a static scenario with multiple colluding eavesdroppers, where the underlay D2D transmitter adopted random power allocation to assist covert communication of the cellular transmitter. However, the integration of UAV deployment, IRS phase shift design, and power control for covert underlay D2D communication in the presence of spatially random eavesdroppers remains unexplored, which motivates us to make the following three main contributions.

- To address the critical yet under-explored threat of randomly distributed and non-colluding eavesdroppers, we propose a novel system model for UAV-IRS-assisted covert communication in a D2D-underlaid cellular network. This model meticulously integrates a full-duplex base station (BS) that transmits artificial noise (AN) to actively create interference. A UAV-IRS is introduced as a mobile relay to dynamically reconfigure the wireless propagation environment. To accurately capture the practical constraints and uncertainties, our model incorporates a bounded log-uniform noise uncertainty model at the eavesdroppers and employs a hybrid channel modeling approach.
- To solve the non-convex and multivariate coupled optimization problem arising from the complex system model, we develop a hierarchical alternating optimization (AO) framework. This algorithm decomposes the original joint optimization problem, like UAV location, IRS phase shifts, D2D transmit power, and AN power, into tractable subproblems. For the subproblems of IRS phase shift and UAV horizontal positioning, we derive closed-form optimal solutions that achieve coherent signal combining and minimize multiplicative path loss, respectively. The power control subproblem is then solved under the worst-case covertness constraint derived from the most capable eavesdropper. By iteratively optimizing these, the algorithm efficiently converges to a solution that jointly maximizes the covert communication rate while strictly satisfying the constraints on detection error probability and cellular link outage, thereby trade off a balance between performance and computational complexity.
- The numerical results demonstrate that the proposed joint optimization scheme effectively improves both communication covertness and covert rate

compared with baseline methods. The simulations validate the theoretical analysis and highlight the importance of simultaneously optimizing transmit power, UAV location, and IRS phase shifts to ensure covert communication under multiple eavesdroppers.

The remainder of this paper is organized as follows. Section 2 introduces the system model. Section 3 analyzes $m$-th Willie's detection, derives key performance metrics. Section 4 analyzed the outage probability of the cellular link. Section 5 presents the optimization problem and the design of an alternating optimization algorithm. Simulation results are discussed in Sect. 6, followed by conclusions in Sect. 7.

## 2 System Model

This section introduces the UAV-IRS-assisted D2D covert communication system, covering the network model, channel model, noise Uncertainty at Willies, and received signals. The optimization problem is then presented.

### 2.1 Network Model

As illustrated in Fig. 1, we consider a UAV-IRS-assisted covert D2D communication network in the presence of multiple wardens (eavesdroppers). The network consists of the following entities: a legitimate D2D transmitter (DT, $t$), a legitimate D2D receiver (DR, $r$), a UAV-IRS ($u$), a base station (BS, $b$), a cellular transmitter (CU, $c$), and $M$ wardens, denoted by Willie $w(m)$, $m \in \{1, 2, \ldots, M\}$. In our considered system, the DT intends to transmit information covertly to the DR with the assistance of a UAV-IRS, while avoiding detection by the Willies. Meanwhile, the system reuses the spectrum resources of the cellular uplink, and the interference generated by the BS further confuses the detection of the Willies. The BS is equipped with two antennas, whereas the DT, DR, CU, and each Willie are equipped with a single antenna. One BS antenna is used for the legitimate uplink, while the other is dedicated to transmitting artificial noise (AN) to enhance covertness.

In addition, we employ a three-dimensional cylindrical coordinate system. The positions of DT, DR, BS, CU, and UAV-IRS are given by $\mathbf{q}_t = (0, 0, 0)$, $\mathbf{q}_r = (x_r, y_r, 0)$, $\mathbf{q}_b = (x_b, y_b, 0)$, $\mathbf{q}_c = (x_c, y_c, 0)$, and $\mathbf{q}_u = (x_u, y_u, H)$, respectively, where $H$ denotes the UAV's altitude. The $M$ Willies are assumed to be independently and uniformly distributed in a circular area with radius $D$ centered at the DT. The location of the $m$-th Willie is denoted as $\mathbf{q}_{w(m)} = (x_{w(m)}, y_{w(m)}, 0)$, which follows a binomial point process (BPP). The IRS is equipped with $K$ passive reflecting elements, with the first element taken as a reference point. The diagonal matrix $\boldsymbol{\Theta} = \text{diag}\{e^{j\theta_1}, e^{j\theta_2}, \ldots, e^{j\theta_K}\}$ represents the effective phase shifts introduced by all reflecting elements of the IRS, where $\theta_k \in [0, 2\pi)$ is the phase shift applied by the $k$-th reflecting element, $k = 1, 2, \ldots, K$.

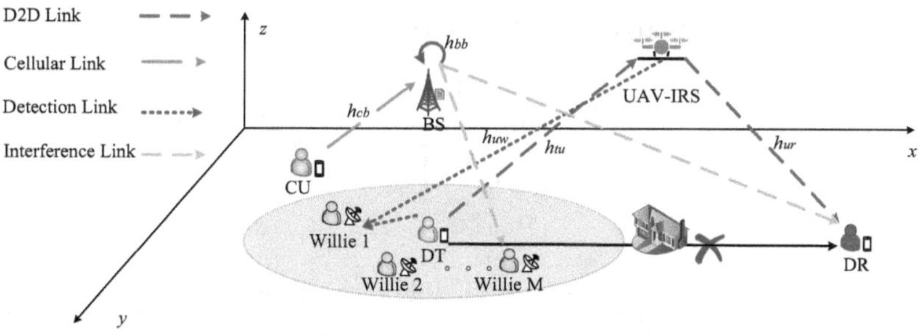


**Fig. 1.** A UAV-IRS-assisted D2D covert communication network.

## 2.2 Channel Models

The UAV-IRS is assumed to hover at a fixed altitude in an obstruction-free environment, thereby maintaining LoS links with ground users. The channel gain vector $\mathbf{h}_{tu} \in \mathbb{C}^{K\times 1}$ can be expressed as

$$\mathbf{h}_{tu} = \sqrt{\beta d_{tu}^{-\alpha}} \left[1, e^{-j\frac{2\pi}{\lambda} d\phi_{tu}}, \ldots, e^{-j\frac{2\pi}{\lambda}(K-1)d\phi_{tu}}\right], \tag{1}$$

where $\beta$ denotes the channel power gain at a reference distance of 1 m, and $\alpha$ denotes the path loss exponent. $\phi_{tu}$ is the cosine of the angle of departure for the link from DT to UAV-IRS. The parameter $\lambda$ represents the carrier wavelength, and $d < \lambda$ is the distance between adjacent reflective elements. The distance between DT and UAV-IRS is

$$d_{tu} = \sqrt{\|\mathbf{q}_u - \mathbf{q}_t\|^2} = \sqrt{\|\mathbf{q}_u\|^2}. \tag{2}$$

Similarly, the channel gain $\mathbf{h}_{ur} \in \mathbb{C}^{1\times K}$ from the UAV-IRS to DR is

$$\mathbf{h}_{ur} = \sqrt{\beta d_{ur}^{-\alpha}} \left[1, e^{-j\frac{2\pi}{\lambda} d\phi_{ur}}, \ldots, e^{-j\frac{2\pi}{\lambda}(K-1)d\phi_{ur}}\right], \tag{3}$$

where $d_{ur} = \sqrt{\|\mathbf{q}_r - \mathbf{q}_u\|^2}$ and $\phi_{ur}$ is the cosine of the angle of departure for the UAV-IRS–DR link.

Due to the UAV's mobility and the passive nature of the Willies, it is difficult for legitimate nodes to determine their precise locations. To capture this uncertainty and the lack of a LoS path, the UAV-IRS–Willie channels are modeled as Rayleigh fading. The channel gain $\mathbf{h}_{uw(m)} \in \mathbb{C}^{1\times K}$ from the UAV-IRS to the $m$-th Willie is expressed as

$$\mathbf{h}_{uw(m)} = \sqrt{\beta d_{uw(m)}^{-\alpha}}\, \mathbf{g}_{uw(m)}, \tag{4}$$

where each element of $\mathbf{g}_{uw(m)}$ follows i.i.d. complex Gaussian distribution, i.e., $\mathbf{g}_{uw(m)}(k) \sim \mathcal{CN}(0, \sigma_{uw(m)}^2)$, $\forall k \in \{1, 2, \ldots, K\}$. The distance between UAV-IRS and the $m$-th Willie is

$$d_{uw(m)} = \sqrt{\|\mathbf{q}_{w(m)} - \mathbf{q}_u\|^2}. \tag{5}$$

The overall channel matrix from UAV-IRS to all Willies is

$$\mathbf{H}_{uw} = \begin{bmatrix} \mathbf{h}_{uw(1)} \\ \mathbf{h}_{uw(2)} \\ \vdots \\ \mathbf{h}_{uw(M)} \end{bmatrix} \in \mathbb{C}^{M \times K}. \tag{6}$$

We assume that all ground-to-ground channels are subject to Rayleigh fading, i.e., CU–BS, BS–DR, BS–Willie, DT–BS, and DT–Willie. The channel gains $h_{ij}$ are expressed as

$$h_{ij} = \sqrt{\beta d_{ij}^{-\alpha}} g_{ij}, \tag{7}$$

where $d_{ij}$ denotes the distance between node $i$ and node $j$, and the small-scale fading coefficient is modeled as $g_{ij} \sim \mathcal{CN}(0, \sigma_{ij}^2)$. The index pairs $ij \in \{tw(m), bw(m), cb, tb, br\}$ correspond to DT–Willie, BS–Willie, CU–BS, DT–BS, and BS–DR, respectively.

### 2.3 Noise Uncertainty at Willies

Due to environmental variations and receiver calibration errors, each Willie cannot know its exact noise power. We adopt a bounded noise uncertainty model: the actual noise power $\sigma_{w(m)}^2$ at the $m$-th Willie lies in a multiplicative interval around a nominal value $\tilde{\sigma}_{w(m)}^2$, i.e.,

$$\sigma_{w(m)}^2 \in \left[\frac{1}{\rho}\tilde{\sigma}_{w(m)}^2,\ \rho\tilde{\sigma}_{w(m)}^2\right], \quad \forall m \in \{1, 2, \dots, M\}, \tag{8}$$

where $\rho \geq 1$ is the noise uncertainty coefficient. Following the commonly adopted log-uniform model, the PDF of $\sigma_{w(m)}^2$ at the $m$-th Willie is

$$f_{\sigma_{w(m)}^2}(x) = \begin{cases} \dfrac{1}{2\ln(\rho)\, x}, & \text{if } \frac{1}{\rho}\tilde{\sigma}_{w(m)}^2 \leq x \leq \rho\tilde{\sigma}_{w(m)}^2, \\ 0, & \text{otherwise.} \end{cases} \tag{9}$$

### 2.4 Received Signals

After reflection and adjustment by the IRS, the received signal $y_r[n]$ at the DR can be written as

$$y_r[n] = \sqrt{P_t}\mathbf{h}_{ur}\boldsymbol{\Theta}\mathbf{h}_{tu}x_t[n] + \sqrt{P_b}h_{br}x_b[n] + n_r[n], \tag{10}$$

where $x_t[n]$ is the covert signal transmitted by the DT with power $P_t$, $x_b[n]$ is the artificial noise from the BS with power $P_b$, $\mathbb{E}[|x_t[n]|^2] = 1$, and $\mathbb{E}[|x_b[n]|^2] = 1$. The AWGN at the DR is denoted by $n_r[n] \sim \mathcal{CN}(0, \sigma_r^2)$. Here $n = 1, 2, \dots, N$, and $N$ is the total number of channel uses.

The received signal $y_{w(m)}[n]$ at the $m$-th Willie is given by

$$y_{w(m)}[n] = \begin{cases} \sqrt{P_b} h_{bw(m)} x_b[n] + n_{w(m)}[n], & \mathcal{H}_0, \\ \sqrt{P_t}\left(\mathbf{h}_{uw(m)} \boldsymbol{\Theta} \mathbf{h}_{tu} + h_{tw(m)}\right) x_t[n] \\ + \sqrt{P_b} h_{bw(m)} x_b[n] + n_{w(m)}[n], & \mathcal{H}_1, \end{cases} \tag{11}$$

where $\mathcal{H}_0$ denotes that DT remains silent and Willies only observe interference plus noise, while $\mathcal{H}_1$ denotes that DT transmits covert signals and Willies observe a superposition of covert signals, interference, and noise. The noise is modeled as $n_{w(m)}[n] \sim \mathcal{CN}(0, \sigma_{w(m)}^2)$. Each Willie performs a binary hypothesis test between $\mathcal{H}_0$ and $\mathcal{H}_1$ to detect the presence of covert transmission.

Accordingly, the signal-to-interference-plus-noise ratio (SINR) at the DR can be expressed as

$$\gamma_r = \frac{P_t \left| \mathbf{h}_{ur} \boldsymbol{\Theta} \mathbf{h}_{tu} \right|^2}{P_b |h_{br}|^2 + \sigma_r^2}, \tag{12}$$

and the achievable transmission rate between DT and DR is

$$R = \log_2 \left(1 + \gamma_r\right). \tag{13}$$

Without loss of generality, we adopt the transmission rate $R$, subject to the covertness constraint, as a measure of communication quality. For clarity and ease of reference, the key parameters used in our system model are summarized in Table 1.

**Table 1.** Summary of Key System Parameters and Notations

| Parameter | Symbol | Value/Description |
|---|---|---|
| DT Location | $\mathbf{q}_t$ | $(0, 0, 0)$ |
| DR Location | $\mathbf{q}_r$ | $(x_r, y_r, 0)$ |
| BS Location | $\mathbf{q}_b$ | $(x_b, y_b, 0)$ |
| CU Location | $\mathbf{q}_c$ | $(x_c, y_c, 0)$ |
| UAV-IRS Location | $\mathbf{q}_u$ | $(x_u, y_u, H)$ |
| UAV Altitude | $H$ | 100 m |
| Willie Distribution | $\mathbf{q}_{w(m)}$ | in a circle centered at the DT |
| Path Loss Exponent | $\alpha$ | Defines large-scale fading |
| Reference Channel Gain | $\beta_0$ | Reference channel gain at unit distance |
| Number of IRS Elements | $K$ | umber of reflecting elements on the IRS |
| IRS Phase Shift Matrix | $\boldsymbol{\Theta}$ | $\mathrm{diag}\{e^{j\theta_1}, \ldots, e^{j\theta_K}\}$ |

# 3 Detection Analysis of Willies

In this section, we adopt $m$-th Willie's minimum detection error probability as the metric to measure the covertness requirement.

## 3.1 Covertness Measurement

Based on the received signal at a time slot from Eqn. (11), the $m$-th Willie makes a binary decision by comparing the average power $Y_{w(m)}$ of the received signals with the preset power detection threshold $\tau_{(m)}$, and the decision rule can be given by

$$Y_{w(m)} \underset{\mathcal{D}_0}{\overset{\mathcal{D}_1}{\gtrless}} \tau_{(m)}, \tag{14}$$

where $\mathcal{D}_0$ and $\mathcal{D}_1$ denote the results of Willies' detections. When $Y_{w(m)} > \tau_{(m)}$, Willies supports the decision $\mathcal{D}_1$ and believes that DT is transmitting to DR, when $Y_{w(m)} < \tau_{(m)}$, Willies is in favor of $\mathcal{D}_0$ and considers that DT is not transmitting to DR. Combined with Eqns. (11) and (14), Willies' average power $Y_{w(m)}$ is

$$Y_{w(m)} = \frac{1}{N} \sum_{n=1}^{N} |y_{w(m)}(n)|^2. \tag{15}$$

Assuming an infinite number of channel uses per time slot, i.e., $N \to \infty$, is justified by the fact that the available communication bandwidth determines the number of transmittable symbols within a time slot. With sufficiently large bandwidth, the number of channel uses can be made large enough to approximate the infinite case. Therefore, combining Eqn. (11) and Eqn. (15), $Y_{w(m)}$ in the case of $\mathcal{H}_0$ and $\mathcal{H}_1$ can be derived as

$$Y_{w(m)} = \begin{cases} P_b|h_{bw(m)}|^2 + \sigma^2_{w(m)}, & \mathcal{H}_0, \\ P_t\left|\mathbf{h}_{uw(m)}\boldsymbol{\Theta}\mathbf{h}_{tu} + h_{tw(m)}\right|^2 & \\ +P_b|h_{bw(m)}|^2 + \sigma^2_{w(m)}, & \mathcal{H}_1. \end{cases} \tag{16}$$

## 3.2 Detection Performance at Willie

According to Eqn. (16), there exist two error situations in the binary hypothesis testing. The first is that Willies makes a ($\mathcal{D}_1$) decision when DT keeps silent ($\mathcal{H}_0$), called the false alarm probability $P_{FA}$. Conversely, Willies performs a ($\mathcal{D}_0$) decision when DT is transmitting ($\mathcal{H}_1$), named the missed detection probability $P_{MD}$. And the total error detection probability of $m$-th Willie can be denoted as

$$\xi_{(m)} = \begin{cases} 1, & \tau_{(m)} < \frac{1}{\rho}\tilde{\sigma}^2_{w(m)}, \\ P_{FA} + P_{MD}, & \frac{1}{\rho}\tilde{\sigma}^2_{w(m)} \le \tau_{(m)} \le \rho\tilde{\sigma}^2_{w(m)}, \\ P_{MD}, & \tau_{(m)} > \rho\tilde{\sigma}^2_{w(m)}. \end{cases} \tag{17}$$

When $\tau_{(m)} < \frac{1}{\rho}\tilde{\sigma}^2_{w(m)}$, the probability of false alarm $P_{FA}$ becomes high, which is undesirable from the Willies' perspective. On the other hand, when $\tau_{(m)} > \rho\tilde{\sigma}^2_{w(m)}$, the probability of missed detection $P_{MD}$ dominates and increases, which again prevents minimizing the overall detection error probability. Therefore, to balance between $P_{FA}$ and $P_{MD}$, the feasible region for the optimal detection threshold $\tau_{(m)}$ should lie within

$$\frac{1}{\rho}\tilde{\sigma}^2_{w(m)} \leq \tau_{(m)} \leq \rho\tilde{\sigma}^2_{w(m)}. \tag{18}$$

Assume that the apriori probability of hypotheses either $\mathcal{H}_0$ or $\mathcal{H}_1$ being true is 0.5, thus $\xi_{(m)}$ can be also rewritten as

$$\xi_{(m)} = 1 - \mathcal{P}(\tau_{(m)} - P_t\mathcal{B} - P_b\mathcal{A} < \sigma^2_{w(m)} < \tau_{(m)} - P_b\mathcal{A}), \tag{19}$$

where $\mathcal{A} = |h_{bw(m)}|^2$ and $\mathcal{B} = \left|\mathbf{h}_{uw(m)}\boldsymbol{\Theta}\mathbf{h}_{tu} + h_{tw(m)}\right|^2$. Then, the average error detection probability conditioned on $\tau_{(m)}$ can be denoted by

$$\overline{\xi}_{(m)}(\tau) = 1 - \int_{\max(\frac{1}{\rho}\tilde{\sigma}^2_{w(m)}, \tau_{(m)} - P_t\mathcal{B} - P_b\mathcal{A})}^{\min(\rho\tilde{\sigma}^2_{w(m)}, \tau_{(m)} - P_b\mathcal{A})} f_{\sigma^2_{w(m)}}(x)\, dx. \tag{20}$$

Then, for the upper bound, it is obvious that

$$\min(\rho\tilde{\sigma}^2_{w(m)}, \tau_{(m)} - P_b\mathcal{A}) = \tau_{(m)} - P_b\mathcal{A}, \tag{21}$$

where $\tau_{(m)} \leq \rho\tilde{\sigma}^2_{w(m)}$, and $P_b\mathcal{A}$ is a positive number.

And for the lower bound, we consider two cases, when $\tau - P_t\mathcal{B} - P_b\mathcal{A} \leq \frac{1}{\rho}\tilde{\sigma}^2_{w(m)}$, the lower bound is $\frac{1}{\rho}\tilde{\sigma}^2_{w(m)}$, and the conditional error probability becomes

$$\begin{aligned} \overline{\xi}_{(m)}(\tau) &= 1 - \int_{\frac{1}{\rho}\tilde{\sigma}^2_{w(m)}}^{\tau_{(m)} - P_b\mathcal{A}} \frac{1}{2\ln(\rho)x}\, dx \\ &= 1 - \frac{1}{2\ln(\rho)} \ln\left(\frac{\tau_{(m)} - P_b\mathcal{A}}{\frac{1}{\rho}\tilde{\sigma}^2_{w(m)}}\right). \end{aligned} \tag{22}$$

And when $\tau_{(m)} - P_t\mathcal{B} - P_b\mathcal{A} > \frac{1}{\rho}\tilde{\sigma}^2_{w(m)}$, the lower bound is $\tau_{(m)} - P_t\mathcal{B} - P_b\mathcal{A}$, and the conditional error probability can be given as

$$\begin{aligned} \overline{\xi}_{(m)}(\tau) &= 1 - \int_{\tau_{(m)} - P_t\mathcal{B} - P_b\mathcal{A}}^{\tau_{(m)} - P_b\mathcal{A}} \frac{1}{2\ln(\rho)x}\, dx \\ &= 1 - \frac{1}{2\ln(\rho)} \ln\left(\frac{\tau_{(m)} - P_b\mathcal{A}}{\tau_{(m)} - P_t\mathcal{B} - P_b\mathcal{A}}\right). \end{aligned} \tag{23}$$

To find the optimal threshold $\tau^*_{(m)}$ that minimizes $\overline{\xi}_{(m)}(\tau)$, we analyze the derivative of $\overline{\xi}_{(m)}(\tau)$ with respect to $\tau_{(m)}$. For $\tau_{(m)} \leq P_t\mathcal{B} + P_b\mathcal{A} + \frac{1}{\rho}\tilde{\sigma}^2_{w(m)})$, we have

$$\frac{\partial \overline{\xi}_{(m)}(\tau)}{\partial \tau_{(m)}} = -\frac{1}{2\ln(\rho)} \frac{1}{\tau_{(m)} - P_b \mathcal{A}} < 0, \tag{24}$$

indicating that $\overline{\xi}_{(m)}(\tau)$ is decreasing with $\tau_{(m)}$.

For $\tau_{(m)} > P_t \mathcal{B} + P_b \mathcal{A} + \frac{1}{\rho}\tilde{\sigma}^2_{w(m)}$, we can derive as

$$\frac{\partial \overline{\xi}_{(m)}(\tau)}{\partial \tau} = -\frac{1}{2\ln(\rho)} \left( \frac{1}{\tau_{(m)} - P_b \mathcal{A}} - \frac{1}{\tau_{(m)} - P_t \mathcal{B} - P_b \mathcal{A}} \right) > 0, \tag{25}$$

indicating that $\overline{\xi}_{(m)}(\tau)$ is increasing with $\tau_{(m)}$.

Therefore, the minimum error probability occurs at

$$\tau^*_{(m)} = P_t \mathcal{B} + P_b \mathcal{A} + \frac{1}{\rho}\tilde{\sigma}^2_{w(m)}. \tag{26}$$

Considering the constraint in (18), the optimal detection threshold is

$$\tau^*_{(m)} = \min\left( P_t \mathcal{B} + P_b \mathcal{A} + \frac{1}{\rho}\tilde{\sigma}^2_{w(m)}, \rho\tilde{\sigma}^2_{w(m)} \right). \tag{27}$$

Then, we derive the optimal detection threshold $\tau^*_{(m)}$ to minimize the average error detection probability at $m$-th Willie. The minimum $\overline{\xi}_m(\tau^*)$ can be denoted as

$$\begin{aligned} \overline{\xi}_{(m)}(\tau^*) &= 1 - \int_{\frac{1}{\rho}\tilde{\sigma}^2_{w(m)}}^{P_t \mathcal{B} + P_b \mathcal{A} + \frac{1}{\rho}\tilde{\sigma}^2_{w(m)} - P_b \mathcal{A}} \frac{1}{2\ln(\rho)x} dx \\ &= \begin{cases} 1 - \frac{1}{2\ln(\rho)} \ln\left(1 + \frac{\rho P_t \mathcal{B}}{\tilde{\sigma}^2_{w(m)}}\right), & \mathcal{V} \le \tilde{\sigma}^2_{w(m)}\left(\rho - \frac{1}{\rho}\right), \\ 0, & \mathcal{V} > \tilde{\sigma}^2_{w(m)}\left(\rho - \frac{1}{\rho}\right). \end{cases} \end{aligned} \tag{28}$$

where $\mathcal{V} = P_t \mathcal{B} + P_b \mathcal{A}$. Following the above analyses, we observe that when $\mathcal{V} > \tilde{\sigma}^2_{w(m)}\left(\rho - \frac{1}{\rho}\right)$, the $\overline{\xi}_{(m)}(\tau^*) = 0$, which means that Willies can detect DT's transmission. Hence, We consider case of $\mathcal{V} \le \tilde{\sigma}^2_{w(m)}\left(\rho - \frac{1}{\rho}\right)$, and can be derived as

$$\xi^*_{(m)} = \mathbb{E}_{\mathcal{B}}[\overline{\xi}_{(m)}(\tau^*)] = \int \overline{\xi}_{(m)}(\tau^*) f_{\mathcal{B}}(b) db. \tag{29}$$

It is noteworthy that, because Willies employs an optimal detector, the BS's interference signal power $P_b \mathcal{A}$ is eliminated in the final expression of his error probability $\xi_{(m)}$. Consequently, $\xi_{(m)}$ depends solely on the DT's covert signal power $P_t \mathcal{B}$.

Considering that the instantaneous information about $h_{uw(m)}$ or $h_{tw(m)}$ is not available, Willies only knows $\mathbf{h}_{uw(m)} \sim \mathcal{CN}(0, \sigma^2_{uw(m)})$ and $\mathbf{h}_{tw(m)} \sim$

$\mathcal{CN}(0, \sigma^2_{tw(m)})$, the combined channel $\mathbf{h}_{uw(m)}\boldsymbol{\Theta}\mathbf{h}_{tu} + h_{tw(m)}$ is a complex Gaussian distribution $\mathcal{CN}(0, z)$ with variance $z = \sigma^2_{uw(m)}(\sum_{k=1}^{K} h^k_{tu}) + \sigma^2_{tw(m)}$. Therefore, the $\xi^*_{(m)}$ can be derived as

$$\begin{aligned}\xi^*_{(m)} &= \int_0^{\frac{\tilde{\sigma}^2_{w(m)}}{\rho}(\rho - \frac{1}{\rho})} \left[1 - \frac{2\ln\rho}{\ln\left(1 + \frac{\rho P_b b}{\tilde{\sigma}^2_{w(m)}}\right)}\right] \frac{1}{\mathbb{E}[\mathcal{D}]} e^{-b/\mathbb{E}[\mathcal{D}]}\, db \\ &= 1 - \frac{1}{2\ln(\rho)} \exp\left(\frac{1}{\rho\gamma_{w(m)}}\right) \left[\mathrm{Ei}\left(-\frac{\rho}{\gamma_{w(m)}}\right) - \mathrm{Ei}\left(-\frac{1}{\rho\gamma_{w(m)}}\right)\right], \end{aligned} \tag{30}$$

where $\mathcal{D} = \beta_0 d^{-\alpha}_{uw(m)} d^{-\alpha}_{tu} K + \beta_0 d^{-\alpha}_{tw(m)}$, and $\gamma_{w(m)} = \frac{\mathcal{D} P_t}{\tilde{\sigma}^2_{w(m)}}$. Ei$(x)$ denotes the exponential integral function.

Since the eavesdroppers operate in a non-colluding manner in our system, the covert transmission is considered unsuccessful once any single eavesdropper manages to detect the communication. Hence, the system performance should be evaluated under the worst-case scenario. Specifically, among the $M$ Willies, we identify the most threatening one, i.e., the Willie that achieves the lowest minimum detection error probability. This Willie determines the overall covertness of the system, as it represents the strongest detector from the legitimate users' perspective. Specifically, the covertness constraint is given by

$$\min_{m \in \{1,\ldots,M\}} \xi^*_{(m)} \geq 1 - \epsilon, \tag{31}$$

where $\xi^*_{(m)}$ is the minimum error probability of the $m$-th Willie, and $\epsilon \in (0, 1)$ is a small tolerance parameter. Due to non-collusive eavesdropping, as long as the worst-case Willie satisfies the constraints, all Willies satisfy them.

## 4 Performance of Cellular Links

To measure the performance of cellular in our work, we explore the probability of outage in this section. The received signals at BS is expressed as

$$\begin{aligned} y_b[n] =& \sqrt{P_c} h_{cb} x_c[n] + \sqrt{P_t}(\mathbf{h}_{ub}\boldsymbol{\Theta}\mathbf{h}_{tu} + h_t b) x_t[n] \\ &+ \sqrt{\varphi P_b} h_{bb} x_b[n] + n_b[n], \end{aligned} \tag{32}$$

where $x_c[n]$ is the transmit signal of CU with power $P_c$, and $\mathbb{E}[|x_c[n]|^2] = 1$. The AWGN at the BS is denoted by $n_b[n] \sim \mathcal{CN}(0, \sigma^2_b)$, and $\varphi$ is the self-interference coefficient..

Then the SINR at BS can be given by

$$\gamma_b = \frac{P_c |h_{cb}|^2}{P_t |\mathbf{h}_{ub}\boldsymbol{\Theta}\mathbf{h}_{tu} + h_{tb}|^2 + \varphi P_b |h_{bb}|^2 + \sigma^2_b}. \tag{33}$$

Combined with the Eqn. (33), the outage probability of the cellular link can be expressed as

$$P_{cout} = \mathcal{P}\{\gamma_b \leq 2^{R_c} - 1\}. \tag{34}$$

We assume that $|h_{cb}|^2$, $|\mathbf{h}_{ub}\boldsymbol{\Theta}\mathbf{h}_{tu} + h_{tb}|^2$, and $|h_{bb}|^2$ follow exponential distributions, the Eqn. (34) can be derived as

$$P_{cout} = 1 - \exp\left(-\frac{\eta\sigma^2}{P_c}\right) \frac{1}{\left(1 + \frac{\eta P_t}{P_c}\right)\left(1 + \frac{\eta\varphi P_b}{P_c}\right)}, \tag{35}$$

where $\eta = 2^{R_c} - 1$.

We investigate the dependence of $P_{cout}$ on $P_c$, $P_t$, and $P_b$ by deriving its first-order derivatives with respect to these parameters. The results of these three derivatives are obtained as follows

$$\begin{aligned} \frac{\partial P_{cout}}{\partial P_c} &= -\exp\left(-\frac{\eta\sigma^2}{P_c}\right) \frac{1}{\left(1 + \frac{\eta P_t}{P_c}\right)\left(1 + \frac{\eta\varphi P_b}{P_c}\right)} \\ &\left(\frac{\eta\sigma^2}{P_c^2} + \frac{\eta P_t}{P_c(P_c + \eta P_t)} + \frac{\eta\varphi P_b}{P_c(P_c + \eta\varphi P_b)}\right) < 0, \end{aligned} \tag{36}$$

$$\frac{\partial P_{cout}}{\partial P_t} = \exp\left(-\frac{\eta\sigma^2}{P_c}\right) \frac{\eta}{\left(1 + \frac{\eta P_t}{P_c}\right)^2\left(1 + \frac{\eta\varphi P_b}{P_c}\right) P_c} > 0, \tag{37}$$

$$\frac{\partial P_{cout}}{\partial P_b} = \exp\left(-\frac{\eta\sigma^2}{P_c}\right) \frac{\eta\varphi}{\left(1 + \frac{\eta P_t}{P_c}\right)\left(1 + \frac{\eta\varphi P_b}{P_c}\right)^2 P_c} > 0. \tag{38}$$

It can be concluded that $P_{cout}$ increases with $P_t$ and $P_b$, but decreases with $P_c$. Therefore, the monotonicity indicates that increasing $P_c$ improves the reliability of the cellular link by reducing the outage probability, whereas increasing $P_t$ or $P_b$ has the opposite effect.

## 5 Covert Performance Optimization for UAV-IRS Assisted D2D Communications

In this section, the covert transmission rate $R$ is maximized by jointly designing the transmit power of DT $P_t$, the transmit power of BS $P_b$, the phase shift matrix $\boldsymbol{\Theta}$ of IRS and the UAV location $\mathbf{q}_u$, with the covertness requirement, the outage probability constraint of the cellular link, the maximum transmit power constraint at DT and BS, and the phase shift constraint of IRS.

### 5.1 Problem Formulation

To maximize the covert transmission rate with the constraints, the optimization problem can be formulated as

$$\max_{P_t, P_b, \boldsymbol{\Theta}, \mathbf{q}_u} \quad \log\left(1 + \frac{P_t \left|\mathbf{h}_{ur}\boldsymbol{\Theta}\mathbf{h}_{tu}\right|^2}{P_b \left|h_{br}\right|^2 + \sigma_r^2}\right) \tag{39}$$

$$\begin{aligned} \text{s.t.} \quad & \xi_{(m)} \geq 1 - \epsilon, \quad m \in \{1, ..., M\}, && \text{(39a)} \\ & P_{cout} \leq \delta, && \text{(39b)} \\ & 0 < P_t < P_t^{\max}, && \text{(39c)} \\ & 0 < P_b < P_b^{\max}, && \text{(39d)} \\ & \theta_k \in [0, 2\pi), \quad k \in \{1, ..., K\}. && \text{(39e)} \end{aligned}$$

Constraint (39a) guarantees the covertness requirement, i.e., the minimum detection error probability at all potential eavesdroppers is no smaller than $1-\epsilon$. Constraint (39b) ensures that the outage probability of the cellular link does not exceed the reliability threshold $\delta$. The power budget constraints (39c) and (39d) restrict the transmit powers $P_t$ and $P_b$ within their respective maximum allowable limits. Finally, constraint (39e) specifies the feasible range of the IRS phase shifts, which are bounded within $[0, 2\pi)$ for each reflecting element.

### 5.2 Optimization of Phase Shift and UAV Location

For fixed transmit powers $P_t$ and $P_b$, we optimize the UAV location $\mathbf{q}_u$ and IRS phase shift matrix $\boldsymbol{\Theta}$ to maximize the covert communication rate while satisfying constraints (39a)-(39e).

**Phase shift design for fixed $\mathbf{q}_u$** For fixed $\mathbf{q}_u$, we can observe that Eq. (30) and Eq. (35) are independent of $\boldsymbol{\Theta}$. Following Eq. (39), the objective function can be rewritten as

$$\max_{\boldsymbol{\Theta}} \left|\mathbf{h}_{ur}\boldsymbol{\Theta}\mathbf{h}_{tu}\right|^2. \tag{40}$$

Then the $\left|\mathbf{h}_{ur}\boldsymbol{\Theta}\mathbf{h}_{tu}\right|^2$ can be equivalently written as

$$\left|\mathbf{h}_{ur}\Theta\mathbf{h}_{tu}\right|^2 = \left|\sum_{k=1}^{K} \left[\mathbf{h}_{ur}\right]_k e^{j\theta_k} \left[\mathbf{h}_{tu}\right]_k\right|^2. \tag{41}$$

This is maximized when all phase terms are aligned, therefore, the $k$-th optimal phase shift of IRS can be expressed as

$$\theta_k^* = \arg\left([\mathbf{h}_{ur}]_k\right) - \arg\left([\mathbf{h}_{tu}]_k\right) + \phi_0, \quad \forall k, \tag{42}$$

where $\phi_0$ is a common phase shift.

**Phase shift design for fixed $\mathbf{q}_u$** Combined with Eq. (42), the objective function can be expressed as

$$R \approx \log_2 \left(1 + \frac{P_t \beta_0^2 K^2}{d_{tu}^{\alpha} d_{ur}^{\alpha} \left(P_b |\mathbf{h}_{br}|^2 + \sigma_r^2\right)}\right). \tag{43}$$

Thus, the objective function can be written equivalently as function can be expressed as

$$\min_{\mathbf{q}_u} d_{tu}^{\alpha} d_{ur}^{\alpha}, \tag{44}$$

where

$$d_{tu} = \sqrt{\|\mathbf{q}_u - \mathbf{q}_t\|^2 + H^2} = \sqrt{x_u^2 + y_u^2 + H^2}, \tag{45}$$

$$\begin{aligned} d_{ur} &= \sqrt{\|\mathbf{q}_u - \mathbf{q}_r\|^2 + H^2} \\ &= \sqrt{(x_u - x_r)^2 + (y_u - y_r)^2 + H^2}. \end{aligned} \tag{46}$$

Based on the locations of DT, DR, and UAV, the objective function can be expressed as

$$f(x) = \left(x_u^2 + H^2\right)\left((d_{tr} - x_u)^2 + H^2\right), \tag{47}$$

where $d_{tr}$ is the distance between DT and DR. We introduce a normalized variable $\zeta = x_u / d_{tr}$, which represents the fraction of the distance from DT to the UAV. Thus, $x_u = \zeta d_{tr}$. We also define the height-to-distance ratio coefficient $\iota = H/d_{tr}$. Substituting $\zeta$ and $\iota$ into the expressions for the squared distances, and the $d_{tu}^2$ and $d_{ur}^2$ can be derived as

$$d_{tu}^2 = (\zeta d)^2 + H^2 = d^2(\zeta^2 + \tau^2), \tag{48}$$

$$d_{ur}^2 = (d - \zeta d)^2 + H^2 = d^2\left((1 - \zeta)^2 + \tau^2\right). \tag{49}$$

The objective function $f(x)$ can now be rewritten in terms of $\zeta$ and $\iota$ as

$$f(\zeta) = \left(\zeta^2 + \iota^2\right)\left[(1 - \zeta)^2 + \iota^2\right]. \tag{50}$$

To find the minimum, we take the derivative of $f(\zeta)$ with respect to $\zeta$ and set it to zero. After simplification, the derivative leads to a cubic equation whose solutions are given by

$$\zeta^* = \begin{cases} \frac{1}{2} \pm \sqrt{\frac{1}{4} - \iota^2}, & \text{if } \iota < \frac{1}{2}, \\ \frac{1}{2}, & \text{if } \iota \geq \frac{1}{2}. \end{cases} \tag{51}$$

The condition $\iota < 1/2$ (i.e., $H < d_{tr}/2$) is practical in most scenarios, as the UAV altitude is typically much smaller than the horizontal separation between ground users, The optimal horizontal location of the UAV-IRS is $\mathbf{q}_u^* = (\zeta^* d_{tr}, 0)$.

### 5.3 Overall Algorithm Design

To address the non-convex optimization problem formulated in Eq. (39), we propose an efficient alternating optimization (AO) based algorithm that decomposes the original problem into three tractable subproblems. The algorithm iteratively optimizes one set of variables while keeping the others fixed, gradually improving the objective function until convergence. The overall algorithm structure is designed as Algorithm 1.

---

**Algorithm 1.** Joint Optimization for UAV-IRS Assisted Covert Communication

---

**Require:** System parameters: $\mathbf{q}_t, \mathbf{q}_r, \mathbf{q}_b, \mathbf{q}_c, H, K, M, \epsilon, \delta, P_t^{\max}, P_b^{\max}, \rho, \sigma^2$.
Initialize $P_t^{(0)}, P_b^{(0)}, \boldsymbol{\Theta}^{(0)}, \mathbf{q}_u^{(0)}$; $i \leftarrow 0$
**while** $|R^{(i+1)} - R^{(i)}| > \eta$ **do**
  **Fix** $P_t^{(i)}, P_b^{(i)}$**:**
  Optimize IRS phase shift: $\theta_k = \arg([\mathbf{h}_{ur}]_k) - \arg([\mathbf{h}_{tu}]_k) + \phi_0, \forall k$;
  Optimize UAV location: $\mathbf{q}_u^{(i+1)} \leftarrow (\zeta^* d_{tr}, 0, H)$.
  **Fix** $\boldsymbol{\Theta}^{(i+1)}, \mathbf{q}_u^{(i+1)}$**:**
  **for** each Willie $m$ in $1, \ldots, M$ **do**
    Calculate $\xi^*_{(m)}$ using Eq. (30).
  **end for**
  Find worst-case Willie: $m^* \leftarrow \arg\min_m \xi^*_{(m)}$;
  Solve power optimization with constraint $\xi^*_{(m^*)} \geq 1 - \epsilon$;
  Update $P_t^{(i+1)}, P_b^{(i+1)}$;$i \leftarrow i + 1$;
  Calculate $R^{(i)}$;
**end while**
**Return** $R^*$.

---

The algorithm operates in two layers, i.e., the inner layer optimizes the UAV location and IRS phase shifts to enhance the D2D channel quality, while the outer layer performs power control under the worst-case covertness constraint derived from multiple eavesdroppers. This structure not only reduces computational complexity but also explicitly accounts for the spatial randomness of eavesdroppers by identifying and suppressing the most detrimental Willie in each iteration. The proposed method achieves a complexity of $O(K+M)$, which is significantly lower than that of exhaustive search with $O(L^{(K+4)}M)$, where $L$ is defined as the number of discretization levels used for each continuous optimization variable in an exhaustive search strategy. Moreover, the proposed AO algorithm shows good scalability, as its computational complexity increases approximately linearly with the number of IRS elements $K$ and eavesdroppers $M$, ensuring practical feasibility even in large-scale scenarios.

## 6 Numerical Results

In this section, we verify the proposed scheme and analyze the effects of key parameters on covertness, cellular link performance, and D2D covert communication rate. Without loss of generality, the location is set to be unity, that is

$\mathbf{q}_t = (0, 0, 0)$, $\mathbf{q}_r = (300, 0, 0)$, and $\mathbf{q}_b = (100, 100, 0)$ and the path loss exponent is $\alpha = 4$. The UAV hovers at the altitude $H = 100$ m. Besides, the $\iota = 1/3$, where $\iota$ is the ratio of $H$ to $d_{tr}$. Where $D$ is the maximum detection radius, and $D = 80$ m. Furthermore, without losing generality, assuming that the received noise variance is the same, i.e., $\sigma_w^2 = \sigma_r^2 = \sigma_c^2 = 5$ dB, $\beta_0 = -20$ dB.

### 6.1 $m$-Th Willie's Minimum Error Detection Probability

As shown in Fig. 2(a), it illustrates the relationship between the detection threshold $\tau_{(m)}$ and the minimum error detection probability $\xi_{(m)}$. The results show that the function $\xi_{(m)}$ exhibits a "convex-downward" behavior, i.e., there exists a unique optimal detection threshold $\tau_{(m)}^*$ that minimizes the error probability to $\xi_{(m)}^*$. When $\tau_{(m)} < \tau_{(m)}^*$, the false alarm probability $P_{FA}$ dominates, causing $\xi_{(m)}$ decrease with increasing $\tau$. Whereas when $\tau_{(m)} > \tau_{(m)}^*$, the missed detection probability $P_{MD}$ becomes the dominant factor, leading to an increase in $\xi_{(m)}$ as $\tau_{(m)}$ grows. In particular, a comparison among the three power configurations reveals that, with the AN power fixed at $P_b = 23$ dB, reducing the covert transmit power $P_t$ from 15 dB to 10 dB increases the $\xi_{(m)}^*$, indicating enhanced covertness of the system. Conversely, when $P_t$ is fixed at 15 dB, reducing $P_b$ from 23 dB to 20 dB decreases $\xi_{(m)}^*$, which implies that $m$-th Willie's detection capability is improved and the system covertness is weakened. These results validate the correctness of the theoretical derivations and provide important insights for the joint optimization of $P_t$ and $P_b$ to maximize covert communication performance.

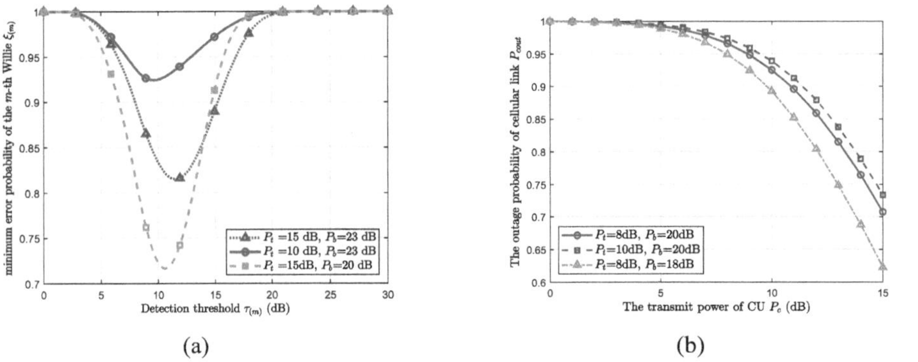


**Fig. 2.** (a) $m$-th Willie's error detection probability $\xi_{(m)}$ versus detection threshold $\tau_{(m)}$ with $\sigma_w^2 = 5$ dB. Three distinct power configurations are considered: $P_t = 15$ dB with $P_b = 23$ dB, $P_t = 10$ dB with $P_b = 23$ dB, and $P_t = 15$ dB with $P_b = 20$ dB. (b) Transmit power of CU $P_c$ versus outage probability of cellular link $P_{\text{cout}}$. Three cases are given: $P_t = 8$ dB with $P_b = 20$ dB, $P_t = 8$ dB with $P_b = 18$ dB, and $P_t = 10$ dB with $P_b = 20$ dB, where $P_c^{\max} = 15$ dB, $\varphi = 0.5$, $R_c = 1$, and $\sigma_c^2 = 5$ dB.

### 6.2 Outage Probability of Cellular Link

Figure 2(b) shows the relationship between the cellular outage probability $P_{\text{cout}}$ versus the transmit power of the cellular user $P_c$, under three different configurations of $P_t$ and $P_b$. The results demonstrate that $P_{\text{cout}}$ decreases monotonically with increasing $P_c$ across all configurations, which aligns perfectly with the theoretical analysis derived from Eq. (35). A higher $P_t$ (e.g., from 8 dB to 10 dB) raises $P_{\text{cout}}$ due to increased interference, while lowering the $P_b$ (e.g., from 20 dB to 18 dB) reduces $P_{\text{cout}}$ by easing self-interference. These results highlight the need to carefully balance $P_t$ and $P_b$ to maintain both covertness and cellular reliability.

### 6.3 UAV-IRS-Assisted D2D Covert Communication Rate

This section analyzes the overall covert communication performance of the UAV-IRS-assisted D2D system. Specifically, we compared the covert communication rate $R_r$ under different configurations, investigated the impact of key optimization variables on system performance, and evaluated various optimization strategies.

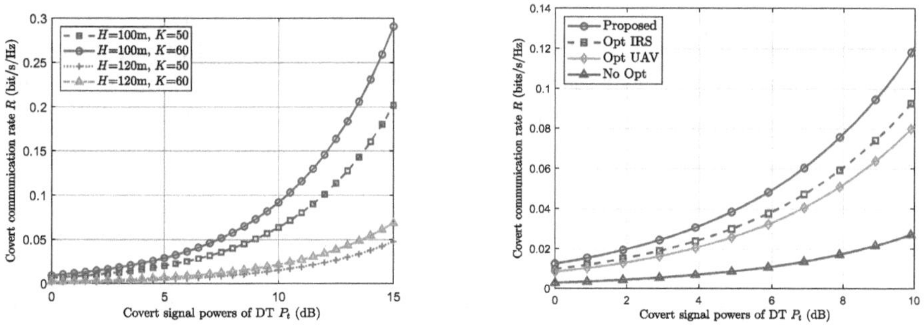


(a) (b)

**Fig. 3.** (a) Covert communication rate $R$ versus transmit power $P_t$ for different UAV flight altitudes and IRS element numbers. The parameters are set as $\beta_0 = -20$ dB, $d_{tr} = 300$ m, $P_b = 25$ dB, $\sigma_r^2 = 5$ dB, and $\alpha = 4$. (b) Comparison of $R_r$ under different schemes, where $P_t^{max} = 10$ dB, $P_b = 20$ dB, $K = 50$, $\sigma_w = 5$ dB, $\beta_0 = -20$ dB, $\epsilon = 0.1$, and $\gamma = 0.2$.

Figure 3(a) illustrates the covert communication rate $R$ as a function of the transmit power $P_t$ for different UAV flight altitudes $H$ and numbers of IRS reflecting elements $K$. Increasing the UAV altitude slightly enlarges the transmission distance $d_{tu}$ and $d_{ur}$, resulting in a lower rate. Similarly, a small increase in the number of IRS elements from 50 to 60 brings gain under the current channel parameters. These results indicate that, in long-distance and high-loss scenarios, enhancing the IRS scale or reducing the UAV altitude would be essential to achieve a noticeable covert rate.

Figure 3(b) compares the covert communication rates $R$ under four strategies, i.e., joint UAV+IRS optimization (Proposed), only IRS optimization (Opt IRS), only UAV optimization (Opt UAV), and no optimization. Results show that the baseline without optimization performs the worst, while both Opt UAV and Opt IRS bring noticeable improvements. Among them, the joint UAV+IRS scheme achieves the highest covert rate across all transmit powers, confirming the effectiveness of combining UAV mobility and IRS phase adjustment in scenarios involving multiple eavesdroppers.

## 7 Conclusion

In this paper, we proposed a UAV-IRS-assisted D2D covert communication framework against multiple spatially random eavesdroppers. By integrating UAV mobility, IRS phase reconfiguration, and AN generation at the base station, the system is able to enhance covertness while maintaining reliable cellular performance. To address the non-convex joint optimization problem, a hierarchical alternating optimization algorithm was developed, yielding efficient solutions for UAV location, IRS phase shifts, and power allocation. Analytical results demonstrate that the proposed scheme effectively improves the covert communication rate compared with baseline methods, and highlight the importance of jointly optimizing UAV and IRS parameters in interference-limited spectrum-sharing networks. It is also worth noting that the proposed optimization relies on certain CSI assumptions, and future research will focus on developing robust schemes under imperfect or statistical CSI to improve practical applicability.

## References

1. Bash, B.A., Goeckel, D., Towsley, D.: Limits of reliable communication with low probability of detection on awgn channels. IEEE J. Sel. Areas Commun. **31**(9), 1921–1930 (2013). https://doi.org/10.1109/JSAC.2013.130923
2. Chen, X., An, J., Xiong, Z., Xing, C., Zhao, N., Yu, F.R., Nallanathan, A.: Covert communications: A comprehensive survey. IEEE Communications Surveys & Tutorials **25**(2), 1173–1198 (2023). https://doi.org/10.1109/COMST.2023.3263921
3. Chen, X., Chang, Z., Liu, M., Zhao, N., Hämäläinen, T., Niyato, D.: Uav-irs assisted covert communication: Introducing uncertainty via phase shifting. IEEE Wireless Communications Letters **13**(1), 103–107 (2024). https://doi.org/10.1109/LWC.2023.3321957
4. Jiang, Y., Wang, L., Chen, H.H.: Covert communications in d2d underlaying cellular networks with antenna array assisted artificial noise transmission. IEEE Trans. Veh. Technol. **69**(3), 2980–2992 (2020). https://doi.org/10.1109/TVT.2020.2966538
5. Jiang, Y., Wang, L., Chen, H.H.: Covert communications with randomly distributed adversaries in wireless energy harvesting enabled d2d underlaying cellular networks. IEEE Trans. Inf. Forensics Secur. **18**, 5401–5415 (2023). https://doi.org/10.1109/TIFS.2023.3307931

6. Jiang, Y., Wang, L., Chen, H.H., Shen, X.: Physical layer covert communication in b5g wireless networks–its research, applications, and challenges. Proc. IEEE **112**(1), 47–82 (2024). https://doi.org/10.1109/JPROC.2024.3364256
7. Jiang, Y., Wang, L., Zhao, H., Chen, H.H.: Covert communications in d2d underlaying cellular networks with power domain noma. IEEE Syst. J. **14**(3), 3717–3728 (2020). https://doi.org/10.1109/JSYST.2020.2967089
8. Jiang, Y., Wang, Y., Wu, H., Liu, Y., Hu, L.: Energy-efficient covert offloading in blockchain-enabled iot: Joint artificial noise and computation resource allocation. IEEE Internet Things J. **12**(6), 6889–6901 (2025). https://doi.org/10.1109/JIOT.2024.3491431
9. Qian, Y., Yang, C., Mei, Z., Zhou, X., Shi, L., Li, J.: On joint optimization of trajectory and phase shift for irs-uav assisted covert communication systems. IEEE Trans. Veh. Technol. **72**(10), 12873–12883 (2023). https://doi.org/10.1109/TVT.2023.3271461
10. Shahidinejad, A., Abawajy, J.: Decentralized lattice-based device-to-device authentication for the edge-enabled iot. IEEE Syst. J. **17**(4), 6623–6633 (2023). https://doi.org/10.1109/JSYST.2023.3319280
11. Sobers, T.V., Bash, B.A., Guha, S., Towsley, D., Goeckel, D.: Covert communication in the presence of an uninformed jammer. IEEE Trans. Wireless Commun. **16**(9), 6193–6206 (2017). https://doi.org/10.1109/TWC.2017.2720736
12. Sun, R., Yang, B., Shen, Y., Jiang, X., Taleb, T.: Covertness and secrecy study in untrusted relay-assisted d2d networks. IEEE Internet Things J. **10**(1), 17–30 (2023). https://doi.org/10.1109/JIOT.2022.3201021
13. Wang, C., Chen, X., An, J., Xiong, Z., Xing, C., Zhao, N., Niyato, D.: Covert communication assisted by uav-irs. IEEE Trans. Commun. **71**(1), 357–369 (2023). https://doi.org/10.1109/TCOMM.2022.3220903
14. Wang, F., Swindlehurst, A.L.: Applications of absorptive reconfigurable intelligent surfaces in interference mitigation and physical layer security. IEEE Trans. Wireless Commun. **23**(5), 3918–3931 (2024). https://doi.org/10.1109/TWC.2023.3312693
15. Wang, S., Yang, B., Wang, W., Shen, S., Jiang, X.: On uav-irs-aided covert communication of d2d-enabled cellular networks. In: 2023 International Conference on Networking and Network Applications (NaNA). pp. 58–63 (2023). https://doi.org/10.1109/NaNA60121.2023.00018
16. Yang, B., Taleb, T., Fan, Y., Shen, S.: Mode selection and cooperative jamming for covert communication in d2d underlaid uav networks. IEEE Network **35**(2), 104–111 (2021). https://doi.org/10.1109/MNET.011.2000100
17. Yang, Y., Yang, B., Shen, S., She, Y., Jiang, X., Taleb, T.: Covert communications for intelligent reflecting surface-enabled d2d networks. IEEE Transactions on Mobile Computing pp. 1–13 (2025). https://doi.org/10.1109/TMC.2025.3583779
18. Zuo, Y., Jiao, J., Sun, R., Shen, Y., Chen, Y., Yang, W., Jiang, X.: Covert communication in d2d underlaying cellular networks with multiple colluding wardens. IEEE Internet Things J. **12**(11), 16559–16573 (2025). https://doi.org/10.1109/JIOT.2025.3533481

# Credibility Mechanism Enabled Trusted Radio Environment Map Construction with Improved Kriging Estimation

Liubi Huang[1(✉)], Wei Wang[2], Xiaolong Hu[3], and Yiliang Liu[4]

[1] College of Electronic and Information Engineering, Nanjing University of Aeronautics and Astronautics, Nanjing 211106, China
huanglb@nuaa.edu.cn

[2] School of Information and Communication Engineering, Xi'an Jiaotong University, Xi'an 710049, China
w25wang@xjtu.edu.cn

[3] Air and Missile Defense School, Air Force Engineering University, Xi'an 710051, Shaanxi, China
huxiaolong0@126.com

[4] School of Cyber Science and Engineering, Xi'an Jiaotong University, Xi'an 710049, China
liuyiliang@xjtu.edu.cn

**Abstract.** Existing Radio Environment Map (REM) estimation methods face unreliable perception results due to data forgery and tampering, as well as significant estimation errors. To address these issues, we propose an improved Kriging estimation method based on a reputation mechanism, enhance the accuracy of REM, under malicious and non-uniform nodes distributions. First, when selecting a set of trustworthy nodes, both reputation value and geographical locations are considered to mitigate large estimation errors caused by the non-uniform trustworthy node distribution. Second, a credibility update mechanism and the adaptive credibility threshold are employed to continuously select high-credibility nodes to join the trustworthy set. Simulation results demonstrate that the proposed method can maintain low estimation errors even under non-uniform nodes distributions.

**Keywords:** Radio Environment Map · Kriging Estimation Method · Reputation

## 1 Introduction

The Radio Environment Map (REM) has emerged as an essential framework for characterizing spatial spectrum conditions, thereby facilitating dynamic spectrum access, interference detection, and efficient resource allocation [1–5]. Since spectrum states cannot be directly measured at all spatial locations, REM construction generally relies on interpolation techniques that exploit data collected


Y. Liu et al. (Eds.): ChinaCom 2025, LNICST 711, pp. 208–220, 2027.
https://doi.org/10.1007/978-3-032-33662-0_16

from a limited set of sensing nodes. Developing and maintaining an accurate REM is of critical importance for enhancing spectrum utilization and enabling efficient dynamic spectrum sharing [6].

Among spatial interpolation techniques, Kriging interpolation has become the predominant method for REM construction because of its ability to accurately model spatial correlation [7]. Prior studies have confirmed the effectiveness of Kriging in wireless communication scenarios [8]. For example, [9] employed Kriging to estimate shadow fading components and combined the results with path loss parameters inferred through a Bayesian hierarchical model, leading to the construction of a high-accuracy REM. Similarly, [10,11] applied Kriging to estimate network coverage and predict the signal strength of primary users, thereby improving the accuracy of spectrum databases. The advantages of Kriging were further demonstrated in [12].

Although effective, Kriging requires a large number of widely distributed sensing nodes, while deploying such large-scale systems involves high costs. To reduce deployment expenses and expand sensing coverage, crowdsensing systems have been introduced into REM construction. In [13], a crowdsourcing mechanism was first applied to REM construction, where incentive schemes were designed to encourage terminals participation and Kriging was used for spatial modeling of the crowdsensed data. However, in open environments, the reliability of crowdsensing nodes poses a significant challenge. Some nodes may submit false or malicious data, which can severely compromise REM estimation.

To address this issue, existing research has mainly adopted two types of approaches: machine learning–based methods and reputation–based methods. For instance, [14] proposed a stacking model–based malicious terminals detection approach that utilized ensemble learning to classify terminals. In [15], an intelligent machine learning model was developed to identify and cluster malicious cognitive radio IoT (CR-IoT) terminals, and a blockchain-based framework was introduced to enhance spectrum security and sharing efficiency. A reputation-based solution was presented in [16], where nodes with reputation values above a defined threshold were considered trustworthy and included in the trusted dataset.

Nevertheless, most of these studies assume that trusted nodes are evenly distributed in space, while in practice the sensing nodes are usually randomly distributed, resulting in local estimation bias and reducing the overall quality of the REM. This study proposes a REM estimation method considering malicious nodes. By introducing a node selection mechanism and a dynamic reputation threshold adjustment strategy, the proposed approach effectively mitigates estimation bias caused by falsified data in open environments. The method achieves a balance between estimation accuracy and system robustness. The main contributions are as follows:

- An REM estimation framework integrating geographic information and dynamic reputation evaluation is constructed. A dual verification mechanism, combining spatial distribution rationality and reputation reliability,

is employed to enable accurate spectrum state estimation in the presence of malicious nodes.
- A reputation-based node selection method is developed, by jointly considering the geographic distribution density of nodes and the credibility of historical data.
- An adaptive reputation threshold adjustment algorithm based on estimation error feedback is proposed, which adaptively adjusts the selection range, thereby improving system robustness while maintaining estimation accuracy.

## 2 System Model

As shown in Fig. 1, the REM estimation system consists of a data fusion center and multiple sensing terminalss distributed in different geographic locations. Operating in an open wireless environment, the fusion center is responsible for collecting spectrum sensing data reported by the terminals and constructing the REM for the target area. In this system, each sensing terminal observes the received spectrum power at its current location and uploads the measurement to the fusion center. However, some malicious nodes may provide falsified information, which can degrade the accuracy of REM estimation. To address this, the fusion center evaluates the credibility of each terminal based on its historical behavior and dynamically computes reputation values. It then selects trustworthy and spatially well-distributed nodes by jointly considering reputation and spatial distribution. Finally, spectrum data from these selected nodes are utilized for spatial interpolation, through which the REM of the target area is iteratively estimated. This system architecture lays the foundation for the subsequent algorithm design and performance analysis.

The operation of the proposed system is driven by two core processes. First, trustworthy nodes are selected by combining a dynamic reputation mechanism

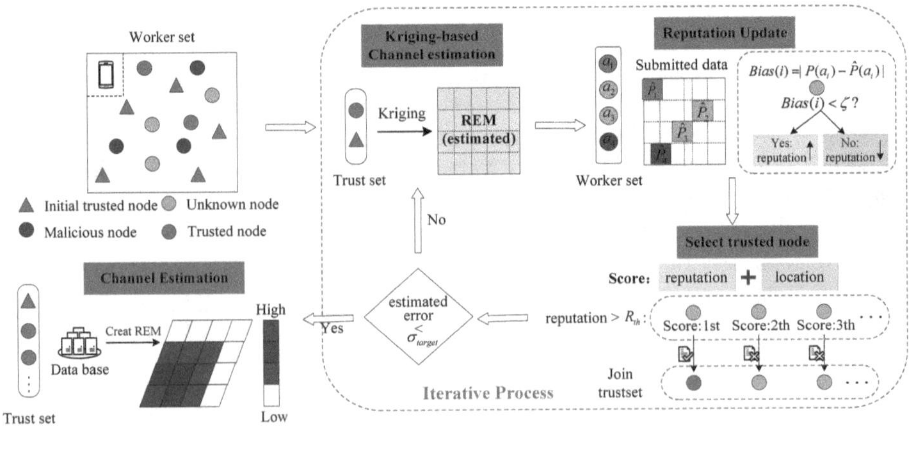


**Fig. 1.** System model.

with geographic location prioritization, ensuring both spatially representative distribution and data reliability. Second, the fusion center performs spatial spectrum state estimation using the Kriging interpolation method based on the set of trustworthy nodes. The estimation error is then calculated and used to dynamically adjust the reputation threshold, thereby enabling robust REM construction.

To provide a systematic description of the proposed mechanism, this study presents two main components: (1) the selection of trustworthy nodes based on reputation values and spatial locations, and (2) the construction of an accurate REM through iterative interpolation using the selected nodes. The overall operational flow of the REM estimation process is illustrated in Fig. 1.

## 3 Trusted Node Selection

In open sensing networks, some terminals may intentionally upload falsified spectrum data, which may compromise the accuracy of REM estimation. To enhance estimation robustness, a trustworthy node selection mechanism is introduced prior to REM estimation. This mechanism selects a high-quality set of nodes for interpolation by jointly considering the historical data credibility and spatial distribution characteristics of each node.

### 3.1 Radio Propagation and Attack Models

In the radio propagation model, the location of sensing terminal $s_i$ is defined as $s_i = (x_i, y_i)$, and the received signal power is denoted by $P(s_i)$. The data vector used for REM interpolation can then be expressed as

$$\mathbf{y} = \big(P(s_1),\, P(s_2),\, \ldots,\, P(s_N)\big)^{\mathsf{T}}. \tag{1}$$

Assume that the primary user (PU) transmitter is located at $s_T = (x_T, y_T)$. The received signal power at a terminal located at position $s$ can be written as

$$P(s) = P_T - L(s) + W, \tag{2}$$

where $P_T$ is the transmit power of the PU, $L(s)$ denotes the path loss between the terminal at $s$ and the PU transmitter at $s_T$, and $W$ represents the shadowing effect, which follows a log-normal distribution with standard deviation $\sigma$.

The spatial correlation of the shadowing component is assumed to follow a typical model [9,16]:

$$\begin{aligned} \rho_{i,j} &= \frac{\mathbb{E}\big[\big(W(s_i) - \mathbb{E}[W(s_i)]\big)\big(W(s_j) - \mathbb{E}[W(s_j)]\big)\big]}{\sigma_i \sigma_j} \\ &\approx \exp\!\left(-\frac{\|x_i - x_j\| \ln 2}{d_{\mathrm{cor}}}\right), \end{aligned} \tag{3}$$

where $\|\cdot\|$ denotes the Euclidean distance, $\sigma_i$ is the standard deviation of the shadowing $W(s_i)$, and $d_{\mathrm{cor}}$ is the correlation distance, defined as the distance at which $\rho_{i,j} = 0.5$.

In open crowdsensing environments, sensing devices are heterogeneous, and some nodes may be attacked, compromised, or manipulated to upload falsified data for malicious purposes. Such erroneous datasets may cause significant errors in REM estimation. This type of attack is referred to as a data falsification attack, where malicious terminals manipulate their sensed spectrum power to contaminate the database. In this paper, a classical data falsification attack strategy is adopted. Specifically, a malicious terminal launches an attack with a probability $P_a$, during which the attack index $\delta$ is multiplied with the sensed power and the falsified value is reported to the database. The reported power of a malicious terminal can be expressed as:

$$P_i = \begin{cases} \delta \cdot P_i^s, & \text{attacks with probability } P_a, \\ P_i^s, & \text{otherwise}, \end{cases} \tag{4}$$

where $P_i^s$ denotes the actual sensed power of terminal $i$, and $P_i$ represents the reported sensing power. Typical attack behaviors include signal amplification ($\delta > 1$) and signal attenuation ($\delta < 1$). This model assumes that attack events occur randomly and that the degree of attack is unpredictable, thereby reflecting the uncertainty of malicious node behavior in real-world environments.

### 3.2 Selection of Trusted Node Set

In wireless shadow fading environment construction, the selection of trusted nodes directly affects the estimation accuracy of Kriging interpolation. Specifically, node selection faces the following two core challenges: (1) Malicious nodes may introduce interpolation errors; (2) Uneven spatial distribution of nodes may lead to estimation bias. As shown in Fig. 1, the selection strategy proposed in this paper comprehensively considers both the data reliability and the spatial distribution characteristics of nodes, ensuring the accuracy of the interpolation results through a dual-objective optimization approach.

After normalization, the trustworthiness $\tilde{R}_i$ and spatial priority $\tilde{D}_i$ of each node jointly determine its evaluation score, which is defined as:

$$Score_i = \alpha \cdot \tilde{R}_i + (1 - \alpha) \cdot \tilde{D}_i, \quad (0 \leq \alpha \leq 1), \tag{5}$$

where $\alpha$ is an adjustable weight factor used to balance the relative importance of the two indicators.

During the trusted node selection process, normalization is applied to unify the scales of trust values and spatial priority indices. The calculation and update of the trust value $R_i$ for terminal $i$ is given in Sect. 4.2. Through linear transformation, the trust value is mapped to $[0, 1]$:

$$\tilde{R}_i = \frac{R_i - R_{\min}}{R_{\max} - R_{\min}}, \tag{6}$$

where $R_{\max}$ and $R_{\min}$ denote the maximum and minimum trust values among candidate nodes, respectively.

The spatial priority index is computed via a grid-based density mechanism. First, the region is divided into $K \times K$ grids. Then, for the grid $g(i)$ containing node $i$, the number of candidate trusted nodes is denoted by $n_{g(i)}$. The spatial priority is then defined as:

$$D_i = \frac{1}{n_{g(i)} + 1}. \tag{7}$$

Finally, normalization is performed as:

$$\tilde{D}_i = \frac{D_i - D_{\min}}{D_{\max} - D_{\min}}, \tag{8}$$

where $D_{\max}$ and $D_{\min}$ are the maximum and minimum spatial priority values among candidate nodes.

These two normalized indicators are fused to form the final comprehensive score. The weight factor $\alpha$ allows adjusting the relative importance of data reliability and spatial coverage uniformity according to the specific requirements of the environment.

**Algorithm 1:** Trusted Node Set Selection

**Input**: Candidate node set $V$, required node count $k$, weight $\alpha$, reputation value $R_i$, geographical location $s_i$
**Output**: Trusted node set $S$
Initialize $S \leftarrow \varnothing$, grid counter $n_{\sigma(i)} \leftarrow 0$;
**while** $|S| < k$ **do**
  **for** *each* $s_i \in V \setminus S$ **do**
    Calculate $\bar{R}_i$ according to (6);
    Query $n_{\sigma(i)}$ in current grid;
    Compute $\tilde{D}_i$ according to (8);
    Calculate $Score_i$ according to (5);
  **end**
  Select node $s^*$ with the highest $Score_i$ to join the trusted set $S \leftarrow S \cup \{s^*\}$;
  Update $n_{\sigma(i)}$;
**end**

# 4 REM Estimation Against Malicious Attacks

## 4.1 Kriging Estimation

Kriging estimation is the mainstream method for constructing the REM. The interpolation formula for estimating the received signal power at an unknown location $s_j$ is given as:

$$\hat{P}(s_j) = \sum_{i=l}^{N} \omega(i) P(s_i), \tag{9}$$

where $\omega(i)$ denotes the interpolation weight, and $P(s_i)$ represents the received signal power at node $s_i$.

Ordinary kriging assumes that the expectation of the random field $P(s_i)$ within the measurement region is constant, and the spatial variability of $P(s_i)$ (variance function) remains homogeneous across the region. According to (2) and (9), for the target $s_j$, the shadowing component $W(s_j)$ and the interpolation estimate $\hat{P}(s_j)$ satisfy the Kriging equation:

$$P(s_j) = P_T - 10\eta \log_{10} \|s_j - s_T\| + \sum_{i=1}^{N} \omega(x_i) \cdot \Big(P(x_i) - (\hat{P}_T - 10\eta \log_{10} \|x_i - s_T\|)\Big), \tag{10}$$

where $P_T$ and $\eta$ denote the estimated transmit power and the path loss exponent, respectively.

The optimal interpolation estimate of the unknown point $s_j$, denoted $\hat{P}(x_j)$, is obtained through the weighted combination of observed values $P(s_i)$ at the sampling nodes, with the weights $\omega(i)$ determined to guarantee unbiasedness. Specifically, the weights must satisfy the normalization constraint: $\sum_{i=1}^{N} \omega(i) = 1$.

This constraint ensures that the interpolation result is not affected by systematic bias. The optimization objective of ordinary Kriging is to minimize the estimation variance $\sigma_i^2$,

$$\min \sigma_i^2 = Var[\hat{P}(s_j) - P(s_j)], \tag{11}$$

so as to achieve the best linear unbiased estimation of the true value $P(s_j)$.

To solve for the optimal weights under this constraint, a Lagrange multiplier $\mu$ is introduced. The objective function can be expressed as

$$\phi(\omega(i), \mu) = \sigma_i^2 - 2\mu \left( \sum_{i=1}^{N} \omega(i) - 1 \right). \tag{12}$$

Taking the derivative of the objective function yields the analytical solution of the weights. The semivariogram function is defined as

$$\gamma(d_{i,j}) = \tfrac{1}{2} Var\left[W(x_i) - W(x_j)\right], \tag{13}$$

where $d_{i,j} = \|s_i - s_j\|$. Thus, the estimation variance can be expressed as

$$\sigma_i^2 = \sum_{i=1}^{N} \sum_{j=1}^{N} \omega_i \omega_j \gamma(d_{i,j}) - 2 \sum_{i=1}^{N} \omega_i \gamma(d_{i,j}) + 2 \sum_{i=1}^{N} \omega_i \mu. \tag{14}$$

Based on (12), the analytical solution of the weights $\omega(i)$ can be derived accordingly,

$$\begin{pmatrix} \boldsymbol{\omega} \\ \mu \end{pmatrix} = \begin{pmatrix} \mathbf{A} & \mathbf{1} \\ \mathbf{1}^{\mathrm{T}} & 0 \end{pmatrix}^{-1} \begin{pmatrix} \mathbf{g} \\ 1 \end{pmatrix} \tag{15}$$

$$\text{where} \quad \mathbf{A}_{ij} = \gamma(d_{i,j}), \quad \mathbf{g}_i = \gamma(d_{i,j}), \quad \mathbf{1} = (1 \cdots 1)^{\mathrm{T}}$$

To evaluate the entire communication region, the global average prediction error can be expressed as

$$\varepsilon_k = \sqrt{\frac{1}{M}\sum_{j=1}^{M}\sigma^2(s_j)}, \tag{16}$$

where $M$ denotes the number of grid points in the region to be estimated.

### 4.2 Reputation-Based REM Estimation

Using the available dataset $\mathcal{S}$, the received power at estimation node $s_i$ can be predicted as $\hat{P}(s_i)$. The absolute deviation between the reported value $P_{s_i}$ and the estimated value $\hat{P}_{s_i}$ at iteration $k$ is given by

$$\mathrm{Bias}_k(i) = \left|P_{s_i} - \hat{P}_{s_i}\right|. \tag{17}$$

To normalize the deviation, we define

$$\mathrm{Bias}_k(i) = \frac{\mathrm{Bias}_k(i) - \min_k}{\max_k - \min_k}, \tag{18}$$

where $\max_k$ and $\min_k$ denote the maximum and minimum deviation at iteration $k$, respectively.

In order to mitigate the adverse impact of abnormal nodes with excessive deviations, an additional normalization is applied to eliminate such nodes. The normalized deviation degree of node $s_i$ is calculated as

$$o_k(i) = \frac{\mathrm{Bias}_k(i) - \mu_k}{\sigma_k}, \tag{19}$$

where $\mu_k$ and $\sigma_k$ denote the mean and standard deviation of deviations at iteration $k$, respectively. If $o_k(i) > \theta$, where $\theta$ is a predefined threshold, node $s_i$ is regarded as an abnormal node and excluded from the normalization process.

Based on the normalized deviation, the reputation value is updated according to

$$R_{k+1}(i) = \begin{cases} R_k(i) + \alpha, & \text{if } \mathrm{Bias}_k(i) < \zeta, \\ R_k(i) - \beta, & \text{otherwise,} \end{cases} \tag{20}$$

where $\alpha$ and $\beta$ denote the reward step size and the penalty step size, respectively, and $\zeta$ is the tolerance threshold for deviation. In order to incentivize nodes to provide truthful sensing reports, the reward step size is generally designed to be smaller than the penalty step size, $\beta > \alpha$.

**Algorithm 2:** Reputation-Based REM Estimation

```
Input: Initial trusted node set S_init, candidate node set S_0, initial reputation
       threshold R_th, target error σ_target, maximum iteration number K_max,
       grid size M, redefined threshold θ.
Output: Optimal REM estimation result.
Initialization: count = 0, pre_σ = ∞ ;
for k = 1 to K_max do
    Select trusted node set S_trust according to Algorithm 1 ;
    Compute REM using (10) and (15) ;
    Compute current estimation error ε_k using (14) and (16) ;
    if ε_k < σ_target then
        return REM ;
    end
    if |ε_k − pre_σ| < ε then
        count = count + 1 ;
    end
    else
        count = 0 ;
    end
    for each node i in S_0 do
        Compute deviation Bias_k(i) and o_k(i) using (17) and (18) ;
        Update reputation using (20) ;
    end
    if count > 5 then
        R_th = 0.9 · R_th ;
        count = 0 ;
    end
end
return REM ;
```

A reputation-based algorithm for REM estimation is proposed, aiming to achieve high-precision map construction through dynamic reputation evaluation and iterative optimization. The procedure of the algorithm can be summarized as follows: Firstly, the power deviation of each node is calculated. Abnormal data are filtered using standardization and normalization techniques, and the reputation values of nodes are dynamically updated through a reward-and-penalty mechanism. Secondly, nodes with higher reputation are selected to perform Kriging interpolation during each iteration. Finally, the estimation error is evaluated. If the target accuracy is not achieved, the credibility threshold is gradually decrease to expand the candidate set until the desired accuracy is attained or the maximum iteration count is reached. The proposed algorithm integrates statistical detection, reputation assessment, and spatial interpolation within a unified framework. A closed-loop feedback mechanism ensures convergence of estimation errors, while differentiated reward and penalty strategies enable intelligent evaluation of data quality. Ultimately, the algorithm provides reliable results that satisfy the properties of optimal linear unbiased estimation. The specific procedure is detailed in Algorithm 2.

## 5 Simulation Results and Discussions

In this section, simulations are conducted to validate the effectiveness of the proposed algorithm, the simulation parameters are shown in Table 1.

**Table 1.** Simulation Parameters

| Parameter | Value |
|---|---|
| Transmission power $P_t$ | 29 dBm |
| Shadowing standard deviation $\sigma_i$ | 6 |
| Correlation distance $d_{cor}$ | 20 m |
| Attack factor of malicious terminals $\sigma$ | 0.6 |
| Attack probability of malicious terminals $P_a$ | 0.7 |
| Proportion of malicious terminals | 0.3 |
| Initial reputation $R_0$ | 1 |
| Reward step size $\alpha$ | 0.1 |
| Penalty step size $\beta$ | 0.3 |
| Grid size for training data $K$ | $5 \times 5$ |
| Grid size for estimation region $M$ | $20 \times 20$ |

To validate the superiority of the proposed trustworthy node selection method in scenarios with uneven node distribution, we compare its performance

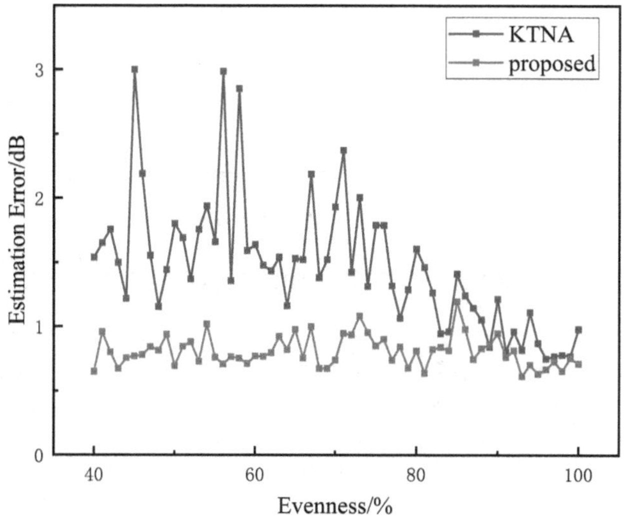


**Fig. 2.** Estimation error varies with node distribution evenness.

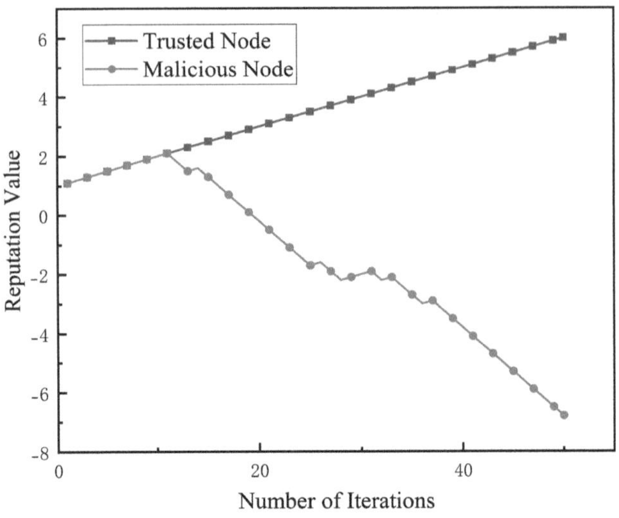


**Fig. 3.** The reputation value of a node changes with the number of iterations.

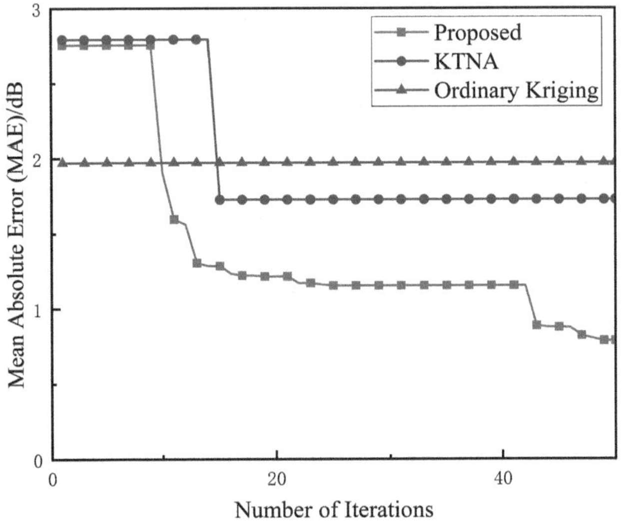


**Fig. 4.** Estimation error varies with the number of iterations.

with the KTNA method [16]. Figure 2 compares the estimation error performance of both methods. The results show that they perform similarly when the nodes are evenly distributed. However, under uneven distribution, the proposed method has significantly lower estimation error than KTNA.

To validate the effectiveness of the proposed reputation mechanism in dynamic environments, we evaluate the node reputation and REM estimation accuracy. Figure 3 illustrates the variation pattern of node reputation values during iterations. It can be observed that the reputation values of trustworthy nodes continuously increase, while those of malicious nodes significantly decrease, demonstrating that the proposed method can effectively distinguish and punish malicious nodes. Additionally, Fig. 4 compares the average estimation error with the proposed method, the KTNA method, and ordinary Kriging. Due to the absence of a reputation mechanism, ordinary Kriging maintains a consistently high estimation error. In contrast, the proposed method accumulates a sufficient number of high-reputation nodes to form a trustworthy set by the 14th iteration, resulting in a marked reduction in average estimation error. Throughout the entire iteration process, the proposed method consistently maintained a lower estimation error level.

## 6 Conclusion

In this paper we have proposed an improved Kriging estimation method to achieve trusted radio environment map construction. By integrating historical data reliability assessment, and a dynamic adjustment strategy, the method effectively enhances the accuracy of radio environment mapping. Experimental results demonstrate that this method maintains stable estimation performance, even with malicious nodes and non-uniform nodes distributions. It significantly reduces estimation errors caused by unreliable data and uneven spatial sampling.

## References

1. Li, Z., Wang, W., Wu, Q., Wang, X.: Multi-operator dynamic spectrum sharing for wireless communications: a consortium blockchain enabled framework. IEEE Trans. Cognitive Commun. Networking (TCCN) **9**(1), 3–15 (2023)
2. Chen, W., Wang, W., Li, Z., Ye, Q., Wu, Q.: Joint pricing and task allocation for blockchain empowered crowd spectrum sensing. Peer-to-Peer Networking Appl. **15**, 783–792 (2022)
3. Huang, L., Wang, W., Cao, P., Liu, Y.: Joint spectrum sensing and resource allocation mechanism with untrusted sensing nodes. Chinese Journal on Internet of Things (2025). accepted
4. Q. Wu, W. Wang, Z. Li, B. Zhou, Y. Huang, and X. Wang: SpectrumChain: a disruptive dynamic spectrum-sharing framework for 6G. Sci. China Inf. Sci. **66**(3), 130302 (2023)
5. Zhao, Y., Morales, L., Gaeddert, J., Bae, K.K., Um, J.-S., J.H.: Reed: applying radio environment maps to cognitive wireless regional area networks. In: 2nd IEEE International Symposium on New Frontiers in Dynamic Spectrum Access Networks, pp. 115–118 (2007)
6. Katagiri, K., Fujii, T.: Radio environment map updating procedure considering change of surrounding environment. In: 2020 IEEE Wireless Communications and Networking Conference Workshops (WCNCW), pp. 1–6 (2020)
7. Alaya-Feki, A.B.H., Jemaa, S.B., Sayrac, B., Houze, P., Moulines, E.: Informed spectrum usage in cognitive radio networks: interference cartography. In: IEEE 19th International Symposium on Personal, Indoor and Mobile Radio Communications, pp. 1–5 (2008)

8. Achtzehn, A., Riihijärvi, J., Vargas, G.M., Petrova, M., Mähönen, P.: Improving coverage prediction for primary multi-transmitter networks operating in the TV whitespaces. In: 2012 9th Annual IEEE Communications Society Conference on Sensor, Mesh and Ad Hoc Communications and Networks (SECON), pp. 623–631. (2012)
9. Xia, H., Zha, S., Huang, J., Liu, P.: Radio environment map construction by residual kriging based on bayesian hierarchical model. In: 2023 IEEE 7th International Symposium on Electromagnetic Compatibility (ISEMC), pp. 1–6 (2023)
10. Phillips, C., Ton, M., Sicker, D., Grunwald, D.: Practical radio environment mapping with geostatistics. In: 2012 IEEE International Symposium on Dynamic Spectrum Access Networks, pp. 422–433 (2012)
11. Achtzehn, A., Riihijärvi, J., Mähönen, P.: Improving accuracy for TVWS geolocation databases: results from measurement-driven estimation approaches. In: 2014 IEEE International Symposium on Dynamic Spectrum Access Networks (DYSPAN), pp. 392–403 (2014)
12. Ying, X., Kim, C.W., Roy, S.: Revisiting TV coverage estimation with measurement-based statistical interpolation. In: 2015 7th International Conference on Communication Systems and Networks (COMSNETS), pp. 1–8 (2015)
13. Ying, X., Roy, S., Poovendran, R.: Incentivizing crowdsourcing for radio environment mapping with statistical interpolation. In: 2015 IEEE International Symposium on Dynamic Spectrum Access Networks (DySPAN), pp. 365–374 (2015)
14. Benazzouza, S., Ridouani, M., Salahdine, F., Hayar, A.: A novel prediction model for malicious users detection and spectrum sensing based on stacking and deep learning. Sensors **22**(17), 6477 (2022)
15. Miah, M.S., Hossain, M.S., A.G.: Armada: machine learning-based malicious users detection in blockchain-enabled CR-IoT network for secured spectrum access. In: 2022 IEEE International Symposium on Broadband Multimedia Systems and Broadcasting (BMSB), pp. 1–6 (2022)
16. Gao, Y., Fujii, T.: Kriging-based trust nodes aided REM construction under threatening environment. In: 2022 IEEE 96th Vehicular Technology Conference (VTC2022-Fall), pp. 1–7 (2022)

# Air-Ground Networking and Low-Altitude Intelligent Systems

# Interference-Aware Resource Scheduling for UAVs-Assisted Agriculture Monitoring

Yining Zhang, Lili Chen(✉), Wenbin Sun, Qian Xu, Haochen Liu, and Ling Wang

Northwestern Polytechnical University, Xi'an, China
yiningzhang@mail.nwpu.edu.cn,
{lilichen,sunwenbin,qianxu,haochenliu,lingwang}@nwpu.edu.cn

**Abstract.** Unmanned aerial vehicles (UAVs) offer a versatile platform for real-time data collection in smart agriculture, where clusters of ground sensors monitor environmental variables across distributed field plots. This paper proposes an interference-aware resource scheduling framework for UAV-assisted agriculture monitoring, jointly optimizing UAV allocation, cluster-level node selection, and collaborative beamforming weight design under energy and practical constraints. Leveraging zero-forcing beamforming, the framework shapes each cluster's uplink transmission to nullify interference at non-target UAVs while maintaining coherent gain at the intended receiver. We formulate the problem as a mixed-integer program that balances SINR-based throughput, scheduling conflicts, and sensor energy consumption, and develop a lightweight distributed algorithm integrating coordinated scheduling with iterative weight computation. Numerical results demonstrate that our scheme consistently outperforms baselines. It reduces data-collection latency as UAV numbers scale, and sustains high network capacity across varying UAV deployment densities.

**Keywords:** Agriculture monitoring · Unmanned aerial vehicle · Collaborative beamforming · Inter-cluster interference

## 1 Introduction

Unmanned aerial vehicles (UAVs) have emerged as an effective solution for data collection in wireless sensor networks (WSNs) in recent years, particularly in scenarios involving disaster recovery, emergency response, and environmental monitoring [1–3]. UAVs offer significant advantages such as high mobility, flexible coverage, and reduced infrastructure requirements [4,5]. By leveraging these characteristics, UAVs have gained significant traction in the domain of smart agriculture, where timely and fine-grained monitoring of soil moisture, temperature, crop health and microclimate is critical for optimizing irrigation, fertilization and pest control [6,7]. By overflying large fields or greenhouse complexes,


Y. Liu et al. (Eds.): ChinaCom 2025, LNICST 711, pp. 223–235, 2027.
https://doi.org/10.1007/978-3-032-33662-0_17

UAVs can collect data from spatially distributed sensor clusters more flexibly and rapidly than fixed towers or satellite links, while dramatically reducing deployment cost and response latency.

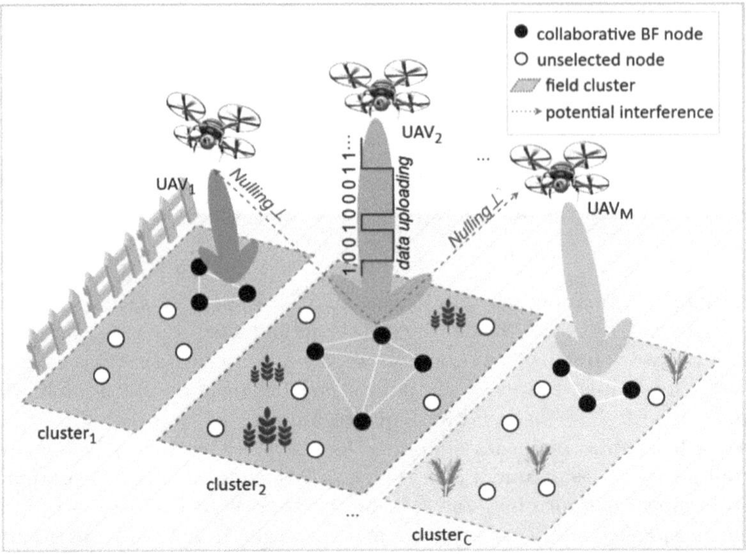


**Fig. 1.** Illustration of the proposed interference-aware collaborative beamforming and scheduling framework in agriculture monitoring scenario.

Most existing UAV-assisted agriculture monitoring systems adopt a cluster-based data-collection paradigm in which ground sensors are organized into per-field or per-plot clusters, and a single cluster head aggregates and uplinks the measurements to the UAV [8–10]. Although this simplifies medium access and reduces control overhead, the single-link uplink often suffers from limited spatial diversity and low reliability when the cluster head's channel to the UAV is obstructed by foliage or terrain irregularities. Motivated by these shortcomings, several recent studies about distributed data collection have begun to replace single-node uplinks with collaborative beamforming [11–13]. Collaborative beamforming allows multiple distributed sensor nodes to synchronously transmit the same symbol after phase-and-amplitude pre-compensation, so that they form a virtual antenna array and their signals add coherently at the UAV [14]. In practice, this approach typically requires that all participating nodes within a cluster hold identical data, which can be achieved via a local data synchronization step prior to uplink transmission. As the energy cost of such short-range, intra-cluster data exchange is negligible compared to the air-to-ground transmission cost, local synchronization does not significantly impact the overall energy consumption or network lifetime. Although collaborative beamforming boosts the received SNR and enlarges the communication range, most existing

UAV-aided collaborative beamforming studies assume single-cluster activation or orthogonal resources, overlooking the inter-cluster interference that occurs when multiple clusters share the same channel. In dense agricultural deployments where adjacent field plots correspond to neighboring clusters, simultaneous collaborative beamforming transmissions on the same frequency incur severe inter-cluster interference.

Motivated by these considerations, we propose a joint optimization framework that simultaneously determines UAV–cluster scheduling, intra-cluster node selection, and collaborative zero-forcing beamforming weights under constraints on node energy, UAV availability and interference. At the start of each time slot, UAVs exchange large-scale channel state information (CSI), residual data and node-energy information to cooperatively schedule one cluster per UAV. Each selected cluster's head then picks a subset of its sensor nodes based on their large-scale gains and remaining energy. The serving UAV triggers a short pilot phase to measure the small-scale uplink channels of those nodes, constructs the interference matrix, and computes zero-forcing beamforming weights that null out signals at unintended UAVs. Finally, the chosen nodes transmit data with their assigned weights, the UAVs decode the payload and update each cluster's remaining data and nodes' energy levels before the next slot. As illustrated in Fig. 1, sensor nodes within each cluster cooperatively transmit synchronized signals to their designated UAV, with only a selected subset (highlighted by circles) participating in beamforming; dashed red arrows denote representative potential inter-cluster interference (only a subset of all possible interference links is shown for clarity). By orthogonalizing each cluster's transmit beam with respect to the channel subspaces of non-intended UAVs via zero-forcing, the proposed framework suppresses inter-cluster interference and enhances the reliability and throughput at the intended UAVs.

The main contributions of this paper are summarized as follows:

- We propose an interference-aware system model for UAV-assisted agriculture monitoring data collection that jointly designs UAV scheduling, intra-cluster node selection, and collaborative beamforming weights under energy and scheduling constraints.
- We formulate a mixed-integer optimization problem that maximizes SINR-based throughput while penalizing scheduling conflicts and energy consumption.
- We develop a lightweight algorithm based on zero-forcing beamforming and coordinated scheduling, demonstrating via simulations a significant throughput gain and interference suppression compared to other baseline schemes.

The remainder of the paper is organized as follows. Section 2 presents the detailed system model and problem formulation. Section 3 describes the proposed interference-aware scheduling and beamforming algorithm. Simulation results are provided and discussed in Sect. 4, followed by conclusions and future research directions in Sect. 5.

## 2 Model Setup and Problem Formulation

We consider a UAV-assisted wireless sensor network deployed for smart agriculture monitoring over a farmland. A total of $N$ ground sensor nodes, each equipped with a single omni-directional antenna, are randomly deployed over several agricultural field plots and grouped into $C$ disjoint clusters $\{S_1, \ldots, S_C\}$, with each cluster representing the sensors within a particular plot and $|S_c| \ll N$. Each cluster $c$ is responsible for monitoring a specific agricultural variable, such as soil moisture, temperature, or crop health, and holds an initial data backlog $D_{c,0}$ bits representing the measurement data to be collected. Prior to data collection, nodes within each cluster have performed local data synchronization so that all members hold identical measurement data, enabling subsequent collaborative beamforming for uplink transmission. Since the energy cost of intra-cluster data exchange over short distances is negligible compared to the high energy required for air-to-ground communications, this synchronization does not significantly impact the overall network lifetime. The system operates on a single carrier of bandwidth $B$ Hz. $M$ UAVs hover at a fixed altitude $H$ and, in each time slot, each UAV collects data from one selected sensor cluster via uplink collaborative beamforming. The data collection process is completed once the UAVs have jointly gathered all the measurement data from every cluster in the field. Such deployment is typical in smart farming scenarios, where fine-grained, real-time data from various plots supports smart irrigation and crop management.

### 2.1 Model Setup

Let $h_{m,n,t}$ denote the channel gain between node $n$ and UAV $m$ at time slot $t$. To reduce signaling overhead, CSI is acquired in two layers. First, a slowly varying large-scale gain $h_{u,n}^{(\mathrm{L})}$ is obtained from node and UAV positions together with a path-loss model; this estimate is exchanged only occasionally. Second, whenever a cluster $c$ is scheduled in slot $t$, its cluster head selects a subset of nodes $S_{c,t} \subseteq S_c$ based on large-scale gains and local energy, then requests those nodes to transmit a short pilot for the serving UAV $u(c)$ to measure the small-scale coefficients $\{h_{u(c),n,t}\}_{n \in S_{c,t}}$.

Scheduling proceeds as follows. All UAVs first exchange the large-scale gains, residual data volumes $D_{c,t}$ and node energies $E_n$, then cooperatively decide which cluster each UAV will serve, yielding binary variables $x_{u,c,t} \in \{0,1\}$ (with $x_{u,c,t} = 1$ if UAV $u$ serves cluster $c$ in slot $t$, and 0 otherwise). After receiving the scheduling decision, each scheduled cluster head selects a subset of nodes $S_{c,t} \subseteq S_c$ for beamforming participation, based on large-scale CSI and residual energy. Selecting only a subset of nodes, rather than involving all cluster members, helps to limit the cumulative energy consumption of the network and reduces the stringent synchronization overhead required for collaborative beamforming across many geographically dispersed nodes. In addition, restricting the number of active nodes ensures that the zero-forcing beamforming design remains tractable, particularly when the available pilot resources are limited.

The selected nodes then transmit uplink pilot sequences, enabling the serving UAV $u(c)$ to estimate the corresponding small-scale air-to-ground channels $\{h_{u(c),n,t}\}_{n\in S_{c,t}}$. Based on these channel estimates, the UAV computes the collaborative beamforming weights $\{w_{n,c,t}\}_{n\in S_{c,t}}$ by imposing a zero-forcing constraint, such that

$$\sum_{n\in S_{c,t}} w_{n,c,t}\, h_{u',n,t} = 0,\ \forall (u',c') \neq (u(c),c), (u',c') \in \mathcal{A}_t,$$

where $\mathcal{A}_t = \{(u',c') \mid x_{u',c',t} = 1\}$ denotes the set of all active UAV–cluster pairs in the current time slot. The beamforming weights $\{w_{n,c,t}\}$ are complex-valued coefficients, with both amplitude and phase jointly adjusted at each node to enable constructive signal combining at the intended UAV and destructive interference at non-target UAVs.

The weights $\{w_{n,c,t}\}$ are then distributed to the participating nodes, which collaboratively upload their data using the assigned weights. Specifically, each active node $n \in S_{c,t}$ applies its assigned weight $w_{n,c,t}$ to modulate the data symbol $s_{c,t}$, and synchronously transmits $x_{n,t} = w_{n,c,t}\, s_{c,t}$ in the uplink. Precise timing and frequency synchronization among participating nodes are assumed to enable effective collaborative beamforming.

### 2.2 Problem Formulation

For any scheduled pair $(u,c) \in \mathcal{A}_t$, the received signal-to-interference-plus-noise ratio (SINR) at UAV $u$ is

$$\mathrm{SINR}_{u,c,t} = \frac{\left|\sum_{n\in S_{c,t}} w_{n,c,t}\, h_{u,n,t}\right|^2}{N_0 + \sum\limits_{\substack{(u',c')\in\mathcal{A}_t \\ c'\neq c}} \left|\sum\limits_{n'\in S_{c',t}} w_{n',c',t}\, h_{u,n',t}\right|^2},$$

where $N_0$ is the noise power. The data rate achieved in slot $t$ is

$$R_{u,c,t} = B\,\Delta\,\log_2\bigl(1 + \mathrm{SINR}_{u,c,t}\bigr),$$

with slot duration $\Delta$.

In time slot $t$, the energy consumed by node $n \in S_{c,t}$ is given by

$$P_{n,c,t} = \Delta |w_{n,c,t}|^2.$$

We introduce binary variables $y_{n,c,t} = 1$ if node $n$ participates in cluster $c$ at time $t$. The decision variables $\{x_{u,c,t}, y_{n,c,t}, w_{n,c,t}\}$ are subject to:

*UAV Scheduling Constraint*: Each UAV can serve at most one cluster per time slot:

$$\sum_{c\in C} x_{u,c,t} \leq 1, \quad \forall u \in U, \forall t.$$

*Cluster Scheduling Constraint*: Each cluster can be served by at most one UAV at a time:

$$\sum_{u \in U} x_{u,c,t} \leq 1, \quad \forall c \in C, \forall t,$$

ensuring no cluster is simultaneously assigned to multiple UAVs.

*Node Participation Constraint*: A node can participate in collaborative beamforming only if its cluster is scheduled on some UAV in that slot:

$$y_{n,c,t} \leq \sum_{u \in U} x_{u,c,t}, \quad \forall n \in S_c, \forall c, \forall t.$$

This ensures nodes only transmit when their cluster is actively being served by a UAV.

*Transmit Power Constraint*: The transmit power of each node is limited by its maximum capability. Equivalently, the magnitude of the beamforming weight for node $n$ cannot exceed the limit set by its maximum power $P_n^{\max}$:

$$|w_{n,c,t}|^2 \leq P_n^{\max} y_{n,c,t}, \quad \forall n \in S_c, \forall c, \forall t,$$

where $P_n^{\max}$ is the maximum transmission power of node $n$.

*Interference Mitigation Constraint*: When multiple clusters transmit in the same slot on the same frequency, their beamforming weights must satisfy interference nulling conditions. Specifically, for any two clusters $c$ and $c'$ scheduled concurrently ($x_{u(c),c,t} = 1$ and $x_{u(c'),c',t} = 1$ with $c' \neq c$), the transmit beams are designed so that cluster $c$'s signal causes no interference at UAV $u(c')$, and vice versa. In mathematical terms:

$$\sum_{n \in S_{c,t}} w_{n,c,t} \, h_{u(c'),n,t} = 0, \quad \forall c' \neq c \text{ active in time } t \,,$$

where $u(c')$ denotes the UAV serving cluster $c'$ in that slot. If a cluster does not have enough participating nodes to satisfy all such orthogonality constraints, this constraint can be relaxed to minimize the interference.

Our objective is to maximise the total network throughput over all $T$ slots while penalising cluster-scheduling conflicts and total energy expenditure:

$$\max_{x,y,w} \sum_{t=1}^{T} \sum_{(u,c) \in \mathcal{A}_t} R_{u,c,t} - \lambda \sum_{t,c} \Big(\sum_{u} x_{u,c,t} - 1\Big)_+ - \gamma \sum_{t,n,c} P_{n,c,t},$$

where $(\cdot)_+ = \max\{0, \cdot\}$ and $\lambda, \gamma > 0$ balance throughput, conflict avoidance and energy efficiency.

## 3 Algorithm Design

We propose an iterative, slot-by-slot algorithm that jointly performs UAV scheduling, intra-cluster node selection, zero-forcing beamforming weight computation, conflict detection, and resource updates. The algorithm proceeds for each time slot $t = 1, \ldots, T$ as follows.

*UAV Scheduling:* At the beginning of each time slot $t$, every UAV $u$ evaluates a priority metric for each cluster $c$ within its coverage region. Specifically, for cluster $c$, UAV $u$ computes

$$\text{Priority}_{u,c,t} = \alpha_1 \cdot \frac{1}{|S_c|} \sum_{n \in S_c} h_{u,n}^{(L)} + \alpha_2 D_{c,t} + \alpha_3 \cdot \frac{1}{|S_c|} \sum_{n \in S_c} E_n,$$

where $h_{u,n}^{(L)}$ is the large-scale channel gain between UAV $u$ and node $n$, $D_{c,t}$ is the remaining data in cluster $c$, $E_n$ is the residual energy of node $n$, and $\alpha_1, \alpha_2, \alpha_3$ are weighting coefficients reflecting the relative importance of channel quality, data backlog, and energy.

Each UAV selects the cluster with the highest priority score within its coverage area as its preferred target. UAVs then exchange their selections to identify any scheduling conflicts (i.e., cases where two or more UAVs prefer the same cluster). Conflicts are resolved by assigning the contested cluster to the UAV with the highest priority score for that cluster, while the others defer to their next-best choices according to their computed metrics. This process continues iteratively until all assignments are conflict-free.

*Node Selection:* The node selection process is based on two main criteria: (i) large-scale channel gain $h_{u(c),n}^{(L)}$ from node $n$ to UAV $u(c)$, and (ii) sufficient residual energy $E_n$ of node $n$ to support the intended transmission.

The cluster head ranks all nodes $n \in S_c$ according to a weighted score:

$$\text{Score}_n = \beta_1 h_{u(c),n}^{(L)} + \beta_2 E_n,$$

where $\beta_1, \beta_2$ are weight factors. The cluster head then selects the top $|S_{c,t}|$ nodes with the highest scores, subject to

$$E_n \geq E^{\min}, \quad \forall n \in S_{c,t},$$

where $E^{\min}$ is a minimum energy threshold for participation.

To ensure that zero-forcing beamforming is feasible, the number of selected nodes must satisfy

$$|S_{c,t}| \geq 1 + N_{\text{int}},$$

where $N_{\text{int}}$ is the number of interference nulls to be placed (i.e., the number of non-target UAVs active in the current slot). This guarantees that there are enough spatial degrees of freedom to support both the desired signal and the required interference suppression.

*Pilot-Based CSI Acquisition and Beamforming Weight Computation:* Once $S_{c,t}$ is fixed, UAV $u(c)$ requests a short uplink pilot from each node $n \in S_{c,t}$. From the pilot echoes, it obtains the instantaneous small-scale CSI $\{h_{u(c),n,t}\}$. These coefficients can be arranged into channel vector

$$\mathbf{h}_{u(c),c,t} = \left[h_{u(c),n,t}\right]_{n \in S_{c,t}} \in \mathbb{C}^{|S_{c,t}|}.$$

**Algorithm 1.** Interference-Aware Scheduling & Beamforming

**for** $t = 1$ **to** $T$ **do**

**UAV scheduling:** each UAV computes $\text{score}_{u,c} = f(h^{(L)}_{u,n}, D_{c,t}, E_n)$, exchanges scores, and sets $x_{u,c,t}$ to avoid conflicts.

**Node selection:** each scheduled cluster $c$ chooses $S_{c,t} \subseteq S_c$ based on large-scale CSI and $E_n$.

**CSI estimation:** UAV $u(c)$ pilots $n \in S_{c,t}$ to measure $h_{u(c),n,t}$ and build $H_{\text{int}}$.

**Weight design:**

$$\begin{aligned} P_{\text{null}} &= I - H^H_{\text{int}}(H_{\text{int}}H^H_{\text{int}})^{-1}H_{\text{int}}, \\ \tilde{\mathbf{w}}_{c,t} &= P_{\text{null}}\mathbf{h}_{u(c),c,t}, \\ w_{n,c,t} &= \sqrt{P^{\max}_n}\frac{[\tilde{\mathbf{w}}_{c,t}]_n}{|[\tilde{\mathbf{w}}_{c,t}]_n|}, \ \forall n \in S_{c,t}. \end{aligned}$$

**Transmission:** nodes in $S_{c,t}$ transmit with $w_{n,c,t}$; UAV measures $\text{SINR}_{u,c,t}$ and computes

$$R_{u,c,t} = B\Delta \log_2(1 + \text{SINR}_{u,c,t}).$$

**Conflict detection and coordination:** For each $c$, if $\sum_u x_{u,c,t} > 1$, record conflict and penalize corresponding $(u, c)$ in next slot.

**Update:**

$$\begin{aligned} D_{c,t+1} &\leftarrow \max(D_{c,t} - R_{u,c,t}, 0), \\ E_n &\leftarrow \max(E_n - |w_{n,c,t}|^2\Delta,\ 0). \end{aligned}$$

**if** all $D_{c,t+1} = 0$ **then**

**break**

**end if**

**end for**

The UAV then computes the unnormalized zero-forcing beamforming vector

$$\tilde{\mathbf{w}}_{c,t} = \left(I - H^H_{\text{int}}(H_{\text{int}}H^H_{\text{int}})^{-1}H_{\text{int}}\right)\mathbf{h}_{u(c),c,t},$$

where $H_{\text{int}}$ denotes the cross-cluster channel matrix

$$H_{\text{int}} = \left[\mathbf{h}^H_{u',c',t}\right]_{(u',c')\in\mathcal{A}_t,\ c'\neq c} \in \mathbb{C}^{(|\mathcal{A}_t|-1)\times|S_{c,t}|}.$$

After normalizing each entry to respect the per-node power constraint $P^{\max}_n$ the beamforming weights are obtained:

$$w_{n,c,t} = \sqrt{P^{\max}_n}\,\frac{[\tilde{\mathbf{w}}_{c,t}]_n}{|[\tilde{\mathbf{w}}_{c,t}]_n|}.$$

*Uplink Transmission and SINR Measurement:* In the scheduled slot, all selected nodes $n \in S_{c,t}$ collaboratively transmit their data symbols, each modulated by its assigned complex beamforming weight $w_{n,c,t}$. The serving UAV $u(c)$ receives the aggregated signal, estimates the resulting SINR, and subsequently decodes the transmitted data.

*Conflict Detection and Coordination:* At the end of each time slot, all UAVs broadcast their measured SINR values and scheduling outcomes to the network. Any remaining scheduling conflicts, i.e., instances where $\sum_u x_{u,c,t} > 1$ for any cluster $c$, or observed high-interference events, are detected and logged. The corresponding UAV–cluster pairings are then flagged to prevent simultaneous scheduling in subsequent slots, thereby enhancing the overall system stability and interference management.

*Resource Update and Termination Check:* Each cluster's remaining data is updated via

$$D_{c,t+1} = \max\bigl(D_{c,t} - R_{u(c),c,t}, 0\bigr),$$

and each participating node's energy is decremented by $\Delta|w_{n,c,t}|^2$. Nodes with depleted energy or clusters with $D_{c,t+1} = 0$ are removed from future scheduling. The algorithm terminates when all clusters' data backlogs reach zero or the maximum slot $T$ is reached.

The proposed algorithm achieves efficient spatial reuse by explicitly incorporating zero-forcing constraints into the beamforming weight design, thereby suppressing inter-cluster interference during each transmission slot. Its adaptive, slot-wise scheduling jointly considers both traffic backlog and residual node energy, ensuring energy-aware and throughput-oriented resource allocation. As demonstrated in Section IV, simulation results confirm that this interference-aware scheduling and beamforming framework significantly enhances aggregate network throughput and link reliability compared to baseline approaches.

## 4 Numerical Results

The simulation scenario investigates an agricultural monitoring scenario where sensor nodes are organized into 6 clusters, each containing 20 nodes distributed within square areas of varying sizes ($800\times800\,\mathrm{m}^2$, $1000\times1000\,\mathrm{m}^2$, or $1200\times1200\,\mathrm{m}^2$). Multiple UAVs, ranging from 2 to 6, hover at a fixed altitude of 100 m to provide connectivity services. The wireless channel between ground nodes and UAVs is modeled using a log-distance path loss with a 2.8 exponent, combined with Rayleigh small-scale fading to capture realistic propagation effects. The system operates over a 5 MHz channel bandwidth under typical thermal noise conditions. Each cluster generates 200-400 Mbits of data to be transmitted to the UAVs, with individual nodes limited to a maximum transmission power of 0.1 W. Each cluster generates between 200 and 400 Mbits of data to be uploaded, and each node has a maximum transmission power of 0.1 W. The simulations run for 30 to 80 time slots, with each slot corresponding to one second of network operation.

The performance evaluation compares three transmission schemes. Direct transmission serves as a baseline in which each UAV collects data from one cluster at a time, using only the single node with the strongest channel for uplink transmission. Round-Robin scheduling employs a fixed cyclic assignment of UAVs to clusters, with each selected cluster utilizing maximum ratio transmission among multiple nodes, but without consideration for inter-cluster interference. The results of these two baseline methods are compared against the proposed interference-aware collaborative beamforming and scheduling approach.

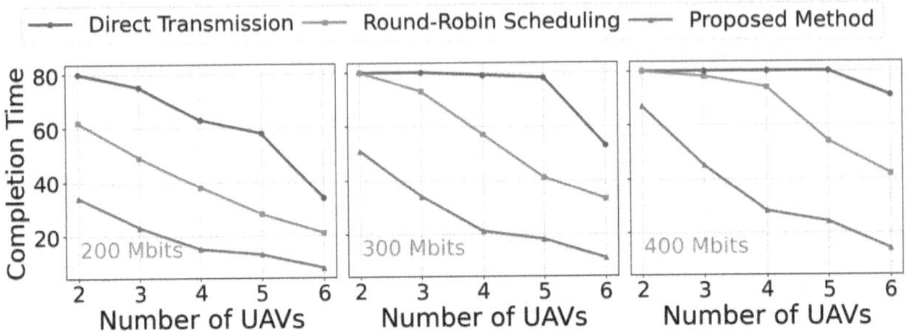


**Fig. 2.** Completion time vs number of UAVs deployed.

Figure 2 presents the completion time required to transfer varying per-cluster data volumes (200, 300, and 400 Mbits per cluster) as a function of the number of UAVs deployed. Across all data sizes, the proposed method consistently achieves significantly lower completion times compared to both the direct transmission and Round-Robin scheduling baselines. This performance advantage becomes increasingly pronounced with larger data volumes. For example, when transmitting 400 Mbits with 6 UAVs, the proposed method completes the task in approximately 15 slots, whereas Round-Robin scheduling and direct transmission require about 43 and 70 slots, respectively. The widening performance gap with increasing data size highlights the scalability of the proposed scheme under heavier traffic loads. In addition, all methods benefit from a greater number of UAVs, exhibiting a clear decrease in completion time as the UAV count increases from 2 to 6. The diminishing returns observed for the proposed method at higher UAV densities (e.g., the smaller improvement from 4 to 6 UAVs compared to 2 to 4 UAVs at 400 Mbits) suggest that the system approaches its spatial multiplexing limit, beyond which additional UAVs yield limited further gains.

Figure 3 compares the system throughput achieved by the three transmission schemes under varying UAV densities and field sizes. Across all configurations, the proposed method consistently outperforms both direct transmission and Round-Robin scheduling, demonstrating superior spectral efficiency and interference management. In the 800 $m^2$ field, where clusters are densely deployed, all schemes achieve relatively high throughput, resulting in only a marginal performance difference between the proposed method and the baselines. Furthermore, increasing the number of UAVs in this compact environment provides limited additional gain for any scheme, as spatial reuse is inherently constrained by cluster proximity. Theoretically, denser UAV deployments could intensify inter-cluster interference; however, the proposed method's interference-aware scheduling and beamforming design effectively mitigate such effects, maintaining robust

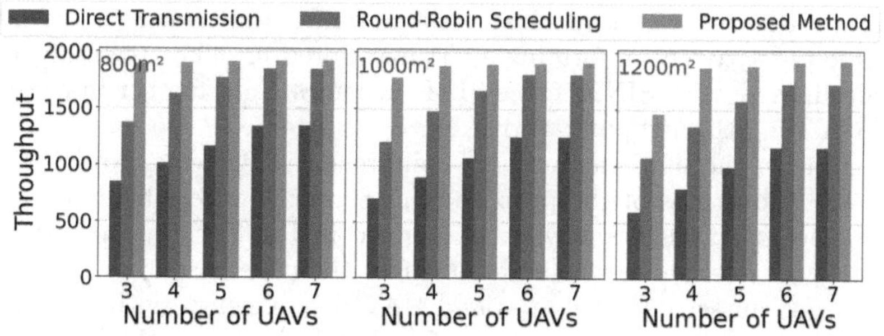


**Fig. 3.** Throughput comparison under different UAV density settings.

throughput even as UAV density increases. As the field size increases, clusters are farther apart, naturally reducing baseline interference and allowing both direct transmission and Round-Robin scheduling to achieve larger incremental improvements as UAV density grows. Despite this, the proposed method retains its advantage: it achieves higher throughput and maintains a roughly constant performance gap over the baselines across all densities and field sizes. These results demonstrate that the proposed method consistently outperforms baseline methods across all tested UAV densities and field sizes.

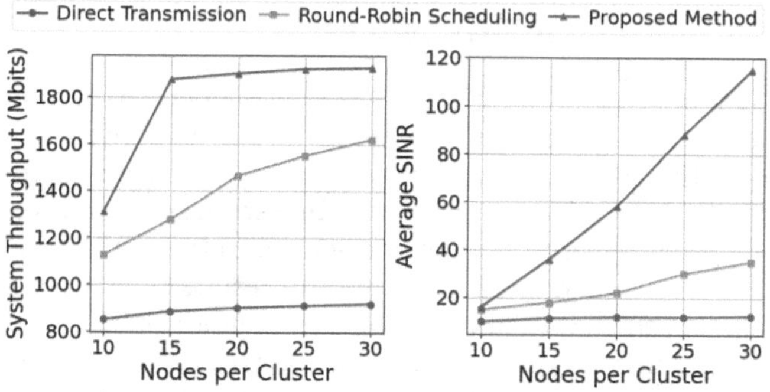


**Fig. 4.** Throughput/SINR vs node quantity per cluster.

Figure 4 examines how increasing the total number of nodes in each cluster (while keeping the number of selected beamforming participants fixed by design) affects both aggregate throughput and average SINR. In the right-hand plot, average SINR for the proposed method rises sharply as more nodes become available, since the beamformer can draw on greater spatial diversity and tighter nulling of interference. However, as shown on the left, throughput gains taper off for all schemes once the cluster size exceeds roughly 20–25 nodes. This is because although each cluster grows, only a subset is activated for collaborative beamforming, so the effective array size increases more slowly than the total node count. Beyond a certain cluster size, adding additional idle nodes does not enlarge the active beamforming aperture. Moreover, The instantaneous rate grows sub-linearly with SINR. Once SINR becomes high, further improvements yield diminishing throughput returns.

In summary, the numerical results comprehensively demonstrate the effectiveness and robustness of the proposed interference-aware scheduling and collaborative beamforming framework. As shown in Fig. 2, the proposed method consistently achieves shorter completion times than the baseline schemes across a range of per-cluster data volumes and UAV deployments, with its advantage becoming increasingly prominent under heavier data loads or higher UAV densities. Figure 3 further confirms that the proposed approach maintains superior system throughput under diverse UAV density and field size settings. While all methods benefit from an increased number of UAVs, the proposed scheme achieves a sustained performance advantage across both dense and sparse deployments, highlighting its adaptability to different operational scenarios. Finally, Fig. 4 the proposed interference-aware method delivers a pronounced improvement in both system throughput and average SINR as the number of nodes per cluster increases, far exceeding the gains of baseline schemes. This highlights the ability of our framework to fully exploit spatial diversity and collaborative transmission opportunities. Collectively, these results verify that the proposed framework offers significant improvements in spectral efficiency, scalability, and reliability for UAV-assisted data collection in smart agriculture.

## 5 Conclusion and Future Work

In this paper, we propose an interference-aware collaborative beamforming and scheduling framework tailored to UAV-assisted precision agriculture monitoring. By jointly optimizing UAV–cluster assignment, intra-cluster node selection and zero-forcing beamforming weights under realistic energy and scheduling constraints, our approach effectively nulls inter-cluster interference while preserving coherent gain at each intended UAV. Numerical results show that our approach significantly accelerates data collection as the number of UAVs increases and improves aggregate throughput and link reliability. It also maintains high network capacity under different UAV deployments, demonstrating scalability and robustness for precise agriculture monitoring.

While our current model assumes fixed, non-overlapping clusters corresponding to distinct field plots, practical agricultural landscapes often feature heterogeneous, partially overlapping sensor deployments (e.g. soil moisture sensors shared between adjacent plots). Future work will address dynamic and overlapping clustering, in which node–cluster associations adapt in real time to changing crop patterns, UAV trajectories and task priorities. We also plan to investigate robust beamforming designs that account for imperfect CSI and UAV mobility, as well as lightweight scheduling algorithms to reduce coordination overhead.

**Acknowledgement.** This work is supported by National Natural Science Foundation of China under Grant No. 62472355 and No. 62301433.

## References


1. Wang, Y., Chen, W., Luan, T.H., Su, Z., Xu, Q., Li, R., Chen, N.: Task offloading for post-disaster rescue in unmanned aerial vehicles networks. IEEE/ACM Trans. Networking **30**(4), 1525–1539 (2022)
2. Yang, Z., Miao, X., Ding, L., Pan, G., Wang, S., An, J.: Optimal swipt transmission in ris-based air-ground wireless communication. IEEE Trans. Aerosp. Electron. Syst. **60**(4), 4310–4322 (2024)
3. Liu, K., Zheng, J.: Uav trajectory optimization for time-constrained data collection in uav-enabled environmental monitoring systems. IEEE Internet Things J. **9**(23), 24300–24314 (2022)
4. Bai, Y., Zhao, H., Zhang, X., Chang, Z., Jäntti, R., Yang, K.: Toward autonomous multi-uav wireless network: A survey of reinforcement learning-based approaches. IEEE Commun. Surv. Tutorials **25**(4), 3038–3067 (2023)
5. Zeng, Y., Wu, Q., Zhang, R.: Accessing from the sky: A tutorial on uav communications for 5g and beyond. Proc. IEEE **107**(12), 2327–2375 (2019)
6. Victor, N., et al.: Remote sensing for agriculture in the era of industry 5.0–a survey. IEEE J. Sel. Top. Appl. Earth Observ. Remote Sensing **17**, 5920–5945 (2024)
7. Shaikh, F.K., Karim, S., Zeadally, S., Nebhen, J.: Recent trends in internet-of-things-enabled sensor technologies for smart agriculture. IEEE Internet Things J. **9**(23), 23583–23598 (2022)
8. Yao, Y.-D., Li, X., Cui, Y.-P., Wang, J.-J., Wang, C.: Energy-efficient routing protocol based on multi-threshold segmentation in wireless sensors networks for precision agriculture. IEEE Sens. J. **22**(7), 6216–6231 (2022)
9. Uddin, M.A., Mansour, A., Le Jeune, D., Aggoune, E.H.M.: Agriculture internet of things: Ag-iot. In: 2017 27th International Telecommunication Networks and Applications Conference (ITNAC), pp. 1–6 (2017)
10. Latino, M.E., Menegoli, M., Corallo, A.: Agriculture digitalization: A global examination based on bibliometric analysis. IEEE Trans. Eng. Manage. **71**, 1330–1345 (2024)
11. Feng, T., Xie, L., Yao, J., Xu, J.: Uav-enabled data collection for wireless sensor networks with distributed beamforming. IEEE Trans. Wireless Commun. **21**(2), 1347–1361 (2022)
12. Mao, Z., Hu, F., Wu, W., Wu, H., Shen, X.: Joint distributed beamforming and backscattering for uav-assisted wpsns. IEEE Trans. Wireless Commun. **22**(3), 1510–1522 (2023)
13. Li, J., Sun, G., Duan, L., Wu, Q.: Multi-objective optimization for uav swarm-assisted iot with virtual antenna arrays. IEEE Trans. Mob. Comput. **23**(5), 4890–4907 (2024)
14. Wentz, M., Chowdhury, K.R.: Intra-network synchronization and retrodirective distributed transmit beamforming with uavs. IEEE Trans. Veh. Technol. **73**(2), 2017–2031 (2024)

# Flexible and Efficient Air-Ground Collaborative Intelligence in Low-altitude Intelligent Networking

Jiyuan Xie(✉), Yuben Qu, Chao Dong, Lei Zhang, and Qihui Wu

Nanjing University of Aeronautics and Astronautics, Nanjing 211100, China
{xiejiyuan,quyuben}@nuaa.edu.cn

**Abstract.** The rapid development of the Low Altitude Intelligent Networking (LAIN) has accelerated the integration of deep neural networks (DNNs) with unmanned aerial vehicles (UAVs), which greatly enhances their capabilities in perception, decision-making, and autonomous operation. However, the computational demands of complex DNNs often exceed the limited onboard resources of UAVs. Traditional approaches either deploy lightweight models on UAVs or offload raw data to ground stations. The former offers low latency but suffers from limited accuracy, while the latter achieves high accuracy at the cost of significant latency. Both struggle to strike a balance between accuracy and latency. In this paper, we investigate dynamic switching between lightweight onboard inference and complex air-ground collaborative processing. We propose Flexible and Efficient Collaborative Intelligence (FECI), an adaptive solution that employs an enhanced Multi-Agent Deep Deterministic Policy Gradient (MADDPG) algorithm to learn optimal inference strategies. Simulation results demonstrate that FECI significantly improves inference efficiency, latency, and accuracy compared with several baseline methods, providing a robust solution for UAV intelligence in LAIN environments.

**Keywords:** UAVs · edge computing · collaborative inference · multi-agent reinforcement learning (MARL) · air–ground coordination

## 1 Introduction

With the development of the low-altitude economy, the rapid integration of Unmanned Aerial Vehicles (UAVs) with Artificial Intelligence (AI), especially Deep Neural Networks (DNNs), has greatly expanded their application potential in mission-critical scenarios in the Low Altitude Intelligent Networking (LAIN), such as environmental monitoring [1], disaster response [2], urban surveillance [3], and infrastructure inspection [4]. In particular, the rise of low-altitude economy has driven increasing demand for onboard data processing with high accuracy and low latency. Although AI-powered UAVs enable enhanced perception, decision-making, and autonomy, the intrinsic resource limitations of UAVs,


Y. Liu et al. (Eds.): ChinaCom 2025, LNICST 711, pp. 236–255, 2027.
https://doi.org/10.1007/978-3-032-33662-0_18

including constraints in memory, computation, and energy, present fundamental challenges to the real-time deployment of DNN-based inference tasks.

To overcome these limitations, previous studies have explored two primary strategies: fully local inference and complete offloading to ground station (GS). However, neither approach is optimal. Localized inference using lightweight DNNs on UAVs typically achieves low latency but suffers from reduced accuracy [5]. In contrast, full offloading to GS [6] enables high-accuracy inference, but incurs significant latency, particularly under constrained air-ground communication links. To address this issue, researchers have proposed model partitioning, which splits complex DNNs between UAVs and GS and transmits intermediate feature representations via air-ground links, thereby enabling collaborative inference [7]. While this approach helps mitigate transmission-induced latency to some extent, it remains insufficient. Recently, researchers have explored integrating the advantages of lightweight and complex DNNs within UAV swarms [8], enabling dynamic switching based on real-time task demands. Although the idea of dynamic collaboration in UAV swarms is promising, there remains a gap in current research regarding its application in air–ground scenarios.

However, while effective in UAV swarm applications, this approach encounters notable challenges when extended to broader air-ground scenarios, particularly those involving multiple UAVs. First, unlike inter-UAV communication in swarms, air-ground links are subject to more severe variability due to dynamic topologies and environmental interference, which significantly complicates decisions on model execution and task offloading. Second, as the number of UAVs increases, the contention for limited air-ground communication bandwidth and centralized ground computing resources becomes more intense, making coordinated resource allocation more difficult than in distributed swarm settings. Third, achieving consistent and low-latency inference across heterogeneous UAVs requires real-time adaptation to diverse flight states and mission-specific requirements, which is more demanding than coordination among homogeneous swarm nodes. These factors collectively present substantial obstacles to building a robust and scalable air-ground collaborative inference system.

Motivated by these challenges, this paper focuses on how to realize accurate and low-latency collaborative inference of DNN streams between multiple UAVs and the GS, subject to stringent latency constraints. We formulate this problem as a joint optimization task that aims to maximize the total normalized task utility, which considers both inference accuracy and latency, under a given time threshold while satisfying constraints on memory, computation, and other resource requirements. To address this, we propose an adaptive solution named Flexible and Efficient air-ground Collaborative Intelligence (FECI). This solution enables each UAV to make effective decisions for several actions, enabling stream-level collaborative inference.

The main contributions of this work are summarized as follows:

- To the best of our knowledge, this is the first work to explore accurate and low-latency inference in multi-UAV air-ground collaborative systems through dynamic switching between lightweight and complex DNN models across multiple task streams.

- To address this problem, we propose FECI, which formulates the problem as a multi-agent Markov Decision Process (MDP) and leverages an enhanced multi-agent reinforcement learning (MARL) algorithm to enable UAVs to jointly learn real-time strategies for model selection, DNN partitioning, bandwidth allocation, and ground resource scheduling.
- Extensive simulation experiments have shown that FECI achieves an average improvement of over 18% in overall system rewards compared to several baselines. Specifically, it improves inference accuracy by 89.98% while meeting latency thresholds, highlighting its exceptional adaptability, efficiency, and scalability under different conditions.

## 2 Related Work

### 2.1 Model Compression

The main goal of DNN model compression is to reduce the size and complexity of large-scale models and convert them into smaller and lighter versions for efficient deployment on UAVs with limited computing resources. Common model compression techniques include pruning, quantization and knowledge distillation. Lee et al. [9] proposed a holistic network pruning method that jointly optimizes both weights and network architectures, enabling automatic pruning without the need for layer-specific hyperparameters. Their approach effectively compresses network parameters and reduces computational cost while maintaining prediction accuracy. Gong et al. [10] accelerated the quantization process using parameterized probabilistic estimation and template-based derivative computation, achieving minimal accuracy loss during DNN compression. Xu et al. [11] employed knowledge distillation to generate high-accuracy lightweight models suitable for deployment on UAVs, facilitating efficient inference.

### 2.2 Collaborative Inference for UAV Systems

Early investigations into collaborative inference involving UAVs primarily focused on deploying a single, complex DNN model across multiple edge devices. The main objective was to enable high-accuracy inference in resource-constrained environments by partitioning the model effectively among UAVs or edge nodes, thus facilitating efficient deployment. Li et al. [12] proposed a DNN model partitioning strategy, where the inference process is divided between local IoT devices and edge servers in the Mobile Edge Computing (MEC) network. By assigning multiple cloud-side threads to handle different parts of the model concurrently, their approach significantly accelerates model inference. Liang et al. [13] introduced a Dynamic Adaptive DNN Surgery (DADS) scheme, which enables joint processing of partitioned DNNs across edge and cloud nodes. Their method optimally partitions the model according to varying network conditions, thereby improving inference efficiency under dynamic environments.

Recent advancements have increasingly focused on the integration of heterogeneous models, where lightweight and complex DNNs coexist and are orchestrated according to environmental dynamics. Li et al. [8] were among the first to explore dynamic switching between lightweight and complex DNN models for enabling edge intelligence in UAV swarm, where lightweight models are executed by individual UAVs and complex models are collaboratively processed by multiple UAVs. Building on this foundation, Qu et al. [14] extended the concept to air–ground networks by proposing a unified optimization framework for model selection and partitioning across a single UAV and GS, thereby minimizing overall latency in cooperative environments. While existing approaches perform well in single-stream tasks, they lack scalability and adaptability for multi-DNN inference scenarios involving concurrent processing. Li et al. [15] took a critical step forward by extending such strategies to multi-stream scenarios within UAV swarms, enabling adaptive model switching under multi-stream conditions and offering key insights into collaborative inference.

Building upon this foundation, our work generalizes the research into a comprehensive air–ground collaborative solution that supports multi-DNN streams processing. For each stream, the system dynamically switches between lightweight and complex models according to real-time conditions. Furthermore, we propose a decentralized, learning-driven coordination mechanism that enables UAVs to collaboratively make real-time decisions on model selection, partitioning, and resource allocation. This design significantly enhances system responsiveness, scalability, and air–ground coordination in dynamic environments.

## 3 System Model

In Fig. 1, a group of $N$ mission drones, denoted as $\mathcal{N} = \{U_1, U_2, \ldots, U_i, \ldots, U_N\}$, cooperates with the GS to form an air–ground intelligent system for collaborative inference, where $U_i$ represents the $i$th UAV. Each UAV carries optical cameras for real-time image capture. Given the strict accuracy and latency requirements of processing tasks, and considering each UAV's varying storage and computing capacity, a flexible approach is necessary. To address these variations, each UAV is preloaded with two models: a lightweight DNN model for fast local processing and a complex DNN model. The GS, on the other hand, deploys a single complex model, identical to the one on the UAVs. This configuration allows tasks to be processed locally using the lightweight model for quick execution or offloaded to the GS to achieve higher accuracy through model partitioning.

We divide the mission period into $T$ time slots, each with a duration of $\tau_{\max}$, which are represented as $\mathcal{T} = \{1, 2, \ldots, T\}$. We assume that each $U_i$ receives its respective inference request $r_i[t]$ from the DNN streams $\mathcal{R} = \{r_1, r_2, \ldots, r_N\}$ at each time slot $t \in \mathcal{T}$. Each UAV makes a dynamic decision on the execution mode for each incoming task, selecting between local lightweight inference and collaborative inference using the complex model. If the lightweight model is chosen, the entire inference is completed onboard and the final result is transmitted to GS. Alternatively, when the complex model is selected, a partition point is

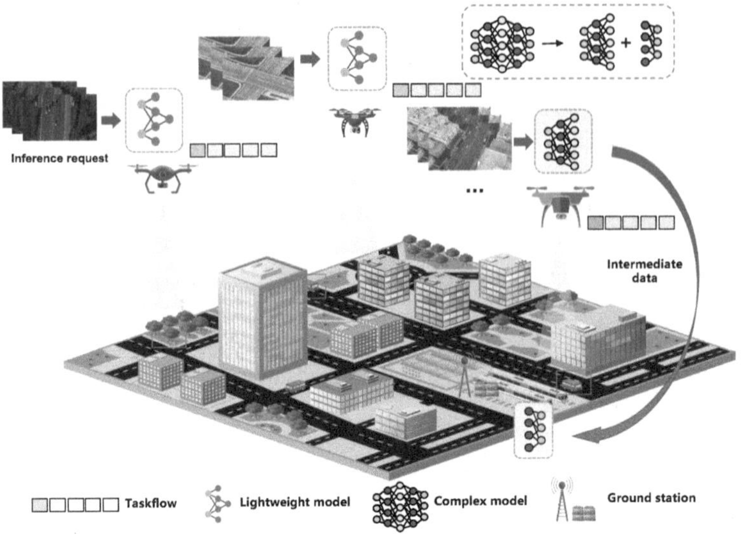


**Fig. 1.** Illustration of several DNN streams performing inference with lightweight and complex models.

determined to split the model execution: the initial layers are processed on the UAV, and the resulting intermediate features are transmitted to GS, where the remaining layers are completed. This hybrid execution strategy enables flexible adaptation to real-time system conditions and resource availability.

### 3.1 Communication Model

To enable inference result transmission and collaborative execution, we model the UAV-to-Ground (U2G) link as a Line-of-Sight (LoS) wireless channel, while inter-UAV communication is omitted. Each UAV communicates directly with the GS over this LoS link, whose channel power gain is modeled as

$$h_i[t] = g_0 \cdot (d_i[t])^{-2}, \tag{1}$$

where $g_0$ denotes the channel gain at the reference distance (1 m), and $d_i[t]$ is the 3D Euclidean distance between UAV $i$ and GS at time $t$, calculated by

$$d_i[t] = \sqrt{(x_i[t] - x_g)^2 + (y_i[t] - y_g)^2 + (z_i[t] - z_g)^2}. \tag{2}$$

The total available bandwidth $W$ is shared among all UAVs and allocated using Orthogonal Frequency-Division Multiple Access (OFDMA), which prevents intra-system interference by design [16]. Specifically, OFDMA divides the spectrum into multiple orthogonal subcarriers and assigns non-overlapping sub-bands to each UAV, enabling simultaneous transmissions without mutual interference. Let $w_i[t]$ denote the bandwidth allocated to the $i$th UAV at time $t$.

Then, the transmission rate is given by

$$R_i[t] = w_i[t] \cdot \log_2\left(1 + \frac{P_i h_i[t]}{w_i[t] N_0}\right), \tag{3}$$

which is derived from the Shannon capacity formula based on the Signal-to-Noise Ratio (SNR) over the allocated bandwidth. Here, $P_i$ is UAV $i$'s fixed transmit power (W), $h_i[t]$ captures the time-varying channel gain (including path loss and fading), and $N_0$ denotes the noise power spectral density (W/Hz).

As shown in (3), the transmission rate $R_i[t]$ is jointly determined by the allocated bandwidth $w_i[t]$ and the channel gain $h_i[t]$, which varies with the UAV's position relative to GS. Due to UAV mobility and limited spectral resources, transmission conditions fluctuate over time and across agents. These dynamics highlight the necessity of real-time, adaptive bandwidth scheduling to maintain efficient air-ground collaboration under constrained radio environments.

### 3.2 Latency Model

We consider two types of inference modes: lightweight local inference and collaborative inference between UAVs and GS. At each time slot $t$, UAV $i$ selects an execution strategy $\eta_i[t] = (\alpha_i[t], \beta_i[t], w_i[t], c_i[t])$, where $\alpha_i[t] \in \{0, 1\}$ indicates the model type (0 for lightweight, 1 for complex), $\beta_i[t]$ denotes the partition point within the complex model, $w_i[t]$ is the bandwidth allocated for transmission, and $c_i[t]$ is the computational resource assigned by the GS.

1) Lightweight Model ($\alpha_i[t] = 0$)

In this mode, the lightweight model is executed entirely onboard without partitioning, and we set $\beta_i[t] = 0$ by default. The total latency consists of the cumulative computation time across all layers and a small transmission delay for sending the final output to the GS:

$$L_i[t] = \sum_{j=1}^{l_{\max}} \frac{\sigma_j}{P_i} + \frac{\theta_{l_{\max}}}{\bar{R}}. \tag{4}$$

Here, $\sigma_j$ represents the computational workload (in FLOPs) required for layer $j$, while $\theta_{l_{\max}}$ denotes the output data size (in bits) from the final layer $l_{\max}$. Since the final output of the lightweight model is typically small, its transmission is modeled with a constant nominal rate $\bar{R}$, independent of dynamic bandwidth allocation. Consequently, the corresponding bandwidth consumption is considered negligible and is excluded from the system-wide bandwidth constraint.

2) Complex Model with Partitioning ($\alpha_i[t] = 1$)

In this case, inference is collaboratively executed between the UAV and GS. The total latency $L_i[t]$ consists of three components: (i) UAV-side computation for the first $\beta_i[t]$ layers, (ii) transmission of the intermediate feature map, and (iii) GS-side computation for the remaining layers. This process is modeled as

$$L_i[t] = \sum_{j=1}^{\beta_i[t]} \frac{\sigma_j}{P_i} + \frac{\theta_{\beta_i[t]}}{R_i[t]} + \sum_{j=\beta_i[t]+1}^{L_{\max}} \frac{\sigma_j}{c_i[t]}, \tag{5}$$

where $\theta_{\beta_i[t]}$ indicates the intermediate feature map size (in bits) at partition layer $\beta_i[t]$. The choice of $\beta_i[t]$ directly affects both communication and computation delays. Consequently, the total latency is highly sensitive to the UAV's computing capability and the quality of U2G communication link.

### 3.3 Problem Formulation

For the DNN streams $\mathcal{R} = \{r_1, r_2, \ldots, r_N\}$, the completion time of each task is constrained to the current time slot $t \in \mathcal{T}$ to ensure real-time processing. To simultaneously optimize the inference accuracy and execution latency across all UAVs, we formulate the following joint optimization objective:

$$\max_{\{\alpha_i[t], \beta_i[t], w_i[t], c_i[t]\}} \quad (\lambda_1 \cdot \text{AvgAcc} - \lambda_2 \cdot \text{AvgLat}), \tag{6}$$

where AvgAcc and AvgLat respectively denote the average normalized inference accuracy and latency across all UAVs and time steps, defined as

$$\text{AvgAcc} = \frac{1}{NT} \sum_{i=1}^{N} \sum_{t=1}^{T} \text{NormAcc}_i[t], \quad \text{AvgLat} = \frac{1}{NT} \sum_{i=1}^{N} \sum_{t=1}^{T} \text{NormL}_i[t]. \tag{7}$$

We assign normalized trade-off weights $\lambda_1$ and $\lambda_2$ to balance inference accuracy and latency, and we constrain them such that $\lambda_1 + \lambda_2 = 1$. In practice, these weights are determined via grid search or sensitivity analysis to meet application-specific requirements, subject to

$$L_i[t] \leq \tau_{\max}, \forall\, i \in N, \forall\, t \in \mathcal{T}, \tag{8}$$

$$\sum_{i=1}^{N} \alpha_i[t] \cdot w_i[t] \leq W, \forall\, t \in \mathcal{T}, \tag{9}$$

$$\sum_{i=1}^{N} \alpha_i[t] \cdot c_i[t] \leq P_g, \forall\, t \in \mathcal{T}, \tag{10}$$

$$\alpha_i[t] \cdot \sum_{j=1}^{\beta_i[t]} \sigma_j \leq P_i, \quad \forall i \in N, \; \forall t \in \mathcal{T}, \tag{11}$$

$$\alpha_i[t] \cdot \sum_{j=1}^{\beta_i[t]} m_j \leq M_{i,\max}, \quad \forall i \in N, \; \forall t \in \mathcal{T}. \tag{12}$$

Constraint (8) stipulates that the task of the $i$th UAV ($i \in N$) in time slot $t \in \mathcal{T}$ must be completed within the slot duration. To ensure fairness in resource allocation, constraint (9) requires that the total bandwidth assigned to all UAVs in each slot does not exceed the system-wide limit $W$. Constraint (10) guarantees that the computational workload allocated to GS remains within its maximum processing capacity. Similarly, Constraint (11) bounds the computational load assigned to each UAV when executing complex models, ensuring it does not exceed their respective capabilities. Finally, Constraint (12) enforces that the memory usage of each UAV stays within its onboard memory limits.

# 4 Algorithm Design

## 4.1 Problem Reformulation

Building upon the constrained optimization problem formulated in Sect. 3, we now examine the structural complexity and decision dependencies inherent in real-time inference scheduling for multiple UAVs. Specifically, At each time step $t$, the $i$th UAV must select four key decision variables. Notably, both communication and computation resources are globally shared across all UAVs, which introduces strong inter-agent dependencies. The action taken by one UAV affects not only its own inference performance but also the feasible action spaces of others. This results in a coupled, non-stationary, and time-evolving environment that renders classical scheduling techniques or single-agent approximations ineffective.

Among these decision variables, $\alpha_i[t]$ and $\beta_i[t]$ are discrete, while $w_i[t]$ and $c_i[t]$ are continuous-valued. These collectively form a structured hybrid action space. The continuous variables are effective only when the complex model is selected, in which case offloading and resource scheduling are required. Otherwise, they are set to zero and do not impact system-level constraints.

Then, we formally define the global action space and analyze its structural properties. Over $N$ agents and $T$ time steps, the global joint action space is defined as

$$\mathcal{A}_{\text{global}} = \left(\{0,1\} \times \{1,\ldots,L_{\max}\} \times \mathbb{R}_w \times \mathbb{R}_c\right)^{N\cdot T}, \tag{13}$$

subject to the conditional resource constraints defined in (10) and (11). Here, $\mathbb{R}_w$ and $\mathbb{R}_c$ denote the bounded continuous domains for bandwidth and computation allocation, respectively, i.e., $w_i[t] \in [0, W]$ and $c_i[t] \in [0, P_g]$.

The discrete portion of the action space alone grows exponentially with the number of agents and time steps:

$$|\mathcal{A}_{\text{disc}}| = \left(2 \cdot L_{\max}\right)^{N\cdot T}. \tag{14}$$

This already suggests a substantial level of complexity, even before considering the continuous decision variables.

The continuous action subspace, governed by constraints (10) and (11), involves two interrelated resource allocation decisions: bandwidth and ground computation. Although these variables span the continuous domains $\mathbb{R}_w$ and $\mathbb{R}_c$, which are theoretically uncountable and infinitely granular, they are practically bounded by the total system resources and only activated when the complex model is selected. Due to the shared nature of these resources and the dynamic number of active UAVs at each time step, the feasible solution space becomes highly entangled and difficult to characterize analytically.

As a result, the joint action space exhibits a hybrid and structurally coupled nature: the discrete portion expands exponentially with system size, while the continuous portion remains high-dimensional and globally constrained. This inherent complexity makes classical combinatorial optimization and tabular reinforcement learning methods impractical. To address this, we reformulate the problem as a multi-agent MDP, as detailed in the following section.

### 4.2 Multi-agent MDP Formulation

The above formulation leads to a high-dimensional, combinatorial optimization problem that couples discrete and continuous variables under stringent time constraints. The inter-agent dependencies further exacerbate the problem complexity, as each agent's decision dynamically influences the global resource landscape. These characteristics render conventional optimization solvers and heuristic-based approaches inadequate, especially when faced with the exponentially large and non-stationary decision space inherent to multi-agent scenarios.

To overcome the curse of dimensionality and adapt to resource constraints, we reformulate the problem as a multi-agent MDP. Each UAV is modeled as an independent agent that sequentially interacts with the environment to learn a decentralized policy. We adopt a centralized training and decentralized execution (CTDE) paradigm, implemented via an enhanced Multi-Agent Deep Deterministic Policy Gradient (MADDPG) algorithm [17].

The core elements of the multi-agent formulation are defined as follows.

1. **Agent:** Each agent corresponds to a task UAV responsible for dynamically selecting the processing model, partition point, bandwidth allocation, and computational resource usage to complete its assigned tasks while satisfying system constraints.
2. **Observation:** The $i$th UAV serving as an agent receives a local observation $o_i[t]$ containing only its own task and status information:

$$\mathbf{o}_i[t] = \{r_i[t],\ P_i[t],\ M_{i,\text{avail}}[t],\ d_i[t],\ \eta_i[t-1]\}\,, \tag{15}$$

   where $r_i[t]$ denotes the inference request assigned to the $i$th UAV, $P_i[t]$ and $M_{i,\text{avail}}[t]$ are its onboard computational and memory states. This partial local view supports decentralized policy execution.
3. **State:** At time step $t$, the global state $\mathbf{s}_t$ aggregates the observations from all UAVs and is accessible only to the centralized critic during training:

$$\mathbf{s}_t = \{\mathbf{o}_i[t] \mid i \in \mathcal{N}\}\,. \tag{16}$$

   This reflects the CTDE paradigm, with global observability in training and local observability in execution.
4. **Action**: The joint action vector $a_i[t]$ selected by each agent comprises four variables:

$$\mathbf{a}_i[t] = \{\alpha_i[t], \beta_i[t], w_i[t], c_i[t]\}, \tag{17}$$

where $\alpha_i[t] \in \{0, 1\}$ indicates the model type, $\beta_i[t]$ is the partition layer (if complex model is selected), $w_i[t]$ is the allocated bandwidth, and $c_i[t]$ is the computation assignment from the GS.

5. **Reward:** To ensure consistency with the optimization objective defined before, we design the reward function at each time step $t$ as a UAV-level metric aggregated into a system-wide signal. Specifically, the local reward for each agent (i.e., the $i$th UAV) is given by

$$r_i[t] = \lambda_1 \cdot \text{NormAcc}_i[t] - \lambda_2 \cdot \text{NormL}_i[t], \tag{18}$$

where $\text{NormAcc}_i[t]$ and $\text{NormL}_i[t]$ denote the normalized inference accuracy and latency as defined in (7) and (8). The global reward used by the centralized critic is the mean of all local rewards:

$$\tilde{r}[t] = \frac{1}{N} \sum_{i=1}^{N} r_i[t]. \tag{19}$$

This formulation ensures that the reward signal directly reflects both the per-agent inference quality and system-level efficiency.

### 4.3 Algorithm Process

To address the high-dimensional, resource-constrained multi-agent scheduling problem introduced above, we adopt the MADDPG algorithm under the CTDE paradigm. This framework enables each UAV agent to learn a hybrid inference strategy that integrates discrete decisions (model type $\alpha_i$ and partition point $\beta_i$) and continuous decisions (bandwidth $w_i$ and computation $c_i$ allocations), while a centralized critic coordinates learning during training.

The training process is summarized in Algorithm 1. At the beginning of each episode, the environment is reset and the initial joint state $\mathbf{s}_0 = \{\mathbf{o}_1[0], \ldots, \mathbf{o}_N[0]\}$ is observed. At each time step $t$, the $i$th UAV receives its local observation $\mathbf{o}_i[t]$ and outputs action logits $\mathbf{P}_i[t]$ from its actor network $\mu_i(\mathbf{o}_i[t])$.

To generate actions from the hybrid action space defined in (19), which includes two discrete variables $(\alpha_i, \beta_i)$ and two continuous variables $(w_i, c_i)$, we adopt a dual-branch architecture in the actor network. The discrete branch employs the Gumbel-Softmax reparameterization [18] to produce differentiable one-hot vectors for $\alpha_i$ and $\beta_i$:

$$\mathbf{a}_i[t] = \text{one\_hot}\left(\arg\max_k \left[\log(\tilde{P}_i^{(k)}) + G_k\right]\right), \\ \text{where } G_k \sim \text{Gumbel}(0, 1). \tag{20}$$

The continuous components $w_i[t]$ and $c_i[t]$ are produced by applying sigmoid activations to the actor's output layer. To enforce system constraints, action

**Algorithm 1.** The FECI Algorithm

**Input:** UAV set $\mathcal{N}$, task set $\mathcal{R}$, time horizon $T$, GS capacity $M$.
**Output:** Learned policy $\mu_i$ for each UAV agent.
Initialize environment, actor networks $\mu_i$, centralized critic $Q^{\psi}$, target networks, and prioritized replay buffer.
**for** each episode $= 1$ to $E$ **do**
  Reset environment; obtain initial joint state $\mathbf{s}_0 = \{\mathbf{o}_1[0], \ldots, \mathbf{o}_N[0]\}$.
  **for** each time step $t = 0$ to $T-1$ **do**
    **for** each agent $i \in \mathcal{N}$ **do**
      Compute action logits $\mathbf{P}_i[t] \leftarrow \mu_i(\mathbf{o}_i[t])$
    **end for**
    Apply action masking and normalize $(w_i[t], c_i[t])$ to satisfy (8)-(12);
    Sample actions $\mathcal{A}_t = \{\mathbf{a}_i[t]\}$ (22);
    Execute joint action $\mathcal{A}_t$ in environment;
    Observe reward $\tilde{r}[t]$ and next joint state $\mathbf{s}_{t+1}$;
    Store $(\mathbf{s}_t, \mathcal{A}_t, \tilde{r}[t], \mathbf{s}_{t+1})$ into buffer.
    **if** buffer size $\geq$ batch size **then**
      Sample mini-batch $\{(\mathbf{s}^{(j)}, \mathcal{A}^{(j)}, \tilde{r}^{(j)}, \mathbf{s}'^{(j)})\}$.
      **for** each agent $i$ **do**
        Update critic $Q^{\psi}$ via TD loss (24);
        Update actor $\mu_i$ using (26);
        Apply gradient clipping.
      **end for**
      Soft update target networks (27);
      Update priorities.
    **end if**
    $\mathbf{s}_t \leftarrow \mathbf{s}_{t+1}$
  **end for**
  Decay learning rate.
**end for**

masking assigns large negative values to invalid logits before sampling. This ensures that all selected actions lie within the valid action set, defined as

$$\mathcal{A}_{\text{valid}} = \{\mathbf{a}_i = (\alpha_i, \beta_i, w_i, c_i) \mid (8)\text{–}(12)\} \tag{21}$$

After executing joint actions $\mathcal{A}$, agents receive the global reward $\tilde{r}$ and observe the next joint state $\mathbf{s}'$. Each transition tuple $(\mathbf{s}, \mathcal{A}, \tilde{r}, \mathbf{s}')$ is stored in a prioritized replay buffer for off-policy learning. When sufficient experience has been collected, a mini-batch is sampled and the networks are updated. The centralized critic $Q^{\psi}$ is trained by minimizing the Temporal-Difference (TD) loss:

$$\mathcal{L}(\psi) = \frac{1}{N}\sum_{j=1}^{N}\left(\hat{y}^{(j)} - Q^{\psi}(\mathbf{s}^{(j)}, \mathbf{a}_1^{(j)}, \ldots, \mathbf{a}_N^{(j)})\right)^2, \tag{22}$$

where the TD target is

$$\hat{y}^{(j)} = \tilde{r}^{(j)} + \gamma Q^{\psi'}(\mathbf{s}'^{(j)}, \mathbf{a}'_1, \ldots, \mathbf{a}'_N), \quad \mathbf{a}'_i = \mu'_i(\mathbf{o}'_i). \tag{23}$$

Here, $\mu_i'$ and $Q^{\psi'}$ are target actor and critic networks, respectively, and $\gamma$ is the discount factor. Each actor $\mu_i$, parameterized by $\omega_i$, is then updated using the deterministic policy gradient:

$$\nabla_{\omega_i} \mathcal{J}_i \approx \frac{1}{N} \sum_{j=1}^{N} \nabla_{\omega_i} \mu_i(\mathbf{o}_i^{(j)}) \cdot \nabla_{\mathbf{a}_i} Q^{\psi}(\mathbf{s}^{(j)}, \mathbf{a}_1^{(j)}, \ldots, \mathbf{a}_N^{(j)}), \quad \text{with } \mathbf{a}_i = \mu_i(\mathbf{o}_i^{(j)}) \tag{24}$$

This update encourages each agent to adjust its policy in a direction that improves the expected joint action value. To prevent gradient explosion and ensure numerical stability during backpropagation, gradient clipping is applied to the actor network during this step. Target networks are softly updated using exponential moving average:

$$\omega_i' \leftarrow \tau\omega_i + (1-\tau)\omega_i', \quad \psi' \leftarrow \tau\psi + (1-\tau)\psi', \tag{25}$$

where $\tau \ll 1$ (typically $\tau = 0.01$). A learning rate decay schedule is applied at the end of each episode to promote convergence.

Through centralized training and decentralized execution, UAV agents learn robust, resource-aware inference strategies that adapt to dynamic environments and heterogeneous constraints. During training, the centralized critic guides joint policy learning. Once training is complete, each UAV independently applies its actor policy $\mu_i$ using local observations only, enabling decentralized execution without inter-agent coordination. This design effectively bridges the gap between joint optimization complexity and real-time decision-making, enabling scalable and coordinated inference scheduling under strict resource constraints.

## 5 Simulation Results

### 5.1 Simulation Settings

In this section, we conduct a comprehensive evaluation of the performance of our proposed system under varying computational capabilities. As detailed in Table 1, the UAVs are equipped with BeagleBone AI, Raspberry Pi 3B+, and Jetson Xavier NX modules. Specifically, the BeagleBone AI features a 1.5 GHz dual-core ARM Cortex-A15 processor and 1 GB of RAM; the Raspberry Pi 3B+ is equipped with a 1.4 GHz quad-core Broadcom BCM2837B0 processor and 1 GB of RAM; and the Jetson Xavier NX includes a 1.9 GHz six-core ARM v8.2 Carmel CPU and 8 GB of LPDDR4 RAM. The Jetson AGX Xavier, deployed at the GS, offers a powerful 2.26 GHz eight-core ARM v8.2 Carmel CPU and 32 GB of LPDDR4x RAM, making it ideal for offloaded computation and complex model inference.

The computational power of the BeagleBone AI and the Raspberry Pi 3B+ is obtained from [19]. Following the methodology described in [19], the available memory of each device is defined as half of its physical memory, and the computational power is estimated as one-tenth of the total CPU clock cycles, assuming that a multiplication operation is completed every 10 clock cycles. Based on this estimation, the computational power of the Jetson Xavier NX and the Jetson AGX Xavier, the latter of which is used to handle the computational tasks of the GS in the simulations of this paper, was similarly derived. This estimation reflects the practically available compute capacity for real-time inference, rather than peak theoretical performance. The computational and storage capacities of these four devices are summarized in Table 1.

**Table 1.** Memory (MB) and computation capacities ($10^6$ multiplications/s) of various devices.

| Device | $M_{i,\max}$ | $P_i$ |
|---|---|---|
| BeagleBone AI | 512 | 300 |
| Raspberry Pi 3B+ | 512 | 560 |
| Jetson Xavier NX | 4096 | 1140 |
| Jetson AGX Xavier | 32768 | 71952 |

To assess the impact of model complexity on algorithm performance, we adopt two high-capacity DNNs, namely VGG16 and ResNet152, along with a lightweight baseline model, AlexNet. These models allow us to analyze how increasing inference complexity affects decision behaviors. On the ImageNet dataset, VGG16 contains approximately 138 million parameters and achieves a top-5 classification accuracy of 91.90%, while the deeper ResNet152 improves this to 94.29% [20]. In contrast, the compact AlexNet comprises around 62 million parameters and reaches an accuracy of 84.60%. UAV trajectories are generated from real-world flight datasets provided in [21].

To further evaluate the performance of the proposed FECI framework, three baseline algorithms are introduced: (1) **DMS** [8], a genetic algorithm-based model assignment method, which we re-implement under our simulation settings for fair comparison; (2) **Random-select**, which randomly selects a model while retaining the MADDPG-learned strategies for partitioning and resource allocation; and (3) **Aver-band**, which enforces uniform allocation of total air-to-ground communication bandwidth among collaborating UAVs, while all other decisions remain learned through FECI.

Unless otherwise specified, we adopt normalized trade-off weights $\lambda_1 = 0.75$ and $\lambda_2 = 0.25$, ensuring $\lambda_1 + \lambda_2 = 1$. Since the system model already enforces a latency threshold $\tau_{\max}$, the optimization can focus more on improving accuracy. In UAV applications like surveillance, reliable decisions typically outweigh minor delays, as accuracy improvements often bring greater benefits than marginal latency reductions. Preliminary experiments show this configuration ensures stable convergence, making it the default for all experiments.

### 5.2 Algorithm Evaluation

To demonstrate the genuine convergence and stability of the proposed algorithm, we first examine the training behavior of FECI under varying task loads. Specifically, we deploy three UAVs equipped with Raspberry Pi 3B+ and set the total communication bandwidth to 10 MHz. Each UAV processes a DNN stream consisting of 10 consecutive tasks. As illustrated in Fig. 2, the cumulative reward rapidly increases across all task settings and generally converges after approximately 800 training episodes. Furthermore, as the number of tasks increases, the cumulative reward exhibits a roughly proportional upward trend. This consistent convergence pattern highlights the effectiveness and robustness of the proposed multi-agent policy learning mechanism in guiding the system toward near-optimal and stable inference decisions.

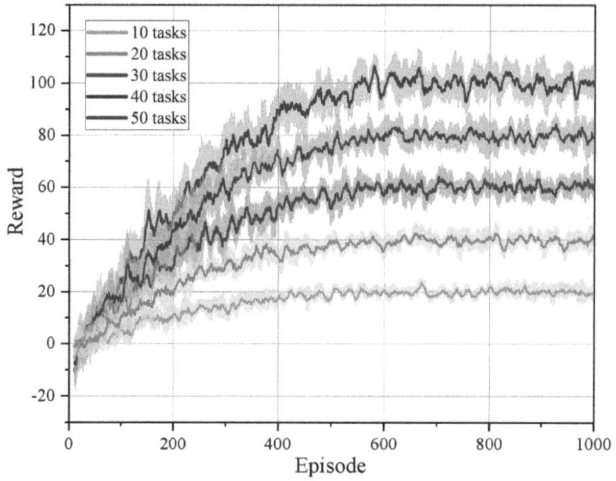


**Fig. 2.** Training curves of FECI for varying numbers of tasks.

### 5.3 Results Analysis

Following the rigorous validation of the FECI algorithm, its comparative performance under more complex scenarios is investigated in detail against several representative baseline approaches. Unless otherwise specified in the experimental groups, the default setting involved three UAVs equipped with Jetson Xavier NX platforms, each assigned to process a DNN stream comprising 10 tasks. The total communication bandwidth was set to 10 MHz, and the latency threshold for each individual task was fixed at 1.1 s.

The system rewards of FECI and the three baseline algorithms are first evaluated for different numbers of tasks, as shown in Fig. 3, where the complex model in (a) is set to VGG16, and the complex model in (b) is set to ResNet152.

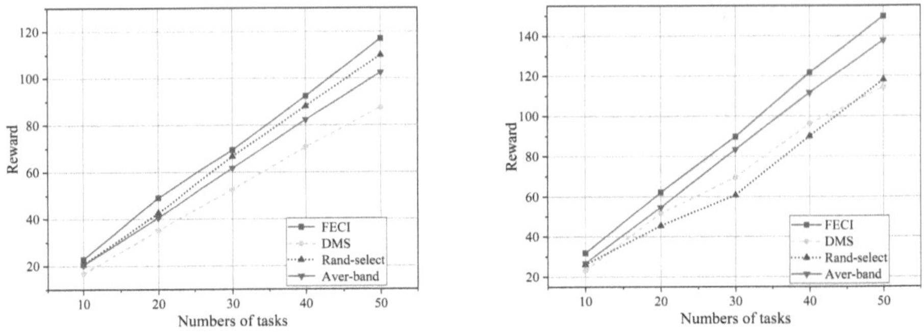


(a) AlexNet and VGG16 (b) AlexNet and ResNet152

**Fig. 3.** Performance of algorithms under different numbers of tasks.

Across all task loads from 10 to 50, FECI achieves the highest reward, with its advantage becoming more apparent as task density increases. For example, under 50 tasks, FECI reaches an average reward of 117.01 with VGG16, outperforming Rand-select, DMS, and Aver-band by 6.3%, 14.2%, and 33.4%, respectively. This performance gain reflects FECI's capacity for coordinated optimization across model selection, inference partitioning, bandwidth allocation, and ground resource scheduling. By contrast, DMS suffers from limited adaptability due to its fixed search strategy, while Rand-select degrades under pressure from increased load due to its lack of task-awareness. Aver-band, constrained by uniform bandwidth allocation, fails to address task heterogeneity.

When the complex model is upgraded to ResNet152, all methods benefit from improved feature extraction, yielding higher rewards. Even with this more demanding setup, FECI maintains the highest performance, outperforming Aver-band, DMS and Rand-select by an average of 11.52%, 28.35% and 33.6%, respectively. This result confirms that FECI can effectively manage increased computational and communication burdens by adapting its decision-making process in real time, achieving a robust balance between accuracy and latency.

Building upon the evaluation presented in Fig. 3, we further validate the performance of the FECI algorithm. Given that a joint optimization objective was adopted, it is necessary to assess the algorithm's effectiveness in simultaneously optimizing both latency and inference accuracy after convergence. To this end, based on the configurations in Fig. 3(a), we conducted a quantitative analysis of the average task latency and inference accuracy under varying task loads. The results are summarized in Table 2 and Table 3. The results show that the proposed FECI is significantly superior to all baseline methods in the comprehensive two performance dimensions. Notably, since the reward function is designed to prioritize accuracy over latency, FECI achieves the highest accuracy across all task configurations. In terms of latency, although FECI exhibits slightly higher latency than a specific baseline algorithm in a few cases, its significantly greater accuracy advantage amply compensates for this minor drawback.

**Table 2.** Average latency (s) under different numbers of tasks.

| Algorithm | Number of Tasks | | | | |
|---|---|---|---|---|---|
| | 10 | 20 | 30 | 40 | 50 |
| FECI | 1.01 | 0.94 | 0.98 | 0.95 | 0.97 |
| DMS | 0.82 | 0.97 | 0.88 | 0.94 | 0.92 |
| Random-select | 0.71 | 1.02 | 0.91 | 1.09 | 0.81 |
| Aver-band | 0.74 | 1.08 | 0.95 | 1.07 | 0.92 |

**Table 3.** Average accuracy (%) under different numbers of tasks.

| Algorithm | Number of Tasks | | | | |
|---|---|---|---|---|---|
| | 10 | 20 | 30 | 40 | 50 |
| FECI | 89.98 | 89.86 | 89.91 | 89.72 | 89.94 |
| DMS | 87.76 | 87.40 | 87.51 | 87.89 | 87.86 |
| Random-select | 87.76 | 88.15 | 88.38 | 88.37 | 88.31 |
| Aver-band | 88.25 | 88.57 | 88.39 | 88.43 | 88.40 |

To further investigate the scalability of the proposed framework, we analyze how the system reward varies with the number of UAVs involved in the collaborative inference process. Figure 4(a) compares the system reward under varying numbers of UAVs, ranging from 3 to 9. FECI consistently achieves the highest reward across all configurations, indicating strong scalability and robustness in distributed task management. On average, it surpasses Rand-select, DMS, and Aver-band by 14.67%, 6.35%, and 14.45%, respectively. As the number of UAVs increases, competition for bandwidth and ground-side computation becomes more intense, resulting in a slight decline in overall system performance. However, FECI maintains the most stable reward trajectory, reflecting its superior adaptability to dynamic resource conditions. With increasing task complexity, Rand-select exhibits a more significant performance drop due to its unguided decision-making. Meanwhile, Aver-band, which rigidly enforces equal bandwidth distribution, exposing its shortcomings in flexible resource scheduling. This further confirms that FECI remains resilient and efficient in high-load, high-complexity collaborative inference scenarios.

In Fig. 4(b), when ResNet152 is used in place of VGG16 as the complex model, FECI consistently outperforms all baseline methods across different UAV configurations. On average, it achieves improvements of 24.09%, 13.49%, and 15.2% over Rand-select, DMS, and Aver-band, respectively. These results are generally aligned with those observed in Fig. 4(a). However, unlike in Fig. 4(a), Rand-select lags behind the other baselines more substantially when applied with ResNet152. This is mainly due to the higher risk associated with random model selection under increased model complexity, which can lead to greater

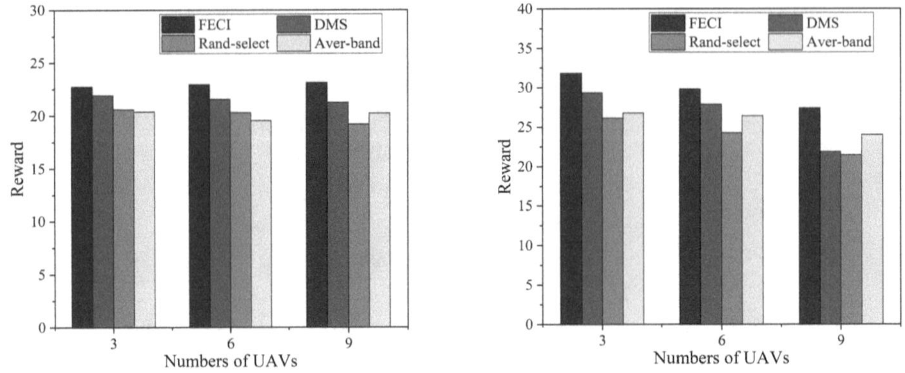


(a) AlexNet and VGG16 (b) AlexNet and ResNet152

**Fig. 4.** Performance of algorithms with different numbers of UAVs.

penalties in both latency and accuracy. Overall, these findings further confirm the effectiveness of FECI in multi-UAV collaboration scenarios.

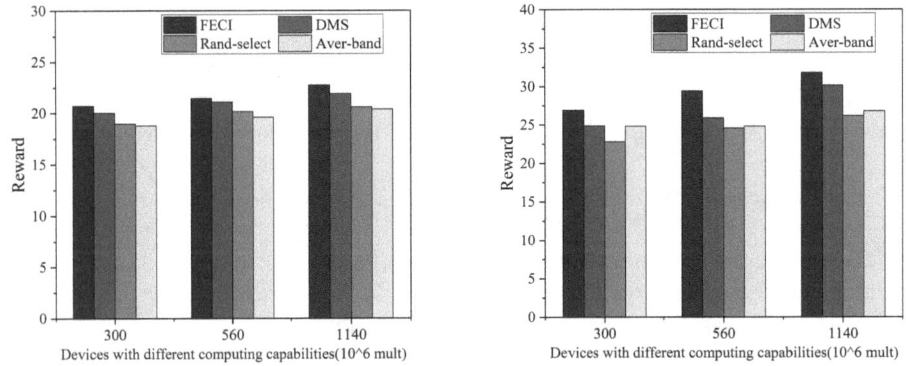


(a) AlexNet and VGG16. (b) AlexNet and ResNet152.

**Fig. 5.** Performance of algorithms with different devices.

We further evaluate how heterogeneous hardware affects performance. Figure 5(a) evaluates system reward across UAVs equipped with embedded devices of varying computational capacities (300, 560, and 1140 $\times$ $10^6$ multiplications per second), using VGG16 as the complex model. As device computing power increases, all methods show a general upward trend in reward. FECI achieves the most pronounced and consistent gains across all settings, with average improvements of 8.79%, 3%, and 10.55% over Rand-select, DMS, and Aver-band, respectively. These results highlight the adaptability of FECI under different computing conditions. FECI's adaptability is evident, especially on high-performance devices (e.g., 1140M), where it maintains significant gains while others show marginal improvements. This stems from FECI's dynamic model partitioning and resource scheduling, which better utilize available compute resources. In contrast, Aver-band's fixed bandwidth allocation and Rand-select's random decisions fail to leverage hardware heterogeneity effectively.

Figure 5(b) extends the evaluation by replacing the complex model from VGG16 to ResNet152 while keeping device configurations unchanged. As model complexity and system load increase, similar to Fig. 5(a), across all hardware platforms, FECI consistently achieves higher system rewards than the baselines and demonstrates improved effectiveness as computational capacity increases. This fine-grained balancing is unachievable by baselines like DMS, which lack adaptive coordination under mixed-resource constraints. Notably, Rand-select suffers from significant performance degradation due to random model choices that often misalign with resource availability, amplifying latency penalties. In summary, FECI demonstrates superior resource awareness and scheduling intelligence under heterogeneous hardware conditions, further validating its applicability in collaborative UAV systems operating across diverse platform constraints.

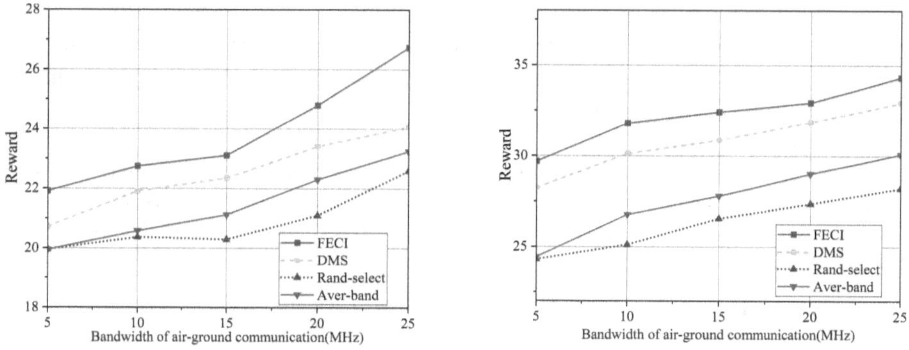


(a) AlexNet and VGG16.

(b) AlexNet and ResNet152.

**Fig. 6.** Performance of algorithms with different bandwidth settings.

Finally, we assess system responsiveness under communication constraints by testing various bandwidth settings. Figure 6(a) shows the impact of air-ground bandwidth (5–25 MHz) on system reward under the AlexNet + VGG16 model. All algorithms exhibit rising rewards with increasing bandwidth. FECI consistently achieves the highest reward, improving from 21.91 to 26.736, outperforming Rand-select, DMS, and Aver-band by 14.22%, 5.93%, and 11.19% on average. This demonstrates FECI's effective dynamic resource scheduling. In contrast, Aver-band and Rand-select show flatter trends due to static or random strategies. While DMS benefits from higher bandwidth, its limited adaptability under constraints leads to inferior performance compared to FECI.

Figure 6(b) compares performance using ResNet152 as the complex model. The increased computational demand heightens sensitivity to bandwidth availability, making communication capacity more critical for overall performance. While all methods show higher rewards than the VGG16-based scenario, FECI maintains a clear advantage. From 5 MHz to 25 MHz, it achieves nearly 25% higher reward, substantially outperforming baselines. On average, FECI surpasses Rand-select, DMS, and Aver-band by 22.55%, 4.59%, and 16.9% respectively. These results demonstrate FECI's effectiveness in bandwidth-constrained environments, especially under high-load inference. Its bandwidth-aware design enables efficient coordination and stable performance in dynamic scenarios.

## 6 Conclusion

In this work, we propose FECI, a flexible and efficient approach for collaborative inference in multi-UAV air-ground systems under strict latency and resource constraints. To handle the hybrid action space, we employ an enhanced MADDPG algorithm under CTDE, enabling UAVs to learn scalable and coordinated strategies. Extensive experiments demonstrate FECI's superior performance in accuracy, latency, and system reward, validating its effectiveness for joint optimization in LAIN. Future work includes real-world deployment on embedded platforms, intra-swarm cooperation, and extending the framework to handle more complex tasks and multimodal data, advancing practical deployment of collaborative intelligence in LAIN.

**Acknowledgement.** This work is supported by the National Natural Science Foundation of China under Grant No. 62427801, and Grant No. 62431014, and Stable Support for Fundamental Research Project in GF Characteristic Disciplines under Grant No. ILF240071A24.

## References

1. Asadzadeh, S., de Oliveira, W.J., de Souza Filho, C.R.: UAV-based remote sensing for the petroleum industry and environmental monitoring: State-of-the-art and perspectives. J. Petrol. Sci. Eng. **208**, 109633 (2022)
2. Sun, G., et al.: Joint task offloading and resource allocation in aerial-terrestrial UAV networks with edge and fog computing for post-disaster rescue. IEEE Trans. Mobile Comput. **23**(9), 8582–8600 (2024)
3. Butilă, E.V., Boboc, R.G.: Urban traffic monitoring and analysis using unmanned aerial vehicles (UAVs): a systematic literature review. Remote Sens. **14**(3), 620 (2022)
4. Aela, P., Chi, H.L., Fares, A., Zayed, T., Kim, M.: UAV-based studies in railway infrastructure monitoring. Autom. Constr. **167**, 105714 (2024)
5. Sun, H., et al.: All-sky autonomous computing in UAV swarm. IEEE Trans. Mobile Comput. **23**(12), 13258–13274 (2024)
6. Qu, Y., et al.: Service provisioning for UAV-enabled mobile edge computing. IEEE J. Sel. Areas Commun. **39**(11), 3287–3305 (2021)

7. Dong, C., et al.: UAVs as an intelligent service: boosting edge intelligence for air-ground integrated networks. IEEE Netw. **35**(4), 167–175 (2021)
8. Li, Y., Qu, Y., Dong, C., Zhou, F., Zhang, L., Wu, Q.: Dynamic DNN model switching for collaborative edge intelligence in UAV swarm. In: Proceedings of the IEEE International Conference on Wireless Communication Signal Processing (WCSP), pp. 923–929 (2023)
9. Lee, G., Lee, K.P: DNN compression by ADMM-based joint pruning. Knowl.-Based Syst. **239**, 107988 (2022)
10. Gong, C., Chen, Y., Lu, Y., Li, T., Hao, C., Chen, D.: VecQ: minimal loss DNN model compression with vectorized weight quantization. IEEE Trans. Comput. **70**(5), 696–710 (2020)
11. Xu, J., Yao, H., Zhang, R., Mai, T., Guizani, M.: Low latency and accuracy-guaranteed DNN inference for UAV-assisted IoT networks. IEEE Trans. Cogn. Commun. Netw. (2025). early access
12. Li, J., Liang, W., Li, Y., Xu, Z., Jia, X., Guo, S.: Throughput maximization of delay-aware DNN inference in edge computing by exploring DNN model partitioning and inference parallelism. IEEE Trans. Mobile Comput. **22**(5), 3017–3030 (2023)
13. Liang, H., et al.: DNN surgery: accelerating DNN inference on the edge through layer partitioning. IEEE Trans. Cloud Comput. **11**(3), 3111–3125 (2023)
14. Qu, Y., et al.: Adaptive switching of lightweight and complex DNNs for air-ground collaborative intelligence. In: Chen, X., Min, G., Guo, D., Xie, X., Pu, L. (eds.) NPC 2024. LNCS, vol. 15528, pp. 249–260. Springer, Singapore (2025). https://doi.org/10.1007/978-981-96-2864-3_20
15. Y. Li, Y. Qu, C. Dong, Z. Qin, L. Zhang, Wu, Q.: Adaptive model switching of collaborative inference for multi-CNN streams in UAV swarm. Chin. J. Aeronaut. (2025). https://doi.org/10.1016/j.cja.2025.103564
16. Wu, Q., Zhang, R.: Common throughput maximization in UAV-enabled OFDMA systems with delay consideration. IEEE Trans. Commun. **66**(12), 6614–6627 (2018)
17. Lowe, R., Wu, Y., Tamar, A., Harb, J., Abbeel, P., Mordatch, I.: Multi-agent actor-critic for mixed cooperative-competitive environments. In: Advance Neural Information Processing System (2017)
18. Jang, E., Gu, S., Poole, B.: Categorical reparameterization with Gumbel-Softmax. In: Proceedings of the International Conference on Learning, Representations (ICLR) (2017)
19. Disabato, S., Roveri, M., Alippi, C.: Distributed deep convolutional neural networks for the internet-of-things. IEEE Trans. Comput. **70**(8), 1239–1252 (2021)
20. Kandel, I., Castelli, M.: Transfer learning with convolutional neural networks for diabetic retinopathy image classification: a review. Appl. Sci. **10**(6), 2021 (2020)
21. Fonder, M., Van Droogenbroeck, M.: Mid-Air: a multi-modal dataset for extremely low altitude drone flights. In Proceedings of the IEEE/CVF Conference on Computer Vision Pattern Recognition Workshops (CVPRW), Long Beach, CA, USA, vol. 2019, pp. 553–562 (2019)

# Research on UAV Dynamic Trajectory Prediction Based on Deep Learning

Tianci Huang, Zirui Zhuang(✉), Qi Qi, and Jingyu Wang

State Key Laboratory of Networking and Switching Technology, Beijing University of Posts and Telecommunications, Beijing 100876, China

zhuangzirui@bupt.edu.cn

**Abstract.** Accurate trajectory prediction for Unmanned Aerial Vehicles (UAVs) is paramount for ensuring operational safety and efficiency in increasingly crowded airspace. However, conventional prediction models struggle to forecast the complex, non-linear paths generated by modern Reinforcement Learning (RL)-based navigation policies. To address this challenge, this paper introduces TC-Former, a novel hybrid deep learning architecture that synergistically integrates a Temporal Convolutional Network (TCN) with a Transformer encoder. The model is designed to capture both local temporal features and long-range global dependencies within UAV motion data. We developed a high-fidelity simulation environment using Gazebo and ArduPilot SITL to generate a comprehensive dataset of a UAV performing obstacle avoidance missions guided by a Twin Delayed Deep Deterministic Policy Gradient (TD3) agent. Experimental results demonstrate that TC-Former achieves state-of-the-art performance, attaining a Coefficient of Determination ($R^2$) of 0.9980 and an Average Displacement Error (ADE) of $5.1748 \times 10^{-4}$ m. This significantly outperforms established baselines, including standalone TCN and Transformer models, validating that our hybrid approach provides a more robust and precise solution for predicting the trajectories of RL-driven autonomous systems.

**Keywords:** UAVs · Trajectory prediction · Deep learning

## 1 Introduction

The increasing integration of Unmanned Aerial Vehicles (UAVs) into complex, low-altitude airspace establishes accurate trajectory prediction as a critical technology for ensuring operational safety and enabling next-generation Unmanned Traffic Management (UTM) systems [1,6,7,21,25]. Historically, trajectory prediction relied on model-based methods, such as Kalman filters, which often fall short in capturing the highly non-linear dynamics of modern autonomous UAVs [3,9,20]. This limitation catalyzed a paradigm shift towards data-driven approaches, which have evolved from Recurrent Neural Networks


Y. Liu et al. (Eds.): ChinaCom 2025, LNICST 711, pp. 256–266, 2027.
https://doi.org/10.1007/978-3-032-33662-0_19

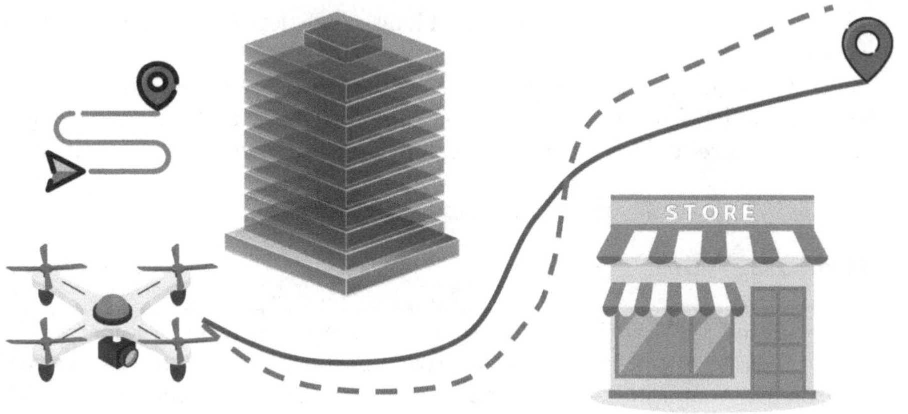


**Fig. 1.** Real flight trajectory in drone reinforcement learning trajectory planning (blue solid line) and trajectory fitted by prediction algorithm (orange dashed line). (Color figure online)

(RNNs) and Long Short-Term Memory (LSTM) networks to more advanced architectures like Temporal Convolutional Network (TCN) and the Transformer, both demonstrating superior capabilities in modeling complex temporal dependencies [5,14,16,18,19].

Despite these significant advancements, accurately forecasting the intricate movements of autonomous agents remains a formidable challenge [12,22]. This difficulty is vividly illustrated in Fig. 1, where a noticeable deviation often emerges between the predicted trajectory and the actual ground truth, even when using sophisticated models. Such prediction errors, especially in critical avoidance maneuvers, can directly compromise system safety and mission success.

This challenge is particularly acute for the next generation of UAVs navigated by Reinforcement Learning (RL) algorithms [4]. The majority of existing studies focus on predicting human-piloted or kinematically simple trajectories, thereby failing to address the unique characteristics of RL-generated paths [23]. Trajectories produced by policies like the Twin Delayed Deep Deterministic Policy Gradient (TD3) are inherently reactive and non-linear, presenting a distinct challenge to conventional prediction models [17,24]. Furthermore, the potential of synergistically combining the hierarchical feature extraction of TCN with the global attention mechanism of Transformers to specifically tackle this class of trajectories remains largely unexplored.

1. First, we formulate the problem of predicting trajectories for a UAV operating under a fixed TD3-based obstacle avoidance policy and generate a benchmark dataset in a high-fidelity Gazebo/Software-in-the-Loop (SITL) simulation.
2. Second, we propose a novel hybrid deep learning architecture, TC-Former, which integrates a TCN to extract hierarchical temporal features from raw

sensor data and a Transformer to model long-range dependencies among these features.
3. Finally, through extensive comparative experiments, we demonstrate that our proposed model achieves state-of-the-art performance, setting a new benchmark for the prediction of complex, algorithmically-generated UAV trajectories.

## 2 Related Work

The literature on UAV trajectory prediction has evolved from classical model-based methods to sophisticated data-driven paradigms [22]. Initial research centered on Kalman Filters (KF) and their non-linear extensions (e.g., EKF, UKF), which rely on predefined motion models like Constant Velocity (CV) or Constant Acceleration (CA) [11,27]. While computationally efficient, these methods exhibit limited capacity to capture the complex, non-linear dynamics inherent in agile or reactive UAV flight, particularly for trajectories governed by learned policies rather than simple kinematics. This fundamental limitation catalyzed the adoption of deep learning for trajectory prediction [9,10]. Early data-driven approaches widely employed RNNs, specifically LSTM and Gated Recurrent Unit (GRU) architectures, to model temporal dependencies [15,26]. Enhancements such as Bidirectional LSTMs and hybrid CNN-LSTM models offered improved context modeling and feature extraction [13]. Nevertheless, these recurrent models are often hampered by difficulties in capturing very long-range dependencies and are susceptible to gradient instability.

To overcome these limitations, recent research has shifted towards more advanced architectures. The TCN utilizes dilated causal convolutions to build a large receptive field, enabling robust long-range dependency modeling with stable gradients and parallel computation [2]. Concurrently, the Transformer architecture, with its self-attention mechanism, has proven highly effective by allowing the model to weigh the importance of all past states globally, irrespective of their temporal distance [15]. Despite the individual successes of the above models, the literature predominantly focuses on validating them against human-piloted or kinematically smooth trajectories. Consequently, a distinct research gap exists in predicting the highly non-linear, reactive trajectories generated by Reinforcement Learning (RL) agents [4,8,28]. The synergistic potential of integrating TCN and Transformer architectures to specifically address this challenging class of algorithmically-generated trajectories remains a compelling and underexplored avenue of research.

## 3 Methodology

This section details our proposed framework for UAV trajectory prediction, encompassing the problem formulation, data generation pipeline, and the proposed TC-Former model architecture.

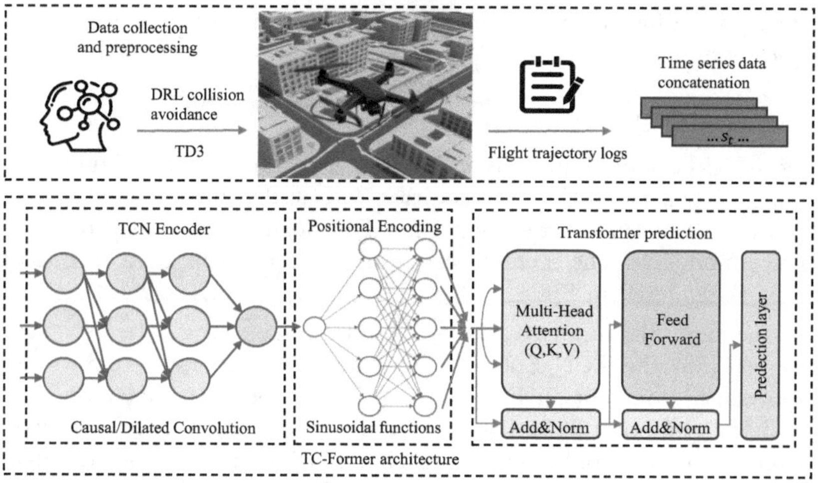


**Fig. 2.** Architecture of the proposed TC-Former scheme.

### 3.1 Problem Formulation

The task of UAV trajectory prediction is formulated as a sequence-to-sequence problem. Given a historical sequence of the UAV's motion states over a time window $T_{in}$, denoted as $X = (s_{t-T_{in}+1}, ..., s_t)$, the objective is to predict the future sequence of its 3D coordinates over a horizon $T_{out}$, denoted as $Y = (p_{t+1}, ..., p_{t+T_{out}})$. The state vector $s_t \in \mathbb{R}^D$ at each time step comprises multimodal sensor data, including Inertial Measurement Unit (IMU) readings, attitude, velocity, and acceleration. Our model, represented by a mapping function $f(X; \Theta)$, is trained to predict $\hat{Y} = f(X; \Theta)$ by minimizing the Mean Squared Error (MSE) loss between the predicted and actual ground truth:

$$\mathcal{L}(\Theta) = \frac{1}{T_{out}} \sum_{i=1}^{T_{out}} ||p_{t+i} - \hat{p}_{t+i}||^2, \tag{1}$$

where $\Theta$ are the learnable model parameters.

### 3.2 Dataset Generation and Preprocessing

A high-fidelity simulation environment was established using Gazebo and SITL with the ArduPilot stack to generate a realistic trajectory dataset. As shown in Fig. 2, trajectories were produced by a fixed, pre-trained TD3 agent executing an autonomous obstacle avoidance task. This approach yields a consistent and reproducible dataset of complex, reactive, and non-linear flight paths.

The raw time-series data underwent two preprocessing steps. First, all input features were normalized to a [0, 1] range using Min-Max scaling to stabilize training. Second, the continuous data was segmented into input-output pairs

$(X, Y)$ using a sliding window of size $T_{in} + T_{out}$ with a fixed stride, creating a supervised learning dataset.

### 3.3 Proposed TC-Former Architecture

We propose TC-Former, a novel hybrid architecture designed to predict complex, algorithmically-generated UAV trajectories. The model synergistically integrates a TCN for robust feature extraction with a Transformer-based module for global dependency modeling. The architecture processes sequential data through three key stages, as depicted in Fig. 2.

1. TCN Encoder: The input sequence of multimodal sensor data, $X \in \mathbb{R}^{T_{in} \times D}$, is first fed into the TCN Encoder. This module is composed of stacked 1D dilated causal convolution blocks. Its primary role is to act as a powerful and efficient temporal feature extractor. By leveraging a large receptive field achieved through exponentially increasing dilation factors, the TCN captures hierarchical patterns and long-range dependencies directly from the raw time-series data. This process transforms the input sequence into a sequence of high-level feature embeddings, $H_{TCN} \in \mathbb{R}^{T_{in} \times D_{model}}$, where $D_{model}$ is the dimensionality of the model's hidden space.
2. Positional Encoding: Since the subsequent Transformer module is permutation-invariant and does not inherently process sequential order, we must inject positional information. Following the standard Transformer methodology, we add positional encodings to the feature embeddings produced by the TCN. The resulting sequence, $H_{PE} = H_{TCN} + P$, where $P \in \mathbb{R}^{T_{in} \times D_{model}}$ are the sinusoidal positional encodings, now contains both the feature information from the TCN and the explicit temporal order of the sequence.
3. Transformer Prediction Module: The positionally-encoded feature sequence $H_{PE}$ is then passed to the Transformer Prediction Module. This module consists of a standard Transformer Encoder followed by a prediction head. The core of this module is a stack of Transformer Encoder layers. Each layer applies a multi-head self-attention mechanism, allowing the model to weigh the importance of all time steps in the input sequence when computing the representation for each step. This global attention mechanism is particularly effective at modeling complex, non-local interactions and identifying critical motion cues, even those distant in time. The encoder processes the entire sequence to produce a contextually-rich output, $H_{Trans} \in \mathbb{R}^{T_{in} \times D_{model}}$. To generate the final forecast, we isolate the representation of the last time step from the encoder's output, $H_{Trans}^{T_{in}}$. This vector, which encapsulates the most relevant information from the entire input history, is fed into a linear layer. This final layer projects the high-dimensional feature vector into the desired output shape, yielding the predicted future trajectory $\hat{Y} \in \mathbb{R}^{T_{out} \times 3}$.

By structuring the model in this way, the TC-Former effectively delegates the task of low-level temporal feature learning to the TCN, while the Transformer focuses on high-level contextual reasoning and prediction, creating a powerful and specialized architecture for the task.

# 4 Experiments

This section presents a rigorous empirical evaluation of the proposed TC-Former model. We first detail the experimental setup and evaluation metrics, then provide a comprehensive quantitative and qualitative analysis against representative baselines to validate the effectiveness of our approach.

## 4.1 Experimental Setup

**Dataset.** As shown in Fig. 3, the trajectory dataset was generated within a high-fidelity simulation environment using Gazebo 11 and ArduPilot SITL. A quadrotor UAV, navigated by a fixed, pre-trained TD3 agent, performed 50 distinct obstacle avoidance missions, resulting in a time-series dataset of approximately 70,000 time steps sampled at 10 Hz. Each data point contains a multimodal feature vector of IMU, attitude, and kinematic states. The prediction task is to forecast the UAV's 3D position for the subsequent 4 steps ($T_{out} = 4$, 0.4 s horizon) based on the preceding 10 steps of its state history ($T_{in} = 10$). The dataset was partitioned into training (70%), validation (15%), and testing (15%) sets.

**Fig. 3.** Simulation Environment for UAV Flight Trajectory Dataset.

**Baselines and Implementation Details.** We benchmarked our TC-Former against a diverse set of models: a canonical LSTM, a simple MLP, an encoder-only Transformer, a hybrid CNN-LSTM, and a standalone TCN. All models were implemented in PyTorch and trained on an NVIDIA RTX 2070 GPU. We used the Adam optimizer with an initial learning rate of $1 \times 10^{-4}$ and a batch size of 256. In 100 epochs of training, an Early Stopping mechanism (patience=5 epochs) was employed to prevent overfitting, with the best-performing model on the validation set saved for testing.

### 4.2 Evaluation Metrics

We assessed model performance using three standard metrics:

1. Coefficient of Determination ($R^2$): Measures the proportion of variance in the ground truth that is predictable from the model. A value closer to 1 indicates a better fit.
2. Average Displacement Error (ADE): The mean L2 distance between predicted and ground truth positions over the entire prediction horizon, measuring the average per-step error.

$$\text{ADE} = \frac{1}{N \cdot T_{out}} \sum_{i=1}^{N} \sum_{j=1}^{T_{out}} \|p_{i,j} - \hat{p}_{i,j}\|_2. \quad (2)$$

3. Maximum Displacement Error (MDE): The maximum L2 distance between the predicted and ground truth positions across all predicted time steps for a given trajectory, averaged over all test samples. It quantifies the worst-case prediction error.

$$\text{MDE} = \frac{1}{N} \sum_{i=1}^{N} \max_{j \in \{1,..,T_{out}\}} \|p_{i,j} - \hat{p}_{i,j}\|_2, \quad (3)$$

where $N$ is the number of test samples, and $p$ and $\hat{p}$ are the ground truth and predicted positions, respectively.

### 4.3 Results and Analysis

**Quantitative Comparison.** Table 1 presents the quantitative results. Our proposed TC-Former achieves superior overall performance, attaining the highest $R^2$ score (0.9980) and the lowest ADE ($5.1748 \times 10^{-4}$ m). This demonstrates that our model provides the most accurate predictions on average across the entire trajectory horizon, affirming the effectiveness of its hybrid architecture.

An insightful observation arises from the MDE metric. While TC-Former performs competitively, the standalone Transformer model records a slightly lower MDE ($1.8292 \times 10^{-2}$ m vs. $1.9717 \times 10^{-2}$ m). This nuanced result suggests a trade-off between average accuracy and worst-case error mitigation. The Transformer's global self-attention mechanism appears exceptionally adept at preventing a single, large deviation at a specific point in the future. However, our TC-Former, by integrating the TCN's hierarchical feature extraction, excels at minimizing the cumulative error throughout the sequence. This leads to a trajectory that is, on average, more faithful to the ground truth, as evidenced by its dominant ADE and $R^2$ scores. For many safety-critical applications, a lower average error (better overall path fidelity) is arguably more valuable than a slightly better single-point worst-case error, making TC-Former a more robust choice overall.

Consistent with recent literature, both TCN and Transformer significantly outperform RNN-based baselines (LSTM, CNN-LSTM), underscoring the limitations of recurrent models in capturing the abrupt dynamics of RL-generated flight paths.

**Table 1.** Quantitative comparison on the test set. Best results are in bold. For $R^2$, higher is better; for ADE and MDE, lower is better.

| Model | $R^2$ ↑ | ADE ($10^{-4}$ m) ↓ | MDE ($10^{-2}$ m) ↓ |
|---|---|---|---|
| LSTM | 0.7825 | 15.2631 | 9.0444 |
| MLP | 0.9833 | 23.0477 | 2.4461 |
| CNN-LSTM | 0.6688 | 32.4147 | 11.0968 |
| Transformer | 0.9890 | 13.2081 | **1.8292** |
| TCN | 0.9918 | 8.7123 | 2.2034 |
| **TC-Former (Ours)** | **0.9980** | **5.1748** | 1.9717 |

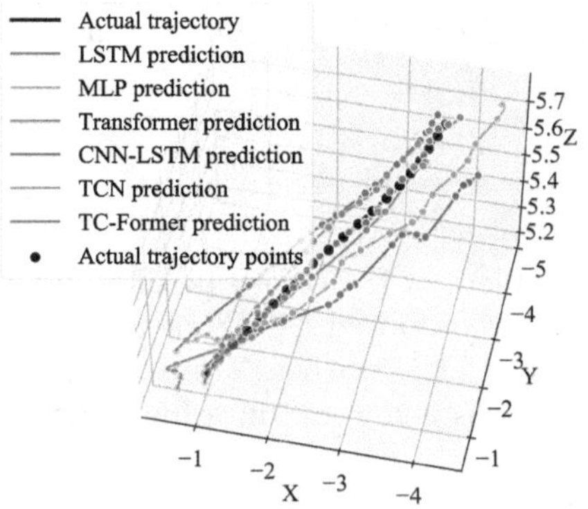


(a) Case 1: Near-Linear Flight Path.

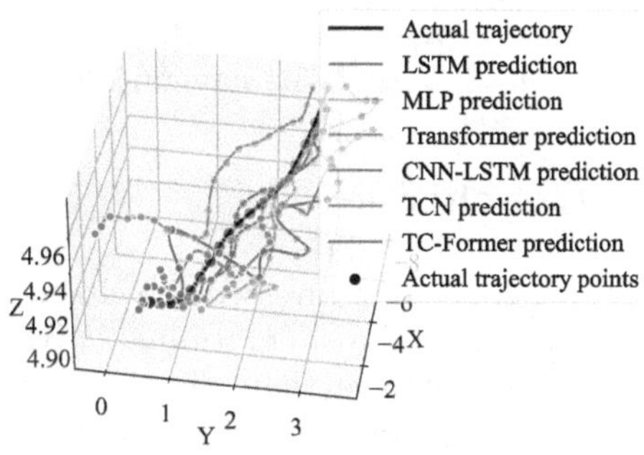


(b) Case 2: Continuous High-Curvature Maneuvers.

**Fig. 4.** Predicted trajectories for two distinct scenarios.

**Qualitative Analysis.** To provide intuitive insights into model performance, Fig. 4 visualizes predicted trajectories for two distinct scenarios from the test set, representing different dynamic regimes.

Case 1: Near-Linear Flight Path. This scenario evaluates the models' ability to maintain stability and precision during a relatively straight trajectory with minor corrections. As shown in Fig. 4a, while most models perform adequately, simpler architectures like LSTM tend to exhibit slight oscillatory noise or drift. In contrast, our TC-Former generates a trajectory that is exceptionally stable and closely aligned with the ground truth, demonstrating its robustness in forecasting low-frequency dynamics and its ability to avoid generating spurious artifacts on simple paths.

Case 2: Continuous High-Curvature Maneuvers. This more challenging scenario involves a segment of continuous, successive turns, testing the models' capability to capture complex, high-frequency dynamics. Figure 4b reveals significant performance disparities. RNN-based models produce heavily over-smoothed paths, completely failing to capture the turning geometry. The standalone Transformer and TCN models offer improvements but still exhibit noticeable lag and underestimation of the turn radius. Our TC-Former, however, excels in this scenario. It accurately predicts the initiation, apex, and completion of each turn in the sequence, maintaining high fidelity to the complex path. This highlights the strength of its hybrid architecture: the TCN effectively extracts the underlying temporal features of the rapid maneuvers, while the Transformer models the global dependencies between turns, resulting in a significantly more accurate and dynamically consistent forecast.

These qualitative results corroborate our quantitative findings. TC-Former demonstrates superior performance across both simple and complex dynamic scenarios, proving its versatility and its advanced capability to understand the underlying intent of the navigation policy.

## 5 Conclusion

In this paper, we addressed the challenging problem of trajectory prediction for UAVs navigated by a deterministic RL policy. We proposed TC-Former, a novel hybrid architecture that effectively integrates a TCN with a Transformer to accurately forecast complex, non-linear flight paths generated in a high-fidelity simulation environment.

Our extensive experiments demonstrated the clear superiority of the proposed model. Quantitatively, TC-Former achieved the highest overall accuracy, with an $R^2$ score of 0.9980 and the lowest ADE of $5.1748 \times 10^{-4}$ m, surpassing all evaluated baselines. An insightful finding was the trade-off between average and worst-case error; while a standalone Transformer yielded a marginally better MDE, TC-Former's dominant ADE highlights its superior ability to maintain high fidelity across the entire trajectory. Qualitative analysis further corroborated these results, showing that our model excels at predicting both near-linear flight and continuous high-curvature maneuvers where other models typically fail.

The success of TC-Former validates our central hypothesis: the synergy between TCN's hierarchical temporal feature extraction and the Transformer's global context modeling provides a powerful mechanism for understanding the intent behind RL-driven behaviors. This work represents a significant step towards developing more reliable predictive tools for ensuring safety in dynamic environments. Future research will focus on validating the TC-Former on real-world flight data to assess its sim-to-real transferability, extending the framework to handle stochastic policies and multi-agent scenarios, and exploring architectural optimizations for on-board deployment.

**Acknowledgments.** This work was supported in part by the National Key Research and Development Program of China under Grant 2024YFE0200800, in part by the National Natural Science Foundation of China under Grants (62171057, U23B2001, 62201072, 62101064, 62321001, 62471055), in part by the National Postdoctoral Program for Innovative Talents under Grant BX20230052, in part by the China Postdoctoral Science Foundation (2023TQ0039), in part by the Ministry of Education and China Mobile Joint Fund (MCM20200202, MCM20180101), in part by the Beijing University of Posts and Telecommunications-China Mobile Research Institute Joint Innovation Center.

## References

1. Bahari, M., Saadatnejad, S., Farsangi, A.A., Moosavi-Dezfooli, S.M., Alahi, A.: Certified human trajectory prediction. arXiv preprint arXiv:2403.13778 (2025)
2. Bai, S., Kolter, J.Z., Koltun, V.: An empirical evaluation of generic convolutional and recurrent networks for sequence modeling. arXiv preprint arXiv:1803.01271 (2018)
3. Becker, S., Hug, R., Huebner, W., Arens, M., Morris, B.T.: Generating versatile training samples for UAV trajectory prediction. In: Galambos, P., Kayacan, E., Madani, K. (eds.) Robotics, Computer Vision and Intelligent Systems. CCIS, pp. 208–229. Springer, Cham (2022). https://doi.org/10.1007/978-3-031-19650-8_11
4. Chung, S., Niekum, S., Krueger, D.: Predicting future actions of reinforcement learning agents. arXiv preprint arXiv:2410.22459 (2024)
5. Huang, T., Wu, H., Tao, X., Wei, Z.: Prediction-based trajectory anomaly detection in UAV system with GPS spoofing attack. Chin. J. Aeronaut. **38**(10), 103478 (2025). https://doi.org/10.1016/j.cja.2025.103478
6. Jia, Z., et al.: NFV-enabled service recovery in space-air-ground integrated networks: a matching game based approach. IEEE Trans. Netw. Sci. Eng. **12**(3), 1732–1744 (2025). https://doi.org/10.1109/TNSE.2025.3538614
7. Jia, Z., et al.: Distributionally robust optimization for aerial multi-access edge computing via cooperation of UAVs and haps. IEEE Trans. Mob. Comput. **24**(10), 10853–10867 (2025). https://doi.org/10.1109/TMC.2025.3571023
8. Jia, Z., He, S., Zhu, Q., Wang, W., Wu, Q., Han, Z.: Trusted routing for blockchain-empowered UAV networks via multi-agent deep reinforcement learning. IEEE Trans. Commun. (2025). https://doi.org/10.1109/TCOMM.2025.3597655., early access
9. Kim, J., Yoon, H., Yoon, S., Kwon, Y., Lee, K.: A deep learning-based trajectory and collision prediction framework for safe urban air mobility. Drones **9**(7), 460 (2025). https://doi.org/10.3390/drones9070460
10. Li, D., Du, B., Bai, Z.: Deep reinforcement learning-enabled trajectory and bandwidth allocation optimization for UAV-assisted integrated sensing and covert communication. Drones **9**(3), 160 (2025). https://doi.org/10.3390/drones9030160
11. Liang, W., et al.: Are hybrid approaches combining EKF-UKF and artificial neural networks key to unlocking the full potential of sustainable energy technologies and reducing environmental footprint? Heliyon **10**(18), e36746 (2024)
12. Liu, Y., Yang, Z., Chai, S., Wang, X., Zhou, Y., Zhou, D.: Autonomous penetration trajectory control for unmanned aerial vehicle based on reinforcement learning. In: 2024 2nd International Conference on Artificial Intelligence and Automation Control (AIAC), pp. 213–219 (2024). https://doi.org/10.1109/AIAC63745.2024.10899596

13. Ma, L., Tian, S.: A hybrid CNN-LSTM model for aircraft 4D trajectory prediction. IEEE Access **8**, 134668–134680 (2020)
14. Messaoud, K., Cord, M., Alahi, A.: Towards generalizable trajectory prediction using dual-level representation learning and adaptive prompting. arXiv preprint arXiv:2501.04815 (2025)
15. Ouyang, L., Zheng, T., Xu, X., Zhang, H., Zhang, Z.: A transformer-based trajectory prediction method for a near-space flight vehicle. In: 2024 43rd Chinese Control Conference (CCC), pp. 4000–4005 (2024). https://doi.org/10.23919/CCC63176.2024.10662821
16. Pei, M., Shi, S., Zhang, L., Li, P., Shen, S.: Goirl: graph-oriented inverse reinforcement learning for multimodal trajectory prediction. arXiv preprint arXiv:2506.21121 (2025)
17. Shen, F., Yang, B., Zhang, J., Xu, C., Chen, Y., He, Y.: Td3-based trajectory optimization for energy consumption minimization in UAV-assisted MEC system. Comput. Netw. **255**, 110882 (2024)
18. Sheng, Z., Xu, Y., Xue, S., Li, D.: Graph-based spatial-temporal convolutional network for vehicle trajectory prediction in autonomous driving. IEEE Trans. Intell. Transp. Syst. **23**(10), 17654–17665 (2022). https://doi.org/10.1109/TITS.2022.3155749
19. Sönmez, S., et al.: Reinforcement learning-based PD controller gains prediction for quadrotor UAVs. Drones **9**(8), 581 (2025). https://doi.org/10.3390/drones9080581
20. Souli, N., et al.: An onboard UAV multi-task system for trajectory prediction and state estimation employing transformer- and reservoir-based networks. ACM J. Auton. Transport. Syst. **2**(4), 18 (2025). https://doi.org/10.1145/3725893
21. Tang, R., Ng, K.K., Li, L., Yang, Z.: A learning-based interacting multiple model filter for trajectory prediction of small multirotor drones considering differential sequences. Transp. Res. Part C Emerg. Technol. **174**, 105115 (2025). https://doi.org/10.1016/j.trc.2025.105115
22. Xiang, J., Chen, J.: Data-driven probabilistic trajectory learning with high temporal resolution in terminal airspace. arXiv preprint arXiv:2409.17359 (2024)
23. Xiang, J., Essick, D., Bautista, L.G., Xie, J., Chen, J.: Landing trajectory prediction for UAS based on generative adversarial network. arXiv preprint arXiv:2411.14403 (2024)
24. Xie, J., Hao, H.: Trajectory prediction and decision optimization for UAV-assisted VEC networks: an integrated LSTM-td3 framework. Information **16**(8), 646 (2025)
25. Zhang, J., Meng, Z., Liu, S., Ji, J., He, J.: A novel trajectory prediction method for UAV air combat based on QCNet-3D. Def. Technol. (2025). https://doi.org/10.1016/j.dt.2025.07.007
26. Zhang, Y., Jia, Z., Dong, C., Liu, Y., Zhang, L., Wu, Q.: Recurrent LSTM-based UAV trajectory prediction with ads-b information. In: GLOBECOM 2022 - 2022 IEEE Global Communications Conference, pp. 1–6 (2022). https://doi.org/10.1109/GLOBECOM48099.2022.10000919
27. Zhao, J., et al.: An improved unscented Kalman filter applied to positioning and navigation of autonomous underwater vehicles. Sensors **25**(2), 551 (2025)
28. Zhou, T., Liu, Z., Jin, W., Han, Z.: Intelligent maneuver decision-making for UAVs using the TD3-LSTM reinforcement learning algorithm under uncertain information. Front. Robot. AI **12**, 1645927 (2025)

# DRL-Based Jointly Trajectory Planning and Beamforming Optimization in STAR-RIS Assisted UAV-NOMA System

Xingyuan Lv[1(✉)], Qian Xu[1], Xin Yang[1], Haochen Liu[1], Yingtai Shao[2], and Ling Wang[1]

[1] Northwestern Polytechnical University, Xian, China
lvxingyuan@mail.nwpu.edu.cn
[2] China Satellite Network Group Co., Ltd, Beijing, China

**Abstract.** This paper investigates the non-orthogonal multiple access (NOMA) communication system of unmanned aerial vehicle (UAV) assisted by simultaneously transmitting and reflecting reconfigurable intelligent surface (STAR-RIS) in the presence of imperfect channel state information (CSI). Specifically, the UAV serves as an aerial base stations (BS) to provide communication services for multiple ground users employing NOAM. Through the STAR-RIS, the transmitted signal can be transmitted to users, who are randomly distributed on both sides of the surface, providing full spatial coverage. In order to maximize the communication sum-rate, the UAV's trajectory, beamforming, as well as the STAR-RIS coefficients are jointly optimized. At same time, the flight safety of the UAV, maximum flight time, and minimum communication rate for each user were also considered. Deep reinforcement learning (DRL) based online decision-making framework is proposed for dynamic scenes with imperfect CSI. The simulation results have verified that the algorithm outperforms other baseline schemes in terms of sum rate.

**Keywords:** Non-orthogonal multiple access (NOMA) · Unmanned aerial vehicle (UAV) · simultaneously transmitting and reflecting reconfigurable intelligent surface (STAR-RIS) · Deep reinforcement learning (DRL)

## 1 Introduction

The excellent maneuverability, flexible deployment capability, and low cost have led to the widespread application and attention of unmanned aerial vehicles (UAVs) in recent years [1, 2]. Compared to ground wireless communication, the maneuverability of UAVs allows them to dynamically adjust their position to best adapt to the environment [3]. Consequently, UAVs are expected to serve as different platforms such as airborne base stations, mobile relays, and mobile users, bringing enormous potential for the next generation of wireless communication [4]. Specifically, using UAVs as aerial BSs can fully utilize the flexible movement of UAVs to provide important line of sight (LoS)


Y. Liu et al. (Eds.): ChinaCom 2025, LNICST 711, pp. 267–279, 2027.
https://doi.org/10.1007/978-3-032-33662-0_20

links, thereby enhancing coverage areas and communication throughput [5]. Due to the above advantages, extensive research has been conducted on UAV communication systems from different perspectives, mainly focusing on UAV's trajectory optimization and launch beamforming design [6].

In addition, It is believed that future wireless networks will face unprecedented and highly diverse user and service demands, and their differentiated demands will further exacerbate the constraints of spectrum scarcity on UAV communication. On this basis, non-orthogonal multiple access (NOMA) technique that supports concurrent transmission from multiple users is considered a highly promising innovative solution aimed at achieving high spectral efficiency [7]. NOMA abandons the traditional OMA's orthogonal resource allocation scheme and allows multiple users to transmit on the same time-frequency resources. Specifically, NOMA sends multiple data streams in parallel at different power levels to simultaneously serve multiple users, thereby introducing mutual interference between users; At the receiving end, each user utilizes successive interference cancellation (SIC) to sequentially decode and remove interference, thereby extracting their desired signal. This technique has five major advantages: significantly improving spectrum efficiency, enhancing user fairness, reducing transmission latency, expanding cell edge throughput, and relaxing the demand for channel feedback accuracy [8].

Despite the excellent maneuverability of UAVs, the air ground link in low altitude urban scenarios is still easily blocked by sudden obstacles. Therefore, reconfigurable intelligent surfaces (RIS) technology has been introduced to reshape the propagation environment [9]. And due to the need for NOMA to manage the orthogonality between user signals by controlling their power levels, the ability of RIS to fine tune user channels has attracted NOMA based communication systems. RIS is composed of numerous low-cost, programmable passive units [10]. By dynamically adjusting their amplitude and phase responses, it can intelligently enhance the desired signal and suppress interference, significantly improving system robustness and universality. In addition, RIS is almost entirely composed of passive components, which have the dual advantages of economic efficiency and green energy conservation. However, traditional reflective RIS can only achieve a single-sided 180° coverage range, which means that in practical applications, there may be service blind spots/blind spots in the transmission area, causing users in that area to be unable to access the network. To overcome this drawback, simultaneously transmitting and reflecting reconfigurable intelligent surface (STAR-RIS) has gained prominence in recent research, a groundbreaking technology that can multiplex incident signals through simultaneous reflection and transmission. The key to implementing "STAR" is that each component must have independent control over current and magnetic field. This collaborative control of electromagnetic characteristics is the basis for synchronously decomposing incident signals into transmitted and reflected beams, and performing independent wavefront manipulation. For simplicity, this paper models STAR-RIS as an independent phase shift model [11].

However, despite assuming that the phase shift coefficient can be independently adjusted in this simple scenario, the optimal strategy for designing UAV's trajectory, beamforming, and the STAR-RIS coefficients effectively and reasonably is challenging for optimizing communication performance due to the high coupling between UAV's trajectory planning, beamforming, and STAR-RIS phase shift configuration [12]. Fortunately, deep learning (DL) has made breakthrough progress in many fields with its ability to extract deep representations and intrinsic patterns from large-scale data. Among them, deep reinforcement learning (DRL) abandons its dependence on offline annotated datasets and instead approaches the optimal decision strategy online through continuous interaction between agents and the environment, thus having natural adaptability to high dynamic and non-stationary wireless channels [13]. In recent years, DRL based optimization paradigms have been widely introduced into STAR-RIS assisted wireless communication systems to solve non convex coupling problems that are difficult to handle with traditional methods [14, 15].

This article studies a NOMA communication system for unmanned aerial vehicles based on STAR-RIS, in which the UAV act as an aerial BS to provide communication services to multiple ground users using NOMA. Given the outstanding potential of deep reinforcement learning (DRL) in uncertain scenarios, this paper aims to propose a joint strategy driven by DRL to achieve the dual goals of ensuring perceptual performance and maximizing communication and rate under the condition of only imperfect channel state information (CSI). And the effectiveness of the proposed algorithm in terms of maximum communication rate was verified through experimental results.

## 2 System Model

As illustrated in Fig. 1, a STAR-RIS assisted UAV system with NOMA was proposed, where the UAV as an aerial BS provides communication services. There are also a passive STAR-RIS and $K$ outdoor mobile users. Furthermore, the UAV features a uniform linear array (ULA) of $M$ antennas and the STAR-RIS is configured as a uniform planar array (UPA) composed of $N = N_x \times N_y$ elements. Let $\mathcal{K} \triangleq \{1, \ldots, K\}$ and $\mathcal{N} \triangleq \{1, \ldots, N\}$ denote the set of mobile users and the element index of STAR-RIS, respectively. These elements are uniformly arranged at half wavelength intervals in both horizontal and vertical directions. Due to significant path loss, signals reflected twice or more by STAR-RIS are ignored.

### 2.1 UAV's Trajectory

Assuming that the entire flight duration is $T$, dividing $T$ evenly into $L$ time slots, utilizing $\delta_t$ to represent each independent time slot, then $t = l\delta_t, \forall\, l \in \mathcal{L} \triangleq \{1, \ldots, L\}$. The static coordinates of the STAR-RIS is $\mathbf{q}_R = (x_R, y_R, z_R)^T$, and the real-time coordinates of the user can be represented as $\mathbf{q}_k[l] = (x_k[l], y_k[l], z_k[l])^T$. Assuming the UAV's flight altitude is $H$, the instantaneous coordinates of the UAV in the $l$-th time slot can be represented as $\mathbf{q}_U[l] = (x_U[l], y_U[l], H)^T$. In practical operation, the flight trajectory of the UAV needs to satisfy the constraints of its initial position $\mathbf{q}_i$ and final position $\mathbf{q}_f$, namely:

$$\mathbf{q}[1] = \mathbf{q}_i, \mathbf{q}[L] = \mathbf{q}_f \tag{1}$$

Where $\mathbf{q}_i$ and $\mathbf{q}_f$ corresponding to the initial and final positions of the UAV respectively.

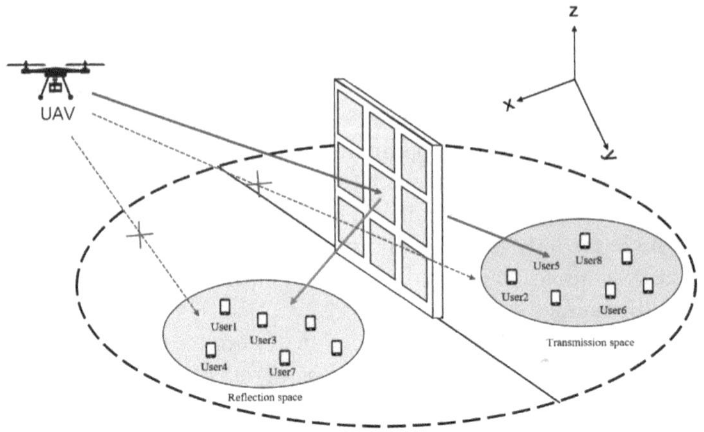


**Fig. 1.** System model: a STAR-RIS assisted UAV system with NOMA.

In urban low altitude environments, unexpected obstacles such as buildings, tower cranes, and elevated bridges are densely distributed, posing a significant threat to the flight safety of the UAV. Therefore, trajectory planning must introduce explicit obstacle avoidance constraints. Specifically, UAVs rely on airborne millimeter wave radar, LiDAR, or stereo vision sensors to perceive the environment in real-time; Let its maximum reliable detection radius be $R$, the minimum distance between the UAV and any obstacle $q \in O$ is defined as the safety distance that must be followed, which can be obtained

$$\|\mathbf{q}_U[l] - \mathbf{q}_o\| \geq d_{\min} \tag{2}$$

Where $d_{\min}$ denotes the safety distance, in order to ensure the safety of UAV, needs to meet $d_{\min} \leq R$, which means a flight restricted zone is designated around the obstacle.

## 2.2 Communication Model

Let $s_k[l] \in \mathbb{C}^{K \times 1}$ and $\mathbf{w}_k[l] \in \mathbb{C}^{M \times 1}$ denote the transmit communication signal vector for mobile user $k$ and the corresponding transmit beamforming vector for user $k$ in each time slot $l$. Assuming that communication signal is an independent and identically distributed (i.i.d.) Gaussian random variable with zero mean and unit variance. Then the signal transmitted by the UAV at time slot $l$ can be modeled as

$$\mathbf{x}[l] = \sum_{k=1}^{K} \mathbf{w}_k[l] s_k[l]. \tag{3}$$

Under the premise that STAR-RIS has independent control over the amplitude and phase of each component, the incident signal will be decomposed into reflection and transmission components, and enter two half spaces respectively. As shown in the figure, the key characteristic of the system is that its role in reflection and transmission space is dynamic: it always defines the side where the UAV is located as the reflection space and the other side as the transmission space. Therefore, when the UAV moves from the $x > 0$ area to the $x < 0$ area, the functions of the two spaces are swapped and switched in real time. The relative UAV-user geometry governs the fundamental criterion for assigning the user to either the reflection or transmission space of the STAR-RIS. Specifically, if the user and the UAV are located on the same side, they receive reflected signals; otherwise, they receive transmitted signals. In addition, we believe that mobile users are randomly distributed in two areas and will not move to another area. The phase shift coefficients of the $n$-th sub-surface of the STAR-RIS in time slot $l$-th can be represented by $\theta_n^r[l] = \sqrt{\beta_n^r[l]}e^{j\phi_n^r[l]}, \forall n \in \mathcal{N}$ and $\theta_n^t[l] = \sqrt{\beta_n^t[l]}e^{j\phi_n^t[l]}, \forall n \in \mathcal{N}$, respectively, where $\beta_n^r[l], \beta_n^t[l] \in [0, 1], \forall n \in \mathcal{N}$ and $\phi_n^r[l], \phi_n^t[l] \in [0, 2\pi), \forall n \in \mathcal{N}$ corresponding to the amplitude and phase shift adjustment applied to the incident signal respectively. Then, we have $\mathbf{\Theta}_r[l] = \text{diag}\big(\theta_1^r[l], \theta_2^r[l], \ldots, \theta_N^r[l]\big)$ and $\mathbf{\Theta}_t[l] = \text{diag}\big(\theta_1^t[l], \theta_2^t[l], \ldots, \theta_N^t[l]\big)$ denote the phase shift coefficients matrices, respectively, with $\mathbf{\Theta}_\gamma[l]$, $\gamma \in [t, r]$ representing the set of transmission coefficient and reflection coefficient matrices. According to the law of conservation of energy, the energy of the signal incident on STAR-RIS should not exceed the sum of the energy of its reflected and transmitted signals. For simplicity, we assume that STAR-RIS will not cause energy loss, i.e. $\beta_n^r[l] + \beta_n^t[l] = 1, \forall n \in \mathcal{N}, \forall l \in \mathcal{L}$.By adjusting the energy distribution ratio appropriately, each sub surface of STAR-RIS can operate in total reflection, total transmission, and mixed modes. For simplicity, we set $\beta_n^r[l] = \beta_n^t[l] = 0.5, \forall n \in \mathcal{N}, \forall l \in \mathcal{L}$, which means equal energy splitting. Furthermore, traditional RIS can also be regarded as STAR-RIS in total reflection mode.

We utilize $\mathbf{H}_{U,R}[l] \in \mathcal{C}^{N\times M}$ and $\mathbf{H}_{R,k}[l] \in \mathcal{C}^{N\times 1}$ to represent the channel matrix from the UAV to the STAR-RIS and the channel matrix from the STAR-RIS to users $k$, respectively. Among them, $\mathbf{H}_{U,R}[l]$ and $\mathbf{H}_{R,k}[l]$ are the Rayleigh fading channel models adopted considering the presence of LoS components. The channel modeling is

$$\mathbf{H}_{U,R}[l] = \sqrt{L_{U,R}}\left(\sqrt{\frac{R}{1+R}}\mathbf{H}_{U,R}^{LoS}[l] + \sqrt{\frac{1}{1+R}}\mathbf{H}_{U,R}^{NLoS}[l]\right) \tag{4}$$

where $L_{U,R}$ represents the channel fading parameters, $\mathbf{H}_{U,R}^{LoS}[l]$ and $\mathbf{H}_{U,R}^{NLoS}[l]$ denotes the LoS and NLoS components, respectively. In which, $\mathbf{H}_{U,R}^{\text{LoS}}[l] = \mathbf{a}_R\big(\psi_{U,R}[l], \zeta_{U,R}[l]\big)\mathbf{a}_U^H\big(\psi_{U,R}[l], \zeta_{U,R}[l]\big)$, where $\psi_{U,R}[l]$ and $\zeta_{U,R}[l]$ are the departure angles (in azimuth and elevation) from the UAV to the STAR-RIS. And $\mathbf{H}_{U,R}^{NLoS}[l]$ is NLoS components. Furthermore, $\mathbf{a}_R(\psi, \zeta)$ and $\mathbf{a}_U(\psi, \zeta)$ can be
expressed as

$$\mathbf{a}_R(\psi, \zeta) = \left[1, \ldots, e^{j\pi(N_x-1)\sin(\psi)\sin(\zeta)}\right]^T \otimes \left[1, \ldots, e^{j\pi(N_y-1)\cos(\zeta)}\right]^T, \tag{5}$$

$$\mathbf{a}_U(\psi, \zeta) = \left[1, \ldots, e^{j(M-1)\pi\sin(\psi)\cos(\zeta)}\right]^T. \tag{6}$$

Additionally, we have

$$\mathbf{H}_{R,k}[l] = \sqrt{L_{R,k}}\left(\sqrt{\frac{R}{1+R}}\mathbf{H}_{R,k}^{LoS}[l] + \sqrt{\frac{1}{1+R}}\mathbf{H}_{R,k}^{NLoS}[l]\right). \tag{7}$$

Then we can mathematically denotes the channel matrix from UAV to user $k$ through STAR-RIS as

$$\mathbf{h}_k^H[l] = \mathbf{h}_{R,k}^H[l]\boldsymbol{\Theta}_{t,r}[l]\mathbf{H}_{U,R}[l], \tag{8}$$

according to the PD-NOMA principle, in time slot $l$, assuming that the relative channel strengths among users are modeled by the relationship: $\left\|\mathbf{h}_1^H\right\| \leq \left\|\mathbf{h}_2^H\right\| \leq \cdots \leq \left\|\mathbf{h}_K^H\right\|$. Therefore, the power gain needs to satisfy

$$\left|\mathbf{h}_k^H\mathbf{w}_1\right|^2 \geq \left|\mathbf{h}_k^H\mathbf{w}_2\right|^2 \geq \cdots \geq \left|\mathbf{h}_k^H\mathbf{w}_K\right|^2. \tag{9}$$

Correspondingly, we define the communication rate for NOMA user $k$ in time instant $t$ as:

$$R_k(t) = \log_2\left(1 + \min_{i=k,\ldots,K}\left\{\frac{\left|\mathbf{h}_i^H\mathbf{w}_k\right|^2}{\sum\limits_{k'=k+1}^{K}\left|\mathbf{h}_i^H\mathbf{w}_{k'}\right|^2 + \sigma_k^2}\right\}\right). \tag{10}$$

Note that during UAV flight, the strength relationship of channel gain between users is not simply from small to large, but dynamically changes with UAV and user positions as well as STAR-RIS phase shift configuration. Therefore, real-time adjustment of power allocation coefficients is required.

## 3 Sum Rate Problem Formulation and Algorithm Design

This section first proposes a joint optimization problem, whose objective is to maximize users sum rate while optimizing UAV's trajectory, active beamforming, and the STAR-RIS passive coefficients. Then, we formalize the joint optimization problem as a Markov decision process. Finally, the DRL algorithm exploited was introduced.

### 3.1 Problem Formulation

The instantaneous communication rate of mobile users mainly depends on three key factors: UAV's position, beamforming vector, and passive beamforming configuration of STAR-RIS. To evaluate the performance gain of STAR-RIS on UAV communication performance, our goal is to maximize the sum rate of all users by jointly optimizing the UAV's trajectory $\mathbf{Q}$, the beamforming matrix $\mathbf{W}$, and the STAR-RIS coefficient matrices

$\mathbf{\Theta}_{\gamma}[l]$ under imperfect CSI conditions. This problem can be formalized as:

$$\begin{aligned}
\mathcal{P}: \max_{\mathbf{Q},\mathbf{\Theta}_{\gamma}[l],W} & \sum_{l=1}^{L}\sum_{k=1}^{K} R_k[l] \\
\text{s.t.} \forall l \in \mathcal{L}, \\
& \mathbf{q}[1] = \mathbf{q}_i, \mathbf{q}[L] = \mathbf{q}_f, \\
& \|q_U[l] - q\| \geq d_{\min}, \forall l \in \mathcal{L}, \\
& R_k[l] \geq R_k^{\min}, \forall k \in \mathcal{K}, \forall l \in \mathcal{L}, \\
& \mathrm{Tr}\{\mathbf{W}[l]\mathbf{W}[l]^H\} \leq P_{\max}, \forall l \in \mathcal{L}, \\
& \beta_n^t[l], \beta_n^r[l] \in [0, 1], \forall l \in \mathcal{L}, \\
& \beta_n^r[l] = \beta_n^t[l] = 0.5, \forall n \in \mathcal{N}, \forall l \in \mathcal{L}, \\
& \theta_n^t[l], \theta_n^r[l] \in [0, 2\pi), \forall l \in \mathcal{L}, \\
& |\mathbf{h}_k^H \mathbf{w}_1|^2 \geq |\mathbf{h}_k^H \mathbf{w}_2|^2 \geq \cdots \geq |\mathbf{h}_k^H \mathbf{w}_K|^2.
\end{aligned} \tag{11}$$

Among them, the first four constraints are for the UAV flight process; the fifth constraint states that the data rate of user $k$ should be greater than the minimum data rate represented as $R_k^{min}$; the sixth constraint states that the total transmission power of the UAV should be less than the maximum transmission power; the following constraints are the STAR-RIS phase shift and amplitude constraints, as well as the NOMA power constraint. The above optimization problem is a multi-objective problem that mainly focuses on communication performance.

The inherent non convex nature of the problem arises from the nonlinear coupling effect between multiple variables, significantly increasing the computational burden. Given the close coupling relationship between UAV flight trajectories and active/passive beamforming vectors, achieving multivariable joint optimization faces significant challenges. Therefore, we adopt a twin delayed deep deterministic policy gradient algorithm (TD3) to solve this problem, which is used to generate beamforming, STAR-RIS coefficients, and UAV trajectories. Compared with traditional schemes, this framework effectively reduces the dimensionality of the policy search space through variable decoupling. TD3 is used as a DRL agent, which is an improved algorithm based on the DDPG algorithm. Next, we will first model the problem as an MDP framework, and then provide a detailed introduction to the TD3 algorithm.

### 3.2 MDP Model

In this section, the problem is modeled as a Markov Decision Process (MDP), which is a commonly used model for developing such environmental interaction systems. The temporal nature of this problem determines that it can be modeled as a multi-stage continuous decision-making process, that is, determining the next single time step based on the current environmental interaction. Let $\langle \mathcal{S}, \mathcal{A}, \mathcal{P}, \mathcal{R}, \gamma \rangle$ denotes the MDP framework, they respectively represent the state space, action space, state transition matrix, reward value, and discount factor.

DRL agents learn strategies through interaction with the environment, guided by the principle of maximizing long-term cumulative returns, which is reflected in the optimization of the state value function $Q_{\pi}(s)$. Mathematically, it can be expressed as

$$\pi^*(s, a) = \arg\max_{\pi} Q_{\pi}(s), \tag{12}$$

where $\pi^*(s, a)$ is the optimal policy.

This strategy is mathematically a mapping from the state to the probability of selecting each possible action, and the state value function is the expected cumulative discount return that the agent receives from the current state, which is

$$Q_\pi(s) = \mathbb{E}_\pi[G_l S_l = s] = \mathbb{E}_\pi\left[\sum_{k=0}^{\infty} \gamma^k R_{l+k+1} S_l = s\right], \quad \forall s \in S, \tag{13}$$

where $\mathbb{E}_\pi$ represents the expected value of the random variable when the agent follows the transition strategy in the $l$-th time step, and $\gamma \in [0, 1]$ represents the discount factor, which determines the degree to which the agent values future rewards during the learning process. The discount factor approaching 0 will make the agent "short-sighted" and only focus on immediate rewards; and approaching 1 encourages "far sighted" behavior, making it more focused on long-term returns. In addition, $G_l = \sum_{k=0}^{\infty} \gamma^k R_{l+k+1}$ can be represented as the action of maximizing the total discount rewards obtained during the learning process.The following provides a detailed description of the state, actions, rewards, and state transitions of the developed MDP.

1. State Space: The state space of DRL encompasses environmental observation information and state transitions caused by historical actions. Therefore, the joint optimization of coupled variables highly relies on the continuous real-time interaction between the intelligent agent and this dynamic channel environment. Therefore, in the $l$-th time slot, we represent the state space as $\mathbf{S}_l = \{\mathbf{q}[l], \mathcal{D}[l], R_{\text{sum}}[l-1], H[l]\}$, which includes the position of the UAV, the obstacle position perceived by the UAV, the reward value, and the channel state information. In addition, to enable the agent to learn the optimal strategy in scenarios containing only imperfect channel state information (CSI), this study further injects random perturbations into the channel gain set to realistically depict CSI errors. The above mechanism ensures that the system can approach and maximize the rate even under non ideal CSI conditions.
2. Action Space: The action space includes UAV flight direction, beamforming, and STAR-RIS transmission/reflection phase shift coefficient configuration decisions. We use DRL to decouple UAV trajectories and other optimization variables. Then we have $A_l = \{\text{Re}\{\mathbf{W}\}, \text{Im}\{\mathbf{W}\}, \text{Re}\{\mathbf{\Theta}_\gamma[l]\}, \text{Im}\{\mathbf{\Theta}_\gamma[l]\}, x_l, y_l\}$.
3. Reward: The core objective of this study is to maximize the total speed of all mobile users during the drone service period. Given that the behavior of reinforcement learning agents is driven by reward functions, their design must be closely aligned with the above objectives. Therefore, we directly map the reward function to the achievable total rate under a given strategy

$$R_l = \sum_{k=1}^{K} R_k[l] - K_1 p_e - K_2 p_u - K_3 p_k \tag{14}$$

where $p_e$, $p_u$, and $p_k$ respectively represent penalties for not meeting the maximum transmission power constraint of the UAV, penalties for violations during the UAV flight, and penalties for not meeting user QoS.

Within the established MDP framework, the UAV position, STAR-RIS phase shift, and sudden obstacles all exhibit significant randomness, and decision-makers can only formulate strategies based on partially observable information. More importantly, the system transition probability matrix is unknown, making traditional model-based methods difficult to apply. Deep reinforcement learning (DRL) precisely eliminates the dependence on precise environmental models, allowing agents to learn optimal control strategies online through continuous interaction with the environment. The next section will elaborate on the DRL algorithm used.

### 3.3 TD3 Algorithm

The twin delayed deep deterministic (TD3) algorithm is currently the mainstream deep reinforcement learning method for continuous action spaces, as shown in the figure. As a systematic improvement to DDPG, TD3 introduces three core technologies to address the training instability and susceptibility to local optima caused by overestimation of Q values and accumulation of estimation errors in the latter.

(1) Dual Critic Architectur: Maintain two sets of Actor Critic networks in parallel, and target the smaller of their Q values to effectively suppress overestimation;
(2) Delay policy update: The parameter update of the Actor network lags behind that of the Critic network, significantly reducing the bias in the policy gradient and improving overall stability;
(3) Smooth regularization of target strategy: Injecting controllable white noise into the output of the target strategy to achieve a smooth approximation of the target Q value, further suppressing error propagation and accelerating convergence.

## 4 Numerical Results

The core work of this section is based on the TD3 algorithm, which systematically evaluates its comprehensive performance in the considered system by jointly optimizing multi coupled variables.

Our simulation scenario is set as follows: the initial position of the drone's mission is set to (30, 20, 30) m, and the final position is set to (30, 20, 30) m. In addition, STAR-RIS is statically arranged at (0, 0, 12.5) m. The initial number of STAR-RIS elements is set to 16, and the number of UAV antennas is set to 4. Assuming each mobile user randomly trains in STAR-RIS and moves at a fixed speed during UAV flight. The following table lists the hyperparameters of the Agent during training (Table 1).

In Fig. 2, we present the evolution curves of four algorithms, NOMA-TD3, OMA-TD3, NOMA-DDPG, and OMA-DDPG, in the STAR-RIS assisted UAV-NOMA scenario, for the training period (episode) and total system rate (summary rate). The following phenomena can be observed:

(1) Multiple access gain: Regardless of the DRL algorithm used, the average total rate of the NOMA scheme after convergence is significantly higher than that of the corresponding OMA scheme. This is because NOMA effectively improving spectral efficiency; However, OMA is limited by orthogonal resource partitioning, making it difficult to fully tap into the reuse potential of high channel correlation users.

**Table 1.** Hyperparametes for TD3.

| Hyperparameters | Values |
|---|---|
| Agent size | 1024 * 512 * 512 * 256 |
| Actor learning rate | 0.0001 |
| Critic learning rate | 0.0005 |
| Number of episodes | 500 |
| Time step | 100 |
| Batch size | 128 |
| Replay memory size | 50000 |

(2) Algorithm stability and convergence speed: TD3 series curves can quickly climb in the early stages of training and tend to stabilize after about 300–400 episodes; In contrast, the DDPG series curves exhibit significant oscillations, slow convergence speed, and generally lower final performance than TD3. This difference is mainly due to the improvement of TD3 on the DDPG algorithm.
(3) Robustness performance: When the CSI error increases or obstacles randomly appear, the curve fluctuation of NOMA-TD3 is the smallest, indicating that it has stronger robustness to uncertain environments; However, the performance of NOMA-DPG slightly decreases under the same disturbance.

Overall, Fig. 2 not only verifies the spectral efficiency advantage of NOMA over OMA, but also demonstrates the excellent convergence and robustness of TD3 in continuous, high-dimensional, and non convex resource allocation problems, providing theoretical support for its deployment in actual low altitude complex urban scenarios.

Figure. 3 shows the UAV's trajectory generated by the TD3 strategy during the online deployment phase. As shown in the figure, UAVs can rely entirely on onboard sensors and real-time channel feedback to autonomously avoid static obstacles in the presence of unknown obstacle distributions, always maintaining a distance of no less than the preset safety threshold from the nearest obstacle, thereby ensuring the physical safety of low altitude flight. Further observation reveals that, constrained by the maximum endurance time, the overall heading of the UAV always points towards the mission endpoint, but exhibits a mixed shape of "line arc" in both horizontal and vertical dimensions. This is because by moderately extending laterally, the UAV actively maintains the maximum direct path (LoS) distance between different STAR-RIS panels to reduce path loss and improve the received signal-to-noise ratio.

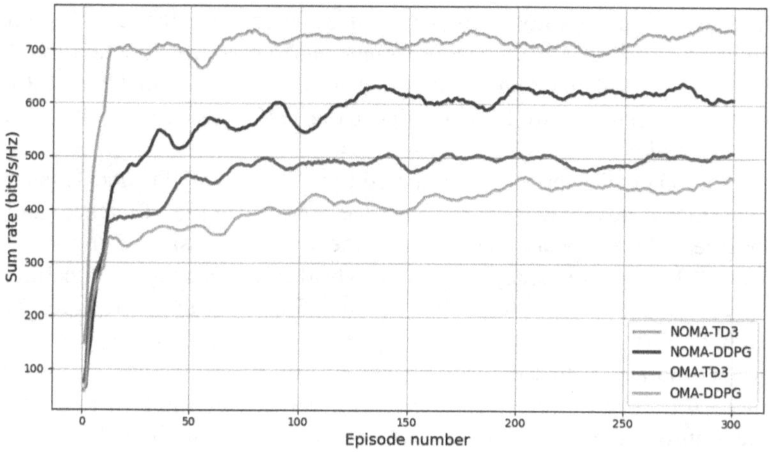


**Fig. 2.** Performance comparison among NOMA-TD3, OMA-TD3, NOMA-DDPG and OMA-DDPG.

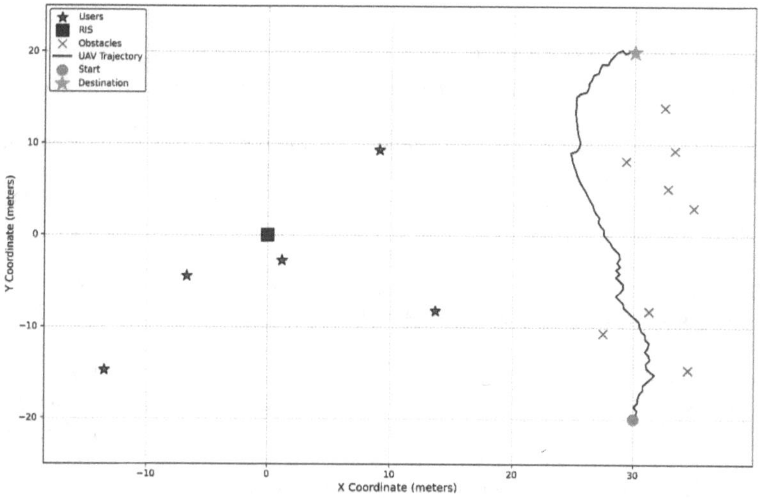


**Fig. 3.** Optimal trajectory map of UAV trained with TD3.

## 5 Conclusion

This study proposes a STAR-RIS assisted UAV-NOMA integrated framework that fully integrates the high maneuverability of unmanned aerial vehicles with STAR-RIS's programmable reconstruction capability for wireless propagation environments, aiming to simultaneously improve spectral efficiency and coverage robustness. We take the overall system speed as the optimization objective and explicitly incorporate 1) three-dimensional obstacle avoidance safety for unmanned aerial vehicles in the constraint set; 2) Maximum flight duration; 3) The minimum achievable rate for mobile users is used to construct a complex non convex optimization problem that couples unmanned aerial vehicle trajectories, onboard beamforming, and STAR-RIS reflection/transmission phase shifts. To cope with uncertain factors such as imperfect Channel State Information (CSI) and random obstacles, we further propose the TD3 algorithm to achieve real-time online decision-making.

The simulation results show that compared to traditional DDPG and TD3 baselines, TD3 has significant advantages in convergence speed, sample efficiency, and disturbance robustness. Future work may include the following aspects: introducing millimeter wave/THz high-frequency band and hybrid beamforming architecture, studying the impact of STAR-RIS phase shift quantization error and hardware non ideality on system performance; considering integrated communication and sensing (ISAC) indicators, incorporating radar detection accuracy and target positioning error into the reward function to achieve joint communication perception optimization; Adopting a multi-agent reinforcement learning framework, supporting multi UAV collaboration and multi STAR-RIS joint regulation, further exploring large-scale distributed resource management in air ground air heterogeneous networks.

## References

1. Pandey, G.K., Gurjar, D.S., Yadav, S., Jiang, Y., Yuen, C.: UAV-assisted communications with RF energy harvesting: a comprehensive survey. IEEE Commun. Surv. Tutor. **27**(2), 782–838 (2025)
2. Mao, K., et al.: A survey on channel sounding technologies and measurements for UAV-assisted communications. IEEE Trans. Instrum. Meas. **73**, 1–24 (2024)
3. Lu, Z., Jia, Z., Wu, Q., Han, Z.: Joint trajectory planning and communication Design for Multiple UAVs in intelligent collaborative air–ground communication systems. IEEE Internet Things J. **11**(19), 31053–31067 (2024)
4. Maeng, S.J., Park, J., Guvenç, İ.: Analysis of UAV radar and communication network coexistence with different multiple access protocols. IEEE Trans. Commun. **71**(11), 6578–6592 (2023)
5. Bai, L., Huang, Z., Feng, T., Cheng, X.: A non-Stationary Channel model for 6G multi-UAV cooperative communication. IEEE Trans. Wirel. Commun. **23**(2), 949–961 (2024)
6. Wu, P., Yuan, X., Hu, Y., Schmeink, A.: Joint power allocation and trajectory design for UAV-enabled covert communication. IEEE Trans. Wirel. Commun. **23**(1), 683–698 (2024)
7. Naeem, M.K., Abozariba, R., Asaduzzaman, M., Patwary, M.: Mobility support for MIMO-NOMA user clustering in next-generation wireless networks. IEEE Trans. Mob. Comput. **22**(10), 6011–6026 (2023)
8. Chauhan, A., Jaiswal, A.: A novel multi-carrier quadrature NOMA with $\alpha$–$\mu$ fading channel for multi-user scenario. IEEE Trans. Commun. **72**(3), 1474–1486 (2024)
9. Saif, M., Valaee, S.: RIS alignment via virtual partitioning for resilient uplink multi-RIS-assisted UAV communications. IEEE Trans. Commun. **73**(8), 6764–6779 (2025)
10. Khan, N., et al.: Design of STAR-RIS assisted uplink NOMA for maximum fairness. IEEE Trans. Veh. Technol. **74**(3), 5223–5228 (2025)
11. Su, Y., Pang, X., Lu, W., Zhao, N., Wang, X., Nallanathan, A.: Joint location and beamforming optimization for STAR-RIS aided NOMA-UAV networks. IEEE Trans. Veh. Technol. **72**(8), 11023–11028 (2023)
12. Zhang, X., Zhang, H., Sun, L., Wang, X., Long, K., Leung, V.C.M.: STAR-RIS-aided UAV communication for next generation multiple access with resource allocation. IEEE J. Sel. Top. Sig. Process. **18**(7), 1222–1234 (2024)

13. Ye, X., Mao, Y., Yu, X., Fu, L.: Intelligent Omni-surface-aided integrated sensing and communications based on deep reinforcement learning with knowledge transfer. IEEE Trans. Wirel. Commun. **24**(5), 4344–4360 (2025)
14. Tian, B., et al.: UAV-assisted wireless cooperative communication and coded caching: a multiagent two-timescale DRL approach. IEEE Trans. Mob. Comput. **23**(5), 4389–4404 (2024)
15. Zhao, J., Zhu, Y., Mu, X., Cai, K., Liu, Y., Hanzo, L.: Simultaneously transmitting and reflecting reconfigurable intelligent surface (STAR-RIS) assisted UAV communications. IEEE J Sel Areas Commun. **40**(10), 3041–3056 (2022)

# Rapid Resource Allocation in UAV-Assisted Multi-band Relay Networks

Jihao Cai and Haichao Wang(✉)

Army Engineering University of PLA, Nanjing 210007, China
whcw10919@sina.com

**Abstract.** This paper studies the resource allocation in a UAV-assisted multi-band relay network. The communication channels and transmission rates per hop are optimized to maximize the expected throughput. A solution to the mixed integer nonlinear programming problem is derived through alternating optimization. For the rate optimization subproblem, we utilize a greedy-based searching algorithm to find a local optimal solution. For the channel optimization subproblem, we formulate an equivalent assignment problem and employ the Hungarian algorithm to obtain the optimal solution. Simulation results show that proposed approach is able to have decent performance with quick convergence.

**Keywords:** Multi-band network (MBN) · Unmanned aerial vehicle (UAV) · Relay network · Resource allocation · Alternating optimization (AO)

## 1 Introduction

Modern applications (e.g., industrial IoT, autonomous vehicles) demand ultra-reliable low-latency communications with throughput exceeding 1 Gbps [10]. Due to the inherent limitations in available bandwidth and coverage, single-band networks (SBNs) struggle to meet the stringent communication requirements. To overcome these challenges, multi-band network (MBN) has emerged as a promising approach, aggregating heterogeneous frequency resources to enhance capacity and reliability [1,4]. However, user devices are power-limited and cannot maintain reliable communication over long distances-even when utilizing multiple bands. This limitation motivates the use of relay to extend coverage and improve link quality. Owing to the favorable characteristics of line-of-sight channels, an unmanned aerial vehicle (UAV) serving as a relay can effectively enhance the transmission quality for ground users [6]. Therefore, this paper studies the

Supported in part by the Natural Science Foundation of Jiangsu Province under Grants BK20212001, BK20240200, BE2023022, and BE2023022-4; and in part by the National Natural Science Foundation of China under Grants 62271501 and 62521003.


Y. Liu et al. (Eds.): ChinaCom 2025, LNICST 711, pp. 280–288, 2027.
https://doi.org/10.1007/978-3-032-33662-0_21

communication channel and transmission rate optimization in a UAV-assisted multi-band relay network.

Compared to decode-and-forward (DF), truncated-decode-and-forward (TDF) relay scheme offers higher transmission speeds but requires more communication channels than DF [3]. The TDF scheme initiates forwarding of a partially decoded bit sequence before completion of the frame reception by truncating the decoding process through convolutional coding and Virerbi decoding and therefore allows all relay nodes to transmit simultaneously [3]. The MBN, with its larger number of channels, is ideal for implementing TDF to boost transmission speed, in contrast to SBNs.

References [5,7–9] studied the resource allocation in TDF-based MBNs employing methods such as optimization, game theory, and reinforcement learning. A drawback of these works is the assumption that channel state information (CSI) is perfectly known. Frequent channel probing incurs additional energy costs. This overhead is significantly higher in MBNs due to their far greater number of channels compared to SBNs, making the probing process even more costly. To this end, we investigate resource allocation under statistical CSI, avoiding channel probing by optimizing for the expected throughput.

The main contributions of this paper are as follow: This work investigates resource allocation in a UAV-assisted MBN, where UAVs act as TDF relays to enhance transmission reliability. An efficient joint channel and rate selection strategy is derived via alternating optimization (AO), maximizing the expected throughput under statistical CSI. Simulation results demonstrate the superiority of the proposed scheme over conventional approaches.

## 2 System Model and Problem Formulation

As shown in Fig. 1, we consider a UAV-assisted MBN consisting of an information source $S$, $N$ hovering UAVs, an information destination $D$, and $L$ communication bands. The UAV serves as relays and $S \to R_1 \to R_2 \to \cdots \to R_N \to D$ is the communication path. Each band is characterized by a distinct carrier frequency, number of orthogonal channels, and channel bandwidth. Each UAV is equipped with $L$ antennas with each antenna working on a frequency band. We assume each UAV uses two of the $L$ antennas for communication, i.e., one antenna for reception from its previous node and the other antenna for transmission to its next node. The TDF relay protocol [8] is employed, i.e., all hops transmit at the same time and the communication channel of each hop is different to eliminate intra-hop interference. We assume the number of channels are no less than that of hops to ensure the implementation of TDF. We also assume each hop transmits at a fixed data rate to reduce the cost of obtaining the instantaneous CSI.

The carrier frequency, bandwidth, and number of channels of band $l$ are denoted by $f_l$, $b_l$, and $m_l$, respectively. Denote $\mathcal{C}_l = \{c_{l,1}, c_{l,2}, \cdots c_{l,m_l}\}$ as the set of channels of band $l$. Therefore, $\mathcal{C} = \bigcup_{l=1}^{L} \mathcal{C}_l$ is the set of channels in all bands and $M = \sum_{l=1}^{L} m_l$ is the number of channels in all bands. For notational brevity,

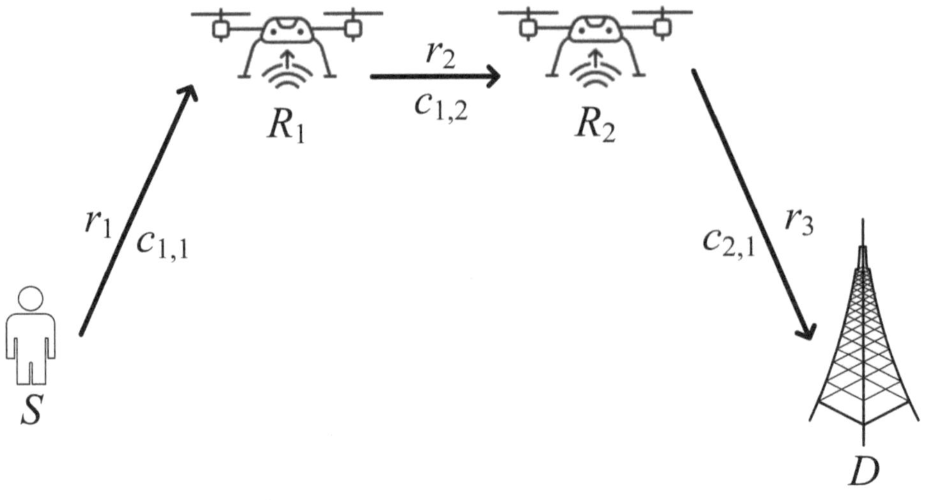


**Fig. 1.** An example of a two-UAV multi-band relay network.

the $k$-th hop denotes the transmission from $R_{k-1}$ to $R_k$. The selected channel and transmission rate of the $k$-th hop are denoted by $c_k$ and $r_k$, respectively.

Due to the change of wireless channels, we adopt the block fading Alpha-Beta-Gamma (ABG) channel model [2], i.e., the channel gain remains unchanged in a time slot and varies independently at different slots. The channel gain of the $k$-th hop in band $l$ is as follows:

$$h_k^l = 10^{\frac{-10\alpha \log_{10} d_k - \beta - 10\gamma \log_{10} f_l - X_\sigma^{ABG}}{10}}, \tag{1}$$

where $d_k$ is the Euclidean distance between $R_{k-1}$ and $R_k$. $\alpha$, $\beta$, $\gamma$, and $\sigma$ are environment-related parameters. $f_l$ in GHz is the carrier frequency of the band $l$. $X_\sigma^{ABG} \sim N\left(0, \sigma^2\right)$ represents the shadow fading.

Since different hops occupy different channels, there is no mutual interference between different hops. Hence, the channel capacity of the $k$-th hop in a channel in band $l$ is as follows:

$$C_k^l = b_l \log_2\left(1 + \frac{p_k h_k^l}{N_0 b_l}\right), \tag{2}$$

where $p_k$ is the transmit power of $R_{k-1}$ and $N_0$ is the power spectral density of additive gaussian white noise (AWGN).

Since the $k$-th hop transmits with fixed rate $r_k$, the successful transmission probability is the probability that the transmission rate is no great than the channel capacity:

$$\begin{aligned} F_k^l\left(r_k\right) &= \Pr\left\{r_k \le C_k^l\right\} \\ &= 1 - Q\left\{\frac{-A_k - 10\log_{10}\left[B_k\left(2^{\frac{r_k}{b_l}} - 1\right)\right]}{\sigma}\right\}, \end{aligned} \tag{3}$$

where $Q(x) = \int_x^{\infty} \frac{e^{-t^2}}{\sqrt{2\pi}} dt$, $A_k = 10\alpha \log_{10} d_k + \beta + 10\gamma \log_{10} f_l$, and $B_k = \frac{N_0 b_l}{p_k}$. The derivation of (3), being a straightforward application of fundamental probability theory, is omitted here.

According to the TDF scheme, all hops transmit simultaneously. Therefore, the expected throughput is as follows:

$$T(\mathbf{R}, \mathbf{C}) = \left( \prod_{k=1}^{N+1} F_k^{l(c_k)}(r_k) \right) \times \left( \min_{1 \leq k \leq N+1} r_k \right), \tag{4}$$

where $\mathbf{R} = [r_1, r_2, \cdots, r_{N+1}]$ and $\mathbf{C} = [c_1, c_2, \cdots, c_{N+1}]$ represent the transmission rate and the selected channel on each hop, respectively. $l(c_k)$ denotes the band of the selected channel of the $k$-th hop. The first term in (4) denotes the overall successful transmission probability, while the second term denotes the overall equivalent data rate.

We aim to maximize the expected throughput through channel and transmission rate optimization:

$$\mathrm{P1}: \max_{\mathbf{R}, \mathbf{C}} \; T(\mathbf{R}, \mathbf{C}) \tag{5a}$$

$$s.t. \; r_k > 0, \forall k \in \{1, 2, \cdots, N+1\}, \tag{5b}$$

$$c_k \in \mathcal{C}, \forall k \in \{1, 2, \cdots, K+1\}, \tag{5c}$$

$$c_i \neq c_j, \forall i, j \in \{1, 2, \cdots, K+1\}, \tag{5d}$$

where (5b) is the transmission rate constraint. (5c) and (5d) is the channel access constraint.

## 3 Problem Solution

Since Problem P1 is a mixed-integer nonlinear programming (MINLP) problem, it is generally challenging to solve. To derive an efficient solution, we adopt an AO framework by solving the rate subproblem (P2) and channel subproblem (P3) iteratively.

### 3.1 Rate Optimization Subproblem

In P2, the channels per hop $\mathbf{C}$ is fixed. We aim to maximize the expected throughput though appropriate transmission rate optimization:

$$\mathrm{P2}: \max_{\mathbf{R}} \; T(\mathbf{R}, \mathbf{C}) \tag{6a}$$

$$s.t. \; r_k > 0, \forall k \in \{1, 2, \cdots, N+1\}, \tag{6b}$$

According to (3), the successful transmission probability is a monotonically decreasing function of the transmission rate. It can thus be proven by contradiction that the transmission rates must be equal across all hops at the optimal solution. Specifically, if the rate of a preceding hop exceeds that of a subsequent hop, reducing the former to match the latter can increase the product of the success probabilities without reducing the end-to-end rate, thereby improving the overall expected throughput. The detailed derivation is omitted due to space constraints.

This simplification reduces the original multi-variable problem to a tractable single-variable optimization. Although the theoretical convexity of the objective function is difficult to establish due to its structure as a product of the rate and the success probabilities of all hops, extensive simulations across various parameter settings demonstrate that it is empirically convex. Therefore, we employ the gradient ascent-based Algorithm 1 to efficiently obtain a near-optimal solution.

**Algorithm 1.** Transmission Rate Optimization via Gradient Ascent

**Require:** $\Delta r$: Step size for numerical gradient computation
  $\eta$: Learning rate (step size for gradient ascent)
  $\text{itr}_{\text{max}}$: Maximum number of iterations
  $\epsilon$: Convergence threshold

**Initialization:**
$r \leftarrow 0$ {Initial transmission rate}
**for** $i = 1$ **to** $\text{itr}_{\text{max}}$ **do**
  Compute numerical gradient:
  $dT \leftarrow \dfrac{T(r + \Delta r) - T(r)}{\Delta r}$
  Update rate: $r_{\text{new}} \leftarrow r + \eta \cdot dT$
  **if** $|T(r_{new}) - T(r)| > \epsilon$ **then**
    $r \leftarrow r_{\text{new}}$ {Accept the update}
  **else**
    **break** {Stop if change is negligible}
  **end if**
**end for**
**return** $r$ {Optimized transmission rate}

### 3.2 Channel Optimization Subproblem

In P3, the transmission rate per hop $r$ is fixed. We aim to maximize the expected throughput through channel selection. The channel assignment problem is a combinatorial optimization problem with factorial complexity, for which exhaustive search becomes computationally prohibitive as the number of hops or channels grows large. To address this, we formulate the channel optimization problem as an equivalent assignment problem by adding virtual hops and use the Hungarian algorithm to find the optimal channel allocation scheme.

**Algorithm 2.** Channel Assignment via the Hungarian Algorithm

**Require:** $\mathbf{W}$: The $K \times K$ weight matrix calculated from (8)
**Initialization:**
Reduce rows: For each row $i$, set $\mathbf{W}[i,:] \leftarrow \mathbf{W}[i,:] - \min(\mathbf{W}[i,:])$
Reduce columns: For each column $j$, set $\mathbf{W}[:,j] \leftarrow \mathbf{W}[:,j] - \min(\mathbf{W}[:,j])$
Cover all zeros with the minimum number of lines (horizontal or vertical).
**while** number of covering lines $\neq K$ **do**
  Find $\delta \leftarrow \min(\mathbf{W}[i,j])$ for all uncovered elements $(i,j)$
  Subtract $\delta$ from all uncovered rows:
    For each uncovered row $i$, $\mathbf{W}[i,:] \leftarrow \mathbf{W}[i,:] - \delta$
  Add $\delta$ to all covered columns:
    For each covered column $j$, $\mathbf{W}[:,j] \leftarrow \mathbf{W}[:,j] + \delta$
  Cover all zeros with the minimum number of lines.
**end while**
Select $K$ zeros such that each row and column contains exactly one selected zero.
**return** the assignment: a set of $(i,j)$ pairs indicating hop $i$ is assigned to channel $j$.

$$\text{P3}: \min_{\mathbf{X}} \sum_{j=1}^{K}\sum_{i=1}^{K} x_{i,j} w_{i,j} \tag{7a}$$

$$s.t.\ x_{i,j} \in \{0,1\}, \forall i,j \in \{1,2,\cdots,K\}, \tag{7b}$$

$$\sum_{i=1}^{K} x_{i,j} = 1, \forall j \in \{1,2,\cdots,K\}, \tag{7c}$$

$$\sum_{j=1}^{K} x_{i,j} = 1, \forall i \in \{1,2,\cdots,K\}, \tag{7d}$$

where $K = \max\{M, N+1\}$. $\mathbf{X}_{K\times K}$ is the channel allocation profile with $x_{i,j} = 1$ means that the $i$-th hop chooses the $j$-th channel and $x_{i,j} = 0$ if otherwise. The channels from the 1st to the $m_1$-th belong to band 1. Similarly, the $(m_1+1)$-th to the $(m_1+m_2)$-th channels belong to band 2, and so on. The channel selection constraints, given in (7b), (7c), and (7d), enforce that no two hops share the same channel. $\mathbf{W}_{K\times K}$ is the weight matrix constructed as follows:

$$w_{i,j} = \begin{cases} -\ln\left[F_i^{l(j)}(r)\right], & \text{if } \begin{cases} i \in \{1,2,\cdots,N+1\}, \\ j \in \{1,2,\cdots,M\} \end{cases} \\ C, & \text{otherwise} \end{cases} \tag{8}$$

where $C$ is a large positive number. The first case in (8) corresponds to the objective function of the original problem P1. This equivalence holds because applying the logarithm to a positive function preserves the location of its maximum, and maximizing a function is equivalent to minimizing its negative. The second case in (8) are the virtual hops/channels, established to satisfy the standard formulation of the assignment problem.

Since P3 is a standard assignment problem, it can be efficiently solved using the Hungarian algorithm, which has a time complexity of $\mathcal{O}(K^3)$, as summarized in Algorithm 2.

## 4 Simulations and Discussions

As shown in Fig. 2, the source, 3 relays, and the destination are located in a square with a side length 500 m. $(0, 0, 0)$ and $(500, 500, 0)$ are the locations of $S$ and $D$, respectively. The 3 relay nodes are uniformly distributed along the line segment between $S$ and $D$, with their z-coordinates uniformly distributed in the interval $[10, 50]$. The transmit power of each node follows a truncated Gaussian distribution, i.e., $p \sim \max\{-10, N(10, 4)\}$ dBm. 4 frequency bands are simulated, i.e., LoRa (863 MHz, 1 channel, $b_1 = 125$ kHz) [11], LTE Band 3 (1.8 GHz, 2 channels, $b_2 = 15$ MHz), WiFi 2.4G (2.4 GHz, 3 channels, $b_3 = 20$ MHz), and WiFi 5G (5.17 GHz, 4 channels, $b_4 = 40$ MHz). The power spectral density of AWGN is $N_0 = -174$ dBm/Hz. The ABG channel parameters are $\alpha = 3.4$ dB, $\beta = 19.2$ dB, $\gamma = 2.3$ dB, and $\sigma = 6.5$ dB.

The proposed scheme is evaluated against two benchmarks: the Exhaustive Search Scheme (ESS) and the Single-Band Scheme (SBS).

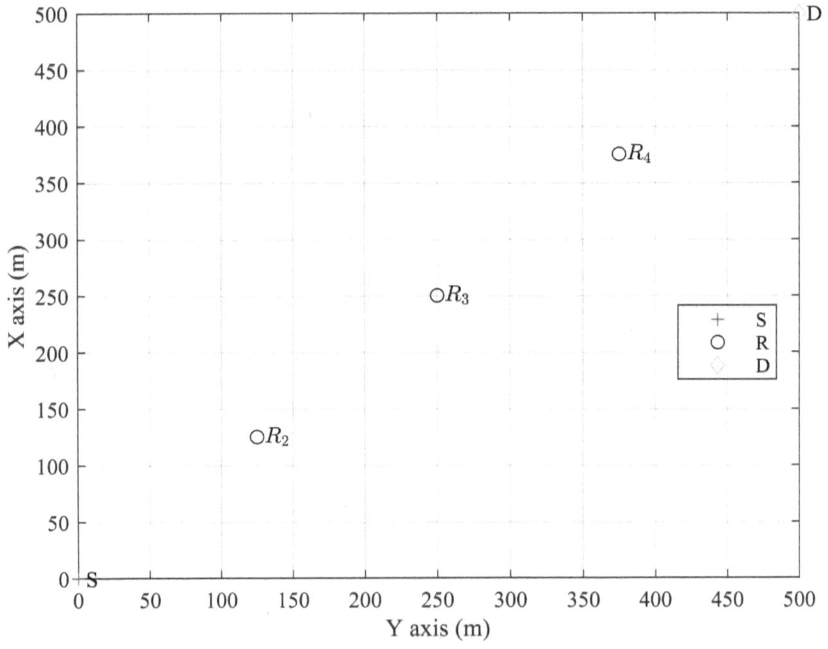


**Fig. 2.** Topology projection onto the x-y plane.

In the exhaustive search scheme, all possible channel assignments are exhaustively enumerated. For each candidate channel assignment, the corresponding transmission rate is determined using Algorithm 1. The solution that yields the highest utility is selected.

In the single-band scheme, all hops are restricted to channels within Band 4, and the transmission rate is optimized via Algorithm 1.

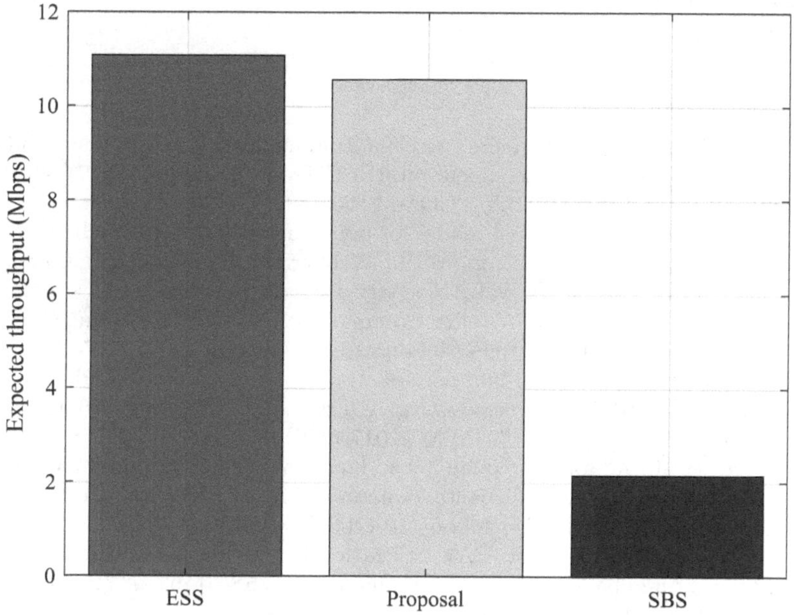


**Fig. 3.** Performance comparison of different algorithms.

Figure 3 compares the performance of the evaluated algorithms. The Exhaustive Search Scheme (ESS) achieves the highest performance, while the proposed scheme closely approximates it, attaining about 95% of the ESS performance. The Single-Band Scheme yields the lowest result. More importantly, the proposed scheme achieves near-optimal performance with significantly fewer iterations than ESS, demonstrating its capability for rapid convergence to a high-quality solution.

## 5 Conclusions

In this paper, we investigate the joint optimization of channel assignment and transmission rate in a UAV-assisted multi-band relay network. Owing to the heterogeneity in bandwidth and channel fading across different frequency bands, the optimization variables are tightly coupled. To address this challenge, an alternating optimization framework is adopted, decomposing the original expected throughput maximization problem into two manageable subproblems. The multi-variable rate optimization is simplified into an equivalent single-variable problem. A gradient ascent algorithm is employed to efficiently compute a near-optimal transmission rate. The channel selection subproblem is formulated as an equivalent assignment problem and solved optimally using the Hungarian algorithm. By iteratively solving these two subproblems, a locally optimal solution is attained. Simulation results demonstrate the superiority of the proposed scheme over existing baseline methods.

## References

1. Aboagye, S., et al.: Multi-band wireless communication networks: fundamentals, challenges, and resource allocation. IEEE Trans. Commun. **72**(7), 4333–4383 (2024). https://doi.org/10.1109/TCOMM.2024.3366816
2. Docomo, N., et al.: 5G channel model for bands up to 100 GHz. Tech. rep. (2016)
3. Egashira, N., Yano, K., Tsukamoto, S., Webber, J., Kumagai, T.: Low latency relay processing scheme for WLAN systems employing multiband simultaneous transmission. In: 2017 IEEE Wireless Communications and Networking Conference (WCNC), pp. 1–6 (2017). https://doi.org/10.1109/WCNC.2017.7925714
4. Fadlullah, Z.M., et al.: Multi-hop wireless transmission in multi-band WLAN systems: proposal and future perspective. IEEE Wirel. Commun. **26**(1), 108–113 (2019). https://doi.org/10.1109/MWC.2017.1700148
5. Hanyu, A., et al.: Adaptive frequency band and channel selection for simultaneous receiving and sending in multiband communication. IEEE Wirel. Commun. Lett. **8**(2), 460–463 (2019). https://doi.org/10.1109/LWC.2018.2876258
6. Liu, D., et al.: Opportunistic UAV utilization in wireless networks: motivations, applications, and challenges. IEEE Commun. Mag. **58**(5), 62–68 (2020). https://doi.org/10.1109/MCOM.001.1900687
7. Mughal, B., Fadlullah, Z.M., Fouda, M.M., Ikki, S.: Optimizing packet forwarding performance in multiband relay networks via customized reinforcement learning. IEEE Open J. Commun. Soc. **3**, 973–985 (2022). https://doi.org/10.1109/OJCOMS.2022.3183172
8. Mughal, B., Fadlullah, Z.M., Ikki, S.: Centralized versus heuristic-based distributed channel allocation to minimize packet transmission delay for multiband relay networks. IEEE Networking Lett. **2**(4), 180–184 (2020). https://doi.org/10.1109/LNET.2020.3030870
9. Mughal, B., Fadlullah, Z.M., Fouda, M.M., Ikki, S.: Applying game theory to relay resource selection in hybrid-band wireless systems. IEEE Sens. J. **22**(23), 23552–23564 (2022). https://doi.org/10.1109/JSEN.2022.3213731
10. Schott, A., Ichkov, A., Beckmann, N., König, N., Simić, L.: Mm-wave connectivity in industrial environments: a measurement study at 28 and 60 GHz. In: GLOBECOM 2024 - 2024 IEEE Global Communications Conference, pp. 4262–4267 (2024). https://doi.org/10.1109/GLOBECOM52923.2024.10901259
11. Vejlgaard, B.: Coverage and capacity analysis of Sigfox, LoRa, GPRS, and NB-IoT. In: VTC Spring, pp. 1–5 (2017). https://doi.org/10.1109/VTCSpring.2017.8108666

# Research on Intelligent Distributed and Self-adaptive Networking Technology for Manned/Unmanned Collaboration

Mengfan Wang, Tengfei Li(✉), Jufeng Fei, Mingqi Li, and Jiajian Pan

Shanghai Radio Equipment Research Institute, Shanghai Shanghai 201109, China
1136929716@qq.com

**Abstract.** With the rapid advancement of unmanned aerial vehicle (UAV) technology, UAVs are widely used in surveying and mapping, geographic information systems, agricultural protection, security, emergency response, logistics, and transportation. They play an increasingly significant role, particularly in unmanned combat operations. The increasing technical requirements for autonomy, intelligence, efficiency, and collaboration in UAV missions have accelerated the shift toward multi-UAV operations. As one of the key technologies enabling collaborative missions, distributed data link adaptive networking technology must be enhanced to improve the capability of intelligent collaborative operations in manned/unmanned systems. Therefore, to address the sudden changes in information volume during multi-UAV missions and meet the demands of dynamically varying service data during transmission and relay among nodes in a collaborative network data link, this paper proposes a resource allocation method based on service requirements. This approach ensures quality of service (QoS) for multi-node and multi-service concurrency under limited bandwidth resources. The proposed method significantly improves bandwidth utilization while maintaining low algorithmic complexity, making it suitable for practical engineering applications.

**Keywords:** Unmanned Aerial Vehicle (UAV) · Adaptive Networking · Collaboration · Resource Allocation

## 1 Introduction

In recent years, the rapid advancement of unmanned aerial vehicle (UAV) technology has led to their widespread application across various fields. UAVs are now extensively used not only in surveying and mapping, geographic information systems, agricultural protection, and logistics but also play an increasingly critical role in un-manned combat operations.[1, 2] Moreover, as technical requirements for autonomy, intelligence, efficiency, and collaboration in UAV missions continue to rise, single-drone systems are gradually being replaced by multi-UAV operations.[3] Collaborative unmanned systems exhibit a more robust distributed architecture and are widely employed in combat scenarios for services such as situation recognition, situational reconstruction, cooperative mission execution, and autonomous navigation and positioning.[4, 5]


Y. Liu et al. (Eds.): ChinaCom 2025, LNICST 711, pp. 289–296, 2027.
https://doi.org/10.1007/978-3-032-33662-0_22

The ongoing development of UAV-related technologies has resulted in increasingly diverse system configurations, with enhanced capabilities in sensing, computing, and mobility control for individual units.[6] However, the data link communication networking—which serves as the critical link between UAVs themselves, as well as between manned and unmanned systems has become a significant bottleneck restricting further advancement. This challenge has attracted growing attention from researchers.[7] To improve the performance of collaborative operations, it is essential to establish distributed networks within the cluster to share reconnaissance and identification information, thereby enhancing the joint operational capability and strike effectiveness of the swarm.

Distributed data link adaptive networking technology is one of the key enablers for cooperative operations. A collaborative swarm data link refers to a tactical system in which all network nodes operate under a unified architecture, using specified communication protocols and message formats to transmit digital information in real time.[8] Through such cooperative data links, the swarm system accomplishes information exchange among its various units. However, networking communication also faces challenges such as a sharp increase in data transmission volume, inefficient static spectrum allocation, and degradation of swarm system performance.[9] To address the resource allocation problem within bandwidth-constrained network systems, a service demand-based resource allocation method is proposed, which significantly improves bandwidth utilization.

## 2 Network Architecture for Manned-Unmanned Teaming (Mum-T)

Swarm networking is typically required for complex operational missions, necessitating the establishment of a robust and flexible network architecture. A swarm combat system generally consists of a ground control station (GCS) and a cluster of unmanned aerial vehicles (UAVs). The ground station can monitor the status of the aerial UAV swarm and can also control the UAVs nodes remotely, allowing human intervention when the swarm is unable to make autonomous decisions. Based on preloaded mission objectives and real-time situational awareness within the operational area, the UAV swarm performs autonomous decision-making and control.

Various network architectures have been developed for UAV swarms. As shown in Fig. 1, the star topology has evolved from single-UAV operational systems. In this architecture, the ground station establishes point-to-point links with each UAV node, forming one-to-one connections.[10] UAV nodes receive control commands directly from the ground station. This structure is suitable for small-scale swarms and is maintained by the ground station. However, the system may fail when operating over long distances or if the ground station malfunctions. Figure 2 illustrates a clustered architecture, which is more suitable for large-scale UAV swarms. In this topology, communication between any two nodes does not necessarily rely on the ground station. Nodes within each cluster can communicate directly, while nodes from different clusters communicate via cluster heads. This network architecture offers greater robustness and flexibility, making it more adapted to large-scale networks and complex mission scenarios with frequent topological changes.[11]

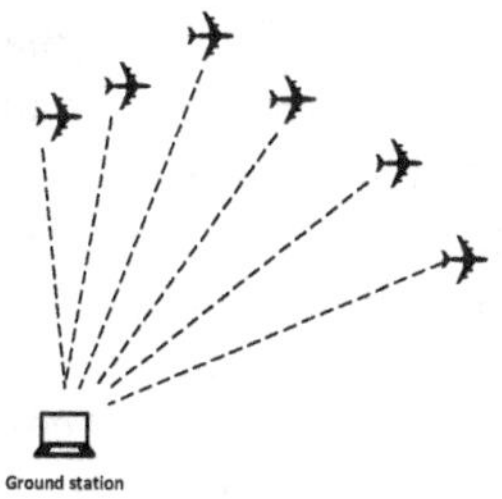


**Fig. 1.** Star Architecture

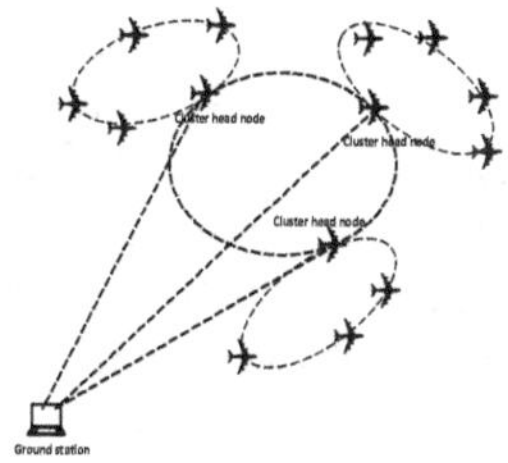

**Fig. 2.** Clustered Architecture

## 3 Resource Allocation Algorithm

The proposed algorithm is designed for a cluster-based network architecture. When a large number of nodes operate within the network, various unpredictable conditions may lead to sudden increases or decreases in service demands from individual nodes. Therefore, a strategy is required to rationally manage resource occupancy across the entire network, enhancing flexibility and optimizing bandwidth utilization. Under the constraint of limited total network bandwidth, a service demand-based resource allocation method is adopted to achieve dynamic time slot allocation. The resource allocation process is illustrated in Fig. 3.

After the data link is activated, the network self-organizes by electing a master node, followed by other UAVs gradually completing the network establishment process to achieve distributed adaptive networking. Based on a pre-defined time slot framework, which satisfies the basic communication requirements of all UAVs in the system, idle time slots are dynamically reserved. These reserved slots can be requested and occupied by UAVs handling services with high demands for real-time transmission, such as situational awareness and autonomous navigation and positioning. This approach maximizes time slot utilization while ensuring low latency for critical service transmission.

The resource allocation method for the UAV swarm based on service demand operates as follows:

(1) Predefined Basic Time Slot Allocation: During the initial establishment of the distributed network, each UAV occupies a fixed time slot at a fixed position to broadcast service data. Even if a node currently has no data to transmit, it will still occupy its preassigned time slot to broadcast network status information.

(2) Dynamic Reallocation of Unused Base Slots: If the number of nodes predefined in the network exceeds the number of actively operating nodes in the current swarm, the time slots originally allocated to non-existent nodes are dynamically reassigned to the active nodes. This improves the utilization efficiency of the basic time slots.
(3) Dynamic Resource Allocation: Different payloads within the swarm perform different tasks, resulting in varying data transmission demands over time. When a node experiences a sudden increase in service demand, its link layer calculates the required volume of data, determines the number of time slots needed, and assesses the priority level of the service. It then sends a request to the master node. The master node collects and aggregates requests from all nodes (including slot quantity and priority), and allocates time slots accordingly. Each node, based on the feedback from the master node, decides whether the allocated resources meet its current traffic demand and continues to monitor flows in real time to determine if additional requests are necessary. When a node's service demand decreases, it promptly adjusts its request and actively releases the dynamically allocated time slots. This process of continuous monitoring and dynamic adjustment continues throughout the mission.
(4) Periodic Request and Synchronized Adjustment: At each allocation cycle, every node must submit its resource request. The master node aggregates all requests within the cycle, and all nodes synchronously adjust their allocations at the beginning of the next cycle. This ensures that even if link instability or other unexpected issues cause abnormal allocation in one cycle, the system can recover in the following cycle through renewed information exchange, significantly enhancing the robustness of the dynamic allocation mechanism.
(5) Ground Station Monitoring and Remote Configuration: The ground station can monitor telemetry data from the swarm in real time. By observing the distribution of time slot occupancy, human operators can determine whether intervention is necessary. If the current allocation of time slots does not optimally support higher-priority information, remote control commands can be issued to adjust the allocation.

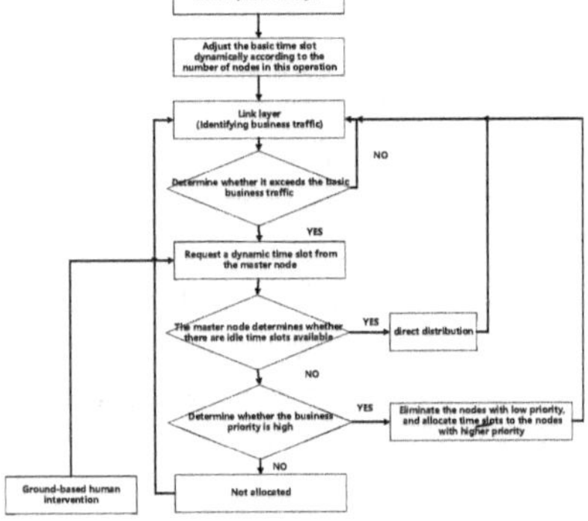


**Fig. 3.** Clustered Resource Allocation Flowchart

## 4 Simulation Experiment

To validate the effectiveness of the proposed service demand-based resource allocation method, this study simulated scenarios with varying service demands, including dynamic time slot requests. The request process was functionally simulated using Vivado. A four-node self-organizing network was constructed, comprising Node 1, Node 2, Node 3, and Node 4. The network was configured with a time slot length of 5 ms, a cycle duration of 500 ms, and a total of 100 time slots per cycle, including 80 basic time slots and 20 dynamic time slots. Multiple scenarios were designed to verify the feasibility of the algorithm. The total available bandwidth was set to 2 Mbps.

Simulation Setup and Scenarios:

- Time Period 0–5 s: No node requested dynamic time slots.
- Time Period 6–8 s: Node 1 requested all 20 dynamic time slots.
- Time Period 9–10 s: Node 1 and Node 3 each requested half of the dynamic time slots (10 slots each).

The simulation recorded the allocation of the 20 dynamic time slots and the transmission volume of each node at various time points. In the simulation:

- slot_type = 0x06 indicates a dynamic time slot.
- dynamic_trans_user_mac records the node ID occupying each dynamic time slot.
- phy_send_gate1 to phy_send_gate4 represent the transmit gate signals for Nodes 1 to 4, respectively. A raised signal indicates the node is transmitting in its allocated slot; otherwise, it remains in receive mode.
- phy_recv_gate1 to phy_recv_gate4 represent the receive gate signals for Nodes 1 to 4, respectively.
- Simulation Results:
- During 0–5 s, all dynamic slots remained unallocated. All nodes stayed in receive mode, and no transmission occurred over the dynamic slot channel.
- During 6–8 s, all 20 dynamic time slots were assigned to Node 1. Accordingly, phy_send_gate1 was raised in these slots, while other nodes' receive gates remained active.
- During 9–10 s, 10 dynamic slots were assigned to Node 1 and 10 to Node 3. Both phy_send_gate1 andphy_send_gate3 were raised in their respective slots, with other nodes receiving in those intervals.

The simulation functionally verified that the resource allocation mechanism correctly responds to dynamic service requests, efficiently assigning time slots based on demand and enabling explicit transmit/receive switching per node.

(1) Scenario with No Dynamic Slot Requests: When no node requests dynamic time slots, the variable dynamic_trans_user_mac shows that no node occupies any slot where slot_type is 0x06 (a dynamic time slot). During this period, all four nodes remain in receive mode. In this case, the bandwidth occupied by each node is 400 kbps (Fig. 4).

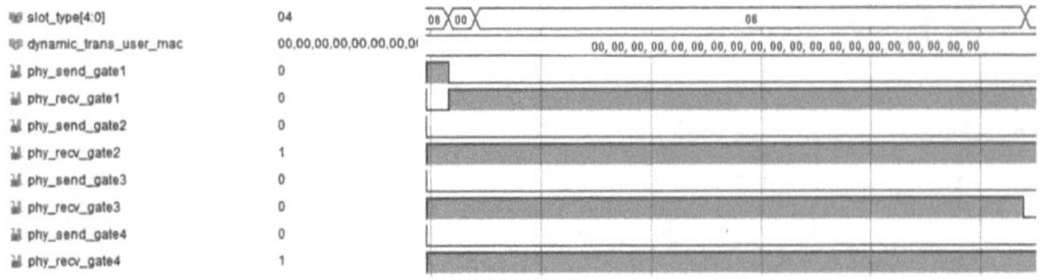


**Fig. 4.** Allocation Diagram When No Node Requests Dynamic Time Slots

(2) Scenario with One Node (Node 1) Requesting All Dynamic Time Slots:When Node 1 requests all available dynamic time slots, the allocation behavior can be observed as follows:

Dynamic Slot Occupancy: The variable dynamic_trans_user_mac shows that all 20 dynamic time slots (identified by slot_type = 0x06) are occupied by Node 1.

Transmit/Receive Status: Throughout the allocation period, the transmit gate of Node 1 (phy_send_gate1) remains consistently raised in these dynamic slots, indicating active data transmission. Meanwhile, the other nodes (Nodes 2–4) remain in receive mode, with their receive gates (phy_recv_gate2 to phy_recv_gate4) active.

Bandwidth Allocation: Node 1 occupies a total bandwidth of 800 kbps, which includes both its predefined basic bandwidth and the additionally allocated dynamic bandwidth. The remaining nodes (Nodes 2–4) each utilize only the basic bandwidth of 400 kbps. Divide the region by using the above samples. Based on the minimization of Bayesian risk, the final optimal decision-making area map is obtained, which is shown in Fig. 5. Among them, the green area indicates no interference, the black area indicates multipath interference, the red area indicates deception interference, and the blue area indicates suppression interference.

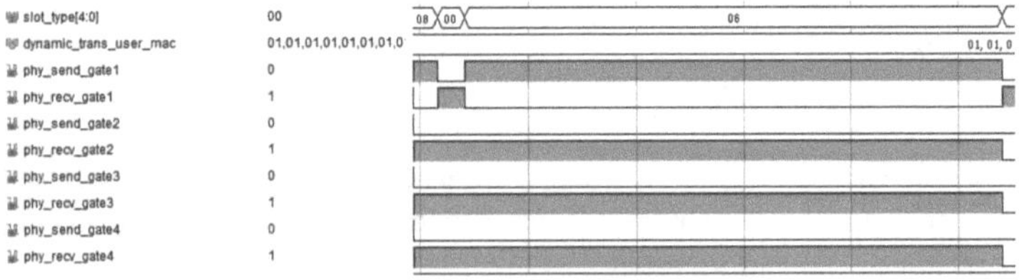


**Fig. 5.** Allocation Diagram When One Node Requests All Dynamic Time Slots

(3) Scenario with Two Nodes (Node 1 and Node 3) Each Requesting Half of the Dynamic Time Slots: When Node 1 and Node 3 each request half of the available dynamic time slots, the allocation results are as follows:

Dynamic Slot Occupancy: The variable dynamic_trans_user_mac shows that the 20 dynamic time slots (identified by slot_type = 0x06) are equally divided, with 10 slots assigned to Node 1 and 10 slots to Node 3.

Transmit/Receive Status: During their respectively allocated dynamic slots, the transmit gates of Node 1 (phy_send_gate1) and Node 3 (phy_send_gate3) are raised, indicating active data transmission. Nodes 2 and 4 remain in receive mode throughout the dynamic slot period, with their receive gates (phy_recv_gate2 and phy_recv_gate4) active and transmit gates inactive.

Bandwidth Allocation: Node 1 and Node 3 each occupy a total bandwidth of 600 kbps, which includes their basic bandwidth allocation plus the additional dynamically assigned slots. Nodes 2 and 4 continue to use only the basic bandwidth of 400 kbps each (Figs. 6 and 7).

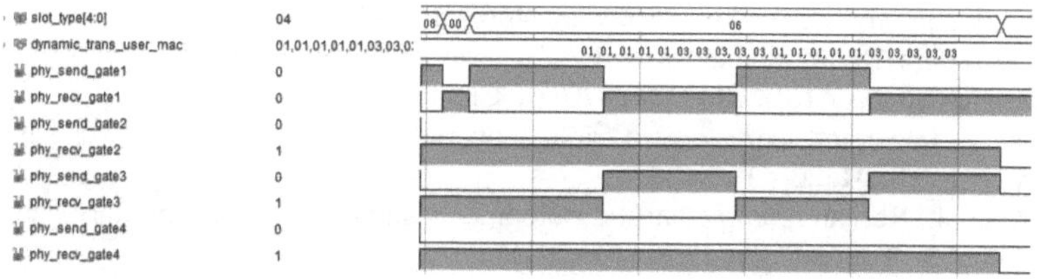


**Fig. 6.** Allocation Diagram When Two Nodes Each Request Half Of The Dynamic Time Slots

The data transmission volume of each node during different time periods, as they request and occupy dynamic time slots, is shown in the figure below.

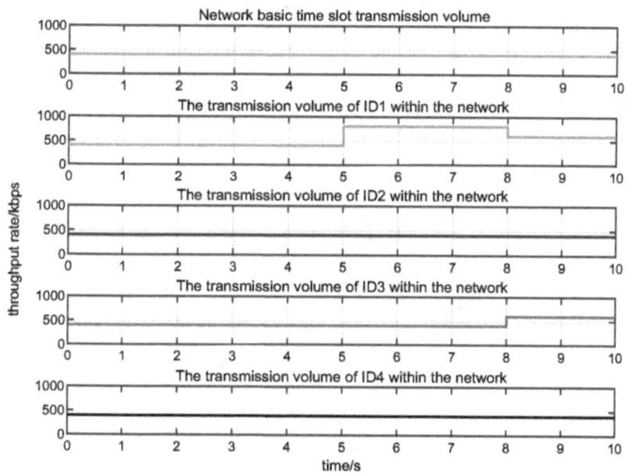


**Fig. 7.** The Data Transmission Volume of Each Node.

## 5 Conclusions

Under the constraint of limited total network bandwidth, this paper proposed a service demand-based resource allocation method. The algorithm features low computational complexity, making it suitable for practical engineering implementation. Simulation results verify that the proposed approach can effectively allocate resources in a dynamic manner, significantly improving bandwidth utilization.

## References


1. C., Z., H., L., F., G.: Integrated sensing, communication, and computing for low-altitude UAV networks: a Base Station-centric approach. Mob. Commun. **48**(9), 57–63 (2024)
2. H., Y., et al.: Intelligent communication and networking key technologies for manned/unmanned cooperation: states-of-the-art and trends. J. Commun. **45**(01), 1–17 (2024)
3. Y.L., H.U., et al.: A survey on UAV-enabled integrated sensing and communication networking and technologies. J. Electro. Inf. Technol. **47**(04), 859–875 (2025)
4. W., H., J., C., Y., L.: Technology survey and development forecast on unmanned aerial vehicle ad hoc networks. Telecommin. Eng. **62**(1), 138–146 (2022)
5. L., H., X., X.: Dynamic time slot allocation algorithm applicable to the data link of missile swarm collaborative networking. Software. **46**(01), 74–78 (2025)
6. X.K., W., et al.: Miniature fixed-wing UAV swarm: review and outlook. Acta Aeronautica et Aeronautica Sinica. **41**(4), 023732 (2020) (in Chinese)
7. J., S., et al.: Integrated space-ground-triple network intelligent adaptive networking technology. Artif. Intell. **01**, 26–41 (2025)
8. M., W., et al.: Research on the latest developments and trends in U.S military data links. J. Mil. Commun. Technol. **37**(04), 86–91 (2016)
9. W., C., K., C.: Data link Technology for Unmanned Cluster. J. command and control. **6**(01), 43–49 (2020)
10. Y., L., et al.: Comprehensive survey on topology control for flying ad-hoc network. J. Commun. **44**(08), 195–214 (2023)
11. J., L.: Design and network simulation verification of large-scale UAV swarm networking. Modern Navigation. **15**(05), 346–351 (2024)

# Fine-Grained Discrimination of Low-Altitude UAV Targets Based on Radar and Remote ID

Ziqi Zheng, Yuben Qu(✉), Haonan Chen, Jie Li, Lei Zhang, Chao Dong, and Qihui Wu

The Key Laboratory of Dynamic Cognitive System of Electromagnetic Spectrum Space, Ministry of Industry and Information Technology, Nanjing University of Aeronautics and Astronautics, Nanjing 211106, China
quyuben@nuaa.edu.cn

**Abstract.** With the rapid growth of the low-altitude economy, low-altitude Unmanned Aerial Vehicles (UAVs) applications have become widespread. Meanwhile, more and more illegal use of UAVs also poses threats to societal safety. Consequently, the development of robust UAVs surveillance is imperative. While Remote ID (RID) provides identity and position for cooperative UAVs mandatorily mounted with RID modules, it cannot detect non-cooperative targets. In contrast, radar can detect moving targets, but cannot distinguish their cooperative status. Mapping RID broadcasts to radar tracks could enable the fine-grained discrimination of low-altitude UAVs (distinguishing between cooperative and non-cooperative UAVs, and further distinguishing among cooperative UAVs), leading to more efficient surveillance, which however remains seldom studied so far. In this paper, we study how to achieve fine-grained discrimination of low-altitude UAVs based on joint radar and RID. Specifically, we map RID broadcasts and radar tracks into a common coordinate system. Then mapping problem is solved via the global nearest neighbor approach. It can be modeled as a constrained bipartite minimum-weight matching problem. We solve it using the Hungarian algorithm. Real-world experimental results demonstrate that, compared to three baselines, our method effectively suppresses interference from cooperative targets during mapping, with microsecond-scale latency that meets the demands of real-time UAV surveillance.

**Keywords:** Remote ID · radar · target mapping · UAVs surveillance

This work is supported in part by the National Key R&D Program of China No. 2022YFB3104500, in part by the National Natural Science Foundation of China under Grant No. 62431014, and in part by Stable Support for Fundamental Research Project in GF Characteristic Disciplines under Grant No. ILF240071A24.


Y. Liu et al. (Eds.): ChinaCom 2025, LNICST 711, pp. 297–310, 2027.
https://doi.org/10.1007/978-3-032-33662-0_23

# 1 Introduction

With the continuous advancement of chip computing power and sensor accuracy, unmanned aerial vehicles (UAVs) technology has developed rapidly in recent years. The high mobility and compact size of UAVs give them many advantages that traditional technologies do not possess, enabling a wide range of applications [1]. The low-altitude economy with low-altitude UAVs is becoming an integral part of digital economy and smart city initiatives nowadays. However, its rapid development has also introduced new public security risks [2]. Since UAVs can be remotely controlled, illegal operators can exploit them for unlawful activities without exposing themselves, such as unauthorized surveillance of sensitive facilities, executing attacks on mass gatherings and the transport of dangerous goods. Apart from posing security threats in physical spaces, UAVs can also disrupt social order in cyberspace. Therefore, with the fast-paced growth of the low-altitude economy, there is a pressing need to enhance the technologies of UAVs surveillance.

To address the security concerns posed by UAVs, governments worldwide have implemented various regulations [3]. For instance, many regulations mandate that UAVs be equipped with Remote ID (RID) systems. The RID system broadcasts the corresponding UAV's real-time position data for both the aircraft and its operator, which can then be monitored by authorized ground receivers. UAVs equipped with RID are usually defined as cooperative ones, while those without RID are deemed non-cooperative and remain invisible to RID-based systems. Besides, radar is also used to monitor UAVs [4]. It offers a complementary surveillance capability, detecting moving targets within its range, including both cooperative and non-cooperative UAVs, as well as clutter such as avians. However, while radar provides comprehensive detection, it cannot inherently distinguish a target's cooperative status. Intuitively, it could achieve the discrimination of UAVs by mapping RID targets with radar-detected targets, which enables more efficient and comprehensive regulation of UAVs: non-cooperative UAVs pose higher security risks since they are unregistered, so more resources can be allocated to monitor them. Fine-grained discrimination can also enhance cooperative UAVs surveillance: if a UAV broadcasts false location information, we can find it via linked radar data. To our knowledge, how to achieve fine-grained discrimination of low-altitude UAVs based on radar and RID has been rarely studied in existing works. Yest, to achieve it, two key issues need to be solved: the non-uniformity of the two coordinate systems (CSs) and target mapping under positioning errors.

In this work, we jointly utilize radar and RID to monitor UAVs, enabling fine-grained discrimination of low-altitude UAVs. Specifically, targets detected by radar are discriminated as cooperative or non-cooperative, while cooperative targets are further mapped to their corresponding RID targets. First, to address coordinate inconsistency, we establish the East-North-Up (ENU) CS centered at the radar as the common reference frame. Targets from both radar and RID are then mapped to this common CS using the solution of Orthogonal Procrustes Problem (OPP) [5] and coordinate transformation relationships between the different CSs. Second, for the target mapping issue under localization errors, we compute the distance between each RID target and each radar target within the common ENU CS. This distance serves as the mapping error, forming an error matrix. Subsequently, the global nearest neighbor approach is employed to find the mapping matrix that minimizes the global mapping error. This process ultimately maps RID targets to radar targets, achieving the fine-grained discrimination of low-altitude UAVs. The key contributions of this work are summarized as follows:

- We study how to use radar and RID data to accurately and fast discriminate whether the monitored UAVs are cooperative or non-cooperative. To achieve the aforementioned goal, two key issues must be addressed: non-unified CSs from Radar and RID and error-aware target mapping.
- For the CSs consistency, we obtain the local-to-common rotation matrix by solving the OPP, and the coordinates of the RID targets in the common CS through the mapping relationship between different CSs. For error-aware target mapping, we apply the global nearest neighbor strategy to find the optimal mapping. Then the mapping problem is modeled as a constrained bipartite minimum-weight matching problem and solved using the Hungarian algorithm [6].
- We designed three sets of real-world experiments to validate the effectiveness of the proposed method. Results show that our method effectively suppresses mapping interference caused by cooperative targets. When all interference originates from cooperative targets, our method achieves an accuracy of 99.1%, 94.6%, and 76.8% at UAV separations of 10 m, 7.5 m, and 5 m, respectively—representing an improvement of at least 4.2%, 7.5%, and 6.2% over the best-performing baseline algorithm. And the latency of proposed method is at the microsecond level.

## 2 Related Work

To regulate UAVs operations, governments have mandated that UAVs broadcast real-time information. While this broadcasting mechanism strengthens airspace monitoring capabilities, it also raises serious concerns regarding the potential leakage of sensitive information belonging to UAVs operators and pilots [7]. These privacy issues present challenges to the practical enforcement of RID regulations, prompting researchers to explore more privacy-preserving deployment strategies. Wisse et al. [8] proposed a RID protocol that supports anonymous direct authentication, aiming to address both the timeliness and energy consumption of anonymous UAVs identification. Alsoliman et al. [9] introduced a privacy-preserving authentication framework by dividing flight plans into multiple "flight zones"—each bounded spatiotemporally and associated with a unique key. Brighente et al. [10] proposed a three-layer architecture combining DiPrID (Differentially-Private Remote ID), ICARUS (Invasion Detection and Privacy-Preserving UAVs Tracking) and TTP (Trusted Third Party) verification. This approach balances trajectory privacy with regulatory effectiveness. Svaigen et al. [11] were the first to propose a comprehensive location privacy protection framework for the Internet of UAVs. Wu et al. [12] developed a blockchain-enabled four-layer privacy protection architecture for UAVs. This architecture improves anti-forgery resilience and collaborative security within UAVs swarms.

In addition to RID-based UAVs regulation, a significant body of research has focused on radar-based UAVs detection. Liu et al. [13] experimentally validated the capability of domestically developed active electronically scanned array (AESA) radar to effectively detect small UAVs. Fu et al. [14] proposed the LSTM-ALRO model, which bypasses the conventional image-based processing paradigm by directly utilizing millimeter-wave RCS signatures for UAVs classification. To address the low detection rate of small UAVs, Gong et al. [15] introduced a novel detector based on Doppler Signal-to-Clutter Ratio (DSCR), which significantly improves weak signal detection and reduces missed alarms. Nuss et al. [16] pioneered the application of MIMO-OFDM radar for UAVs detection. Their system achieves long-range, real-time and 3D positioning even in low-RCS and high-clutter environments, offering a validated solution for all-weather counter-UAVs systems. Wang et al. [17] developed a novel fast 3D constant false alarm rate (CFAR) detection algorithm aimed at minimizing computational complexity.

Although extensive research has been conducted on UAVs surveillance using RID and radar individually, few studies have explored the integration of these two modalities for UAVs surveillance. Our main work is to propose a method for fine-grained discrimination of low-altitude UAV targets based on radar and RID.

## 3 Problem Formulation and Proposed Solution

### 3.1 Problem Formulation

We utilize both radar and RID for the joint surveillance of UAVs, as illustrated in Fig. 1. UAVs with black-filled icons represent non-cooperative targets, while those without fill represent cooperative targets. RID receives the positional information and corresponding timestamps broadcast by cooperative UAVs via wireless links. Meanwhile, the radar scans the surveillance area and provides the positions of all moving targets along with millisecond-level timestamps. To align the data from radar and RID, we employ timestamp-based synchronization. Specifically, the radar timestamps are rounded to the nearest second and then matched with the RID data. The radar timestamp is taken as the reference time, and the true position of the UAV at that moment is used as the reference position.

The reference position is indicated by a UAV icon. The positions detected by radar are marked as blue coordinate points, while the positions reported by RID at the associated time are shown as green coordinate points. The errors in the radar-detected positions mainly stem from detection inaccuracies, which are represented by blue arrows and denoted as $\mathbf{e_{radar}}$. In the RID-reported

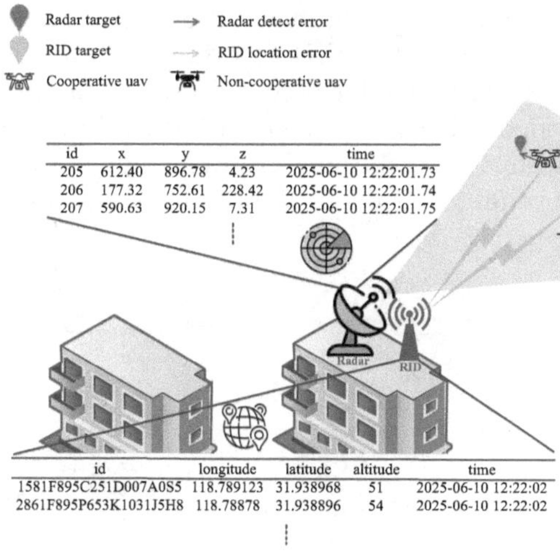


**Fig. 1.** Illustration of the problem scenario involving multiple low-altitude UAVs.

data, the timestamp resolution is on the second level. Therefore, the position reported by RID deviates from the reference position due to two factors: temporal error (denoted as $\mathbf{e_t}$) and localization error (denoted as $\mathbf{e_{rid}}$). In Fig. 1, the total deviation between the RID-reported position and the reference position is illustrated by green arrows. Both $\mathbf{e_{radar}}$ and $\mathbf{e_{rid}}$ are modeled as random variables representing the respective sensing uncertainties, and $||\mathbf{e_{radar}}|| \in [0, 10]$, $||\mathbf{e_{rid}}|| \in [0, 5]$. The $\mathbf{e_t}$ is denoted as: $\mathbf{e_t} = \mathbf{v} \cdot \Delta t$, where $\Delta t$ is the time difference between the radar timestamp and the RID timestamp.

According to the above analysis, we can conclude that in order to map RID targets to radar-detected targets, two key issues need to be considered: (1) The coordinate of radar-detected targets and the coordinates received via RID are not in the same CS. (2) Both the radar-detected coordinates and the RID coordinates contain errors. As a result, even if they are transformed into the same CS, they do not coincide exactly.

### 3.2 Proposed Framework

The target positions detected by the radar are represented in a local CS, where the radar is located at the origin. In this system, The x-axis points right, the y-axis points forward, and the z-axis points upward relative to the radar. In contrast, the position information provided by RID for cooperative UAVs is expressed in geodetic coordinates (latitude, longitude, altitude). To enable the mapping from cooperative UAVs from RID to radar-detected targets, it is essential to convert both sets of coordinates into a common CS.

In this paper, we adopt a local ENU CS centered at the radar as the unified reference frame. The workflow is divided into two stages: the calibration phase and the mapping phase. During the calibration phase, referring to the approach of Graff et al. [18], we formulate the problem of obtaining the rotation matrix from a local coordinate frame to the ENU coordinate frame as an OPP. During the mapping phase, both the radar-detected target positions and the RID-reported positions of cooperative UAVs are transformed into this common ENU frame. Then, a global nearest-neighbor algorithm is applied to map RID targets to radar targets. The overall workflow of the proposed method is illustrated in Fig. 2.

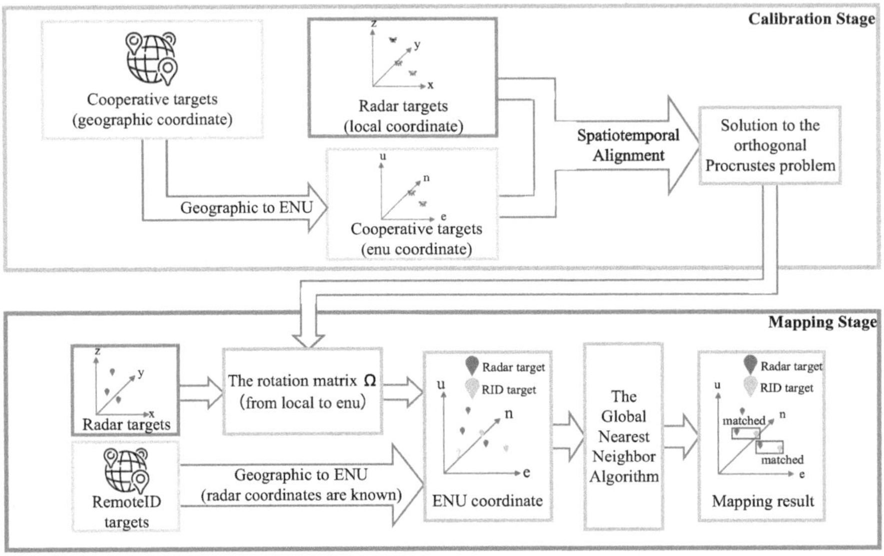


**Fig. 2.** Workflow of The Proposed Method.

**Conversion of Cooperative Targets from Geodetic Coordinates to the Common Reference Frame.** We are given the radar's centimeter-level geodetic coordinates ($\text{lon}_{radar}$, $\text{lat}_{radar}$, $\text{alt}_{radar}$) and the cooperative UAV's geodetic coordinates ($\text{lon}_{rid}$, $\text{lat}_{rid}$, $\text{alt}_{rid}$) provided by RID. We model the Earth using the WGS84 ellipsoid, with the semi-major axis $a = 6378137.0\,\text{m}$ and flattening $f = 1/298.257223563$. We first convert the geodetic coordinates to ECEF coordinates using the following method:

$$\mathrm{N} = \frac{\mathrm{a}}{\sqrt{1 - \mathrm{e}^2 \sin^2(\mathrm{lat})}} \tag{1}$$

$$x = (\mathrm{N} + \mathrm{alt}) cos(\mathrm{lat}) cos(\mathrm{lon}) \tag{2}$$

$$y = (\mathrm{N} + \mathrm{alt}) cos(\mathrm{lat}) \sin(\mathrm{lon}) \tag{3}$$

$$z = [\mathrm{N}(1 - e^2) + \mathrm{alt}] \sin(\mathrm{lat}) \tag{4}$$

where $e = \sqrt{2f - f^2}$ denotes the first eccentricity, and $(x, y, z)$ represents the coordinate in the ECEF frame. Here lon, lat, and alt denote longitude, latitude, and altitude, respectively. After this transformation, we obtain the ECEF coordinates of the radar and cooperative UAV: $(x_{\text{radar}}, y_{\text{radar}}, z_{\text{radar}})$ and $(x_{\text{c}}, y_{\text{c}}, z_{\text{c}})$. Then, we compute the distance vector $\mathbf{d}_{\text{radar2rid}}$ between the two coordinates:

$$\mathbf{d}_{\text{radar2rid}} = \left[\Delta x,\ \Delta y,\ \Delta z\right]^{\top} \tag{5}$$

$$\Delta x = x_c - x_{radar} \tag{6}$$

$$\Delta y = y_c - y_{radar} \tag{7}$$

$$\Delta z = z_c - z_{radar} \tag{8}$$

Multiplying the distance vector by the ECEF-to-ENU rotation matrix (right-multiplication) yields the target's coordinates in the common CS:

$$\left[e_{\text{c}},\ n_{\text{c}},\ u_{\text{c}}\right]^{\top} = \mathbf{R}\,\mathbf{d}_{\text{radar2rid}} \tag{9}$$

$$\mathbf{R} = \begin{pmatrix} -\sin(\text{lon}) & \cos(\text{lon}) & 0 \\ -\sin(\text{lat})\cos(\text{lon}) & -\sin(\text{lat})\sin(\text{lon}) & \cos(\text{lat}) \\ \cos(\text{lat})\cos(\text{lon}) & \cos(\text{lat})\sin(\text{lon}) & \sin(\text{lat}) \end{pmatrix} \tag{10}$$

where lon and lat denote the longitude and latitude of the radar, respectively. And $[e_c, n_c, u_c]^{\top}$ denotes the position vector of a cooperative target in the ENU CS.

**Calibration Stage.** To obtain the rotation matrix that transforms coordinates from the radar's local frame to the common reference frame, we adopt the solution to the OPP [5]:

$$\begin{aligned} &\min_{\boldsymbol{\Omega}} \|\mathbf{A}\boldsymbol{\Omega} - \mathbf{B}\|_F \\ &\text{s.t. } \boldsymbol{\Omega}^{\top}\boldsymbol{\Omega} = \mathbf{I} \end{aligned} \tag{11}$$

where $\boldsymbol{\Omega}$ is the rotation matrix that transforms coordinates from the radar's local frame to the common reference frame. And matrix $\mathbf{A}$ represent the positions of cooperative UAVs as detected by the radar, expressed in the radar's local CS. Here, $\mathbf{A} \in \mathbf{R}^{n \times 3}$, where $n$ denotes the number of samples, and each row of $\mathbf{A}$ contains the $(x, y, z)$ coordinates of a UAV. Similarly, matrix $\mathbf{B}$ represents the corresponding positions of the same UAV in the ENU CS centered at the radar. The values in $\mathbf{B}$ can be calculated using Eq. (9), and the dimensions of $\mathbf{A}$ and $\mathbf{B}$ are identical.

However, $\mathbf{A}$ and $\mathbf{B}$ cannot be directly obtained from raw data, as they require strict correspondence between radar and RID measurements. Specifically, each pair $(\mathbf{A}_{i,:}, \mathbf{B}_{i,:})$ must represent the same UAV at the same time. We establish radar-RID correspondence through spatiotemporal alignment. Matched pairs are accepted only when a unique radar target spatiotemporally matches an RID target. Due to the existence of errors, multiple matched pairs are collected to increase the robustness of the rotation estimation.

**Conversion of Radar Targets from Local Coordinates to the Common Reference Frame (Mapping Stage).** The coordinate vector of a radar target is transformed to the ENU CS via right-multiplication by the rotation matrix $\boldsymbol{\Omega}$, yielding:

$$[e_a, n_a, u_a]^\top = \boldsymbol{\Omega}[x_a, y_a, z_a]^\top \tag{12}$$

where $[x_a, y_a, z_a]^\top$ denotes the coordinate vector of a radar target in the local CS, and $[e_a, n_a, u_a]^\top$ represents the corresponding coordinate vector in the ENU frame after transformation.

**Mapping Methodology (Mapping Stage).** In the previous steps, both RID targets and radar targets were transformed into the common CS. This enables the computation of the Euclidean distance between any RID target and any radar-detected target. We define a error matrix $\mathbf{D}$:

$$\mathbf{D} = \begin{pmatrix} d_{11} & \cdots & d_{1n} \\ \vdots & \ddots & \vdots \\ d_{m1} & \cdots & d_{mn} \end{pmatrix} \tag{13}$$

where $d_{ij}$ represents the distance between the coordinate of the $i$-th cooperative target and that of the $j$-th radar-detected target. Meanwhile, we define an mapping matrix $\mathbf{P}$:

$$\mathbf{P} = \begin{pmatrix} p_{11} & \cdots & p_{1n} \\ \vdots & \ddots & \vdots \\ p_{m1} & \cdots & p_{mn} \end{pmatrix} \tag{14}$$

where $p_{ij}$=0/1, when $p_{ij}$=0, it indicates that the $i$-th cooperative target and the $j$-th radar-detected target are not the same object. Conversely, $p_{ij}$=1 indicates that they refer to the same physical target. Thus, the mapping problem can be formulated as:

$$\begin{aligned} &\min < \mathbf{D}, \mathbf{P} >_F \\ &\text{s.t.} \quad \sum_{j=1}^{n} p_{ij} = 1, \quad \forall i, \\ &\qquad \sum_{i=1}^{m} p_{ij} \in \{0, 1\}, \quad \forall j. \end{aligned} \tag{15}$$

where $\sum_{j=1}^{n} p_{ij} = 1$ ensures that each cooperative target is assigned to exactly one radar-detected target, $\sum_{i=1}^{m} p_{ij} \in \{0, 1\}$ ensures that each radar-detected target is assigned to at most one cooperative target. This problem constitutes a constrained bipartite minimum-weight matching problem, falling within the domain of discrete optimization. Furthermore, in this context, the condition $m \leq n$ holds, which exactly conforms to the standard formulation of the assignment problem. This problem can be efficiently solved using the Hungarian algorithm.

# 4 Experimental Verification

## 4.1 Hardware Platform and Experimental Setup

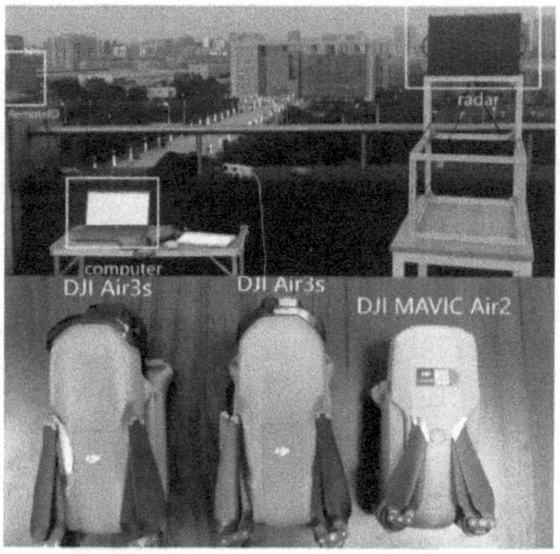


**Fig. 3.** Hardware Platform for Experiments.

To validate the effectiveness of the proposed method, we conducted a series of experiments. The hardware platform used in our experiments includes a 2D active phased-array pulse-Doppler radar, a RID receiving device, two DJI Air 3 s UAVs, one DJI MAVIC Air 2 UAV and a laptop with an Intel i5-1135G7 CPU serving as the control center. The radar operates at a refresh rate of 1 Hz, with a distance error of no more than 10 m and an angular error of no more than 0.5°. Two DJI Air 3 s UAVs serve as cooperative targets, and one DJI MAVIC Air 2 UAV acts as a non-cooperative target. The devices are shown in Fig. 3. We investigate how the detection accuracy of the proposed algorithm changes as the distance between targets decreases, and how the algorithm performs in terms of real-time capability as the number of targets increases. The detection accuracy is defined as the proportion of cooperative targets that are correctly mapped to radar targets among all cooperative targets. The real-time performance is evaluated based on the time consumed by the algorithm. To ensure the comprehensiveness of the experiments, we designed multiple sets of experiments, as shown in Table 1.

**Table 1.** Experimental Configuration

| Experiment | UAVs Configuration | Distance (m) |
|---|---|---|
| I | Air 3 s*1, MAVIC Air 2*1 | 20, 15, 10, 8, 5 |
| II | Air 3 s*2 | 20, 15, 10, 8, 5 |
| III | Air 3 s*2, MAVIC Air 2*1 | 20, 15, 10, 8, 5 |

Due to the limited resolution of our radar, it becomes incapable of distinguishing between two targets when the UAVs are too close to each other, resulting in a lack of valid experimental data. To address this issue, the original data were collected when the UAVs were positioned far apart. We then generated data for close-range scenarios at distances of 20 m, 15 m, 10 m, 8 m, and 5 m by spatially shifting the recorded positions of the UAVs.

We select the following three methods as baseline algorithms for comparison:

**Range-Only** : This method directly performs mapping based on the distance between the target and the radar.

**One-by-One** : This method selects the closest radar target for each, while ensuring a one-to-one correspondence between cooperative and radar targets.

**Distance-Shortest** : This method directly maps each cooperative target to the nearest radar target based solely on distance.

## 4.2 Experimental Results

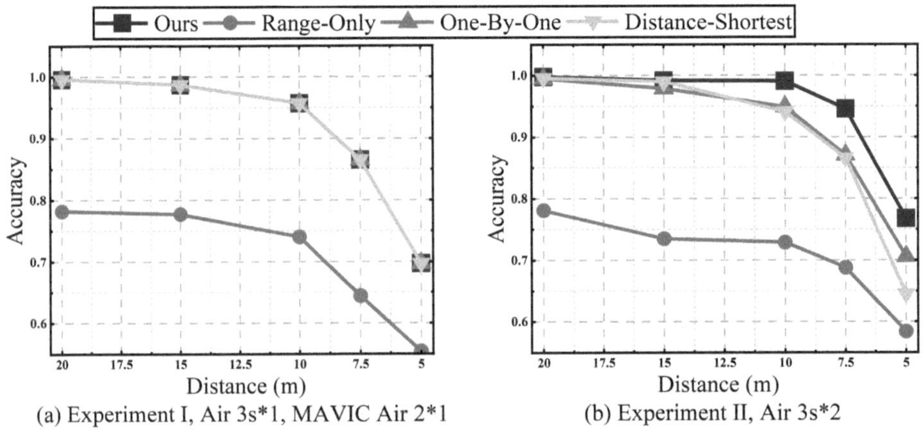


**Fig. 4.** Accuracy Results of Experiment I And II.

Figure 4 illustrates the variation of mapping accuracy with decreasing distance in Experiment I and II. The specific accuracy rates for Experiment I and II can be found in Tables 2 and 3, respectively. In Experiment I, the proposed method achieves nearly the same accuracy as One-by-one and Distance-shortest. This is because Experiment I involves only a single cooperative target, in which case all three methods aim to map the radar target closest to the UAV itself.

Since their strategies are effectively identical under this condition, the resulting performance is similar. In Experiment II, the proposed method outperforms the others. Compared with the method achieving the second-highest accuracy, our approach achieves improvements of 4.2%, 7.5%, and 6.2% at distances of 10 m, 7.5 m, and 5 m, respectively. This is primarily due to the presence of two cooperative UAVs. When mapping cooperative targets to radar detections, the main source of interference is the other cooperative UAVs. The proposed method takes into account the mapping errors of both UAVs simultaneously and thus produces a globally optimal mapping result. In contrast, the other methods do not consider the global context, which leads to a higher likelihood of incorrect decisions. **In other words, the proposed method exhibits a stronger ability to suppress interference caused by cooperative targets during the mapping process.**

**Table 2.** Accuracy Results of Experiment I

| Distance (m) | Ours | Range-only | One-by-one | Distance-shortest |
|---|---|---|---|---|
| 20 | 0.996 | 0.782 | 0.996 | 0.996 |
| 15 | 0.987 | 0.777 | 0.987 | 0.987 |
| 10 | 0.957 | 0.740 | 0.957 | 0.957 |
| 7.5 | 0.865 | 0.644 | 0.865 | 0.865 |
| 5 | 0.697 | 0.554 | 0.697 | 0.697 |

**Table 3.** Accuracy Results of Experiment II

| Distance (m) | Ours | Range-only | One-by-one | Distance-shortest |
|---|---|---|---|---|
| 20 | **0.998** | 0.781 | 0.995 | 0.996 |
| 15 | **0.994** | 0.735 | 0.979 | 0.990 |
| 10 | **0.991** | 0.729 | 0.949 | 0.941 |
| 7.5 | **0.946** | 0.688 | 0.871 | 0.866 |
| 5 | **0.768** | 0.584 | 0.706 | 0.645 |

Figure 5 illustrates the variation of mapping accuracy with decreasing distance in Experiment III. The specific accuracy rates for Experiment III can be found in Table 4. In Experiment III, the mapping interference for cooperative UAVs originates from both cooperative and non-cooperative UAVs. The proposed method demonstrates superior suppression of interference caused by cooperative UAVs, and thus consistently outperforms other approaches in terms of mapping accuracy. Compared with the method achieving the second-highest accuracy, our approach achieves improvements of 2.1%, 3.8%, and 4.1%

**Table 4.** Accuracy Results of Experiment III

| Distance (m) | Ours | Range-only | One-by-one | Distance-shortest |
|---|---|---|---|---|
| 20 | **0.997** | 0.751 | 0.993 | 0.994 |
| 15 | **0.993** | 0.730 | 0.992 | 0.992 |
| 10 | **0.964** | 0.712 | 0.943 | 0.939 |
| 7.5 | **0.925** | 0.604 | 0.872 | 0.887 |
| 5 | **0.706** | 0.485 | 0.665 | 0.624 |

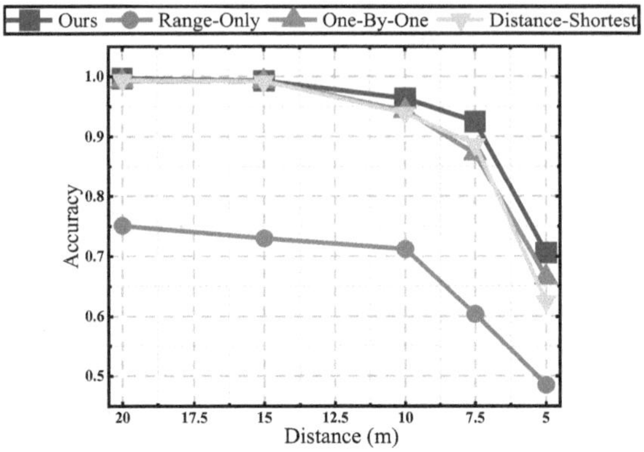


**Fig. 5.** Accuracy Results of Experiment III (Air 3s*2, MAVIC Air 2*1).

at distances of 10 m, 7.5 m, and 5 m, respectively. **It is worth noting that although the method with the second-best accuracy varies across different distances, our proposed method consistently achieves the highest accuracy.**

**Table 5.** Real-time Performance of Experiments($\mu s$)

| Experiment | Ours | Range-only | One-by-one | Distance-shortest |
|---|---|---|---|---|
| I | 93.89 | 291.14 | 67.52 | 50.61 |
| II | 130.54 | 555.42 | 76.27 | 57.39 |
| III | 156.38 | 815.43 | 84.24 | 64.09 |

Table 5 shows the real-time performance of different methods in the experiment. It can be seen that Distance-shortest is the fastest. However, the proposed method's delay is not significantly higher than that of Distance-shortest. Moreover, in practical scenarios, the radar update rate is 1 Hz, whereas the proposed method operates at the microsecond level, which is much faster than the radar update rate. Therefore, overall, the proposed method demonstrates performance improvements compared to the other methods.

## 5 Conclusion

In this paper, to achieve more efficient and comprehensive surveillance, we propose a method to accomplish the fine-grained discrimination of low-altitude UAVs based on RID and radar. First, we align information from RID and radar, transform them into a common CS. Then, we apply a global nearest-neighbor approach to map RID targets to radar targets. Finally, we validate the effectiveness of our proposed method through three sets of field experiments. The results show that proposed method outperforms other methods in handling mapping interference from other cooperative targets. Additionally, our algorithm exhibits low latency, which can meet the real-time requirements. In future work, we will conduct further analysis on the statistical characteristics of radar and navigation positioning errors to mitigate mapping interference from non-cooperative UAVs.

## References


1. Muchiri, G., Kimathi, S.: A review of applications and potential applications of UAV. In: Proceedings of the Sustainable Research and Innovation Conference, pp. 280–283 (2022)
2. Pyrgies, J.: The UAVs threat to airport security: risk analysis and mitigation. J. Airline Airport Manag. **9**(2), 63–96 (2019)
3. Belwafi, K., Alkadi, R., Alameri, S.A., Al Hamadi, H., Shoufan, A.: Unmanned aerial vehicles' remote identification: a tutorial and survey. IEEE Access **10**, 87577–87601 (2022)
4. Khawaja, W., Ezuma, M., Semkin, V., Erden, F., Ozdemir, O., Guvenc, I.: A survey on detection, classification, and tracking of UAVs using radar and communications systems. IEEE Commun. Surv. Tutorials (2025)
5. Schönemann, P.H.: A generalized solution of the orthogonal procrustes problem. Psychometrika **31**(1), 1–10 (1966)
6. Kuhn, H.W.: The Hungarian method for the assignment problem. Nav. Res. Logist. **52**(1–2), 7–21 (2010)
7. Svaigen, A.R., Boukerche, A., Ruiz, L.B., Loureiro, A.A.: Is the remote id a threat to the drone's location privacy on the internet of drones? In: Proceedings of the 20th ACM International Symposium on Mobility Management and Wireless Access, pp. 81–88 (2022)
8. Wisse, E., Tedeschi, P., Sciancalepore, S., Di Pietro, R.: A 2 rid–anonymous direct authentication and remote identification of commercial drones. IEEE Internet Things J. **10**(12), 10587–10604 (2023)
9. Alsoliman, A., Rabiah, A.B., Levorato, M.: Privacy-preserving authentication framework for UAS traffic management systems. In: 2020 4th Cyber Security in Networking Conference (CSNet), pp. 1–8. IEEE (2020)
10. Brighente, A., Conti, M., Sciancalepore, S.: Hide and seek: privacy-preserving and FAA-compliant drones location tracing. In: Proceedings of the 17th International Conference on Availability, Reliability and Security, pp. 1–11 (2022)
11. Svaigen, A.R., Boukerche, A., Ruiz, L.B., Loureiro, A.A.: Design guidelines of the internet of drones location privacy protocols. IEEE Internet Things Mag. **5**(2), 175–180 (2022)

12. Wu, Y., Dai, H.N., Wang, H., Choo, K.K.R.: Blockchain-based privacy preservation for 5G-enabled drone communications. IEEE Network **35**(1), 50–56 (2021)
13. Liu, Y.H., Chen, C.Y., Tsai, C.L., Zhuang, H.Z., Chen, C.H.: Enhancing small drone detection with active electronically scanned array radar. In: 2024 International Symposium on Intelligent Signal Processing and Communication Systems (ISPACS), pp. 1–3. IEEE (2024)
14. Fu, R., Al-Absi, M.A., Kim, K.H., Lee, Y.S., Al-Absi, A.A., Lee, H.J.: Deep learning-based drone classification using radar cross section signatures at mmWave frequencies. IEEE Access **9**, 161431–161444 (2021)
15. Gong, J., Yan, J., Hu, H., Kong, D., Li, D.: Improved radar detection of small drones using doppler signal-to-clutter ratio (DSCR) detector. Drones **7**(5), 316 (2023)
16. Nuss, B., Sit, L., Fennel, M., Mayer, J., Mahler, T., Zwick, T.: MIMO OFDM radar system for drone detection. In: 2017 18th International Radar Symposium (IRS), pp. 1–9. IEEE (2017)
17. Wang, S., Herschel, R.: Fast 3D-CFAR for drone detection with MIMO radars. In: 2021 18th European Radar Conference (EuRAD), pp. 209–212. IEEE (2022)
18. Graff, D., Anderson, B., Buck, D., Peterson, C.K., McLain, T.W., Warnick, K.F.: Online calibration for networked radar tracking of UAS. J. Intell. Robot. Syst. **110**(4), 163 (2024)

# MK-SPMA: A Markov-Chain-Based Priority Escalation Protocol for Multi-class UAV Communications

Yiran Yan[1](✉), Da Wang[2], Feiyu Mu[2], Xiang Zhang[2], and Xin Yang[1]

[1] Northwestern Polytechnical University, Xian, China
yanyiran@mail.nwpu.edu.cn
[2] China Satellite Network Group Co., Ltd, Beijing, China

**Abstract.** Unmanned aerial vehicle (UAV) clusters in post-disaster emergency communications require reliable and low-latency multiple access mechanisms to ensure real-time data delivery under dynamic network conditions. This paper introduces a Markov-based Statistical Priority Multiple Access (MK-SPMA) scheme, which incorporates a priority-aware Markov chain into the conventional SPMA framework. By dynamically upgrading data packets to higher-priority classes once the retransmission count reaches a predefined threshold, MK-SPMA enables adaptive priority escalation beyond the initial assignment, ensuring that persistently delayed packets gain increased transmission opportunities. By adaptively adjusting transmission probabilities based on both priority levels and historical transmission outcomes, MK-SPMA achieves more efficient channel access control and resource utilization. Analytical results provide closed-form expressions for state transition probabilities, steady-state distributions, throughput, delay, success probability, and slot utilization. Extensive MATLAB simulations demonstrate that, under identical configurations, MK-SPMA consistently outperforms traditional SPMA in terms of throughput, latency, and slot efficiency, particularly in dense multi-priority scenarios. These results highlight the potential of Markovian adaptation with priority-upgrade mechanisms to enhance mission-critical UAV communications, offering a promising solution for reliable and efficient post-disaster network access.

**Keywords:** UAV · MAC Protocol · SPMA · Markov chain

## 1 Introduction

In the aftermath of large-scale natural disasters such as earthquakes [1], floods, or hurricanes, hundreds of unmanned aerial vehicles (UAVs) are often rapidly deployed to form an emergency communication and sensing network [2].These UAV ad hoc networks play a vital role in real-time reconnaissance, disaster assessment, and search-and-rescue operations. However, the network traffic in such scenarios is highly heterogeneous: high-priority services [3] include emergency rescue commands, survivor location and


Y. Liu et al. (Eds.): ChinaCom 2025, LNICST 711, pp. 311–325, 2027.
https://doi.org/10.1007/978-3-032-33662-0_24

SOS signals, and real-time medical telemetry.Low-priority services include environmental monitoring, logistics support, network management, and post-disaster analysis [4]. Although these services have relatively low real-time requirements, they still play a crucial role in maintaining network stability, ensuring resource coordination, and supporting rescue decision-making [5].

Traditional medium access control (MAC) protocols in UAV ad hoc networks primarily focus on ensuring the timely delivery of high-priority data while often neglecting the cumulative importance of low-priority flows [6]. This can lead to severe consequences: delayed environmental data may impair situational awareness, outdated routing information can cause network fragmentation, and the overall system robustness may degrade if low-priority nodes experience persistent transmission failures [7, 8].

Statistical Priority-based Multiple Access (SPMA) protocols were introduced to address priority differentiation in heterogeneous networks. However, most existing SPMA schemes rely on fixed or heuristically tuned access parameters [7] and fail to capture the stochastic nature of channel contention dynamics under highly dynamic UAV networks [9]. In particular, they lack a rigorous analytical framework to model the interaction between different priority classes and time-varying contention windows [10].

Research on SPMA mainly focuses on mechanism optimization and performance analysis. In [6], a PF-MAC protocol for UAV-assisted Internet of Things (IoT) systems was proposed with an adaptive backoff mechanism to improve delay and throughput; however, the work lacks a rigorous analytical foundation. A spatio-temporal analytical framework combining stochastic geometry and queueing theory was presented in [9, 10] investigated spatial performance metrics and parameter impacts; nevertheless, both assume relatively static network topologies. In [11], the SPMA protocol was modeled using a preemptive M/G/1 queue for high-speed mobile ad hoc networks, but the threshold configuration still relied on heuristic tuning. Finally, [12] combined theoretical modeling with simulation correction for threshold optimization, yet spatial interference and multi-hop effects were not considered.

The main contributions of this paper can be summarized as follows:

(1) Failure-Count–Driven Markov Modeling for Priority Access (with Priority Upgrade).We develop a discrete-time Markov chain explicitly tracking each packet's failure-retransmission count $N$ and its priority class (0 being the highest). When the retransmission count reaches its maximum $N_{\max}$, the packet is promoted to a higher-priority class, ensuring urgent packets gradually escalate in priority. The model derives steady-state attempt/idle probabilities and busy/collision dynamics without any contention window notion, capturing per-class behavior under varying loads.
(2) Adaptive N-Policy Access Control Guided by the Markov Model. Rather than adjusting a contention window, we design an N-aware adaptive mechanism that dynamically tunes attempt probabilities and retry thresholds per class based on collision/busy statistics inferred from the Markov model. This ensures low latency for high-priority flows while regulating network load and improving service for lower-priority traffic.

(3) Enhanced Performance for Large-Scale Disaster-Response UAV Networks. Extensive simulations confirm that MK-SPMA meets real-time requirements for high-priority traffic, significantly improves success rates of lower-priority flows under dense network conditions, and provides reliable connectivity in large-scale disaster-response scenarios.

## 2 Protocol Description

### 2.1 System Model

We consider a post-disaster UAV-assisted communication network consisting of $n$ UAVs and multiple ground terminals. The UAVs act as airborne relays, forming a wireless multi-hop topology to deliver heterogeneous traffic. The system operates over $C$ orthogonal channels, each with identical bandwidth and time-slotted access. High-priority packets are allocated channel access with the highest probability, while medium- and low-priority packets share the remaining resources based on SPMA scheme. The priority levels are indexed by $i \in \{0, 1, \ldots, m - 1\}$, where $i = 0$ denotes the highest priority (e.g., survivor location, emergency commands), and larger $m$ values correspond to lower-priority tasks (e.g., environmental monitoring, logistics). Each UAV dynamically selects channels according to its traffic priority and local queue state, enabling differentiated quality of service while maintaining high overall throughput and fairness under heavy traffic conditions (Figs. 1 and 2).

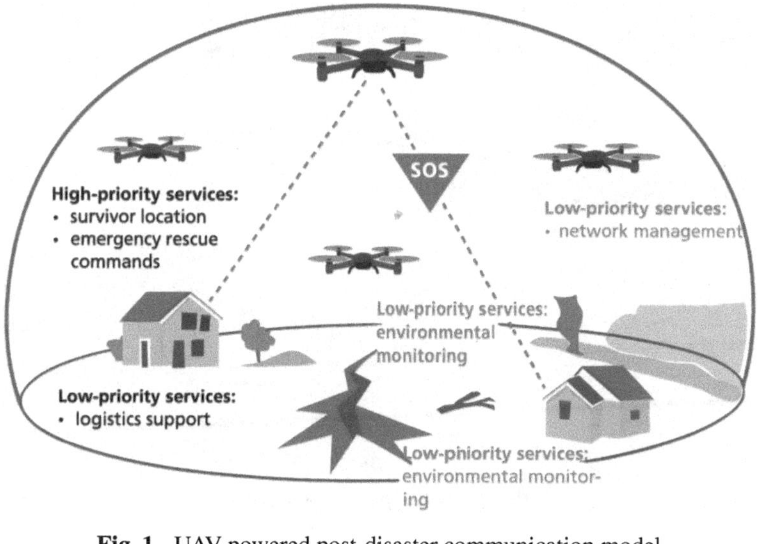


**Fig. 1.** UAV-powered post-disaster communication model

### 2.2 MAC Protocol Structure

Upon packet arrival, the packet is categorized into $m$ priority classes $i \in \{0, 1, \ldots, m - 1\}$ (with $i = 0$ the highest). Each packet enters the access process at state $(i, 0)$, where

$k$ counts failures within the current class. A successful attempt completes transmission; otherwise $k = k + 1$ .While $k < N_{\max}$, the packet remains in class $i$ and retransmits $(i, k) \rightarrow (i, k + 1)$. When $k \geq N_{\max}$, cross-class escalation is triggered: if $i > 0$, set $i = i - 1$ and reset to $(i, 0)$;if already at $i = 0$, the packet self-loops in the highest class until success. The design dispenses with a backoff window and instead uses a "failure counting → priority escalation" mechanism: parameters are fixed within each class, and escalation at the threshold $N_{\max}$ preserves timeliness for high-priority traffic while preventing prolonged blockage of low-priority packets, thereby improving overall fairness and accessibility.

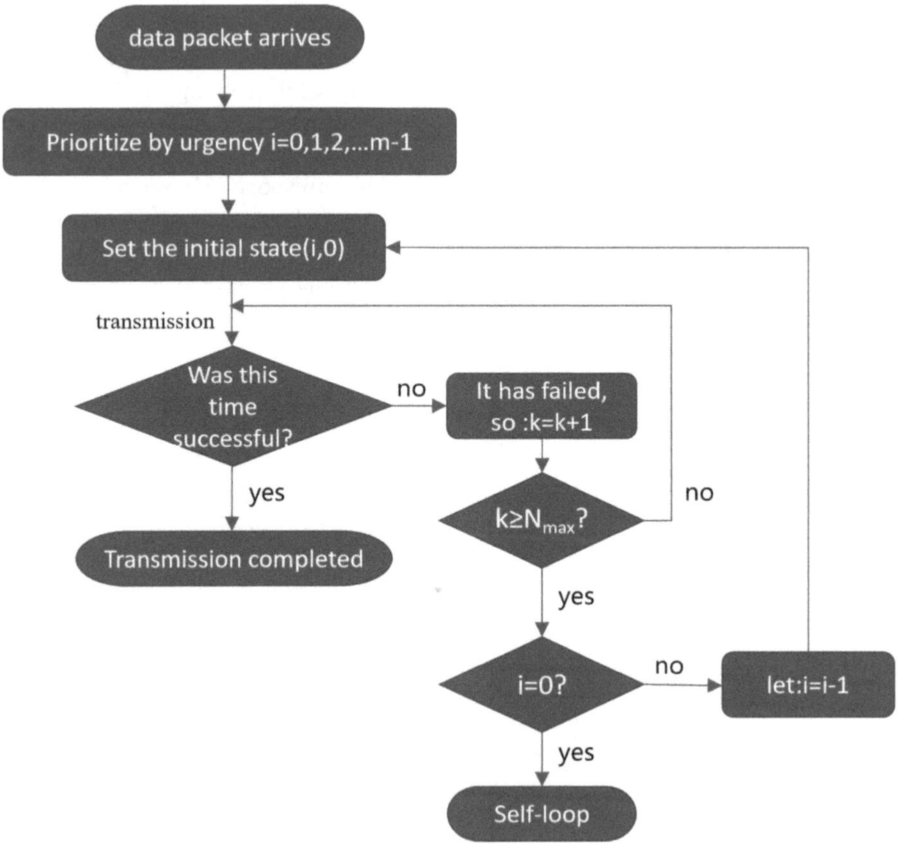


**Fig. 2.** MK-SPMA flowchart

## 2.3 Parameter Selection and Design Justification

After defining the overall system model and the detailed MAC protocol structure, the core parameters of the proposed MK-SPMA algorithm are further specified. In particular, two parameters—the number of priority levels $m$ and the maximum failure count

$W_{max}$—play critical roles in determining priority differentiation, escalation frequency, and overall network performance. Their selection is based on both theoretical reasoning and empirical optimization, as discussed below.

The selected parameters $m = 8$ and $W_{max} = 4$ collectively ensure that MK-SPMA achieves balanced performance among timeliness, fairness, and computational efficiency, making it well suited for large-scale UAV-assisted post-disaster communication networks.

### A. Number of Priority Levels($m = 8$)

In the proposed MK-SPMA scheme, the number of priority classes $m = 8$ is selected to balance differentiation granularity and computational tractability. This configuration is consistent with widely adopted priority frameworks such as IEEE 802.11e EDCA and DiffServ, which typically define four to eight service categories [13].

In UAV-assisted post-disaster networks, eight priority levels are sufficient to represent diverse mission-critical and supportive traffic types, including emergency command dissemination, medical telemetry, real-time video, situational monitoring, mapping, environmental sensing, logistics coordination, and network management. From an analytical perspective, the number of Markov states grows approximately as $O(m \times W_{max})$; increasing $m$ beyond eight results in rapidly rising complexity with diminishing throughput and delay gains.

Simulation evaluations also demonstrate that when $m \geq 8$, both throughput and latency improvements saturate, indicating that eight levels provide adequate differentiation while maintaining manageable state complexity. Therefore, $m = 8$ represents an optimal trade-off between modeling accuracy and algorithmic efficiency.

### B. Maximum Failure Count ($W_{max} = 4$)

Unlike conventional SPMA protocols relying on backoff windows, MK-SPMA employs a failure-count-based retransmission mechanism. Each packet remains in state $(i, k)$ until either a successful transmission occurs or the failure count $k$ reaches the threshold $W_{max}$, triggering an upgrade to a higher-priority class. The value of $W_{max}$ directly controls the system's tolerance to transmission failures and the frequency of cross-priority escalation.

A small $W_{max}$ may cause excessive escalation and congestion at higher priorities, whereas a large $W_{max}$ could prolong low-priority waiting times. Analytical steady-state evaluations and parameter sweeps show that $W_{max} \in [3, 5]$ achieves near-optimal trade-offs between throughput, fairness, and latency. Empirically, setting $W_{max} = 4$ provides the best overall performance, improving low-priority success rate by approximately 7–8% compared with $W_{max} = 3$ and reducing average delay by about 11% compared with $W_{max} = 5$ [14].

Moreover, this value aligns with the retransmission limits (4–7 attempts) specified in IEEE 802.11 MAC standards, ensuring realistic physical-layer compatibility. Consequently, $W_{max} = 4$ is adopted as the default configuration, justified by both analytical modeling and simulation evidence.

# 3 Analysis of mac Protocol MODELING

## 3.1 Markov Chain Modeling

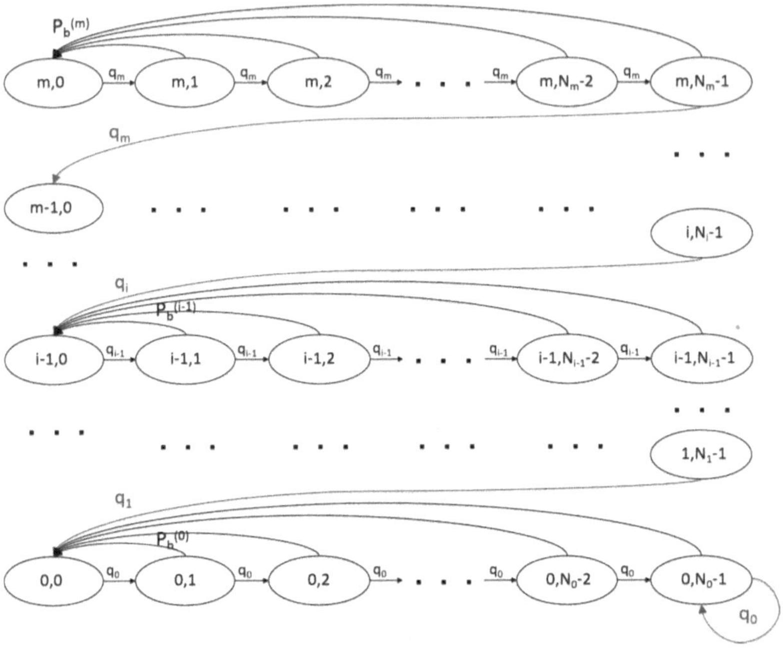


**Fig. 3.** Finite-state multi-priority Markov retrial chain

To analyze the internal transmission dynamics of the proposed MK-SPMA protocol, each packet is modeled as a finite-state Markov chain with multi-priority coupling.A state is denoted by $(i, k)$, where $i \in [0, m - 1]$ is the priority level (0 = highest priority) and $k \in [0, N_i - 1]$ represents the consecutive failure counter.

At every slot within level $i$, a packet either succeeds with probability $P_b^{(i)}$ (the probability that the channel is idle or transmission succeeds) or fails with probability $q_i$ (the probability that the channel is busy or collision occurs), satisfying $P_b^{(i)} + q_i = 1$.If the transmission succeeds, the packet returns to the start of its current level $(i, 0)$; if it fails and $k < N_i - 1$,it moves to $(i, k + 1)$; and if the failure counter reaches $k = N_i - 1$, the packet is upgraded to the next higher priority level $(i - 1, 0)$.For the highest priority $i = 0$, the packet continues retrying within the same level.

This modeling structure captures both intra-level retransmissions and cross-priority promotions, which are unique features of MK-SPMA compared with conventional SPMA schemes.

Top level $m$:

$$\begin{gathered}P\{(m,k)\rightarrow(m,0)\}=P_b^{(m)},0\le k\le N_m-1,\\P\{(m,k)\rightarrow(m,k+1)\}=q_m,0\le k<N_m-1,\\P\{(m,N_m-1)\rightarrow(m-1,0)\}=q_m.\end{gathered}\quad(1)$$

Intermediate level $i$ ($0 < i < m$):

$$\begin{cases}P\{(i,k)\rightarrow(i,0)\}=P_b^{(i)},0\le k\le N_i-1,\\P\{(i,k)\rightarrow(i,k+1)\}=q_i,0\le k<N_i-1,\\P\{(i,N_i-1)\rightarrow(i-1,0)\}=q_i.\end{cases}\quad(2)$$

Lowest level 0:

$$\begin{cases}P\{(0,k)\rightarrow(0,0)\}=P_b^{(0)},0\le k\le N_0-1,\\P\{(0,k)\rightarrow(0,k+1)\}=q_0,0\le k<N_0-1,\\P\{(0,N_0-1)\rightarrow(0,N_0-1)\}=q_0.\end{cases}\quad(3)$$

In this formulation, $P_b^{(i)}$ governs the successful return path (black arrow) and $q_i$ represents the failed transition (red arrow) that may eventually trigger an inter-level promotion.

Let a visit denote the time interval from entering $(i, 0)$ until the packet leaves level $i$.During a visit, the process sequentially traverses states $(i, 0)$, $(i, 1)$, …, $(i, N_i - 1)$.Each failure increases the counter by 1, while success resets it to 0 and ends the visit.

The probability that a visit reaches state $(i, k)$ is simply:

$$P\{\text{reach}(i,k)\}=q_i^k,\quad 0\le k\le N_i-1.\quad(4)$$

The expected number of slots spent in one visit equals the expected number of consecutive trials before success or upgrade:

$$E[T_i]=\sum_{k=0}^{N_i-1}q_i^k=\frac{1-q_i^{N_i}}{1-q_i}=\frac{1-q_i^{N_i}}{P_b^{(i)}}.\quad(5)$$

Hence, the conditional steady-state distribution within level i is truncated geometric:

$$\phi_{i,k}=\frac{P\{\text{reach}(i,k)\}}{E[T_i]}=\frac{(1-q_i)q_i^k}{1-q_i^{N_i}}=\frac{P_b^{(i)}q_i^k}{1-q_i^{N_i}},\quad 0\le k\le N_i-1.\quad(6)$$

The intra-level success and upgrade probabilities are:

$$\sigma_i=1-q_i^{N_i},\quad u_i=q_i^{N_i},\quad \sigma_i+u_i=1.\quad(7)$$

Intuitively, $\sigma_i$ measures the chance of successful transmission before the retry limit, while $u_i$ represents the likelihood of escalation to a higher priority.

Let $\Lambda_i$ be the total inflow rate into level $i$,composed of external arrivals $A_i$ and upgraded flows $U_{i+1}$ from the lower level. The flow relationships are:

$$\begin{aligned} \Lambda_i &= A_i + U_{i+1}, \\ U_i &= \Lambda_i u_i = \Lambda_i q_i^{N_i}, \\ D_i &= \Lambda_i \sigma_i = \Lambda_i \left(1 - q_i^{N_i}\right), \\ \Lambda_{i-1} &= A_{i-1} + U_i, \quad i = 1, \ldots, m-1. \end{aligned} \tag{8}$$

$D_i$denotes the successfully transmitted flow from level $i$,while $U_i$ corresponds to the upgraded packets entering level $i - 1$.These equations ensure flow conservation and quantify the coupling among adjacent priority levels.

According to renewal theory, the fraction of time the system spends in level $i$ is proportional to the product of its inflow rate and mean residence time:

$$\Theta_i = \frac{\Lambda_i E[T_i]}{\sum_{r=0}^{m-1} \Lambda_r E[T_r]}, \qquad E[T_i] = \frac{1 - q_i^{N_i}}{P_b^{(i)}}. \tag{9}$$

Combining intra-level and inter-level results, the global steady-state probability of being in state $(i, k)$ is:

$$\pi_{i,k} = \Theta_i \phi_{i,k} = \frac{\Lambda_i E[T_i]}{\sum_r \Lambda_r E[T_r]} \cdot \frac{P_b^{(i)} q_i^k}{1 - q_i^{N_i}} = \frac{\Lambda_i q_i^k}{\sum_r \Lambda_r E[T_r]}. \tag{10}$$

This compact form highlights that the probability of occupying state $(i, k)$ depends on the traffic inflow and the per-level failure statistics.

## 3.2 Performance Parameters

### A. **Throughput (S)**

Throughput represents the average number of packets successfully transmitted per slot. For each priority level $i$, the successful transmission probability within a slot is given by

$$S_i = \Lambda_i \left(1 - q_i^{N_i}\right) \tag{11}$$

where $\Lambda_i$ denotes the total packet arrival rate to level $i$, and $q_i$ represents the failure probability of a single attempt.Hence, the overall system throughput can be written as

$$S_{total} = \sum_{i=0}^{m-1} S_i = \sum_{i=0}^{m-1} \Lambda_i \left(1 - q_i^{N_i}\right) \tag{12}$$

B. **Average Delay(D)**

The average delay, denoted as $\overline{D}_j$, measures the expected number of time slots consumed from packet arrival to successful transmission.

It includes both intra-priority retransmission and inter-priority upgrade. For a packet initially belonging to priority level $j$:

$$E\left[T_j^{(e2e)}\right] = E\left[T_j\right] + u_j E\left[T_{j-1}\right] + u_j u_{j-1} E\left[T_{j-2}\right] + \cdots + \left(\prod_{\ell=1}^{j} u_{j-\ell+1}\right) E[T_0] \quad (13)$$

where the expected number of transmissions within priority $i$ is

$$E[T_i] = \frac{1 - q_i^{N_i}}{P_b^{(i)}}. \quad (14)$$

and $u_i = q_i^{N_i}$ is the upgrade probability, $T_{\text{slot}}$ is the slot duration.Thus, the average delay is

$$\overline{D}_j = E\left[T_j^{(e2e)}\right] \cdot T_{slot} \quad (15)$$

C. **Slot Utilization($\eta$)**

The slot utilization ratio, denoted as $\eta$, characterizes the fraction of time slots actively occupied by transmissions (either successful or collided).It measures how efficiently the channel resource is utilized.

$$\eta = S_{\text{total}} + P_{\text{fail}} \quad (16)$$

Where $P_{\text{fail}}$ is the aggregated per-slot probability of collisions or busy-channel failures.

Alternatively, using the steady-state probabilities $\pi_{i,\,k}$ and per-state transmission probability $p_{tx}^{(i,k)}$:

$$\eta = \sum_{i=0}^{m-1} \sum_{k=0}^{N_i-1} \pi_{i,k} p_{tx}^{(i,k)} \quad (17)$$

## 4 Simulations Results

In this section, we evaluate the performance improvement of the proposed MK-SPMA protocol through extensive simulations under identical network settings (Table 1). (Fig. 3, Fig. 4, Fig. 5, Fig. 6, Fig. 7 and Fig. 8) illustrate the comparison between the traditional SPMA and the proposed MK-SPMA in terms of throughput, average delay, successful packet count, throughput vs. number of nodes, latency vs. number of nodes, and slot utilization vs. number of nodes.

**Table 1.** Parameters used in discussion and simulation

| Parameters | Values |
|---|---|
| Number of Nodes | 36 |
| Number of Channels | 8 |
| Channel Transmission Rate | 2 Mbit/s |
| Time Slot | 0.5 ms |
| Maximum Fail Count | 4 |
| Payload Length | 1000 bit |
| Preamble Length | 100 bit |
| PHY Rate | 2e6 bps |
| Base Transmission Probabilities | 0.12 → 0.05 (m = 8) |
| Physical Success Probabilities | 0.78 → 0.95 (m = 8) |
| Max Transmission Probability | 0.25 |

### 4.1 Performance Comparison of SPMA and MK-SPMA Across Priority Levels

As illustrated in Fig. 4, the throughput of both SPMA and MK-SPMA gradually decreases as the priority index i increases from 0 to 7, which is consistent with the design principle that high-priority traffic (e.g., i = 0–2) should enjoy higher transmission probability and shorter access delay. Across all priority levels, MK-SPMA (solid line) consistently achieves higher throughput than traditional SPMA (dashed line). The improvement is most evident in the mid-to-low priority classes (i = 3–6*), where the throughput gap reaches about 10–15%. This advantage stems from the Markov-chain-driven retransmission mechanism, which dynamically adjusts access probability according to each packet's failure state, thereby reducing persistent collisions and idle slots. Moreover, the smooth and nearly linear descent of MK-SPMA demonstrates that the proposed scheme achieves both throughput enhancement and balanced degradation across priorities, ensuring fairness while preserving the required priority differentiation.

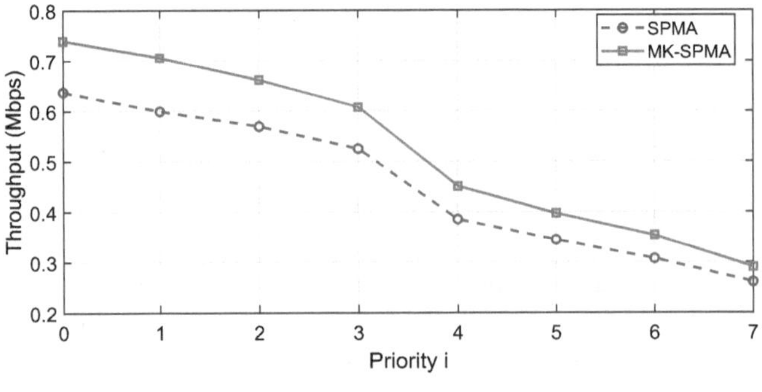


**Fig. 4.** Throughput vs. Priority Level

Figure. 5 presents the variation of average delay with respect to the priority level i. As expected, average delay increases monotonically from high- to low-priority traffic, reflecting the scheduling hierarchy in contention-based access. Compared with SPMA, MK-SPMA yields consistently shorter delays for all priority classes. The reduction is most pronounced for higher priorities (i $\leq$ 3*), where the delay decreases by approximately 8–12%, while even the lowest priority traffic (i = 7*) benefits from an observable reduction of about 5%. This performance gain verifies that the adaptive probability control based on retransmission states effectively reduces backoff waiting time and improves transmission efficiency. Additionally, MK-SPMA exhibits a smoother growth trend, implying greater temporal stability and predictable latency characteristics, which are crucial for delay-sensitive UAV communication services such as command and control or real-time telemetry.

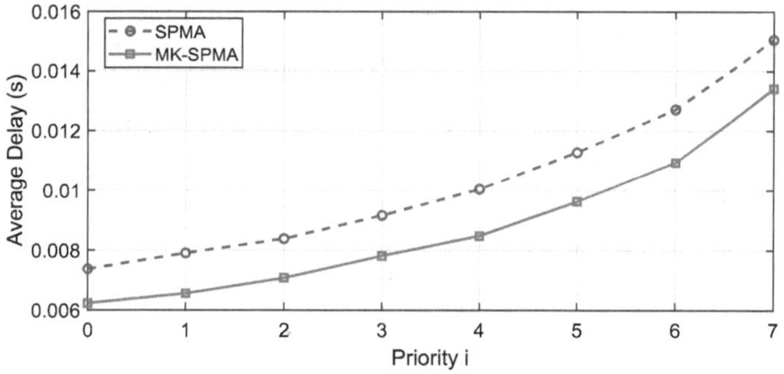


**Fig. 5.** Average Delay vs. Priority Level

As shown in Fig. 6, the number of successfully transmitted packets declines as the priority level i increases, which aligns with the throughput and delay trends observed earlier. High-priority traffic achieves the largest volume of successful transmissions due to its higher access probability and shorter retransmission path, while low-priority traffic experiences a gradual decline as competition intensifies. Nevertheless, MK-SPMA significantly improves the overall success count across all priority levels compared with traditional SPMA. The enhancement is especially evident in the mid-priority range ($i = 3 - 5$), where the number of successful packets increases by roughly 15–20%. This confirms that MK-SPMA not only enhances average throughput but also improves transmission reliability by reducing the probability of consecutive failures and premature packet drops. Consequently, the scheme achieves higher overall channel efficiency and more balanced resource utilization among multiple service classes.

## 4.2 Performance Comparison of SPMA and MK-SPMA under Increasing Node Density

As shown in Fig. 7, the overall throughput of both SPMA and MK-SPMA protocols increases monotonically with the number of nodes, indicating that the proposed mechanism scales effectively as network density grows. High-priority classes (0–3) consistently achieve higher throughput than low-priority ones (4–7), confirming that priority

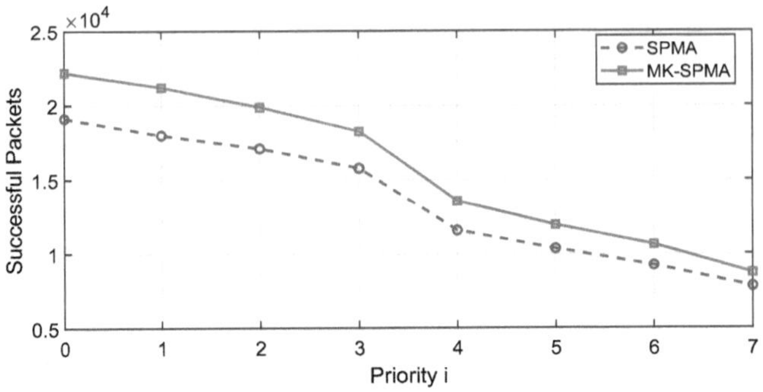


**Fig. 6.** Number of successful packets vs. priority level

differentiation is preserved under multi-channel contention. More importantly, MK-SPMA (solid lines) exhibits a clear throughput advantage over the traditional SPMA (dashed lines) across all priority levels. This improvement becomes most pronounced in medium-to-high-load regions (20–40 nodes), where collisions are frequent. For instance, at 50 nodes, MK-SPMA achieves approximately 6%–12% higher throughput for high-priority classes and 4%–9% for lower ones. The gain originates from the Markov-chain-driven retransmission mechanism, which adaptively adjusts the transmission probability according to the failure count k, thereby reducing idle and collided slots. Furthermore, the hierarchical ordering among priorities remains intact even at dense node populations, demonstrating that MK-SPMA enhances network capacity without sacrificing the service-level separation inherent in SPMA.

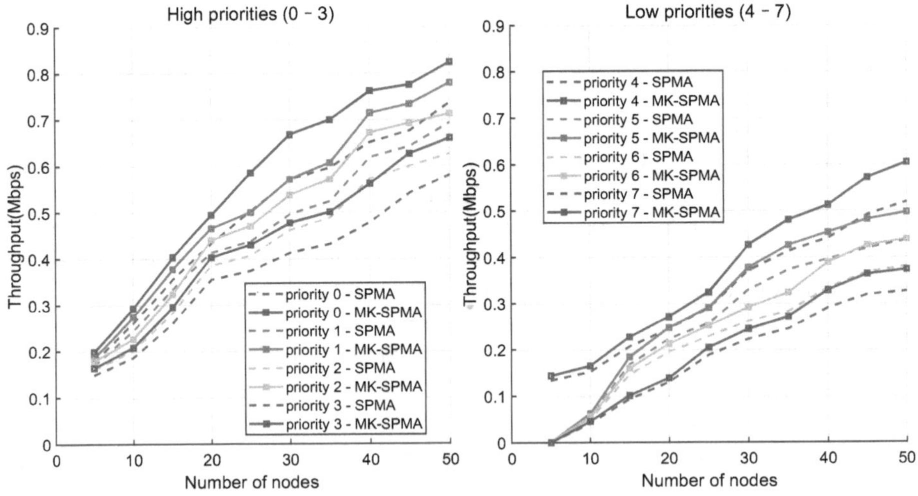


**Fig. 7.** Throughput vs. Number of Nodes

Figure. 8 illustrates the variation of average transmission latency with the number of nodes. As expected, latency increases gradually with network load due to rising queue lengths and retransmission delays. Nevertheless, MK-SPMA consistently achieves lower latency than traditional SPMA across all priority levels, validating its efficiency in collision mitigation and scheduling balance. In the high-priority group (0–3), the latency reduction reaches 7%–12% under heavy load, while for the low-priority group (4–7), the reduction remains around 5%–10%. The difference is especially evident in the moderate-load region (10–30 nodes), where adaptive probability control effectively allocates channel access to active nodes, shortening average waiting time. Additionally, the MK-SPMA curves are smoother and more stable, implying that its performance degradation with load growth is more predictable and controlled. This stability ensures that even in large-scale UAV ad-hoc deployments, real-time and delay-sensitive data streams can maintain bounded latency, which is essential for emergency coordination and control tasks.

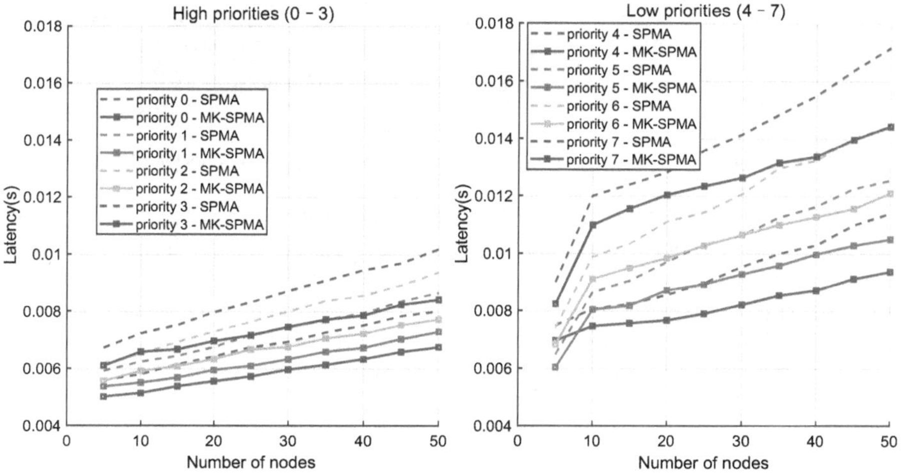


**Fig. 8.** Latency vs. number of nodes

In Fig. 9, the slot utilization ratio is plotted as a function of the number of nodes. Both protocols show an upward trend as node density increases, reflecting more active channel access attempts. High-priority traffic exhibits greater utilization, consistent with its higher access probability p_tx, while low-priority slots remain comparatively underloaded. However, MK-SPMA achieves significantly higher utilization than traditional SPMA across all priorities—an improvement of roughly 8%–20% depending on network load and priority index. This confirms that MK-SPMA allocates time-slot resources more efficiently by reducing idle and collision periods. Notably, under congested conditions (30–50 nodes), the utilization of lower-priority classes in SPMA drops sharply, whereas MK-SPMA maintains steady growth, indicating a better fairness-throughput trade-off. The enhanced utilization directly corresponds to the throughput gain observed in Fig. 7, revealing that MK-SPMA not only improves transmission success but also ensures that each slot contributes more effectively to network throughput, thereby achieving superior overall spectral efficiency.

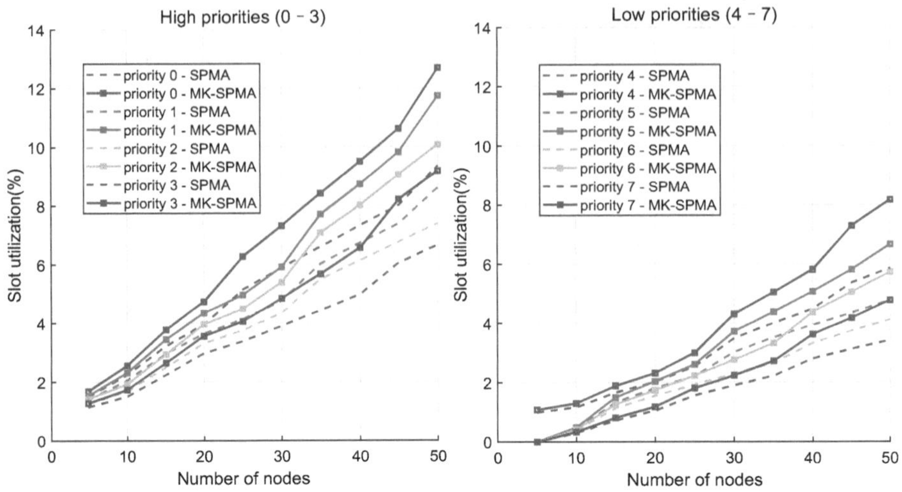


**Fig. 9.** Slot utilization vs. number of nodes

### 4.3 Quantitative Performance Comparison of SPMA and MK-SPMA

Quantitatively, the throughput of MK-SPMA increases from 3.630 Mbps to 4.208 Mbps, achieving a 15.9% improvement, while the average delay decreases from 9.538 ms to 8.102 ms, corresponding to a 15.1% reduction. These results clearly demonstrate that MK-SPMA significantly enhances transmission efficiency and reduces latency compared to the baseline SPMA. Moreover, MK-SPMA achieves a slightly higher success rate (98.59% vs. 97.00%), confirming its overall performance advantages.

## 5 Conclusion

This paper addresses the need for reliable, low-latency communications in disaster rescue networks by proposing a finite-state multi-priority Markov retrial chain. Closed-form steady-state distributions and key metrics such as throughput and collision probability were derived, revealing how retransmission limits and priority strategies affect performance. Results show that the model enables effective trade-offs between reliability and delay in wireless networks. The framework generalizes classical single-priority models and offers practical insights for protocol optimization. Future work will integrate adaptive backoff schemes and time-varying channels to broaden applicability in ultra-reliable low-latency communications (URLLC) scenarios.

## References

1. Zhang, J., Wang, Z., Wu, H., Li, W.: Ordered submodularity-based value maximization of UAV data collection in earthquake areas. IEEE Trans. Netw. Sci. Eng. **11**(5), 4886–4897 (2024)
2. Matracia, M., Kishk, M.A., Alouini, M.-S.: UAV-aided post-disaster cellular networks: a novel stochastic geometry approach. IEEE Trans. Veh. Technol. **72**(7), 9406–9418 (2023)

3. Cao, H., Zhu, W., Chen, Z., Sun, Z., Wu, D.O.: Energy-delay Tradeoff for dynamic trajectory planning in priority-oriented UAV-aided IoT networks. IEEE Transact. Green Commun. Network. **7**(1), 158–170 (2023)
4. Wang, D., Cao, Y., Lam, K.-Y., Hu, Y., Kaiwartya, O.: Authentication and key agreement based on three factors and PUF for UAV-assisted post-disaster emergency communication. IEEE Internet Things J. **11**(11), 20457–20472 (2024)
5. Khalid, R., Shah, Z., Naeem, M., Ali, A., Al-Fuqaha, A., Ejaz, W.: Computational efficiency maximization for UAV-assisted MEC networks with energy harvesting in disaster scenarios. IEEE Internet Things J. **11**(5), 9004–9018 (2024)
6. Khisa, S., Moh, S.: Priority-aware fast MAC protocol for UAV-assisted industrial IoT systems. IEEE Access. **9**, 57089–57106 (2021)
7. Wu, J., Zhou, J., Yu, L., Gao, L.: MAC optimization protocol for cooperative UAV based on dual perception of energy consumption and channel gain. IEEE Trans. Mob. Comput. **23**(10), 9851–9862 (2024)
8. Xie, T., Zhao, H., Xiong, J., Sarkar, N.I.: A Multi-channel MAC protocol with retrodirective array antennas in flying ad hoc networks. IEEE Trans. Veh. Technol. **70**(2), 1606–1617 (2021)
9. Zhang, Y., He, Y., Wang, X., Sun, H., Quek, T.Q.S.: Modeling and performance analysis of statistical priority-based multiple access: a stochastic geometry approach. IEEE Internet Things J. **9**(15), 13942–13954 (2022)
10. Zhang, Y., Sun, H., He, Y., Zhang, Z., Wang, X., Quek, T.Q.S.: A Spatio-temporal analytical model for statistical priority-based multiple access network. IEEE Wirel. Commun. Let. **12**(1), 153–157 (2023)
11. Li, Z., Zhao, J., Han, T.: The performance analysis of SPMA protocol in high speed Mobile ad hoc network. IEEE Access. **11**, 23485–23494 (2023)
12. Li, Z., Guo, J.: A threshold setting method for SPMA protocol. In: 2022 7th International Conference on Signal and Image Processing (ICSIP), Suzhou, China, pp. 691–695 (2022)
13. Khorov, E., Levitsky, I., Akyildiz, I.F.: Current status and directions of IEEE 802.11be, the future Wi-Fi 7. IEEE Access. **8**, 88664–88688 (2020). https://doi.org/10.1109/ACCESS.2020.2993448
14. Xin, L., Starobinski, D.: Countering cascading denial of service attacks on Wi-Fi networks. IEEE/ACM Trans. Network. **29**(3), 1335–1348 (2021). https://doi.org/10.1109/TNET.2021.3062363

# An Efficient Communication Method Based on Data Mules in Low-Density Unmanned Aerial Vehicles Networks

Yicheng Zhao[1(✉)], Hai Wang[1], and Zhen Qin[2]

[1] College of Communication Engineering, Army Engineering University of PLA, Nanjing, China
1966945431@qq.com

[2] Department of Information and Communication, Noncommissioned Officer Academy of PAP, Hangzhou, China
xiaonianhua@aeu.edu.cn

**Abstract.** The rapid advances of unmanned aerial vehicle (UAV) technology have fundamentally transformed wide-area monitoring and data transmission for military communications, particularly in battlefield scenarios infrastructure-free. However, as the monitoring area expands, designing and managing UAV networks becomes increasingly complex, which poses a major challenge for efficient long-distance data transmission. The key issue is how to establish reliable, long-distance communication links with a limited number of UAVs, especially under low node density conditions ($< 2$ nodes/k $m^2$), while ensuring efficient end-to-end data transmission. In this study, we propose a cooperative data transport scheme that uses UAVs as "data mules". We also model the positional errors incurred during UAV mobility and self-localization to ensure reliable data delivery. Building on achieving end-to-end communication, we further optimize the scheme to improve link energy efficiency by adjusting UAV quantity, maneuver duration, and communication range. Simulation results show that compared to traditional methods [store-and-forward, multi-hop routing], our scheme reduces transmission delay by 15.2% and 9.3%, respectively, while increasing energy consumption by 5.6% and 13.9%. Furthermore, compared to multi-hop UAV schemes optimized by different algorithms, our approach exhibits superior overall transmission efficiency, particularly in high-interference environments and video transmission scenarios with large data volumes.

**Keywords:** Low-density UAV network · Data transmission · Data mules

## 1 Introduction

In application scenarios of unmanned aerial vehicle(UAV) networks such as border patrol, battlefield data collection, and field scientific research, establishing a

Supported by organization x.


Y. Liu et al. (Eds.): ChinaCom 2025, LNICST 711, pp. 326–345, 2027.
https://doi.org/10.1007/978-3-032-33662-0_25

fully connected network cross large areas remains challenging [1–3].Key barriers include the high cost of dense UAV clusters and performance degradation from inter-node interference. Furthermore, dense UAV clusters in battlefield environments are highly vulnerable to detection and interception. Thus, developing efficient data transmission by low-density UAV networks for these scenarios holds substantial research significance. Existing UAV remote transmission schemes fall into three modes: cellular UAV networks [4], UAV-satellite communication [5], and UAV-assisted multi-hop relaying [6,7]. Each mode exhibits distinct characteristics regarding communication range and application scenarios. For cellular UAV networks, this mode integrates UAVs with ground cellular infrastructure, enabling UAVs to forward data via nearby cellular base stations [4]. This system can significantly expand communication coverage and enhance transmission efficiency. However, its effectiveness heavily relies on cellular base station density—rendering it unsuitable for remote areas lacking cellular infrastructure. For satellite-assisted systems, UAVs equipped with satellite terminals conduct beyond-line-of-sight (BLoS) data transmission via orbital systems [5]. While integrating satellite communication enables wide-area coverage [8], it suffers from high communication costs, large latency ($> 500$ ms), and high weather sensitivity. This performance degradation is particularly severe in harsh weather or areas with complex atmospheric electromagnetic environments [1]. Additionally, the energy consumption and size of satellite terminals restrict its application primarily to large fixed-wing platforms—precluding use in low-cost small rotor UAVs [5]. For UAV-assisted multi-hop transmission, current research focuses on relay mechanisms for UAV trajectory optimization: cluster-based transmission algorithms adopt equidistant path planning to implement delay-tolerant network(DTN) mobile relay schemes, which leverage UAV mobility to enhance transmission flexibility [6]; sparse FANET schemes improve connectivity via adaptive trajectory control [7]. Recent advancements address specific challenges: energy-aware path planning improves message delivery rates in shuttle networks [9]. Prediction-based routing leverages mobility patterns for opportunistic transmission [10].

However, the above research has three limitations: (1) UAV node density requirement: Achieving multi-hop transmission across wide areas requires dense UAV clusters, resulting in high costs, complex transmission mechanism designs, and subsequent system instability. (2) Relay hop count limitation: Most schemes restrict the hop count in UAV relay links to two. Although this reduces link risks, it severely limits the scalability of UAV maneuver ranges [11]. (3) Practicality gap in real-world scenarios: Unless channel conditions are validated via field tests, the simplified simulation models in existing literature fail to capture complex channel dynamics in long-distance communication scenarios.

This creates favorable conditions for applying low-density UAV networks based on data mules (DMs) in wide-area environments [12,22]. In sparse UAV networks, inter-node mutual interference is low, and large-area data collection and long-distance data transportation are achievable by leveraging UAV mobility—thereby effectively reducing UAV costs [13]. In this paper, we propose an end-to-end data transmission strategy for low-density UAV networks based on data mules—one that aims to design an efficient, reliable, and low-complexity UAV relay link for wide-area end-to-end communication, and provides a feasible solution for information circulation in such networks. The main contributions of this paper are as follows:

(1) We have designed an end-to-end data transmission method for low-density UAV networks based on DMs, addressing the end-to-end data transmission challenge in wide-area low-density UAV networks and reducing associated end-to-end delays. This method adaptively adjusts DMs' mobility mode and communication power based on the source-destination distance and the number of available UAVs.
(2) Second, we model position error diffusion during DM maneuvering and construct a historical observation-based positioning error diffusion model, tailored to specific application scenarios. By adjusting DMs' flight status, we ensure the position error of DMs navigating to the data offloading position is controlled with limited prior information—thus mitigating the impact of position error on link data transmission.
(3) We have investigated link optimal energy efficiency under varying transmission distances, data volumes, and external interference intensities, and proposed an iteration-based optimization algorithm for the number of DMs, maneuver time, and speed in end-to-end links—this further improves the scheme's transmission efficiency. Experimental comparisons verify that the proposed strategy exhibits advantages in long-distance, large-capacity data transmission scenarios.

The remainder of this paper is organized as follows: Sect. 2 presents the related work. Section 3 introduces the system model and optimization problem for the target environment. Section 4 describes the analytical solution process and specific workflow of the iterative algorithm for the outlined problem, and presents simulation and numerical results to validate the performance of our scheme. Finally, Sect. 5 discusses and concludes our work.

## 2 Related Work

In low-density UAV networks without ground communication infrastructure, using UAVs as data mules for data transportation is widely adopted [2,11,12]. Similar to modern postal couriers, data mule transmission employs mobile data storage platforms as carriers to enable physical data transportation via the storage-transportation-unloading process [13]. With the advancement of cameras and remote sensing systems, Data mule transmission based on UAVs enjoys broad applicability. A UAV collects data at a sensing location, then flies to a communication location to offload the collected data, representing a typical DM transmission scenario [14]. In the related works, research on DM transmission mainly focuses on the UAV path-planning [13], optimization of data offloading locations [14], and resource allocation in data collection [15].

**Fig. 1.** Mission scenarios of low-density UAV networks

However, the above studies have optimized UAV data transmission strategies based on DMs from various perspectives, but fail to address the construction and optimization of end-to-end links in low-density UAV network. Three fundamental challenges exist for realizing long-range communication via data DMs in low-density UAV networks:

- Discontinuous network topology arising from large-area deployment: some UAV nodes cannot establish stable communication links, requiring reduced inter-node distances by DM cooperative maneuvering to construct intermittent virtual links for relay services.
- Limited UAV battery capacity yet highly energy-intensive long-distance data transportation: this poses a requirement for low-density UAV networks to balance latency and energy consumption while sustaining link connectivity, and identify the transmission mode that maximizes link energy efficiency.
- Position errors in DM maneuvering based on self-perception and prior environmental information: this necessitates developing corresponding positioning models and analytical metrics to ensure data delivery to the specified location within the error threshold.

# 3 System Model and Problem Formulation

## 3.1 Low-Density UAV Network Model and Collaborative Transmission Link Model

This section presents the assumptions, symbols, and definitions used for low-density UAV networks. Nodes in low-density UAV networks are represented by the set $U = \{U_1, U_2, U_3, ..., U_n\}$, where $n$ denotes the number of UAV nodes deployed in the mission area $\bar{A} = N \times N \times N\text{m}^3$. We investigate end-to-end video streaming scenarios in low-density UAV networks [18]. As shown in Fig. 1, during the data collection phase, UAVs are randomly deployed in the mission area to conduct scientific observations and collect image or video data. Upon capturing sensitive information, a UAV enters the data transmission phase and acts as the source node—further collecting information at its current location and transmitting it to the remote ground data center via DMs. All idle UAVs can act as DMs to participate in data transport. All UAV nodes have unique identifiers, each equipped with a camera, an image encoder, a wireless transceiver, and an inertial navigation system. Given the high energy demand of DMs, their communication energy consumption is assumed to mainly include two components: data packet forwarding and reception, with equal initial energy levels. Additionally, all UAVs have the same initial cache size, quantified by the total number of storable data packets.

A notable issue is the impact of DMs' positioning and navigation errors during maneuvering on data offloading. Many studies overlook this issue when focusing on communication problems, failing to account for the impact of communication locations on data transmission. Large deviations between the communication location and preset relay position cause changes in communication distance and environmental factors to significantly affect channel quality during data offloading. Without relying on satellite navigation systems, DMs can achieve autonomous navigation and localization via combining their inertial navigation systems and perception sensors. Unlike research on UAV network node positioning, DMs do not require precise global positioning accuracy during transport—instead, they only need to transmit data with the next node at the offloading location. Drawing on the UAV positioning method in [17], each time a DM maneuvers long distances to the vicinity of the offloading location, it can receive positioning signals sent by the next-hop DM or ground data center via sensor polling and TOF wireless ranging—enabling relative positioning between adjacent DMs in the link.

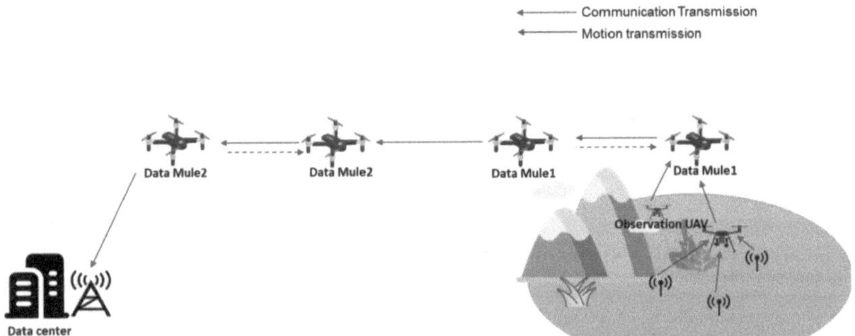


**Fig. 2.** End-to-end data transmission based on data mules

When a observation UAV encounters an emergency during remote inspection, it must transmit video data collected at the incident site to the ground data center promptly—yet lacks access to communication infrastructure (e.g., base stations) along the route. Thus, it can only relay data by transmitting it to a neighboring UAV. As shown in Fig. 2, this is an end-to-end data transmission scenario using DMs. No direct end-to-end data transmission link exists between the observation UAV (serving as the data source) and the ground data center; instead, the observation UAV transmits collected data to a DM equipped with a large-capacity data storage unit. DMs at the current transmission distance perform relay transmission via the store-transport-forward (STF) [14] mode to establish a virtual end-to-end communication link, ultimately transmitting collected data to the ground data center. This scheme is an intermittent data transmission approach involving multiple UAVs, where each DM acts as a transport carrier—maneuvering between data receiving and offloading locations to transport and transmit data from the previous node to the next.

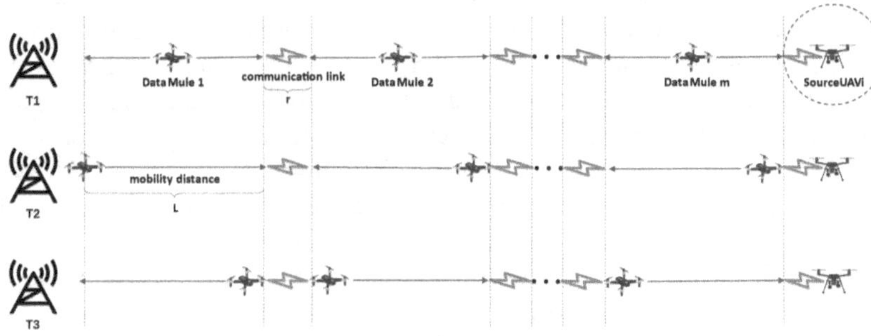


**Fig. 3.** End-to-end data transmission based on data mules

The periodic cooperative transmission process of the proposed scheme is shown in Fig. 3, assuming that there are $m$ DMs (denoted as $DM_1, DM_2, ..., DM_m$) assist the source UAV in end-to-end data transmission to the ground data center over a total distance $D$, and these $m$ DMs divide the route from the source UAV to the ground data center into $m+1$ maneuver segments. The data offloading distance between neighboring DMs is $r$ ($r \leq r_{max}$, where $r_{max}$ denotes the UAV's maximum communication radius). Since data requires $m+1$ downlink communications, the round-trip maneuvering distance for each DM is uniformly calculated as $L = [D - (m+1)r]/m$. Each DM maneuvers at the same speed, ensuring adjacent DMs arrive at the data offloading location simultaneously—thus reducing DM hovering time and balancing energy consumption across all DMs. Phase $T_1$ is the initial deployment phase, where $m$ $DMs$ are deployed at the midpoint of each of the $m+1$ flight path segments. Phases $T_2$ and $T_3$ are stable transmission phases. During $T_2$: odd-labeled $DMs$ move toward the source UAV, while even-labeled $DMs$ move toward the destination node and converge in the data exchange area within UAV communication coverage. They then transmit the carried data to the next-hop relay UAV or destination node. During $T_3$: odd-labeled $DMs$ move toward the destination node, while even-labeled $DMs$ move toward the source UAV; the post-convergence communication process is identical to that in $T_2$. After these three phases, the

UAV link completes a full data transmission and all $DM$ returns to their initial $T_1$ positions—thus completing one transmission cycle and initiating the next cycle.

Since data from the source to the ground data center is transmitted via round-trip coordinated transport by multiple DMs, each DM node avoids long-distance movement and only needs to offload data to the next hop. DM maneuvering distance decreases as the number of nodes increases—thus, the number of UAV nodes required for this transmission method is flexible, offering high adaptability to diverse scenarios. Analysis shows this scheme acts as a transitional mode between single-UAV payload forwarding and multi-hop forwarding in large-scale UAV networks. When only 1 DM is used for end-to-end transmission, the mode switches to single-UAV payload forwarding; when the number of DMs exceeds $D/r_{max}$, DMs can form a multi-hop link between the source and destination nodes without maneuvering—consistent with multi-hop data forwarding in large-scale networks. However, when the number of relay UAVs ($n$) falls in the range $1 < n < D/r_max$, this number is insufficient to form a complete data transmission link—yet exhibits slight redundancy compared to the single-UAV payload forwarding method. The multi-DM collaborative transportation method proposed in this paper is designed for this scenario. Therefore, this scheme is not intended to replace any existing UAV transport scheme in research. Instead, it serves as a complementary approach for wide-area UAV-assisted communication scenarios. It acts as an alternative for end-to-end data transmission when the number of UAVs is insufficient for multi-hop routing, or when a single UAV cannot handle ultra-long-distance data transmission.

### 3.2 Data Mule Positioning Error Diffusion Model

In battlefield environments, frequent self-localization by DMs increases their risk of being detected and shot down by enemy forces. Furthermore, high-precision position information offers no benefit for DM data transportation; instead, it wastes wireless resources and energy. Only the position error of DMs upon reaching the data offloading location needs to be controlled to avoid impacting data unloading. The flight trajectories of DMs during long-distance maneuvering in their respective airway segments are considered the shortest paths between two data offloading points. Since the transportation process is dominated by constant flight speed, DM flight in different airway segments is treated as linear motion. As shown in Fig. 4, drawing on [17], the initial position of a DM is $(x_0, y_0)$. With a linear motion model, it reaches the target position $(x_t, y_t)$ after a time interval $\delta$, and the localization error bound for the new position $PEB_{new}$ can be derived from that of the initial position $PEB_{old}$. It is worth noting that, unlike [17], since DMs in this study undergo prolonged movement, we do not treat their linear motion as ideal uniform linear motion—instead, we further account for velocity sensor measurement errors in the inertial navigation system.

Define the nominal velocity $v = v_0 + \Delta v$, where $v_0$ is the ideal velocity and $\Delta v$ is the velocity error, which is modeled as a zero-mean Gaussian noise, i.e., $\Delta v \sim N(0, \sigma_v^2)$, taking into account the measurement error of the velocity sensor

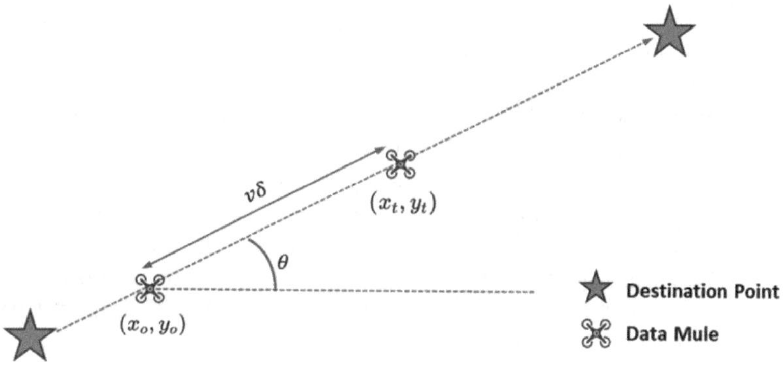


**Fig. 4.** End-to-end data transmission based on data mules

in the inertial navigation system. The state parameter vector of the data mule is denoted as $\Theta = [x_0, y_0, v]^T$, and the current position ($\mathbf{p_{old}} = (x_0, y_0)$) is related to its orientation ($\theta$) with respect to the future position ($\mathbf{p_{new}} = (x_t, y_t)$) as follows: $\theta = \tan^{-1}\left(\frac{y_t - y_0}{x_t - x_0}\right)$. Thus the future position $(x_t, y_t)$ after a time $\delta$ can be written as:

$$\begin{cases} x_t = x_0 + v_0\delta\cos\theta + \Delta x \\ y_t = y_0 + v_0\delta\sin\theta + \Delta y \end{cases} \tag{1}$$

where $\Delta x = \Delta v\delta\cos\theta$, $\Delta y = \Delta\ \mathrm{v}\delta\sin\theta$
So the Fisher information matrix(FIM) of the future position can be expressed as:

$$I_{p_{\text{new}}} = J I_{p_{\text{old}}} J^T + I_v \tag{2}$$

$J = \begin{bmatrix} \frac{\partial x_t}{\partial x_0} & \frac{\partial x_t}{\partial y_0} \\ \frac{\partial y_t}{\partial x_0} & \frac{\partial y_t}{\partial y_0} \end{bmatrix} = \begin{bmatrix} 1 - \frac{v_0\delta}{R_0}\sin^2\theta & \frac{v_0\delta}{R_0}\sin\theta\cos\theta \\ \frac{v_0\delta}{R_0}\sin\theta\cos\theta & 1 - \frac{v_0\delta}{R_0}\cos^2\theta \end{bmatrix}$ is the Jacobian matrix of the future position with respect to the current position, $I_v = \frac{1}{\delta^2\sigma_v^2}\begin{bmatrix} \cos^2\theta & \cos\theta\sin\theta \\ \cos\theta\sin\theta & \sin^2\theta \end{bmatrix}$ is the FIM sub-block corresponding to the velocity error, which reflects the effect of velocity uncertainty on position. The $I_{p_{\text{old}}}$ is the FIM information matrix for the current position. The *Process* of $I_{p_{\text{old}}}$ and $I_v$ is given in Appendix.

The localization performance is benchmarked by the fundamental limits of localization accuracy, called position error bound (PEB), which are derived from the Fisher information matrix. According to (2), the achievable PEB can be derived as:

$$\text{PEB}_{\text{new}} = \sqrt{\text{Trace}(I_{p_{\text{new}}}^{-1})} = \sqrt{\text{PEB}_{\text{old}}^2 \cdot \left(1 - \frac{v\delta}{R_0} + \left(\frac{v\delta}{R_0}\right)^2\right) + \delta^2\sigma_\nu^2} \tag{3}$$

$R_0 = \sqrt{(x_t - x_0)^2 + (y_t - y_0)^2}$ denotes the spatial relationship between the initial position and the future position. $PEB_{old}$ is the initial localization error, and the specific derivation process is detailed in the appendix.

In summary, the localization accuracy model for DMs accounts for two types of errors: (1)The localization error bound of the initial position $PEB_{old}$, which refers to the localization accuracy of UAV nodes in low-density UAV networks upon reaching preset positions, and is determined by TOF measurement noise and NLoS deviation. (2)$PEB_{new}$, which originates from the geometric propagation of initial position errors (related to UAV maneuvering modes) and the temporal accumulation of velocity errors (related to UAV sensors, external wind speeds, interference, and other factors).

### 3.3 Data Mule Wireless Channel and Energy Model

There are two types of communication links in low-density UAV networks, air-ground communication links between DMs and data centers, and air-air communication links between DMs and DMs. The line-of-sight and non-line-of-sight signals in the air-ground link exist with a specific probability, so the channel gain between the DM and the data center is:

$$g^{\text{G2A}} = \frac{|\tilde{g}_{DM,dc}|}{\sqrt{p^{Los} L^{LoS} + (1 - p^{Los}) L^{NLoS}}} \tag{4}$$

where $P^{LoS}$ is the LoS probability and $L^{LoS}$ and $L^{NLoS}$ are the free-space path losses of the LoS and NLoS links, $\tilde{g}_{DM,dc}$ is the channel gain per unit distance between the data mule and the data center.

In the air-air link, the data mule generally does not have obstacle occlusion when unloading data, so only LoS link transmission is considered, so the channel gain of $DM_i$ and $DM_{i+1}$ is expressed as: $g_{i,i+1}^{\text{A2A}} = |\tilde{g}_0| D_{DM}^{-2}$, where $\tilde{g}_0$ indicates the channel power gain per unit distance and $D_{DM}$ is the Euclidean distance for communication between two data mules. The channel transmission rate between data mules [16] can be expressed as:

$$C_i(t) = \begin{cases} B \log_2 \left(1 + \frac{P_i^{TX} \rho_i g_{i,i+1}^{A2A}}{I_i(t) + N}\right), d_{i,i+1}(t) \le r_{max} \\ 0, d_{i,i+1}(t) > r_{max} \end{cases} \tag{5}$$

$B$ is the channel transmission bandwidth, $P_i^{TX}$ denotes the transmit power of $DM_i$, $\rho_i$ is the power control factor, $d_{i,i+1}(t)$ denotes the communication distance between $DM_i$ and $DM_{i+1}$ at the moment $t$, $I_i(t) = \sum\limits_{m \in U \setminus i,i+1} P_m^{TX} \rho_m g_0 d_{i,m}(t)^{-2}$ denotes the interference of $DM_i$ by the surrounding UAVs.

In task execution, whether hovering, flying, or communicating, a DM consumes energy; thus, the energy consumption model essentially determines a DM's maximum task duration. This study focuses on scenarios where rotary-wing UAVs serve as DMs for data transport in low-density UAV networks; their energy consumption is thus categorized into three components: flight energy, hovering energy, and communication energy. As [6] indicates, the propulsion power of such UAVs is calculated as shown in Eq. 6:

$$P(V) = P_0\left(1+\frac{3V^2}{U_{\text{tip}}^2}\right) + P_i\left(\sqrt{1+\frac{V^4}{4\nu_0^4}}-\frac{V^2}{2\nu_0^2}\right)^{\frac{1}{2}} + \frac{1}{2}d_0\rho sAV^3 \tag{6}$$

$P_0$ and $P_i$ denote the rotor spin-stop power and induced power, respectively, $V$ is the flight speed of UAV, $U_{tip}$ is the tip speed of the rotor blade, $\nu_0$ is the average induced speed during the rotor hovering period, $d_0$ is the fuselage drag ratio, $s$ is the solidity of the rotor, $\rho$ is the air density, and $A$ is the area of the rotor disk. When $V = 0$, the hovering energy consumption of the DM is expressed as: $P(V = 0) = P_0 + P_i$. To simplify the energy consumption equation, we make the following approximation:

$$P_0 \triangleq \frac{\delta}{8}\rho sA\Omega^3R^3 \tag{7}$$

$$P_i \triangleq (1+k)\frac{W^{3/2}}{\sqrt{2\rho A}} \tag{8}$$

$R$ is the radius of rotation, $\Omega$ is the blade angular velocity, $W$ is the weight of the vehicle, $\rho$ is the profile resistance coefficient, $k$ is the incremental correction factor for the induced power. Therefore, its motorized energy consumption can be expressed as:

$$E_u^P = \int_0^{t_0} P\left(V(t)\right)dt \tag{9}$$

where $t_0$ is the maneuvering time for the data mule for each segment in the link. And communication energy consumption can be expressed as:

$$E_u^c = P_u^{TX}T_u^c \tag{10}$$

$P_u^{TX}$ is the rated communication power of the data mule, $T_u^c = \sum_{\varphi=1}^{n}\frac{data_\varphi}{C_i(t)}$ is the data transfer time. Here $\varphi = \begin{cases}1, Data \leqslant data \\ \left\lceil \frac{Data}{data}\right\rceil, Data > data\end{cases}$ is denoted as the number of motorized transport cycles of the data mule, related to the total amount of *Data* transferred and the *data* that DMs can carry.

### 3.4 Problem Formulation

We adopt link transmission energy efficiency as the optimization objective—defined as bits transmitted per joule of energy per unit time(unit:bis/s/J)—to balance the relationship among "data transmission volume", "energy consumption", and "time delay". This makes it more suitable for long-distance, large-volume data transmission scenarios, and the energy efficiency model is thus given as follows:

$$EE = \frac{R_{avg}}{E} \tag{11}$$

where $R_{avg} = \frac{\text{Data}}{\text{T}}$ is the average transmission rate of the link, $T$ is the Total time required to transfer $Data$ bits of data, which consists of the data transfer time $T_u^c$ and the flight maneuver time $t$, which can be expressed as:

$$T = (m+1)T_u^c + t = (m+1)\sum_{\varphi=1}^{n} \frac{data_\varphi}{C_i(t)} + t \tag{12}$$

And $E$ is the total link energy consumption, which is the sum of energy consumed by each data mule and can be expressed as:

$$E = E_u^P + E_u^c = m\left(\int_0^{t_0} P\left(V(t)\right) dt + P_u^{TX} T_u^c\right) \tag{13}$$

According to the previous analysis, the default ideal state DMs do a uniform motion with velocity $V$ (ignoring the acceleration and deceleration during the motion) and stay in a hovering state when the data is unloaded, so the total energy consumption can be simplified as:

$$E = m\left(P(V)t + \left(P_u^{TX} + P(0)\right) T_u^c\right) \tag{14}$$

When each DM maneuvers along the preset route, localization is performed while hovering during data offloading to correct positional errors incurred during maneuvering—making each DM's data offloading process also a re-ranging and localization step. From the localization accuracy model, the variation in a DM's localization accuracy is associated with its movement mode and flight time. To ensure DMs can complete data offloading across different transport distances, their positioning error bound is constrained within their own perception range ($R_{range}$), enabling them to detect the next-hop UAV or data center despite a certain positional error. Thus, the following constraint applies: $\text{PEB}_{\text{new}}(v,t) \leq R_{\text{range}}$

Therefore, the optimization problem $P0$ can be expressed as:

$$\begin{aligned} (P0) \quad & \max_{m,t,V} \quad EE \\ & \text{s.t.} C1{:}r \leq r_{max} \\ & C2{:}t > 0, L > 0 \\ & C3: \text{PEB}_{\text{new}} \leq R_{\text{range}} \\ & C4{:}m \leq n, V \leq V_{max}, P_u^{TX} \leq 1 \end{aligned} \tag{15}$$

By optimizing the number of data mules, flight speed and flight time in the link, the optimal link energy efficiency of the link is achieved for different transmission distances, data volumes, and environmental interference intensities. Constraint $C1$ is the UAV communication range constraint, which sets the channel rate to 0 by default when the maximum communication range is exceeded. $C2$ is the DM maneuvering constraint, which guarantees the cooperative transmission mode of DMs. $C3$ is the localization error constraint, which ensures DMs can offload data at the specified location. $C4$ is the UAV hardware constraint, i.e., limiting the number of UAVs, flight speed, and transmit power within a reasonable range.

## 4 Solution and Simulation

The objective function is the energy efficiency ratio (EER), whose main physical meaning is the data transmission rate achievable per unit of energy. To improve the EER, it is necessary to maximize link energy efficiency while increasing the data transmission capacity of DMs. Considering stable transmission rate and power, the EER is essentially equivalent to the ratio of transmission rate to total power. Therefore, balancing power and transmission rate is crucial to maximizing the link's EER. The original optimization problem is a mixed-integer programming problem and is non-convex, making direct solution quite complex. However, for such optimization problems, an iterative approach can be employed to gradually approximate the optimal solution. Typically, to simplify the problem, it is divided into three sub-problems for solution:

Sub-problem 1: Maximizing transmission energy efficiency when maneuvering speed and maneuvering time are fixed in Eq. 16

$$\begin{aligned} (\text{P1}) \quad & \max_{m,t=t_0,V=v_0} \frac{\text{Data}\cdot L(m)^2}{m\left[P(V_0)t_0^2\, L(m)^2 + t_0\,\text{Data}[(m+1)P(V_0)+P_u^{\text{TX}}]L(m)+(m+1)P_u^{\text{TX}}\,\text{Data}^2\right]} \\ \text{s.t.} \quad & r \le r_{\max} \\ & m \le n \end{aligned} \tag{16}$$

Sub-problem 2: Finding the optimal maneuvering time with a fixed number of DMs and a fixed maneuvering speed in Eq. 17

$$\begin{aligned} (\text{P2}) \quad & \max_{m=m_0,t,V=v_0} \frac{\text{Data}\cdot L(t)^2}{m_0[P(V_0)t^2\, L(t)^2 + t\,\text{Data}[(m_0+1)P(V_0)+P_u^{\text{TX}}]L(t)+(m_0+1)P_u^{\text{TX}}\,\text{Data}^2]} \\ \text{s.t.} \quad & r \le r_{\max} \\ & \text{PEB}_{\text{new}} \le R_{\text{range}} \end{aligned} \tag{17}$$

Sub-problem 3: Finding the optimal maneuvering speed with a fixed number of DMs and a fixed maneuvering tiime in Eq. 18

$$\begin{aligned} (\text{P3}) \quad & \max_{m=m_0,t=t_0,V} \frac{\text{Data}\cdot L(V)^2}{m_0\left[P(V)t_0^2\, L(V)^2 + t_0\,\text{Data}[(m_0+1)P(V)+P_u^{\text{TX}}]L(V)+(m_0+1)P_u^{\text{TX}}\,\text{Data}^2\right]} \\ \text{s.t.} \quad & r \le r_{\max} \\ & \text{PEB}_{\text{new}} \le R_{\text{range}} \\ & V \le V_{max} \end{aligned} \tag{18}$$

Sub-problem 1 is an integer programming problem, and within the limited number of UAVs, the optimal solution can be obtained through exhaustive enumeration. Subsequently, the obtained optimal solution $m_0$ is substituted into Sub-problem 2 and Sub-problem 3. Further iterations of sub-problem 2 and 3, although Sub-problem 2 and Sub-problem 3 remains a non-convex optimization problem, the Sequential Convex Approximation (SCA) method can be employed to iteratively approach the optimal solution $t_0$ and $V_0$. The obtained result is then substituted back into Sub-problem 1 for further iteration and solution refinement.

**Algorithm 1.** Data Mule-Based Communication Optimization Process

**Require:** $D$: Distance from source UAV to ground control center, Data: Total data volume to transmit, $n$: Number of idle UAVs , $t_0$: Initial maneuver time of data mules, $V_0$: Initial maneuver speed of data mules, max_iter = 200: Maximum iterations (to exit loop)

**Ensure:** $EE_{\max}$: Maximum energy efficiency, $m^*$: Optimal number of data mules, $t^*$: Optimal maneuver time, $V^*$: Optimal maneuver speed

Initialize $i \leftarrow 0$, $EE_{\text{old}} \leftarrow -\infty$, $t \leftarrow t_0$, $V \leftarrow V_0$
**while** $i <$ max_iter **do**
  $i \leftarrow i + 1$
  **Subproblem 1: Optimize Number of Data Mules** $m$
  Compute feasible range $[m_{\min}, m_{\max}]$ (via $m_{\min} = \lceil \frac{D - r_{\max}}{tV + r_{\max}} \rceil$, $m_{\max} = n$).
  Enumerate $m$ in $[m_{\min}, m_{\max}]$, select $m^*$ with maximum $EE$ (satisfy positioning error $\leq R_{\text{range}}$).
  **Subproblem 2: Optimize Maneuver Time** $t$
  Fix $m^*$, $V$; linearize non-convex terms (e.g., channel rate) via first-order Taylor expansion.
  Solve convexified problem (via CVX) to obtain $t^*$.
  **Subproblem 3: Optimize Maneuver Speed** $V$
  Fix $m^*$, $t^*$; linearize non-convex terms (e.g., flight power) via first-order Taylor expansion.
  Solve convexified problem (via CVX) to obtain $V^*$.
  Compute current energy efficiency $EE_{\text{new}}$ using $m^*$, $t^*$, $V^*$.
  **if** $\left| \frac{EE_{\text{new}} - EE_{\text{old}}}{EE_{\text{old}}} \right| < 10^{-4}$ **and** $EE_{\text{old}} \neq -\infty$ **then**
    **break**
  **end if**
  Update: $EE_{\text{old}} \leftarrow EE_{\text{new}}$, $t \leftarrow t^*$, $V \leftarrow V^*$.
**end while**
Set $EE_{\max} \leftarrow EE_{\text{new}}$.
**return** $EE_{\max}$, $m^*$, $t^*$, $V^*$.

The parameters of the rotary-wing UAVs are set as in Table 1. All UAVs are set to a flight altitude of $H$ and it is assumed that obstacle heights between the source UAV and the ground data center do not exceed $H$. The end-to-end transmission distance is set to 15 km, the number of available UAVs is not more than 15, and the maximum coverage of communication of a single UAV is 600 m. In this case, the traditional UAV multi-hop relay links cannot meet the 15 km communication demand. Taking DMs communicating in the 2.4 GHz as an example, we first evaluate the transmission performance of the Multi-Data Mule Transmission Scheme (MDM) under different conditions, and compare variations in link energy efficiency, energy consumption, and delay across different parameter settings.

Figure 5 illustrates the variation of link energy efficiency with the number of data mules (DMs) across different data volumes. It can be observed that for small transmitted data volumes ([50–100 Mbits]), link energy efficiency increases with the number of DMs. For data volumes of [300500 Mbits], link energy effi-

**Table 1.** Relevant parameters of simulation

| Parameter | Physical Meaning | Value |
|---|---|---|
| $\rho$ | Air Density | $1.225\,\text{kg/m}^3$ |
| $A$ | Rotor disc area | $0.79\,\text{m}^2$ |
| $s$ | Rotor solidity | 0.05 |
| $U_{\text{tip}}$ | Wing tip speed | 200 m/s |
| $d_0$ | Fuselage drag ratio | 0.3 |
| $\nu_0$ | Mean rotor induced velocity in hover | 7.2 m/s |
| $P_0$ | Blade power | Formula 27 |
| $P_i$ | Induced power | Formula 28 |
| $V_{\max}$ | Max aircraft forward speed | 60 m/s |
| $\Omega$ | Blade angular velocity | 400 radians/s |
| $\delta$ | Profile drag coefficient | 0.012 |
| $R$ | Rotor radius in meter | 0.5 m |
| $W$ | Aircraft weight | 100 Newton |
| $k$ | Incremental correction factor to induced power | 0.1 |
| data | Maximum data volume storable by a single UAV | 500 MB |
| $\tilde{g}_0$ | Channel power gain per unit distance | −50 dB |
| $P_u^{\text{TX}}$ | Data mule transmission power | $\leq 1$ W |
| $\rho_i$ | UAV power control coefficient | 0.35 |
| $R_{\text{range}}$ | Positioning sensing radius | 500 m |
| $\sigma_v$ | Sensor random noise coefficient | 0.05 |
| $r_{\max}$ | Max UAV communication radius | 600 m |

ciency first increases and then decreases. For larger data volumes ([10005000 Mbits]), the number of DMs required to achieve optimal link energy efficiency further decreases compared to that for data volumes below 500 Mbits. This indicates that for larger data volumes, DMs' transportation benefits outweigh their communication benefits, and the link favors longer-distance data transmission via a small number of maneuvering DMs. Due to the positioning error constraint limiting each DM's maneuvering distance, when the number of DMs is small ($m < 4$), the link transport distance is excessively long relative to each DM's maneuvering distance plus communication distance. This causes the distance between neighboring DMs to exceed the maximum communication distance, resulting in failed link establishment—thus, link energy efficiency is non-existent for $m < 4$. Figure 5b shows that the scheme achieves a maximum transmission energy efficiency of 118.36 bit/s/J) at a data volume of 2569 Mbits; link energy efficiency then begins to decrease slowly as the data volume increases further.

From Fig. 6, it can be seen that when the link transmits a small amount of data (50 M–100 M), the link transmission delay decreases with the increase in the number of data mules. However, when the data volume is 250 M it can

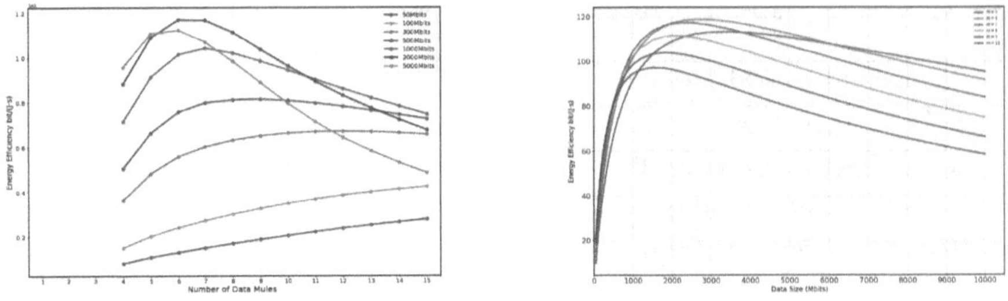


(a) EE changes with number of DMs (b) EE changes with data volume

**Fig. 5.** Transmission energy efficiency variation curve of the MDM link.

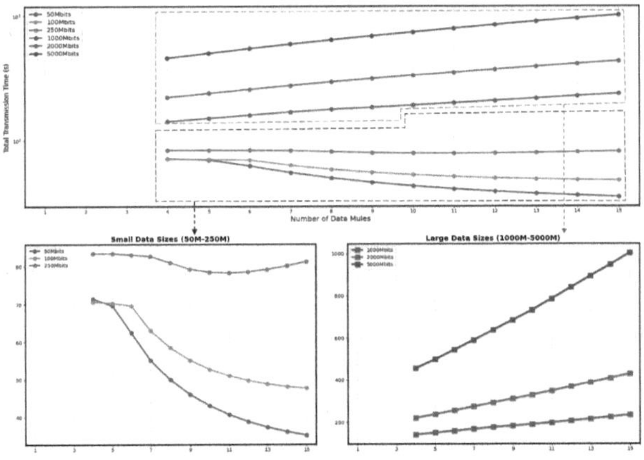


**Fig. 6.** The transmission time changes the curve with the number of data mules.

be observed that as the number of data mules increases, the total transmission delay decreases and then increases. When the link transmits a large amount of data (1000 M–5000 M), it can be observed that the link transmission time increases with the increase in the number of data mules, and the larger the amount of transmitted data the faster the total transmission time grows. The above simulation shows that the number of data mules is not the more the better in long-distance end-to-end links, but the optimal number of data mules needs to be selected according to the size of the transmitted data volume.

From the Fig. 7a, it can be seen that the multi-hop routing and forwarding scheme (MRF)'s transmission energy consumption is better than MDM when the amount of data transmitted in a single transmission is small, but when the amount of transmitted data is more than 1053Mbits, MDM's transmission energy consumption will be better than MRF. Figure 7b further compares the transmission delay of different schemes. DS [21] denotes a dual-stack integration scheme based on MRF; it enables dual-mode UAV communication by integrating millimeter-wave and Bluetooth technologies into MRF, thereby improving communication reliability and efficiency. Thus, DS is an optimized version of MRF.

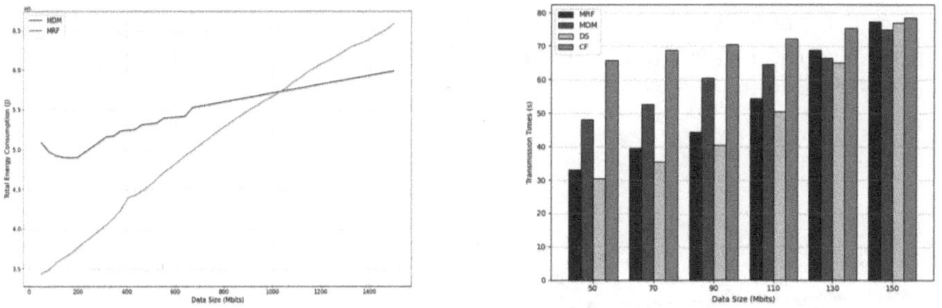


(a) energy consumption of two schemes (b) latency of four schemes

**Fig. 7.** Comparison of different transmission schemes.

It can be observed that although the end-to-end data transmission method proposed by us RM is not as effective as multi-hop forwarding and DS when the data volume is less than 130 M. CF represents the scheme of carrying storage and forwarding. From the Fig. 7b, our proposed MDM scheme exhibits higher transmission delay than MRF and DS for small data volumes, but lower delay than MRF when the data volume reaches 130 Mbits. At 150 Mbits, the MDM scheme outperforms the other three in terms of delay. Owing to the inherent mechanism of multi-hop forwarding schemes (including MRF and DS), even DS has limitations in large-data-volume transmission scenarios. Larger data volumes result in longer transmission times, and after multiple hops, transmission time grows exponentially while energy consumption rises sharply. However, MRF and DS require deploying a large number of UAVs to achieve communication link coverage. Thus, in our target scenario, multi-hop transmission-based schemes incur significantly higher economic and maintenance costs compared to MDM. Additionally, realizing large-scale cooperative transmission for MRF or DS poses significant challenges in low-density UAV mission environments. This is because simultaneous deployment of numerous UAVs introduces complex issues—such as mutual interference and collision avoidance between UAVs. This further indicates that the MDM scheme proposed in this paper has a delay advantage over MRF when the transmitted data volume and link hop count exceed specific thresholds.

Meanwhile, we compare two other proposed schemes, with MRF serving as a static reference multi-hop scheme. One scheme is JTP (Joint Trajectory and Power Allocation), which optimizes the number of drones, their locations, and communication power [19]. The other is APP (Approximate Convex Policy for Association, Power Allocation, and Placement), which optimizes drone transmission power and locations based on the link's minimum transmission rate requirement. It achieves higher link energy efficiency while ensuring transmission link continuity [20]. The Fig. 8 demonstrates the performance of the four transmission schemes across different single-transmission data volumes, revealing that our proposed scheme exhibits lower energy efficiency and poorer performance for smaller single-transmission volumes. However, for larger single-transmission volumes, the energy efficiency of our proposed scheme is significantly higher than that of the other three schemes and exhibits an increasing trend.

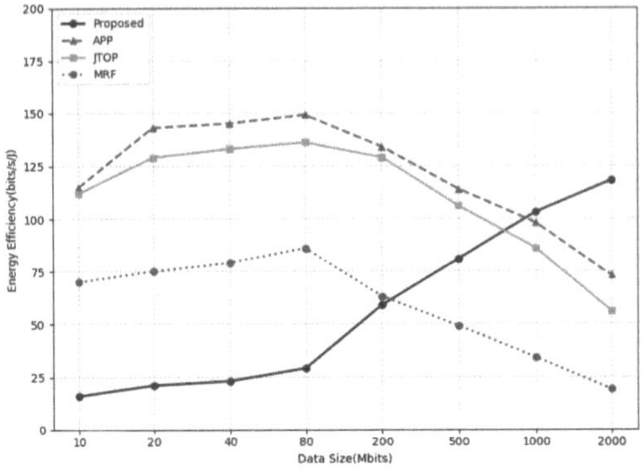


**Fig. 8.** The transmission time changes the curve with the number of data mules.

# 5 Conclusion

In this paper, we propose an end-to-end data transmission scheme for low-density UAVs network based on data mul while considering the variation of the localization error of the data mule. It is suitable for data transmission scenarios where UAV network nodes are sparse. For example, when UAVs perform large-scale patrol missions over wide areas, this scheme can achieve end-to-end transmission of image and video data through several drones without relying on infrastructure. Compared to existing large-scale UAV networks for end-to-end data transmission, this scheme offers more advantages for handling large traffic data and results in lower overall energy consumption and cost. In comparison to existing data transmission schemes for UAV carrying and forwarding, this approach can achieve multiple data transmission links with lower latency, which can better address large-scale remote scenarios, which indicates that our proposed scheme can improve the overall transmission energy efficiency of the system when facing larger data volumes of video streams.

**Acknowledgments.** This work was supported in part by the National Natural Science Foundation of China under Grant 62171465.

# Appendix

## The *Process* of $I_v$

The deviation from future position caused by the velocity error $\Delta v \sim \mathcal{N}(0, \sigma_v^2)$ is $\begin{cases} \Delta x = \Delta v \cdot \delta \cdot \cos\theta \\ \Delta y = \Delta v \cdot \delta \cdot \sin\theta \end{cases}$. When considering the positional errors caused by velocity errors in the direction of motion, let $s = \Delta v \cdot \delta$ then $s \sim \mathcal{N}(0, \delta^2\sigma_v^2)$. The covariance matrix of the positional deviation is: $\mathrm{Cov}(\Delta x, \Delta y) = \mathbb{E}\left[\begin{bmatrix}\Delta x \\ \Delta y\end{bmatrix}\begin{bmatrix}\Delta x & \Delta y\end{bmatrix}\right]$ and substitute the expressions for $\Delta x$ and $\Delta y$:

$$\mathrm{Cov}(\Delta x, \Delta y) = \sigma_v^2 \cdot \delta^2 \cdot \begin{bmatrix}\cos^2\theta & \cos\theta\sin\theta \\ \cos\theta\sin\theta & \sin^2\theta\end{bmatrix}$$

Take the inverse of the covariance matrix $\mathrm{Cov}(\Delta x, \Delta y)$:

$$I_v = \left(\sigma_v^2 \cdot \delta^2 \cdot \begin{bmatrix}\cos^2\theta & \cos\theta\sin\theta \\ \cos\theta\sin\theta & \sin^2\theta\end{bmatrix}\right)^{-1}$$

### The *Process* of $I_{p_{old}}$ and $PEB_{old}$

Assuming that there are $B$ sensors involved in data mule TOF ranging in the vicinity of the relay position, the TOF measurement equation for the $i-th$ sensor is:

$$\tau_i = \frac{\sqrt{(x_0 - x_i)^2 + (y_0 - y_i)^2 + (H_0 - H_i)^2} + \Delta_i}{c}$$

$(x_i, y_i, H_i)$ is the ground sensor position coordinate, $\Delta_i$ is the sensor NLoS deviation. $I_\Theta$ is the FIM of the initial position $(x_0, y_0)$, denoted as:

$$I_\Theta = J_{\tau\to\Theta}^T \Omega^{-1} J_{\tau\to\Theta}$$

where $\Omega = \begin{bmatrix}\omega_1^2 & 0 & \dots & 0 \\ 0 & \omega_2^2 & \dots & 0 \\ \vdots & \vdots & \ddots & \vdots \\ 0 & 0 & \dots & \omega_B^2\end{bmatrix}$ is the covariance matrix of the measurement noise, $\omega_i = \frac{1}{8\pi^2\eta^2\mathrm{SNR}_i}$ The state parameter vector is $\Theta = [x_0, y_0, v, \Delta_1, ..., \Delta_B]^T$, and the Jacobi Matrix $J_{\tau\to\Theta}$ can be expressed as:

$$J_{\tau\to\Theta} = \begin{bmatrix}\frac{\partial\tau_1}{x_o} & \frac{\partial\tau_2}{x_o} & \dots & \frac{\partial\tau_B}{x_o} \\ \frac{\partial\tau_1}{\partial y_o} & \frac{\partial\tau_2}{\partial y_o} & \dots & \frac{\partial\tau_B}{\partial y_o} \\ \frac{\partial\tau_1}{\partial\Delta_1} & \frac{\partial\tau_2}{\partial\Delta_1} & \dots & \frac{\partial\tau_B}{\partial\Delta_1} \\ \vdots & \vdots & \ddots & \vdots \\ \frac{\partial\tau_1}{\partial\Delta_B} & \frac{\partial\tau_2}{\partial\Delta_B} & \dots & \frac{\partial\tau_B}{\partial\Delta_B}\end{bmatrix}$$

$\frac{\partial\tau_i}{\partial x_0} = \frac{x_0 - x_i}{c\cdot r_i}$, $\frac{\partial\tau_i}{\partial y_0} = \frac{y_0 - y_i}{c\cdot r_i}$, $\frac{\partial\tau_i}{\partial\Delta_j} = \begin{cases}\frac{1}{c}, & j = i \\ 0, & j \neq i\end{cases}$, $r_i = \sqrt{(x_0 - x_i)^2 + (y_0 - y_i)^2 + (H_0 - H_i)^2}$.

The matrix $I_\Theta$ can be represented in chunks as

$$I_\Theta = \begin{bmatrix}A_{2\times2} & D_{2\times B} \\ D_{B\times2}^T & C_{B\times B}\end{bmatrix}, \begin{cases}A = \sum_{i=1}^B \frac{1}{\omega_i^2}\begin{bmatrix}\frac{(x_0-x_i)^2}{c^2r_i^2} & \frac{(x_0-x_i)(y_0-y_i)}{c^2r_i^2} \\ \frac{(x_0-x_i)(y_0-y_i)}{c^2r_i^2} & \frac{(y_0-y_i)^2}{c^2r_i^2}\end{bmatrix} \\ D = \frac{1}{c}\begin{bmatrix}\frac{x_0-x_1}{ar_1r_1} & \dots & \frac{x_0-x_B}{\sigma_Br_B} \\ \frac{y_0-y_1}{ar_1r_1} & \dots & \frac{y_0-y_B}{\sigma_Br_B}\end{bmatrix} \\ C = \mathrm{diag}\left(\frac{1}{c^2\sigma_1^2}, \dots, \frac{1}{c^2\sigma_B^2}\right)\end{cases}$$

where $A$ is the FIM sub-block of the position parameters, consisting of the TOF measurement Jacobi matrix and the noise covariance matrix, $D$ is the sub-block of the cross terms of the position and NLoS deviations, and $C$ is the FIM sub-block of the NLoS deviations. The inverse of the sub-block matrix (Schur complement) eliminates the NLoS deviation and obtains the effective FIM of the position parameters:$I_{p_{\mathrm{old}}} = A - DC^{-1}D^{T}$. The localization error bound for the initial position can be expressed as:

$$\mathrm{PEB}_{\mathrm{old}} = \sqrt{\mathrm{tr}\left(l_{p_{\mathrm{old}}}^{-1}\right)} = \frac{c}{\sqrt{\sum_{i=1}^{B} \frac{1}{\omega_i^2} \cdot \frac{(H_0 - H_i)^2}{(x_0 - x_i)^2 + (y_0 - y_i)^2 + (H_0 - H_i)^2}}}$$

## References


1. Azari, M.M., et al.: Evolution of non-terrestrial networks from 5G to 6G: a survey. IEEE Commun. Surv. Tutor. **24**(4), 2633–2672 (2022). https://doi.org/10.1109/COMST.2022.3199901
2. Hosseinalipour, S., Rahmati, A., Dai, H.: Interference avoidance position planning in dual-hop and multi-hop UAV relay networks. IEEE Trans. Wirel. Commun. **19**(11), 7033–7048 (2020). https://doi.org/10.1109/TWC.2020.3007766
3. Mozaffari, M., Saad, W., Bennis, M., Nam, Y.-H., Debbah, M.: A tutorial on UAVs for wireless networks: applications, challenges, and open problems. IEEE Commun. Surv. Tutor. **21**(3), 2334–2360 (2019). https://doi.org/10.1109/COMST.2019.2902862
4. Zeng, Y., Lyu, J., Zhang, R.: Cellular-connected UAV: potential, challenges, and promising technologies. IEEE Wirel. Commun. **26**(1), 120–127 (2019). https://doi.org/10.1109/MWC.2018.1800023
5. Wang, J., Jiang, C., Kuang, L.: High-mobility satellite-UAV communications: challenges, solutions, and future research trends. IEEE Commun. Mag. **60**(5), 38–43 (2022). https://doi.org/10.1109/MCOM.001.2100850
6. Zeng, Y., Zhang, R., Lim, T.J.: Throughput maximization for UAV-enabled mobile relaying systems. IEEE Trans. Commun. **64**(12), 4983–4996 (2016). https://doi.org/10.1109/TCOMM.2016.2611512
7. Agrawal, J., Kapoor, M., Tomar, R.: A novel unmanned aerial vehicle-sink enabled mobility model for military operations in sparse flying ad-hoc network. Trans. Emerg. Telecommun. Technol. **33**(5) (2022). https://doi.org/10.1002/ett.4466
8. Jia, Z., Sheng, M., Li, J., Niyato, D., Han, Z.: LEO-satellite-assisted UAV: joint trajectory and data collection for internet of remote things in 6G aerial access networks. IEEE Internet Things J. **8**(12), 9814–9826 (2021). https://doi.org/10.1109/JIOT.2020.3021255
9. Wang, L., Zhang, X., Deng, P., Kang, J., Gao, Z., Liu, L.: An energy-balanced path planning algorithm for multiple ferrying UAVs based on GA. Int. J. Aerosp. Eng. **2020**, 1–15 (2020). https://doi.org/10.1155/2020/3516149
10. Yoon, J., Lee, A.-H., Lee, H.: Rendezvous: opportunistic data delivery to mobile users by UAVs through target trajectory prediction. IEEE Trans. Veh. Technol. **69**(2), 2230–2245 (2020). https://doi.org/10.1109/TVT.2019.2962391

11. Albinsson, P.-A.: Data mules in future command and control systems – A complement to traditional radio communication through physical transport of data. Report No. FOI-R–5592–SE. Stockholm: FOI (Totalförsvarets forskningsinstitut) (2024). ISSN 1650-1942
12. Shah, R.C., Roy, S., Jain, S., Brunette, W.: Data MULEs: modeling and analysis of a three-tier architecture for sparse sensor networks. Ad Hoc Netw. **1**(2–3), 215–233 (2003)
13. Mertens, J.S., Milotta, G.M., Nagaradjane, P., Morabito, G.: SDN-(UAV)ISE: Applying software defined networking to wireless sensor networks with data mules. In: 2020 IEEE 21st International Symposium on "A World of Wireless, Mobile and Multimedia Networks" (WoWMoM), pp. 323–328. IEEE (2020)
14. Yu, B., Yang, W., Wang, Q., Zhang, R., Cai, Y.: Age of information analysis and optimization in unmanned aerial vehicles-assisted integrated sensing and communication systems. J. Electron. Inf. Technol. **46**(5), 1996–2003 (2024). https://doi.org/10.11999/JEIT231175
15. Cai, Y., Jiang, X., Liu, M., Zhao, N., Chen, Y., Wang, X.: Resource allocation for URLLC-oriented two-way UAV relaying. IEEE Trans. Veh. Technol. **71**(3), 3344–3349 (2022). https://doi.org/10.1109/TVT.2022.3143174
16. Wu, B., Zhang, B., Guo, D., Wang, H., Jiang, H.: Anti-jamming trajectory design for UAV-enabled wireless sensor networks using communication flight corridor. China Commun. **19**(7), 37–52 (2022). https://doi.org/10.23919/JCC.2022.07.004
17. Hussain, W.J., Duggal: utility of aged measurements for localization. In: 2024 IEEE Military Communications Conference (MILCOM). IEEE (2024)
18. Burhanuddin, L.A. binti, Liu, X., Deng, Y., Challita, U., Zahemszky, A.: QoE optimization for live video streaming in UAV-to-UAV communications via deep reinforcement learning. IEEE Trans. Veh. Technol. 71(5), 5358–5370 (2022). https://doi.org/10.1109/TVT.2022.3152146
19. Zhang, G., Yan, H., Zeng, Y., Cui, M., Liu, Y.: Trajectory optimization and power allocation for multi-hop UAV relaying communications. IEEE Access **6**, 48566–48576 (2018). https://doi.org/10.1109/ACCESS.2018.2868117
20. Xiao, H., Wu, C., Jiang, H., Deng, L.-P., Luo, Y., Zhang, Q.-Y.: Energy-efficient resource allocation in multiple UAVs-assisted energy harvesting-powered two-hop cognitive radio network. IEEE Sens. J. **23**(7), 7644–7655 (2023). https://doi.org/10.1109/JSEN.2023.3247436
21. Grieco, L.A., Boggia, G., Piro, G., Jararweh, Y., Campolo, C. (eds.): ADHOC-NOW 2020. LNCS, vol. 12338. Springer, Cham (2020). https://doi.org/10.1007/978-3-030-61746-2
22. Qin, Z., Wang, H., Qin, Z.: An optimized end-to-end data transmission scheme for long-range unmanned aerial vehicles based on resonant-motion. Phys. Commun. **71**, 102689 (2025). https://doi.org/10.1016/j.phycom.2025.102689

# Movable Antennas Assisted Air-Ground Collaborative Network: A DRL Approach for Uplink Sum-Rate Maximization

Shiyu Huang and Shichao Li(✉)

School of Information and Communication, Guilin University of Electronic Technology, Guilin 541004, China

**Abstract.** The deployment of movable antenna (MA) at base station (BS) within air-ground collaborative network constitutes a pivotal enhancement for Internet of things (IoT) wireless communications, as BS-mounted MAs dynamically reconfigure channel propagation conditions through antenna repositioning. Specifically, unmanned aerial vehicle (UAV) mobility enables extended service coverage while BS-deployed MA significantly enhances channel conditions through antenna position relocation. In this paper, we investigate a joint MA position, receive beamforming design at the BS, and UAV trajectory design problem to maximize the uplink sum-rate in the MAs assisted air-ground collaborative (MA-AGC) network. Given that the problem is non-convex and hard to solve by the traditional methods, we convert it into a Markov decision process (MDP) and solve it using a deep reinforcement learning (DRL) approach based on the multi-agent proximal policy optimization (MAPPO) collaborative framework. Simulation results have demonstrated that the proposed approach outperforms existing classical baseline methods in maximizing the uplink sum-rate.

**Keywords:** Uplink sum-rate · Movable antenna (MA) · Unmanned aerial vehicle (UAV) · Deep reinforcement learning (DRL)

## 1 Introduction

With the widespread proliferation of Internet of things (IoT) technology, the massive access of IoT devices in urban environments has precipitated significant high-rate data transmission demands in wireless networks [1]. However, in areas with dense IoT device deployments and complex city layouts, when transmitting data to processing centers, various physical obstacles like buildings and vegetation cause significant signal fading. To solve this problem, the reconfigurable movable antenna (MA) has emerged as a promising solution [2,3]. By leveraging its dynamic reconfiguration capability, the MA enables antennas to be relocated to positions optimal for signal transmission or reception, which mitigates


Y. Liu et al. (Eds.): ChinaCom 2025, LNICST 711, pp. 346–360, 2027.
https://doi.org/10.1007/978-3-032-33662-0_26

multipath fading and co-channel interference by exploiting spatial correlation characteristics, thereby enhancing data transmission rates.

Nevertheless, when MAs are exclusively deployed at terrestrial base stations (BS), their spatial reconfiguration capability becomes geometrically constrained by the BS fixed infrastructure locations [4]. This limitation restricts the effective coverage expansion and path loss mitigation in complex urban scenarios, particularly for IoT devices distributed beyond the BS original service areas. To overcome these constraints, the MAs assisted air-ground collaborative (MA-AGC) network is proposed. Specifically, unmanned aerial vehicle (UAV) mobility enables extended service coverage while BS-deployed MA significantly enhances channel conditions through position relocation.

Recently, MAs serving as a pivotal innovation in 6th-generation (6G) wireless communications, have attracted widespread research. For multi-user communication (MUC) network with MA-aided BS [5–7], the sum-rate of the MUC network is maximized by jointly optimizing the digital beamformer, analog beamformer, and MA position [5]. To maximize the minimum achievable rate in the MUC network, the joint optimization algorithm for MA position, receive combining at the BS, and the transmit power of users was proposed [6]. In order to minimize the transmit power of the BS in the MUC network, the joint optimization problem for beamforming and the positions of MA at both transmitter and receivers was investigated [7]. In the MA-assisted UAV scheme, the achievable data rate of the UAV-enabled MUC network is maximized by jointly optimizing the transmit beamforming, the UAV trajectory, and the positions of the MA [8]. However, the previous research only considers MA-aided terrestrial BS or MA-aided UAV, while neglecting to incorporate MA into air-ground collaborative network. The integration of MA into an air-ground collaborative network establishes a MA-AGC network, leveraging UAV mobility for service coverage extension while BS-deployed MAs improve channel conditions through dynamic antenna repositioning. Therefore, how to make full use of their advantages to improve the MA-AGC network performance is a challenging issue.

In this paper, the maximization of the uplink sum-rate in the MA-AGC network is formulated by joint optimization of MA position, UAV trajectory design, and receive beamforming design at the BS. Since the problem is non-convex, we transform it into a Markov decision process (MDP) and subsequently adopt a deep reinforcement learning (DRL) approach based on the multi-agent proximal policy optimization (MAPPO) algorithm to solve it. Simulation results validate the proposed MAPPO algorithm exhibits favorable convergence characteristics while effectively improving the uplink sum-rate.

## 2 System Model and Problem Formulation

In this section, we first propose the system model of the MA-AGC network, which includes the network model, the transmission model, and the energy consumption model of UAV. Subsequently, a joint MA position, receive beamforming design at the BS, and UAV trajectory design problem is formulated to maximize the uplink sum-rate of the whole network.

### 2.1 Network Model

In this paper, we consider a MA-AGC network as shown in Fig. 1, which consists of one BS, $M$ UAVs, and $K$ IoT devices. Each IoT device employs a single antenna to collect localized scenario data, subsequently transmitting the aggregated information to its serving UAV via uplink connections. Meanwhile, the UAV can collect data from IoT devices and transmit these data to the BS. The BS employs $J$ MAs with reconfigurable spatial positioning within a constrained three-dimensional workspace $\mathcal{D}_s \in [-A, A] \times [-A, A] \times [-A, A]$, where $\mathcal{J} = \{1, ..., j..., J\}$ indexes the MA array. Define the set of UAVs and IoT devices denoted as $\mathcal{M} = \{1, ..., m..., M\}$ and $\mathcal{K} = \{1, ..., k..., K\}$, respectively. Define the IoT devices served by the UAV $m$ as $k_m$ and the set is $\mathcal{K}_m = \{1, ..., k_m..., K_m\}$. The whole time period is divided into $N$ time slots, denoted as $\mathcal{N} = \{1, ..., n, ..., N\}$, and each time slot duration is $\tau$. As the duration of a single time slot is very short, it is denoted that the positions of BS and UAVs remain constant within each time slot. The location of IoT device $k_m$ and the BS is $\boldsymbol{P}_{k_m} = (x_{k_m}, y_{k_m}, z_{k_m})$ and $\boldsymbol{d}_0 = (x_0, y_0, z_0)$, respectively. The location of the UAV $m$ and the MA $j$ at time slot $n$ is $\boldsymbol{q}_m(n) = (x_m(n), y_m(n), z_m(n))$ and $\boldsymbol{d}_j(n) = (x_j(n), y_j(n), z_j(n))^T \in \mathcal{D}_s$, respectively.

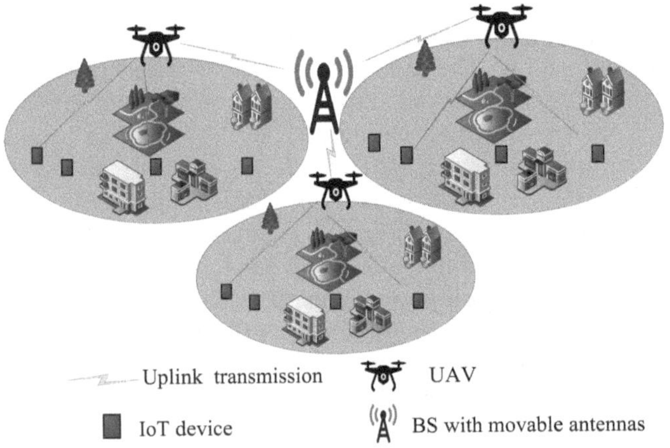


**Fig. 1.** System model.

### 2.2 Transmission Model

We denote the transmission link between the UAV $m$ and IoT devices $k_m$ can be viewed as a LoS link [9], and the channel gain at time slot $n$ can be expressed as

$$h_{k_m,m}(n) = \frac{\beta_0}{\|\boldsymbol{q}_m(n) - \boldsymbol{P}_{k_m}\|^2}, \tag{1}$$

where $\beta_0$ represents the channel gain at a reference distance of 1 m.

For the uplink transmission from IoT devices to UAVs, we consider that each UAV operates over non-overlapping frequency bandwidths. In each UAV coverage area, between IoT devices and the serving UAV employ orthogonal frequency division multiple access (OFDMA). Therefore there is no interference among the IoT devices in the same device cluster. We denote the transmission power of IoT device $k_m$ as $p_{k_m}$, and bandwidth allocated by the UAV $m$ to IoT device $k_m$ as $b_{k_m,m}$. The transmission rate between the UAV $m$ and the IoT device $k_m$ at time slot $n$ can be expressed as

$$R_{k_m,m}(n) = b_{k_m,m} \log_2 \left(1 + \frac{h_{k_m,m}(n) p_{k_m}}{\sigma_0^2}\right), \tag{2}$$

where $\sigma_0^2$ represents the noise power.

In the UAV-BS link, the MA received a signal at the BS at time slot $n$ as $\boldsymbol{y}_{bs}(n) \in \mathbb{C}^{M\times 1}$, which is expressed as

$$\boldsymbol{y}_{bs}(n) = h_{m,bs}(n)\boldsymbol{W}^H(n)\boldsymbol{F}(n)\hat{\boldsymbol{s}}(n) + \boldsymbol{W}^H(n)\boldsymbol{\zeta}, \tag{3}$$

where $h_{m,bs}(n)$ represents the free-space path loss from the UAV $m$ to the BS at time slot $n$. $\boldsymbol{W}(n) \in \mathbb{C}^{J\times M}$ is the receive beamforming matrix at time slot $n$. $\boldsymbol{F}(n) = (\boldsymbol{d}(n), \boldsymbol{\rho}(n)) \in \mathbb{C}^{J\times M}$ denote steering matrix of MAs at time slot $n$. $\boldsymbol{d}(n) = (\boldsymbol{d}_1^T(n), \boldsymbol{d}_2^T(n), \ldots, \boldsymbol{d}_J^T(n))^T \in \mathbb{C}^{J\times 1}$ is the matrix of antenna positions and $\boldsymbol{\rho}(n) = (\boldsymbol{\rho}_1(n),\ \boldsymbol{\rho}_2(n),\ \ldots,\ \boldsymbol{\rho}_M(n)) \in \mathbb{C}^{1\times M}$ is the matrix of steering angles, at time slot $n$, respectively. $\hat{\boldsymbol{s}}(n) = (\hat{s}_1(n), \hat{s}_2(n), ..., \hat{s}_M(n))^T \in \mathbb{C}^{M\times 1}$ is the transmit signal vector with normalized power i.e., $\mathbb{E}\left\{\hat{\boldsymbol{s}}(n)\hat{\boldsymbol{s}}^H(n)\right\} = \boldsymbol{I}_M$ at time slot $n$. Additionally, $\boldsymbol{\zeta} = (\zeta_1, \zeta_2, \ldots, \zeta_J)^T \sim \mathcal{N}(\boldsymbol{0}, \sigma_0^2 \boldsymbol{I}_J)$ denotes the zero-mean additive white Gaussian noise with $\sigma_0^2$ denoting the average noise power.

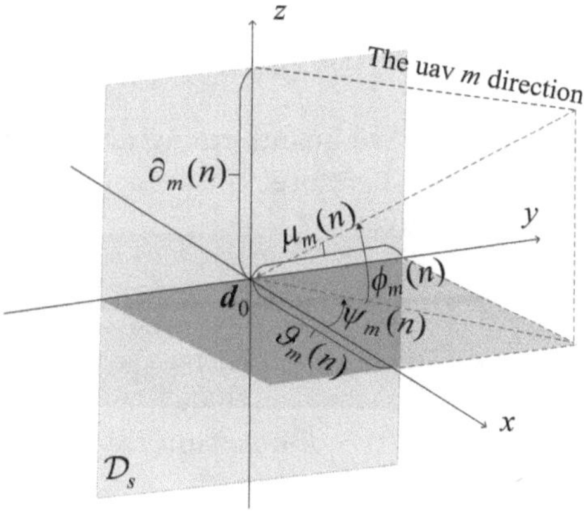


**Fig. 2.** The spatial steering angle between UAV $m$ and BS.

The instantaneous UAV-BS channel response is governed by the azimuth angle of the UAV-BS link and the spatial coordinates of the MAs, with the angle of arrival (AoA) being mathematically represented by the steering angle matrix $\boldsymbol{\rho}(n) \in \mathbb{C}^{1\times M}$ [10]. We denote that the steering angle between UAV $m$ and BS at time slot $n$ as shown in Fig. 2, and the vector of the steering angle is given by

$$\boldsymbol{\rho}_m(n) = \left(\vartheta_m(n),\, \mu_m(n),\, \partial_m(n)\right)^T, \tag{4}$$

$$\vartheta_m(n) = \cos\phi_m(n)\cos\psi_m(n), \tag{5}$$

$$\mu_m(n) = \cos\phi_m(n)\sin\psi_m(n), \tag{6}$$

$$\partial_m(n) = \sin\phi_m(n), \tag{7}$$

where $\phi_m(n)$ and $\psi_m(n)$ represent the elevation and azimuth angles of arrival (AoA) from UAV $m$ to the BS at time slot $n$, respectively. Accordingly, we define the steering vector of UAV $m$ and the BS at time slot $n$ as

$$\boldsymbol{F}\left(\boldsymbol{d}(n), \boldsymbol{\rho}_m(n)\right) = \left(e^{j\frac{2\pi}{\lambda}\boldsymbol{d}_1^T(n)\rho_m(n)}, \ \ldots, \ e^{j\frac{2\pi}{\lambda}\boldsymbol{d}_J^T(n)\rho_m(n)}\right)^T. \tag{8}$$

We consider the UAV $m$ to BS link is the LoS channel, and the channel gain from the UAV $m$ to the BS at time slot $n$ is given by

$$h_{m,bs}(n) = \frac{\beta_0}{\|\boldsymbol{q}_m(n) - \boldsymbol{d}_0\|^2}. \tag{9}$$

All UAVs are denoted to share the entire BS bandwidth during uplink transmission. Therefore, there is interference among UAVs, and the receive signal-to-interference-plus-noise ratio (SINR) of UAV $m$ is given by

$$\gamma_{m,bs}(n) = \frac{h_{m,bs}(n)\left|\boldsymbol{F}^H\left(\boldsymbol{d}(n), \boldsymbol{\rho}_m(n)\right)\boldsymbol{w}_m(n)\right|^2 p_m}{\sum\limits_{\substack{u\in\mathcal{M}\\ u\neq m}} h_{u,bs}(n)\left|\boldsymbol{F}^H\left(\boldsymbol{d}(n), \boldsymbol{\rho}_u(n)\right)\boldsymbol{w}_u(n)\right|^2 p_u + \sigma_0^2}, \tag{10}$$

where $\boldsymbol{w}_m(n)$ is the vector of receive beamforming at the BS, $p_m$ represents the transmission power of UAV $m$. Therefore, the transmission rate between UAV $m$ and the BS at time slot $n$ is given by

$$R_{m,bs}(n) = b_{bs}\log_2\left(1 + \gamma_{m,bs}(n)\right), \tag{11}$$

where $b_{bs}$ represents the bandwidth allocated by the BS to the UAV for uplink data transmission.

Based on the above analysis, the uplink sum-rate of the whole network at time slot $n$ can be formulated as

$$R_{sum}^{up}(n) = \sum_{m\in\mathcal{M}}\sum_{k_m\in\mathcal{K}_m} R_{k_m,m}(n) + \sum_{m\in\mathcal{M}} R_{m,bs}(n). \tag{12}$$

### 2.3 Energy Consumption Model of UAV

In the energy consumption model of this network, we only consider UAV energy consumption, which includes both UAV flight energy and transmission energy.

**Flight Energy:** The flight energy consumption of the UAV $m$ at time slot $n$ is determined by

$$E_m^{flg}(n) = \tau(\lambda_1 v_m^3 + \frac{\lambda_2}{v_m}), \tag{13}$$

where $v_m$ is the flight speed of UAV $m$. $\lambda_1$ and $\lambda_2$ are fixed parameters related to air density, the UAV weight, wing area, and so on.

**Transmission Energy:** The transmission energy consumed by the UAV $m$ for data transmission at time slot $n$ can be expressed as

$$E_m^{tra}(n) = p_m \tau, \tag{14}$$

where $p_m$ is the transmission power of UAV $m$.

**Total Energy Consumption:** Based on the above analysis, the total energy consumed by the UAV $m$ at time slot $n$ can be expressed as

$$E_m^{tot}(n) = E_m^{flg}(n) + E_m^{tra}(n). \tag{15}$$

### 2.4 Problem Formulation

Based on the above models, at time slot $n$, the problem of MA position, receive beamforming design at the BS, and UAV trajectory design to maximize the uplink sum-rate of the network can be formulated as

$$(\mathbf{P1}): \max_{\boldsymbol{Q},\boldsymbol{W},\boldsymbol{d}} R_{sum}^{up}(n) \tag{16}$$

$$\text{s.t.} \quad \|\boldsymbol{q}_m(n+1) - \boldsymbol{q}_m(n)\| \leq v_m \tau, \tag{16a}$$

$$\|\boldsymbol{q}_m(n) - \boldsymbol{q}_u(n)\| \geq q_0, \ m \neq u, \tag{16b}$$

$$E_m^{tot}(n) \leq E_m^{max}(n), \tag{16c}$$

$$\|\boldsymbol{w}_m(n)\| = 1, \tag{16d}$$

$$\boldsymbol{d}_j \in \mathcal{D}_s, \tag{16e}$$

$$\|\boldsymbol{d}_j(n) - \boldsymbol{d}_g(n)\| \geq D_0, \ j \neq g, \tag{16f}$$

$$\sum_{k_m \in \mathcal{K}_m} R_{k_m,m}(n) \leq R_{m,bs}(n), \tag{16g}$$

where $\boldsymbol{Q} = \{\theta_m^p(n), \theta_m^r(n), \theta_m^y(n), \forall m \in \mathcal{M}, \forall n \in \mathcal{N}\}$, $\theta_m^p(n)$, $\theta_m^r(n)$ and $\theta_m^y(n)$ are the pitch angle, roll angle, and yaw angle of the UAV $m$ at time slot $n$, respectively. $\boldsymbol{W} = \{\boldsymbol{w}_1(n), \boldsymbol{w}_2(n), \ldots, \boldsymbol{w}_M(n), \forall m \in \mathcal{M}, \forall n \in \mathcal{N}\}$ is the receive beamforming design at the BS at time slot $n$. $\boldsymbol{d} = \{\boldsymbol{d}_1^T(n), \boldsymbol{d}_2^T(n), \ldots, \boldsymbol{d}_J^T(n), \forall j \in \mathcal{J}, \forall n \in \mathcal{N}\}$ is the position of MA at time slot $n$. $E_m^{max}(n)$ represents the maximum energy of the UAV $m$ at time slot $n$. $q_0$ and $D_0$ represent the minimum safety distance of UAVs and the minimum distance of MA, respectively. Constraints (16a) and (16b) are the UAV trajectory constraints. Constraint (16c) represents the UAV energy constraint. Constraint (16d) implies the receive beamforming vector constrained to satisfy the normalization condition. Constraints (16e) and (16f) represent the MA position constraint. Constraint (16g) is the constraint of the transmission rate. The inherent non-convexity in constraints (16b), (16d), and (16f), combined with the strong coupling among optimization variables, renders the problem (**P1**) is non-convex and difficult to solve.

## 3 System Model and Problem Formulation

In this section, we first reformulate the problem (**P1**) as a MDP, and then, utilize the deep reinforcement learning method to solve it.

### 3.1 MDP Modeling

We transform the problem (**P1**) into a partially observable Markov with $M+1$ agents, where $1 \sim M$ agents correspond to $1 \sim M$ UAVs, respectively, and the $(M+1)$-th agent corresponds to the BS. At time slot $n$, the Markov process of agents is defined by a set of states $\mathcal{S}(n) = \{\boldsymbol{s}_1(n), \ldots, \boldsymbol{s}_M(n), \boldsymbol{s}_{M+1}(n)\}$, a set of actions $\mathcal{A}(n) = \{\boldsymbol{a}_1(n), \ldots, \boldsymbol{a}_M(n), \boldsymbol{a}_{M+1}(n)\}$ and reward $r(n)$. The three elements of the Markov process can be given as

**State:** At time slot $n$, $\mathcal{S}(n)$ represents the joint state space of $M+1$ agents, consisting of all possible configurations and global information available to the agents. Specifically, $\boldsymbol{s}_m(n)$ and $\boldsymbol{s}_{M+1}(n)$ denote the states obtained by UAV $m$ and the BS from the environment at time slot $n$, respectively. For $\boldsymbol{s}_{M+1}(n)$, it contains the real component $g_m(n)$ and imaginary component $f_m(n)$ of the equivalent channel gains from all UAVs to BS. Therefore, at time slot $n$, the state of the BS is

$$\begin{aligned} \boldsymbol{s}_{M+1}(n) = &\{g_1(n), g_2(n), \ldots, g_M(n), \\ &f_1(n), f_2(n), \ldots, f_M(n)\}. \end{aligned} \tag{17}$$

For $\boldsymbol{s}_m(n)$, which includes the position, energy information, and channel gain from IoT devices to UAV $m$. The state of UAV $m$ at time slot $n$ can be expressed as

$$\begin{aligned} \boldsymbol{s}_m(n) = \{&x_m(n), y_m(n), z_m(n), E_m^{\text{tot}}(n), \\ &h_{1,m}(n), \cdots, h_{K_m,m}(n)\}. \end{aligned} \tag{18}$$

**Action:** The action of the BS $\boldsymbol{a}_{M+1}(n)$ comprises the moving size of MA position as well as the receive beamforming. At time slot $n$, $\boldsymbol{a}_{M+1}(n)$ can be expressed as

$$\begin{aligned}\boldsymbol{a}_{M+1}(n) =&\{x_1(n),\ldots,x_J(n),y_1(n),\ldots,y_J(n),\\&z_1(n),\ldots,z_J(n),\boldsymbol{w}_1(n),\ldots,\boldsymbol{w}_M(n)\}.\end{aligned} \tag{19}$$

At time slot $n$, the action of the UAV $m$ is $\boldsymbol{a}_m(n)$ which includes the pitch angle, roll angle, and yaw angle of the UAV $m$. Therefore, $\boldsymbol{a}_m(n)$ can be expressed as

$$\boldsymbol{a}_m(n) =\{\theta_m^p(n),\theta_m^r(n),\theta_m^y(n)\}. \tag{20}$$

**Reward:** The objective of the paper is to maximize the uplink sum-rate of the whole network. The agents in this environment have the same objective and maintain a cooperative relationship, the BS and UAVs share the reward function. Therefore, at time slot $n$, the reward can be expressed as

$$r(n) = \alpha \cdot R_{sum}^{up}(n) + (P_1 + P_2 + P_3 + P_4). \tag{21}$$

To address the excessively large sum-rate values that complicate the joint analysis of penalty and reward mechanisms, a sum-rate scaling factor $\alpha$ is introduced for performance evaluation. Moreover, $P_1 \leq 0$, $P_2 \leq 0$, $P_3 \leq 0$, and $P_4 \leq 0$, are defined, respectively, as follows:

$$P_1 \triangleq \begin{cases}0, & \text{while (16a),(16b) is qualified}\\ \varpi_1, & \text{otherwise}\end{cases} \tag{22}$$

$$P_2 \triangleq \begin{cases}0, & \text{while (16c) is qualified}\\ \varpi_2, & \text{otherwise}\end{cases} \tag{23}$$

$$P_3 \triangleq \begin{cases}0, & \text{while (16e),(16f) is qualified}\\ \varpi_3, & \text{otherwise}\end{cases} \tag{24}$$

$$P_4 \triangleq \begin{cases}0, & \text{while (16g) is qualified}\\ \varpi_4, & \text{otherwise}\end{cases} \tag{25}$$

where the constant $\varpi_1 < 0$ and $\varpi_2 < 0$ is introduced to punish UAV for violating trajectory constrain (16a), (16b) and energy constrain (16c), respectively. The constant $\varpi_3 < 0$ is used to punish MA for violating the position constraint (16e), (16f). The constant $\varpi_4 < 0$ is used to punish UAV for violating the rate constraint (16g).

### 3.2 The MAPPO Algorithm

Given the fully continuous action space requirements of our developed MA-AGC network comprising BS and UAVs, and the strong coupling among optimization variables including UAV trajectory, MA position, and receive beamforming at the BS, we employ the MAPPO algorithm to address the cooperative optimization problem. MAPPO demonstrates environmental adaptability by dynamically adjusting policies online to counteract time-varying channel conditions and interference patterns. The algorithmic architecture is depicted in Fig. 3.

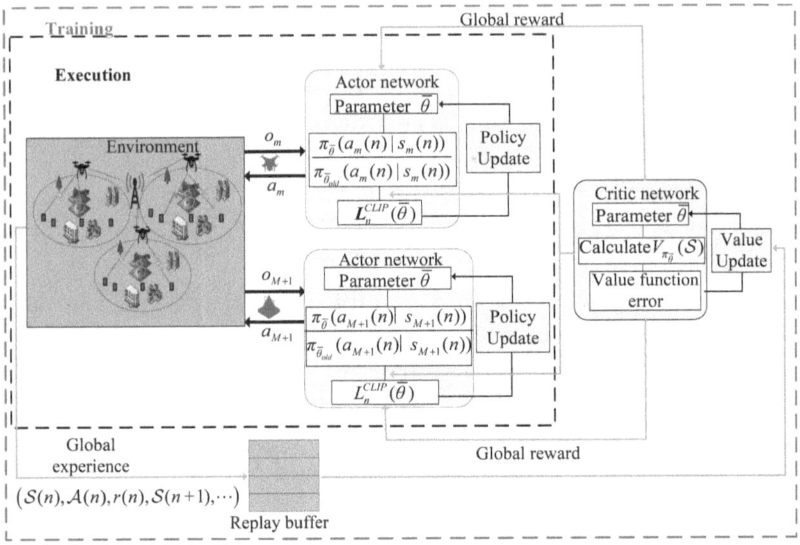


**Fig. 3.** The structure of MAPPO algorithm.

The agents include BS and UAVs in the environment. Each agent has an actor network and all agents share a common critic network. Formally, let $\pi_{\bar{\theta}}$: $\mathcal{S} \rightarrow \mathcal{A}$ denote the parameterized actor network mapping states to actions, and $V_{\bar{\phi}}$: $\mathcal{S} \rightarrow \mathbb{R}$ represent the shared critic network estimating state-value functions, where $\bar{\theta}$ and $\bar{\phi}$ are respective neural network parameters. The MAPPO policy gradient objective with clipped updates is expressed as

$$L_n^{CLIP}(\bar{\theta}) = \mathbb{E}_n \left[ \min \left( \sigma_n(\bar{\theta}), \text{clip} \left( \sigma_n(\bar{\theta}), 1 - \varepsilon, 1 + \varepsilon \right) \right) \widehat{A}(n) \right], \tag{26}$$

where $\sigma_n(\bar{\theta}) = \pi_{\bar{\theta}}(\mathcal{A}(n)|\mathcal{S}(n))/\pi_{\bar{\theta}_{\text{old}}}(\mathcal{A}(n)|\mathcal{S}(n))$ is the importance sampling weight, quantifies policy update magnitudes between iterations, with $\varepsilon$ defined as the trust region clipping threshold. This clipping mechanism serves to enforce policy update stability by constraining $\sigma_n(\bar{\theta}) \in [1 - \varepsilon, 1 + \varepsilon]$, thereby preventing destructive gradient steps. $\widehat{A}(n)$ is the generalized advantage estimator, the $\gamma$ is the discount factor, as show in

$$\widehat{A}(n) \approx r(\mathcal{S}, \mathcal{A}) + \gamma V_{\bar{\phi}}(\mathcal{S}(n+1)) - V_{\bar{\phi}}(\mathcal{S}(n)). \tag{27}$$

The parametric representation of critic, defined through the parameter $\bar{\phi}$, undergoes optimization via gradient-based methods with the following objective function

$$L^{VF}(\bar{\phi}) = \mathbb{E}_n\left[\left(V_{\bar{\phi}}(\mathcal{S}(n)) - y(n)\right)^2\right], \tag{28}$$

where the bootstrapped target estimate is defined as $y(n) = r(n) + \gamma V_{\bar{\phi}}(\mathcal{S}(n+1))$. Consequently, the composite objective function introduces a policy entropy regularization term $X[\pi_{\bar{\theta}}]$ to enhance policy exploration diversity, which can be formulated as

$$L = \mathbb{E}_n\left[L_n^{CLIP}(\bar{\theta}) - c_1 L^{VF}(\bar{\phi}) + c_2 X[\pi_{\bar{\theta}}](\mathcal{S}(n))\right], \tag{29}$$

where $c_1$ and $c_2$ denote coefficients, $X[\pi_{\bar{\theta}}](\mathcal{S}(n))$ quantifies the policy entropy conditioned on the input state $\mathcal{S}(n)$.

In the centralized training stage, the critic network calculates the global action value function $Q(\mathcal{S}, \mathcal{A}\,|\,\bar{\theta}))$ based on the environment. The global action value function can evaluate the action of the actor network and guide the actor network to choose better actions. The critic network subsequently optimizes the parameters $\bar{\theta}$ through loss minimization

$$\text{loss}(\bar{\theta}) = \mathbb{E}\left[\left(Q(\mathcal{S}, \mathcal{A}\,|\,\bar{\phi})) - y^{MAPPO}\right)\right]^2, \tag{30}$$

where the MAPPO target value is defined as $y^{MAPPO} = r(n) + \gamma Q'(\mathcal{S}', \mathcal{A}'\,|\,\bar{\phi}')$, with $\mathcal{S}'$ characterizing the state transitions of the target network and $\bar{\phi}'$ representing the updated evaluation network parameters. The actor network consequently optimizes policy parameters $\bar{\theta}$ through gradient ascent along $\nabla_{\bar{\theta}} J'(\bar{\theta})$, guided by the centralized Q-value estimates from the critic network and local observational inputs. $\nabla_{\bar{\theta}} J'(\bar{\theta})$ is defined as

$$\nabla_{\bar{\theta}} J'(\bar{\theta}) \approx \mathbb{E}\left[\nabla_{\mathcal{A}} Q(\mathcal{S}, \mathcal{A}\,|\,\bar{\phi}) \nabla_{\bar{\theta}} \pi(\mathcal{S}\,|\,\bar{\theta})\right]. \tag{31}$$

During the decentralized inference phase, the critic architecture is deactivated, with solely the optimized actor network executing real-time policy generation derived from localized agent observations. The employed MAPPO algorithm is shown in Algorithm 1.

## 4 Simulation Results

In this section, we illustrate the performance of the MAPPO algorithm. There is 1 BS with 3 MAs, 2 UAVs, and 6 IoT devices in the MA-AGC network. Each UAV serves 3 IoT devices distributed in a 300 m $\times$ 300 m area. The position of the BS is $\boldsymbol{d}_0$ = (150, 150, 20) m. The initial positions of UAVs are (75, 75, 80) m and (225, 225, 85) m, respectively. The bandwidth of BS is 10 MHz, and the bandwidth of each UAV is 3 MHz. The transmission power of UAV $m$ and

**Algorithm 1:** MAPPO Algorithm

Initialize policy network $\pi_{\bar{\theta}}$ and value network $V_{\bar{\phi}}$ let $\pi_{\bar{\theta}'} = \pi_{\bar{\theta}}$ .
Initialize the size of replay memory buffer $\mathcal{D}$, minization bitch size $Z$ and evaluation frequency $f$.
**for** episode = 0 to max-episode-length **do**
  Initialize system state $\mathcal{S}(n)$ and set $r(n) = 0$.
  **for** $N$ steps **do**
    **for** each agent $i$ **do**
      Executes action according to $\pi_{\bar{\theta}'}(\boldsymbol{a}_n^i \mid \boldsymbol{o}_n^i)$.
    **end for**
    Get the reward $r(n)$, the new global state $\mathcal{S}(n+1)$ and obtain new observations $\boldsymbol{O}(n+1)$.
    **for** each agent $i$ **do**
      Store transition $\{\boldsymbol{s}_i(n), \boldsymbol{a}_i(n), r_i(n), \boldsymbol{s}_i(n+1)\}$ into replay buffer $\mathcal{D}$.
    **end for**
    Update global state $\mathcal{S}(n) \leftarrow \mathcal{S}(n+1)$.
  **end for**
  **if** episode/$f = 0$ **then**
    $Z$ experiences are randomly selected from the replay buffer.
    **for** $z = 1$ to $Z$ **do**
      **for** $n = 1$ to $N$ **do**
        Calculate generalized advantage estimator $\widehat{A}(n)$.
      **end for**
    **end for**
    Let $\pi_{\bar{\theta}} = \pi_{\bar{\theta}'}$.
    Update network parameters for each agent based on Eq.(30) and Eq.(31).
  **end if**
**end for**

IoT device $k_m$ is 1 W and 0.01 W, respectively. The flight speed of each UAV is 10 m/s. The time period is 60 s and the duration of each time slot is 1 s. Other simulation parameters are set as shown in Table 1.

To demonstrate the performance of the MAPPO algorithm, the following three algorithms are compared to it.

- Multi-agent Soft Actor-Critic (MASAC) algorithm: The MASAC algorithm is chosen as a strong off-policy, maximum-entropy baseline for continuous multi-agent control. Its entropy bonus and sample efficiency improve exploration under time-varying channels and suit our coupled actions in UAV trajectory, receiving beamforming, MA position.
- Advantage Actor-Critic (A2C) algorithm: The A2C algorithm is selected as a canonical on-policy baseline with synchronous advantage estimation that reduces variance and stabilizes updates. Under centralized training with a decentralized execution (CTDE), it enables deterministic, stable policy learning and offers a complementary contrast to entropy-regularized methods for joint UAV trajectory, receive beamforming, and MA position optimization.

**Table 1.** Simulation parameters.

| Parameter | Notation | Value |
|---|---|---|
| Referenced channel gain | $\beta_0$ | $-50\,\text{dB}$ |
| Noise power | $\sigma_0^2$ | $-80\,\text{dBm}$ |
| Carrier wavelength | $\lambda$ | $0.1\,\text{m}$ |
| Length of sides of receive area | $A$ | $0.15\,\text{m}$ |
| Minimum inter-MA distance | $D_0$ | $0.1\,\text{m}$ |
| Elevation of AoA | $\phi_m(n)$ | $\left(-\frac{\pi}{2}, \frac{\pi}{2}\right)$ |
| Azimuth of AoA | $\psi_m(n)$ | $\left(-\pi, \pi\right)$ |
| Steering-matrix reference point at BS | $\boldsymbol{d}_0$ | (150, 150, 20) |
| UAV weight/wing constants | $\lambda_1, \lambda_2$ | 0.00614, 15.97 |
| Sum-rate scaling factor | $\alpha$ | $10^{-8}$ |
| Discount factor for rewards | $\gamma$ | 0.96 |
| Actor/Critic hidden layers | $L_{\text{act}}/L_{\text{cri}}$ | 2 |
| Hidden units per layer | $d_h$ | 256 |
| Actor/Critic network learning rate | $l_a/l_c$ | $10^{-3}$ |

- MAPPO with fixed position antenna (MAPPO-FPA) algorithm: In this baseline, the BS is equipped with $M$ FPAs instead of MAs. Besides, the UAV trajectory as well as receive beamforming at the BS is under the control of MAPPO.

Figure 4 compares the convergence performance of the four algorithms. It is evident that all algorithms reward consistently increases and stabilizes after 10000 episodes of training. Besides, the network equipped with MAs demonstrates superior convergence performance to the with FPAs baseline. Among MA-assisted network, the proposed MAPPO algorithm achieves higher reward growth and stability compared to A2C algorithm and MASAC algorithm, validating its effectiveness in dynamic MA-AGC network.

Figure 5 shows the relationship between the uplink sum-rate of the MA-AGC network and the total number of IoT devices. Under fixed UAV bandwidth, the uplink sum-rate improves with IoT device density owing to enhanced spectrum utilization but saturates beyond 10 devices as bandwidth orthogonality constraints restrict per-device capacity. Besides, the MAPPO-FPA algorithm yields lower sum-rates than MA-enabled methods. This case shows the critical role of MAs in interference mitigation and channel improvement. The proposed MAPPO algorithm achieves 4.73% and 21.63% higher sum-rates than A2C algorithm and MASAC algorithm respectively at 10 devices saturation, demonstrating superior coordination in a bandwidth-limited MA-AGC network.

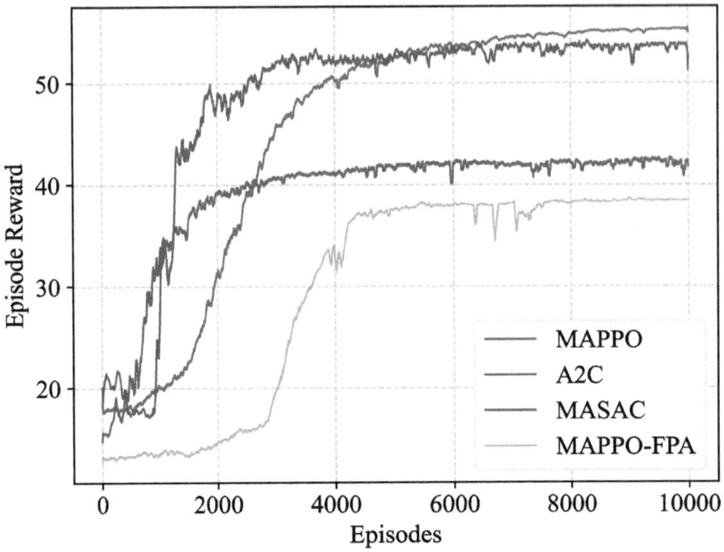


**Fig. 4.** Convergence performance of four algorithms.

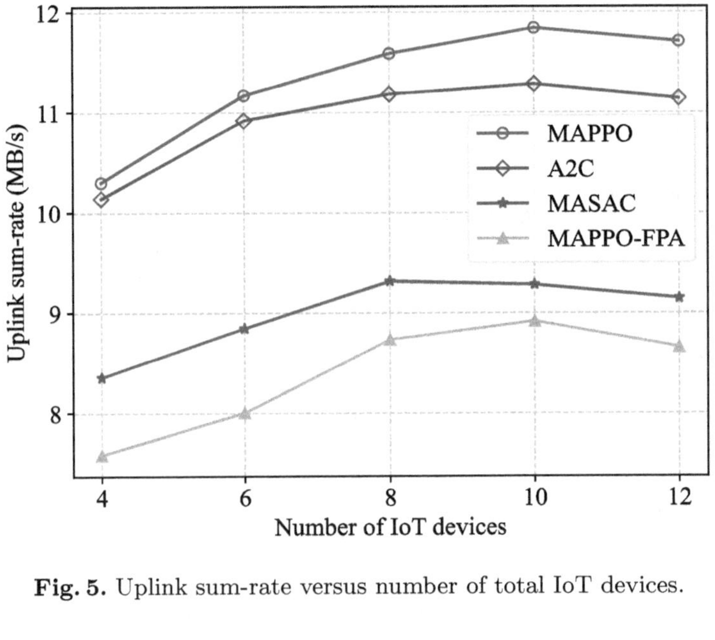


**Fig. 5.** Uplink sum-rate versus number of total IoT devices.

Figure 6 illustrates the relationship between the uplink sum-rate of the MA-AGC network and the number of BS antennas across four algorithms. As shown, all schemes improve in sum-rate as the number of BS antennas increasing due to the enhanced spatial diversity gain and beamforming gain. Moreover, the scheme with FPAs consistently yields lower sum-rates than MA-enabled methods, con-

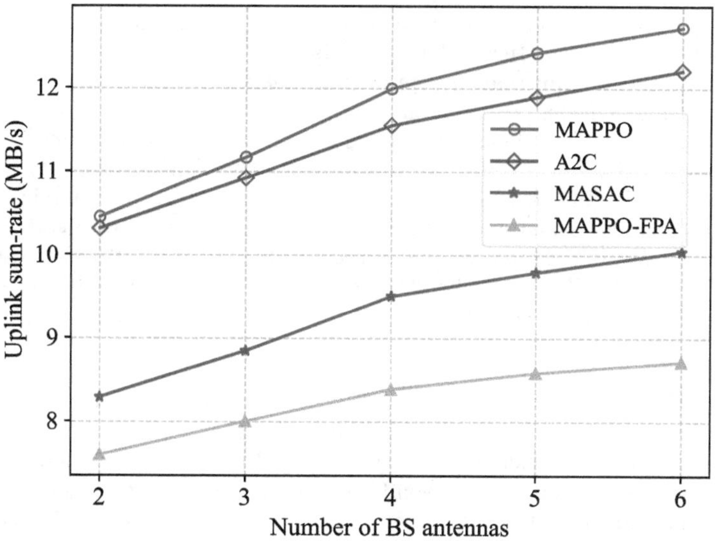


**Fig. 6.** Uplink sum-rate versus number of BS antennas.

firming the essential role of MAs in improving channel conditions. Among MA-enabled methods, the proposed MAPPO algorithm sustains performance advantages over A2C algorithm and MASAC algorithm across all the BS antennas, which demonstrates its superiority in dynamic MA-AGC network.

## 5 Conclusion

In this paper, we formulated the optimization problem focusing on jointly optimizing the UAV trajectory design, MA position, and receive beamforming design at the BS to maximize the uplink sum-rate of the MA-AGC network. To tackle this non-convex problem, we transformed it into a MDP, and subsequently solved using the MAPPO algorithm. Simulation results demonstrated that the proposed MAPPO algorithm can effectively maximize the uplink sum-rate.

**Acknowledgments.** This work was partly supported by the Guangxi Natural Science Foundation (No. 2025GXNSFAA069677); in part by the Project of Guangxi Wireless Broadband Communication and Signal Processing Key Laboratory (No. AD25069102).

## References

1. Li, S., et al.: Joint admission control and resource allocation in edgecomputing for internet of things. IEEE Network **32**(1), 72–79 (2018)
2. Li, N., Wu, P., Ning, B., Zhu, L.: Sum rate maximization for movable antenna enabled uplink NOMA. IEEE Wirel. Commun. Lett. **13**(8), 2140–2144 (2024)

3. Zhu, L., Ma, W., Zhang, R.: Movable antennas for wireless communication: opportunities and challenges. IEEE Commun. Mag. **62**(6), 114–120 (2023)
4. Hu, G., et al.: Two-timescale design for movable antenna array-enabled multiuser uplink communications. IEEE Trans. Veh. Technol. **74**(3), 5152–5157 (2024)
5. Zhang, Y., et al.: Movable antenna-aided hybrid beamforming for multi-user communications. IEEE Trans. Veh. Technol. **74**(6), 9899–9903 (2025)
6. Xiao, Z., Pi, X., Zhu, L., Xia, X.-G., Zhang, R.: Multiuser communications with movable-antenna base station: joint antenna positioning, receive combining, and power control. IEEE Trans. Wirel. Commun. **23**(12), 19744–19759 (2024)
7. Ding, J., Zhu, L., Zhou, Z., Jiao, B., Zhang, R.: Near-field multiuser communications aided by movable antennas. IEEE Wirel. Commun. Lett. **14**(1), 138–142 (2024)
8. Liu, W., Zhang, X., Xing, H., Ren, J., Shen, Y., Cui, S.: UAV-enabled wireless networks with movable-antenna array: flexible beamforming and trajectory design. IEEE Wirel. Commun. Lett. **14**(3), 566–570 (2024)
9. Li, S., Lu, B., Ale, L., Chen, H., Tan, F., Huang, J.: Two-hop partial task offloading and resource allocation in air-ground integrated mobile edge computing network: a DRL-based method. IEEE Internet Things J. **12**(12), 21443–21456 (2025)
10. Ma, W., Zhu, L., Zhang, R.: MIMO capacity characterization for movable antenna systems. IEEE Trans. Wirel. Commun. **23**(4), 3392–3407 (2023)

# Edge Computing

# Research on Resource Management Algorithms for Three-Layer Collaboration in UAV-Assisted MEC

Yang Lou, Pu Zhao, Yu Hong, and Li Wang(✉)

School of Software, Northwestern Polytechnical University, Xi'an, China
{louyang,puzhao,hong_yu}@mail.nwpu.edu.cn, wang.li@nwpu.edu.cn

**Abstract.** Mobile Edge Computing (MEC) enhances service capability by offloading computation to the network edge, providing high bandwidth and low latency. Unmanned Aerial Vehicles (UAVs), with flexible deployment and three-dimensional mobility, further extend MEC coverage. Meanwhile, Federated Learning (FL) enables distributed training with privacy preservation, making it a promising tool for UAV-assisted MEC. However, large-scale deployments face two issues: (i) device heterogeneity in data distribution, communication quality, and computational capacity complicates efficient client selection; and (ii) the coupling among communication and computation resources makes joint allocation difficult. To address these issues, we propose a UAV-assisted MEC framework based on Hierarchical Federated Learning (HFL). First, we design an Adaptive Scoring and Bidirectional Proposal Mechanism (AS-BPM) Based client selection Algorithm by jointly considering data volume, channel quality, and model staleness, with adaptive weight adjustment. Second, we develop a resource allocation algorithm using Deep Deterministic Policy Gradient (DDPG), which jointly optimizes UAV scheduling, transmission power, and computing frequency to minimize latency and energy consumption. Experiments on the CIFAR-10 dataset under both IID and non-IID settings demonstrate that the proposed framework achieves up to 83% model accuracy while reducing the total system cost by as much as 19.3% compared with baseline schemes.

**Keywords:** UAV-assisted MEC · Hierarchical Federated Learning · Client Selection · Resource Allocation

## 1 Introduction

### 1.1 Research Background

MEC enhances service quality by offloading computation and storage to the network edge, enabling low-latency and high-bandwidth support for intelligent

Supported by the National Natural Science Foundation of China under Grant 61901388.


Y. Liu et al. (Eds.): ChinaCom 2025, LNICST 711, pp. 363–377, 2027.
https://doi.org/10.1007/978-3-032-33662-0_27

Internet of Things (IoT) applications [1]. However, the rapid growth of intelligent devices and data-intensive services imposes stringent demands on efficient and scalable resource management, which remains a central challenge for improving MEC performance [2,3].

UAVs, with flexible deployment and three-dimensional mobility, have emerged as promising MEC nodes that can extend coverage and augment communication capacity, particularly in infrastructure-poor or emergency scenarios [4–6]. Nevertheless, UAV-assisted MEC faces two major challenges: (i) strong heterogeneity among clients in terms of data distribution, computing capability, and channel quality [7]; and (ii) the intrinsic complexity of jointly managing communication and computation resources under multi-objective and time-varying conditions [8].

FL has become a promising paradigm for collaborative training that is both privacy-preserving and communication-efficient, as it enables devices to share model updates instead of raw data [9]. To further enhance scalability and reduce communication bottlenecks, HFL extends the conventional FL framework by introducing intermediate aggregation nodes. In UAV-assisted MEC systems, UAVs serve as such intermediaries between the base station (BS) and clients, thereby forming a three-layer BS–UAV–client architecture. This hierarchical design not only improves training efficiency and scalability but also provides greater flexibility in managing distributed resources. Within this architecture, however, robust performance under heterogeneous and dynamic conditions still hinges on three critical aspects: adaptive client selection, UAV scheduling, and joint resource allocation.

Existing studies on MEC resource management range from architectural design to joint optimization of communication, computation, and caching. Representative works have developed offloading and allocation schemes that reduce latency or energy consumption through coordinated use of radio and computing resources [10,11]. In UAV-assisted MEC, optimization and deep reinforcement learning (DRL) have been applied to address UAV mobility, energy limits, and link dynamics, e.g., task offloading and CPU allocation strategies or DRL-based scheduling policies (such as SAC) for energy-efficient service provision [12]. Meanwhile, the integration of FL/HFL with MEC has motivated methods that balance latency–energy trade-offs, improve client scheduling, and enhance scalability. Prior studies have considered probabilistic or data-aware client selection, staleness-aware scheduling, and adaptive participation control [13–15]. More recently, joint optimization of client selection, UAV scheduling, and resource allocation under semi-synchronous aggregation has been formulated as non-convex problems and solved with decomposition or DRL-based techniques such as DDPG [8].

Despite these advances, important gaps remain for UAV-assisted HFL in realistic deployments: (i) the need for client selection and UAV scheduling strategies that explicitly account for heterogeneous data, channels, and model staleness while preserving long-term fairness; and (ii) the need for continuous control policies that jointly allocate communication (uplink power) and computation (CPU frequency) resources to minimize weighted system cost (latency and energy) under mixed integer–continuous constraints and dynamic environments. These challenges motivate this work.

### 1.2 Main Contributions

This paper develops a three-layer cooperative resource management framework for UAV-assisted MEC under HFL. The main contributions are as follows:

1. Hierarchical framework: We construct a BS–UAV–client architecture that integrates adaptive client selection, UAV scheduling, and joint resource allocation to reduce overall system cost.
2. AS-BPM-based client selection: We design an AS-BPM based algorithm that accounts for model staleness, dataset size, and channel quality, thereby improving timeliness, fairness, and efficiency in heterogeneous settings.
3. DDPG-based resource allocation: We propose a fairness-aware resource allocation algorithm based on DDPG that jointly optimizes uplink power and computation frequency, adaptively balancing latency and energy consumption.

### 1.3 Organization

The remainder of this paper is organized as follows. Section 2 presents the system model of UAV-assisted HFL. Section 3 introduces the proposed AS-BPM-based client selection algorithm. Section 4 develops the UAV scheduling and DDPG-based resource allocation algorithm. Section 5 reports simulation results and performance analysis. Finally, Sect. 6 concludes the paper.

## 2 System Model and Problem Formulation

### 2.1 Scenario Description

We consider a UAV-assisted MEC system with HFL, which forms a three-layer cloud–edge–client collaborative architecture. The system consists of a BS, a fleet of UAVs, and a set of distributed clients. This framework enhances training efficiency and resource utilization while ensuring data privacy.

As shown in Fig. 1, the UAV edge layer comprises $K$ UAVs, denoted by $\mathcal{K} = \{1, 2, \ldots, K\}$, while the client layer consists of $N$ clients, denoted by $\mathcal{N} = \{1, 2, \ldots, N\}$. Each client $n \in \mathcal{N}$ holds a private dataset $\mathcal{D}_n$ for local model training. In each round, every UAV $k \in \mathcal{K}$ is associated with a subset of clients $\mathcal{N}_k \subseteq \mathcal{N}$, which perform local training and upload their models to the UAV for aggregation.

For modeling clarity, the HFL workflow is divided into two phases: (i) the client–UAV phase, where local training and UAV aggregation are conducted, and (ii) the UAV–BS phase, where UAVs forward aggregated models to the BS for global aggregation.

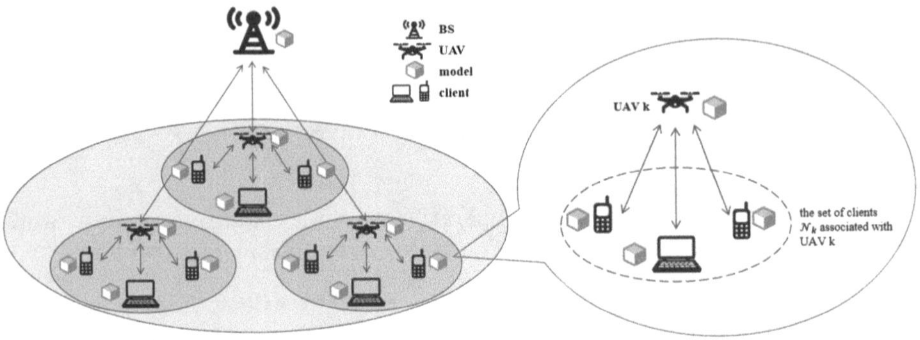


**Fig. 1.** UAV-assisted MEC network scenario.

### 2.2 Client–UAV Phase

In this phase, each client $n$ trains a local model on $\mathcal{D}_n$ by minimizing

$$\mathcal{L}_n(\mathbf{w}_n) = \frac{1}{|\mathcal{D}_n|} \sum_{(\mathbf{x}_i, y_i) \in \mathcal{D}_n} \ell(f(\mathbf{x}_i; \mathbf{w}_n), y_i), \tag{1}$$

where $\mathbf{w}_n$ is the model parameter vector, $\ell(\cdot)$ is the per-sample loss, $\mathbf{x}_i$ represents the input feature vector of the $i$-th sample, and $y_i$ is the corresponding true label associated with $\mathbf{x}_i$. To accelerate convergence, a OneCycleLR learning-rate schedule is applied, and an early-stopping mechanism halts training if, for $P$ consecutive epochs, the accuracy improvement is below a threshold $\varepsilon$:

$$\mathrm{Acc}_i - \max_{j=i-P,\dots,i-1} \{\mathrm{Acc}_j\} < \varepsilon, \tag{2}$$

where $\mathrm{Acc}_i$ is the validation accuracy at epoch $i$.

The training latency and energy consumption of client $n$ are

$$T_n^{\mathrm{train}} = \frac{C_n |\mathcal{D}_n|}{f_n}, \qquad E_n^{\mathrm{train}} = \kappa_n C_n |\mathcal{D}_n| f_n^2 \tag{3}$$

where $C_n$ is the number of CPU cycles per sample, $f_n$ is the CPU frequency, and $\kappa_n$ is the effective switched capacitance.

After local training, each client uploads its model (size $S$ bits) to the associated UAV $k$. Let the horizontal coordinates of client $n$ be $(x_n, y_n, 0)$ and those of UAV $k$ be $(x_k, y_k, h_k)$, where $h_k$ denotes the flight altitude of UAV $k$. The Euclidean distance between client $n$ and UAV $k$ is

$$d_{n,k} = \sqrt{(x_n - x_k)^2 + (y_n - y_k)^2 + h_k^2}. \tag{4}$$

The corresponding channel gain is modeled as

$$h_{n,k} = \frac{h_0}{d_{n,k}^2}, \tag{5}$$

where $h_0$ represents the reference channel power gain at a distance of 1 m. Given client transmit power $P_n$, noise power $\sigma^2$, and effective bandwidth $\eta B$, the achievable uplink rate is

$$R_{n,k} = \eta B \log_2\Big(1 + \frac{P_n h_{n,k}}{\sigma^2}\Big). \tag{6}$$

Thus, the upload latency and energy consumption are

$$T_{n,k}^{\mathrm{up}} = \frac{S}{R_{n,k}}, \qquad E_{n,k}^{\mathrm{up}} = P_n T_{n,k}^{\mathrm{up}}. \tag{7}$$

Upon receiving local models from $\mathcal{N}_k$, UAV $k$ aggregates them as

$$\mathbf{w}_k = \sum_{n\in\mathcal{N}_k} \frac{|\mathcal{D}_n|}{\sum_{j\in\mathcal{N}_k}|\mathcal{D}_j|}\mathbf{w}_n. \tag{8}$$

The latency and energy consumption associated with UAV-side aggregation are given by

$$T_k^{\mathrm{agg}} = \max_{n\in\mathcal{N}_k}\left(T_n^{\mathrm{train}} + T_{n,k}^{\mathrm{up}}\right) + T_k^{\mathrm{proc}}, \tag{9}$$

$$E_k^{\mathrm{agg}} = \sum_{n\in\mathcal{N}_k}\left(E_n^{\mathrm{train}} + E_{n,k}^{\mathrm{up}}\right) + E_k^{\mathrm{proc}}, \tag{10}$$

where $T_k^{\mathrm{proc}}$ and $E_k^{\mathrm{proc}}$ denote the computation delay and energy consumption for model aggregation at UAV $k$. Here, the latency is determined by the slowest client in $\mathcal{N}_k$, as UAV $k$ must wait for all local updates before aggregation, while the energy reflects the total cost of all participating clients and the UAV.

### 2.3 UAV–BS Phase

After completing UAV-side aggregation, the intermediate models are uploaded to the BS for global aggregation, which constitutes the core of the edge–cloud collaboration. To avoid interference among concurrent transmissions, orthogonal frequency-division multiple access (OFDMA) is adopted, and each UAV uses a pre-assigned orthogonal channel. The uplink latency and energy consumption of UAV $k \in \mathcal{K}$ are

$$T_k^{\mathrm{up}} = \frac{S}{R_k^{\mathrm{up}}}, \qquad E_k^{\mathrm{up}} = P_k^{\mathrm{up}} T_k^{\mathrm{up}}, \tag{11}$$

where $S$ is the model size, $R_k^{\mathrm{up}}$ is the achievable UAV–BS uplink rate, and $P_k^{\mathrm{up}}$ is the transmit power of UAV $k$.

Once all uploads are completed, the BS acts as the global coordinator and performs synchronous aggregation, i.e., it waits for all scheduled UAVs before updating the global model. Although synchronous schemes may introduce additional waiting time, the UAV fleet is relatively small and fully controllable, ensuring stable convergence. Let $\mathcal{K}_t$ denote the set of UAVs selected in global round $t$, and define the indicator

$$\delta_k = \begin{cases} 1, & \text{if UAV } k \text{ is scheduled,} \\ 0, & \text{otherwise.} \end{cases} \tag{12}$$

Accordingly, the selected-UAV set can be equivalently represented as $\mathcal{K}_t = \{ k \mid \delta_k = 1 \}$.

The global model update performed at the BS in global round $t$ is obtained by aggregating the models from the selected UAVs, denoted by the set $\mathcal{K}_t$:

$$\boldsymbol{w}_{t+1} = \sum_{k \in \mathcal{K}_t} \frac{D_k}{D_{\text{tot}}(t)} \boldsymbol{w}_{k,t}, \tag{13}$$

where $D_k = \sum_{n \in \mathcal{N}_k} |\mathcal{D}_n|$ denotes the total data volume of clients associated with UAV $k$, and $D_{\text{tot}}(t) = \sum_{k \in \mathcal{K}_t} D_k$ represents the cumulative dataset size of all selected UAVs in round $t$. Here, $\boldsymbol{w}_{k,t}$ is the local model aggregated by UAV $k$ during round $t$, and $\boldsymbol{w}_{t+1}$ is the updated global model after aggregation at the BS.

Since the BS has substantially higher computation and communication capacity than UAVs and clients, the latency and energy consumption of BS-side global aggregation and broadcasting are neglected. Accordingly, the overall system latency and energy consumption in each global round are expressed as

$$T_{\text{total}} = \max_{k \in \mathcal{K}_t} \{ T_k^{\text{up}} + T_k^{\text{agg}} \}, \tag{14}$$

$$E_{\text{total}} = \sum_{k \in \mathcal{K}_t} (E_k^{\text{up}} + E_k^{\text{agg}}). \tag{15}$$

Here, the total latency is determined by the slowest UAV among the selected set $\mathcal{K}_t$, as the BS must wait for all participating UAVs to complete their local aggregation and transmission before initiating the next global round. In contrast, the total energy consumption equals the sum of energy expenditures of all selected UAVs.

## 2.4 Problem Formulation

We next formulate the optimization problem of the UAV-assisted HFL system. The objective is to minimize the total system cost per global round, defined as a weighted sum of latency and energy consumption. Two interdependent tasks are jointly considered: client scheduling and UAV resource allocation.

In this framework, UAVs serve as aerial relays between clients and the BS, responsible for aggregating local updates and forwarding them to the cloud. Due to client heterogeneity and limited system resources, inefficient scheduling may lead to load imbalance, model staleness, and high cost. Thus, we design a joint optimization framework to ensure efficient training and scalability.

According to the system model, the overall objective is to minimize the weighted cost of each global training round, defined as

$$\min_{\boldsymbol{p},\, \boldsymbol{f},\, \{\mathcal{N}_k\}} \quad \Omega = \lambda T_{\text{total}} + (1 - \lambda) E_{\text{total}}, \tag{16}$$

where $\boldsymbol{p}$ and $\boldsymbol{f}$ denote the transmission power and computation frequency allocation strategies, respectively, $\mathcal{N}_k$ represents the set of clients associated with UAV

$k$, and $\lambda \in [0, 1]$ is a trade-off parameter that balances the importance between latency minimization and energy efficiency. This formulation captures the inherent tension between fast convergence (low delay) and sustainable operation (low energy consumption) in UAV-assisted HFL systems.

This optimization problem can be formulated as a mixed-integer nonlinear programming (MINLP) task, which is NP-hard due to the presence of nonlinear functions, maximum operators, and the coupling between discrete scheduling variables and continuous resource allocation variables. To improve tractability, we adopt a modular design and decompose the original problem into two manageable subproblems: (i) adaptive client selection based on the AS-BPM algorithm, and (ii) fairness-aware UAV scheduling and resource allocation based on DDPG algorithm. This decomposition not only reduces computational complexity but also enhances scalability, making the proposed framework more practical for deployment in UAV-assisted HFL systems.

## 3 Client Selection Algorithm

In the scenario shown in Fig. 1, client selection critically affects both global model convergence and resource efficiency. Due to the limited computation and communication capacities of UAVs, it is infeasible for all clients to participate in every round; instead, a representative subset must be chosen. However, strong heterogeneity in client data and network conditions makes conventional random or greedy policies inefficient, often leading to stale models, imbalanced resource use, and degraded training stability.

To address these challenges, we propose an AS-BPM Based Client Selection Algorithm. This scheme jointly considers model staleness, dataset size, and channel quality through a dynamic scoring function, while introducing a bidirectional matching process between clients and UAVs to achieve efficient and fair scheduling.

### 3.1 Evaluation Metric Design

To select appropriate clients in each training round, we design a comprehensive evaluation metric that jointly considers model staleness, data volume, and channel quality. The score of client $n$ in round $t$ is defined as

$$S_n^{(t)} = \left(\alpha^{(t)} \cdot \phi_n^{(t)} + \beta^{(t)} \cdot d_n + \gamma^{(t)} \cdot h_n^{(t)}\right) \cdot \eta^{(t)} \cdot F_n^{(t)}, \quad (17)$$

where $\phi_n^{(t)}$ denotes the model staleness of client $n$, i.e., the number of rounds since its last participation. $d_n$ is the normalized local dataset size. $h_n^{(t)}$ represents the normalized uplink channel gain. $F_n^{(t)}$ is a fairness incentive factor that promotes long-term balanced participation. The weights $\alpha^{(t)}, \beta^{(t)}, \gamma^{(t)}, \eta^{(t)}$ control the relative importance of these factors.

Among them, $\alpha^{(t)}$ and $\gamma^{(t)}$ are dynamically adjusted in each round based on historical training feedback. Specifically, the system records the average model staleness $\overline{\phi}^{(t)}$ and the average channel quality $\overline{h}^{(t)}$ of previously selected clients, and updates the weights as follows:

$$\alpha^{(t+1)} = f\left(\overline{\phi}^{(t)}\right), \quad \gamma^{(t+1)} = g\left(\overline{h}^{(t)}\right), \tag{18}$$

where $f(\cdot)$ and $g(\cdot)$ are adaptive adjustment functions. If the average staleness exceeds a predefined threshold, it indicates that many clients suffer from outdated models, and thus the weight $\alpha^{(t)}$ is increased to prioritize the participation of stale clients. Conversely, if the average channel quality falls below the threshold, the weight $\gamma^{(t)}$ is raised to give higher priority to clients with better links.

This adaptive scoring mechanism ensures that client selection accounts for both short-term efficiency and long-term fairness. Clients with high staleness or low selection frequency receive higher priority through the fairness factor $F_n^{(t)}$, thereby preventing over-concentration on a small subset of clients and improving global training stability.

### 3.2 AS-BPM Based Client Selection Algorithm

To enable efficient client participation scheduling, we propose an AS-BPM based client selection algorithm, which builds upon the scoring function introduced in Sect. 3.1. The objective is to select an optimal subset of clients for each training round under resource constraints. This algorithm not only preserves model performance but also enhances fairness and resource utilization in the HFL system.

The proposed algorithm consists of four main stages:

1. Initialization: Initialize the preference lists of clients toward UAVs, the preference lists of UAVs toward clients, and the client candidate set.
2. Bidirectional Preference Construction:
   (a) Each client evaluates all accessible UAVs using the scoring function, ranking them in descending order to form its preference list. A higher score indicates a stronger inclination to join the corresponding UAV's task.
   (b) Similarly, each UAV evaluates all candidate clients within its coverage area using the same scoring function and constructs its own ranked preference list to guide proposal priority.
3. Proposal–Matching Phase: After preference construction, a two-sided matching process is executed between UAVs and clients through an iterative "proposal–response" mechanism:
   (a) In each round, UAVs that have not yet reached their client quota propose to the highest-ranked unallocated clients on their lists. A client may receive multiple proposals simultaneously.
   (b) Each client accepts the proposal from its most preferred UAV and rejects the others.
   (c) Accepted clients are removed from the candidate set and deleted from all UAV preference lists to prevent duplication.
   (d) Once a UAV fulfills its quota, it exits the process. Iterations continue until all UAVs complete allocation or available resources are exhausted.

This mechanism balances communication quality, data diversity, and model timeliness, ensuring rational, adaptive, and stable client selection.

4. Output: Each UAV obtains a representative subset of clients with sufficient local training capability and reliable channel quality. This subset is used in the subsequent client–UAV training and edge aggregation stage.

# 4 Joint Optimization of UAV Scheduling and Resource Allocation

Resource allocation is critical to achieving efficient training and reducing overall system cost. In the scenario illustrated in Fig. 1, UAVs are responsible for collecting and pre-aggregating local models, and their scheduling strategy directly determines the available communication links as well as the scope of resource allocation in each training round. Consequently, an effective UAV scheduling policy, coupled with optimized resource allocation for the associated clients, is essential for minimizing system overhead.

To this end, we decompose the joint optimization problem into two sequential stages. In the first stage, a UAV scheduling policy determines the subset of UAVs that will participate in the current training round. In the second stage, for the clients covered by the selected UAVs, a DDPG-based algorithm jointly optimizes communication and computation resource allocation, aiming to minimize the total system cost within that round.

## 4.1 Metric Design

In line with the delay and energy definitions in Sect. 2, the efficiency of each training round is evaluated by a weighted sum of latency and energy, while long-term robustness is promoted by a fairness-aware UAV scheduling score.

Firstly, the round-wise cost for UAV $k$ is defined as

$$\mathcal{L}_k^{\mathrm{uav}} = \omega_T T_k^{\mathrm{agg}} + \omega_E E_k^{\mathrm{agg}}, \quad \omega_T, \omega_E \in [0,1], \;\; \omega_T + \omega_E = 1, \tag{19}$$

where $T_k^{\mathrm{agg}}$ and $E_k^{\mathrm{agg}}$ denote the latency and energy incurred by UAV $k$ in the current round, including both client-side training/upload and UAV-side aggregation.

Secondly, to avoid persistently favoring UAVs with lower cost, a fairness-aware scheduling priority is introduced:

$$\eta_k = \frac{1}{\mathcal{L}_k^{\mathrm{uav}} + \varepsilon} \cdot F_k, \quad \varepsilon > 0, \tag{20}$$

where $F_k$ is a fairness factor that escalates the priority of UAVs excluded for multiple consecutive rounds:

$$F_k = \begin{cases} a^{\Delta_k}, & \Delta_k > \theta, \\ 1, & \text{otherwise}, \end{cases} \qquad \Delta_k = r - r_k - 1, \;\; a > 1. \tag{21}$$

Here $r$ is the current round, $r_k$ is the last round UAV $k$ was scheduled, $\theta$ is the fairness threshold, and $a$ controls escalation.

*Scheduling Rule.* Given $K$ candidate UAVs and scheduling ratio $\alpha \in (0, 1]$, the system selects $\max\{1, \lfloor \alpha K \rfloor\}$ UAVs with the highest $\eta_k$ values. After scheduling, the round index of each selected UAV is updated as $r_k \leftarrow r$, and resource allocation is performed for the clients covered by these UAVs.

## 4.2 DDPG-Based Fairness-Oriented Resource Allocation

After UAV scheduling (Sect. 4.1), the system jointly optimizes the uplink transmit power and local computation frequency of the *selected* clients. The goal in each round is to minimize the same weighted round-wise cost used in Eq. (16), while long-term fairness is enforced by the scheduling priority in Eqs. (20)–(21). Given the dynamic and continuous nature of the resource allocation task, conventional convex optimization methods are impractical. We therefore employ the DDPG algorithm, which is well-suited for continuous-control optimization in such environments.

Let $\mathcal{K}_t$ be the scheduled UAV set in round $t$ and $\mathcal{N}_k^{(t)}$ the client set associated with UAV $k \in \mathcal{K}_t$. The UAV controller is the agent, and the closed-loop interaction proceeds as follows.

1. State perception: At the beginning of round $t$, construct

$$s_t = \left[ \{h_{n,k}^{(t)}\}_{k \in \mathcal{K}_t,\, n \in \mathcal{N}_k^{(t)}},\ \{d_n\}_{n \in \cup_k \mathcal{N}_k^{(t)}} \right], \tag{22}$$

where $h_{n,k}^{(t)}$ is the normalized client–UAV channel gain and $d_n = |\mathcal{D}_n|$ is the normalized dataset size of client $n$.

2. Action decision: The Actor maps $s_t$ to a continuous action

$$a_t = \left[ \{p_n^{(t)}\}_{n \in \mathcal{N}_k^{(t)}},\ \{f_n^{(t)}\}_{n \in \mathcal{N}_k^{(t)}} \right], \tag{23}$$

where $p_n^{(t)}$ and $f_n^{(t)}$ are the transmit power and CPU frequency allocated to client $n$. To satisfy system constraints, actions are projected onto the feasible set

$$\mathcal{A} = \left\{ 0 \le p_n^{(t)} \le P_{\max},\ f_{\min} \le f_n^{(t)} \le f_{\max} \right\}, \tag{24}$$

where $P_{\max}$ is the maximum transmit power permitted by client devices and $f_{\max}$ (resp. $f_{\min}$) is the upper (resp. lower) bound of CPU frequency supported by their processors.

3. System execution and feedback: Clients perform local training using $\{f_n^{(t)}\}$ and upload their models with $\{p_n^{(t)}\}$; UAVs then aggregate and forward to the BS. The latency and energy consumption of each scheduled UAV follow the definitions in Sect. 2.
4. Policy update: Form the experience $(s_t, a_t, r_t, s_{t+1})$ and update the Actor–Critic networks via mini-batch sampling and soft target updates.

The immediate reward is defined as the negative round-wise system cost $\Omega_t$:

$$r_t = -\,\Omega_t. \tag{25}$$

This reward formulation explicitly ties the learning signal to the latency–energy trade-off, while fairness in long-term participation is ensured by the UAV scheduling score $\eta_k$ in Sect. 4.1.

# 5 Simulation Results

This section evaluates the performance of the proposed UAV-assisted HFL framework. The experiments aim to verify both the effectiveness and efficiency of the proposed algorithms compared with baseline schemes under different data distribution settings of CIFAR-10. Two partitioning schemes are considered: (i) an IID setting, where data samples from all classes are uniformly distributed across clients; and (ii) a non-IID setting, where each client holds data biased toward a limited subset of classes, reflecting realistic heterogeneity [16].

We simulate a UAV-assisted MEC system consisting of 1 BS, 4 UAVs, and 32 clients uniformly distributed in a 1 km × 1 km area. UAVs act as intermediate aggregation nodes, collecting local updates from their associated clients and forwarding aggregated models to the BS for global fusion. The main simulation parameters are summarized in Table 1.

**Table 1.** Simulation Parameters

| Parameter | Value/Setting |
|---|---|
| Simulation area | 1 km × 1 km |
| Number of UAVs ($K$) | 4 |
| Number of clients ($N$) | 32 |
| Data distribution | IID/non-IID partitions of CIFAR-10 |
| System bandwidth | 10 MHz |
| Noise power spectral density | −174 dBm/Hz |
| Client transmit power | $P_{\max} = 500$ mW |
| Client CPU frequency | $[1.0, 3.0]$ GHz |
| Fairness threshold $\theta$ | 3 rounds |

To illustrate the impact of data heterogeneity, Fig. 2 depicts the IID case, where each client receives a balanced subset of all classes. Figure 3 shows the non-IID case, where clients possess data from only a few classes, resulting in skewed local distributions. These two settings enable a comprehensive evaluation of the proposed algorithms under both balanced and heterogeneous conditions.

## 5.1 Performance of AS-BPM Based Client Selection

To evaluate the effectiveness of the proposed AS-BPM based client selection algorithm, we compare it with two baseline strategies: (i) *random selection*, where participating clients are chosen uniformly at random in each round, and (ii) *greedy selection*, where clients with the smallest distances to UAVs (i.e., with better channel conditions) are always prioritized.

As shown in Fig. 4, under the IID setting the AS-BPM algorithm achieves the lowest average model staleness throughout the training process, significantly outperforming both baselines. This indicates that AS-BPM ensures a more balanced coverage across clients, thereby preventing over-reliance on a small subset and enhancing overall stability and fairness.

In the highly skewed non-IID scenario illustrated in Fig. 5, the superiority of AS-BPM remains evident: its average model staleness consistently stays below that of the random and greedy strategies. These results demonstrate that AS-BPM effectively balances client participation frequencies and mitigates long-term staleness accumulation, which leads to more stable model convergence and improved fairness among clients, even under heterogeneous data distributions.

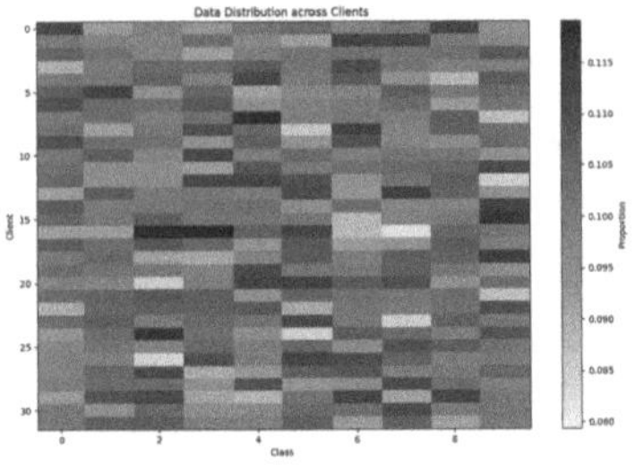


**Fig. 2.** IID partition of CIFAR-10 across clients.

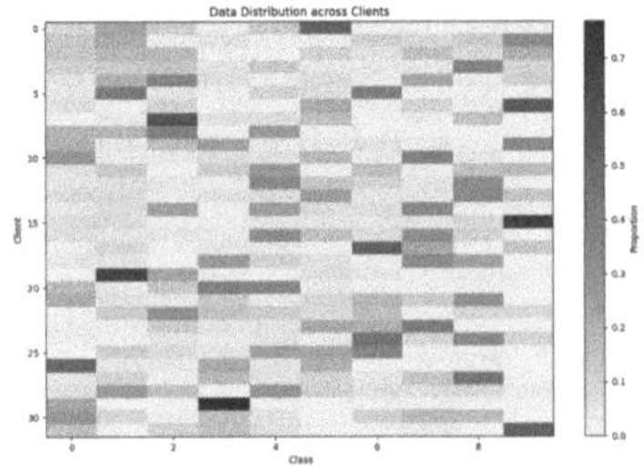


**Fig. 3.** Non-IID partition of CIFAR-10 across clients.

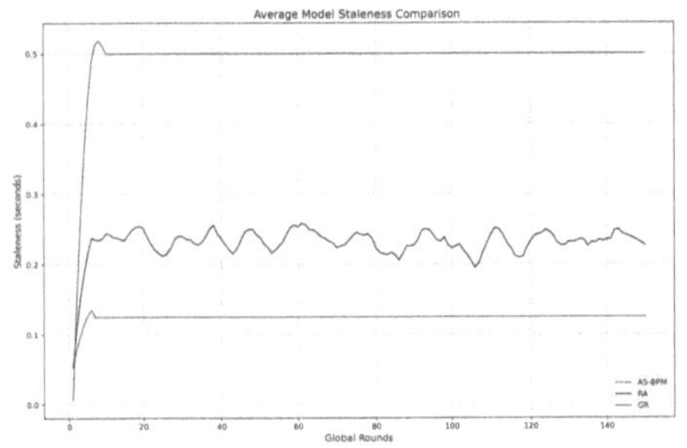


**Fig. 4.** Comparison of Average Model Staleness for User Equipment under Three Algorithms in IID Settings.

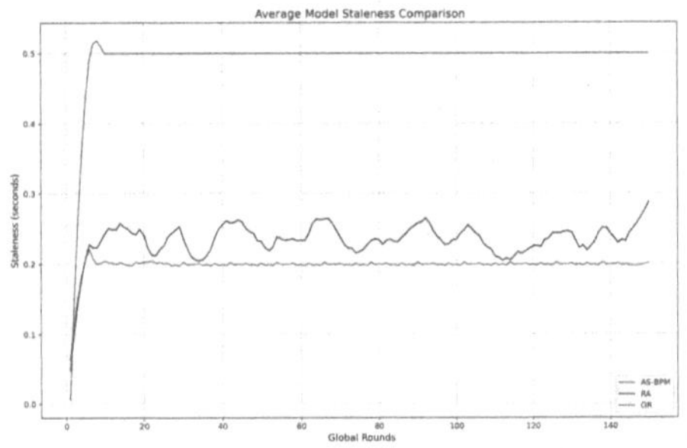


**Fig. 5.** Comparison of Average Model Staleness for User Equipment under Three Algorithms in Non-IID Settings.

### 5.2 Performance of the DDPG-Based Fairness-Aware Resource Allocation

We evaluate the proposed DDPG-based fairness-aware resource allocation against four baselines: (i) *fixed-computation*, with constant CPU frequency; (ii) *fixed-power*, with constant transmit power; (iii) *random allocation*, with uniformly sampled power and frequency; and (iv) a *DQN-based* method using a discrete-action policy [17]. The first three are static or random strategies, while DQN serves as a learning baseline limited by its discretized action space.

Figure 6 shows the total system cost under the IID setting. The proposed method consistently achieves the lowest cost, reducing the average value by about 19.3% compared with the static and random baselines, and by 5.7% relative to DQN once the number of global rounds exceeds 70. This demonstrates the effectiveness of continuous-action control in adapting to dynamic client states.

As shown in Fig. 7, the average per-client cost increases with the number of clients per UAV, yet our method consistently attains the lowest cost. By jointly optimizing transmit power and computation frequency, it captures fine-grained state variations, yielding better resource utilization, smoother convergence, and higher robustness than static and discrete-action approaches.

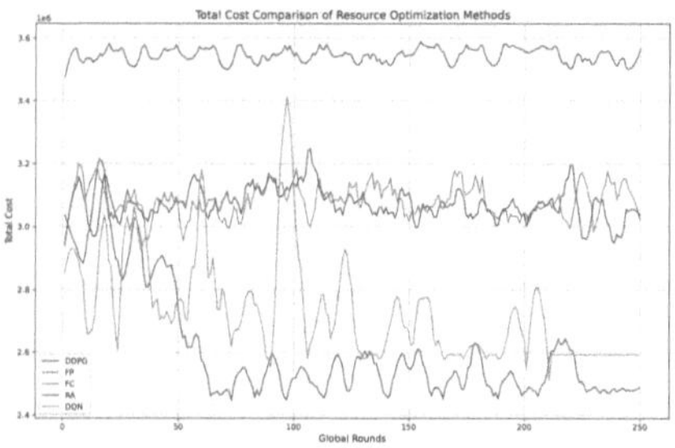


Fig. 6. Total system cost vs. training rounds (IID partition).

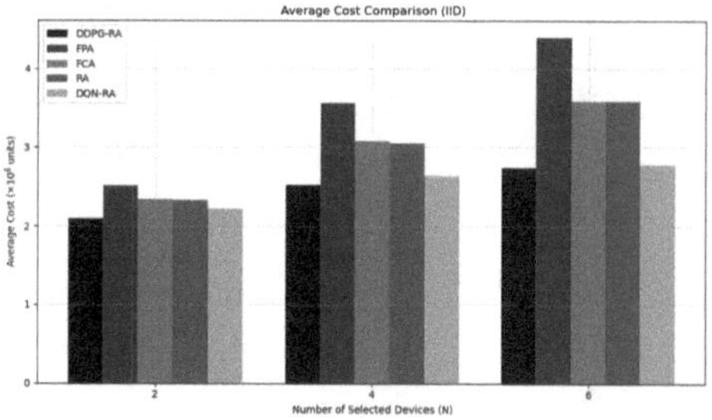


Fig. 7. Number of associated clients per UAV (IID partition).

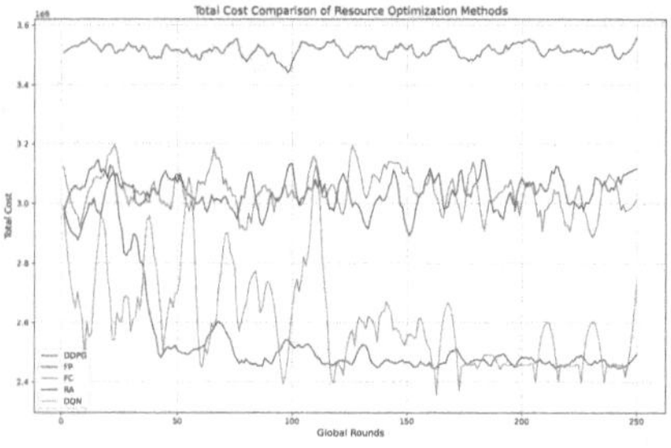


Fig. 8. Total system cost vs. training rounds (Non-IID partition).

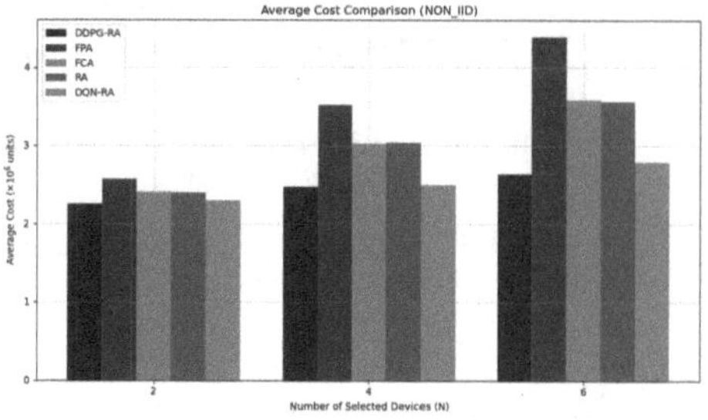


Fig. 9. Number of associated clients per UAV (Non-IID partition).

Under the non-IID partitions (Figs. 8–9), the advantage of the proposed DDPG-based resource allocation algorithm becomes more pronounced. The increased heterogeneity in local data volumes and channel qualities further exposes the limitations of static or discretized control schemes, which cannot flexibly adapt to diverse client conditions. In contrast, our continuous-control approach learns fine-grained adjustments of uplink transmit power and CPU frequency, effectively balancing latency, energy consumption, and fairness.

Overall, these results confirm that the proposed algorithm achieves a lower total system cost than all baselines, particularly under highly heterogeneous environments. The continuous-action learning mechanism enables adaptive resource coordination that better accommodates variability among clients compared with both static/random strategies and the discrete-action DQN baseline.

## 6 Conclusion

This paper investigated the joint optimization of user selection, UAV scheduling, and resource allocation in UAV-assisted MEC networks. To minimize the overall system cost, a unified optimization framework was formulated, integrating a multi-dimensional scheduling mechanism with a DDPG-based continuous control algorithm. Building on this design, an HFL-enabled three-layer collaborative resource management architecture was established across the BS, UAVs, and end clients. Simulation results verified that the proposed framework achieves superior performance over baseline schemes in both improving HFL convergence efficiency and reducing total system cost.

## References

1. Ale, L., Zhang, N., King, S.A., et al.: Empowering generative AI through mobile edge computing. Nat. Rev. Electr. Eng. **1**(7), 478–486 (2024)
2. Kumar, S., Yamsani, N., Kumar, S., et al.: Advancements in IoT-powered smart environment monitoring systems. In: Proceedings of 3rd International Conference on Advancement in Electronics and Communication Engineering (AECE), pp. 299–302. IEEE (2023)
3. Rao, B., Zhang, J., Wu, D., et al.: Privacy inference attack and defense in centralized and federated learning: a comprehensive survey. IEEE Trans. Artif. Intell. (2024)
4. Amodu, O.A., Mahmood, R.A.R., Althumali, H.: A question-centric review on DRL-based optimization for UAV-assisted MEC sensor and IoT applications, challenges, and future directions. Veh. Commun. 100899 (2025)
5. Gu, X., Zhang, G.: A survey on UAV-assisted wireless communications: Recent advances and future trends. Comput. Commun. **208**, 44–78 (2023)
6. Wang, T., Huang, X., Wu, Y., et al.: UAV swarm-assisted two-tier hierarchical federated learning. IEEE Trans. Netw. Sci. Eng. (2023)
7. Tursunboev, J., Kang, Y.S., Huh, S.B., et al.: Hierarchical federated learning for edge-aided unmanned aerial vehicle networks. Appl. Sci. **12**(2), 670 (2022)

8. Wu, B., Fang, F., Wang, X.: Client selection and cost-efficient joint optimization for NOMA-enabled hierarchical federated learning. IEEE Trans. Wirel. Commun. (2024)
9. Abreha, H.G., Hayajneh, M., Serhani, M.A.: Federated learning in edge computing: a systematic survey. Sensors **22**(2), 450 (2022)
10. Mao, Y., You, C., Zhang, J., et al.: A survey on mobile edge computing: the communication perspective. IEEE Commun. Surv. Tutor. **19**(4), 2322–2358 (2017)
11. Wang, S., Zhang, X., Zhang, Y., et al.: A survey on mobile edge networks: convergence of computing, caching and communications. IEEE Access **5**, 6757–6779 (2017)
12. Zhao, X., Zhao, T., Wang, F., et al.: SAC-based UAV mobile edge computing for energy minimization and secure data transmission. Ad Hoc Netw. **157**, 103435 (2024)
13. Tang, J., Nie, J., Zhang, Y.: Multi-UAV-assisted federated learning for energy-aware distributed edge training. IEEE Trans. Netw. Serv. Manag. (2023)
14. Deng, X., Li, J., Ma, C., et al.: Low-latency federated learning with DNN partition in distributed industrial IoT networks. IEEE J. Sel. Areas Commun. **41**(3), 755–775 (2022)
15. Luo, S., Chen, X., Wu, Q., et al.: HFEL: joint edge association and resource allocation for cost-efficient hierarchical federated edge learning. IEEE Trans. Wirel. Commun. **19**(10), 6535–6548 (2020)
16. Cao, L.: Beyond IID: Non-IID thinking, informatics, and learning. IEEE Intell. Syst. **37**(4), 5–17 (2022)
17. Wu, Y.C., Dinh, T.Q., Fu, Y., et al.: A hybrid DQN and optimization approach for strategy and resource allocation in MEC networks. IEEE Trans. Wirel. Commun. **20**(7), 4282–4295 (2021)

# Research on Resource Management Algorithms Based on Federated Learning in UAV-Assisted MEC

Pu Zhao, Yang Lou, Chenyu Meng, and Li Wang(✉)

School of Software, Northwestern Polytechnical University, Xi'an 710072, Shanxi, China
{puzhao,louyang,chenyumeng}@mail.nwpu.edu.cn, wang.li@nwpu.edu.cn

**Abstract.** As Mobile Edge Computing (MEC) becomes increasingly important in edge data processing, Unmanned Aerial Vehicles (UAVs) have emerged as key enablers for MEC due to their flexible deployment and broad coverage. However, UAVs are constrained in computing and communication resources, and the presence of imperfect Channel State Information (CSI) further complicates resource management. Federated Learning (FL) offers a promising solution by enabling efficient coordination between UAVs and base stations. This paper investigates FL-based dynamic resource management in UAV-assisted MEC under imperfect CSI. We model the joint optimization of UAV selection, transmission power, and CPU frequency as a Markov Decision Process (MDP), and apply the Std Q-target (SQT) framework for online policy learning. Our proposed FL-SQT algorithm improves the success rate by 1.98% and the Accuracy-to-Energy (AE) gain by 29.2% compared to traditional methods.

**Keywords:** Federated learning · Deep reinforcement learning · MEC · Unmanned aerial vehicle

## 1 Introduction

The proliferation of User Equipment (UE) and demand for low-latency services have positioned Mobile Edge Computing (MEC) as a critical solution for reducing core network load and enabling localized intelligence. Unmanned Aerial Vehicles (UAVs), with their high mobility and rapid deployment capability, serve as key elements in MEC architectures—especially in areas with inadequate ground infrastructure or for temporary applications such as disaster response and traffic management [1]. However, the rise of edge intelligence also introduces challenges related to data privacy and communication costs. Federated Learning (FL) addresses these issues through distributed, privacy-preserving model training.

---

Supported by the National Natural Science Foundation of China under Grant 61901388.


Y. Liu et al. (Eds.): ChinaCom 2025, LNICST 711, pp. 378–393, 2027.
https://doi.org/10.1007/978-3-032-33662-0_28

Its integration into UAV-assisted MEC enhances collaborative intelligence while adapting to resource-limited and dynamic environments [2].

Nevertheless, UAVs operate under strict energy and hardware constraints, limiting computational and communication capabilities and necessitating efficient resource scheduling. Moreover, the acquisition of channel state information between UAVs and servers relies on regular measurement and feedback mechanisms. Inevitable measurement errors and feedback delays [3] lead to scheduling decisions based on inaccurate channel data, thereby causing deviations in resource allocation. The presence of imperfect CSI further complicates resource allocation and system reliability.

In FL systems, selecting an appropriate number of UAV clients per round is essential: too few impedes model accuracy and convergence, while too many increases energy consumption and delay risks. Thus, optimizing UAV selection and resource allocation to balance training accuracy and energy efficiency remains a complex and significant challenge. The main contributions of this paper are as follows:

*1)* A federated learning resource management optimization algorithm for UAV-assisted MEC (FL-SQT) is proposed. This algorithm is based on the SQT framework and uses a deep reinforcement learning model to learn the dynamic network state space. It achieves joint optimization of UAV selection, transmission power, and computation frequency under imperfect channel state conditions.
*2)* The uncertainty modeling mechanism introduced in the hierarchical federated learning system fully considers the practical issue of estimation errors in channel state information, breaking through the limitations of existing methods that mostly rely on static or ideal channel assumptions. FL-SQT algorithm has online learning and adaptive updating capabilities, enabling it to dynamically respond to changes in the network environment. It continuously adjusts the policy network and resource allocation scheme during training, enhancing the system's robustness to complex environments.
*3)* In strategy optimization, we employs an SQT multi-Q network integration structure and introduces an uncertainty penalty term, effectively suppressing the overestimation bias present in traditional reinforcement learning. This improves the stability and generalization performance of the strategy. Simulation results show that compared with traditional algorithms, the FL-SQT algorithm increases the success rate by 1.98% and achieves a 29.2% improvement in the Accuracy-to-Energy (AE) gain.

The remainder of this paper is structured as follows: Sect. 2 reviews related work on FL and UAV-assisted MEC. Section 3 introduces the system model. Section 4 presents the proposed FL-based dynamic resource management algorithm. Section 5 describes the simulation setup and analyzes experimental results. Finally, Sect. 6 summarizes the paper and discusses future research directions.

## 2 Related Works

This section reviews FL-based resource management methods and their application in UAV-assisted MEC networks.

**FL-Based Resource Management:** FL enables distributed model training while preserving data privacy, with client selection playing a critical role in enhancing efficiency and fairness. Some studies increase the number of participants per round to improve performance, such as FedCS [5] and long-term selection strategies [6]. However, expanding client participation often raises energy consumption. Subsequent works like BEFL [7] and CEFL [8] aim to maintain accuracy while reducing energy use and incorporating cost-aware metrics. These approaches, however, generally assume perfect CSI, which is often unrealistic.

**UAV-Assisted MEC Resource Management:** Leveraging their mobility and computing capability, UAVs are increasingly deployed in MEC. Resource management in such systems focuses on computation offloading, communication allocation, and energy optimization under latency constraints. Studies have used convex optimization [10], multi-agent reinforcement learning [11], and deep reinforcement learning [12] to improve performance in single- and multi-UAV setups. Despite progress, issues such as limited energy and scheduling latency call for more efficient and stable collaboration mechanisms.

In summary, while existing work has advanced FL and UAV-assisted MEC, balancing UAV energy limits and FL resource demands under imperfect CSI remains an open problem. This paper formulates the resource management problem under realistic constraints and proposes an FL-based dynamic resource allocation algorithm to maximize training accuracy while optimizing energy consumption.

## 3 System Model

This paper considers a hierarchical federated learning system as shown in Fig. 1, focusing on the model interaction process between UAVs and hierarchical federated learning servers. The system consists of a base station, $U$ UAVs (represented by the set $\mathcal{U} = [1, 2, \ldots, U]$ ), and several devices. UAVs exchange information with the base station via wireless communication.

### 3.1 System Architecture Model

In a hierarchical federated learning system, both the global model on the server and local models on UAVs are updated each round. Let $\mathcal{T} = [1, 2, \ldots, T]$ denote the maximum number of rounds. Each UAV $u \in \mathcal{U}$ possesses a local dataset $D_{t,u}$ in round $t \in \mathcal{T}$. The key steps of the $t$-th training round are illustrated in Fig. 2.

*1)* UAV Selection and Global Model Distribution: The server selects some appropriate UAVs $I_t (I_t \in \mathcal{U})$ based on the resource request status and sends the global model to the selected UAVs through the downlink.

*2)* Local Model Update and Upload: Each selected UAV u trains the model using its local dataset $D_{t,u}$ and updates the local model parameters . All selected UAVs upload their trained local models to the federated learning server.

*3)* Global Model Aggregation and Update: The server collects the local models from all selected UAVs and aggregates them into a new global model by weighting according to the amount of data.

### 3.2 Communication Process Model

In wireless communication systems, obtaining perfect CSI is very difficult due to the inherent time-varying nature of the wireless channel and the presence of feedback delays [13]. The uncertainty in CSI is manifested in the form of channel estimation errors. Therefore, this paper represents the actual CSI as the sum of the estimated channel value and the channel estimation error [14].

$$g_{t,u}^{up} = \tilde{g}_{t,u}^{up} + e_{t,u}^{up}, \quad g_{t,u}^{down} = \tilde{g}_{t,u}^{down} + e_{t,u}^{down} \tag{1}$$

where $\tilde{g}_{t,u}^{up}$ and $\tilde{g}_{t,u}^{down}$ represent the uplink and downlink channel estimates for UAV $u$ in round $t$, respectively. The corresponding channel estimation errors $e_{t,u}^{up}$ and $e_{t,u}^{down}$ follow a Circularly Symmetric Complex Gaussian (CSCG) distribution with zero mean and variance 0.005. The effective noise incorporates both additive white Gaussian noise and additional noise induced by channel estimation errors. This additional noise is caused by inaccurate channel estimation, so it needs to be considered in the overall noise. Therefore, the lower-bound expressions for the effective uplink and downlink Signal-to-Interference-plus-Noise Ratio (SINR) are derived as follows:

$$\mathrm{SINR}_{t,u}^{up} = \frac{\left|\tilde{g}_{t,u}^{up}\right|^2 p_{t,u}^{up}}{\left|e_{t,u}^{up}\right|^2 p_{t,u}^{up} + b_{t,u}N_0}, \quad \mathrm{SINR}_{t,u}^{down} = \frac{\left|\tilde{g}_{t,u}^{down}\right|^2 p_{t,u}^{down}}{\left|e_{t,u}^{down}\right|^2 p_{t,u}^{down} + b_{t,u}N_0} \tag{2}$$

Here,$p_{t,u}^{up}$ is the uplink transmission power and $p_{t,u}^{down}$ is the downlink transmission power.$b_{t,u}$ represents the bandwidth allocated by the server to UAV u

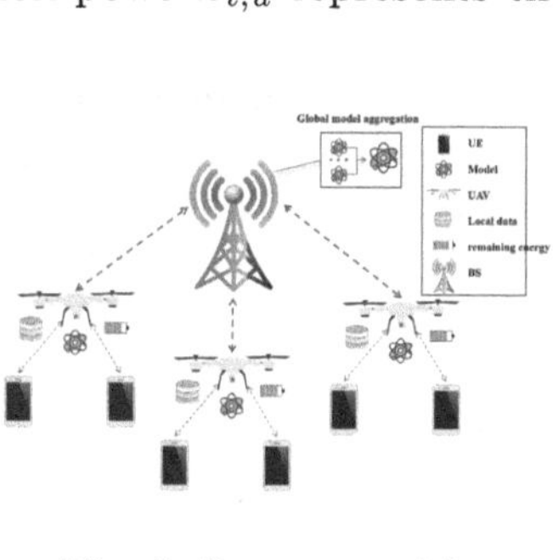


**Fig. 1.** System model.

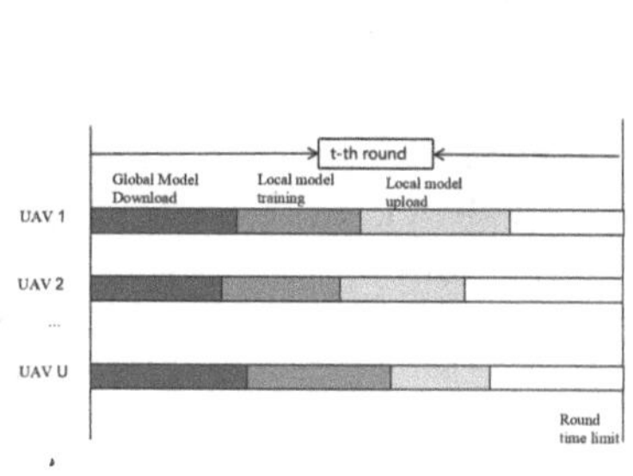


**Fig. 2.** The training process of each round of federated learning.

in the t-th training round.$N_0$ is the power spectral density of noise.Therefore, in this paper, the uplink and downlink transmission rates for UAV u in the t-th round are given by

$$r_{t,u}^{up} = b_{t,u}\log_2\left(1+\mathrm{SINR}_{t,u}^{up}\right), \quad r_{t,u}^{down} = b_{t,u}\log_2\left(1+\mathrm{SINR}_{t,u}^{down}\right) \tag{3}$$

### 3.3 Computation Resource Model

The time required for UAV u to train the local model in the t-th round is jointly determined by the computational resources and the size of the local dataset [15]. Therefore, the time required for UAV u to train the local model in the t-th round can be expressed as

$$\tau_{t,u}^{cmp} = \frac{|D_{t,u}|\, Lc_u}{f_{t,u}} \tag{4}$$

where $c_u$ is the number of CPU cycles required by the UAV to train a single data sample, $L$ is the number of required local training rounds, and $f_{t,u}$ is the CPU frequency of UAV u in the t-th round. The energy consumption of UAV u during local model training in the t-th round can be expressed as

$$E_{t,u}^{cmp} = \xi_u c_u f_{t,u}^2 \,|D_{t,u}|\, L \tag{5}$$

where $\xi_u$ denotes the Effective Capacitance Coefficient (ECC) of UAV $u$. In the federated learning framework, after local training, UAVs upload their models to the server in parallel. The local model $M_{local}$ upload and global model $M_{\mathrm{global}}$ download time for UAV $u$ in round $t$ are given by:

$$\tau_{t,u}^{up} = \frac{M_{local}}{r_{t,u}^{up}}, \quad \tau_{t,u}^{down} = \frac{M_{global}}{r_{t,u}^{down}} \tag{6}$$

In federated learning systems, the server generally has substantial computational resources, hence we assume the time for global aggregation and client selection is negligible. As shown in Fig. 2, the time to complete the $t$-th round of federated learning depends on the slowest UAV.

$$T_t = \max_{u\in I_t}(\tau_{t,u}^{down} + \tau_{t,u}^{cmp} + \tau_{t,u}^{up}) \tag{7}$$

Similarly, because the federated learning server has ample energy, the energy consumed on the federated learning server is not considered. Since this paper mainly focuses on the interaction process between UAVs and the federated learning server, the energy consumed by UAV u for uploading the local model in the t-th round can be expressed as

$$E_{t,u}^{up} = \tau_{t,u}^{up} p_{t,u}^{up} \tag{8}$$

The total energy consumption of the selected UAV u in the t-th round can be expressed as

$$E_{t,u}^{total} = E_{t,u}^{cmp} + E_{t,u}^{up} \tag{9}$$

### 3.4 AE Gain and Problem Description

In federated learning, a comprehensive metric is required for the joint optimization of energy and latency. Training accuracy serves as a frequently used performance metric, directly indicating the model's learning efficacy. The accuracy in round $t$, denoted as $\Gamma_t$, depends on the local dataset size of participating UAVs [16].

$$\Gamma_t = \log\left(1 + \sum_{u=1}^{U} \phi_{t,u}\right) = \log\left(1 + \sum_{u=1}^{U} \mu_u \left|D_{t,u}\right| x_{t,u}\right) \tag{10}$$

Here, $\phi_{t,u}$ denotes the data contribution of UAV $u$ in round $t$, $\mu_u$ is its data quality weight, and $x_{t,u} \in \{0,1\}$ indicates the selection status of UAV $u$. Selecting fewer UAVs saves energy but reduces accuracy, whereas more UAVs improve accuracy at increased energy cost. To balance this trade-off between energy consumption and accuracy [17], we define the Accuracy-Energy (AE) gain as follows:

$$\sum_{t=1}^{T}\left(\Gamma_t - \alpha \sum_{u \in I_t} E_{t,u}^{total}\right) \tag{11}$$

where $\alpha$ is a weight coefficient that balances the relative importance between training energy consumption and federated learning accuracy. When the UAV resources are limited, the value of $\alpha$ should be set to be larger. This will guide the system to focus more on reducing energy consumption during the optimization process, even if this may sacrifice the training accuracy of the model to some extent. On the contrary, when the application scenario has higher requirements for model performance and the energy supply is relatively sufficient, the value of $\alpha$ should be set to be smaller. This allows the system to focus more on improving training accuracy during optimization, permitting higher energy consumption to support more thorough model training, thus obtaining a more optimal global model.

Considering latency constraints and resource limitations, we formulate an optimization problem $P0$ to maximize the AE gain of the federated learning system, thereby identifying the optimal UAV selection and resource allocation strategy for enhanced performance.

$$\text{P0:} \quad \max_{x_{t,u}, p_{t,u}^{up}, f_{t,u}} \sum_{t=1}^{T}\left(\Gamma_t - \alpha \sum_{u \in I_t} E_{t,u}^{total}\right) \tag{12}$$

To ensure the feasibility of the optimization problem and the stability of the federated learning system, the following constraints are introduced:

Transmission Power Constraint: $\forall t \in \mathcal{T}, \forall u \in \mathcal{U}, p_{t,u}^{\min} \leq p_{t,u}^{up} \leq p_u^{\max}$. CPU Frequency Constraint: $\forall t \in \mathcal{T}, \forall u \in \mathcal{U}, f_u^{\min} \leq f_{t,u} \leq f_u^{\max}$. UAV Energy Constraint: $\forall t \in \mathcal{T}, \forall u \in I_t, E_{t,u}^{total} \leq E_{t,u}$. UAV Selection Constraint: $\forall t \in \mathcal{T}, 1 \leq \sum_{u=1}^{U} x_{t,u} \leq |\mathcal{U}|$. Federated Learning Training Accuracy Constraint:

$\forall t \in \mathcal{T}, \Gamma_t \geq \epsilon_0$, $\epsilon_0 \in (0,1]$ is the minimum model accuracy threshold. Total Bandwidth Allocation Constraint: $\forall t \in \mathcal{T}, \sum_{u \in I_t} b_{t,u} \leq B^{\text{total}}$. Time Constraint: $\forall t \in \mathcal{T}, T_t \leq T^{\text{limit}}$.

Problem $P0$ is a Mixed Integer Nonlinear Programming (MINLP) problem. Traditional optimization algorithms are inefficient in handling dynamic resource allocation problems and struggle to adapt to rapidly changing environments and complex, variable resource demands. In this paper, we employ a resource allocation optimization algorithm based on deep reinforcement learning, which effectively addresses dynamic environments within the federated learning framework and maximizes the AE gain.

# 4 FL-SQT Algorihtm

## 4.1 MDP

Deep reinforcement learning (DRL) addresses MDP problems by enabling agents to learn policy functions iteratively, maximize cumulative rewards, and adapt strategies autonomously [18]. In this work, each UAV acts as an independent agent interacting with the federated learning system. While multiple agents in competitive settings may reach local optima, these need not maximize global performance. To solve Problem $P0$, we reformulate the multi-agent scenario as a cooperative game and design a unified reward function to incentivize UAV collaboration and achieve system-wide objective optimization.

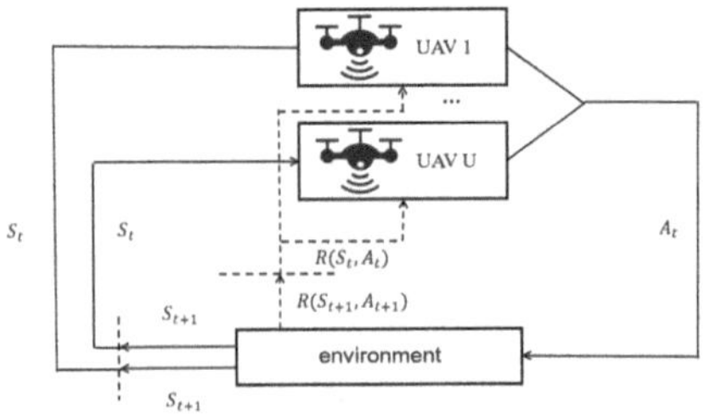


**Fig. 3.** Markov Decision Process model for Joint UAV selection and resource allocation.

In each federated learning round, every UAV acts as an agent, making distributed decisions on UAV selection and resource allocation to maximize the system's AE gain [20]. Thus, optimization problem $P0$ can be modeled as a MDP. Figure 3 illustrates the MDP for joint UAV selection and resource allocation in the federated learning system. The state space, action space, and reward function of the MDP are defined as follows:

State Space: MDPs often require discrete state representations. To obtain a discretized state space for the federated learning system [21], this paper assumes that in the federated learning system, the state space of each UAV in each training round is fixed, but the specific content differs. The state space designed in this paper includes: uplink/downlink channel estimates and their errors, dataset size, bandwidth allocation, and remaining battery energy. The state space for round t can be represented as:

$$S_t = \{ (\tilde{g}_{t,u}^{up}, e_{t,u}^{up}, \tilde{g}_{t,u}^{down}, e_{t,u}^{down}, |D_{t,u}|, b_{t,u}, E_{t,u}) \,|u \in \mathcal{U}\} \tag{13}$$

Action Space: The action space of the MDP consists of the UAV selection variables, the uplink transmission power of the UAVs, and the CPU frequency of the UAVs. The action space for round t can be represented as:

$$A_t = \{x_{t,u}, p_{t,u}^{up}, f_{t,u}|u \in \mathcal{U}\} \tag{14}$$

To address the issue of converting continuous neural network outputs to discrete UAV selection variables $x_{t,u}$ in the context of deep reinforcement learning, a common approach is to use a threshold-based method. Specifically, if the neural network output for a UAV is less than 0.5, the UAV is not selected ($x_{t,u}$=0); if the output is 0.5 or greater, the UAV is selected ($x_{t,u}$=1).

Reward: In this paper, the reward function is defined as the difference between training accuracy and weighted energy consumption to balance these two key metrics. Specifically, the immediate reward for round t is calculated as follows:

$$R(S_t, A_t) = \Gamma_t - \alpha \sum_{u \in I_t} E_{t,u}^{total} \tag{15}$$

## 4.2 SQT Framework

This paper employs the SQT framework to determine optimal actions. As illustrated in Fig. 4, the framework integrates a policy network, value network, agent, replay buffer, and environment. It utilizes the SQT algorithm for model training and decision-making [24], with the goal of maximizing the action-value function. Compared to other deep reinforcement learning algorithms, the SQT framework offers the following advantages:

*1)* The Deep Deterministic Policy Gradient (DDPG) algorithm is prone to overestimation bias, causing it to favor risky actions and impair performance [22]. SQT, built upon the Twin Delayed Deep Deterministic Policy Gradient (TD3) algorithm, employs multiple Q-networks to mitigate this bias.
*2)* While TD3 reduces overestimation via a double Q-network and minimum target selection, it can introduce underestimation bias [23]. SQT addresses this by incorporating the standard deviation of the Q-network as an uncertainty penalty term, correcting overestimation without significant underestimation and yielding more accurate value estimates.
*3)* Through its uncertainty penalty mechanism, SQT enables stable convergence to a near-optimal policy even in complex channel environments. This aligns well with fine-grained control of continuous resource parameters, making it highly suitable for solving problem P0 with continuous action spaces.

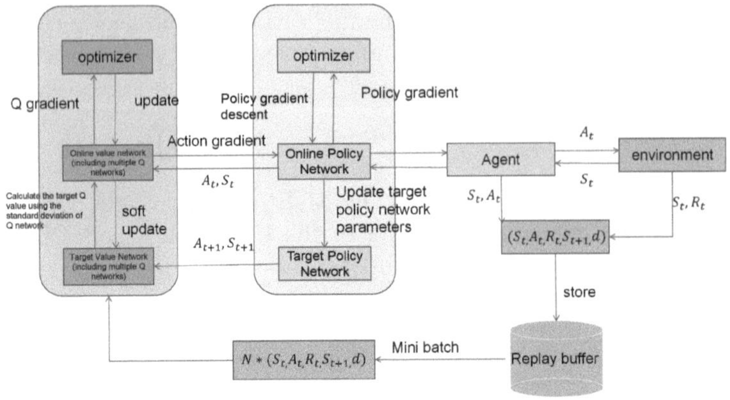


**Fig. 4.** SQT framework.

In the SQT framework, the policy network consists of an online network for model training and a target network to enhance stability by preventing data tampering. The framework utilizes the Deterministic Policy Gradient (DPG) to derive the optimal policy and output actions. Parameters of the online policy network are updated via policy gradient descent, improving both performance and training stability.

$$\theta^{\mu} \leftarrow \frac{1}{N} \sum_{S_t} [\nabla_{\theta^{\mu}}(\pi(S_t; \theta^{\mu})) \nabla_{A_t} Q(S_t, A_t; \theta^{q})]_{A_t = \pi(S_t; \theta^{\mu})} \tag{16}$$

Here, $\theta^{\mu}$ represents the parameters of the online policy network; $N$ is the batch size, and denotes the number of samples used for each update; $\theta^{q}$ is the parameter of the online value network; $\pi(S_t; \theta^{\mu})$ is the policy function; $Q(S_t, A_t; \theta^{q})$is the action-value function.

The value network in the SQT framework comprises multiple online and target Q-networks. By incorporating the standard deviation of these Q-networks as an uncertainty penalty, the algorithm quantifies estimation divergence and mitigates overestimation bias. Specifically, this penalty acts as a stabilizer: when Q-values exhibit high variability (large standard deviation), the target value is reduced. This discourages overoptimistic estimates and promotes more stable and reliable Q-value predictions, leading to reduced overestimation and more stable learning. The standard deviation is calculated as follows:

$$\mathrm{std}_{i=1\ldots n} Q_i(S_t, A_t) = \sqrt{\frac{1}{n} \sum_{i=1}^{n} \left( Q_i(S_t, A_t) - \frac{1}{n} \sum_{j=1}^{n} Q_j(S_t, A_t) \right)^2} \tag{17}$$

$$\mathrm{SQT}[B] = \frac{1}{|B|} \sum_{(S_t, A_t) \in B} \mathrm{std}_{i=1\ldots n} Q_i(S_t, A_t) \tag{18}$$

SQT[$B$] represents the average of the standard deviations of the Q-networks over the batch $B$. $B$ is a batch sampled from the experience replay buffer, containing multiple state-action pairs. $Q_i(S_t, A_t)$is the prediction value of the i-th Q-network for the state-action pair $(S_t, A_t)$. $n$ denotes the total number of Q-networks.

The core idea of the SQT algorithm is to incorporate the standard deviation of the Q-networks as an uncertainty penalty in the Q-target formula. Specifically, the Q-target formula for SQT is as follows:

$$y_t = R(S_t, A_t) + \gamma \mathcal{Q}[Q](S_{t+1}, \mu(S_{t+1}|\theta^q) - \text{sqt\_}\alpha \cdot \text{SQT}[B] \tag{19}$$

$y_t$ is the target Q-value, $R(S_t, A_t)$ is the immediate reward, which is the direct feedback of the action's effect and reflects the agent's performance in the current state. $\gamma \mathcal{Q}[Q](S_{t+1}, \mu(S_{t+1}|\theta^q)$ is the estimate of future rewards, $\mathcal{Q}$ is the ensemble-based Q-value operator. sqt_$\alpha$·SQT[$B$] is the uncertainty penalty term, and sqt_$\alpha$ is a penalty parameter between 0 and 1, controlling the strength of the uncertainty penalty.

### 4.3 Overview of FL-SQT Algorithm and Complexity Analysis

In federated learning implementation, to minimize energy consumption in dynamic environments while maintaining training accuracy, this paper proposes an algorithm named FL-SQT for joint drone selection and resource allocation.

The summary of the FL-SQT algorithm is presented in Algorithm 1, which mainly focuses on drone selection and resource allocation to achieve the training of the SQT network.

The FL-SQT algorithm updates policy and value network parameters based on the SQT method. To assess its computational efficiency, we analyze the complexity of both networks. The policy network has a complexity of $O((l_a - 1)n_a^2)$, where $l_a$ is the number of layers and $n_a$ the number of neurons per layer. The value network consists of $n$ independent sub-networks, each with $l_c$ layers and $n_c$ neurons, yielding a per-sub-network complexity of $O((l_c - 1)n_c^2)$ and total value network complexity of $O(n(l_c - 1)n_c^2)$. Over $T$ training rounds, the overall complexity of FL-SQT is $O(T[(l_a - 1)n_a^2 + n(l_c - 1)n_c^2])$.

## 5 Simulation and Analysis

### 5.1 Simulation Environment Settings

Table 1 provides the simulation basic parameters required for system calculations.

This paper implements FL-SQT in Python 3.8 with PyTorch, simulating a federated learning system comprising one server, 10 drones, and multiple devices. The server conducts 20 training rounds, each with 2,000 steps. For simplicity, both uplink and downlink channel estimates are modeled as Gaussian distributions with mean 0 and variance 1, while their estimation errors follow Gaussian distributions with mean 0 and variance 0.005.

**Algorithm 1.** FL-SQT Algorithm

Initialize the online policy network and the online value network, with parameters $\theta^{\mu}$ and $\theta^{q}$, respectively.
Initialize the target policy network and the target value network.
Initialize the experience replay buffer.
Initialize the discount factor $\gamma$, training rounds T, penalty parameter sqt_$\alpha$, update frequency $m$, update step size$\tau$, exploration noise, and noise range.
**for** t = 1 to T do **do**
  Reset the environment and initialize the state space $S_1$.
  Select action $A_t$ according to the online policy network and add exploration noise.
  The FL server sends the current global model to the selected UAVs based on action $A_t$, and allocates uplink transmission power $p_{t,u}^{up}$ and CPU power $f_{t,u}$.
  The selected UAVs train the local model and then upload it to the FL server.
  Calculate time, energy consumption, and training accuracy according to formulas 7,9 and 10
  Explore $n$ steps with a random strategy, obtain immediate reward $R(S_t, A_t)$, next state $S_{t+1}$, and termination flag $d$; finally, collect and store the $n$-step $(S_t, A_t, R(S_t, A_t), S_{t+1}, d)$ in the experience replay buffer.
  Sample a mini-batch from the experience replay buffer.
  Obtain target action: $A_{t+1} \leftarrow \pi(S_{t+1}, \theta^{\mu})$ + exploration noise.
  Calculate the target value function $Q(S_{t+1}, A_{t+1})$.
  Calculate the standard deviationSQT$[B]$.
  Obtain the target value $y_t$.
  Update $\theta^{q}$ according to the Bellman equation.
  $\frac{1}{N}\sum_{S_t}\left(Q(S_t, A_t, \theta^{q}) - y_t\right)^2$.
  **if** t mod m = 0 **then**
    Update $\theta^{\mu}$ using formula16.
    Update the target networks: $\theta^{\mu'} \leftarrow \tau\theta^{\mu} + (1-\tau)\theta^{\mu'}, \theta^{q'} \leftarrow \tau\theta^{q} + (1-\tau)\theta^{q'}$.
  **end if**
**end for**

The SQT hyperparameters are configured as follows: exploration noise standard deviation is 0.1 with a range of 0.5; experience replay buffer capacity is 10,000 with a batch size of 64; discount factor is 0.9; soft update step size $\tau = 0.005$; policy and value networks update every 2 steps; both networks use a learning rate of $1 \times 10^{-3}$; number of Q-networks is 5; and the uncertainty penalty coefficient sqt_$\alpha = 0.2$.

## 5.2 Algorithm Performance and Comparative Analysis

This paper compares the performance of the FL-SQT algorithm with the TD3 algorithm and the DDPG algorithm. Specifically, the common goal of these schemes is to maximize the AE gain. FL-DDPG employs the DDPG algorithm to train the network, while FL-TD3 utilizes the TD3 algorithm for training. Additionally, similar to FL-SQT, the perfect channel state information scheme uses

**Table 1.** Simulation Environment Settings

| Parameter | Mathematical Expression | Value |
|---|---|---|
| Energy Consumption Weight Coefficient | $\alpha$ | 0.0003 |
| Downlink Transmission Power | $p_{t,u}^{down}$ | [10,50] dBm |
| Minimum Uplink Transmission Power | $p_u^{\min}$ | 0.5 dBm |
| Maximum Uplink Transmission Power | $p_u^{\max}$ | 1.5 dBm |
| Minimum CPU Frequency | $f_u^{\min}$ | 2 GHz |
| Maximum CPU Frequency | $f_u^{\max}$ | 4 GHz |
| Dataset of UAV $u$ | $D_{t,u}$ | [1,10] MB |
| Single Round FL Training Duration | $T^{limit}$ | 45 s |
| Total Bandwidth | $B^{total}$ | 1000 MHz |
| Bandwidth Allocation | $\beta$ | [10,100] kHz |
| Global Model Size | $M_{global}$ | $2 \times 10^5$ bit |
| Local Model Size | $M_{local}$ | $6 \times 10^5$ bit |
| CPU Cycles per Bit | $c_u$ | 50 cycles/bit |
| Effective Capacity Coefficient | $\xi_u$ | $1 \times 10^{-26}$ |
| UAV Weight Coefficient | $\mu_u$ | $2.9 \times 10^{-9}$ |
| Initial Energy of UAV $u$ | $E_{1,u}$ | 800 kJ |
| UAV Selection Variable | $x_{t,u}$ | {0,1} |
| Gaussian Noise | $N_0$ | $1 \times 10^{-8}$ |
| Local training rounds | $L$ | 4 |

the SQT algorithm to train the network, that is, without considering channel errors ( $e_{t,u}^{up}$ and $e_{t,u}^{down}$ ).

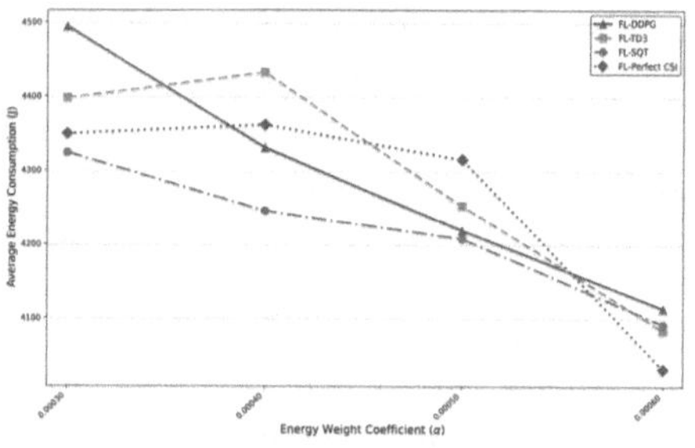


**Fig. 5.** Energy consumption comparison of various algorithms under different energy consumption weight coefficients.

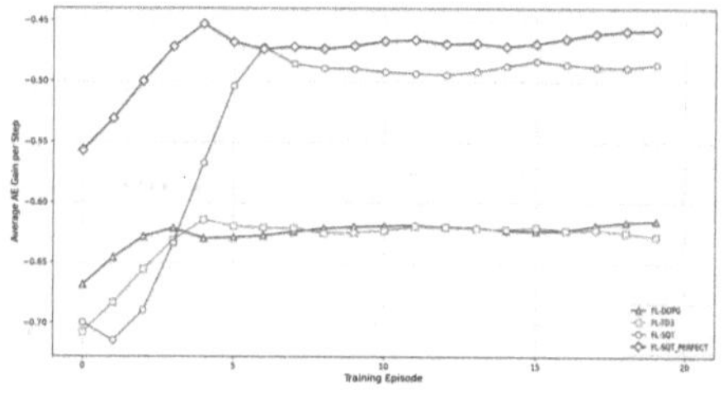


**Fig. 6.** Comparison of AE gains of different algorithms.

Figure 5 compares the energy consumption of various algorithms under different weight coefficients $\alpha$. As $\alpha$ increases, energy consumption decreases, indicating that the system prioritizes energy reduction over accuracy in the optimization objective. As $\alpha$ increases, the system tends to sacrifice some training accuracy in exchange for lower energy consumption, thereby achieving more efficient operation in resource-constrained environments. Overall, compared with the FL-TD3 and FL-DDPG algorithms, the proposed FL-SQT algorithm performs better in terms of energy consumption, achieving a lower level of energy consumption.

Figure 6 compares the AE gain of different algorithms when the energy consumption weight coefficient $\alpha = 0.003$. The proposed FL-SQT algorithm achieves higher AE gain than both FL-TD3 and FL-DDPG. While its performance is slightly lower than that of the perfect CSI scheme(Imperfect CSI can cause a chain reaction of decreased transmission rate, increased latency, and increased energy consumption, leading to a decrease in AE gain)FL-SQT still significantly outperforms the other methods. Overall, FL-SQT improves AE gain by 29.2% and 29% compared to FL-DDPG and FL-TD3, respectively.

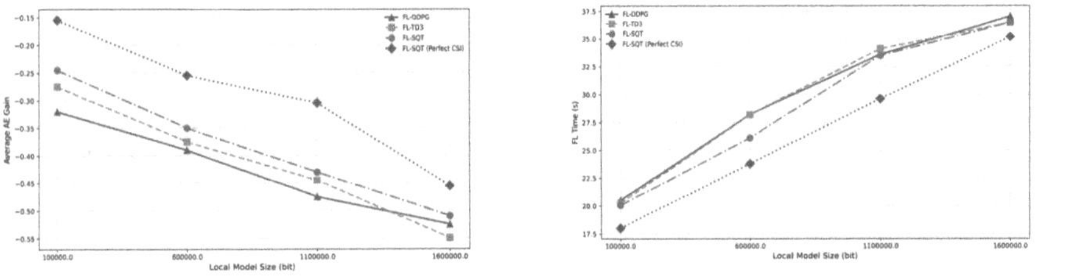


(a) Comparison of AE gains of various algorithms under different local model sizes

(b) Comparison of Federated Learning Time for Various Algorithms under different local model sizes

**Fig. 7.** Comparison of algorithms under different local model sizes.

Figure 7(a) and Fig. 7(b) illustrate the AE gain and federated learning time, respectively, of various algorithms under different local model sizes $M_{\text{local}}$ (from $1 \times 10^5$ to $16 \times 10^5$ bits) with energy consumption weight $\alpha = 0.003$. As $M_{\text{local}}$ increases, the AE gain gradually decreases due to the steep rise in energy consumption from uploading larger models. Concurrently, federated learning time per round increases owing to longer model upload times. Under the same $M_{\text{local}}$, FL-SQT achieves higher AE gain and maintains competitive learning time compared to FL-DDPG and FL-TD3, demonstrating its effectiveness in balancing energy consumption and accuracy through efficient resource management.

Figure 8(a) and Fig. 8(b) show the AE gain and federated learning time, respectively, of different algorithms under increasing dataset sizes $|D_{t,u}|$ (from 1MB to 10MB) with energy weight $\alpha = 0.003$. As $|D_{t,u}|$ grows, AE gain decreases across all algorithms due to the rapid increase in energy consumption from local training on larger datasets, which dominates the AE metric despite limited gains

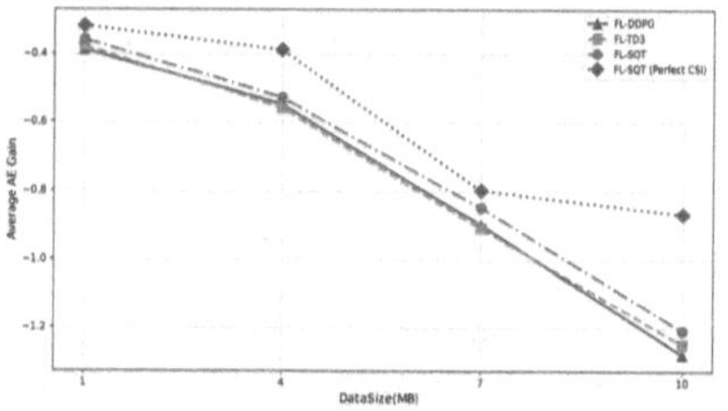


(a) Comparison of AE gains of various algorithms under different local dataset sizes

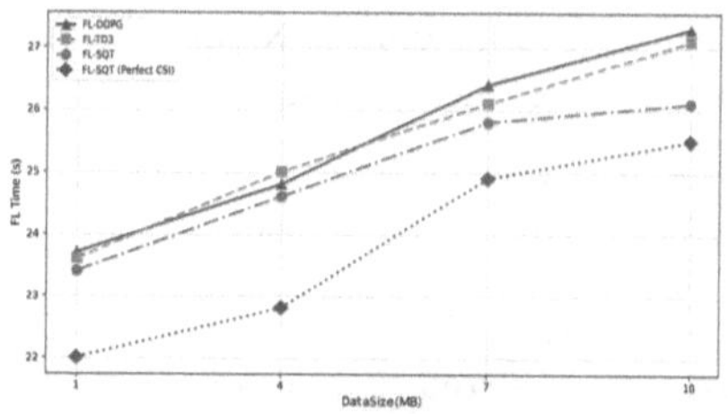


(b) Comparison of Federated Learning Time for Various Algorithms under different local dataset sizes

**Fig. 8.** Comparison of algorithms under different local dataset sizes.

in accuracy. Correspondingly, federated learning time also rises as more time is required for local model training. The proposed FL-SQT algorithm achieves the highest AE gain (excluding perfect channel conditions), demonstrating its effectiveness in balancing energy and accuracy under varying data volumes.

**Table 2.** Success Rates Of Different Algorithms

| $T_{\text{limit}}$ (s) | 10 | 15 | 20 | 25 | 30 |
|---|---|---|---|---|---|
| FL-DDPG | 0.0785 | 0.287 | 0.4905 | 0.597 | 0.6765 |
| FL-TD3 | 0.061 | 0.2635 | 0.4745 | 0.6005 | 0.689 |
| FL-SQT | 0.083 | 0.314 | 0.4905 | 0.606 | 0.694 |
| Perfect CSI | 0.157 | 0.515 | 0.562 | 0.7065 | 0.738 |

To further evaluate the robustness of FL-SQT under imperfect CSI, Table 2 presents its success rate under varying delay constraints. A round is considered successful if completed within the delay limit $T_{\text{limit}}$. As $T_{\text{limit}}$ increases, the success rate rises accordingly, owing to the more relaxed time constraint. Without perfect CSI, FL-SQT achieves the highest overall success rate, outperforming FL-DDPG and FL-TD3 by 1.36% and 1.98%, respectively.

## 6 Conclusion

This paper proposes an FL-SQT algorithm for dynamic resource management in UAV-assisted MEC systems to address resource constraints and imperfect CSI. By formulating a Markov decision process for joint UAV selection, power, and computational resource allocation, and employing the SQT framework for online policy optimization, simulations demonstrate that the proposed method outperforms traditional deep reinforcement learning approaches in both task success rate and AE gain. Future work will focus on validating and refining the algorithm in more complex channel models, end-to-end resource scheduling, and real-world edge networks.

## References


1. Cui, J., Wei, Y., Wang, J., et al.: Joint trajectory design and resource allocation for UAV-assisted mobile edge computing in power convergence network. EURASIP J. Wirel. Commun. Netw. **2025**(1), 4 (2025)
2. Albshaier, L., Almarri, S., Albuali, A.: Federated learning for cloud and edge security: a systematic review of challenges and AI opportunities. Electronics **14**(5), 1019 (2025)
3. Liu, J., Zhang, H.: Outage-aware deployment in multi-UAV-RIS aided networks with imperfect CSI. IEEE Trans. Commun. (2025)
4. Chen, X., Zhou, X., Zhang, H., et al.: Client selection for wireless federated learning with data and latency heterogeneity. IEEE Internet Things J. (2024)
5. Nishio, T., Yonetani, R.: Client selection for federated learning with heterogeneous resources in mobile edge. In: ICC 2019-2019 IEEE International Conference on Communications (ICC), pp. 1–7. IEEE (2019)
6. Li, Q., Miao, J., Zhao, P., et al.: Emulating full client participation: a long-term client selection strategy for federated learning. arXiv preprint arXiv:2405.13584 (2024)
7. Ju, Z., Wei, T., Shen, F.: BEFL: balancing energy consumption in federated learning for mobile edge IoT. arXiv preprint arXiv:2412.03950 (2024)
8. Mehboob, T., Bashir, N., Iglesias, J.O., et al.: CEFL: carbon-efficient federated learning. arXiv preprint arXiv:2310.17972 (2023)
9. Song, Z., Ma, C., Ding, M., et al.: Personalized federated deep reinforcement learning-based trajectory optimization for multi-UAV assisted edge computing. In: 2023 IEEE/CIC International Conference on Communications in China (ICCC), pp. 1–6. IEEE (2023)
10. Wu, Q., Zeng, Y., Zhang, R.: Joint trajectory and communication design for multi-UAV enabled wireless networks. IEEE Trans. Wirel. Commun. **17**(3), 2109–2121 (2018)
11. Peng, H., Shen, X.: Multi-agent reinforcement learning based resource management in MEC-and UAV-assisted vehicular networks. IEEE J. Sel. Areas Commun. **39**(1), 131–141 (2020)
12. Hoang, L.T., Nguyen, C.T., Pham, A.T.: Deep reinforcement learning-based online resource management for UAV-assisted edge computing with dual connectivity. IEEE/ACM Trans. Network. **31**(6), 2761–2776 (2023)
13. Zhong, S., Wang, L., Wu, W., Feng, L.: Joint client selection and resource allocation for federated edge learning with imperfect CSI. Comput. Netw. **257**, 110914 (2025). https://doi.org/10.1016/j.comnet.2024.110914
14. Wang, J., Feng, D., Zhang, S., et al.: Joint computation offloading and resource allocation for MEC-enabled IoT systems with imperfect CSI. IEEE Internet Things J. **8**(5), 3462–3475 (2020)
15. Wu, B., Fang, F., Wang, X., et al.: Client selection and cost-efficient joint optimization for NOMA-enabled hierarchical federated learning. IEEE Trans. Wirel. Commun. **23**(10), 14289–14303 (2024)
16. Khan, L.U., Pandey, S.R., Tran, N.H., et al.: Federated learning for edge networks: resource optimization and incentive mechanism. IEEE Commun. Mag. **58**(10), 88–93 (2020)

17. Zhou, S., Feng, L., Mei, M., et al.: Dynamic resource management for federated edge learning with imperfect CSI: a deep reinforcement learning approach. IEEE Internet Things J. (2024)
18. Gao, Q., Schweidtmann, A.M.: Deep reinforcement learning for process design: review and perspective. Curr. Opin. Chem. Eng. **44**, 101012 (2024)
19. Pollack, M., Steimle, L.N.: The implications of state aggregation in deteriorating Markov Decision Processes with optimal threshold policies. arXiv preprint arXiv:2405.12912 (2024)
20. Zhao, N., Pei, Y., Liang, Y.C., et al.: Multi-agent deep reinforcement learning based incentive mechanism for multi-task federated edge learning. IEEE Trans. Veh. Technol. **72**(10), 13530–13535 (2023)
21. Zheng, J., Li, K., Mhaisen, N., et al.: Exploring deep-reinforcement-learning-assisted federated learning for online resource allocation in privacy-preserving EdgeIoT. IEEE Internet Things J. **9**(21), 21099–21110 (2022)
22. Hwang, U., Hong, S.: Moderate actor-critic methods: controlling overestimation bias via expectile loss. arXiv preprint arXiv:2504.09929 (2025)
23. Ren, Z., Zhu, G., Hu, H., et al.: On the estimation bias in double q-learning. Adv. Neural. Inf. Process. Syst. **34**, 10246–10259 (2021)
24. Soffair, N., Di-Castro, D., Avner, O., et al.: SQT–std $Q$-target. arXiv preprint arXiv:2402.05950 (2024)

# Breaking Information Barriers in Edge Computing: Financing Contracts with Double Asymmetries

Zirun Zhou, Chunxia Su(✉), Jichong Guo, and Zhenping Chen

Suzhou University of Science and Technology, Suzhou 215009, China
suchunxia33@163.com, guojichong@usts.edu.cn

**Abstract.** In edge computing networks, computing service providers (SP) face the issue of insufficient computational power. Consequently, they must offload computing tasks to edge computing nodes (ECNs). ECNs are owned by third parties, leading to information asymmetry between SP and ECNs. This paper aims to incentivize the participation of ECNs in task offloading and to maximize the expected payoff for the SP. This is addressed through the design of an optimal financing contract based on contract theory and an exploration of its incentive mechanisms. Firstly, a model leveraging adverse selection and moral hazard is established. While taking account of incentive compatibility (IC) and individual rationality (IR), this paper aims to maximize the expected payoff of SP. Finally, the optimal financing contract is solved using the Lagrange multiplier method, and the rationality and feasibility of the contract are simulated and verified.

**Keywords:** task offloading · contract theory · financing contract · Lagrange multiplier method

## 1 Introduction

The development of 5G networks leads to a proliferation of terminals that require computational capabilities. The terminals generate a large amount of data that needs to be processed. However, their computation resource and battery life are limited due to the constrained size and cost. Thus, they need to offload these tasks to a more capable computing entity. The cloud possesses a large number of CPUs [1] and is well suited for large-scale data processing [2]. Therefore, it is a common approach to offload computing tasks to the cloud. However, a major disadvantage of cloud computing [3] is its high latency, as it is located far from the terminal. At this time, latency-sensitive tasks such as autonomous car driving, AR real-time rendering, and drone swarm formation require

The work was supported in part by the Natural Science Foundation of the Higher Education Institutions of Jiangsu Province, China, under Grant 23KJB520035 and Grant 23KJB510031; and in part by the Suzhou Science and Technology Plan (Basic Research) Project, under Grant SJC2023002.


Y. Liu et al. (Eds.): ChinaCom 2025, LNICST 711, pp. 394–408, 2027.
https://doi.org/10.1007/978-3-032-33662-0_29

extremely low latency, which obviously cannot be met by cloud servers. Although the computing power of the edge server is weaker than that of the cloud server, it is closer to the terminal, and the end-to-end latency can be controlled at the millisecond level. Under all considerations, the terminal will choose to offload the computing task to the edge server [4, 5].

As mentioned earlier, edge servers benefit from low latency. However, they are constrained by deployment density and hardware costs. These limitations can lead to instantaneous overload. To address this issue, edge servers choose to collaborate with ECNs [6]. It is important to clarify that edge servers are deployed by SP, while ECNs like smart home gateways and charging station computing devices are owned by individuals or third-party enterprises. Although both belong to edge nodes, they are discussed as two separate concepts due to ownership issues.

Since ECNs are owned by third parties, they lack the inherent incentive to proactively complete offloaded tasks to the best of their abilities when collaborating with the SP. Meanwhile, SP needs to utilize ECNs' computing resources to carry out terminal offloaded computing tasks in order to receive payoff. This creates a conflict [7] of interest between the two: On one hand, the SP must offload tasks to capable ECNs due to its own insufficient computing power, aiming for rational resource utilization. On the other hand, it must allocate the remuneration fairly to maximize its returns while incentivizing the ECNs.

The design of this incentive mechanism based on voluntary resource contributions has been recognized as a key research direction in the field of edge computing at present [8]. Nakyoung Kim et al. [9] propose an innovative coded distributed computing (DC) mechanism to complete computing task offloading, aiming to reduce computational latency in Internet of Things (IoT) services through incentives and coding techniques. Ke Zhang et al. [10] propose a vehicle edge computing task offloading scheme based on contract theory to solve the problem of edge server resource allocation and service pricing by designing optimal contract combinations. Hongzhi Guo et al. [11] propose an intelligent task offloading scheme based on machine learning to solve the computing task allocation problem of mobile devices in the edge computing environment through decision tree algorithms. However, these examples are based on the assumption of perfect information between the SP and ECNs. As mentioned earlier, since ECNs are owned by third parties, this assumption does not hold in practice.

To solve this interest game with information asymmetry [13], this paper employs contract theory. This approach designs rational financing contracts based on the principles of incentive compatibility and individual rationality. This design ensures that the SP and ECNs can complete computational tasks fairly and effectively. The model is solved using the Lagrange multiplier method, and the resulting contract parameters—along with the expected utilities of the SP and ECNs—are simulated. These simulations are analyzed to study the incentive mechanisms of the parameters, with the goal of validating their rationality and adaptability in realistic scenarios.

## 2 System Model and Problem Formulation

### 2.1 Financing Contract

This paper introduces a non-cash auction model tailored for the transaction of computational task execution rights in edge computing networks. The core innovation lies in its incorporation of financing contracts, which effectively mitigate long-standing issues stemming from information asymmetry—notably the inefficient completion of computing tasks and the inequitable distribution of rewards among participants. As depicted in Fig. 1, the system model consists of three key entities: Service Providers, Edge Computing Nodes, and terminal devices. SP may encounter scenarios where a sudden influx of compute-intensive tasks from terminals risks overwhelming the edge server's CPU capacity. In response, the SP proactively issues a financing contract to offload part of the computational workload. While this appears to be a simple allocation of execution rights due to insufficient resources, the underlying incentives are more complex. ECNs, serving as independent third-party computing providers, are not concerned with the SP's actual reasons for offloading. Their focus is purely on whether accepting and executing these tasks will result in adequate compensation. Reconciling the differing objectives and strategic behaviors in this multi-stakeholder environment poses a significant challenge. The proposed financing contract, however, serves as a strategic tool to align interests, reduce conflicts, and ensure a fair and efficient distribution of benefits for all parties involved.

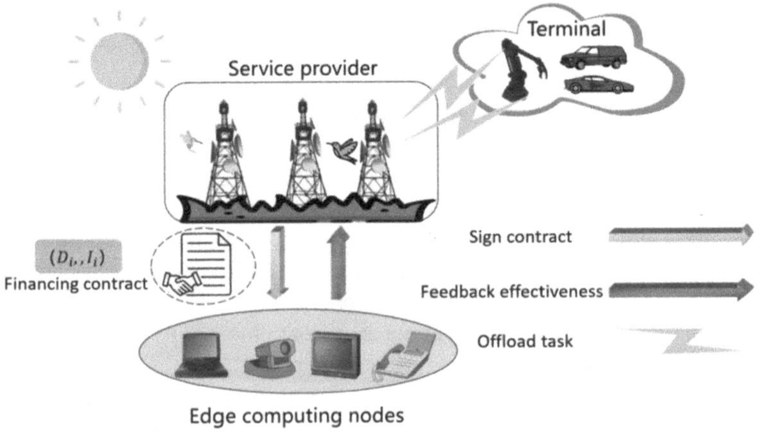


**Fig. 1.** Operational framework of financing-based task offloading in edge computing networks

SP issues a series of financing contracts denoted as $(D_i, I_i)$ for ECNs to select from. Upon signing a contract, an ECN obtains the right to execute the computational task. $D_i$ denotes the down payment that ECNs need to pay immediately after choosing the $i$-th contract. $I_i$ represents the future installment, which is a single lump-sum payment to be made at a later date. By signing a financing contract, an ECN gains the right to execute a computational task by paying a partial down payment. The contract stipulates that upon successful task completion, the ECN will receive the full remuneration from the terminal. A portion of the remuneration received from the terminal can then be allocated by the ECN to pay the subsequent installments. This feature of the financing contract overcomes the drawbacks of traditional non-cash auction transactions. Furthermore, it not only prevents the loss of potential customers who lack sufficient funds to trade but also enhances the motivation of ECNs. Thus, ECNs can actively and efficiently complete computing tasks.

In this paper, the following conditions are assumed. 1. The propagation delay in the process of unloading the computing task is negligible compared to the computational delay. 2. Due to the difference in the computational complexity of various computational tasks, the task amount of the computational task has been specified as a fixed value. Based on the above assumptions, the computational delay model is established as follows

$$T_i = \frac{X_i}{\varepsilon_i {}^* f_i}, \tag{1}$$

where $X_i$ represents the amount of computing tasks assigned by the SP to the ECN when an ECN signs the $i$-th contract with the SP. $f_i$ represents the CPU resources contributed by the ECN of the $i$-th contract to complete the computing task as promised. $\varepsilon_i$ represents the actual contribution ratio of the ECN signed the $i$-th contract. This parameter is influenced by multiple factors. For instance, a contracted ECN may reduce its resource commitment to the task—such as lowering output power or allocating less CPU space—if it becomes occupied with its own computational workloads, or in cases where hardware failure occurs and is not promptly repaired.

In this model, the computational task amount is assumed to be identical for each contract; consequently, the revenue (denoted as R) obtained from the terminal is the same for every ECN. For ECNs to be able to pay off subsequent instalments, $R \geq I_i \geq 0$ is required without violating the provisions of the financing contract. If an ECN fails to complete the computational task, it cannot receive revenue from the terminal or afford the installments of the financing contract. This situation is considered a default, resulting in a net return of zero without considering the down payment. If an ECN completes the computational task, it receives all the revenue from the terminal. Its net return is R - $I_i$ without considering the down payment. In summary, the income of ECNs is $P \in \{0, R - I_i\}$ without considering the down payment.

Therefore, for the normal progress of the contract, ECNs need to be able to successfully complete the calculation task. The threshold for the latency requirement of completing computational tasks is unknown. Specifically, it is unclear how much the latency needs to be reduced to satisfy $T_i < T_{\min}$. However, it is certain that lower computational latency is always better. When the computational latency is sufficiently low, the task can definitely be completed. In the case of a fixed amount of calculation tasks, only two parameters, $\varepsilon_i$ and $f_i$, can affect the calculation delay $T_i$, which we will interpret in the following two models.

## 2.2 Adverse Selection

Adverse selection problem [14] is a typical problem caused by information asymmetry in contract theory, which usually appears before the contract is signed. When an SP signs a contract with ECNs, it typically possesses a clear understanding of the computing tasks to be offloaded, including their relative importance and complexity. However, the SP lacks accurate information about the ECNs themselves. SP does not know which ECNs have more computing power and are more capable of completing the computational tasks that are offloaded to them. As the party that obtains the right to execute tasks, ECNs know their computing power better, but do not understand what computing tasks are more valuable.

This information asymmetry leads to a key problem: since ECNs may inflate computing power to obtain low-priced tasks, SP needs to establish a scientific ECN classification mechanism to screen reliable nodes. Based on this, the computational delay formula indicates that, given a constant actual contribution rate, an increase in $f_i$ leads to a decrease in the computational delay and a higher probability of task completion. Consequently, we define the type of $\mathrm{ECN}_i$ as $\theta_i$. This variable is related to $f_i$ and satisfies

$$\theta_1 < \theta_2 < \ldots < \theta_i < \ldots < \theta_n. \tag{2}$$

In this way, SP classify the type of ECNs according to the CPU prior contributed by completing the compute task, and $\theta \in \{\theta_1, \theta_2, \ldots, \theta_i, \ldots, \theta_n\}$. However, the contributed CPU resources may be misrepresented, making it impossible to accurately determine each ECN's computing power type. Therefore, the SP can only presumptively assume that the probability of an ECN belonging to type $\theta_i$ is $\alpha_i$. This probability satisfies the constraint as follows

$$\sum_{i=1}^{n} \alpha_i = 1. \tag{3}$$

Thus, information asymmetry leads to an adverse selection problem. To mitigate this issue, the SP applies contract theory to design a series of distinct financing contracts corresponding to different ECN types. This approach enables the ECNs to self-select into appropriate contracts.

In the case of adverse selection, ECNs as the information advantaged party, tend to choose contract terms that are most beneficial to themselves, which can prevent SPs from maximizing their expected payoff. At this point, the clever design of financing contracts effectively resolves this dilemma. Financing contracts achieve automatic separation of types of ECNs through differentiated terms: high-capacity but cash-strapped ECNs will choose "low down payment, high installment" financing contracts, while low-capacity ECNs will choose "high down payment, low installment" financing contracts. This design not only ensures the participation possibilities of different types of ECNs but also enables effective screening under conditions of information asymmetry. However, it should be pointed out that this selection method only considers the adverse selection problem and has a one-sided perspective in real scenarios, thus introducing the need for moral hazard issues as a joint constraint.

## 2.3 Moral Hazard

The problem of moral hazard [14] is also a typical problem caused by information asymmetry in contract theory, which occurs after the contract is signed. When SP signs a financing contract with ECNs, it will face a huge problem: how to make ECNs always contribute high CPU resources to complete computing tasks.

Since the execution rights of the computational tasks were transferred to the ECNs upon contract signing, the SP cannot monitor them in real time. Consequently, the SP cannot determine whether the ECNs will engage in shirking behavior. If ECNs engage in resource diversion by reallocating CPU resources to other tasks, they compromise their terminal delivery commitments. This significantly reduces the probability of task completion. This failure directly impacts the SP's expected payoff and jeopardizes the ECN's ability to repay its installments.

To address the issue of moral hazard, SP will implement a series of measures. These measures are designed to either incentivize or penalize ECNs. The goal is to encourage ECNs to sustain a high level of CPU resource contribution. This ensures the successful completion of terminal computing tasks. Here, the behavior of ECNs maintaining high CPU resource contribution needs to be defined as the degree of effort, denoted by $e$. The ECNs need to consume the corresponding computing cost $\Psi$ to complete the computing task. The computing cost $\Psi$ is the convex function of the degree of effort $e$, i.e.,

$$\psi(e) = \frac{\eta}{2}^* e^2. \tag{4}$$

In the equation, $\psi(e)$ represents the computational cost consumed by ECNs to complete the computational task. Since only one variable exists in the equation, this cost is ultimately determined by $e$. $\eta$ represents the computational cost coefficient. As the decisive coefficient for computational cost, its magnitude determines the extent of change induced by variations in the degree of effort. $e$ represents the degree of effort made by ECNs to maintain a high CPU resource contribution. It is related to the $\varepsilon_i$ in the Eq. (1). Additionally, the actual contribution rate of ECNs increases when the level of effort is higher. Furthermore, it can be seen from the cost function calculation that the two are in a quadratic relationship; when $e$ increases, the computation cost rises sharply in a quadratic manner.

Next, the key part of the design in this section is to maintain the balance between $e$ in compliance with financing contracts and the net income of ECNs. Section 2.1 discusses the scenario where ECNs fail to complete computational tasks. This failure means that no income is received, which is considered a breach of contract. Consequently, the SP will terminate the contract, resulting in the ECNs losing their down payment as a form of punishment. Under this constraint, ECNs are compelled to maintain their effort level as high as possible. However, on the other hand, if $e$ is high enough to make computational costs excessive, it will lead to negative net income for ECNs, and thus ECNs will lack the motivation to engage in the task. Therefore, the issue of moral hazard needs to be addressed with the help of individual rationality constraints. Finally, adjust the financing contract parameters by jointly considering adverse selection and moral hazard issues.

## 2.4 Optimization Goals

The ultimate goal of financing contract design is to maximize the SP's payoff. Therefore, the objective function for the optimization problem is the SP's payoff. The payoff of SP comes from the down payment and installments of ECNs, so it needs to get the income function of ECNs first.

From Eq. (1), it can be seen that a larger $\varepsilon_i{}^*f_i$ leads to a shorter time for ECNs to complete the computational task. Once a specific threshold is reached, the terminal task is considered completed, and the remuneration is obtained. Because $\theta_i$ is related to $f_i$, $e_i$ is related to $\varepsilon_i$, so $\theta_i{}^*e_i$ is related to $\varepsilon_i{}^*f_i$. Therefore, the success probability of an ECN completing the calculation task is defined here as $\theta_i{}^*e_i \in (0, 1)$, as shown in Table 1.

**Table 1.** Expected income

| ECNs completed task earnings | Probability of occurrence | Expected return |
|---|---|---|
| 0 | $1 - \theta_i{}^*e_i$ | $(1 - \theta_i{}^*e_i) * 0$ |
| $\mathrm{R} - I_i$ | $\theta_i{}^*e_i$ | $(\theta_i{}^*e_i) * (\mathrm{R} - I_i)$ |

According to Table 1, the expected returns of $\mathrm{ECN}_i$ can be obtained by

$$\theta_i e_i{}^*(\mathrm{R} - I_i) + (1 - \theta_i e_i) * 0 = \theta_i e_i{}^*(\mathrm{R} - I_i), i \in \{1, 2, \ldots, n\}. \tag{5}$$

The final payoff for $\mathrm{ECN}_i$ is derived by recombining Eqs. (4, 5)as follows

$$U_{\mathrm{ECN}_i} = \theta_i e_i{}^*(\mathrm{R} - I_i) - D_i - \frac{\eta}{2}e_i^2, i \in \{1, 2, \ldots, n\}. \tag{6}$$

Therefore, the installment paid to SP by different types of ECNs is $\theta_i e_i{}^*I_i$. Given that the SP's prior belief that ECN is of type $\theta_i$ is $\alpha_i$, the final payoff for the SP is derived as follows

$$U_{\mathrm{SP}} = \sum_{i=1}^{n}\left[\alpha_i{}^*\left(\theta_i e_i{}^*I_i + D_i\right)\right] - \mathrm{c}. \tag{7}$$

That is, the optimization goal can be denoted by

$$\max_{(D_i, I_i)}\left\{\sum_{i=1}^{n}\left[\alpha_i{}^*\left(\theta_i e_i{}^*I_i + D_i\right)\right] - \mathrm{c}\right\}. \tag{8}$$

Where c denotes the rental fee charged by the SP for trading computational task execution rights with ECNs. Its value is fixed. Meanwhile, $D_i$ and $I_i$ constitute the two sets of decision variables to be optimized.

### 2.5 Core Constraints of Contract Design

#### 2.5.1 Incentive Compatibility Constraints

In Sect. 2.2, it is mentioned that ECNs choose the appropriate financing contract according to their own type. In fact, the fundamental reason for achieving this behavior lies in the incentive compatibility constraint: The constraint ensures that ECNs choose the contracts most aligned with their own conditions. The selection results in the maximization of their expected payoff. This resulting value is clearly superior to that of any other contractual alternative, i.e.,

$$\theta_i e_i(\text{R-}I_i) - D_i - \frac{\eta}{2}e_i^2 \geq \theta_i e_i'(\text{R} - I_j) - D_j - \frac{\eta}{2}{e'}^2{}_i, \quad \forall j \neq i, i, j \in \{1, 2, \ldots, n\} \tag{9}$$

where $e_i'$ represents the level of effort required by the ECN to enter into a financing contract that does not conform to its type.

### 2.5.2 Individual Rationality Constraints

In Sect. 2.3, it is mentioned that the balance between $e$'s compliance with financing contracts and the net income of ECNs is fundamentally achieved by individual rationality constraints: This constraint ensures that each ECN obtains at least zero benefit from its selected contract. This provision guarantees that ECNs have sufficient incentive to sustain the contract, i.e.,

$$\theta_i e_i * (\text{R} - I_i) - D_i - \frac{\eta}{2}e_i^2 \geq 0, i \in \{1, 2, \ldots, n\}. \tag{10}$$

# 3 Solution of Optimal Contracts

## 3.1 Construction of Recursive Relationship under Multi-Stage Constraints

Sections 2.4 and 2.5 illustrate the objective function and constraints for solving the optimal financing contract, i.e.,

$$\max_{(D_i, I_i)} \left\{ \sum_{i=1}^{n} [\alpha_i * (\theta_i e_i * I_i + D_i)] - \text{c} \right\}, \tag{11}$$

$$\begin{cases} (\text{IC}) : \theta_i e_i{}^*(\text{R-}I_i) - D_i - \frac{\eta}{2}e_i^2 \geq \theta_i e_i^{,*}(\text{R-}I_j) - D_j - \frac{\eta}{2}e_i^{,2} \\ (\text{IR}) : \theta_i e_i{}^*(\text{R-}I_i) - D_i - \frac{\eta}{2}e_i^2 \geq 0, \forall j \neq i, i, j \in \{1, 2, \ldots, n\} \end{cases}. \tag{12}$$

The presence of only adverse selection or only moral hazard constitutes two distinct extreme scenarios. In reality, both situations usually occur at the same time. Therefore, both must be considered together during the solution process.

By taking the derivative of the function of the final net income for ECNs with respect to $e$, the optimal effort degree of ECNs can be obtained by

$$e_i^* = \frac{1}{\eta}^* \theta_i{}^*(\text{R} - I_i), i \in \{1, \ldots, n\}. \tag{13}$$

The optimal effort level is only reached when an ECN picks a contract that matches its true type. If it lies about its type to choose a different contract, it needs to pay different down payments and installments. But its real type does not change, i.e.,

$$e_i^{,*} = \frac{1}{\eta}^* \theta_i{}^*(\text{R} - I_j), \forall j \neq i, i, j \in \{1, 2, \ldots, n\}. \tag{14}$$

At this time, the optimal degree of effort under different situations is obtained, and the Eqs. (13, 14) can be substituted into the Eqs. (11, 12) as follows

$$\max_{(D_i,I_i)}\left\{\sum_{i=1}^{n}\left[\alpha_i{}^*\left(\frac{1}{\eta}\theta_i^2 I_i(\mathrm{R}-I_i)+D_i\right)\right]-\mathrm{c}\right\}, \tag{15}$$

$$\begin{cases}(\mathrm{IC}):\frac{1}{2\eta}\theta_i^2(\mathrm{R}-I_i)^2-D_i\geq\frac{1}{2\eta}\theta_i^2\left(\mathrm{R}-I_j\right)^2-D_j\\(\mathrm{IR}):\frac{1}{2\eta}\theta_i^2(\mathrm{R}-I_i)^2-D_i\geq 0,\forall j\neq i,i,j\in\{1,2,\ldots,n\}\end{cases}. \tag{16}$$

According to Eq. (16), the number of cases where ECNs choose financing contracts inconsistent with their own types is excessively high. This issue can be resolved through contract theory by implementing the local downward IC constraint and imposing the IR constraint only for the $\theta_1$ condition. The reasons are as follows:

1. According to contract theory [12, 15], the monotonicity of type ordering in Eq. (2) implies that a high-ability ECN may benefit from mimicking a low-ability one, whereas the reverse is not true. Consequently, only the constraints that prevent each type from mimicking its adjacent lower type need to be considered.
2. The SP's objective is to maximize its expected payoff. When the individual rationality constraint is greater than zero, the SP can gradually reduce the IR value until it equals zero. This reduction is achieved by readjusting the down payment and installment parameters while keeping all incentive compatibility constraints unchanged. The adjustment process continues until the SP's payoff is optimized. In this equilibrium state, the payoff of the lowest-type ECN is fully squeezed to zero. Therefore, only this boundary condition needs to be satisfied to attain the SP's optimal solution.

Based on the above analysis, it can be obtained by

$$\max_{(D_i,I_i)}\left\{\sum_{i=1}^{n}\left[\alpha_i{}^*\left(\frac{1}{\eta}\theta_i^2 I_i(\mathrm{R}-I_i)+D\right)\right]-\mathrm{c}\right\}, \tag{17}$$

$$\begin{cases}(\mathrm{IC}):\frac{1}{2\eta}\theta_i^2(\mathrm{R}-I_i)^2-D_i=\frac{1}{2\eta}\theta_i^2(\mathrm{R}-I_{i-1})^2-D_{i-1}\\(\mathrm{IR}):\frac{1}{2\eta}\theta_1^2(\mathrm{R}-I_1)^2-D_1=0,i\in\{2,\ldots,n\}\end{cases}. \tag{18}$$

## 3.2 Optimal Solution Analysis Based on Lagrange Multiplier Method

This optimization problem is solved using Lagrangian multiplier method, with $u_i$ and $v$ as the Lagrangian multipliers. From the objective function and constraints, the Lagrangian equation is derived as follows

$$\begin{aligned}\kappa=&\sum_{i=1}^{n}\left\{\alpha_i{}^*\left[\frac{1}{\eta}\theta_i^2 I_i(\mathrm{R}-I_i)+D_i\right]\right\}-\mathrm{c}+v^*\left\{\frac{1}{2\eta}[\theta_1(\mathrm{R}-I_1)]^2-D_1\right\}\\&+u_i{}^*\left\{\frac{1}{2\eta}[\theta_i(\mathrm{R}-I_i)]^2-\frac{1}{2\eta}\left[\theta_i(\mathrm{R}-I_{i-1})\right]^2+D_{i-1}-D_i\right\}.\end{aligned} \tag{19}$$

With $\frac{d\kappa}{dD_i} = 0$, the solution is derived by classifying cases according to the value of $i$, as follows

$$\begin{cases} \alpha_n = u_n, i = n \\ \alpha_1 = v - u_2, i = 1 \\ \alpha_i = u_i - u_{i+1}, i \in \{2, \ldots, n-1\}. \end{cases} \quad (20)$$

With $\frac{d\kappa}{dI_i} = 0$, the solution is derived by classifying cases according to the value of $i$, as follows

$$\begin{cases} \alpha_n(\mathrm{R} - 2I_n) = -u_n(-\mathrm{R} + I_n), i = n \\ \alpha_1\theta_1^2(\mathrm{R} - 2I_1) = \left(v\theta_1^2 - u_2\theta_2^2\right)(\mathrm{R} - I_1), i = 1 \\ \alpha_i\theta_i^2(\mathrm{R} - 2I_i) = \left(u_i\theta_i^2 - u_{i+1}\theta_{i+1}^2\right)(\mathrm{R} - I_i), i \in \{2, \ldots, n-1\}. \end{cases} \quad (21)$$

Substitution of Eq. (20) into Eq. (21) yields the result as follows,

$$\begin{cases} I_i = 0, i = n \\ I_i = \frac{(u_{i+1}\theta_{i+1}^2 - u_{i+1}\theta_i^2) * \mathrm{R}}{\alpha_i\theta_i^2 + u_{i+1}\theta_{i+1}^2 - u_{i+1}\theta_i^2}, i = \{1, \ldots, n-1\}. \end{cases} \quad (22)$$

Finally, according to the incentive compatibility constraint and the individual rational constraint in Eq. (18), the expression of the decision variable $D_i$ can be obtained by

$$\begin{cases} D_i = \frac{1}{2\eta}\theta_i^2(\mathrm{R} - I_i)^2, i = 1 \\ D_i = \frac{1}{2\eta}\theta_i^2(\mathrm{R} - I_i)^2 - \frac{1}{2\eta}\theta_i^2(\mathrm{R} - I_{i-1})^2 + D_{i-1}, i = \{2, \ldots, n\}. \end{cases} \quad (23)$$

As shown in Eqs (22, 23), when the moral hazard problem is addressed first and the effort level is optimized, the adverse selection problem becomes the primary factor influencing the decision variables. Within the adverse selection framework, both the types of ECNs and their prior probabilities cause variations in these variables. This relationship demonstrates the inherent connection between the two problems. Therefore, only by considering both issues simultaneously can we determine the optimal financing contract parameters and maximize the service provider's expected payoff.

## 4 Simulation Experiments

In Sect. 3.2, the optimization of the expected return of the SP is solved using the Lagrange multiplier method, resulting in functional expressions for the two decision variables: down payment and installment. In this section, to examine the incentive effects of certain variables on the down payment and installment payments, as well as to verify the rationality and feasibility of the financing contract, we will perform multidimensional simulations using MATLAB. The analysis focuses on the influence of different cost coefficients and revenue on the down payment, installment payments, and the final expected payoff.

### 4.1 Analysis of Financing Contract Parameters

In the parameter settings, consider introducing 20 different types of ECNs, i.e., $n = 20$. Secondly, to simplify the model, let $\theta_i = i$ be established, which also meets the monotonicity mentioned earlier. It means that the stronger the capability, the higher the type. When only considering the computation cost coefficient, assume that the distribution of ECN types is uniform, thus $\alpha_i = 1/n$. A three-dimensional waterfall chart is used for simulation here to intuitively show the extent to which the down payment and installment amounts for different types of ECNs are affected by the computation cost coefficient, as shown in Fig. 2:

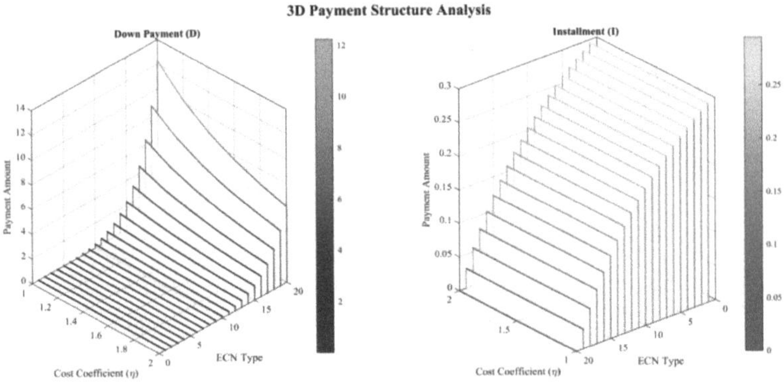


**Fig. 2.** Visualization of multi-dimensional payment mechanisms based on cost coefficients

From the perspective of the distribution of ECN types, changes in the computation cost coefficient have a significant layered impact on the payment structure. The payment behavior of the lowest capability type of ECN remains stable, with the installment payment amount unaffected by fluctuations in the cost coefficient. The down payment amount is relatively low. As a result, despite the presence of a downward trend, it is not obvious and remains largely unchanged. However, as the type of ECN increases, the payment structure begins to exhibit regular variations: All higher types of ECN exhibit installment payments that remain unaffected by the cost coefficient. However, because of their larger down payment amounts, a clearly gradual decreasing trend can be observed. When the highest type of ECN is reached, the installment payment amount drops completely to zero. This reflects the special status of the optimal capability node within the payment mechanism. The structured response of the entire payment system reveals the inherent trade-off mechanism between computation cost and node capability. This result is consistent with the derivations in Eqs. (22, 23): installment payments are unaffected by the computation cost coefficient, while the down payment is influenced by the cost coefficient.

When considering the impact of the revenue, the basic parameters remain unchanged, setting the cost coefficient $\eta = 4$. Using a three-dimensional waterfall chart to visually display the response of the down payment and installment amounts of different types of ECNs as the revenue varies, as shown in Fig. 3:

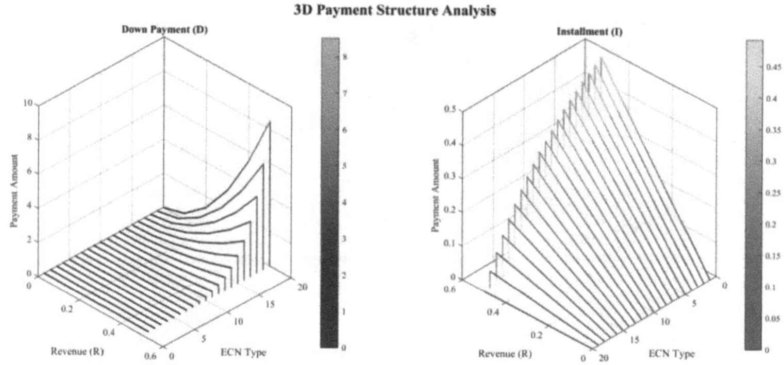


**Fig. 3.** Visualization of a revenue-based multi-dimensional payment mechanism

As the revenue increases, regardless of the type of ECN, the required down payment and installment amount both show a rising trend. This change helps maximize the expected payoff for SP: When other parameters remain constant, an increase in the ECN's revenue results in higher net income. At this point, while ensuring that ECNs still have the incentive to enter into the financing contract, SP can appropriately increase the parameters of the financing contract to enhance its own payoff. It can also be seen that high-type ECNs exhibit the characteristics of "high down payment, zero installment", while low-type ECNs exhibit the characteristics of "zero down payment, high installment". Unlike dealing with the adverse selection problem alone, when addressing the joint moral hazard issue, it is necessary to introduce the optimal level of effort, i.e., Eq. (13). High-type ECNs reduce their effort level when paying high installments, while low-type ECNs are insensitive to such changes. Therefore, to ultimately maximize the expected payoff for SP, it is necessary to force a reduction in the installment payments of high-type ECNs through contract design. This variation in financing contract parameters ultimately better aligns with real-world application scenarios.

### 4.2 Expected Payoff Analysis

This section simulates and visualizes the expected payoff for both the SP and all ECNs. It further investigates how the computational cost coefficient and revenue influence the expected payoff.

The computation cost coefficient $\eta$ is set between 1 and 2, and the revenue R is set between 0 and 0.5. The revenue and the cost coefficient are represented on the x and y axes respectively. The expected returns of the SP and all ECNs are represented by color shades in the resulting heat maps, as shown in Fig. 4 and Fig. 5:

From the Figs. 4 and 5, it can be seen that the expected returns of SP and ECNs show a similar trend of variation. This is because the payoff of the SP come from ECNs. Consequently, an increase in an ECN's expected return prompts the SP to raise the down payment and installment as much as possible. The sole requirement is to preserve the ECN's motivation to complete computational tasks. With a fixed cost coefficient, the payoff of both increase significantly with an increase in the revenue; whereas with R fixed, the payoff decrease as the cost coefficient increases. Further combining the

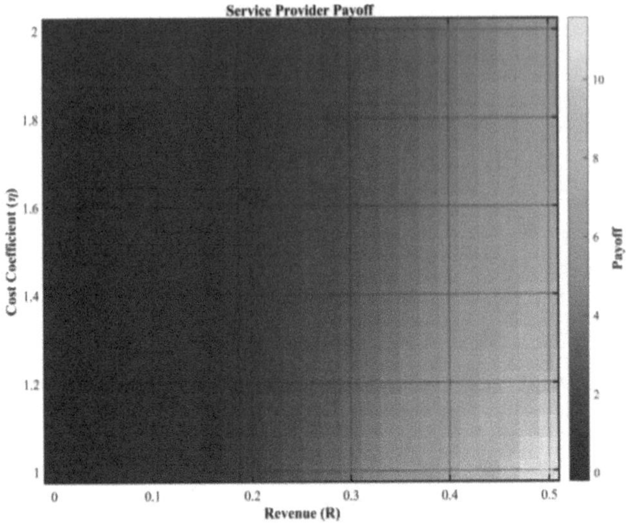


**Fig. 4.** Sensitivity analysis of SP's payoff to cost coefficient and revenue

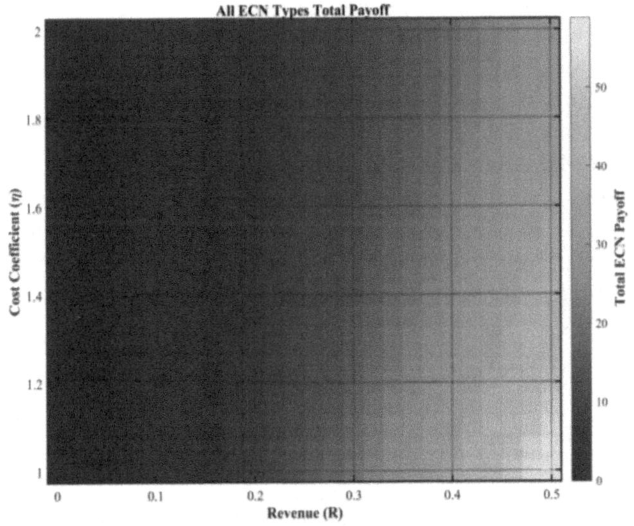


**Fig. 5.** Sensitivity analysis of total ECNs' payoff to cost coefficient and revenue

effects of the two parameters, we can observe from the heatmap that high return areas concentrate in the lower right corner, corresponding to a combination of high revenue and low cost coefficients.

The simulation graphs are plotted, on one hand, to demonstrate the adaptability of the optimal financing contract in real-world scenarios. For instance, if computing device damage causes a sudden rise in the computational cost coefficient or if the ECNs' revenue drops abruptly, the financing contract parameters can be adjusted proactively.

This enables the contract to better adapt to environmental changes and maintain its validity. On the other hand, they demonstrate the incentive effects of revenue and the cost coefficient on the optimal financing contract parameters. This allows us to understand the conditions under which the SP's payoff can be maximized.

## 5 Conclusion

This paper employs contract theory to analyze a scenario involving both adverse selection and moral hazard. The contract parameters are derived using the Lagrange multiplier method, ultimately determining SP's expected payoff. The simulation results clearly reveal the incentive mechanisms through which the cost coefficient and revenue influence the contract parameters and the expected payoff of both the SP and ECNs. These findings support three key conclusions: First, when only adverse selection is considered, high-type ECNs select contracts with low down payment and high installment. However, a realistic model must jointly consider moral hazard, where the introduced concept of effort level significantly impacts parameter selection. Second, the SP's expected payoff is maximized under conditions of high revenue and a low cost coefficient. Third, the framework demonstrates enhanced adaptability to dynamic environments; it allows for timely adjustment of contract parameters prior to agreement finalization in response to external changes, thereby safeguarding the SP's expected payoff.

## References


1. Hua, W., Liu, P., Huang, L.: Energy-efficient resource allocation for heterogeneous edge-cloud computing. IEEE Internet Things J. **11**(2) (2023). https://doi.org/10.1109/jiot.2023.3293164
2. Bitalebi, H., Safaei, F., Ebrahimi, M.: Nearest data processing in GPU. Sustain. Comput. Inform. Syst. **44**, 101047 (2024). https://doi.org/10.1016/j.suscom.2024.101047
3. Ji, Z.: Evaluation and analysis of tail latency performance under mixed workloads in cloud computing environment. Tianjin Univ. (2020). https://doi.org/10.27356/d.cnki.gtjdu.2018.001290
4. Zhang, Z.: A computing allocation strategy for internet of things' resources based on edge computing. Int. J. Distrib. Sens. Netw. (2021). https://doi.org/10.1177/15501477211064800
5. Zhang, Y., Lan, Y., Cai, L.: Efficient computing resource sharing for mobile edge-cloud computing networks. IEEE/ACM Trans. Netw. **28**(3), 1249–1262 (2020). https://doi.org/10.1109/tnet.2020.2979807
6. Zhang, Z., Li, J., Li, Y., He, Y.: Metadata-private resource allocation in edge computing withstands semi-malicious edge nodes. Sensors. **24**(10), 2989 (2024). https://doi.org/10.3390/s24102989
7. Wang, W., Wu, X., Ye, Q., Chen, L., Liao, H.: Electricity market clearing for multiple stakeholders based on the Stackelberg game. Front. Energy Res. **12** (2024). https://doi.org/10.3389/fenrg.2024.1342516
8. Wang, H., Mir, M.: Voluntary resource sharing at the network edge to provide cloud services: a systematic survey. Computing. **107**, 113 (2025). https://doi.org/10.1007/s00607-025-01479-y
9. Kim, N., Kim, D., Lee, J., Niyato, D., Choi, J.K.: Incentive-based coded distributed computing management for latency reduction in IoT services—a game theoretic approach. IEEE Internet Things J. **8**(10), 7915–7927 (2021). https://doi.org/10.1109/jiot.2020.3045277

10. Zhang, K., Mao, Y., Leng, S., Maharjan, S., Vinel, A., Zhang, Y.: Contract-theoretic approach for delay constrained offloading in vehicular edge computing networks. Mob. Netw. Appl. **24**, 1003–1014 (2019). https://doi.org/10.1007/s11036-018-1032-0
11. Guo, H., Liu, J., Lv, J.: Toward intelligent task offloading at the edge. IEEE Netw. **34**(2), 148–155 (2020). https://doi.org/10.1109/mnet.001.1900200
12. Basuchaudhary, A.: [Book Review] Contract theory, by Bolton, P. Dewatripont, M. MIT press: Cambridge and London, 2005. Manag. Decis. Econ. **28**(1), 81–82 (2007). https://doi.org/10.1002/mde.1332
13. Hu, Q., Xie, J., Zhang, G., Liang, L., Xie, J.: Contract design for government incentives to collaborative innovation in sci-tech platforms: a perspective of double information asymmetry. Chin. j. Manag. Sci. (2025). https://doi.org/10.16381/j.cnki.issn1003-207x.2024.0917
14. At, C., Thomas, L.: Optimal tenurial contracts under both moral hazard and adverse selection. Am. J. Agric. Econ. **101**(3), 941–959 (2019). https://doi.org/10.1093/ajae/aay049
15. Gupta, N., Singh, J., Dhurandher, S.K., Han, Z.: Contract-theory-based incentive design mechanism for opportunistic IoT networks. IEEE Internet Things J. **10**(4), 3369–3382 (2023). https://doi.org/10.1109/jiot.2021.3109162

# DRO-Based Computation Offloading and Trajectory Design for Low-Altitude Networks

Guanwang Jiang[1], Ziye Jia[1(✉)], Can Cui[1], Lijun He[2], Qiuming Zhu[1], and Qihui Wu[1]

[1] Key Laboratory of Dynamic Cognitive System of Electromagnetic Spectrum Space, Ministry of Industry and Information Technology, Nanjing University of Aeronautics and Astronautics, Nanjing 211106, Jiangsu, China
{gwjiang,jiaziye,cuican020619,zhuqiuming,wuqihui}@nuaa.edu.cn
[2] School of Information and Control Engineering, China University of Mining and Technology, Xuzhou 221116, Jiangsu, China

**Abstract.** The low-altitude networks (LANs) integrating unmanned aerial vehicles (UAVs) and high-altitude platforms (HAPs) have become a promising solution for the rising computation demands. However, the uncertain task sizes and high mobility of UAVs pose great challenges to guarantee the quality of service. To address these issues, we propose an LAN architecture where UAVs and HAPs collaboratively provide computation offloading for ground users. Moreover, the uncertainty sets are constructed to characterize the uncertain task size, and a distributionally robust optimization problem is formulated to minimize the worst-case delay by jointly optimizing the offloading decisions and UAV trajectories. To solve the mixed-integer min-max optimization problem, we design the distributionally robust computation offloading and trajectories optimization algorithm. Specifically, the original problem is figured out by iteratively solving the outer-layer and inner-layer problems. The convex outer-layer problem with probability distributions is solved by the optimization toolkit. As for the inner-layer mixed-integer problem, we employ the Benders decomposition. The decoupled master problem concerning the binary offloading decisions is solved by the integer solver, and UAV trajectories in the sub-problem are optimized via the successive convex approximation. Simulation results show the proposed algorithm outperforms traditional optimization methods in balancing the worst-case delay and robustness.

This work was supported in part by National Natural Science Foundation of China under Grant 62301251, in part by the Natural Science Foundation on Frontier Leading Technology Basic Research Project of Jiangsu under Grant BK20222001, in part by the Aeronautical Science Foundation of China 2023Z071052007, and in part by the Young Elite Scientists Sponsorship Program by CAST 2023QNRC001.


Y. Liu et al. (Eds.): ChinaCom 2025, LNICST 711, pp. 409–423, 2027.
https://doi.org/10.1007/978-3-032-33662-0_30

**Keywords:** Low-altitude network · computation offloading · unmanned aerial vehicle · trajectory optimization · distributionally robust optimization

## 1 Introduction

The development of the sixth generation communication technology has spawned a large number of on-demand computation services, putting forward urgent requirements for sufficient infrastructure, especially in remote areas. Equipped with computation resources, the low-altitude network (LAN), composed of various aircrafts, can provide services for these demands in infrastructure-limited areas [1]. As a main component of LAN, unmanned aerial vehicles (UAVs) can adapt to dynamic user distributions due to the high flexibility and easy deployment [2,3]. Meanwhile, high-altitude platforms (HAPs) are worth boosting for their stable wide-area coverage, supplementing the limited endurance and coverage of UAVs. Therefore, the cooperation of UAVs and HAPs is expected to provide on-demand and large-coverage computation offloading services for ground users (GUs) [4].

There exist some recent works related with LAN. For example, the authors in [5] optimized the UAV trajectories and task offloading ratios in the multi-UAV mobile edge computing system using the deep reinforcement learning (RL). Authors in [6] leveraged the multi-agent RL to reduce the energy consumption in the scenario where the UAVs and HAP provided cooperative task offloading. [7] investigated the problem of the task assignment and resource optimization in an integrated multi-UAV system, aiming to maximize the sum of detection, tracking, and communication performance. In most existing works, task sizes are assumed to be fixed or predictable. However, due to the users' behaviors and environmental factors, the task sizes exhibit stochastic variations [8,9]. Although the traditional optimization methods offer ideas to deal with the uncertainty, they struggle to balance the optimality and robustness [10]. In contrast, the distributionally robust optimization (DRO) can achieve a better trade-off by uncertainty sets [11].

In this paper, we focus on the joint optimization of the computation offloading decisions and UAV trajectories in LAN where UAVs and one HAP cooperate to provide computation offloading services for GUs. To characterize the uncertain task sizes, we construct uncertainty sets based on the $L_1$ norm metric. Then, a DRO problem is formulated to minimize the worst-case delay, which is in the form of mixed-integer min-max optimization and hard to solve. To deal with the problem, we design the distributionally robust computation offloading and trajectories optimization (DRCOTO) algorithm. Specially, we solve the outer-layer minimization problem and inner-layer maximization problem iteratively. The convex outer-layer problem related with the probability distribution is solved by the optimization solver. To handle the mixed-integer inner-layer problem concerning decisions and trajectories, we employ the Benders decomposition (BD) integrated with the successive convex approximation (SCA). Finally, simulations evaluate the superiority of the proposed DRCOTO algorithm.

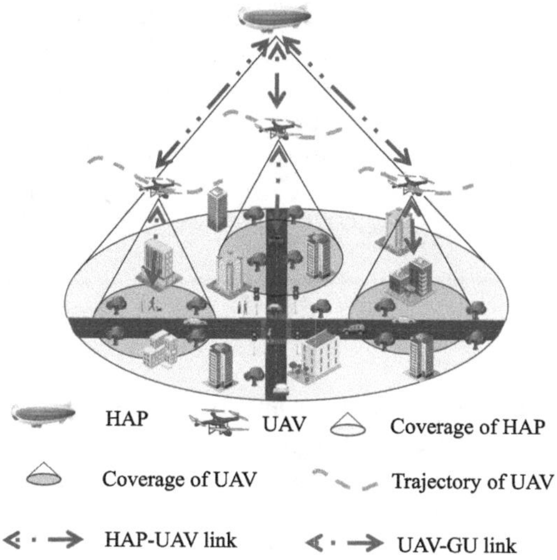


**Fig. 1.** Scenario of LAN.

The rest of this paper is arranged as follows. Section 2 presents the system model and problem formulation. Section 3 details the DRCOTO algorithm. Section 4 provides simulation results. Finally, Sect. 5 concludes the paper.

## 2 System Model and Problem Formulation

As shown in Fig. 1, we consider an LAN composed of GUs, cruising UAVs, and one hovering HAP, denoted as $i \in \mathcal{I} = \{1, 2, ..., I\}$, $j \in \mathcal{J} = \{1, 2, ..., J\}$, and $H$, respectively. Both UAVs and the HAP carry edge servers to provide computing services for GUs. The considered time period $\mathcal{T}$ is divided into $N$ time slots, indexed by $n \in \mathcal{N} = \{1, 2, ..., N\}$, each with a duration of $\tau$. The slot length $\tau$ is small enough so that the flying distance of UAV during each slot is negligible, and the channel gain is regarded as constant in each slot. The three-dimensional Cartesian coordinate is employed to describe the locations of GU $i$, UAV $j$ and HAP $H$ in time slot $n$, denoted as $q_i^g = (q_i^{gx}, q_i^{gy}, 0)$, $q_{j,n}^u = (q_{j,n}^{ux}, q_{j,n}^{uy}, q^{uz})$ and $q^h = (q^{hx}, q^{hy}, q^{hz})$, respectively. Note that UAVs maintain flying with the fixed height $q^{uz}$, and the position of the HAP keeps unchanging.

### 2.1 Uncertainty Set for Task Size

Each GU has a computation-intensive task $\phi_i = \{s_i, c_i\}$ to be processed over the entire time period $\mathcal{T}$. $s_i$ represents the total task size measured in bits, and $c_i$ denotes the required number of CPU cycles per bit. To facilitate processing, each task $\phi_i$ is evenly divided into $N$ parts, with one part processed in each slot. Hence, the data size of task $\phi_i$ to be computed in time slot $n$ is $s_{i,n} = s_i/N$.

In most scenarios, data size $s_i$ of task $\phi_i$ is uncertain, and the probability distribution is unspecified. To model the uncertainty, each task size $s_i$ is supposed to have the same sample space $\Omega$, which contains $K$ possible discrete values of the task volume, i.e., $\Omega = \{s^k|\forall k = 1, 2, ..., K\}$. Meanwhile, $s_i$ follows its respective probability distribution $\mathbb{P}_i = \{p_{i,k}|\forall k = 1, 2, ..., K\}$, where $p_{i,k}$ denotes the probability of sample $s^k$ in the distribution of $s_i$. Besides, the reference distribution of $s_i$ is $\mathbb{P}_i^0 = \{p_{i,k}^0|\forall k = 1, 2, ..., K\}$, denoted as

$$p_{i,k}^0 = \frac{\sum_{q=1}^{Q} \delta^k(s_i)}{Q}, \forall k = 1, 2, ..., K. \tag{1}$$

$Q$ is the number of the historical data and $\sum_{q=1}^{Q} \delta^k(s_i)$ is the total number of historical data size which falls in interval $[d^k, d^{k+1})$. In detail, if $d^k \leq s_i < d^{k+1}$, $\delta^k(s_i)1$, and otherwise $\delta^k(s_i)0$. Moreover, we use the $L_1$ norm metric to quantify the distance between $\mathbb{P}_i^0$ and $\mathbb{P}_i$, defined as

$$d_{L_1}(\mathbb{P}_i^0, \mathbb{P}_i) = ||\mathbb{P}_i^0 - \mathbb{P}_i||_1 = \sum_{k=1}^{K} |p_{i,k} - p_{i,k}^0|. \tag{2}$$

Then, the uncertainty set is $\mathscr{D}_i = \{\mathbb{P}_i|d(\mathbb{P}_i^0, \mathbb{P}_i) \leq \epsilon\}$, where $\epsilon$ is the tolerance value.

### 2.2 Computation Model

In the LAN scenario, GUs can either process their computation task locally or offload them to the UAV. Due to the limited resources, UAVs can compute the collected data or relay them to the HAP for the further processing. The decision variable $x_{i,j,n} \in \{0, 1\}$ is introduced. If $s_{i,n}$ is collected by UAV $j$, $x_{i,j,n} = 1$ and otherwise $x_{i,j,n} = 0$. The delay and energy for GU $i$ computing $s_{i,n}$ locally are

$$T_{i,n}^{gcp} = \frac{\left(1 - \sum\limits_{j=1}^{J} x_{i,j,n}\right) s_{i,n} c_i}{f^{gcp}}, \tag{3}$$

and

$$E_{i,n}^{gcp} = (1 - \sum_{j=1}^{J} x_{i,j,n}) \eta^g s_{i,n} c_i (f^{gcp})^2, \tag{4}$$

respectively. $f^{gcp}$ and $\eta^g$ are the CPU cycles per second and effective capacitance coefficient of GU, respectively. Similarly, binary variable $y_{i,j,n} \in \{0, 1\}$ is defined, and $y_{i,j,n} = 1$ if $s_{i,n}$ is computed by UAV $j$, or $y_{i,j,n} = 0$. The delay and energy for UAV $j$ to compute data $s_{i,n}$ are

$$T_{i,j,n}^{ucp} = \frac{s_{i,n} y_{i,j,n} c_i}{f^{ucp}}, \tag{5}$$

and

$$E_{i,j,n}^{ucp} = \eta^u y_{i,j,n} s_{i,n} c_i (f^{ucp})^2, \tag{6}$$

respectively. $f^{ucp}$ and $\eta^u$ are the CPU cycles per second and effective capacitance coefficient of UAVs, respectively [12]. Besides, $z_{i,j,n} \in \{0,1\}$ is the index binary, and $z_{i,j,n} = 1$ represents $s_{i,n}$ is relayed from UAV $j$ to HAP $H$. The delay and energy for $s_{i,n}$ computed on HAP $H$ are

$$T_{i,j,n}^{hcp} = \frac{s_{i,n} z_{i,j,n} c_i}{f^{hcp}}, \tag{7}$$

and

$$E_{i,j,n}^{hcp} = \eta^h s_{i,n} c_i (f^{hcp})^2 z_{i,j,n}, \tag{8}$$

respectively. $f^{hcp}$ and $\eta^h$ are the CPU cycles per second and effective capacitance coefficient of the HAP, respectively.

### 2.3 Communication Model

**GU to UAV.** The probabilistic line-of-sight (LoS) channel model is leveraged for the mixture of LoS and non-line-of-sight (NLoS) environments between GUs and UAVs [13]. The probability of the LoS link is $P_{LoS}(\theta_{i,j,n}) = \frac{1}{1+aexp(-b(\theta_{i,j,n}-a))}$, where $\theta_{i,j,n} = \arcsin\left(q^{uz}/d_{i,j,n}^{ug}\right)$ is the angle between GU $i$ and UAV $j$ in time slot $n$. $d_{i,j,n}^{ug}$ is the Euclidean distance between GU $i$ and UAV $j$ in slot $n$. $a$ and $b$ are the environment related parameters [6]. The probability of NLoS is $P_{NLoS}(\theta_{i,j,n}) = 1 - P_{LoS}(\theta_{i,j,n})$, and the channel gain between GU $i$ and UAV $j$ in time slot $n$ is $g_{i,j,n}^{ug} = P_{LoS}(\theta_{i,j,n})\beta_0(d_{i,j,n}^{ug})^{-\alpha} + P_{NLoS}(\theta_{i,j,n})\kappa\beta_0(d_{i,j,n}^{ug})^{-\alpha}$, where $\beta_0$, $\alpha$, and $\kappa$ are the path loss parameters. According to the Shannon theory, the data transmission rate from GU $i$ to UAV $j$ in time slot $n$ is

$$R_{i,j,n}^{ug} = B^{ug} \log_2\left(1 + \frac{p^{gtr} g_{i,j,n}^{ug}}{\sigma^2 + I^{ug}}\right). \tag{9}$$

$B^{ug}$ represents the channel bandwidth between GUs and UAVs, $p^{gtr}$ denotes the maximum transmission power of GUs, $\sigma^2$ is the noise power, and $I^{ug}$ is the average interference from other GUs, sharing the same sub-channel [14]. Therefore, the delay for sending data $s_{i,n}$ from GU $i$ to UAV $j$ is

$$T_{i,j,n}^{gutr} = \frac{s_{i,n} x_{i,j,n}}{R_{i,j,n}^{ug}}, \tag{10}$$

and the corresponding energy cost is

$$E_{i,n}^{gutr} = p^{gtr} \sum_{j=1}^{J} T_{i,j,n}^{gutr}. \tag{11}$$

Thus, the total energy consumption of GU $i$ to transmit and compute data $s_{i,n}$ is

$$E_{i,n}^{g} = E_{i,n}^{gutr} + E_{i,n}^{gcp}. \tag{12}$$

**UAV to HAP.** The free space path loss is considered to characterize communication links between UAVs and the HAP, ignoring the fading effects caused by the reflection and diffraction [15]. Besides, we apply the orthogonal frequency division multiplexing technique to UAV-HAP links, and the mutual interference can be avoided [16]. The achievable data transmission rate [17] from UAV $j$ to HAP $H$ in time slot $n$ is

$$R_{j,n}^{uh} = B^{uh} \log_2 \left(1 + \frac{p^{utr} G^{uh} L_l L_j^{uh}(n)}{B^{uh} K_B T_s}\right), \tag{13}$$

where $B^{uh}$ is the bandwidth between the UAVs and HAP, $G^{uh}$ is the antenna gain, $p^{utr}$ is the transmit power of UAVs, $L_l$ is the total path loss, $K_B$ is the Boltzmann constant, $T_s$ is the system noise temperature, and $L_j^{uh}(n) = \left(c/(4\pi d_{j,n}^{uh} f_c^{uh})\right)^2$ is the free-space path loss. $c$ is the speed of light, $d_{j,n}^{uh}$ is the Euclidean distance between the HAP and UAV $j$ in slot $n$, and $f_c^{uh}$ is the central frequency. Then, the delay and energy consumption for sending data $s_{i,n}$ from UAV $j$ to HAP $H$ are

$$T_{i,j,n}^{uhtr} = \frac{s_{i,n} z_{i,j,n}}{R_{j,n}^{uh}}, \tag{14}$$

and

$$E_{i,j,n}^{uhtr} = p^{utr} T_{i,j,n}^{uhtr}, \tag{15}$$

respectively. Hence, the total delay for computing task $s_{i,n}$ is

$$T_{i,n} = T_{i,n}^{gcp} + \sum_{j=1}^{J} \left(T_{i,j,n}^{gutr} + T_{i,j,n}^{uhtr} + T_{i,j,n}^{ucp} + T_{i,j,n}^{hcp}\right). \tag{16}$$

### 2.4 UAV Trajectory Model

The UAV trajectories are constrained within the operation area, i.e.,

$$0 < q_{j,n}^{ux} < X_{max}, \forall j \in \mathcal{J}, n \in \mathcal{N}, \tag{17}$$

and

$$0 < q_{j,n}^{uy} < Y_{max}, \forall j \in \mathcal{J}, n \in \mathcal{N}, \tag{18}$$

where $X_{max}$ and $Y_{max}$ are the horizontal boundaries. UAVs are assumed to cruise with a constant flight speed $v^{uf}$, and the maximum horizontal flight distance during each time slot is limited by

$$||q_{j,n}^{u} - q_{j,n-1}^{u}|| \leq v^{uf} \tau, \forall j \in \mathcal{J}, n \in \mathcal{N}. \tag{19}$$

Considering the aerial safety, the inter-distance between any two UAVs shall be no less than $D_{min}$, i.e.,

$$||q_{j,n}^{u} - q_{j',n}^{u}|| \geq D_{min}, \forall j, j' \in \mathcal{J}, j \neq j', n \in \mathcal{N}. \tag{20}$$

We consider the rotary wing UAV propulsion power model [18] and the flight power $p^{uf}$ of UAV is

$$p^{uf} = P_1 \left(1 + \frac{3||v^{uf}||^2}{U_{tip}^2}\right) + \frac{1}{2} d_0 \varsigma_0 s A ||v^{uf}||^3 + P_2 \left(\sqrt{1 + \frac{||v^{uf}||^4}{4v_0^2}} - \frac{||v^{uf}||^2}{2v_0^2}\right)^{\frac{1}{2}}, \tag{21}$$

where $P_1$ is the power of the UAV blade, $U_{tip}$ represents the blade tip speed, $d_0$ denotes the fuselage drag ratio, $\varsigma_0$ is the air density, $s$ is the rotor solidity, $A$ is the rotor area, $P_2$ is the induced power during hovering, and $v_0$ is the mean velocity of rotors. Moreover, the hovering power consumption of UAVs is

$$p^{uhov} = P_1 + P_2. \tag{22}$$

The flight time for UAV $j$ during time slot $n$ is calculated as

$$T_{u,n}^{fly} = \frac{||q_{j,n}^u - q_{j,n-1}^u||}{v^{uf}}. \tag{23}$$

The propulsion energy cost of UAV $j$ in time slot $n$ is

$$E_{j,n}^{uf} = p^{uf} T_{u,n}^{fly} + p^{uhov}(\tau - T_{u,n}^{fly}). \tag{24}$$

The energy consumption $E_j^u$ of UAV $j$ mainly consists of three parts: the communication cost $E_{i,j,n}^{uhtr}$, computing cost $E_{i,j,n}^{ucp}$, and movement cost $E_{j,n}^{uf}$, i.e.,

$$E_j^u = \sum_{i=1}^{I} \sum_{n=1}^{N} E_{i,j,n}^{uhtr} + \sum_{i=1}^{I} \sum_{n=1}^{N} E_{i,j,n}^{ucp} + \sum_{n=1}^{N} E_{j,n}^{uf}. \tag{25}$$

### 2.5 Problem Formulation

The DRO problem **P0** is formulated on the basis of the constructed uncertainty sets, jointly optimizing the computation offloading strategies and UAV trajectories, to minimize the expected maximum total worst-case delay, i.e.,

$$
\begin{aligned}
\textbf{P0}: & \min_{\boldsymbol{x},\boldsymbol{y},\boldsymbol{z},\boldsymbol{q}} \max_{\boldsymbol{p}} \sum_{i=1}^{I}\sum_{n=1}^{N} \mathbb{E}_{\mathbb{P}_i}\left(T_{i,n}\right) \\
\text{s.t. } & (17) - (20), \\
& \sum_{j=1}^{J} x_{i,j,n} \leq 1, \forall i \in \mathcal{I}, n \in \mathcal{N}, && (26)\\
& \sum_{i=1}^{I} y_{i,j,n} \leq N^u, \forall j \in \mathcal{J}, n \in \mathcal{N}, && (27)\\
& \sum_{i=1}^{I}\sum_{j=1}^{J} z_{i,j,n} \leq N^h, \forall n \in \mathcal{N}, && (28)\\
& y_{i,j,n} + z_{i,j,n} = x_{i,j,n}, \forall i \in \mathcal{I}, j \in \mathcal{J}, n \in \mathcal{N}, && (29)\\
& \mathbb{E}_{\mathbb{P}_i}\left(T_{i,n}\right) \leq \tau, \forall i \in \mathcal{I}, n \in \mathcal{N}, && (30)\\
& \sum_{n=1}^{N} \mathbb{E}_{\mathbb{P}_i}\left(E_{i,n}^{g}\right) \leq E^{gmax}, \forall i \in \mathcal{I}, && (31)\\
& \mathbb{E}_{\mathbb{P}_i}\left(E_{j}^{u}\right) \leq E^{umax}, \forall j \in \mathcal{J}, && (32)\\
& \sum_{i=1}^{I}\sum_{j=1}^{J}\sum_{n=1}^{N} \mathbb{E}_{\mathbb{P}_i}\left(E_{i,j,n}^{hcp}\right) \leq E^{hmax}, && (33)\\
& \mathbb{P}_i \in \mathscr{D}_i, \forall i \in \mathcal{I}, n \in \mathcal{N}, && (34)\\
& x_{i,j,n}, y_{i,j,n}, z_{i,j,n} \in \{0,1\}, \forall i \in \mathcal{I}, j \in \mathcal{J}, n \in \mathcal{N}, && (35)
\end{aligned}
$$

where $\mathbb{E}_{\mathbb{P}_i}\left(T_{i,n}\right)$ represents the expectation of $T_{i,n}$ under the probability distribution $\mathbb{P}_i$. $\boldsymbol{x} = \{x_{i,j,n}, \forall i \in \mathcal{I}, j \in \mathcal{J}, n \in \mathcal{N}\}$, $\boldsymbol{y} = \{y_{i,j,n}, \forall i \in \mathcal{I}, j \in \mathcal{J}, n \in \mathcal{N}\}$, $\boldsymbol{z} = \{z_{i,j,n}, \forall i \in \mathcal{I}, j \in \mathcal{J}, n \in \mathcal{N}\}$, $\boldsymbol{q} = \{q_{j,n}^u, \forall j \in \mathcal{J}, n \in \mathcal{N}\}$, and $\boldsymbol{p} = \{\mathbb{P}_i, \forall i \in \mathcal{I}\}$. Constraint (26) dictates that each task can be collected by at most one UAV during each time slot. Constraints (27) and (28) impose the numbers of GUs served by the UAV and HAP cannot exceed $N^u$ and $N^h$, respectively. Constraint (29) indicates the data flow balancing on the UAV. Constraint (30) specifies that the delay for completing processing data $s_{i,n}$ must not surpass the duration of time slot $\tau$. Constraints (31), (32) and (33) confine the energy consumption of each GU, UAV, and HAP to stay within the maximum capacity limits of $E^{gmax}$, $E^{umax}$, and $E^{hmax}$, respectively. Constraint (34) implies that probability distribution $\mathbb{P}_i$ for task size $s_i$ belongs to uncertainty set $\mathscr{D}_i$.

Note that **P0** is a mix-integer problem, concerning binary variables $\boldsymbol{x}$, $\boldsymbol{y}$, and $\boldsymbol{z}$, as well as continuous variables $\boldsymbol{p}$ and $\boldsymbol{q}$. Since the time complexity is exponential with the problem scale growing, it is intractable to solve **P0** efficiently.

## 3 Algorithm Design

To address the great challenges in solving **P0**, we design the DRCOTO algorithm based the BD and SCA. First, we discretize the sample space into $K$, denoted as $\Omega = \{s^k | \forall k = 1, 2, ..., K\}$, and problem **P0** is reformulated as

$$\begin{aligned} \mathbf{P1}\colon & \min_{\boldsymbol{x},\boldsymbol{y},\boldsymbol{z},\boldsymbol{q}} \max_{\boldsymbol{p}} \sum_{i=1}^{I}\sum_{n=1}^{N}\sum_{k=1}^{K} p_{i,k}T_{i,n,k} \\ & \text{s.t. } (17)-(20), (26)-(35). \end{aligned}$$

Based on the discretization, $s_{i,n}$ in $T_{i,n}$ can be replaced by $s^k$, and $T_{i,n}$ is transformed into $T_{i,n,k}$. With the fixed $p_{i,k}$ of the inner-layer max problem, **P2** is given by

$$\begin{aligned} \mathbf{P2}\colon & \min_{\boldsymbol{x},\boldsymbol{y},\boldsymbol{z},\boldsymbol{q}} \sum_{i=1}^{I}\sum_{n=1}^{N}\sum_{k=1}^{K} p_{i,k}T_{i,n,k} \\ & \text{s.t. } (17)-(20), (26)-(33), (35). \end{aligned}$$

By solving problem **P2**, $\boldsymbol{x}$, $\boldsymbol{y}$, $\boldsymbol{z}$, and $\boldsymbol{q}$ are obtained. With the pre-determined $\boldsymbol{x}$, $\boldsymbol{y}$, $\boldsymbol{z}$, and $\boldsymbol{q}$, **P1** is transformed to **P3**, i.e.,

$$\begin{aligned} \mathbf{P3}\colon & \max_{\boldsymbol{p}} \sum_{i=1}^{I}\sum_{n=1}^{N}\sum_{k=1}^{K} p_{i,k}T_{i,n,k} \\ & \text{s.t. } (30)-(34). \end{aligned}$$

Then, we handle **P1** by addressing **P2** and **P3** through alternating iterations.

To tackle the coupled continuous and integer variables, **P2** is decomposed into a sub-problem **SP** and a master problem **MP** based on the BD. Specifically, given binary variables $\boldsymbol{x}$, $\boldsymbol{y}$, and $\boldsymbol{z}$ generated by **MP** at the $\omega$-th iteration, **SP** is

$$\begin{aligned} \mathbf{SP}\colon & \min_{\boldsymbol{q}} \sum_{i=1}^{I}\sum_{n=1}^{N}\sum_{k=1}^{K} p_{i,k}T_{i,n,k} \\ & \text{s.t. } (17)-(20), (30)-(32). \end{aligned}$$

To deal with non-convex problem **SP**, we design the algorithm based on the SCA to achieve a local optimal solution. Specifically, at the $m$-th iteration of the SCA, we implement the first-order Taylor series expansions of $T_{i,n,k}$ and $E^{uf}_{j,n}$ to obtain the approximated functions $\hat{T}^m_{i,n,k}$ and $\hat{E}^{muf}_{j,n}$, i.e.,

$$\hat{T}^m_{i,n,k} = T_{i,n,k}(\boldsymbol{q}^{m-1}) + \nabla T_{i,n,k}(\boldsymbol{q}^{m-1})(\boldsymbol{q}^m - \boldsymbol{q}^{m-1}), \tag{36}$$

and

$$\hat{E}^{muf}_{j,n} = E^{uf}_{j,n}(\boldsymbol{q}^{m-1}) + \nabla E^{uf}_{j,n}(\boldsymbol{q}^{m-1})(\boldsymbol{q}^m - \boldsymbol{q}^{m-1}), \tag{37}$$

respectively. $\boldsymbol{q}^{m-1}$ is the solution obtained at the $(m-1)$-th iteration of the SCA. $T_{i,n,k}(\boldsymbol{q}^{m-1})$ and $E_{j,n}^{uf}(\boldsymbol{q}^{m-1})$ are values of $T_{i,n,k}$ and $E_{j,n}^{uf}$ at the point $\boldsymbol{q}^{m-1}$, respectively. Additionally, $\nabla f(x)$ represents the derivative of $f(x)$ at $x$. Then, at the $m$-th iteration of the SCA, problem **SP** is transformed into

$$\begin{aligned}\mathbf{SP}'\text{: } &\min_{\boldsymbol{q}} \sum_{i=1}^{I}\sum_{n=1}^{N}\sum_{k=1}^{K} p_{i,k}\hat{T}_{i,n,k}^{m}\\ &\text{s.t. } (17)-(20),(30)-(32).\end{aligned}$$

The Lagrangian function of problem $\mathbf{SP}'$ at the $\omega$-th iteration of the BD is denoted as

$$\begin{aligned}&L\left(\boldsymbol{x}^{\omega-1},\boldsymbol{y}^{\omega-1},\boldsymbol{z}^{\omega-1},\boldsymbol{q}\right)\\ &=\sum_{i=1}^{I}\sum_{n=1}^{N}\sum_{k=1}^{K} p_{i,k}T_{i,n,k}+(\boldsymbol{\lambda}^{\omega})^{T}(G\left(\boldsymbol{x}^{\omega-1},\boldsymbol{y}^{\omega-1},\boldsymbol{z}^{\omega-1},\boldsymbol{q}\right)),\end{aligned} \tag{38}$$

where $\boldsymbol{\lambda}^{\omega}$ is the vector of dual factors, $(\boldsymbol{\lambda}^{\omega})^{T}$ is the transpose of $\boldsymbol{\lambda}^{\omega}$ and $G\left(\boldsymbol{x}^{\omega-1},\boldsymbol{y}^{\omega-1},\boldsymbol{z}^{\omega-1},\boldsymbol{q}\right)$ is the constraint sets for problem $\mathbf{SP}'$, defined as

$$\begin{aligned}&G\left(\boldsymbol{x}^{\omega-1},\boldsymbol{y}^{\omega-1},\boldsymbol{z}^{\omega-1},\boldsymbol{q}\right)=\\ &\left\{\begin{array}{l}-q_{j,n}^{ux},-q_{j,n}^{uy},\forall j\in\mathcal{J},n\in\mathcal{N},\\ q_{j,n}^{ux}-X_{max},q_{j,n}^{uy}-Y_{max},\forall j\in\mathcal{J},n\in\mathcal{N},\\ \|q_{j,n}^{u}-q_{j,n-1}\|-v^{uf}\tau,\forall j\in\mathcal{J},n\in\mathcal{N},\\ D_{min}-\|q_{j,n}^{u}-q_{j'}(n)\|,\forall j,j'\in\mathcal{J},j\neq j',n\in\mathcal{N},\\ \mathbb{E}_{\mathbb{P}_i}\left(T_{i,n,k}\right)-\tau,\forall i\in\mathcal{I},n\in\mathcal{N},\\ \sum_{n=1}^{N}\mathbb{E}_{\mathbb{P}_i}\left(E_{i,n}^{g}\right)-E^{gmax},\forall i\in\mathcal{I},\\ \mathbb{E}_{\mathbb{P}_i}\left(E_{j}^{U}\right)-E^{umax},\forall j\in\mathcal{J}.\end{array}\right\}\end{aligned} \tag{39}$$

After solving **SP**, we obtain the optimality cut at the $\omega$-th iteration, and **MP** at the $\omega$-th iteration is

$$\begin{aligned}\mathbf{MP}\text{: } &\min_{\boldsymbol{x},\boldsymbol{y},\boldsymbol{z}} \xi\\ &\text{s.t. } (26)-(33),(35),\\ &\qquad L(\boldsymbol{x},\boldsymbol{y},\boldsymbol{z},\boldsymbol{q}^{\omega})\leq\xi.\end{aligned} \tag{40}$$

By adding Benders cuts as constraint (40), the search space for the global optimal solution is gradually reduced. Then, we can solve problem **MP** using the optimization tool such as Gurobi.

The overall algorithm of the DRCOTO is summarized in Algorithm 1. First, the decision variables $\boldsymbol{x}^0$, $\boldsymbol{y}^0$, $\mathbf{z}^0$, $\boldsymbol{p}^0$, and $\boldsymbol{q}^0$ are initialized as the arbitrary

**Algorithm 1.** DRCOTO Algorithm

**Initial:** $r = \omega = m = 0$, $D_1^r = D_2^\omega = D_3^m = \text{UB} = +\infty$, $\text{LB} = -\infty$, $\boldsymbol{x}^0$, $\boldsymbol{y}^0$, $\boldsymbol{z}^0$, $\boldsymbol{p}^0$, $\boldsymbol{q}^0$.

1: **repeat**
2: $r = r + 1$.
3: Substitute $\boldsymbol{p}^0$ into **P1** to get **P2**.
4: **repeat**
5: $\omega = \omega + 1$.
6: Substitute $\boldsymbol{x}^0$, $\boldsymbol{y}^0$, and $\boldsymbol{z}^0$ into **P2** to get **SP**.
7: **repeat**
8: $m = m + 1$. Perform the first-order Taylor expansion of $T_{i,n,k}$ and $E_{j,n}^{uf}$ at point $\boldsymbol{q}^0$.
9: Solve **SP**′ to get $\boldsymbol{q}^m$ and the delay $D_3^m$. $\boldsymbol{q}^0 = \boldsymbol{q}^m$.
10: **until** $|D_3^{m-1} - D_3^m| \leq \varrho$ or $m = m^{\max}$.
11: $\text{UB} = \min\{\text{UB}, D_3^m\}$. $\boldsymbol{q}^\omega = \boldsymbol{q}^m$.
12: Calculate the Benders cut according to (40) and then add it to master problem **MP**.
13: Solve **MP** to get $\boldsymbol{x}^\omega$, $\boldsymbol{y}^\omega$, $\boldsymbol{z}^\omega$ and the delay $D_2^\omega$.
14: $\boldsymbol{x}^0 = \boldsymbol{x}^\omega$, $\boldsymbol{y}^0 = \boldsymbol{y}^\omega$, and $\boldsymbol{z}^0 = \boldsymbol{z}^\omega$.
15: $\text{LB} = \max\{\text{LB}, D_2^\omega\}$.
16: **until** $\text{UB} - \text{LB} \leq \delta$ or $\omega = \omega^{\max}$.
17: Substitute $\boldsymbol{x}^\omega$, $\boldsymbol{y}^\omega$, $\boldsymbol{z}^\omega$, $\boldsymbol{q}^\omega$ into **P1** to get **P3**.
18: Solve **P3** by the optimizer to get $\boldsymbol{p}^r$ and the delay $D_3^r$.
19: $\boldsymbol{p}^0 = \boldsymbol{p}^r$.
20: **until** $|D_3^{r-1} - D_3^r| \leq \zeta$ or $r = r^{max}$.

**Output:** $\boldsymbol{x}^\omega$, $\boldsymbol{y}^\omega$, $\boldsymbol{z}^\omega$, $\boldsymbol{q}^\omega$, and $\boldsymbol{p}^r$.

feasible solutions. At the $r$-th iteration, $\boldsymbol{p}^0$ is fixed in **P1** to get problem **P2** (line 3). Then, we substitute $\boldsymbol{x}^0$, $\boldsymbol{y}^0$, and $\boldsymbol{z}^0$ into **P2** to get problem **SP** (line 6). To solve problem **SP**, the SCA is leveraged (lines 7-10). We update the upper bound of problem **P2** with objective value $D_3^m$ of problem **SP**′ (line 11). Then, the Benders cut according to (40) is calculated and added to master problem **MP** (line 12). By solving problem **MP**, the lower bound of problem **P2** is updated (lines 13-15). Repeat the steps 8-15 until the BD is convergent. Besides, **P1** is transformed into **P3** by substituting variables $\boldsymbol{x}^\omega$, $\boldsymbol{y}^\omega$, $\boldsymbol{z}^\omega$, $\boldsymbol{q}^\omega$ and UAV trajectories into problem **P1** (line 17). By solving problem **P3**, the possible distribution of task sizes is updated (lines 18-19). Repeat the steps 2-19 until the DRCOTO converges. Finally, we get the computation offloading related variables and UAV trajectories.

## 4 Simulation Results

We consider an LAN scenario within a $X_{max} \times Y_{max} = 1\text{km} \times 1\text{km}$ ground area. $I = 15$ GUs are randomly distributed. $J = 3$ UAVs and 1 HAP collaboratively provide computation offloading service. The sample space of the task size is $\Omega = \{0.2, 0.5, 1, 1.5, 2\}$Mbit. The radius of the uncertainty set is $\epsilon = 0.3$. The

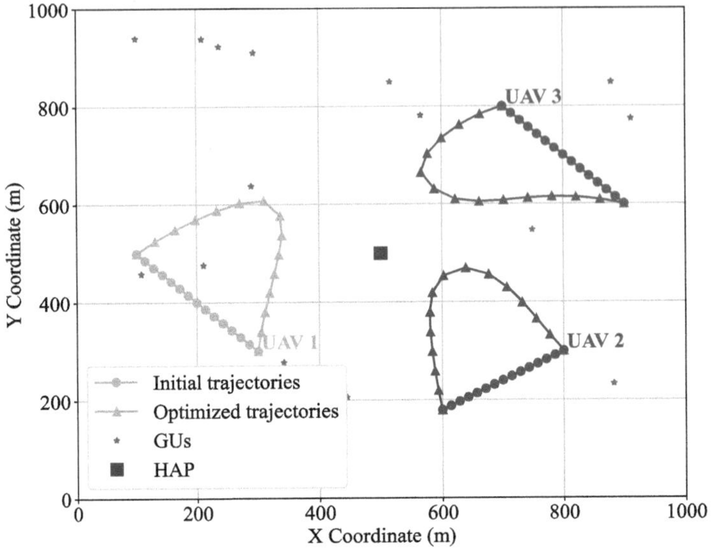


**Fig. 2.** The UAV trajectories and locations of GUs and HAP.

key parameters are set as: $I^{uq} = -90$dBm, $N = 15$, $\tau = 2$s, $D_{min} = 20$ m, $v_u^{fly} = 20$m/s, $Q = 200$, $K = 5$, $q^{uz} = 200$m, $q_H^z = 20$km, $N^u = 3$, and $N^h = 7$. The remaining parameters refer to [6,14,17,19].

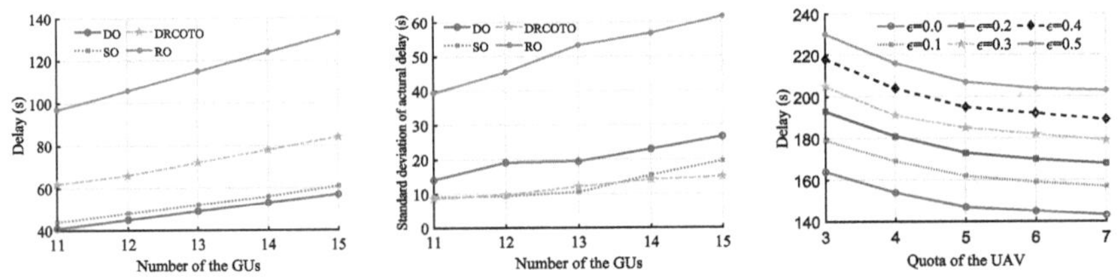


(a) The optimized delay.

(b) The standard deviation of actual delays related to optimized delays.

(c) The relationships between the delay and quota of the UAV.

**Fig. 3.** Comparison of multi-dimensional performance of various optimization methods.

Figure 2 shows the initial and optimized UAV trajectories in LAN. The initial and terminal positions of the UAVs are fixed. It is observed that all the optimized UAV trajectories curve toward the center of the map. This is because the central area of the map has a relatively dense distribution of the GUs and the HAP is also positioned there. Consequently, the UAVs fly toward the center to reduce the transmission delays.

Figure 3 compares results obtained from the deterministic optimization (DO), stochastic optimization (SO), DRCOTO, and robust optimization (RO) to evaluate the performance of the proposed algorithm. In detail, task sizes are treated as deterministic, ignoring the uncertainty entirely in the DO. In the SO, the probability distribution of task sizes is known. In the RO, the maximum potential task sizes is considered.

As shown in Fig. 3a, as the number of GUs increases, the delay derived from all optimization methods shows an upward trend. This is because a larger number of GUs leads to more data to be processed, which in turn causes the higher delay. With the same number of GUs, the optimized delays of the four methods increase in sequence, i.e., DO, SO, DRCOTO, and RO. This indicates that the scenarios considered by these methods become progressively more conservative.

Figure 3b shows the standard deviation of actual delays related to optimized delays. The "actual delays" specifically refers to the measured delays derived from processing five distinct datasets with the optimized computation offloading strategy and UAV trajectories. As illustrated in Fig. 3b, the standard deviation of actual delays increases with the growing number of GUs. This is because the deviation between the actual and optimized task sizes expands gradually with more GUs, thereby leading to a higher standard deviation. Besides, with the same number of GUs, the standard deviations of the RO, DO, SO, and DRCOTO exhibit a sequentially decreasing trend. The DRCOTO method yields the smallest standard deviation, indicating its superior stability. It is concluded that compared with other benchmarks, the DRCOTO achieves the best balance between the delay optimization and robustness.

Figure 3c depicts the relationships between the delay and quota of the UAV. As shown in Fig. 3c, the delay decreases as the quota of UAVs increases. This is attributed to the fact that the computation delay of UAVs is lower than that of GUs. With larger quotas of UAVs, more tasks can be computed on UAVs, thereby reducing the delay. Furthermore, the optimized delay increases with the expanding radius of the uncertainty set. This is because a larger radius covers more adverse possible probability distributions, particularly those with larger task sizes, which ultimately leads to an increment in the delay.

## 5 Conclusions

In this paper, we highlight the cooperation mechanisms of UAVs and HAPs in the LAN to provide offloading services for GUs. The uncertainty sets are established based on the $L_1$ norm metric to measure uncertainties in task sizes. Based on the constructed uncertainty sets, a DRO problem is formulated to minimize the worst case delay by jointly optimizing offloading strategies and UAV trajectories. Subsequently, the DRCOTO algorithm is developed based on the BD and SCA to solve the proposed DRO problem. Simulation results demonstrate the DRCOTO algorithm outperforms the DO, SO, and RO methods in achieving a trade-off between the optimized delay and robustness.

## References

1. Azari, M.M., et al.: Evolution of non-terrestrial networks from 5G to 6G: a survey. IEEE Commun. Surv. Tutor. **24**(4), 2633–2672 (2022). https://doi.org/10.1109/COMST.2022.3199901
2. McEnroe, P., Wang, S., Liyanage, M.: A survey on the convergence of edge computing and AI for UAVs: opportunities and challenges. IEEE Internet Things J. **9**(17), 15435–15459 (2022). https://doi.org/10.1109/JIOT.2022.3176400
3. Jia, Z., et al.: Hierarchical low-altitude wireless network empowered air traffic management. arXiv preprint arXiv:2509.03386 (2025)
4. He, Y., Wang, D., Huang, F., Zhang, R., Gu, X., Pan, J.: Downlink and uplink sum rate maximization for HAP-LAP cooperated networks. IEEE Trans. Veh. Technol. **71**(9), 9516–9531 (2022)
5. Luo, Y., Wang, Y., Lei, Y., Wang, C., Zhang, D., Ding, W.: Decentralized user allocation and dynamic service for multi-UAV-enabled MEC system. IEEE Trans. Veh. Technol. **73**(1), 1306–1321 (2024). https://doi.org/10.1109/TVT.2023.3308589
6. Cao, H., Yu, G., Chen, Z.: Cooperative task offloading and dispatching optimization for large-scale users via UAVs and HAP. In: IEEE Wireless Communication and Networking Conference (WCNC). Glasgow, United Kingdom (2023). https://doi.org/10.1109/WCNC55385.2023.10118722
7. Zhang, X., Wang, K., Li, X., Liu, P., Shin, H.: Joint task chain, power, and UAV trajectory optimization based on an integrated multi-UAV system. IEEE Trans. Veh. Technol. **74**(8), 12907–12920 (2025). https://doi.org/10.1109/TVT.2025.3553874
8. Zhang, S., Yi, N., Ma, Y.: A survey of computation offloading with task types. IEEE Trans. Intell. Transport. Syst. **25**(8), 8313–8333 (2024). https://doi.org/10.1109/TITS.2024.3410896
9. Jiang, G., Jia, Z., He, L., Dong, C., Wu, Q., Han, Z.: Distributionally robust optimization for computation offloading in aerial access networks. In: IEEE Global Communication Conference (GLOBECOM). Cape Town, South Africa (2024). https://doi.org/10.1109/GLOBECOM52923.2024.10901605
10. Beyer, H.G., Sendhoff, B.: Robust optimization - a comprehensive survey. Comput. Method Appl. M. **196**(33–34), 3190–3218 (2007)
11. Pan, K., Guan, Y.: Data-driven risk-averse stochastic self-scheduling for combined-cycle units. IEEE Trans. Ind. Informat. **13**(6), 3058–3069 (2017)
12. Jia, Z., et al.: Distributionally robust optimization for aerial multi-access edge computing via cooperation of UAVs and HAPs. IEEE Trans. Mob. Comput. **24**(10), 10853–10867 (2025). https://doi.org/10.1109/TMC.2025.3571023
13. El Hammouti, H., Benjillali, M., Shihada, B., Alouini, M.S.: Learn-as-you-fly: a distributed algorithm for joint 3D placement and user association in multi-UAVs networks. IEEE Trans. Wirel. Commun. **18**(12), 5831–5844 (2019). https://doi.org/10.1109/TWC.2019.2939315
14. Fan, W., et al.: Joint task offloading and resource allocation for vehicular edge computing based on V2I and V2V modes. IEEE Trans. Intell. Transp. Syst. **24**(4), 4277–4292 (2023). https://doi.org/10.1109/TITS.2022.3230430
15. Mrema, D.D., Shimamoto, S.: Performance of quadrifilar helix antenna on EAD channel model for UAV to LEO satellite link. In: International Conference on Collaboration Technology and System (CTS). Denver, CO, USA (2012). https://doi.org/10.1109/CTS.2012.6261045

16. Pu, L., Chen, X., Mao, G., Xie, Q., Xu, J.: Chimera: an energy-efficient and deadline-aware hybrid edge computing framework for vehicular crowdsensing applications. IEEE Internet Things J. **6**(1), 84–99 (2019). https://doi.org/10.1109/JIOT.2018.2872436
17. Jia, Z., Wu, Q., Dong, C., Yuen, C., Han, Z.: Hierarchical aerial computing for Internet of Things via cooperation of HAPs and UAVs. IEEE Internet Things J. **10**(7), 5676–5688 (2023). https://doi.org/10.1109/JIOT.2022.3151639
18. Zeng, Y., Xu, J., Zhang, R.: Energy minimization for wireless communication with rotary-wing UAV. IEEE Trans. Wirel. Commun. **18**(4), 2329–2345 (2019). https://doi.org/10.1109/TWC.2019.2902559
19. Peng, S., Li, B., Liu, L., Fei, Z., Niyato, D.: Trajectory design and resource allocation for multi-UAV-assisted sensing, communication, and edge computing integration. IEEE Trans. Commun. **73**(4), 2847–2861 (2025). https://doi.org/10.1109/TCOMM.2024.3478115

# Sensing and Localization

# Indoor Mapping Based on Virtual Anchors with a Single Base Station

Mengling Geng[1(✉)], Ze Li[1,2], Zengshan Tian[1], and Xuesha Shi[1]

[1] School of Communications and Information Engineering, Chongqing University of Posts and Telecommunications, Chongqing 400065, China
{S230101035,S230101126}@stu.cqupt.edu.cn, {lize,tianzs}@cqupt.edu.cn

[2] Key Laboratory of Industrial Internet of Things and Networked Control, Ministry of Education, Chongqing University of Posts and Telecommunications, Chongqing 400065, China

**Abstract.** Traditional indoor mapping methods typically rely on multiple base stations (BSs) and sensor fusion, resulting in high costs and limited flexibility. Although single-BS mapping in low-bandwidth, single-input single-output (SISO) networks has attracted significant research interest, it remains challenging. This paper proposes a virtual anchor (VA)-based mapping method using only a single BS, enabling accurate map generation without prior knowledge of indoor geometry. First, we propose an iterative maximum likelihood delay estimation (IMLDE) algorithm that accurately estimates the time of flight (ToF) while reducing computational complexity. Then, a deep neural network (DNN) is employed to model the nonlinear relationship between user locations and VA locations. To refine VA estimates, we introduce an iterative ToF-based selection algorithm. In each iteration, theoretical ToFs for VA-reflected paths are derived under geometric constraints, and the most consistent estimated ToFs are selected to retrain the DNN, progressively improving accuracy. Finally, simulations using commercial-grade wireless ray propagation modeling software show that the proposed method achieves high-precision indoor mapping in resource-constrained scenarios.

**Keywords:** indoor mapping · virtual anchor · time of flight · deep neural network

## 1 Introduction

With the popularization of smart devices and the growing demand for indoor localization, indoor mapping technologies have gained significant attention in applications such as robot navigation, augmented reality (AR), and security monitoring [1]. Traditional methods primarily rely on technologies like ultra-wideband (UWB), LiDAR, and RGB-based visual sensors, which often face challenges including complex calibration procedures, high deployment complexity, and limited adaptability to diverse environments.


Y. Liu et al. (Eds.): ChinaCom 2025, LNICST 711, pp. 427–440, 2027.
https://doi.org/10.1007/978-3-032-33662-0_31

Recently, the concept of virtual anchors (VAs), which model the environment exploiting the multipath components (MPCs) of wireless signals, has attracted increasing attention. As shown in Fig. 1, for specular reflection, VAs are the mirror images of the base station (BS) with respect to the surfaces that create first-order reflections. The geometry of VAs reveals the spatial configuration of dominant reflectors, enabling environment mapping without prior structural knowledge [2]. Previous studies have demonstrated the feasibility of estimating VA locations from channel state information (CSI) [2,3] or time of flight (ToF) measurements [3,4], and constructing indoor maps using VA-based models [2–5], even with a single BS and commodity hardware.

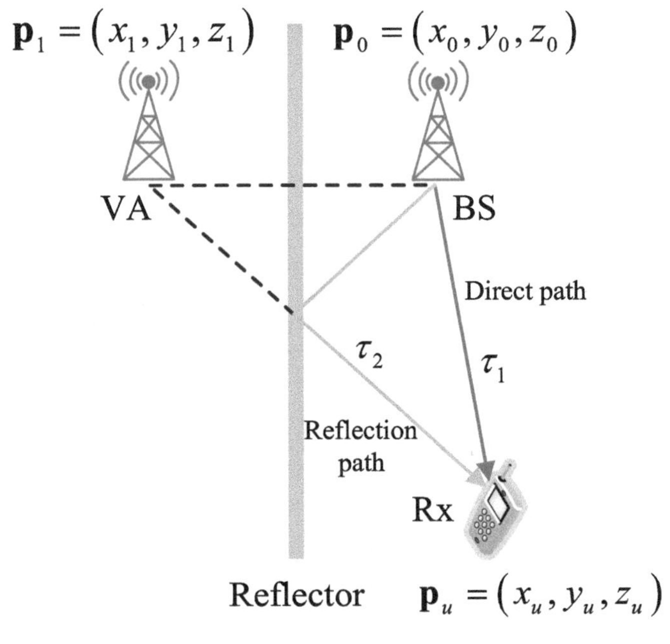


**Fig. 1.** Virtual anchor geometric model under specular reflection.

Despite these advancements, VA-based mapping still faces significant challenges. Most existing methods rely on a combination of ToF and angle of arrival (AoA) to estimate VA locations. However, obtaining AoA information requires multi-antenna arrays, which significantly increases system complexity and cost [6]. In many practical scenarios, such as IoT devices, smartphones, and low-end WiFi equipment, the hardware is typically limited to a single antenna and constrained bandwidth, making reliable AoA estimation infeasible. Therefore, localizing VAs using only ToF (i.e., range-only measurements) under conditions without angular information and limited bandwidth holds significant practical relevance. Nevertheless, in complex indoor environments, multipath propagation and non-line-of-sight (NLoS) often cause ambiguous range measurements, complicating accurate VA estimation. To solve these problems, researchers have proposed various solutions, such as employing multiple hypothesis models to identify the correct propagation path [7,8]. For instance, the efficient distributed particle filter (EDPF) in [8] decomposes the simultaneous localization and mapping (SLAM) problem into multiple low-dimensional sub-filters with joint weight updates, effectively reducing multipath ambiguity. However, EDPF may converge to incorrect hypotheses, leading to error accumulation, and its computational complexity hinders real-time performance on resource-constrained devices. Additionally, the successive tap removal (STR) method proposed in [9] improves VA estimation through an iterative grid search-based process using range-only measurements. However, its performance is limited by the trade-off between grid resolution and complexity, and estimation bias may arise in complex environments due to path association failures. In contrast, deep learning-based methods utilize large-scale datasets to train neural networks that can automatically learn complex relationships between multipath components and VA locations without predefined hypothesis models. For example, the encoder-decoder model in [3] jointly estimates user and VA locations from CSI. Similarly, the variational inference-based model in [10] utilizes ToFs and amplitudes to estimate user and VA locations from single-anchor measurements, achieving high accuracy in challenging scenarios. However, it still relies on AoA information extracted from wideband antenna arrays in certain configurations.

Inspired by the above works, this paper proposes a VA-based indoor mapping method using range-only measurements from a single BS. First, we introduce the iterative maximum likelihood delay estimation (IMLDE) algorithm, a two-stage refinement method that improves ToF estimation accuracy while reducing computational complexity. Next, the Hungarian algorithm [11] optimizes the association between multipath components and VAs, enabling more effective training of a deep neural network (DNN) to map user locations to VA locations. To further refine VA estimates, we introduce an iterative ToF-based selection algorithm. In each iteration, estimated ToFs are compared with theoretical ToFs of VA-reflected paths derived under geometric constraints, and the most consistent ones are selected to retrain the DNN. The simulation experiment is conducted in an underground garage scenario using the commercial electromagnetic propagation simulation software Wireless InSite. The results demonstrate that the proposed method significantly improves VA estimation accuracy, thereby contributing to more accurate indoor mapping.

## 2 System Design

### 2.1 Parameter Estimation

In low-bandwidth systems, the limited frequency resolution restricts the accuracy of ToF estimation. Moreover, multipath propagation and NLoS interference introduce signal aliasing and overlapping ToFs, undermining the robustness of environment mapping. These challenges are especially pronounced in resource-constrained scenarios, such as single-BS, single-antenna systems, where a low-complexity yet accurate ToF estimation algorithm is essential.

Traditional super-resolution methods, such as the multiple signal classification (MUSIC) algorithm, suffer from subspace estimation bias in the presence of strong direct paths, often leading to the suppression of weaker reflected components. Although Rap-MUSIC partially alleviates this problem by modifying the signal subspace, it requires a densely sampled ToF grid, resulting in high computational complexity. In low-bandwidth conditions, the limited frequency resolution further impairs its ability to resolve closely spaced paths. Orthogonal matching pursuit (OMP), which adopts a greedy dictionary-matching strategy, exhibits strong robustness to noise. However, it involves an exhaustive search across dictionary atoms in each iteration, leading to increased computational complexity and slower convergence.

To solve these problems, we propose an iterative maximum likelihood delay estimation (IMLDE) algorithm that achieves accurate ToF estimation with reduced computational cost. IMLDE is formulated within the maximum likelihood estimation (MLE) framework and incorporates a modified space-alternating generalized expectation-maximization (SAGE) structure. It performs ToF estimation in two stages: a coarse search with large step sizes to rapidly identify candidate ToFs, followed by fine-grained local refinement to enhance estimation accuracy. This hierarchical strategy significantly reduces the search space and accelerates convergence.

We consider a single-input single-output (SISO) system. The channel frequency response (CFR) under multipath propagation conditions can be expressed as

$$h\left(f\right)=\sum_{l=1}^{L}\alpha_{l}e^{-j2\pi f\tau_{l}} \tag{1}$$

where $L$ is the number of propagation paths, $\alpha_l$ and $\tau_l$ represent the amplitude and ToF of the $l$-th path, respectively, and $f$ is the subcarrier frequency.

Assuming that the orthogonal frequency division multiplexing (OFDM) signal contains $N$ subcarriers, the CSI is sampled at discrete frequencies, and represented as

$$\mathbf{H}=\left[h_1,h_2,\cdots,h_N\right]^T \tag{2}$$

To estimate the ToF, the CSI matrix is given by

$$\mathbf{X}=\mathbf{A}\left(\tau\right)\mathbf{s}\left(\alpha\right)+\mathbf{W} \tag{3}$$

where $\mathbf{X}$ is the CSI observation vector, $\mathbf{s}\left(\alpha\right)$ is the attenuation vector of length $L$, $\mathbf{W}$ is an additive white Gaussian noise vector, and the steering matrix $\mathbf{A}\left(\boldsymbol{\tau}\right)$ is defined as

$$\mathbf{A}(\boldsymbol{\tau})=\left[\mathbf{a}(\tau_1),\mathbf{a}(\tau_2),\cdots,\mathbf{a}(\tau_L)\right] \tag{4}$$

where $\mathbf{a}(\tau)$ represents the array manifold vector about ToF, which is given by

$$\mathbf{a}(\tau)=\left[1,e^{-j2\pi\Delta f\tau},\cdots,e^{-j2\pi(N-1)\Delta f\tau}\right]^T \tag{5}$$

where $\Delta f$ is the frequency spacing between adjacent subcarriers.

To estimate the ToF vector $\boldsymbol{\tau} = [\tau_1, \tau_2, \ldots, \tau_L]$, we construct the following maximum likelihood objective function:

$$\hat{\boldsymbol{\tau}} = \arg\min_{\boldsymbol{\tau}} \|\mathbf{X} - \mathbf{A}(\boldsymbol{\tau}) \cdot \mathbf{s}(\boldsymbol{\alpha})\|^2 \tag{6}$$

The IMLDE algorithm employs an alternating iterative update strategy, where interference from other paths is suppressed at each iteration to enhance the ToF estimation accuracy. The specific steps are as follows.

*Step 1:* Initialize the ToF vector $\boldsymbol{\tau}^{(0)} = \left[\tau_1^{(0)}, \tau_2^{(0)}, \cdots, \tau_L^{(0)}\right]$, and set the iteration counter $t = 1$.

*Step 2:* For the $l$-th path, calculate the residual signal by removing the contributions from other paths as follows:

$$\gamma_l = \mathbf{X} - \sum_{n \neq l} \alpha_n{}^{(0)} \cdot \mathbf{a}\left(\tau_n^{(0)}\right) \tag{7}$$

Then, within the coarse search range $\tau \in [\tau_{\min}, \tau_{\max}]$, obtain the initial ToF estimate by

$$\hat{\tau}_l^{(0)} = \arg\max_{\tau} |\langle \gamma_l, \mathbf{a}(\tau) \rangle| \tag{8}$$

*Step 3:* At the $t$-th iteration, update the residual signal as

$$\gamma_l^{(t)} = \mathbf{X} - \sum_{n=1}^{L} \alpha_n^{(t-1)} \cdot \mathbf{a}\left(\tau_n^{(t-1)}\right) \tag{9}$$

Restore the contribution of the $l$-th path by

$$\gamma_l^{(t),new} = \gamma_l^{(t)} + \alpha_l^{(t-1)} \cdot \mathbf{a}\left(\tau_l^{(t-1)}\right) \tag{10}$$

Then, within the local search range $\tau \in \left[\hat{\tau}_l^{(t-1)} - \Delta\tau, \hat{\tau}_l^{(t-1)} + \Delta\tau\right]$, where $\Delta\tau$ denotes the local step size, refine the ToF as

$$\hat{\tau}_l^{(t)} = \arg\max_{\tau} \left|\left\langle \gamma_l^{(t),new}, \mathbf{a}(\tau) \right\rangle\right| \tag{11}$$

*Step 4:* For all $l = 1, 2, \ldots, L$, if the following convergence condition is satisfied:

$$\left|\hat{\tau}_l^{(t)} - \hat{\tau}_l^{(t-1)}\right| < \epsilon \tag{12}$$

where $\epsilon$ is a convergence threshold, the iteration terminates and the final ToF estimates for all paths are obtained. Otherwise, set $t = t+1$ and return to Step 3.

## 2.2 VA Location Estimation Based on DNN

We design a DNN to learn the nonlinear mapping from user locations to VA locations, aiming to capture the dominant reflection geometry in indoor environments. Using an underground parking garage as a representative scenario, we observe that wireless signals predominantly reflect off the surrounding walls and the regularly spaced columns on either side. These columns can be collectively modeled as two continuous vertical reflective surfaces. In contrast, the ceiling and floor generally produce weaker reflections due to their material and structural properties. Therefore, we focus on estimating VAs associated with the major structural components (e.g., walls and columns), while omitting contributions from weaker reflectors (e.g., ceilings and floors). Despite this simplification, the retained VAs effectively capture the key geometrical features required for accurate indoor mapping.

Given the relatively stable spatial relationship between users and nearby reflectors in structured indoor environments, the user's location inherently contains valuable information for inferring VA locations. Let the 3D coordinates of the $j$-th user be denoted as $\mathbf{p}_u^{(j)}$. The DNN, parameterized by $\theta$, is trained to learn a nonlinear function $f_\theta$ that maps the user's location to the predicted VA locations as follows:

$$\mathbf{VA} = f_\theta\left(\mathbf{p}_u^{(j)}\right) \tag{13}$$

where $\mathbf{VA} = \left\{\mathbf{p}_i^{(j)}\right\}_{i=1}^{M}$ represents the coordinates of $M$ predicted VAs for the $j$-th user, with $M = 6$ in this paper.

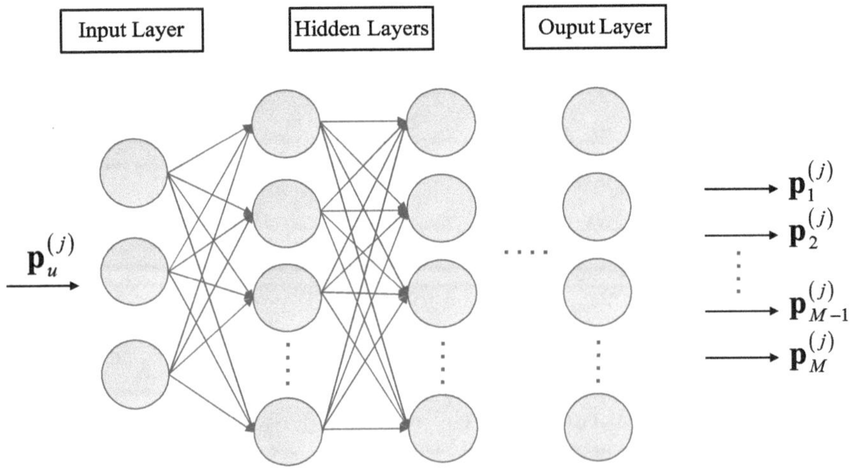


**Fig. 2.** DNN architecture for VA prediction. The network maps a 3-dimensional user location to a $3M$-dimensional output representing the coordinates of $M$ predicted VAs, with multiple ReLU-activated hidden layers modeling nonlinear transformations.

The network is implemented as a multilayer perceptron (MLP), which is well-suited for modeling complex nonlinear relationships. Rectified linear unit (ReLU) activation functions are employed in the hidden layers to facilitate efficient training and mitigate the vanishing gradient problem. The model parameters are optimized through gradient descent with backpropagation to minimize the prediction error. The architecture of the proposed network is illustrated in Fig. 2.

To supervise the DNN training, we avoid directly using absolute ToF, which may contain systematic offsets caused by phase errors. Instead, we calculate the relative time of flight (rToF) between each reflection path and the direct path. Specifically, we assume that $\tau_1$ corresponds to the direct path, and $\tau_l$ $(l = 2, ..., L)$ represents the $(l-1)$-th reflection path. The rToF is defined as $\tau_l - \tau_1$ and can be converted into a relative distance via $d_{l-1} = (\tau_l - \tau_1) \cdot C$, where $C$ is the speed of light. For a training batch of size $N_b$, the resulting reference distance set is denoted as $\mathcal{D} = \{d_1, d_2, \cdots, d_J\}$, where $J = (L-1) \times N_b$. This set provides geometric supervision that enforces consistency between the predicted VA locations and their expected mirror locations relative to the BS.

For each user-VA pair, we calculate the predicted relative distance as

$$I_{u,i}^{(j)} = \left| \|\mathbf{p}_u^{(j)} - \mathbf{p}_i^{(j)}\| - \|\mathbf{p}_u^{(j)} - \mathbf{p}_0\| \right| \tag{14}$$

where $\mathbf{p}_0$ denotes the location of the BS. For each user, this yields $M$ predicted distances, forming the predicted set $\mathcal{I} = \{I_1, I_2, \cdots, I_K\}$ across the batch, where $K = M \times N_b$.

Since there is no predefined one-to-one correspondence between the reference set $\mathcal{D}$ and the predicted set $\mathcal{I}$, directly matching them by index is inappropriate. To solve this, we apply the Hungarian algorithm to determine the optimal one-to-one assignment that minimizes the total matching error. We construct a cost matrix $\mathbf{C} \in \mathbb{R}^{J \times K}$, where each entry $C_{jk} = |d_j - I_k|$ quantifies the error between the $j$-th reference distance and the $k$-th predicted distance. The objective is to find a binary assignment matrix $\mathbf{A} = \{a_{jk}\}$ that minimizes the total cost:

$$\min \sum_{j=1}^{J} \sum_{k=1}^{K} C_{jk} a_{jk} \tag{15}$$

where $a_{jk} \in \{0, 1\}$ indicates whether $d_j$ is matched with $I_k$. Once the optimal assignment is determined, the residual error for each matched pair is calculated as $\Delta\Gamma_{jk} = I_k - d_j$. To ensure robustness during training, we apply the smooth L1 loss (also known as the Huber loss), which is defined as

$$\mathcal{L} = \sum_{j,k} \rho(\Delta\Gamma_{jk}) \tag{16}$$

where $\rho(\cdot)$ denotes the smooth L1 function. This loss function combines the advantages of L2 loss for small errors and L1 loss for large errors, leading to stable convergence and robustness against outliers.

To mitigate prediction noise and improve reliability, we apply K-Means clustering to VA predictions obtained through repeated inferences. The resulting cluster centers serve as the final estimates of those dominant VA locations, corresponding to major reflective surfaces in the environment.

**Algorithm 1** Indoor Mapping via VA Estimation

**Require:** CSI matrix $\mathbf{H}$; user locations $\{\mathbf{p}_u\}$.
**Ensure:** Generated indoor map $\mathcal{M}$.
**Stage 1: ToF Parameter Estimation via IMLDE**
Initialize ToF vector $\boldsymbol{\tau}^{(0)}$, and set iteration counter $t = 1$.
**for** $l = 1$ to $L$ **do**
  Calculate residual $\gamma_l$ and initial ToF $\hat{\tau}_l^{(0)}$ using (7)-(8).
**end for**
**repeat**
  **for** $l = 1$ to $L$ **do**
    Update residual $\gamma_l^{(t)}$ using (9).
    Restore path contribution $\gamma_l^{(t),new}$ using (10).
    Refine ToF estimate $\hat{\tau}_l^{(t)}$ using (11).
  **end for**
**until** convergence condition in (12) is satisfied
**Stage 2: Initial VA Estimation via DNN**
Train DNN model $f_\theta$ to learn the mapping: $\{\mathbf{p}_u\} \rightarrow \{\hat{\mathbf{p}}_i\}$.
Obtain initial VA estimates $\{\hat{\mathbf{p}}_i^{(0)}\}$ using $f_\theta$ and K-Means.
**Stage 3: Iterative VA Refinement via ToF Selection**
Set the iteration counter $k = 1$.
**repeat**
  Calculate theoretical ToFs $\{\tau_i^{\text{geo},(k)}\}$ based on current VA estimates $\{\hat{\mathbf{p}}_i^{(k-1)}\}$ using (17).
  Construct discrepancy matrix $\mathbf{B}^{(k)}$ and calculate consistency scores $\{\delta_l^{(k)}\}$ using (18)-(19).
  Select top $Q$ estimated ToFs $\{\tau_l^{\text{sel},(k)}\}$ with smallest consistency scores.
  Retrain $f_\theta$ with $\{\tau_l^{\text{sel},(k)}\}$ to update $\{\hat{\mathbf{p}}_i^{(k)}\}$.
**until** convergence condition in (21) is satisfied
Final refined VA locations: $\{\hat{\mathbf{p}}_i^*\}$.
**Stage 4: Indoor Map Generation**
Construct the map $\mathcal{M}$ based on $\{\hat{\mathbf{p}}_i^*\}$.

## 2.3 Optimizing VA Estimation via ToF-Based Selection

To further enhance the accuracy of VA estimation, we propose an iterative ToF-based selection algorithm that leverages the geometric relationship between VAs and their associated first-order reflection paths. Since VAs represent the mirror images of the BS with respect to the dominant reflective surfaces, accurate VA estimation is crucial for generating reliable indoor maps.

However, the VA locations initially predicted by the DNN may be affected by measurement noise, multipath interference, and estimation errors. To mitigate these problems, our algorithm employs an iterative refinement procedure.

First, it calculates theoretical ToFs based on the geometric constraints between the user's location and the current VA estimates. Next, the algorithm evaluates the consistency between these theoretical and estimated ToFs, selecting high-confidence estimates with minimal geometric deviation to supervise DNN retraining. This iterative process progressively improves VA prediction accuracy. The specific steps are as follows.

*Step 1:* Let $\{\hat{\mathbf{p}}_i^{(0)}\}_{i=1}^{M}$ denote the initial VA locations predicted by the DNN, where $M$ is the number of VAs. Set the iteration counter $k = 1$.

*Step 2:* At the $k$-th iteration, based on the current VA estimates $\{\hat{\mathbf{p}}_i^{(k-1)}\}_{i=1}^{M}$ and the known user location $\mathbf{p}_u$, the theoretical ToF for the $i$-th VA is calculated as

$$\tau_i^{\text{geo},(k)} = \frac{\left\| \mathbf{p}_u - \hat{\mathbf{p}}_i^{(k-1)} \right\|}{C} \tag{17}$$

The set $\{\tau_i^{\text{geo},(k)}\}_{i=1}^{M}$ represents the expected ToFs corresponding to first-order specular reflections.

Meanwhile, a set of estimated ToFs $\{\tau_l^{\text{est}}\}_{l=1}^{L}$ is obtained using the parameter estimation algorithm described in Sect. 2.1. To assess the consistency between estimated and theoretical ToFs, we construct a discrepancy matrix $\mathbf{B}^{(k)} \in \mathbb{R}^{L \times M}$, where each element is defined as

$$B_{l,i}^{(k)} = \left| \tau_l^{\text{est}} - \tau_i^{\text{geo},(k)} \right| \tag{18}$$

*Step 3:* For each estimated ToF $\tau_l^{\text{est}}$, the minimum discrepancy with respect to the theoretical ToFs is calculated as

$$\delta_l^{(k)} = \min_i B_{l,i}^{(k)} \tag{19}$$

where $\delta_l^{(k)}$ serves as a consistency score indicating the likelihood that the $l$-th estimated ToF corresponds to a valid first-order reflection. A smaller score implies a higher degree of geometric consistency.

Subsequently, the consistency scores $\{\delta_l^{(k)}\}_{l=1}^{L}$ are sorted in ascending order, and the top $Q$ ToFs with the smallest discrepancies are selected to form a high-confidence ToF set $\{\tau_l^{\text{sel},(k)}\}_{l=1}^{Q}$. These selected ToFs are then used as supervisory signals to retrain the DNN, leading to updated VA predictions.

*Step 4:* After retraining, the updated VA estimates $\{\hat{\mathbf{p}}_i^{(k)}\}_{i=1}^{M}$ are obtained. The average locational change between consecutive iterations is measured by

$$\Delta^{(k)} = \sqrt{\frac{1}{M} \sum_{i=1}^{M} \left\| \hat{\mathbf{p}}_i^{(k)} - \hat{\mathbf{p}}_i^{(k-1)} \right\|^2} \tag{20}$$

The iterative refinement process continues until the following convergence condition is satisfied:

$$\Delta^{(k)} < \beta \tag{21}$$

where $\beta$ is a convergence threshold. If this condition holds for $S$ consecutive iterations, the refinement process is terminated, and the final VA estimates $\{\hat{\mathbf{p}}_i^*\}_{i=1}^M$ are considered stable. Otherwise, set $k = k+1$ and return to Step 2.

This iterative ToF-based selection algorithm ensures that the DNN is progressively trained with geometrically consistent supervisory signals, leading to significantly improved VA estimation accuracy. Algorithm 1 illustrates our overall method in detail.

# 3 Simulation Results

## 3.1 Simulation Setup

We construct a simulation environment using the electromagnetic propagation simulation software Wireless InSite [12] to simulate the experimental scenario. The dataset includes first-order and higher-order reflections, as well as diffraction and diffuse scattering effects. As shown in Fig. 3, the experimental setting is situated in an underground parking garage, with dimensions of $40 \times 30\,\text{m}^2$ and a height of 4 m. The green dot represents the location of the BS with a height of 2 m. We only consider the SISO scenario. The transmitted OFDM signal operates at a frequency of 2.4 GHz with a bandwidth of 100 MHz. To generate the CSI data, the number of subcarriers of the signal is set to 64. To ensure mapping stability, only reflections from static structures (e.g., walls and columns) are considered, while dynamic objects like cars are excluded duc to their variable locations and unstable reflections.

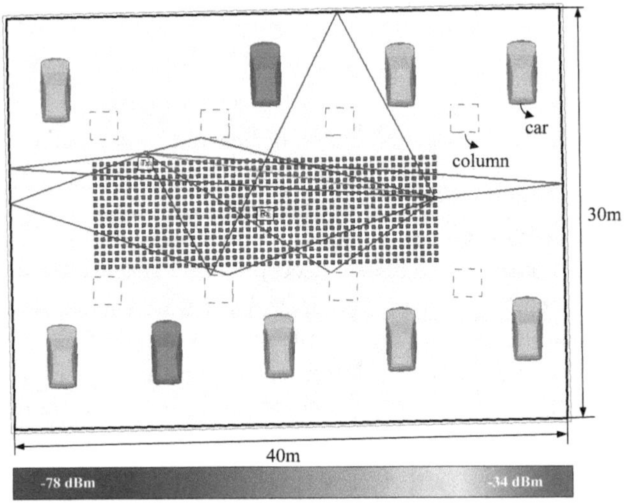


**Fig. 3.** Underground parking garage simulation scenario. Car colors (blue and gray) are used only for visual distinction and do not indicate any functional differences. (Color figure online)

### 3.2 Overall Mapping Accuracy

Since the locations of VAs reflect the spatial distribution of the primary reflective surfaces, they can be utilized to construct the geometric structure of the indoor environment. To evaluate the accuracy of map generation, we use precision as the primary metric, following prior literature. The ground-truth map is constructed using true VA locations and overlaid with a $1\,\text{m} \times 1\,\text{m}$ grid. Each grid cell that overlaps any portion of the map is labeled as an *occupied* cell, while others are labeled as *vacant* cells. The same procedure is applied to the generated map $\mathcal{M}$ based on estimated VA locations. Precision is defined as the proportion of occupied cells in the generated map grid that correctly match the corresponding occupied cells in the ground-truth map grid, thereby reflecting the accuracy of map generation. Since most indoor mapping applications focus on horizontal layouts, we compare planar maps constructed from true and estimated VA locations, as shown in Fig. 4. Solid lines represent the garage's surrounding walls, and dashed rectangles denote columns. The results show that the generated map achieves a precision of 99.5%, demonstrating the high accuracy of the proposed method.

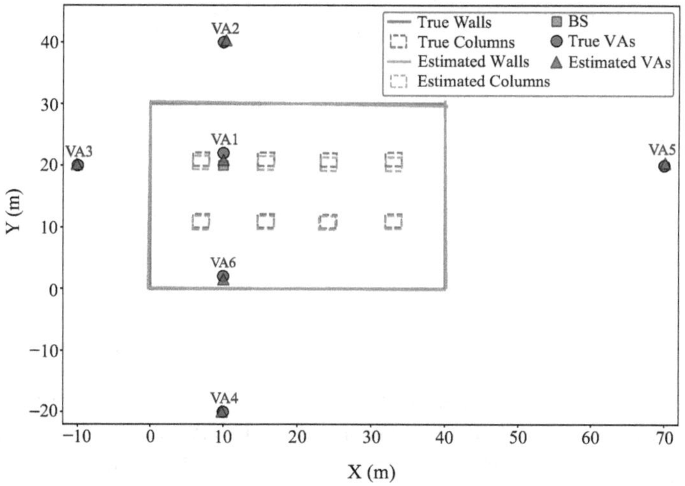


**Fig. 4.** Comparison of planar maps constructed from true and estimated VAs. VA2VA5 correspond to reflections from surrounding walls, while VA1 and VA6 are associated with reflections from columns.

### 3.3 Performance of ToF-Based Selection Optimization Method

To evaluate the effectiveness of the proposed ToF-based selection algorithm, we analyze the root mean squared error (RMSE) trajectory of VA location estimates during the iterative refinement process, as shown in Fig. 5. Within the first seven iterations, the RMSE decreases significantly from an initial 1.93 m (corresponding to the baseline DNN without ToF-based selection) to 1.12 m. Thereafter, it tends to stabilize, indicating a 42.0% reduction in estimation error. Meanwhile, the precision of the generated map improves from 93.8% to 99.5%. These results demonstrate that the ToF-based selection algorithm, combined with DNN retraining, significantly enhances VA estimation accuracy and thereby improves the reliability of map generation.

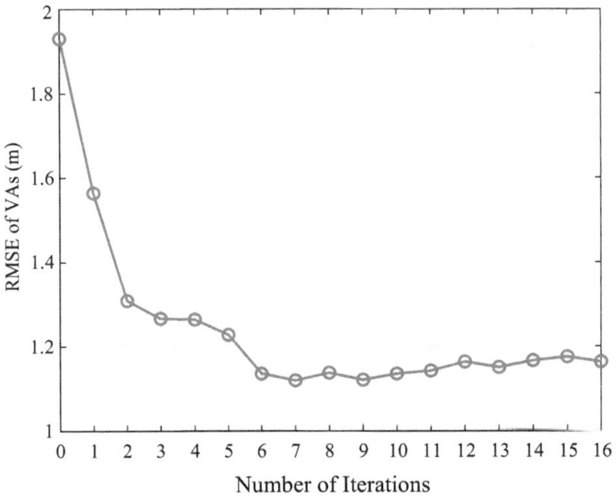


**Fig. 5.** RMSE of VAs over iterations.

### 3.4 Impact of Bandwidth on VA Estimation: IMLDE vs. OMP

To fairly compare the performance of IMLDE and OMP under different bandwidths, we evaluate the estimation errors of each VA at 100 MHz and 200 MHz without applying the ToF-based selection algorithm. As shown in Fig. 6, increasing the bandwidth improves the time resolution for both algorithms, thereby reducing estimation errors. It is worth noting that IMLDE achieves RMSE reductions of 35.5% and 38.8% over OMP at 100 MHz and 200 MHz, respectively. This improvement is mainly attributed to its coarse-to-fine search and iterative interference suppression, which enhance ToF resolution and accuracy. Overall, IMLDE outperforms OMP, with greater bandwidth further amplifying its advantage in indoor mapping accuracy.

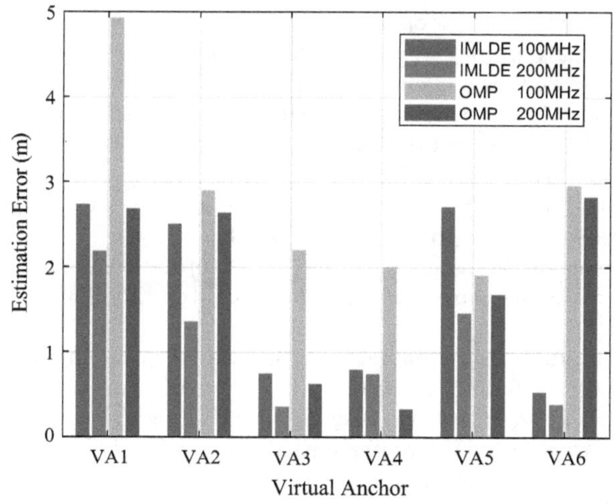


**Fig. 6.** Per-VA error distribution under different algorithms and bandwidths.

# 4 Conclusion

This paper proposes a hybrid VA estimation framework that integrates a DNN with a geometry-guided ToF selection algorithm, enabling accurate map generation without requiring prior knowledge of indoor geometry. The proposed IMLDE algorithm enhances ToF estimation accuracy while reducing computational complexity. Additionally, the ToF-based selection algorithm iteratively refines VA estimates by retraining the DNN with geometry-consistent ToFs. Simulation results show that the proposed method reduces RMSE by 42.0% compared to the baseline DNN model without ToF-based refinement and achieves a mapping accuracy of 99.5%, highlighting its effectiveness and efficiency in resource-constrained wireless indoor mapping scenarios.

# References

1. Show, S.E., Pu, C.-H., Kadim, Z.: 3D mapping and indoor navigation for an indoor environment of the university campus. In: IEEE Symposium on Wireless Technology and Applications (ISWTA), pp. 163–168 (2023)
2. Palacios, J., Bayraktar, M., González-Prelcic, N., Chen, H.: High accuracy device localization in indoor mmWave networks exploiting channel sparsity and virtual anchor mapping. In: IEEE International Conference on Acoustics, Speech and Signal Processing (ICASSP), pp. 13411–13415 (2024)
3. Kadambi, S.: Neural RF SLAM for unsupervised positioning and mapping with channel state information. In: IEEE International Conference on Communications, pp. 3238–3244 (2022)
4. Leitinger, E., Meyer, F., Hlawatsch, F., Witrisal, K., Tufvesson, F., Win, M.Z.: A belief propagation algorithm for multipath-based SLAM. IEEE Trans. Wirel. Commun. **18**(12), 5613–5629 (2019)

5. Naseri, H., Koivunen, V.: Cooperative simultaneous localization and mapping by exploiting multipath propagation. IEEE Trans. Sig. Process. **65**(1), 200–211 (2017)
6. Kim, H., Granström, K., Gao, L., Battistelli, G., Kim S., Wymeersch, H.: 5G mmWave cooperative positioning and mapping using multi-model PHD filter and map fusion. IEEE Trans. Wirel. Commun. **19**(6), 3782–3795 (2020)
7. Herranz, F., Llamazares, A., Molinos, E., Ocaña, M.: A comparison of SLAM algorithms with range only sensors. In: IEEE International Conference on Robotics and Automation (ICRA), pp. 4606–4611 (2014)
8. Xiong, J., Cheong, J.W., Ding, Y., Xiong, Z., Dempster, A.G.: Efficient distributed particle filter for robust range-only SLAM. IEEE Internet Things J. **9**(21), 21932–21945 (2022)
9. Amiri, R., et al.: Indoor environment learning via RF-Mapping. IEEE J. Sel. Areas Commun. **41**(6), 1859–1872 (2023)
10. Wang, T., Li, Y., Liu, J., Hu, K., Shen, Y.: Multipath-assisted single-anchor localization via deep variational learning. IEEE Trans. Wirel. Commun. **23**(8), 9113–9128 (2024)
11. Zhang, X., He, S., Liu, K., Zhao, J.: Unsupervised learning of neural semantic mappings with the Hungarian algorithm for compositional semantics. In: IEEE International Conference on Acoustics, Speech and Signal Processing (ICASSP), pp. 9971–9975 (2024)
12. Remcom, Wireless InSite. http://www.remcom.com/wireless-insite-em-propagation-software. Accessed 8 Sep 2024

# High-Precision Angle Estimation Method of UWB Signals Based on IAA Algorithm

Jie Lei(✉), Shuliang Gui, Zengshan Tian, Zhaoyu Li, and Chenglin Huang

School of Communication and Information Engineering, Chongqing University of Posts and Telecommunications, 400065 Chongqing, China
s230132053@stu.cqupt.edu.cn, {guisl,tianzs,lizhaoyu}@cqupt.edu.cn

**Abstract.** Ultra-wideband (UWB) technology has become a research hotspot for high-precision positioning due to its high temporal resolution and robustness against multi-path interference. However, traditional angle estimation algorithms are limited in accuracy. To address this issue, this study proposes a high-precision angle estimation algorithm for UWB signals based on an iterative adaptive approach (IAA). By establishing a mathematical model of the received signal from an array antenna, a theoretical framework is derived, and an iterative optimization mechanism is designed to achieve precise parameter convergence. Experiments using the YunSDR Y750 demonstrate that the IAA algorithm significantly outperforms the multiple signal classification (MUSIC) algorithm, achieving an angle estimation error of less than 4.5° in 90% of cases (compared to less than 5.5° for the MUSIC algorithm). This algorithm effectively improves the accuracy and robustness of UWB signal angle estimation.

**Keywords:** ultra-wideband · iterative adaptive method · angle estimation

## 1 Introduction

With its excellent time resolution and strong anti-multipath interference capability, UWB technology has shown broad application prospects in high-precision positioning, indoor navigation and other fields [1]. In the UWB multi-base station positioning system [2], the angle estimation is the core link for building spatial geometric constraints. It effectively improves the ill-conditioned nature of the positioning equations by providing target orientation information. The measurement accuracy of angle estimation directly determines the theoretical upper limit of system performance. In recent years, various angle estimation methods have been proposed, such as machine learning-based models [3–5], single antenna technology [6], and low-complexity TOA/AOA joint algorithms [7–9]. Although these methods have improved traditional methods, they still face huge challenges when processing UWB signals. In complex indoor environments,


Y. Liu et al. (Eds.): ChinaCom 2025, LNICST 711, pp. 441–456, 2027.
https://doi.org/10.1007/978-3-032-33662-0_32

multipath effects (such as reflections from walls and furniture) will interfere with angle estimation; in environments with severe electromagnetic interference such as factories or hospitals, the signal-to-noise ratio (SNR) may be lower than − 10 dB, and the impact of noise on the signal is dominant. As a result, the angle estimation error will increase sharply, making it difficult to meet the needs of high-precision positioning. Machine learning-based angle estimation methods perform poorly when the training environment differs from the actual deployment environment. In unseen environments, the median angle estimation error of the machine learning model can reach 14°, which is much higher than its performance in the training environment. This requires retraining or transfer learning in each new environment, which increases the complexity and cost of deployment. Although the single-antenna angle estimation method reduces the hardware cost, its estimation accuracy is limited and has high requirements for antenna design and calibration. Only 58%–66.8% of the estimation errors are less than 15°, which is much lower than the performance of the multi-antenna system. In addition, the single-antenna method is highly dependent on antenna design and requires carefully designed antennas to obtain good angle estimation resolution, which increases the complexity and calibration difficulty of the system and limits its practicality.

To address the aforementioned challenges, this paper proposes a high-precision angle estimation algorithm for UWB signals based on an iterative adaptive approach. As a non-parametric spectral estimation technique, IAA reconstructs the signal's covariance matrix and power spectrum by iteratively optimizing a weighted least-squares criterion. Its uniqueness and advantage lie in the fact that, unlike subspace methods such as MUSIC that require prior knowledge of the number of signal sources, IAA does not require such prior information. Instead, it adaptively estimates the signal power in all potential directions. More importantly, its iterative purification concept effectively handles coherent signals caused by UWB multipath effects, overcoming the limitations of traditional subspace methods. Furthermore, as a model-driven approach, IAA exhibits superior environmental adaptability and generalization capabilities compared to machine learning models reliant on extensive environment-specific training data. Through its iterative optimization mechanism, the algorithm achieves high-precision spatial spectrum estimation, delivering super-resolution performance surpassing traditional beamforming methods even under single-snapshot conditions.

The rest of this paper is organized as follows. Section 2 introduces the system design, including the UWB signal model and preprocessing pipeline. Section 3 details the core principles and implementation of the IAA-based angle estimation algorithm. Section 4 presents the experimental setup, performance evaluation, and a discussion of the study limitations. Finally, Sect. 5 concludes this paper.

## 2 System Design

In this section, we design and implement a UWB signal angle estimation system based on the proposed IAA algorithm. Figure 1 shows the system model, which consists of three core modules: UWB signal generation and reception, preprocessing and data collection, and angle estimation using the IAA algorithm.

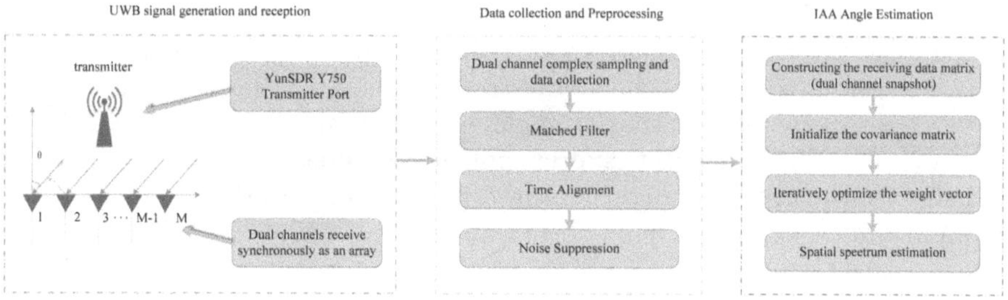


**Fig. 1.** IAA Angle Estimation System Framework.

## 2.1 Analysis Of UWB Signal Characteristics

UWB signals are usually defined as signals with an absolute bandwidth greater than 500 MHz or a relative bandwidth greater than 20%. It is characterized by extremely short pulses in the time domain. This unique time-frequency domain characteristic significantly affects the angle estimation performance of UWB signals. The UWB system based on the IEEE 802.15.4z standard can achieve a ranging accuracy of about 15 cm within a 1 GHz bandwidth [10], fully demonstrating its potential in high-precision positioning applications. The mathematical model of the UWB signal can be expressed as follows:

$$s(t) = \sum_{j=1}^{N_p} A_j w(t - jT_f - c_j T_c - \delta) \tag{1}$$

where $w(t)$ represents the UWB pulse waveform, typically a Gaussian pulse or its derivative; $N_p$ denotes the number of pulses per symbol; $T_f$ denotes the frame duration; $c_j$ denotes the time-hopping code; $T_c$ denotes the chip time; $\delta$ denotes the modulation delay. Due to its ultra-wideband characteristics, the propagation characteristics of UWB signals are significantly different from those of narrowband signals, showing stronger anti-multipath and penetration capabilities. These unique propagation characteristics must be considered in the design of the angle estimation algorithm.

## 2.2 Angle Estimation Mathematical Model Construction

The angle estimation problem based on the UWB system can be mathematically expressed by constructing an array receiving signal model. Consider a uniform linear array (ULA) consisting of $M$ elements. When $L$ UWB signal sources are incident from different angles $\theta_1$, $\theta_2$, ..., $\theta_L$, the signal vector $x(t)$ received by the array at the $t$-th sampling instant can be expressed as:

$$x(t) = A(\theta)s(t) + \mathbf{n}(t), t = 1, 2, \cdots, N \tag{2}$$

where $\mathbf{n}(t)$ is the additive noise vector, $A(\theta) = [a(\theta_1), a(\theta_2), \cdots, a(\theta_l)]$ is the array manifold of $M \times l$, and the array structure requires that the direction vector $a(\theta_l)$ corresponds to the spatial angle $\theta_l$. $s(t) = [s_1(t), s_2(t), \cdots, s_l(t)]^T, t = 1, 2, \cdots, N, A(\theta)$ has different expressions for different geometric arrays.For UWB signals, the array manifold vector $\mathbf{a}(\theta)$ needs to consider frequency correlation and can be expressed as:

$$\mathbf{a}(\theta) = \frac{1}{L} \sum_{l=1}^{L} \mathbf{a}(f_l, \theta) \tag{3}$$

where $L$ is the number of frequencies considered, $f_l$ is the $l$-th frequency, $\mathbf{a}(f_l, \theta)$ is the array manifold vector at this frequency point. The angle estimation problem is the process of recovering the signal arrival angle $\theta_l(l = 1, 2, ..., \mathrm{L})$ from the observed signal $x(t)$. This is a typical inverse problem that requires special algorithms to solve effectively.

### 2.3 Signal Preprocessing

Preprocessing and data collection are the core preliminary steps for UWB signal angle estimation. They extract high-quality data from the raw signals received by the dual channels, providing reliable input for subsequent algorithms.

The YunSDR Y750 device synchronously collects UWB signals through dual channels and generates complex baseboard data. Assuming the received signals are $r_1(t)$ and $r_2(t)$, after orthogonal down-conversion and analog-to-digital conversion, a discrete complex sampling sequence is obtained:

$$\begin{cases} x_1[n] = I_1[n] + jQ_1[n] \\ x_2[n] = I_2[n] + jQ_2[n] \end{cases} \tag{4}$$

where $n = 1, 2, \ldots, N$ is the sampling point index, $I$ and $Q$ are the in-phase and quadrature components respectively. The data is stored by channel as a matrix $\mathbf{X} \in \mathbb{C}^{N \times 2}$, and each column corresponds to the sampling sequence of a channel.

To improve the signal-to-noise ratio (SNR), the conjugate time reversal of the transmitted signal $s(t)$ is used as the matched filter coefficient. The filter output is:

$$y_i[n] = \sum_{k=0}^{L-1} x_i[k] s^*[L - 1 - (n - k)], \quad i = 1, 2, \tag{5}$$

where $L$ is the length of the transmitted signal, and $s^*[\cdot]$ represents the complex conjugate. The filtered signal $\mathbf{Y} = [y_1, y_2]$ retains the main signal energy star and suppresses out-of-band noise.

Because the dual-channel signals have a time delay $\tau$ due to the difference in propagation paths. The time delay is estimated by the cross-correlation method and interpolated and aligned, so the discrete cross-correlation function is defined as:

$$R_{12}[\tau] = \sum_{n=0}^{N-1} y_1[n] \cdot y_2^*[n+\tau], \quad \tau \in [-T_{\max}, T_{\max}], \tag{6}$$

where $T_{\max}$ is the preset maximum delay range.

Then, for peak detection and delay compensation, the peak position of the cross-correlation function $\tau_{\max} = \arg\max_\tau |R_{12}[\tau]|$ is extracted, and cubic spline interpolation compensation is performed on $y_2[n]$. The compensated signal is:

$$y_2'[n] = \sum_{m=-\infty}^{\infty} y_2[m] \cdot \operatorname{sinc}\left(\frac{n-m-\tau_{\max}}{\Delta t}\right)$$

where $\Delta t$ is the sampling interval. Ensure that the data of the two channels are phase synchronized.

In order to further suppress the residual noise, we can use an adaptive Wiener filter to eliminate the residual noise. Assume that the signal and noise power spectral densities are $P_s(f)$ and $P_n(f)$ respectively. The filter transfer function is:

$$H(f) = \frac{P_s(f)}{P_s(f) + P_n(f)} \tag{7}$$

The signal after frequency domain filtering is:

$$\mathbf{Z}_i = \mathcal{F}^{-1}\left\{H(f) \cdot \mathcal{F}(\mathbf{y}_i)\right\}, \quad i = 1, 2, \tag{8}$$

where $\mathcal{F}$ and $\mathcal{F}^{-1}$ are discrete Fourier transform (DFT) and inverse transform (IDFT) respectively

The aligned and denoised dual-channel data are arranged in snapshot form as a received data matrix $\mathbf{R} \in \mathbb{C}^{N\times 2}$, where each row represents the simultaneous sampling value of the dual channels, that is:

$$\mathbf{R} = \begin{bmatrix} x(1)^{\mathrm{T}} \\ x(2)^{\mathrm{T}} \\ \vdots \\ x(N)^{\mathrm{T}} \end{bmatrix} \tag{9}$$

where $N$ is the number of snapshots, $x(t) = \begin{bmatrix} z_1[t] \\ z_2[t] \end{bmatrix}$

## 3 UWB Signal Angle Estimation Based On IAA Algorithm

IAA is a non-parametric super-resolution spectrum estimation technology based on the weighted least squares criterion. Through its unique iterative optimization framework, it can achieve single-snapshot high-precision angle estimation of UWB signals. The core advantages of this technology are: its non-parametric characteristics can adaptively process an unknown number of signal sources in the UWB multipath environment; at the same time, it has the flexibility of array configuration and can be compatible with various UWB antenna topologies; more importantly, its alternating update mechanism effectively guarantees stable convergence performance under UWB wideband conditions, making it an effective method for solving the problem of UWB signal angle estimation in complex scenarios.

### 3.1 IAA Algorithm Core Principle

Assume $P$ is a $L \times L$ diagonal matrix, the diagonal elements are the signal energy at each angle on the scanning grid, and the covariance matrix of interference and noise is $Q(\theta_l) = R - P_l a(\theta_l) a^{\mathrm{H}}(\theta_l)$, where $R = A(\theta) P A^{\mathrm{H}}(\theta)$. Here the weighted least squares cost function is given by

$$\sum_{t=1}^{N} \|x(t) - s_l(t)\boldsymbol{a}(\theta_l)\|_W^2 \tag{10}$$

where $\|A\|_w^2 = A^H W A$,$s_l(t)$ represents the complex amplitude of the signal at the $t$th snapshot $\theta_l$.

In order to obtain accurate estimation results, the following formula is given:

$$J_W(s_l(t)) = (x(t) - \hat{s}_l(t)a(\theta_l))^{\mathrm{H}} W \cdot (x(t) - \hat{s}_l(t)a(\theta_l)) \tag{11}$$

When (11) reaches its minimum value, $\hat{s}_l(t)$ becomes the least squares weighted quantity, $W$ becomes the weighted matrix, and when $W = I$, it is a non-weighted least squares estimate.

Taking the partial derivative of (11) with respect to $\hat{s}_l(t)$ and setting the result equal to zero, we get the least squares estimator:

$$\hat{s}_l(t) = \frac{a^{\mathrm{H}}(\theta_l) W x(t)}{a^{\mathrm{H}}(\theta_l) W a(\theta_l)} \tag{12}$$

then the variance matrix of the estimation error is:

$$\begin{aligned} &E\{[s_l(t) - \hat{s}_l(t)][s_l(t) - \hat{s}_l(t)]^{\mathrm{H}}\} = \\ &(a^{\mathrm{H}}(\theta_l) W a(\theta_l))^{-1} a^{\mathrm{H}}(\theta_l) W E(n(t) n^{\mathrm{H}}(t)) \\ &W a(\theta_l)(a^{\mathrm{H}}(\theta_l) W a(\theta_l))^{-1} = \\ &(a^{\mathrm{H}}(\theta_l) W a(\theta_l))^{-1} a^{\mathrm{H}}(\theta_l) W Q(\theta_l) \cdot \\ &W a(\theta_l)(a^{\mathrm{H}}(\theta_l) W a(\theta_l))^{-1} \end{aligned} \tag{13}$$

where $a(\theta_l)$ and $Q(\theta_l)$ are known. The literature [11] points out how to select the weighting matrix to minimize the above equation.

Assume $A, B$ are any two matrices of $M \times K$ and $K \times L$, respectively, and the inverse matrix of $AA^{\mathrm{H}}$ exists, then the matrix inequality:

$$B^{\mathrm{H}}B \geqslant (AB)^{\mathrm{H}}(AA^{\mathrm{H}})^{-1}(AB) \tag{14}$$

when:

$$\begin{aligned} A &= a^{\mathrm{H}}(\theta_l)Q(\theta_l)^{-\frac{1}{2}}, B = Q(\theta_l)^{-\frac{1}{2}}C^{\mathrm{H}} \\ C &= (a^{\mathrm{H}}(\theta_l)Wa(\theta_l))^{-1}a^{\mathrm{H}}(\theta_l)W \end{aligned} \tag{15}$$

The following can be concluded:

$$\begin{aligned} &\boldsymbol{C}\boldsymbol{Q}(\theta_l)\boldsymbol{C}^{\mathrm{H}}(a^{\mathrm{H}}(\theta_l)C^{\mathrm{H}})^{\mathrm{H}}(a^{\mathrm{H}}(\theta_l)Q(\theta_l)^{-1}a(\theta_l))^{-1}\cdot \\ &(a^{\mathrm{H}}(\theta_l)C^{\mathrm{H}}) = \\ &(\boldsymbol{C}\boldsymbol{a}(\theta_l))(\boldsymbol{a}^{\mathrm{H}}(\theta_l)\boldsymbol{Q}(\theta_l)^{-1}\boldsymbol{a}(\theta_l))^{-1}(\boldsymbol{C}\boldsymbol{a}(\theta_l))^{\mathrm{H}} = \\ &(\boldsymbol{a}^{\mathrm{H}}(\theta_l)\boldsymbol{Q}(\theta_l)^{-1}\boldsymbol{a}(\theta_l))^{-1} \end{aligned} \tag{16}$$

The left side of the above equation is exactly equation (13), and the right side is exactly the variance matrix of the estimation error when $W = Q(\theta_l)^{-1}$. It can be concluded that:

$$E\{[s_l(t) - \hat{s}_l(t)][s_l(t) - \hat{s}_l(t)]^{\mathrm{H}}\} \geqslant (a^{\mathrm{H}}(\theta_l)Q(\theta_l)^{-1}a(\theta_l))^{-1} \tag{17}$$

Therefore, When $W = Q(\theta_l)^{-1}$, the variance matrix of the estimation error is minimized, and the optimal weighted least squares estimator can be obtained.

$$\hat{s}_l(t) = \frac{a^{\mathrm{H}}(\theta_l)Q(\theta_l)^{-1}x(t)}{a^{\mathrm{H}}(\theta_l)Q(\theta_l)^{-1}a(\theta_l)} \tag{18}$$

According to the matrix inversion theorem [12], we can obtain:

$$\hat{s}_l(t) = \frac{a^{\mathrm{H}}(\theta_l)R^{-1}x(t)}{a^{\mathrm{H}}(\theta_l)R^{-1}a(\theta_l)} \tag{19}$$

### 3.2 Angle Estimation

Based on the core principles of the aforementioned IAA algorithm, its iterative optimization framework and adaptive weighting mechanism provide theoretical support for UWB signal angle estimation.

The core process first discretizes the spatial azimuth into a fine scanning grid $\{\theta_l\}_{l=1}^{L}$, initializes the signal power matrix $P^{(0)}$ to the identity matrix (i.e. $P^{(0)} = I$), and calculates the empirical covariance matrix based on the preprocessed data matrix $\mathbf{R}$:

$$\hat{R} = \frac{1}{N}\sum_{t=1}^{N} x(t)x^{\mathrm{H}}(t) \tag{20}$$

Each snapshot $x(t)$ has been processed by matched filtering, time alignment and noise suppression to ensure its phase consistency and high signal-to-noise ratio.

Based on the updated $\hat{R}$, calculate the complex amplitude of the signal at each angle $\theta_l$ according to (19), and then update the power spectrum:

$$P^{(t+1)}(\theta_l) = \frac{|\boldsymbol{a}^{\mathrm{H}}(\theta_l)\hat{R}^{-1}x|^2}{|\boldsymbol{a}^{\mathrm{H}}(\theta_l)\hat{R}^{-1}\boldsymbol{a}(\theta_l)|^2} \tag{21}$$

Then calculate the relative change of the power spectrum of adjacent iterations, When $\epsilon < \xi$, the iteration is terminated and the final spatial spectrum is output:

$$P_{IAA}(\theta_l) = P^{(t+1)}(\theta_l) \tag{22}$$

Perform peak search on the converged spatial spectrum, that is:

$$\hat{\theta}_l = \arg\max_{\theta_l} P_{IAA}(\theta_l), \quad l = 1, ..., L \tag{23}$$

Therefore, by accurately estimating the signal power distribution at different angles and observing the peak position in the power spectrum, the estimated arrival angle can be obtained.

Through the above process, the algorithm can achieve high-precision, low-latency angle estimation in UWB dense multipath environments, providing theoretical support for real-time positioning in complex scenarios.

The algorithm 1 is summarized as follows:

### 3.3 Computational Complexity And Real-Time Feasibility Analysis

To assess the engineering feasibility of the proposed IAA-based framework, we provide a computational complexity analysis. Let the number of array elements be $M$, the number of grid points be $L$, the number of temporal snapshots be $N$, and the number of algorithmic iterations be $T$. The computational burden per iteration can be decomposed as follows:

1. **Sample covariance matrix construction**: Constructing the sample covariance requires multiplying and averaging $N$ data snapshots, which incurs a complexity of $\mathcal{O}(NM^2)$.
2. **Covariance matrix inversion (or factorization)**: A direct matrix inversion involves $\mathcal{O}(M^3)$ operations. In practice, more efficient decomposition methods (e.g., Cholesky factorization) may slightly reduce the constant factor but not the asymptotic order.
3. **Grid-based power update**: For each of the $L$ candidate directions, computing $\mathbf{a}^H\hat{\mathbf{R}}^{-1}\mathbf{x}$ requires $\mathcal{O}(M^2)$ operations, leading to $\mathcal{O}(LM^2)$ over all grid points.

Combining these terms, the overall per-iteration complexity is approximately

$$\mathcal{O}\big(NM^2 + M^3 + LM^2\big). \tag{24}$$

Therefore, the total computational complexity of the algorithm is given by

$$\mathcal{O}\big(T(NM^2 + M^3 + LM^2)\big), \tag{25}$$

**Algorithm 1.** Iterative Signal Processing

**procedure** ITERATIVEESTIMATION($\mathbf{x}, \mathbf{A}(\theta), \epsilon$)
  **Initialization:**
  **for all** $l \in \{1, \dots, L\}$ **do**
    Compute initial signal estimate:

$$s_l^{(0)} \leftarrow \frac{\mathbf{a}^H(\theta_l)\mathbf{x}}{\mathbf{a}^H(\theta_l)\mathbf{a}(\theta_l)}$$

  **end for**
  **for** $t = 1, 2, \dots, T_{\max}$ **do**
    Form power vector:

$$\mathbf{p} \leftarrow \left[|s_1^{(t-1)}|^2, |s_2^{(t-1)}|^2, \dots, |s_L^{(t-1)}|^2\right]^T$$

    Reconstruct covariance matrix:

$$\hat{R} = \frac{1}{N}\sum_{t=1}^{N} x(t)x^{\mathrm{H}}(t)$$

    **for all** $l \in \{1, \dots, L\}$ **do**
      Update signal components:

$$s_l^{(t)} \leftarrow \frac{\mathbf{a}^H(\theta_l)\hat{R}^{-1}\mathbf{x}}{\mathbf{a}^H(\theta_l)\hat{R}^{-1}\mathbf{a}(\theta_l)}$$

    **end for**
    Update power estimates:

$$\hat{p}_l^{(t)} \leftarrow |s_l^{(t)}|^2 \quad \forall l$$

    Check convergence:
    **if** $\|\hat{\mathbf{p}}^{(t)} - \hat{\mathbf{p}}^{(t-1)}\|_2 < \epsilon$ **then**
      **break**
    **end if**
  **end for**
  **return** $\hat{\mathbf{p}}^{(t)}, \{s_l^{(t)}\}$
**end procedure**

where $T$ is typically moderate due to the empirical fast convergence of IAA.

It should be emphasized that although the asymptotic complexity appears significant, the dominant term depends on the problem scale: for large arrays ($M$ large) the $M^3$ term becomes critical, whereas for fine angular grids ($L$ large) the $LM^2$ term dominates. Nevertheless, with modern parallel computation platforms, the proposed algorithm remains feasible for real-time or near-real-time applications.

# 4 Experimental Verification

## 4.1 Experimental Setup And Parameter Selection

To comprehensively evaluate the performance of the IAA algorithm for ultra-wideband angle estimation, a Y750 ultra-wideband hardware system experimental platform based on a software-defined radio architecture was constructed in an indoor hall, as shown in Fig. 2, the experiments were conducted in a typical indoor hall measuring approximately 10 m × 20 m. Various objects were placed in the environment, potentially causing signal reflections and multipath effects. To ensure the validity of the experimental results, a clear line-of-sight path was maintained between the transmit and receive antennas during testing. During the experiments, no one was moving around in the environment to reduce channel variations caused by dynamic objects. While the environment contained potential interference sources in the 2.4GHz/5GHz bands, such as multiple Wi-Fi routers, the 3.8GHz center frequency of the UWB system was minimally affected. These settings were designed to simulate a reasonably complex indoor scenario close to real-world applications. The distance between the transmitter and receiver was set to 5 m. On the receiver side, the system was configured as a two-element uniform linear array, with the element spacing set to half a wavelength corresponding to the center frequency of 3.8 GHz. This configuration maximizes the effective aperture of the array while ensuring reliable angle estimation, thereby improving directional resolution. The transmitter uses the YunSDR Y750 to send Gaussian second-order derivative pulses.

To ensure the accuracy of clock synchronization and delay measurement, the dual Y750 device configuration used in the experiment is shown in Fig. 3. This design greatly improves the stability of data acquisition and the accuracy of measurement results through the collaborative work between hardware. Specific parameters are shown in Table 1 below.

**Table 1.** Experimental Parameters.

| Parameters | value |
|---|---|
| Carrier Number of array elements | 2 |
| Element spacing | $\lambda/2$ |
| Center frequency | 3.8 GHz |
| Signal bandwidth | 500 MHz |
| Sampling rate | 1 GS/s |
| Signal Type | Gaussian second derivative pulse |
| IAA Iterations | 1, 5, 10, 15 |
| Angle search step | $-90^\circ \sim 90^\circ$ |
| Transmitter gain | 8dB, 14dB, 20dB |

**Fig. 2.** Experimental scenario.

**Fig. 3.** Schematic diagram of dual Y750 equipment.

### 4.2 Performance Analysis Under Different Algorithms

In the CDF analysis, Fig. 4 shows the performance comparison of the absolute deviation of angle estimation between the IAA algorithm and the MUSIC algorithm. By analyzing the CDF curves of the two in detail, the performance differences between the two in terms of estimation accuracy, consistency and robustness can be evaluated.

First, the CDF curve of the IAA algorithm shows a steeper upward trend. When the deviation is less than about 1.8°, the cumulative probability reaches 0.5, meaning that 50% of the estimated deviations are less than 1.8°; when the deviation is less than 4.5°, the cumulative probability reaches 0.9, meaning that 90% of the estimated deviations are less than 4.5°. When the deviation reaches

8°, the curve tends to be stable and the cumulative probability is close to 1.0, indicating that the deviation rarely exceeds 8°, reflecting that the IAA algorithm has high estimation accuracy and strong consistency in the range of -90° to 90°, and the error distribution is relatively concentrated, highlighting its superior performance in UWB signal processing. In contrast, the CDF curve of the MUSIC algorithm has a relatively gentle upward trend, and The median deviation is less than 2.5°, meaning that 50% of the estimated deviations are less than 2.5°, and 90% of the estimated deviations are less than 5.5°. When the curve reaches a deviation of about 10°, the cumulative probability approaches 1.0, indicating that while most deviations are within 5.5°, some can be as large as 10°. Compared with the IAA algorithm, the CDF curve of the MUSIC algorithm has a more gentle upward trend, indicating that the probability distribution consistency of its estimated deviation is lower and the error distribution is more dispersed. Therefore, the IAA algorithm is more robust in dealing with the complex challenges of UWB signals (such as large bandwidth and high resolution requirements).

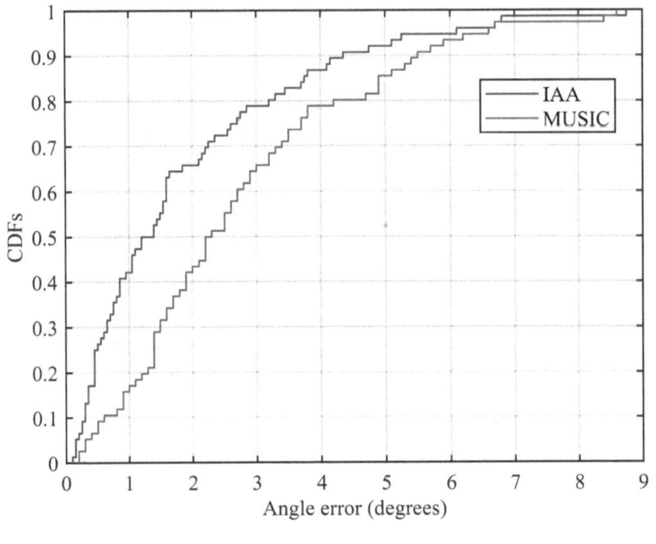


**Fig. 4.** Comparison between IAA and MUSIC.

Figure 5 shows the CDF comparison of angle estimation performance for the IAA algorithm under different numbers of iterations (1, 5, 10, and 15). The analysis reveals that the algorithm's performance shows significant dependence on the number of iterations: when the number of iterations increases to 15, the CDF curve exhibits the steepest upward trend, with the median error stabilizing at 1.8° and the 90th percentile error being less than 5°, reflecting a highly concentrated error distribution. Notably, 10 iterations achieve similar convergence, with error statistics similar to those of 15 iterations (median error of 1.8°

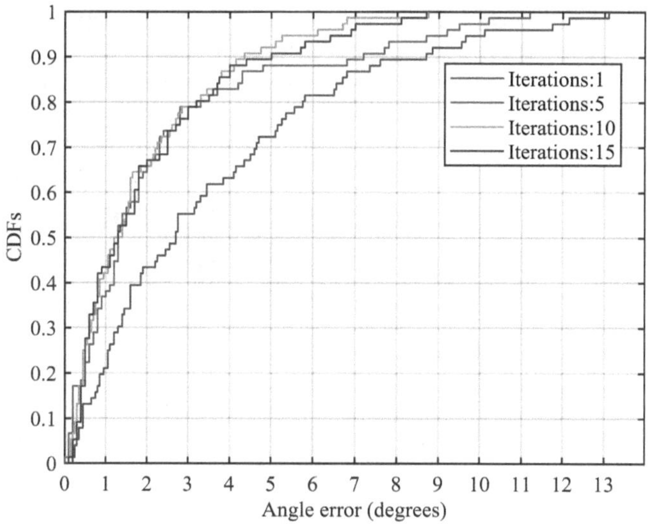


**Fig. 5.** Comparison of different iteration numbers.

and 90th percentile error of 4.2°), indicating that the algorithm reaches a stable convergence stage after 10 iterations.

In comparison, the performance with fewer iterations is significantly different. With 5 iterations, although the median error (2.3°) is comparable to that of higher iteration counts, the 90th percentile error increases to 7.5°, reflecting a wider spread in the error distribution. Particularly noteworthy is the extreme case of a single iteration, whose CDF curve rises the most slowly, with a median error of 2.8° and a 90th percentile error of 6.8°, demonstrating the critical role of the iteration mechanism in improving the algorithm's accuracy.

### 4.3 Comparison Of CDF Under Different TX Gains

Figure 6 shows the systematic impact of transmitter gain on the CDF of angle estimation in the IAA algorithm for UWB signal processing. Experimental results show that as the TX gain decreases from 20 dB to 14 dB and then to 8 dB, the CDF curves exhibit a clear trend of gradual performance degradation: the CDF curve for 20 dB gain shows the best performance, with a median error of 1.3° and a 90th percentile error of 4.2°. In comparison, the median error increases by 40% and the 90th percentile error by 31% at 14 dB gain, and by 62% and 46%, respectively, at 8 dB gain. This nonlinear response stems from the variation in SNR due to changes in TX gain: under low SNR conditions, increased noise interference makes it difficult for the IAA algorithm to accurately estimate signal parameters during iteration, leading to a wider spread in the angle estimation errors. Therefore, higher transmission gain leads to better estimation accuracy for the IAA algorithm. However, beyond a certain threshold, the performance

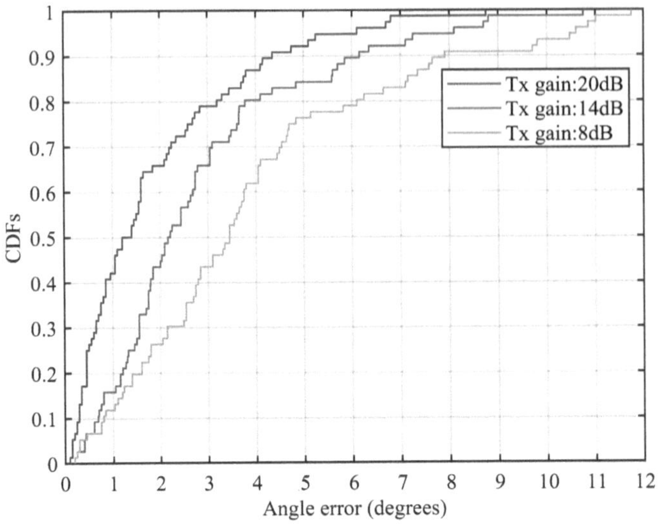


**Fig. 6.** Comparison of different TX gains.

improvement exhibits diminishing returns. As a high-resolution parameter estimation method, the IAA algorithm is particularly well-suited to the wide-band nature of UWB signals, exhibiting excellent performance, especially under high signal-to-noise ratio conditions.

### 4.4 Limitations And Scalability

While this study validated the effectiveness of the IAA algorithm for UWB angle estimation, several limitations remain, suggesting directions for future research. These limitations are due to three factors:

1. **Array Aperture Limitation**: The experimental platform was based on two YunSDR Y750 devices operating in dual-channel mode. Due to device limitations, a dual-channel configuration minimizes system complexity and facilitates reliable synchronization and error diagnosis, which are critical for method validation. While IAA has demonstrated superior performance to MUSIC in this configuration, the limited physical aperture of the dual-element array inherently limits its spatial resolution and interference mitigation capabilities.
2. **Single Source Scenario**: This experiment was conducted primarily in a single-source line-of-sight (LOS) propagation environment. In practical applications, multiple UWB sources may operate simultaneously, or multipath effects may generate multiple virtual sources in non-LOS propagation environments. This study did not fully evaluate the algorithm's resolution capabilities in these multi-source or strong multipath interference scenarios.

3. **Real-time Evaluation**: While we analyze the computational complexity of the algorithm, we do not report its actual runtime latency on an embedded platform or specific hardware. For certain high-dynamic tracking applications, the algorithm's real-time processing capability is a key consideration.

To fully evaluate the scalability of the proposed framework, we recommend expanding the experiments in future work as follows:

- Expand the experimental platform to 4- or 8-element uniform linear or planar arrays to systematically evaluate the effect of array size on the performance of the IAA algorithm (including accuracy, resolution, and robustness). Compare the estimation accuracy and computational latency of IAA with benchmarks such as root-MUSIC and OMP.
- Conduct experiments under multi-source coexistence and typical NLoS scenarios (such as corner occlusion and through-wall propagation) to test the resolution limit and robustness of the IAA algorithm.
- Study algorithm optimization strategies for specific hardware platforms (such as FPGA) to reduce computing latency, quantify their processing time and resource consumption in real systems, and evaluate their feasibility for real-time applications.

## 5 Conclusion

In order to solve the technical bottleneck of insufficient accuracy of traditional methods in UWB signal angle estimation, this paper proposes a UWB signal angle estimation algorithm based on iterative adaptive method. Different from traditional methods, the IAA algorithm iteratively optimizes the signal power and covariance matrix, thereby enhancing the accuracy and robustness without relying on the restrictive assumption of signal subspace separation or prior knowledge of the number of sources. Experiments based on the Yun SDR Y750 platform show that the accuracy and performance of the IAA algorithm in angle estimation in UWB systems are higher than those of the MUSIC algorithm, verifying the effectiveness of the IAA algorithm in UWB signal angle estimation. Therefore, the significance of this study is to provide an effective and practical solution for high-precision angle estimation in UWB positioning systems, and to provide important theoretical and application value for emerging fields such as high-precision indoor positioning and intelligent transportation.

## References


1. Jang, B.-J., et al.: Principles and trends of UWB positioning technology. J. Korean Inst. Electromagnetic Eng. Sci. **33**(1), 1–11 (2022)
2. Qiu, L., Li, B., Zhao, S., Wang, H.: Multi-base-station UWB time difference positioning system. In: 2021 International Conference on Microwave and Millimeter Wave Technology (ICMMT), pp. 1–3. IEEE (2021)

3. Alam, A.M., Ayna, C.O., Biswas, S.: Deep learning-based direction-of-arrival estimation with covariance reconstruction. In: 2024 IEEE Radar Conference (RadarConf24), pp. 1–6. IEEE (2024)
4. Naseri, M., Shahid, A., Gordebeke, G.J., et al.: Machine learning-based angle of arrival estimation for ultra-wide band radios. IEEE Commun. Lett. **26**(6), 1273–1277 (2022)
5. Zheng, S., Yang, Z., Shen, W., et al.: Deep learning-based DOA estimation. IEEE Trans. Cogn. Commun. Netw. **10**(3), 819–835 (2024)
6. Zhang, X., Wang, W., Xiao, X., Yang, H., Zhang, X., Jiang, T.: Peer-to-peer localization for single-antenna devices. In: Proceedings of the ACM on Interactive, Mobile, Wearable and Ubiquitous , Vol. 4, no. (3), pp. 1–25 (2020)
7. Ho, K.C., Le, T.K.: Integrating AOA with TDOA for joint source and sensor localization. IEEE Trans. Signal Process. **71**, 2087–2102 (2023)
8. Chandra, M.L.R., Bhargavi, K.V.N.A., Dilli, R.: Localization in 6G communication networks using low complex time of arrival (TOA) and time difference of arrival (TDOA) techniques. In: 2025 International Conference on Machine Learning and Autonomous Systems (ICMLAS), pp. 1604–1611. IEEE (2025)
9. Li, X., Xing, Y., Zhang, Z.: A Hybrid AOA and TDOA-Based Localization Method Using Only Two Stations. Int. J. Antennas Propagation **2021**(1), 5512395 (2021)
10. Sedlacek, P., Slanina, M., Masek, P.: An overview of the IEEE 802.15.4z standard its comparison and to the existing UWB standards. In: 2019 29th International Conference Radioelektronika (RADIOELEKTRONIKA), pp. 1–6. IEEE (2019)
11. Levy, B.C.: Principles of signal detection and parameter estimation. Springer Science & Business Media (2008)
12. Stoica, P., Moses, R.L.: Spectral analysis of signals, vol. 452, Citeseer (2005)

# Research on Far-Near Effect in Cooperative Integrated Sensing and Communication

Xiaoqian Wang, Rongyan Xi(✉), Hongjun He, Tao Jiang, Liang Xia, and Guangyi Liu

China Mobile Research Institute, Beijing, China
xirongyan@chinamobile.com

**Abstract.** The integrated sensing and communication (ISAC) system is a key research direction for 6G, where it faces multiple challenges in both communication and radar functionalities. In this paper, we investigate the near-far effect (FNE) problem in an orthogonal frequency division multiplexing (OFDM)-based ISAC system. Firstly, a cooperative ISAC prototype platform is built to confirm the specific impact of FNE. Based on the experimental results, it is found that the FNE is caused by the main and side lobes of a target with strong power in 2D-fast Fourier transform (2D-FFT) matrix when the received power is not saturated. It can be suppressed using environmental clutter elimination and moving target detection (MTD). In addition, we model the FNE problem as a 2D sinc function and derive a theoretical FNE threshold. The ideal theoretical FNE threshold is 13 dB when considering only the first side lobe, and the measured FNE threshold is about 8 dB. This difference is attributed to the received bottom noise, signal randomness and environmental factors.

**Keywords:** Integrated sensing and communication · far-near effect · 6G · environmental clutter elimination

## 1 Introduction

Integrated sensing and communication (ISAC) is a new technology that merges communication function and radar function. It utilizes communication signals for radar sensing, which is expected to support multiple emerging 6G services such as driverless cars and unmanned aerial vehicle (UAV) while reducing deployment costs [1–3].

ISAC needs to balance the functions of radar and communication. Communication requires high spectral efficiency, whereas radar requires high spatial resolution. They both require signals with good autocorrelation, large signal bandwidth, large dynamic range and resistance to large Doppler shift. Therefore, designing an ISAC system that combines orthogonal frequency division


Y. Liu et al. (Eds.): ChinaCom 2025, LNICST 711, pp. 457–468, 2027.
https://doi.org/10.1007/978-3-032-33662-0_33

multiplexing (OFDM) waveform has become a hot area in recent years [4]. Current studies on ISAC waveform mainly focus on two types, one is combining the radar signals and communication signals, such as the time-division multiplexing (TDM) form of linear frequency modulation (LFM) signals and OFDM signals, and the other is to use only communication signals for sensing, such as the downlink reference signals like channel state information reference signal (CSI-RS) and physical downlink shared channel demodulation reference signal (PDSCH-DMRS). The latter approach provides sensing while maintaining a better data rate.

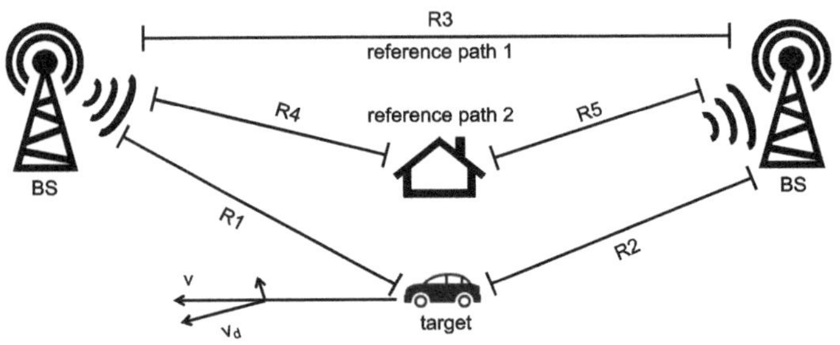


**Fig. 1.** A reference path-based cooperative ISAC system.

According to the deployment of base station (BS), ISAC is categorized into single-BS mode and multi-BS mode [5]. The former refers to the transmitting and receiving of the sensing signals is performed by one BS, while the latter refers to the reception of the sensing signals is performed by different BSs respectively. The latter mode is also called cooperative ISAC [6]. Cooperative ISAC requires precise time-frequency synchronization between BSs. In practice, the time-frequency synchronization between multiple BSs can be ensured using global positioning system (GPS) timing and other hardware methods. Additionally, wireless signal calibration provides a more accurate method [7,8]. The use of air-interface signals is also referred to as the reference path.

In an air-interface calibration-based cooperative ISAC system, the problem of the far-near effect (FNE) is easy to occur due to the different choices of reference paths. In a typical communication scenario, users closer to the BS have stronger signal strength than users further away. In this case, the stronger signal interferes with the weaker signal, resulting in the weaker signal being overwhelmed. The same problem also occurs in ISAC, where a closer or stronger reflecting target interferes with a farther or weaker target. The ISAC FNE may cause bit overflow of analog-to-digital converter (ADC) sampling, increases of receiver bottom noise or leads to error in target measurement. Since the power of reference path is usually higher and more stable, it is more likely to affect the weak target detection results. Furthermore, since the reflected power is passive, managing ISAC FNE is more challenging than managing its in communications.

To investigate the impact of FNE in ISAC, we first build an indoor cooperative ISAC prototype, which help us to confirm the existence of the FNE. In addition, the causes and power thresholds of the FNE are initially determined. Subsequently, we derive a mathematical model based on the test results and find that it is consistent with the experimental data. These relevant conclusions are helpful in solving the problems in ISAC beamforming design and multi-target detection.

The rest of this paper is organized as follows. Firstly, the system model of a brief cooperative ISAC is built to illustrate the prototype platform. In Sect. 3, a cooperative ISAC platform is built to test the specific impacts of FNE. Finally, the mathematical model of FNE is derived in Sect. 4, and the conclusions are drawn in Sect. 5.

## 2 Cooperative ISAC Transmission System

Consider a cooperative ISAC system consisting of two BSs, each of which has the ability to send and receive sensing signals. In addition to the target needs to be detected, there are direct path or strong reflective paths from stationary objects in the environment that can be identified, and these are the potential reference paths mentioned in the previous section. The RX BS uses the direct path as the reference path to complete time-frequency synchronization using a priori information of the reference path. The normal velocity of the target with respect to the RX BS is denoted as $v_d$, and the corresponding Doppler frequency is denoted as $f_d$, as shown in Fig. 1.

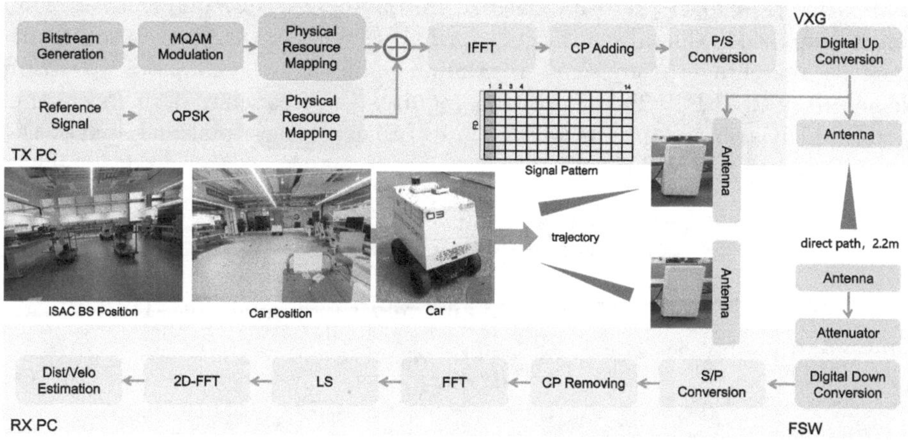


**Fig. 2.** Block diagram and environment of indoor cooperative ISAC testing system.

The transmitted time domain OFDM signal can be written as:

$$x(t) = \sum_{l=0}^{L-1} \sum_{k=0}^{K-1} X(k,l) e^{j2\pi f_k t} rect\left(\frac{t - lT_{sym}}{T_{sym}}\right) \tag{1}$$

where $L$ and $K$ is the number of OFDM symbol and subcarrier. $x(\cdot)$ is the modulated complex signal on the $k$th subcarrier of $l$th symbol. $f_k$ is the frequency of the corresponding subcarrier, and the time length of one symbol is denoted as $T_{sym}$. The time-domain rectangular window function is denoted as $rect(\cdot)$. After reflection from the target, the time domain received signal of the BS can be written as:

$$y(t) = \sum_{l=0}^{L-1} \sum_{k=0}^{K-1} A(k,l) X(k,l) e^{j2\pi f_k \left(t - \frac{R_1+R_2}{c}\right)} e^{j2\pi f_d t} \times \\ rect\left(\frac{t - lT_{sym} - \frac{R_1+R_2}{c}}{T_{sym}}\right) + n(t) \tag{2}$$

where $A(\cdot)$ represents the overall channel gain in the frequency domain, incorporating the target's radar cross section (RCS), path loss and a reflected random phase. It can be written as:

$$A(k) = \frac{\lambda^2 G_t G_r \sigma_{RCS}}{(4\pi)^3 R_1^2 R_2^2} \tag{3}$$

$n(t)$ is the additive white Gaussian noise (AWGN) and $c$ is the light speed. $R_1$ and $R_2$ are the distances from the transmitter and receiver to the target, respectively. $f_d$ is the Doppler shift, which is caused by the projected velocity in the normal direction of receiver.

C. Sturm et al. investigated the OFDM radar detection and proposed a 2D-fast Fourier transform (2D-FFT) algorithm on the basis of frequency domain channel matrix [4]. The distance and normal velocity of target are then determined by searching the index of maximum value in delay-Doppler spectrum calculated by 2D-FFT. This algorithm requires the frequency domain channel matrix, which is obtained using least square (LS) channel estimation based on the transmitted and received signals.

$$H(k,l) = \frac{Y(k,l)}{X(k,l)} \tag{4}$$

In cooperative mode, the distance and velocity obtained by 2D-FFT algorithm are estimated as:

$$R_1 + R_2 = \frac{m_{\max} c}{\Delta f \cdot K} \tag{5}$$

$$v = \frac{n_{\max} \lambda}{2NT_P} \tag{6}$$

where $m_{max}$ and $n_{max}$ are the indices corresponding to the column and row of maximum value of delay-Doppler matrix, respectively. $T_P$ is the time interval between two ISAC signals. $N$ is the total number of ISAC signals. $\Delta f$ is the subcarrier spacing and $\lambda$ is the wavelength of carrier.

## 3 Cooperative ISAC Platform and FNE Test

To validate the effect of the FNE, an indoor cooperative ISAC prototype platform is built in the Wi-Fi frequency band. The time-frequency synchronization is achieved via the direct path. By controlling the power of the direct path, the FNEs of target located at different distances can be estimated. The experimental setup of the cooperative ISAC platform is shown in Fig. 2, where the target is a $1\,\text{m} \times 1\,\text{m} \times 0.5\,\text{m}$ car. The transmitter is a vector signal generator (VXG, Keysight M9484C) and the receiver uses a signal and spectrum analyzer (FSW, Rohde&Schwarz FSW50). VXG transmits the pre-set OFDM time domain signals cyclically and FSW performs the sampling and sends the baseband time domain I/Q sampling points to PC via TCP/IP protocol. In addition, the Wi-Fi antennas used in the prototype are single-polarized plate antennas. The antenna gain is approximately 14 dBi and its major lobe width is around 40°. And all antennas are approximately 0.66 m high.

Two power dividers are used at the RX side and TX side to separate the power of the direct path and the target. Power control of the direct path is realized using a step attenuator at the receiver. Thus, this system can be equated to the mode of a multi-beam single antenna channel system. Additionally, the transceiver antennas of the reflection path are oriented in the same direction in order to maximize the power of the return signal.

The transmitted ISAC signal is a slot which consists of one channel state information reference signal (CSI-RS) and 13 random 16 quadrature amplitude modulation (QAM) data. The CSI-RS is used not only as a time synchronization sequence but also as the bearer signal for ISAC. It is generated using the 5G new radio (NR) physical layer protocol [9,10]. Different from the protocol, the frequency domain density of the CSI-RS pattern is set to 1 for simplicity. The PC receives the time-domain signal and performs the time synchronization using time-domain correlation. The received I/Q sampling data is represented in 32-bit floating point format. The receiver then completes the serial-parallel transform, removes the cyclic prefix (CP), performs FFT and LS channel estimation. The CSI-RS locations are then extracted to form a new matrix. A 2D-FFT operation is then performed on this matrix to determine the velocity of the direct path at the 0-distance location. The relevant parameters for the experiment are configured as shown in the table below (Table 1). In addition, each time the radar image is refreshed, the FSW needs to sample the data of 20 slots. The cell ID of the TX is set to 0. The working frequency point is set to 2.2 GHz, and the slot time length ($T_p$) is 0.25 ms.

Due to the complex indoor wireless environment, the target's echo power can easily become obscured by background clutter, leading to missed detection and misjudgment. Therefore, it is difficult to locate the target directly by searching the maximum power of the distance-velocity matrix. The clutter cancellation is required. For cooperative ISAC, the reference path is one example of the clutter that needs to be eliminated. As the power of the reference path is typically higher, the FNE is also more significant and closely related to the performance

**Table 1.** Experiment Parameters Setting

| Parameter Setting | Value | Parameter Setting | Value |
|---|---|---|---|
| Subcarrier Spacing | 60 KHz | CP Length | 288 |
| Data Type | 16QAM | VXG Attenuation | 0 dB |
| TX Sample Rate | 245.76 MHz | Signal Bandwidth | 200 MHz |
| RB Number | 264 | IFFT Points | 3168 |
| VXG TX Power | 0 dBm | Central Frequency | 2.2 GHz |
| RX Sample Rate | 245.76 MHz | FSW Attenuation | 0 dB |
| FSW Amplifier | 0 dB | Target Dist | 6–8 m |
| Target Velocity | 0 m/s | Step Attenuator | 0–15 db |

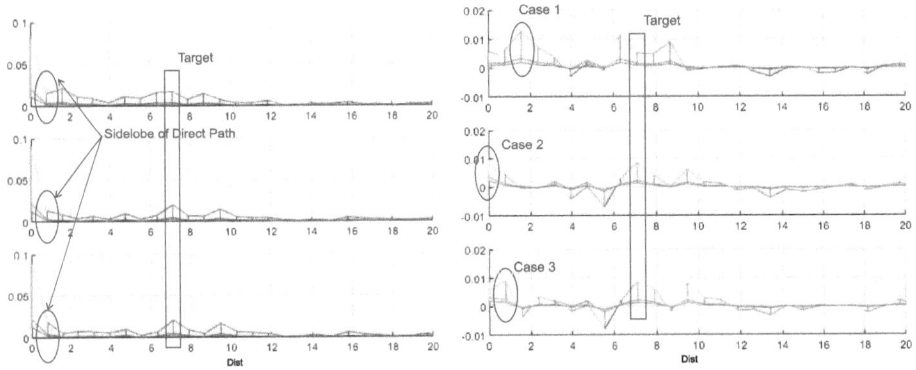


(a) Power of 2D-FFT matrix.

(b) Power of 2D-FFT matrix after environmental cluster elimination.

**Fig. 3.** The case of environmental cluster elimination when strong target (direct path) exists, where the x-axis represents the distance and y-axis is the linear modules of 2D-FFT. A total of 3 calculations are performed.

of clutter elimination algorithms. The commonly used clutter cancellation algorithms include moving target indication (MTI) and environment reconstruction.

In this work, a statistical averaging method is used to reconstruct the multipath power in the environment. The environmental information is the 2D-FFT power matrix obtained after time-frequency calibration, and the formula is as follows:

$$abs\left(\mathbf{M}_{2D-FFT,env}\right)=\frac{1}{I}\sum_{i=1}^{I}abs\left(\mathbf{M}_{2D-FFT,i}\right) \tag{7}$$

where matrix $M$ denotes the distance-velocity matrix computed by 2D-FFT and $I$ is the total number of statistics of environmental information.

Figure 3 shows the effect of clutter elimination and FNE on a car located in an indoor environment. The car is stationary 8 m away and its trajectory is on the height of an isosceles triangle. The number of clutter environment statistics is 50 times. The step attenuator attenuates 9 dB, and the length of the direct path is 2.2 m. Therefore, the target is located near 7 m in Fig. 3 after the calibration of the direct path. Following the elimination of environmental clutter, three types of misjudgment can be identified. The first is computational misjudgement caused by insufficient received echo power, the second is misjudgement caused by insufficient direct path power elimination, and the third is misjudgement caused by side lobe power. The probability of these three cases increases with increasing direct path power.

Figure 4 depicts the effect of the FNE on distance estimation when the car stops at 6 m, 7 m and 8 m along the trajectory, respectively. By controlling the step attenuator, the power of the direct path can be adjusted and used to evaluate different FNEs. As shown in Fig. 4(a), when the attenuation value is too large, a synchronization error occurs and the error rate quickly rises to 100% because the direct path power falls below that of the target. However, the estimation error also occurs when the direct path power is high. This phenomenon is illustrated in Fig. 3. The estimated results also show that the error data are near the direct path.

Since the power of main and side lobes of the strong echo power still remains after the environmental elimination, the moving targets detection (MTD) algorithm proves to be an effective method for dealing with this problem. In addition, the target can be found using constant false alarm rate detector (CFAR) and clustering algorithms. However, due to the threshold set by CFAR, the false alarm caused by the residual power cannot be entirely eliminated. On the basis of Fig. 4(a), Fig. 4(b) shows the estimation results using MTD, where values within one distance resolution of the direct path are filtered out in the 2D-FFT matrix. It can be noticed that the error rate is significantly reduced.

Therefore, our experimental results indicate that the ISAC FNE increases with the variance of the power of strong echo targets when the total received power does not reach the ADC saturation threshold. Specifically, the magnitude variance of the 2D-FFT linear power is larger for targets with strong echo power, which may be caused by hardware or bottom noise enhancement. Even with environmental reconstruction, there is still a high probability of residual power. When the residual power exceeds the weak target power, misclassification and missed detection readily occur.

To determine the power threshold of ISAC FNE, it is necessary to separate the power of the direct path and target path. We move the platform to an outdoor, open scenario and use FSW to obtain the average power of the direct and target paths. The target reflected powers at 6 m, 7 m and 8 m are −58.65 dBm, −59.68 dBm and −61.83 dBm, and the direct path power is −50.35 dBm. Figure 5 presents the estimation accuracy, where the x-axis represents the power ratio of the direct path to the target path, derived by converting the attenuator attenuation values used in Fig. 4(a). It can be seen that the error rate increases significantly when the power ratio is less than 0 dB for 6 m and 7 m. This is due to a synchronization error, which equates to an incorrect selection of reference path. In the case of 8 m, the threshold is −3 dB, which may be due to the indoor-outdoor measurement errors or the complexity of the indoor environment. Even if the synchronization error occurs when the ratio is smaller than 0 dB, there is still a probability of calculating 8 m due to the possible presence of multiple reflections in the environment at 16 m. As indicated in Fig. 3(a), a significant power appears at 16 m, which may be consider as a target after direct path calibration.

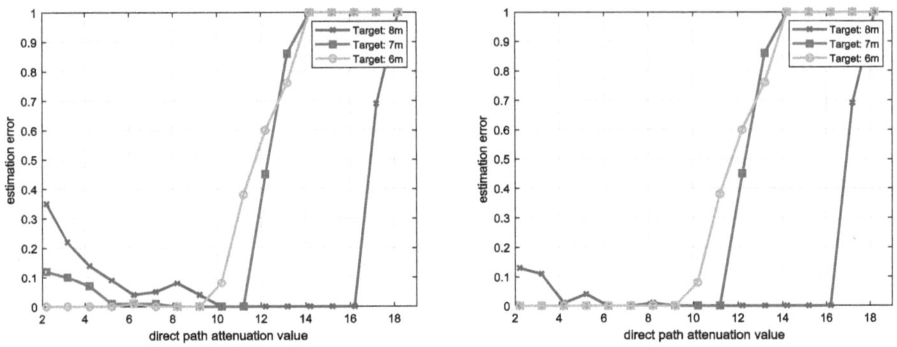


(a) The accuracy of distance estimation using environmental clutter elimination.

(b) The accuracy of distance estimation using MTD filtering..

**Fig. 4.** The effect of FNE on distance estimation at different power ratios, where 100 measurements are counted separately for different attenuation values. The attenuation range of the step attenuator is from 0–16 dB. The inherent loss of step attenuator and line is approximately 2.2 dB, and the number of environment reconstruction times is 50. The car is located on the trajectories at 6 m, 7 m and 8 m respectively. For subfigure 4(b), totally one distance resolution is filtered by MTD.

If the required error rate is less than 10%, the power threshold is approximately from 0 dB to 8 dB. When the power threshold is estimated using free-space propagation loss, the results are also similar. The power threshold increases further to 0 to 12 dB when the MTD algorithm is adopted.

## 4 Mathematical Model of FNE

Based on the above experimental results, it is known that the power of the main and side lobes of a strong target determines how its FNE affects other weak targets. These lobes are introduced due to the IFFT and FFT operations, which are equivalent to adding rectangular windows to a finite length signal. According to Eq. (4), the frequency domain channel matrix can be written as follows:

$$H(k,l) = A(k)\mathrm{e}^{-j2\pi f_k \frac{R_1+R_2}{c}} e^{j2\pi f_d t} + N(k) \tag{8}$$

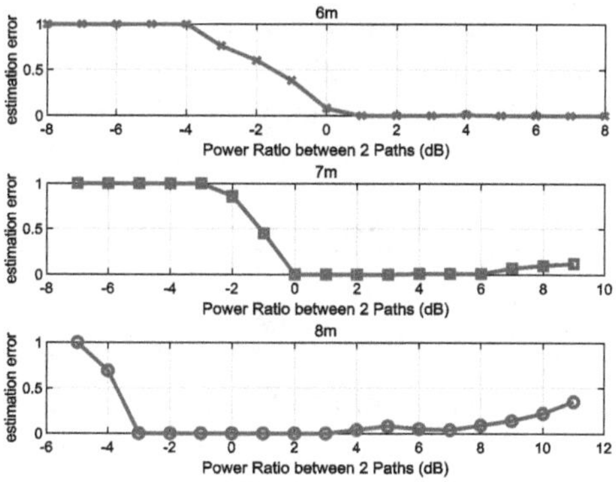


**Fig. 5.** The impact of the direct path power to target echo power ratio on the accuracy of distance estimation.

For simplicity, the channel gain magnitude is normalized to 1 in this section. Applying an $N_r$-point IFFT along the subcarrier dimension to Eq. (8) is equivalent to multiplying the frequency-domain channel $H(k)$ by a rectangular window.

$$h(m) = \text{sinc}\,(m - m_d)\, e^{j2\pi f_d t} \tag{9}$$

where

$$\text{sinc(x)} = \frac{\sin(\pi x)}{\pi x} \tag{10}$$

Similarly, applying an $N_v$-point FFT along the OFDM symbol dimension to Eq. (9) is equivalent to multiplying the time domain sequence $h(m)$ by a rectangular window. When velocity and distance are independent, the 2D-FFT matrix can be modeled as a two-dimensional sinc function as:

$$S(m,n) = \text{sinc}\,(m - m_d)\,\text{sinc}\,(n - n_d) \tag{11}$$

where

$$m_d = \frac{(R_1 + R_2)\cdot \Delta f \cdot K}{c}, n_d = \frac{2v_d f_c}{c} N T_P = \frac{2 v_d N T_P}{\lambda} \tag{12}$$

and

$$m = \Delta f \cdot K \cdot \frac{d}{c}, n = \frac{2vNT_P}{\lambda} \tag{13}$$

Since the velocity and distance are assumed to be independent, the locations of the zero points of the sinc function can be analyzed in terms of the distance dimension. The $p$-th zero point of distance dimension is $m = m_d \pm p, p = 1, 2, 3, \ldots$. When converted to distance, the zero points are located at $\pm\frac{c\cdot p}{\Delta f\cdot K}$, corresponding to the distance resolution intervals. Similarly, in the velocity dimension, the zero points are located at $\pm\frac{\lambda\cdot q}{2NT_P}, q = 1, 2, 3, \ldots$, which is also the velocity resolution.

The locations of zero points remain unchanged when $N_r > K$ and $N_v > N$, but the required MTD filtering range needs to be adjusted accordingly. In addition to the main lobe power, the power of the first and second side lobes also affect the FNE. The coordinates of the side lobe peaks can be determined by finding the zeros of first derivative of magnitude of Eq. (11). For the standard one-dimensional sinc function in Eq. (10), the zero points can be calculated as:

$$\operatorname{sinc}(x)' = \frac{\pi x \cos(\pi x) - \sin(\pi x)}{\pi x^2} = 0 \tag{14}$$

$$\pi x = \tan(\pi x) \overset{u=\pi x}{\rightarrow} u = \tan(u) \tag{15}$$

The locations of the peak values of the side lobes can be found by solving the transcendental equation given in Eq. (15). This is usually accomplished using Newton's iterative method, where the locations of first and second lobe are $u_1 = 4.3924$ and $u_2 = 7.7253$, respectively. The corresponding modulus of the side lobe is:

$$|\operatorname{sinc}(x)| = |\cos u| = \frac{1}{\sqrt{u^2+1}} \tag{16}$$

Therefore, the modules of the first and second lobes are $-13.26\,\text{dB}$ and $-17.83\,\text{dB}$, respectively. In the case of two-dimensional sinc function, the power of the side lobe along the x-axis (y = 0) or y-axis (x = 0) is the same as in one-dimension. In OFDM ISAC system, the power distribution is primarily analyzed along these two axes. In the other directions, the side lobe power is much lower due to the mismatch of the physical magnitudes of the ISAC.

Therefore, in the ideal case of no environmental clutter elimination or MTD, the FNE threshold should be the side lobe power. To model the FNE threshold after environmental clutter elimination, the residual side lobe power is approximated as follows:

$$P'_{s,i} = \beta \cdot P_{s,l}, \beta \propto P_m \tag{17}$$

where $P_{s,i}$ is the suppression factor, dependent on the main lobe power of strong target echo. $\beta$ is the elimination factor, which is determined by the main lobe power of the target echo power. High reference path power degrades the environmental reconstruction performance due to the increased background noise, hardware nonlinearities and other factors. This leads to higher residual power after elimination, effective lowering the achievable FNE threshold. As indicated in Fig. 4(c), the theoretical FNE threshold (considering only the first side lobe) is approximately 13 dB, where the car is located at 8 m. After environmental clutter elimination, the error rate remains high (around 50%) even at a 13 dB power ratio, which implies that environmental elimination can suppress the side lobe power to some extent. With MTD, the FNE is further suppressed and the correct rate is significantly improved.

## 5 Conclusions

This paper investigated the far-near effect (FNE) in cooperative integrated sensing and communication (ISAC) systems. The main contributions are summarized as follows:

- Firstly, an indoor cooperative ISAC prototype platform was developed to experimentally confirm the existence of the FNE and its specific impacts. Tests demonstrated that the FNE arises primarily from the residual power in the main and side lobes of strong targets within the 2D-FFT matrix when receiver power saturation is avoided. This residual power can affect weaker targets, leading to significant errors in distance estimation.
- Secondly, some effective methods for suppressing FNE were identified and validated. Environmental clutter elimination, based on statistical averaging of background multi-path signatures, combined with moving target detection (MTD) filtering around the locations of strong targets, significantly mitigates FNE and improves target detection accuracy. The experimental results clearly showed the substantial reduction in estimation error rate.
- Thirdly, a mathematical model characterizing FNE was established. It is modeled using a two-dimension sinc function. Based on this model, the theoretical FNE threshold determined by the first side lobe power was derived to be approximately 13 dB. The measured threshold was found to be approximately 8 dB, notably lower than the theoretical 13 dB. This reason is attributed to practical factors including bottom noise, signal randomness, and environmental complexity, which degrade the effectiveness of environmental clutter elimination and increase residual lobe power.

The analysis of the power ratio threshold provides crucial guidance for future 6G ISAC system design.

## References

1. Wei, Z., Qu, H., Wang, Y., et al.: Integrated sensing and communication signals toward 5G-A and 6G: a survey. IEEE Internet Things J. **10**(13), 11068–11092 (2023)
2. Liu, F., Masouros, C., Petropulu, A.P., et al.: Joint radar and communication design: applications, state-of-the-art, and the road ahead. IEEE Trans. on Commun. **68**(6), 3834–3862 (2020)
3. Liu, A., Huang, Z., Li, M., et al.: A survey on fundamental limits of integrated sensing and communication. IEEE Commun. Surv. Tutor. **24**(2), 994–1034 (2022)
4. Sturm, C., Wiesbeck, W.: Waveform design and signal processing aspects for fusion of wireless communications and radar sensing. Proc. IEEE **99**(7), 1236–11259 (2011)
5. Zhang, J.A., et al.: Enabling joint communication and radar sensing in mobile networks a survey. IEEE Commun. Surv. Tutor. **24**(1), 306–345 (2022)
6. Wang, X., Jin, S., Tao, J., et al.: A method of inter-base station synchronization for cooperative integrated sensing and communications in indoor 2.2GHz scenarios. In: Proc 19th EAI International Conference on Communications and Networking in China, pp. 1–12 (2024)
7. Tao, K., Masouros, C., Petropulu, A.P., Hanzo, L.: Cooperative ISAC networks: performance analysis, scaling laws, and optimization. IEEE Trans. Wireless Commun. **24**(2), 877–892 (2025)
8. Liu, M., et al.: Performance analysis and power allocation for cooperative ISAC networks. IEEE Internet Things J. **10**(7), 6336–6351 (2023)

9. 3GPP TS 38.211: Physical channels and modulation (Release 17) (2021)
10. 3GPP TS 38.213: Physical layer procedures for control (Release 17) (2021)

# MM-HAR: Human Activity Recognition with mmWave Radar Micro-Doppler Features

Xiaohang Zhang, Yajun Zhang(✉), Kun Liang, and Chunhong Yue

School of Software, University of Xinjiang, Urumqi 830091, China
zyj@xju.edu.cn

**Abstract.** Human Activity Recognition (HAR) has wide applications in scenarios such as smart healthcare and human-computer interaction. However, traditional vision-based methods often rely on lighting conditions and pose the risk of user privacy leakage. In contrast, millimeter-wave (mmWave) radar has gradually attracted widespread attention due to its contactless nature, insensitivity to lighting conditions, and strong privacy protection. This paper proposes a HAR system based on mmWave radar. First, the system combines Range-FFT and Doppler-FFT algorithms to extract micro-Doppler features from the echo signals. Subsequently, this paper proposes a lightweight model by integrating channel topology and Convolutional Neural Networks. In this model, efficient and lightweight local feature extraction is achieved through the proposed multi-channel branch convolution. Meanwhile, the model introduces dilated depthwise convolution to expand the receptive field, thereby maintaining lightweight characteristics and enhancing global perception capability. Experimental results demonstrate that the system achieves an average accuracy of 97.6% in HAR tasks, highlighting its excellent robustness and effectiveness, and providing strong support for practical applications.

**Keywords:** Human Activity Recognition · mmWave Radar · Micro-Doppler Features · Convolutional Neural Networks.

## 1 Introduction

In recent years, HAR has become an important research direction in the fields of intelligent perception and artificial intelligence. In scenarios such as healthcare monitoring [1], smart homes [2], and human-computer interaction [3], HAR can provide users with a higher quality of life and personalized services. Traditional HAR research mainly relies on computer vision and wearable devices. Among them, computer vision-based

Supported by the Key Research and Development Program of Xinjiang Uygur Autonomous Region (2024B03028, 2022A03016), and the Natural Science Foundation of Xinjiang Uygur Autonomous Region (2022D01C54).


Y. Liu et al. (Eds.): ChinaCom 2025, LNICST 711, pp. 469–482, 2027.
https://doi.org/10.1007/978-3-032-33662-0_34

methods [4] recognize actions by capturing and analyzing human motion patterns in images through cameras. Although this method can capture rich visual information, it is sensitive to occlusion and lighting conditions and is prone to raising user privacy concerns. Methods based on wearable devices equipped with sensors such as accelerometers and gyroscopes [5] may cause user discomfort. Although these methods have achieved certain results, they still have limitations in practical applications.

**Fig. 1.** Experimental setup for HAR based on mmWave radar

Unlike vision-based and wearable device-based methods, mmWave radar technology has gradually attracted attention due to its advantages of contactless sensing, user privacy protection, and insensitivity to lighting conditions. Moreover, compared with methods based on WiFi [6] and RFID [7], mmWave radar can achieve higher spatial resolution and capture finer motion features. Therefore, in complex scenarios, mmWave radar-based methods demonstrate excellent robustness and monitoring capability, showing great potential in the field of HAR.

Although mmWave radar has many advantages, there are still numerous challenges in achieving HAR. First, the motion features of similar actions are often easily confused, which places higher demands on feature selection and extraction capabilities. Second, how to effectively integrate temporal and spatial features in mmWave signals remains a key issue affecting action recognition performance. Finally, to enhance the scalability and generalizability of the system, developing efficient and lightweight neural network models remains a critical challenge. To address the aforementioned challenges, this paper makes the following main contributions:

- This paper proposes a HAR system based on micro-Doppler features from mmWave radar signals. As shown in Fig. 1, the system perceives changes in human motion features through commercial mmWave radar. Even for similar human actions, the system can recognize them accurately and efficiently.

- In the signal preprocessing module, this paper proposes a micro-Doppler feature extraction algorithm. Unlike existing methods [8] that extract features from one-dimensional temporal signals, this algorithm enriches the feature representation of mmWave radar signals by performing visual mapping and spatial modeling of the Doppler features of actions [9].
- This paper proposes a lightweight model based on channel topology and a large receptive field. To achieve efficient and lightweight local feature extraction, this paper proposes a multi-channel branch convolution (MCB-Conv) in the Multi-Branch Local Feature (MBLF) Block. Meanwhile, to enhance the model's receptive field and global perception capability, this paper proposes a Multi-Scale Perception (MSP) block based on dilated depthwise convolution. The model achieves more robust HAR through the collaborative fusion of local and global features.

## 2 Related Work

With the development of artificial intelligence, edge computing, and multimodal sensors, HAR has gradually become a core research problem in fields such as smart healthcare [10], autonomous driving [11], and smart surveillance [12]. Its goal is to accurately recognize and understand human actions through the analysis of multimodal sensor data, thereby providing more intelligent and human-centered services.

### 2.1 Human Activity Recognition Methods

Existing studies mainly perform HAR through computer vision [13], wearable devices [14], and radio frequency (RF) signals [15]. Vision-based HAR methods are easily affected by lighting variations, occlusion, and privacy issues, thus limiting their deployment in applications such as smart homes and healthcare monitoring. Genc et al. [16] proposed a vision-based HAR model. The model achieved a recognition accuracy of 94.1% by combining CNN and LSTM architectures. However, vision-based methods are easily affected by lighting and occlusion. Dahou et al. [17] proposed a HAR model based on wearable sensors. The model achieves efficient HAR by combining a residual convolutional neural network with 1-D trainable DWT. However, wearable sensor-based methods still face issues regarding long-term wearing comfort and user dependency, limiting their deployment in practical scenarios. Zein et al. [18] proposed a model named HAR-LightCNN based on WiFi signals. The model enhances its generalization capability through convolutional neural networks and data augmentation techniques, achieving effective HAR. Compared with mmWave radar-based methods, WiFi-based methods have low spatial resolution and are easily affected by multipath effects.

Although progress has been made in HAR research, it is still limited by factors such as lighting conditions and wearing comfort. Therefore, this paper aims to improve HAR performance by exploring mmWave radar-based methods that are contactless and insensitive to lighting conditions.

### 2.2 Research Methods of mmWave Radar-Based HAR

Due to its advantages of contactless sensing, insensitivity to lighting conditions, and protection of user privacy, mmWave radar has gradually become an important direction in HAR research. Zhang et al. [19] proposed a HAR system based on mmWave radar point clouds. The system extracts features and centroid coordinates of each point cloud frame through TF-Net and PointNet++, and inputs them into the ST-Transformer layer.

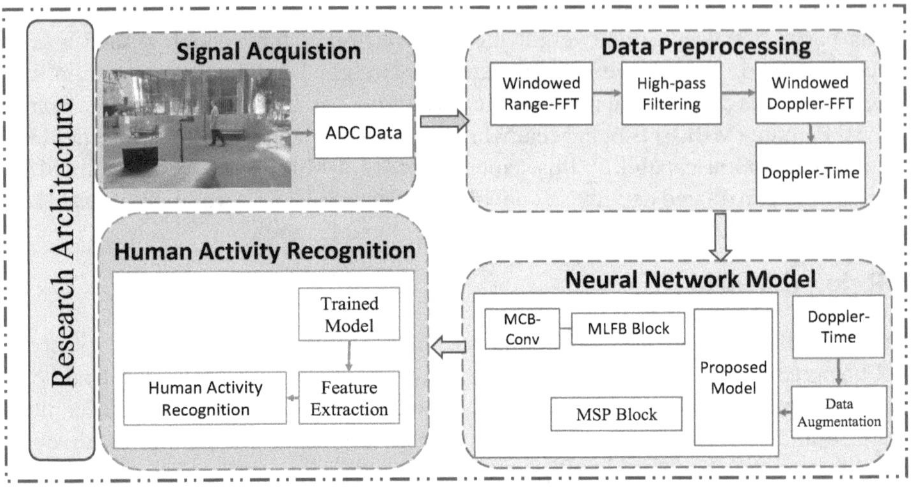


**Fig. 2.** Overall architecture of the system

The model decouples and encodes the spatiotemporal structure of the centroid coordinates through the ST-Transformer layer to capture the spatiotemporal information of actions, thereby achieving HAR. Although point cloud-based methods using mmWave radar can provide spatial structural information, their point cloud resolution is low, making it difficult to finely capture the detailed motion features of the human body. Muaaz et al. [20] proposed a HAR system based on a distributed single-monostatic mmWave radar. The system extracts temporal and frequency domain features from time-varying micro-Doppler signals generated by two orthogonally placed single-monostatic radars and achieves a 6% improvement in accuracy using a support vector machine. However, single-monostatic-based methods tend to lose complex temporal information and spatial correlations, are sensitive to noise and environmental changes, and have limited generalization capability.

This paper proposes a HAR system based on mmWave radar micro-Doppler. The system achieves an efficient and lightweight model design by combining a channel topology-based local feature extraction module with a large receptive field-based global feature extraction module. By extracting high-resolution micro-Doppler features of human activities, the system achieves robust HAR.

## 3 System Architecture and Design

As shown in Fig. 2, the system consists of modules for signal acquisition, data preprocessing, training, and recognition. The system performs Range-FFT on the echo signals to separate targets at different distances. Within the selected range, Doppler-FFT is performed along the slow-time dimension. Meanwhile, to suppress reflection signals from stationary objects such as the ground and walls, a high-pass filter is applied in the experiments to remove static clutter. Finally, the Doppler spectra of consecutive frames are concatenated sequentially to obtain the Doppler-Time representation over time.

In the training module, the proposed model consists of the MLFB block (local feature extraction module) and MSP block (global feature extraction module). Among them, the MLFB block effectively enhances the model's local feature extraction capability through multi-channel branch convolution. The MSP block enlarges the receptive field through large-kernel convolution, enhancing the ability to capture global features. Finally, the system performs HAR in the recognition module.

### 3.1 Construction of Doppler-Time Spectrum

mmWave radar perceives the surrounding environment by transmitting electromagnetic signals and receiving reflected echoes from targets. The transmitted signal T and the received signal S can be expressed as:

$$T = A_i \exp\left(j\left(2\pi ft + \pi Kt^2\right)\right) \tag{1}$$

$$S = A_j \exp\left(j\left(2\pi f(t - t_m) + \pi K(t - t_m)^2\right)\right) \tag{2}$$

Where $A_i$ and $A_j$ represent the amplitudes of the transmitted and received signals, respectively. K and f represent the frequency-modulation slope and the carrier frequency, respectively. $t_m$ is the propagation delay. By performing Range-FFT on each chirp signal, the time-domain beat signal can be transformed into the frequency domain, thereby extracting frequency components corresponding to the target distance. The mathematical transformation of Range-FFT can be expressed as:

$$S(K, a, b) = \sum_{i=0}^{N-1} s(i, a, b)W(i) \exp\left(-j\frac{2\pi Ki}{N}\right) \tag{3}$$

Where s(i, a, b) represents the intermediate frequency signal at the i-th sample point. W(i) represents the Hamming window function. N and K represent the number of sampling points per chirp and the frequency index, respectively. In this study, a high-pass filter is applied to suppress static clutter. The formula for the high-pass filter is:

$$y_n = b_0 x_n + \cdots + b_N x_{n-N} - a_1 y_{n-1} - \cdots - b_M y_{n-M} \tag{4}$$

Where $x_n$ is the n-th sample of the input signal. $y_n$ is the n-th sample of the filtered output signal. N and M represent the orders of the filter. Subsequently, Doppler-FFT is applied to the sequence of multiple chirp signals to obtain the Doppler spectrum of the frame. The algorithm extracts the frequency components of the signal using the Fast Fourier Transform and maps them to the radial velocity of the target. The mathematical transformation of Doppler-FFT can be expressed as:

$$S(A, B, n) = \sum_{i=0}^{C-1} s(A, i, n)W(i) \exp\left(-j\frac{2\pi Bi}{C}\right) \tag{5}$$

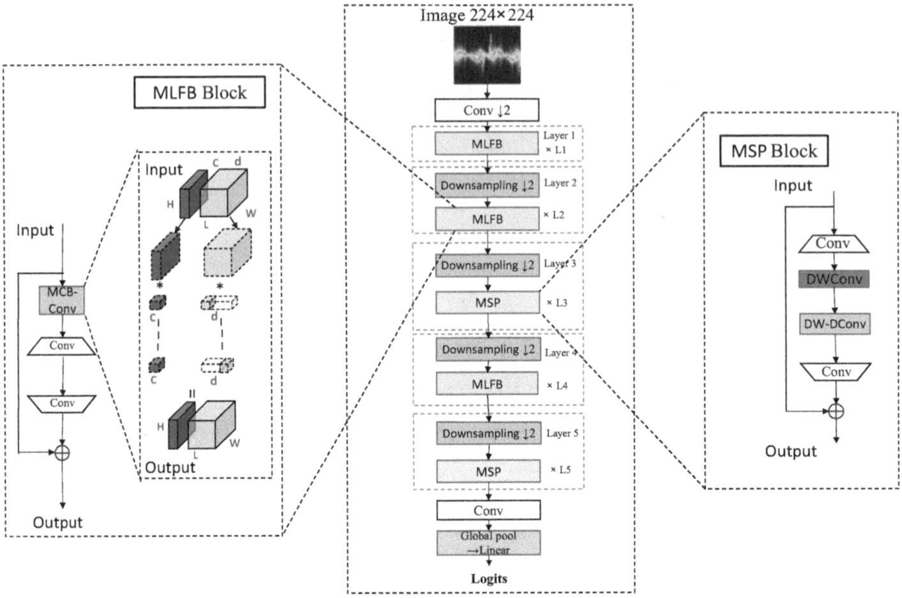


**Fig. 3.** Overall architecture of the model

Where A and B represent the range bin and Doppler bin, respectively. C and W(i) represent the number of chirps and the Hamming window function, respectively. Finally, the Doppler spectra of consecutive frames are concatenated in temporal order. This map can intuitively reflect the motion characteristics of the target person.

## 3.2 Training Module

Figure 3 shows the overview of MM-HAR. The model consists of the MLFB block and MSP block.

**MLFB Block**

To capture local features of the model, this paper proposes the MLFB block. In this module, to reduce the computational overhead caused by redundant information in channels, this paper proposes MCB-Conv. MCB-Conv contains two parallel channel branches, which apply standard convolution and depthwise convolution to different subsets of channels, respectively. Standard convolution is applied to key channels to fully capture the spatial features across channels, while depthwise convolution processes redundant channels to reduce computational overhead. The two feature sets are then concatenated, which not only preserves important spatial structural information but also reduces channel redundancy. Subsequently, pointwise convolution is used to first expand and then reduce the dimensionality. MCB-Conv performs channel optimization and reduces redundant computation on low-dimensional features, while providing more refined feature input for subsequent layers. On this basis, the MLFB block enhances local feature extraction and lightweight capability by preserving key features and introducing cross-layer connections. Let M and N represent the input and output tensors, respectively. The MLFB block can be expressed as:

$$N = C_{2,pw} C_{1,pw} C(M) + M \tag{6}$$

Where C and $C_{i,\,pw}$ represent MCB-Conv and the i-th pointwise convolution, respectively.

**MSP Block**
To capture broader spatial structural information and global patterns, this paper proposes the MSP block. This module first uses a pointwise convolution to expand the dimensionality, enhancing feature representation capability. Subsequently, depthwise convolution and dilated depthwise convolution with a kernel size of 7 are applied on the high-dimensional channels to capture features with a large receptive field. Finally, another pointwise convolution is used for dimensionality reduction, achieving feature compression and integration. The pointwise convolution for dimensionality expansion provides rich feature representation, while the combination of depthwise and dilated depthwise convolutions reduces computational overhead and achieves a larger receptive field. Let M and N represent the input and output tensors, respectively. The MSP block can be expressed as:

$$N = A_{2,p}\big(C\big(B\big(A_{1,p}(M)\big)\big)\big) + M \tag{7}$$

Where B and C represent depthwise convolution and dilated depthwise convolution, respectively, and $A_{i,\,p}$ is the $i$-th pointwise convolution.

## 4 Experiments and Evaluation

### 4.1 Experimental Setup

**Experimental Equipment and Development Environment Configuration**
The experimental scenario is shown in Fig. 1. In this experiment, the IWR1642BOOST and DCA1000EVM data acquisition boards are used to collect raw radar echo signals. The IWR1642BOOST is a 77 GHz radar board equipped with two transmit antennas and four receive antennas. The mmWave radar is connected to a computer with an Intel i7-12700H CPU and an NVIDIA RTX 3070 GPU.

Due to MATLAB's powerful data visualization and efficient matrix computation capabilities, this experiment uses the MATLAB platform for processing in the data acquisition and prediction modules. Meanwhile, the system employs Python 3.9 and the PyTorch framework to develop the training and recognition modules. With Python's

extensive library support and PyTorch's efficient deep learning capabilities, the entire process from model construction to action recognition is realized.

**Fig. 4.** Five human activities for HAR

**Table 1.** IDs and descriptions of five human activities

| IDs | Human Activities |
|---|---|
| A | Walking forward |
| B | Climbing stairs |
| C | Sitting to Standing |
| D | Squatting down |
| E | Falling to the ground |

**Experimental Dataset**

Figure 4 shows the five types of human activities. Table 1 lists the labels and descriptions of these five human activities. In this experiment, a dataset comprising 20 volunteers and five types of human activities was constructed. For each volunteer, each type of human activity was recorded 50 times in each experimental scenario. The dataset was randomly divided into training, validation, and test sets in a ratio of 60%:20%:20%. The experiment includes two scenarios: the baseline scenario, where a single person performs the human activities, and the comparison scenario, where other standing volunteers are present near the target volunteer. The experiment obtained 10,000 human activity samples.

**Evaluation Metrics**

This study uses accuracy and F1-score as evaluation metrics. The calculation formulas for accuracy and F1-score in HAR are:

$$\text{Accuracy} = \frac{\text{TP} + \text{TN}}{\text{TP} + \text{TN} + \text{FP} + \text{FN}} \tag{8}$$

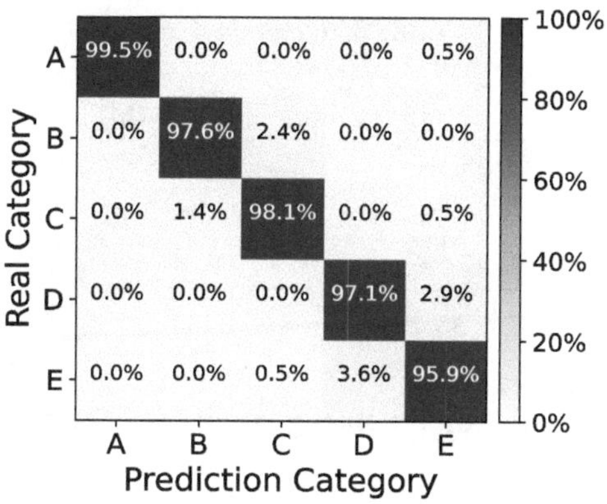


**Fig. 5.** Confusion matrix of the five human activities

$$\text{F1-score} = \frac{2 \times \text{Precision} \times \text{Recall}}{\text{Precision} + \text{Recall}} \tag{9}$$

$$\text{Precision} = \frac{\text{TP}}{\text{TP} + \text{FP}} \tag{10}$$

$$\text{Recall} = \frac{\text{TP}}{\text{TP} + \text{FN}} \tag{11}$$

Where TP and TN represent True Positive and True Negative, respectively. FP and FN represent False Positive and False Negative, respectively.

### 4.2 Performance Evaluation of HAR

To evaluate the system's performance in HAR, this experiment analyzes the five human activities performed by all volunteers. Figure 5 shows the confusion matrix of the human activities. The system achieves an average recognition accuracy of 97.6%. Among them, action E has the lowest recognition accuracy at 95.9%. Compared with the other human activities, action E occurs very quickly, making it difficult to accurately capture motion details, which may result in lower accuracy. The other four human activities all achieve an accuracy higher than 97.1%. The experimental results demonstrate that the system achieves excellent recognition of human activities, with an average accuracy of 97.6%. The system can effectively distinguish similar human activities, demonstrating robustness.

**Table 2.** Key performance metrics of five models

| Model | Accuracy | Params (M) | FLOPs (G) |
|---|---|---|---|
| MobileViT V3 [21] | 95.9% | 5.8 | 1.8 |
| RDNet [22] | 96.6% | 23.8 | 5.0 |

*(continued)*

**Table 2.** *(continued)*

| Model | Accuracy | Params (M) | FLOPs (G) |
|---|---|---|---|
| EfficientViT [23] | 95.3% | 24.3 | 1.6 |
| Swin Transformer [24] | 94.8% | 28.3 | 4.4 |
| (Proposed) MM-HAR | 97.6% | 3.9 | 0.6 |

### 4.3 Performance Evaluation under Background Interference Scenarios

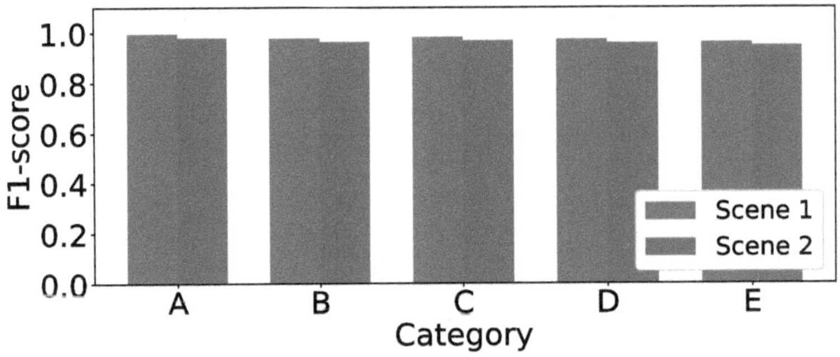


**Fig. 6.** F1-scores of HAR in different scenarios

To evaluate the system's recognition performance under different background interference conditions, this experiment compares Scenario 1 (single person, no interference) and Scenario 2 (other standing volunteers nearby). Figure 6 shows the F1-scores of HAR in the two scenarios described above. Compared with Scenario 2, the average recognition F1-score in Scenario 1 improves by 1.4%. This is because, in the single-person, no-interference scenario, the system can focus entirely on the target user. The radar can clearly capture the human activity features of the target, resulting in a higher average recognition F1-score in Scenario 1. In both scenarios, the F1-score for each action exceeds 94.6%. This indicates that the system can effectively distinguish even similar actions. The experimental results demonstrate that even in the presence of other people's interference, the system can effectively recognize the target user's human activities, highlighting its generalizability and robustness.

### 4.4 Comparison of Performance across Different Models

To evaluate the performance of MM-HAR, this experiment compares its recognition performance with that of several mainstream models. Table 2 lists the key performance metrics of the different models. Among them, the proposed MM-HAR achieves the highest accuracy, reaching 97.6%. The average accuracy of the other four comparison models is 1.95% lower than that of MM-HAR. In terms of computational complexity,

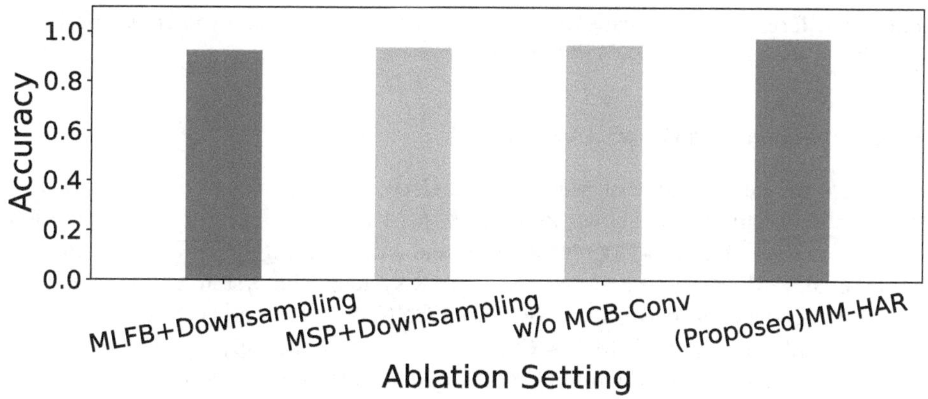


**Fig. 7.** HAR accuracy with different module combinations

**Table 3.** Methods, devices, and accuracy of different studies

| Study | Key Methods | Device | Accuracy |
|---|---|---|---|
| [25] | Autoencoders and CNN | RGB camera | 94.9% |
| [26] | Spatiotemporal attention and multi-layer network | Wearable sensors | 96.5% |
| [27] | Parameter estimation and PDHE-Net | mmWave radar | 96.7% |
| (Proposed) MM-HAR | Doppler-Time, large receptive field, and multi-channel branch convolution | mmWave radar | 97.6% |

MM-HAR has significantly fewer parameters (Params) and floating-point operations (FLOPs) compared with the other models. Compared with RDNet and Swin Transformer, MM-HAR has 19.9 M and 24.4 M fewer Params, respectively. MM-HAR reduces the average FLOPs by 81.3% compared with the other four models. The experimental results indicate that MM-HAR demonstrates excellent lightweight design while maintaining high accuracy.

### 4.5 Ablation Study

This experiment assesses the impact on MM-HAR by progressively removing or replacing key modules within the model. Figure 7 compares the HAR accuracy of different module combinations. When the MLFB block is removed, MM-HAR's local feature extraction and channel optimization capabilities are reduced, resulting in a 3.7% decrease in recognition accuracy. After removing the MSP block, the model's ability to capture large-scale spatial structures and global perception is weakened, leading to a 5.2% decrease in recognition accuracy. Finally, removing MCB-Conv reduces the refinement of redundant channels and the representation of local features, resulting in a 2.5% decrease in recognition accuracy. The experimental results indicate that removing or replacing different modules leads to an average recognition accuracy decrease of 3.8%, highlighting their effectiveness in MM-HAR.

### 4.6 Comparison with Other HAR Methods

To evaluate the performance of MM-HAR in HAR, this experiment compares it with other existing methods. As shown in Table 3, MM-HAR achieves robust recognition performance through micro-Doppler features and a lightweight model architecture.

Jain et al. [25] proposed a vision-based HAR system. The system extracts features using autoencoders and performs HAR with a CNN, achieving an accuracy of 94.9%. Compared with this system, MM-HAR has the advantage of not relying on unobstructed views or lighting conditions, while also effectively protecting user privacy. MM-HAR can reliably recognize human activities in complex environments, making it suitable for a wider range of application scenarios.

Zhang et al. [26] proposed a wearable sensor-based HAR system called Multi-STMT. Multi-STMT acquires motion data through accelerometers and gyroscopes. The system captures the spatiotemporal dependencies of multimodal signals using a multi-layer network with spatiotemporal attention and multi-scale temporal embeddings, achieving an average recognition accuracy of 96.5% across multiple datasets. Compared with Multi-STMT, MM-HAR can acquire motion data under non-contact conditions, avoiding the limitations of wearable devices in terms of comfort and battery life.

Ding et al. [27] proposed a mmWave radar-based HAR model called PDHE-Net. The model combines parameter estimation and deep learning feature extraction modules to recognize the extracted human activity features, achieving an accuracy of 96.7%. Compared with PDHE-Net, MM-HAR captures global perception through a large receptive field and integrates a local feature extraction module, resulting in a more efficient and lightweight model architecture.

The experimental results indicate that MM-HAR not only outperforms other existing methods in recognition accuracy but also fully leverages the advantages of mmWave radar in non-contact sensing, privacy protection, and high generalizability. This further demonstrates its robustness in HAR research.

## 5 Conclusion

This paper proposes a HAR system based on mmWave radar. The system performs Doppler-FFT along the slow-time dimension and sequentially concatenates the Doppler spectra to obtain continuous micro-Doppler features. Subsequently, the system feeds the micro-Doppler features into a lightweight model proposed in this paper, which combines channel topology with convolutional structures. The model employs multi-channel branch convolution and dilated depthwise convolution to achieve a large receptive field and enhance local feature extraction capabilities, respectively. By integrating local feature extraction with global perception, the system effectively enhances HAR performance. Experimental results show that the system achieves an accuracy of 97.6% on HAR tasks, demonstrating excellent robustness and effectiveness.

In future research, we will explore real-time HAR to provide more efficient and reliable technical support for practical applications such as smart medical monitoring and human-computer interaction. It is hoped that this study will provide a positive impetus for the development of HAR and sensing technologies.

## References


1. Gao, M., Yang, Z., Choi, J., et al.: Triboelectric nanogenerators for preventive health monitoring. Nano. **14**(4), 336 (2024)
2. Perumal, T., Ramanujam, E., Suman, S., et al.: Internet of things centric-based multiactivity recognition in smart home environment. IEEE Internet Things J. **10**(2), 1724–1732 (2022)
3. Heinisch, J.S., Kirchhoff, J., Busch, P., et al.: Physiological data for affective computing in human-robot interaction with anthropomorphic service robots: the AFFECT-HRI data set. Sci. Data. **11**(1), 333 (2024)
4. Venkatachalam, K., Yang, Z., Trojovský, P., et al.: Bimodal HAR—an efficient approach to human activity analysis and recognition using bimodal hybrid classifiers. Inf. Sci. **628**, 542–557 (2023)
5. Tseng, Y.H., Wen, C.Y.: Hybrid learning models for inertial measurement unit-based human activity recognition with feature analysis and data correction. Sensors. **23**(18), 7802 (2023)
6. Liang, W., Tang, R., Jiang, S., et al.: LiWi-HAR: lightweight WiFi-based human activity recognition using distributed AIoT. IEEE Internet Things J. **11**(1), 597–611 (2023)
7. Wang, Z., Chen, Y., Zheng, H., et al.: Body RFID skeleton-based human activity recognition using graph convolutional neural network. IEEE Trans. Mob. Comput. **23**(6), 7301–7317 (2023)
8. Hao, Z., Wang, Y., Li, F., et al.: Mmwave-RM: a respiration monitoring and pattern classification system based on millimeter-wave radar. Sensors. **24**(13), 4315 (2024)
9. Bhola, G., Vishwakarma, D.K.: A review of vision-based indoor human activity recognition: state-of-the-art, challenges, and future prospects. Multimed. Tools Appl. **83**(1), 1965–2005 (2024)
10. Serpush, F., Menhaj, M.B., Masoumi, B., et al.: Wearable sensor-based human activity recognition in the smart healthcare system. Comput. Intell. Neurosci. **2022**(1), 1391906 (2022)
11. Tammvee, M., Anbarjafari, G.: Human activity recognition-based path planning for autonomous vehicles. SIViP. **15**(4), 809–816 (2021)
12. Thamba Meshach, W., Hemajothi, S., Mary Anita, E.A.: Smart affect recognition system for real-time biometric surveillance using hybrid features and multilayered binary structured support vector machine. Comput. J. **65**(4), 897–917 (2022)
13. Gaya-Morey, F.X., Manresa-Yee, C., Buades-Rubio, J.M.: Deep learning for computer vision-based activity recognition and fall detection of the elderly: a systematic review. Appl. Intell. **54**(19), 8982–9007 (2024)
14. Sharen, H., Anbarasi, L.J., Rukmani, P., Gandomi, A.H., Neeraja, R., Narendra, M.: WISNet: a deep neural network based human activity recognition system. Exp. Syst. Appl. **258**, 124999 (2024)
15. Sun, X., Wang, Y., Zhang, C., et al.: LoDiHAR: a low-cost distributed human activity recognition system based on RFID. In: 2024 21st Annual IEEE International Conference on Sensing, Communication, and Networking (SECON), pp. 1–9. IEEE, New York (2024)
16. Genc, E., Yildirim, M.E., Yucel, B.S.: Human activity recognition with fine-tuned CNN-LSTM. J. Electr. Eng. **75**(1), 8–13 (2024)
17. Dahou, A., Al-Qaness, M.A.A., Elaziz, M.A., Helmi, A.M.: MLCNNwav: multilevel convolutional neural network with wavelet transformations for sensor-based human activity recognition. IEEE Internet Things J. **11**(1), 820–828 (2024)

18. El Zein, H., Mourad-Chehade, F., Amoud, H.: CSI-based human activity recognition via lightweight CNN model and data augmentation. IEEE Sensors J. **24**(15), 25060–25069 (2024)
19. Chang, Z., Lou, S.: Efficient human action recognition with fine-grained spatiotemporal feature extraction from millimeter-wave point clouds. IEEE Sensors J. (2025)
20. Muaaz, M., Waqar, S., Pätzold, M.: Orientation-independent human activity recognition using complementary radio frequency sensing. Sensors. **23**(13), 5810 (2023)
21. Wadekar, S. N., Chaurasia, A.: MobileViTv3: Mobile-friendly vision transformer with simple and effective fusion of local, global and input features. arXiv preprint https://arxiv.org/abs/2209.15159 (2022)
22. Kim, D., Heo, B., Han, D.: DenseNets reloaded: paradigm shift beyond ResNets and vision transformers. In: Proceedings of the European Conference on Computer Vision (ECCV), pp. 395–415. Springer, Heidelberg (2024)
23. Cai, H., Li, J., Hu, M., Gan, C., Han, S.: EfficientViT: lightweight multi-scale attention for high-resolution dense prediction. In: Proceedings of the IEEE/CVF International Conference on Computer Vision (ICCV), pp. 17302–17313. IEEE, New York (2023)
24. Liu, Z., et al.: Swin transformer: hierarchical vision transformer using shifted windows. In: Proceedings of the IEEE/CVF International Conference on Computer Vision (ICCV), pp. 10012–10022. IEEE, New York (2021)
25. Jain, S., Garg, A., Nigam, S., et al.: Convolutional autoencoder for vision-based human activity recognition. In: International Conference on Intelligent Human Computer Interaction, pp. 93–104. Springer, Cham (2023)
26. Zhang, H., Xu, L.: Multi-STMT: multi-level network for human activity recognition based on wearable sensors. IEEE Trans. Instrum. Meas. **73**, 1–12 (2024)
27. Ding, C., Guo, S., Cui, G., et al.: A parameter estimation and deep learning hybrid extraction network for multi-directional human activity recognition based on millimeter-wave radar. IEEE Internet Things J. (2024)

# Federated Learning with Sensing Enhancement for CSI-Based Gait Recognition

Haoyu Liang(✉), Jiayuan Lei, Juntao Yang, Zuan Qin, and Dongqi Hou

School of Computer Science and Technology, Xi'an University of Posts and Telecommunications, Xi'an 710121, Shaanxi, China
haoyuliang@stu.xupt.edu.cn

**Abstract.** Gait recognition systems based on CSI (Channel State Information) measurements face dual challenges in practical applications: individual differences among users and scene diversity. Individual differences make it difficult for a unified model to accurately capture personalized features, while environmental variations cause systematic shifts in the CSI measurement distribution of the same user across different scenes. We propose UniSense, a universal sensing enhancement module that ensures prototype alignment and cross-scene consistency through collaborative class feature prototype modeling. UniSense integrates into local models agnostically, mitigating environmental interference and enhancing robustness via prototype sharing in a federated learning manner, without requiring raw data upload or centralized model training. Experiments in two real-world environments (S1, S2) show UniSense improves recognition accuracy by 3.48% points under scene and model heterogeneity. Intra-scene experiments with non-overlapping user sets further show a 3.25% point accuracy improvement, highlighting UniSense's adaptability and generalizability.

**Keywords:** CSI · Gait Recognition · Model Heterogeneity · Cross-Scene · Federated Learning

## 1 Introduction

With the rapid advancement of wireless sensing technology, Channel State Information (CSI) has gradually emerged as a powerful tool for identity recognition and activity sensing due to its high sensitivity to subtle human movements, non-contact nature, and penetration capability [1–3]. Particularly in long-term stability tasks such as gait recognition, CSI can maintain stable outputs under complex conditions involving lighting variations and occlusions, demonstrating stronger robustness compared to vision-based approaches [4,5].

In real-world scenarios, differences in physiological and behavioral factors such as height, weight, body shape, stride frequency, and BMI are nonlinearly


Y. Liu et al. (Eds.): ChinaCom 2025, LNICST 711, pp. 483–494, 2027.
https://doi.org/10.1007/978-3-032-33662-0_35

mapped to their corresponding CSI measurements gait signals. These individual characteristics lead to pronounced inter-user specificity in CSI measurements, posing challenges for a unified model to effectively capture discriminative features across all users due to structural adaptation difficulties [6,7]. For certain users, CSI signals exhibit stable features and concentrated distributions, enabling lightweight networks to achieve satisfactory recognition performance. In contrast, other users generate signals with complex dynamic variations that require deep networks to capture higher-order time-frequency patterns. As system deployment scales up, these differences in model architecture requirements among individuals become increasingly pronounced. Designing and searching for an optimal model architecture for each user, followed by independent training and deployment, would incur significant overhead in model design, parameter tuning, resource management, and maintenance, severely limiting the scalability and practicality of CSI-based gait recognition systems in large-scale, multi-user, and multi-scene settings.

On the other hand, cross-scene adaptability remains a core challenge for CSI-based gait recognition. CSI signals are highly dependent on multipath propagation characteristics in the environment, making them extremely susceptible to factors such as spatial layout, obstruction distribution, and building materials. This leads to systematic distributional shifts in CSI gait signals for the same user across different scenes. Compounding this challenge, real-world multi-user systems often employ heterogeneous local models for personalized modeling due to terminal heterogeneity or resource constraints. This dual heterogeneity—both in models and in scenes leads to highly inconsistent sensing capabilities across models in response to environmental perturbations, and even locally trained models struggle to achieve stable generalization and robust recognition.

To address the system generalization degradation caused by the combination of model heterogeneity and scene heterogeneity in CSI-based gait recognition, this paper proposes a unified sensing enhancement system, UniSys, which is designed based on the principles of federated learning. Without requiring raw data sharing or a unified model architecture, the framework supports users to flexibly select model structures according to local data characteristics for personalized training, and introduces a unified semantic space to facilitate cross-model knowledge collaboration and representation optimization. Considering that the gait pattern of a specific user exhibits relatively stable spatial-temporal characteristics in CSI measurements, lightweight networks are often sufficient to achieve accurate recognition by capturing user-specific signal dynamics with limited parameters. This property enables efficient on-device deployment while preserving discriminative capability. The core module, UniSense, is a lightweight fully connected structure that can be embedded into any model. It receives locally extracted gait features during training and constructs shared semantic representations across users and scenes based on class prototype aggregation. The updated representations are then synchronized and injected into the corresponding local model layers to replace the original classification head, enabling feature sharing and semantic alignment across heterogeneous models. In cross-scene generalization scenarios, UniSys leverages the assumption that the same users participate in data collection under different environments, and explicitly aligns the class prototypes extracted from multiple scenes to mitigate performance degradation caused by CSI signal distribution shifts. In within-domain recognition scenarios, although user identities are disjoint, UniSense can still aggregate class prototypes across different users under the same environment to learn shared scene representations, thereby enhancing the robustness to physical disturbances such as multipath effects and improving the modeling capability for scene-specific gait patterns.

**Contributions:** The contributions of this paper are summarized as follows:

1. To address the performance degradation in CSI-based gait recognition caused by model heterogeneity + scene heterogeneity, this paper proposes UniSys, a universal sensing enhancement system based on the idea of federated learning. UniSys operates without raw data sharing or unified architectures, and improves recognition accuracy of heterogeneous models under cross-scene conditions through prototype alignment and feature prototype sharing mechanisms.
2. This paper proposes the UniSense module, which can be integrated into any local model to enable cross-scene prototype sharing and sensing consistency modeling among multiple models. While preserving each model's personalized adaptation capability, UniSense performs collaborative representation learning across users and environments under the federated learning paradigm, thereby mitigating system performance degradation in CSI-based gait recognition caused by user feature differences and environmental changes.

## 2 Related Work

In recent years, to improve the representation capability of CSI measurements in intelligent sensing and address the issue of cross-domain generalization, researchers have proposed various deep modeling and transfer strategies to mitigate the impact of environmental changes on CSI-based measurements gait recognition performance. On one hand, existing work explores effective strategies for CSI measurements feature representation and cross-domain generalization to address performance degradation caused by different environments; on the other hand, aiming at the characteristics of model heterogeneity and data decentralization, studies focus on enhancing sensing performance under flexible model architectures. This paper, based on the current research progress, elaborates from two perspectives: cross-domain generalization of CSI measurements and sensing enhancement under model heterogeneity.

***Cross-Domain Generalization Based on CSI Measurements***

Liang et al. [8] proposed MaP-SGAN, which address distribution discrepancies between source and target domains through a Consistency Maintenance Module, aDiversity Enhancement Module, and Multi-anchor Point Metrics. He et al. [9]

proposed the CNN-ABLSTM model combining CNN, BLSTM, and attention mechanism, which improves cross-domain performance by pretraining on the source domain and fine-tuning on the target domain. Yan et al. [10] proposed the Wi-SFDAGR framework, which optimizes feature structures using unsupervised clustering and an attraction-dispersion mechanism to enhance generalization. Although these methods mitigate the impact of environmental changes on CSI recognition to some extent, most existing approaches adopt a single model architecture and fail to fully consider feature differences across users and devices, limiting their adaptability under personalized scenarios.

***Sensing Enhancement under Model Heterogeneity***

Zhang et al. [11] introduced WiFed-CHAR, which builds a feature extraction knowledge base in the cloud to guide rapid inheritance of appropriate feature knowledge in new environments and reduce the need for training samples. Huang et al. [12] introduced FCCL, which achieves general representation learning among heterogeneous models through self-supervised learning and public data. Although these methods improve model collaboration to some extent, they primarily rely on feature alignment between specific architectures. Even when supporting heterogeneous modeling, significant model structure differences or substantial environmental changes make effective alignment of feature prototypes challenging, which lead to low knowledge-sharing efficiency and poor cross-domain performance. There remains a lack of a universal enhancement mechanism capable of spanning different model structures.

To address the challenges caused by model heterogeneity and environmental differences in cross-domain CSI measurements based gait recognition, this paper proposes a universal sensing enhancement system UniSys. The framework integrates and optimizes knowledge across different model architectures by sharing high-level category prototype information, supporting flexible use of heterogeneous models for diverse data characteristics, and enhancing both personalization adaptability and cross-scene generalization capability of models.

# 3 Methodology

## 3.1 Overview of UniSys

Figure 1 shows the proposed unified sensing enhancement framework, UniSys, and its core module, UniSense, which aims to address the degradation of generalization performance in CSI measurements-based gait recognition caused by individual differences and scene variations. Grounded in the federated learning paradigm, UniSys supports users in locally selecting and training the most suitable personalized models to meet heterogeneous modeling requirements. To enable efficient collaboration and knowledge sharing among heterogeneous models without requiring raw data exchange, this paper proposes a general sensing enhancement module, UniSense, which is essentially a lightweight fully connected layer that can be embedded into any local model. During training, each local model extracts CSI gait features of the local user, which are uploaded and fused into the global UniSense module to achieve unified semantic alignment. The fused UniSense replaces the corresponding fully connected layer in the local models, effectively improving recognition performance under different scene and user conditions while preserving data privacy and model autonomy, in line with federated learning principles.

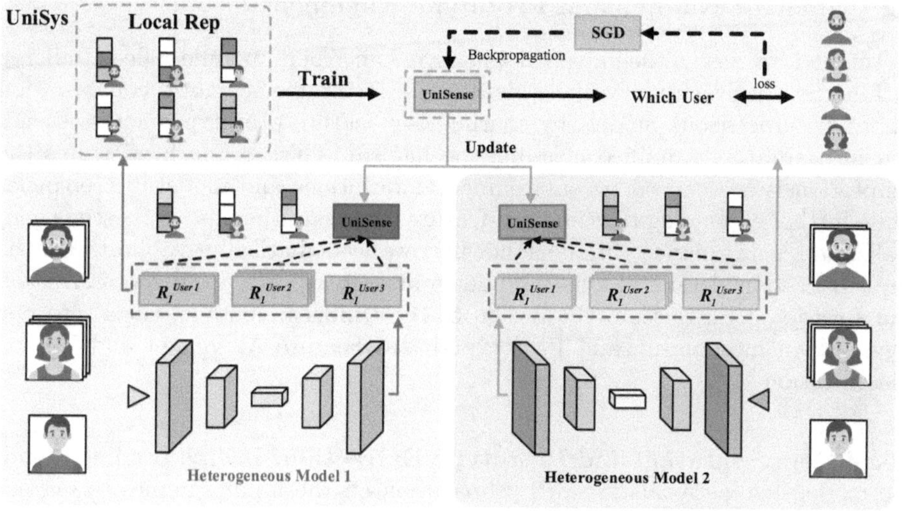


**Fig. 1.** The framework of UniSys.

In the cross-domain generalization scenario, UniSense leverages the fact that the same users participate in data collection in both physical scene S1 and S2, explicitly aligning the feature prototypes of the same user across different scenes, thereby achieving cross-environment semantic sharing and prototype alignment. In this way, UniSense effectively mitigates the performance degradation caused by distribution shifts in CSI data and enhances the model's generalization ability across environments.

In the intra-domain scenario, although the user groups are disjoint in identity, the data collected from the same scene share consistent environmental characteristics. UniSense aggregates the feature prototypes of different user groups to learn a shared environmental representation, thereby weakening the noise interference caused by physical disturbances such as multipath effects. This enhances the model's ability to capture scene-specific gait patterns and improves its recognition robustness within a single environment.

The following sections will detail the implementation of CSI gait feature sharing and UniSense module training within the federated UniSys framework. Specifically, we describe the federated feature aggregation and update process, where each user independently performs local representation learning and prototype extraction, followed by centralized aggregation and distribution of the semantic prototypes through UniSense. This process enables privacy-preserving collaboration across heterogeneous models and scenes. The method is elaborated through the following components: Local Representation and Prototype Extraction, UniSense Module, Prototype Aggregation, and Prototype-based Feature Alignment and Unified Classification.

### 3.2 UniSense Module and Prototype Alignment

To this end, we design the universal sensing enhancement module called UniSense within the UniSys framework. This module facilitates semantic collaboration among heterogeneous models by sharing user feature prototypes across scenes and incorporating a unified classifier mechanism. This approach mitigates the adaptation issues caused by environmental variations and model discrepancies while further enhancing personalized feature representation and cross scene generalization performance. In the following, we systematically elaborate on the implementation details of this module from four aspects: local representation and Prototype Extraction, the design of the UniSense module, the Prototype Aggregation mechanism, and Prototype-based Feature Alignment and Unified Classification.

**Local Reprcsentation and Prototype Extraction.** In each training round, the model first performs forward propagation on the input samples to extract their local representations. These representation vectors, obtained through network mapping, reflect the characteristics of the samples. To abstract the representative features of each class, we construct class prototypes (Prototype), defined as the mean of representations of samples belonging to the same class:

$$p_i^c = \frac{1}{|D_i^c|} \sum_{x_j \in D_i^c} f_i(x_j) \tag{1}$$

where $D_i^c$ denotes the sample set of class $c$ on group $i$, and $p_i^c$ is the local representation of that class. In the actual implementation, we extracts the prototype of each class from the training set. The prototype construction process is lightweight, requiring no storage of all sample features and is accomplished solely through the aggregation of class representations, effectively reducing computational overhead. During the prototype extraction process, a weighted averaging strategy is introduced to enhance the robustness of prototypes against dynamic environmental variations.

**UniSense Module.** The UniSense Module is a simple but effective fully connected layer that takes input features $p_i^c \in \mathbb{R}^d$ and outputs a prediction probability vector of length $C$, where $C$ is the total number of global classes. Its definition is as follows:

$$g(p;\theta) = Wp + b \tag{2}$$

where the parameters $\theta = \{W, b\}$, $W$ is the weight matrix with each row corresponding to a class, and $b$ is the bias term. This module is responsible for guiding the representation space of groups at the local representation level.

And use the standard cross-entropy loss to train the UniSense Module, ensuring accurate classification of class prototypes uploaded by groups, with the formula given as:

$$\mathcal{L}_{\text{cap}} = -\sum_{i \in S_t} \sum_{c \in Y_i} \log \left( \frac{\exp\left(g(p_i^c)_c\right)}{\sum_{k=1}^{C} \exp\left(g(p_i^c)_k\right)} \right) \tag{3}$$

where $S_t$ is the set of selected groups in the $t$-round, $Y_i$ is the label set on group $i$, and $g(p_i^c)_c$ represents the model's score on the true label of prototype $p_i^c$. During the training process, we use the SGD optimizer with momentum and add gradient clipping to stabilize the optimization process:

$$\theta \leftarrow \theta - \eta \cdot \text{Clip}(\nabla_\theta \mathcal{L}_{\text{unisense}}, \text{max\_norm} = 50) \tag{4}$$

After optimization is completed, sending the updated UniSense Module parameters as the global UniSense to all groups.

**Prototype Aggregation.** Due to statistical differences in CSI measurements gait data caused by channel environments, collection devices, and individual gait styles, the extracted features exhibit significant non-independent and identically distributed characteristics. Traditional feature-sharing methods struggle to directly align the semantic space. To alleviate this issue, the UniSense module introduces a prototype-based semantic aggregation mechanism to enforce consistency constraints on global class representations.

Let the set of class prototypes be $\mathcal{P} = \{p_c^m \mid c \in \mathcal{C}_m\}$, where $p_c^m$ denotes the class prototype for class $c$ extracted by model $m$. The global semantic anchor for class $c$ is computed as:

$$p_c = \frac{1}{|\mathcal{M}_c|} \sum_{m \in \mathcal{M}_c} p_c^m \tag{5}$$

where $\mathcal{M}_c$ is the set of models containing class $c$ samples. This anchor models the common semantic features of class $c$ and helps to offset semantic shifts caused by individual modeling differences.

During UniSense training, all prototypes $p_c^m$ are projected into a unified semantic space and aligned using the standard cross-entropy loss:

$$\mathcal{L}_{\text{cls}} = -\sum_{m} \sum_{c \in \mathcal{C}_m} \log P(c \mid g(p_c^m; \theta)) \tag{6}$$

where $\theta$ are the parameters of the UniSense module and $P(c \mid \cdot)$ denotes the predicted probability of class $c$.

Additionally, to quantify semantic shift across models, the Prototype Dispersion metric is introduced:

$$\mathcal{D}_c = \frac{1}{|\mathcal{M}_c|} \sum_{m \in \mathcal{M}_c} \|p_c^m - \bar{p}_c\|^2 \tag{7}$$

which reflects the representation differences of the same class across models. As training proceeds and UniSense parameters are optimized, $\mathcal{D}_c$ converges, indicating the gradual establishment of global semantic consistency.

This aggregation mechanism effectively mitigates semantic shifts caused by model heterogeneity and improves the system's stability and generalization ability under non-dependent and identically conditions. The inference process is formulated as:

$$\hat{y} = g(f_i(x); \theta) \tag{8}$$

where the local feature extractor $f_i(\cdot)$ is combined with the global classifier $g(\cdot; \theta)$, enabling semantic sharing despite structural heterogeneity.

**Prototype-Based Feature Alignment and Unified Classification.** By performing supervised training on class prototype representations, the UniSense module undertakes the tasks of unified semantic space projection and global class discrimination, serving as a unified classification module to execute cross-model feature alignment. In each training round, prototype information is mapped into a unified semantic space to enable supervised control and mitigate feature distribution discrepancies across different models. After updating the UniSense module, its weights are utilized as the unified classification module for inference. In each model, the current local feature extractor is combined with the global UniSense to form the final model:

$$f_{\text{final}}(x) = h(f_{\text{local}}(x)) \tag{9}$$

This integration preserves the feature extraction capability of local models while achieving semantic sharing at the classification layer. After multiple training rounds, the prototypes of the same class from different models tend to converge, effectively capturing common patterns among multiple users even when data are non-overlapping, thereby significantly improving model generalization and multi-scene recognition performance.

## 4 Experiments

### 4.1 Experimental Setup

This experiment aims to validate the effectiveness and robustness of the UniSys for CSI-based gait recognition under conditions of multi-user diversity and environmental variations. CSI measurements gait data from 20 users were collected across two real-world physical scenes, S1 and S2, totaling 400 samples. Each sample represents a gait action trajectory containing continuous motion information captured through Wi-Fi CSI streams. The dataset was collected using a TP-Link WDR7500 wireless router as the transmitter and a mini-PC equipped with an Intel 5300 NIC as the receiver. Both devices were configured with three antennas, forming a $3 \times 3$ transceiver antenna pair setup. Each transceiver pair records CSI measurements over 30 subcarriers at a sampling rate of 1000 Hz, resulting in 270 CSI streams per frame. The transmitter sends one packet per millisecond, and the receiver records 1000 packets per second for each CSI stream. To simulate the decentralized and heterogeneous nature of user data in practical distributed training environments, users were divided into 4 groups (5 users per group). For each scene, data were split 50% : 50% into training and testing sets, encompassing variations in gait temporal features, frequency-domain energy distributions, as well as statistical differences induced by environmental noise and multipath effects.

The experiments are based on four typical heterogeneous models: CNN, VGG19, ShuffleNet, and ResNet18. Ours first evaluate their independent performance on domains S1 and S2 without the UniSys enhancement mechanism, serving as baseline comparisons. Then, two types of enhancement experiments are designed: the first is the cross-scene experiment, which verifies the generalization ability of UniSys under environmental changes by performing feature sharing and prototype alignment across different environments; the second is the same-domain enhancement experiment, where in a single scenario, user groups are non-overlapping across groups. By aggregating feature prototypes from multiple user groups, this experiment evaluates the effectiveness of UniSys in modeling scene-specific gait patterns and improving local representation capability, i.e., environmental adaptability. For all heterogeneous models, the learning rate is set to 1e−5, the batch size to 10, and the training is conducted for 200 epochs with an early stopping strategy applied when the training accuracy does not improve for 20 consecutive epochs.

### 4.2 Baseline

The baseline experiment aims to evaluate the independent performance of each heterogeneous model without the UniSense and analyze the impact of environmental differences on gait recognition, providing a comparative basis for the performance improvement brought by UniSys. The experiments are conducted by training and testing CNN, VGG19, ShuffleNet, and ResNet18 models separately in the S1 and S2 scenarios, using only local scenario data. The data in S1 is collected in a relatively enclosed corridor environment with many obstacles, which is more susceptible to multipath effects and channel fluctuations. In contrast, S2 data is collected in an open hall with fewer environmental interferences and more stable channel conditions. Although the data in both S1 and S2 comes from the same users, differences in environments and deployment scenarios significantly affect gait recognition accuracy. The results are shown in Table 1.

The results show that the average accuracy of the S2 scenario is 0.908 higher than that of the S1 scenario 0.858, which is attributed to the lower environmental interference and more stable channel conditions in S2, while S1 is more

**Table 1.** Baseline accuracy of each group in S1 and S2

| Scene | Group 1 | Group 2 | Group 3 | Group 4 | Avg |
|---|---|---|---|---|---|
| S1 | 0.842 | 0.796 | 0.868 | 0.926 | 0.858 |
| S2 | 0.898 | 0.926 | 0.960 | 0.848 | 0.908 |

affected by multipath effects and channel fluctuations. The baseline experiment reveals the significant impact of different environments on gait recognition performance, highlighting the challenge of environmental adaptability and providing a foundation for validating the superiority of UniSys.

### 4.3 Cross-Scene Recognition with UniSense Module

To verify the generalization capability UniSense Module in handling CSI measurements data distribution shift caused by scene variations, experiments are conducted between two different scenes, S1 and S2. Through the UniSense module, category feature prototypes are shared and aggregated to promote prototype alignment and feature transfer across different scenes, without requiring additional data transmission or labeling. This mechanism enhances the personalized gait representation of models in local scenes and improves the recognition accuracy and robustness under cross-scene conditions, effectively mitigating the problem of data distribution shift. The results are shown in Table 2.

**Table 2.** Accuracy comparison of each groups in S1 and S2 under Baseline and UniSys settings

| Scene | Method | Group 1 | Group 2 | Group 3 | Group 4 | Avg |
|---|---|---|---|---|---|---|
| S1 | Baseline | 0.842 | 0.796 | 0.868 | 0.926 | 0.858 |
| | UniSys | 0.858 | 0.796 | 0.908 | 0.944 | 0.877 |
| S2 | Baseline | 0.898 | 0.926 | 0.960 | 0.848 | 0.908 |
| | UniSys | 0.930 | 0.972 | 0.972 | 0.928 | 0.959 |

In the S1 scenario, the average accuracy of models is improved from 0.858 to 0.877, with an increase of about 1.9% points; in the S2 scenario, the accuracy increases from 0.908 to 0.959, with an improvement of about 5.05% points. Notably, in the S2 scenario, the accuracy of the ResNet18-based model significantly increases from 0.848 to 0.928. These results show that the UniSys, through the sharing of feature prototypes and the introduction of the UniSense module, significantly enhances the feature representation capability of heterogeneous models and effectively improves the ability to capture stable gait features and environment-specific characteristics, thereby achieving robust improvement in recognition accuracy under cross-scene conditions.

### 4.4 Intra-scene Collaboration with UniSense Module

To further verify the performance improvement brought by UniSense within a single scene, an intra-scene prototype sharing experiment is designed. In this setting, users in different groups are non-overlapping, and UniSense is utilized to share environment-specific features within the scene to mitigate the impact of multipath effects. After training models independently for four user groups, the extracted category feature prototypes are uploaded to UniSense to construct a shared prototype representation space across groups. Prototype alignment optimization is performed through UniSense, which enhances the models' ability to represent data features within the scene and effectively captures scene-specific gait patterns and environment-dependent features. The experimental results are shown in Fig. 2.

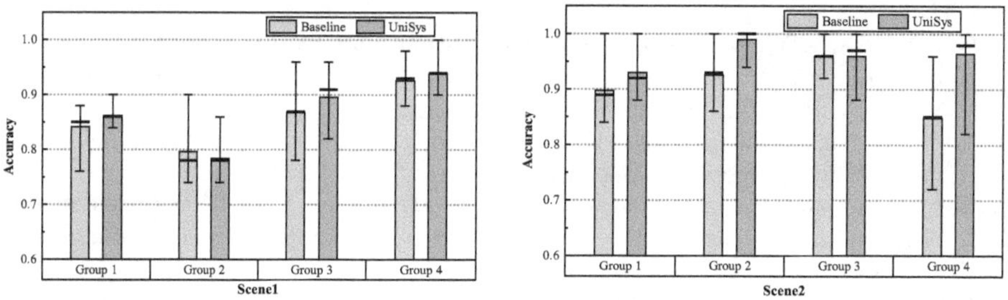


(a) Comparison of accuracy between Baseline and UniSys in S1

(b) Comparison of accuracy between Baseline and UniSys in S2

**Fig. 2.** Accuracy of groups under intra-domain collaborative setting with UniSense module.

In the S1 scene, the average recognition accuracy increases from 0.858 to 0.870, with an improvement of about 1.2% points; in the S2 scene, it increases significantly from 0.908 to 0.961, with an improvement of 5.3% points. The results show that the UniSense module can enhance the recognition performance of heterogeneous models within a single scenario by sharing prototype information and effectively capturing stable gait patterns and environmental features. This result further verifies that UniSense, by constructing a unified prototype space, optimizes the feature representation capability of models under single-scene conditions, showing its robustness and effectiveness within a single scenario.

## 5 Conclusion

This paper addresses the performance degradation problem in CSI-based gait recognition under cross-domain generalization and heterogeneous model collaboration. We propose a universal sensing enhancement module, UniSense, and integrate it into the federated UniSys framework. Grounded in federated learning principles, UniSense achieves prototype alignment and collaborative modeling of environmental sensing across local models through a structure-agnostic prototype sharing mechanism, without relying on raw data transmission or unified model architectures. Experimental results show that UniSys, when locally trained and tested in two distinct scenarios, improves the average recognition accuracy by 3.48% points across both domains, significantly enhancing cross-scenario generalization. Moreover, under the condition of heterogeneous modeling with non-overlapping users in the same scenario, the average recognition accuracy of each local model is improved by 3.25% points, verifying the effectiveness of the proposed method in enhancing model robustness and environmental adaptability in a privacy-preserving, federated learning setting.

## References

1. Cui, Y., Kang, Y.: Multi-modal gait recognition via effective spatial-temporal feature fusion. In: Proceedings of the IEEE/CVF Conference on Computer Vision and Pattern Recognition, pp. 17949–17957 (2023)
2. Wang, C., Li, Z., Sarpong, B.: Multimodal adaptive identity-recognition algorithm fused with gait perception. Big Data Min. Anal. **4**(4), 223–232 (2021)
3. Luo, Y., et al.: Intelligent carpet: inferring 3D human pose from tactile signals. In: Proceedings of the IEEE/CVF Conference on Computer Vision and Pattern Recognition, pp. 11255–11265 (2021)
4. Liang, Y., et al.: WiAi-ID: Wi-Fi-based domain adaptation for appearance-independent passive person identification. IEEE Internet Things J. **11**(1), 1012–1027 (2023)
5. Wang, X., Li, F., Xie, Y., Yang, S., Wang, Yu.: Gait and respiration-based user identification using Wi-Fi signal. IEEE Internet Things J. **9**(5), 3509–3521 (2021)
6. Meng, Z., et al.: Gait recognition for co-existing multiple people using millimeter wave sensing. In: Proceedings of the AAAI Conference on Artificial Intelligence, vol. 34, pp. 849–856 (2020)
7. Meneghello, F., Garlisi, D., Dal Fabbro, N., Tinnirello, I., Rossi, M.: Sharp: environment and person independent activity recognition with commodity IEEE 802.11 access points. IEEE Trans. Mob. Comput. **22**(10), 6160–6175 (2022)
8. Liang, Y., Li, H., Wenjie, W., Pengfei, X.: MaP-SGAN: multi-anchor point Siamese GAN for Wi-Fi CSI-based cross-domain gait recognition. Expert Syst. Appl. **251**, 124083 (2024)
9. He, Z., Bouazizi, M., Gui, G., Ohtsuki, T.: A cross-subject transfer learning method for CSI-based wireless sensing. IEEE Internet Things J. **12**(13), 23946–23960 (2025)
10. Yan, H., et al.: Wi-SFDAGR: WiFi-based cross-domain gesture recognition via source-free domain adaptation. IEEE Internet Things J. **12**(13), 24159–24173 (2025)
11. Zhang, S., Jia, H., Jiang, T., Wu, S., Ding, X., Zhong, Y.: Federated learning framework for Wi-Fi-based cross-environment human action recognition. Measurement, 117821 (2025)
12. Huang, W., Ye, M., Du, B.: Learn from others and be yourself in heterogeneous federated learning. In: Proceedings of the IEEE/CVF Conference on Computer Vision and Pattern Recognition, pp. 10143–10153 (2022)

# DeepEVO: Towards Robust Visual Odometry via Attention-Based Events and Video Fusion

Xucheng Guo[1], Bowen Du[2], Hongkai Wen[3], and Yiran Shen[1](✉)

[1] School of Software, Shandong University, Jinan 250100, China
xucheng.guo@mail.sdu.edu.cn, yiran.shen@sdu.edu.cn
[2] School of Computer Science and Technology, Tongji University, Shanghai, China
bowendu@tongji.edu.cn
[3] The Department of Computer Science, University of Warwick, Coventry CV4 7AL, U.K.
hongkai.wen@warwick.ac.uk

**Abstract.** Visual odometry (VO) is one of the fundamental tasks for vision-based navigation on mobile robots. It estimates the position and rotation of the camera by investigating the translation between consecutive video frames or other visual signals. However, traditional video-based odometry suffers from the issues of blur and overexposure under fast movement or challenging light conditions, which weaken the robustness of the visual odometry approach. Event-based cameras are new bio-inspired sensors that capture changes in image intensity asynchronously across all pixels on the camera, which introduce better performance in capturing scenes of fast-moving and high dynamic range over the standard cameras. These advantages allow event cameras to complement standard RGB cameras for robust visual odometry. In this paper, We propose an end-to-end learning approach, DeepEVO, which adopts a mixed attention module to fuse events and video for robust motion estimation. The video cameras provide rich semantic information while the events complement the visual odometry on solving the problem of motion blur and lighting conditions. Through extensive experiments, the results show that the DeepEVO can greatly improve the pose estimation accuracy compared with the approaches that only use a standard camera in a variety of scenarios by automatically adopting dominant information from different sources.

**Keywords:** Visual Odometry · Event Camera · Multi-modal Vision

## 1 Introduction

Nowadays, navigation plays an increasingly important role in widespread mobile robots such as cars, drones, underwater robots, and Mars rovers. For accurate navigation, robots rely on different kinds of sensors and a broad and precise


Y. Liu et al. (Eds.): ChinaCom 2025, LNICST 711, pp. 495–510, 2027.
https://doi.org/10.1007/978-3-032-33662-0_36

perception of the environment. Vision sensors, inertial sensors and lidars have been widely equipped to sense the environment for robots. However, different types of sensors have their unique advantages and limitations. For example, the performance of vision sensors will degrade when the weather is foggy or during the night, but inertial sensors can perform as usual in such challenging environments. In contrast, vision sensors generally outperform inertial sensors under suitable light conditions. The most promising approach to maintaining high-accurate navigation is to fuse the data from different types of sensors and decide which sensor should dominate the process in the current environment.

Event cameras, as an emerging bio-inspired vision platform, have a lot of unique advantages over standard cameras, providing a better performance of vision tasks under some challenging conditions. Compared with standard cameras, event cameras can capture an intensity change at each pixel with microseconds' time resolution. Due to its asynchronous operation, event cameras can cope with high-speed movement or challenging light conditions. There has been a limited number of work applying event cameras in visual odometry (VO) tasks, such as event-based visual inertial odometry (EVIO) [24]. It is a purely geometric method of real-time, 6-DOF parallel tracking and mapping with an event camera in natural scenes. However, this method requires a complex process of feature extraction, feature matching, and motion estimation (Fig. 1).

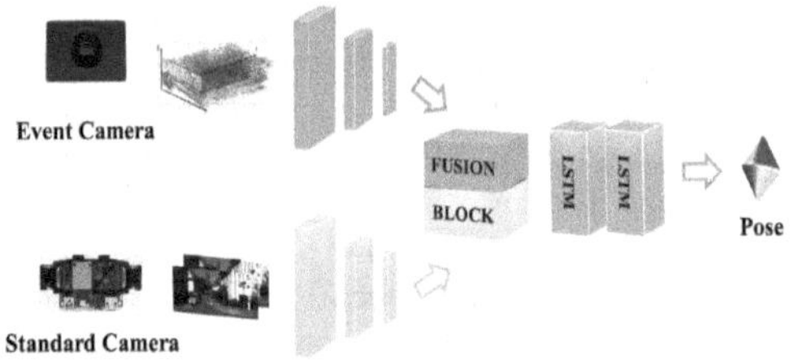


**Fig. 1.** The DeepEVO fuses a standard camera and an event camera coupled with a deep neural network model to accurately and robustly estimate 6-DOF ego-motion. The standard camera and the event camera are suitable for different scenarios, even challenging environments.

In order to explore the potential of both event cameras and standard cameras for visual odometry estimation, and take advantage of deep learning, we propose an end-to-end model to estimate ego-motion by fusing the standard frames and the event stream (the output of event cameras). We design two learnable fusion blocks to enable the network to automatically choose the suitable feature combination between the standard image and event stream. Moreover, inspired by EV-FlowNet [25], we convert the event stream to image-like inputs to align the event stream with images, after which we can use a standard image-based neural network to extract features from the event stream. At last, to obtain enough samples for training and evaluation, V2E [8] is utilized to convert videos to event streams from the classic VO dataset KITTI [6] which has been used frequently for benchmarking the visual odometry approaches. In order to fully demonstrate the advantages of our DeepEVO on real world event stream datasets, we conduct experiments on an extremely challenging dataset (the UZH-FPV Drone Racing dataset [3]). The main technical contributions of this paper can be summarised as follows:

- We design two mixed fusion modules to select the dominant features from both frames and event streams under different working conditions, enabling our approach better facilitate the potential of the two vision modalities to adapt to more complex scenarios.
- Based on the mixed fusion modules, two end-to-end approaches are designed to estimate the ego-motion of the platforms producing both event streams and video frames.
- we conduct extensive evaluations using transformed KITTI datasets and the UZH-FPV Drone Racing dataset, including the visualization of the attention module's weights to validate its effectiveness. The results highlight that DeepEVO can autonomously adapt through sensor interaction, successfully mitigating the impact of motion blur and extreme illumination variations on accuracy.

## 2 Related Work

Since frames and events are complementary, a number of recent efforts have been proposed to revolve challenging vision tasks around them, such as joint events and frames for depth estimation [5], feature tracking [4], image deblurring [14], 6-DoF Object Motion tracking [11] and Simultaneous Localization and Mapping (SLAM) [16]. For visual odometry, there are many pure event-based visual odometry methods, as well as visual odometry methods that combines events with other modalities.

### 2.1 Pure Event-Based VO

The event-based particle filter is the first approach using events to estimate poses [22]. Haram Kim [10] proposed a method for estimating rotational motion using only event cameras. EVO [15] uses the methods of image-to-model alignment for trajectory tracking. The optimal motion parameters also can be computed by maximizing contrast in 3D [20]. Chengxi Ye and Anton Mitrokhin [23] proposed a low-parameter method to simultaneously generate optical flow, depth map, and ego-motion. They introduced a new lightweight high-performance network architecture – ECN.

### 2.2 Event Assisted VO

Many studies combine an event-based camera with other sensors to estimate poses. Event-based and RGB-D sensors are integrated to lag-free track the

motion, it can represent the motion of the system in a continuous manner [21]. Daniel Gehrig's method [4] extracts frame features and then tracks them asynchronously using events, thus making full use of both types of data to track visual features. A. Censi and D. Scaramuzza [2] Integration of event and absolute brightness information to estimate relative motion. Yi-Fan Zuo and Jiaqi Yang [26] proposed a new approach that combines depth steam and event steam. The addition of events makes pipelines better at handling fast movements. J Hidalgo-Carri [7] proposed the first method that combines frames and events with a direct approach to estimate the 6-DOF pose. Samuel Bryner [1] uses classical dense 3D reconstruction algorithms to build 3D maps of optical flow, tracking the 6-DOF pose of the Event Camera. Antoni Rosinol Vidal and Henri RebecqHis [16] proposed pipeline incorporate an event Camera, conventional camera, and IMU for state estimation. Good robustness, high accuracy, and can work properly under large sudden changes in ambient light, and high-speed motion.

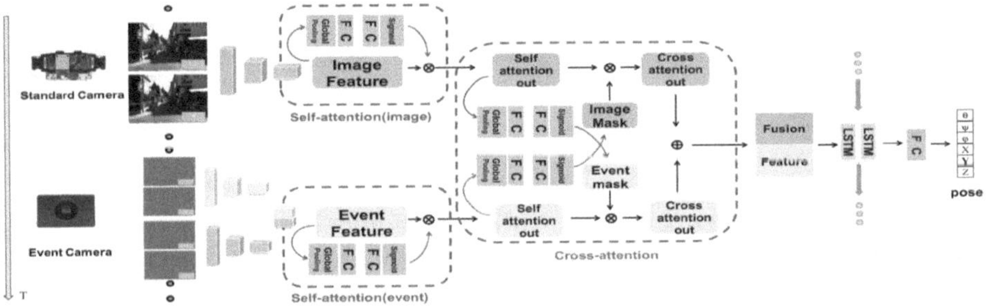


(a) DeepEVO-Mask

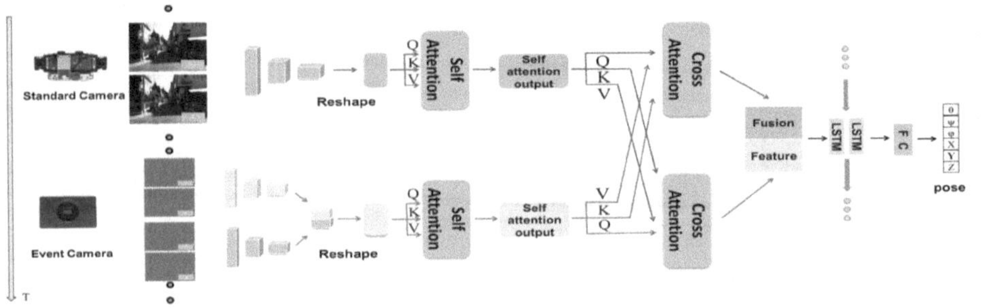


(b) DeepEVO-Multihead

**Fig. 2.** The proposed network architectures. (a) DeepEVO with the mask-based attention mechanism. (b) DeepEVO with the multi-head attention mechanism.

## 3 Network Architecture

In this section, we provide a comprehensive overview of the DeepEVO architecture, as illustrated in Fig. 2. The network's primary input consists of event streams and video frames. To extract meaningful features from these inputs, we employ encoders equipped with multiple convolutional layers. These layers serve to capture relevant information from both the event streams and video frames. Following feature extraction, we employ two distinct attention mechanisms: mask-based attention and multi-head attention. These mechanisms facilitate the fusion of features derived from the two modalities. Ultimately, the DeepEVO model employs a trained LSTM component to estimate the poses. It is important to emphasize that an event's format is defined as $(t, x, y, p)$, where $t$ denotes the timestamp of the event's generation, while $x$ and $y$ represent the pixel coordinates of the event. The variable $p$ denotes the event's polarity, with values of $p$ being either $+1$ or $-1$.

### 3.1 Events and Image Alignment

Conventional cameras operate by capturing frames at regular intervals, thereby providing a sequence of discrete images. In contrast, event cameras exhibit the capability to densely record event streams, offering a substantially higher temporal resolution compared to traditional video frames. This unique characteristic of event cameras imparts them with the ability to capture inter-frame information that is beyond the reach of standard cameras. For the purpose of estimating the camera's motion, it becomes imperative to align these two distinct data sources: the image frames and the event streams. During the model training process, a specific approach is employed to establish this alignment. Two consecutive image frames are selected as a foundational reference point, and the neighboring events are subsequently synchronized with respect to these selected frames. This synchronization process enables the integration of event data with the temporal context provided by image frames, facilitating accurate motion estimation.

Concretely, when two image frames are captured at $T_n$ and $T_{n+1}$, respectively, the events generated in intervals $[(T_{n-1}+T_n)/2,\ T_n]$ and $[T_n,\ (T_n+T_{n+1})/2]$ are packed and converted into event frames $E_n^1$ and $E_n^2$. Similarly, the events in intervals $[(T_n+T_{n+1})/2,\ T_{n+1}]$ and $[T_{n+1},\ (T_{n+1}+T_{n+2})/2]$ are used to form the frames $E_{n+1}^1$ and $E_{n+1}^2$. $E_n^1$, $E_n^2$, $E_{n+1}^1$ and $E_{n+1}^2$ are concatenated as $F_n$ and $F_{n+1}$, respectively. Figure 3 demonstrates the alignment process.

In this way, a pair of image frames and the aligned pairs of event frames are obtained, which are further employed to estimate the motion of the camera.

### 3.2 Feature Encoder

The primary objective of the feature encoder network is to extract essential features for the purpose of ego-motion estimation, drawing from both the images and the event stream. Our approach takes inspiration from the work of EV-FlowNet [25], which utilizes a learning-based method for computing optical flow

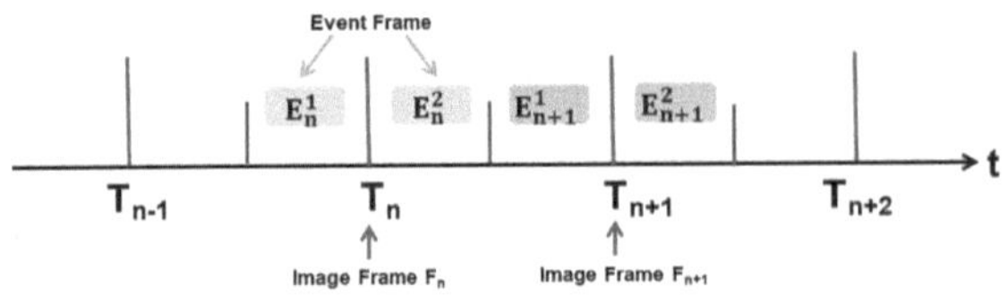


**Fig. 3.** Alignment of events and video frames.

using event stream data. In alignment with this methodology, we employ the same structural framework as FlowNet-simple to encode event-related features, further leveraging the pre-trained weights of FlowNet's convolutional neural network (CNN) component. It is noteworthy that the event data, when converted into image format, exhibits a single channel. To accommodate this structure for compatibility with the FlowNet architecture, we duplicate this single channel into three channels, which are then employed as input to the FlowNet structure.

The FlowNet, specifically its CNN component, is composed of a sequence of convolutional layers. These layers exhibit a progressive reduction in the sizes of their respective receptive fields, transitioning from initial dimensions of $7 \times 7$ and $5 \times 5$ to culminate at $3 \times 3$. This reduction in receptive field size is deliberate, as it aids in capturing more meaningful features. Additionally, the number of channels within the network undergoes a systematic increase, progressing from 6 channels at the outset, to 64, 128, 256, 512, and ultimately reaching 1024 channels. This augmentation in the number of channels enables the network to learn and represent a diverse array of features, contributing to the efficacy of the feature extraction process.

### 3.3 Self-attention Module

The original design of self-attention is to solve the long-range feature interdependence problem in machine translation, and here it is used to select dominant features of standard images and event frames, respectively. Two different attention modules, mask-based attention and multi-head attention, are designed to automatically select the more valuable features, and the corresponding neural network are names as DeepEVO-Mask (MK) and DeepEVO-Multihead (MD).

**DeepEVO-MK:** The output of the feature encoder network is fed into the self-attention module. This module computes the weight at each channel of the features by calculating the correlation between each channel and taking their weighted average in the embedding space. Assuming that $e$ is the feature vector of events, a non-local operation [19] is:

$$y_i = Sigmoid(\sum_{\forall_j} f(e_i, e_j)) \tag{1}$$

where $e_i$ and $e_j$ denotes the $i^{th}$ channel and the $j^{th}$ channel in the vector $e$, and $f(e_i, e_j)$ is the function that calculates the similarity between $e_i$ and $e_j$, which can be represented as

$$f(e_i, e_j) = (W_i e_i)^T (W_j e_j) \tag{2}$$

where $W_i$ and $W_j$ denote learnable weight matrices that project $e_i$ and $e_j$ to embedding spaces. Finally, function $g(e_j)$ projects original feature $e_i$ to a new embedding space associated with the self-attention. The attended features $\widetilde{e_i}$ which are given by

$$\widetilde{e_i} = Sigmoid((W_i e_i)^{\mathrm{T}} W_j e_j) g(e_i) \tag{3}$$

**DeepEVO-MD:** The self-attention module operates on the feature map after encoding. The feature map passes through three $1 \times 1$ convolution structures to generate query, key, and value matrices. The channel of query and key is reduced to $\frac{1}{8}$ of the original. The channels of value remain unchanged. Query is transposed and multiplied by key. After softmax normalization, an attention map of [H×W, H×W] is obtained. Multiply the attention map with the value matrix to get a [H×W, C] feature map. Finally reshape the output to [H, W, C].

$$\begin{aligned}[Q_e, K_e, V_e] &= W_{qkv} e \\ \widetilde{e_i} &= Sigmoid(\frac{Q_e^T K_e}{\sqrt{d_k}}) V_e\end{aligned} \tag{4}$$

where $W_{qkv}$ is learnable weight matrix that used to generate query $Q_e$, key $K_e$, and value $V_e$ the feature vector of events $e$, $d_k$ is the dimension of $K_e$ and $\widetilde{e_i}$ is the attended features.

### 3.4 Cross-Attention Module

The self-attention module focuses on the dominant features from the same sensor, while the cross-attention module focuses on the features from different sensors in different scenarios. This cross-attention module aims to fusion the data from different sensors complementary.

**DeepEVO-MK:** Given two features $e$ and $f$ from two different sensors after self-attention module, two corresponding cross-attention masks can be computed as:

$$\begin{aligned}m_{f \to e} &= Sigmoid((W_{f \to e} e_i)^{\mathrm{T}} W_{f \to e} e_j) \\ m_{e \to f} &= Sigmoid((W_{e \to f} f_i)^{\mathrm{T}} W_{e \to f} f_j)\end{aligned} \tag{5}$$

Two features multiply the corresponding masks via element-wise operation, after which two attended features are concatenated together as the input of LSTM for pose regression.

$$\widetilde{V_{ef}} = [m_{f \to e} \odot e; m_{e \to f} \odot f] \tag{6}$$

**DeepEVO-MD:** The cross-attention follows self-attention and considers the influence of the relationship between the two modalities on the output. The update of event and image feature maps can be represented by the following formula.

$$\begin{aligned} f &= Q_f K_f^T V_f + Q_f K_e^T V_e \\ e &= Q_e K_e^T V_e + Q_e K_f^T V_f \end{aligned} \tag{7}$$

### 3.5 Pose Regression

LSTM can model dependencies in sequences, and current estimates are also related to previous states. This is very suitable for the VO problem because the VO problem is to get the motion changes of the camera from the image sequence. Estimating the pose change of the current image frame takes into account not only the input frame but also the previous state and the information of the previous frame. However, LSTM is not suitable for direct learning from the initial image, and it is necessary to use CNN to extract features before continuing to learn. Two LSTM layers were stacking for better performance. The last two fully connected layers make the output 6 dimensions $(x, y, z, \Theta, \Psi, \varphi)$.

**Table 1.** Results on testing sequences of the KITTI dataset. Bold indicates the best performance among the blurred image methods for each sequence.

| Seq. | DeepEVO-MK | | DeepEVO-MD | | DeepVO | | ESP-VO | | DeepVO (Clear) | | ESP-VO (Clear) | |
|---|---|---|---|---|---|---|---|---|---|---|---|---|
| | $r_{rel}$ | $t_{rel}$ | $r_{rel}$ | $t_{rel}$ | $r_{rel}$ | $t_{rel}$ | $r_{rel}$ | $t_{rel}$ | $r_{rel}$ | $t_{rel}$ | $r_{rel}$ | $t_{rel}$ |
| 03 | 7.77 | 12.23 | **2.89** | **3.44** | 6.52 | 11.17 | 3.57 | 5.62 | 9.00 | 11.11 | 5.40 | 8.10 |
| 04 | 3.64 | **9.48** | 3.58 | 10.48 | 5.02 | 11.18 | **3.10** | 10.06 | 3.44 | 10.52 | 2.87 | 8.06 |
| 05 | **2.44** | **6.37** | 4.22 | 10.15 | 6.06 | 13.71 | 3.82 | 10.13 | 4.02 | 10.22 | 2.27 | 5.86 |
| 06 | 3.46 | 11.18 | **3.35** | **10.96** | 5.09 | 14.80 | 4.75 | 14.61 | 3.36 | 9.54 | 3.28 | 9.41 |
| 07 | 4.81 | 8.07 | **3.10** | **4.11** | 5.56 | 8.92 | 10.68 | 14.52 | 6.90 | 9.43 | 4.70 | 6.67 |
| 10 | 4.80 | 14.15 | **3.81** | **10.71** | 5.05 | 12.52 | 4.54 | 12.10 | 4.26 | 9.25 | 3.30 | 8.80 |
| **Mean** | 4.48 | 10.24 | **3.49** | **8.31** | 5.56 | 12.05 | 5.07 | 11.17 | 5.16 | 10.01 | 3.63 | 7.81 |

$r_{rel}$: Rotational RMSE (degrees/100 m); $t_{rel}$: Translational RMSE drift (%) over segments of 100–800 m.

## 4 Experiment

### 4.1 Experiment Settings

Due to limited memory of GPU, we did not use the original resolution of the images as DeepVO(1280 × 384) [17] and ESP-VO(1280 × 384) [18], but resized the image to 640 × 192. The mean square error (MSE) loss is employed, and the Adam optimizer was used to train the network with an initial learning rate of 0.0001. The learning rate is reduced to half of the original value for every 20 epochs, and the result is obtained by training 200 epochs. There is no intervention in the training process. The batch size is set to 8 to get better generalization performance.

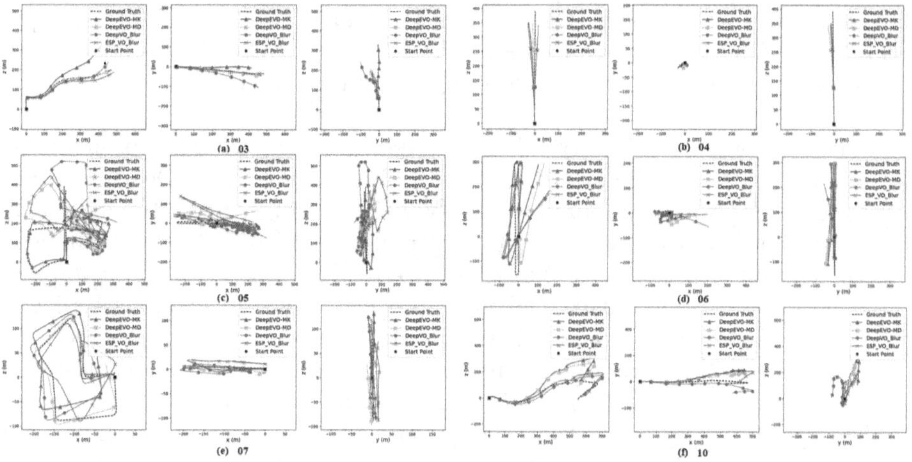


**Fig. 4.** Trajectories of VO results on the testing Sequence 03, 04, 05, 06, 07 and 10 of the KITTI VO benchmark.

### 4.2 Results on The KITTI Dataset

KITTI dataset [6] has 11 sequences with the groundtruth, and the maximum speed in the dataset reaches 85 km/h. There are three types of environments: urban, country and highway.

Here, sequences 00, 02, 08, and 09 are used for training since they are relatively long, and the sequence 03, 04, 05, 06, 07, and 10 are used for evaluation.

We use the open-source method (V2E [8]) to convert video to the event stream. In order to clearly reflect the advantages of our methods, the KITTI dataset [6] is actively added with a lot of motion blur. The frame rate of KITTI dataset is 10 Hz, we use Superslomo [9] to interpolate frames to reach 60 hz. After that, we averaged 6 consecutive images to generate a blurred frame by considering gamma correction [12]. In this way, the dataset is restored to the original 10hz.

The DeepVO [17] and the ESP-VO [18] are selected as baselines, both of which only use video frames. We test the performance of both methods on blurred and clear datasets. DeepEVO uses additional event streams to the blurred dataset.

As demonstrated by the results presented in Table 1, where $t_{rel}$ represents the average translational RMSE drift (%) over distances ranging from 100 m to 800 m, and $r_{rel}$ denotes the average rotational RMSE drift (°/100 m) over the same distance range, it becomes evident that performance on blurred frames alone falls short of the quality achieved with clear frames. However, with the inclusion of the event stream and the associated fusion module, significant improvements are realized.

In particular, the introduction of the event stream and fusion module yields a noteworthy reduction in rotational drift for DeepEVO-MK, with a decrease of

1.08°/100 m in comparison to DeepVO, and a reduction of 0.59°/100 m relative to ESP-VO. Moreover, the average translational drift for DeepEVO-MK exhibits a decrease of 1.81% in comparison to DeepVO and a reduction of 0.93% relative to ESP-VO.

In the case of DeepEVO-MD, the improvements are even more pronounced, with a reduction in rotational drift by 2.07°/100 m compared to DeepVO, and a decrease of 1.58°/100 m compared to ESP-VO. The average translational drift for DeepEVO-MD demonstrates a substantial reduction of 3.74% when compared to DeepVO, and a reduction of 2.86% relative to ESP-VO.

Furthermore, a comparative analysis between DeepEVO-MK and DeepEVO-MD reveals that the latter consistently outperforms in both translation and rotation estimation. These experiments underscore the efficacy of the event stream in complementing the information lacking in blurred frames, while the fusion module effectively highlights the salient characteristics from both the frames and the event data, thereby enhancing overall performance.

We further visualized the experimental results in Fig. 4. Each test sequence demonstrates translation changes from three viewpoints. The black dotted line in each picture represents the ground truth. The closer to the black dotted line, the better the result. On the four test sequences of 03, 05, 06, and 07, it can be clearly seen that DeepEVO is closer to the black dotted line than DeepVO.

### 4.3 Results on The UZH-FPV Drone Racing Dataset

Compared with the KITTI dataset, the UZH-FPV Drone Racing dataset [3] is more challenging. Large accelerations, rotations, and apparent motion in vision sensors make aggressive trajectories difficult for state estimation. The trajectories in this dataset include fast laps around a racetrack with drone racing gates, as well as free-form trajectories around obstacles, both indoor and outdoor, and four scenarios are included: indoor forward facing, indoor 45-degree downward facing, outdoor forward facing, outdoor 45-degree downward facing.

**Table 2.** Results on testing sequences of the UZH-FPV Drone Racing Dataset. Bold indicates the best performance for each sequence.

| Sequence | DeepEVO-MK | | DeepEVO-MD | | DeepVO [17] | | ESP-VO [18] | | Pure-Event [13] | |
|---|---|---|---|---|---|---|---|---|---|---|
| | $r_{rel}$ | $t_{rel}$ | $r_{rel}$ | $t_{rel}$ | $r_{rel}$ | $t_{rel}$ | $r_{rel}$ | $t_{rel}$ | $r_{rel}$ | $t_{rel}$ |
| Indoor_forward_5 | 18.64 | **4.01** | 33.30 | 4.56 | 33.49 | 9.80 | **14.74** | 8.94 | 20.51 | 6.63 |
| Indoor_45_9 | 19.47 | 3.23 | 19.50 | **2.74** | 22.66 | 2.97 | 22.20 | 2.82 | **14.96** | 3.67 |
| Outdoor_forward_5 | **19.38** | **33.80** | 30.97 | 33.87 | 22.76 | 35.01 | 22.89 | 34.81 | 38.75 | 51.10 |
| **Mean** | **19.16** | **13.68** | 27.92 | 13.72 | 26.30 | 15.92 | 19.94 | 15.52 | 24.74 | 20.46 |

We choose the sequence 3, 6, 7, 9, 10 of indoor forward facing, the sequence 2, 4, 12, 13, 14 of indoor 45-degree downward facing and the sequence 1, 3 of outdoor forward facing as the training dataset and indoor_forward_5_davis, indoor_45_9_davis, outdoor_forward_5_davis are utilized for evaluation. Outdoor 45-degree downward facing has only one sequence with ground truth, and the sequence is too short to be used for training. Therefore, it is not used in the experiments.

We used the evaluation method from The UZH-FPV Drone Racing dataset website. The Pure-Event approach [13] are selected as baselines, which only use event frames. The relative pose errors at the sub-trajectory of lengths 40, 60, 80, 100, 120 m are computed. The results are shown in the Table 2. $t_{rel}$ denotes average translational RMSE drift (%) on length of (40 m, 60 m, 80 m, 100 m, 120 m). $r_{rel}$ denotes average rotational RMSE drift (°/100 m) on length of (40 m, 60 m, 80 m, 100 m, 120 m). We further visualized the experimental results in Fig. 5 Each test sequence demonstrates translation changes from three viewpoints.

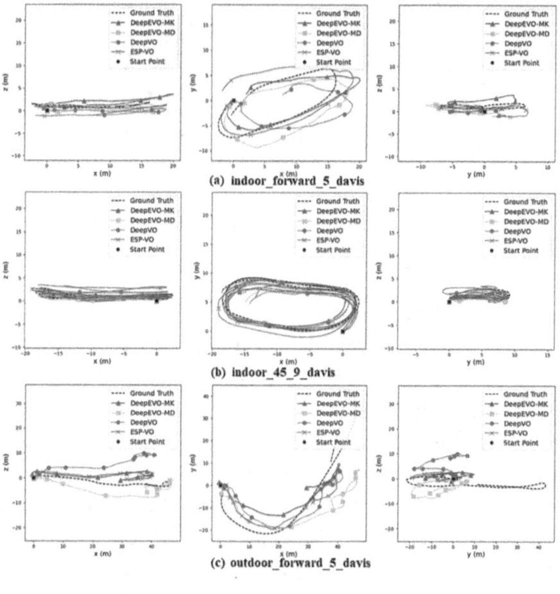


**Fig. 5.** Trajectory descriptions from three perspectives on the test set.

In the evaluation of the test sequence indoor_forward_5_davis, DeepEVO demonstrates superior performance compared to DeepVO and ESP-VO. As illustrated in Fig. 6(a), this experiment takes place in an indoor environment characterized by low room lighting, with certain regions, such as doors and windows, exhibiting notably high brightness levels. Consequently, in the video frame, many fine details are inadequately captured due to the overwhelming impact of the intense illumination. In sharp contrast, the event camera's exceptional dynamic range, boasting a remarkable 140 dB in comparison to the 60 dB of standard cameras, enables it to preserve a greater amount of detail without succumbing to the challenges posed by intense lighting conditions.

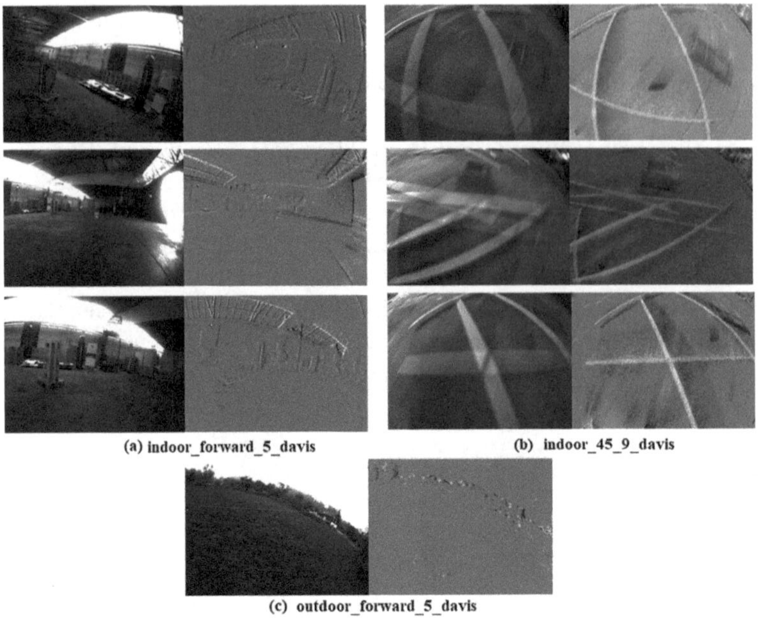


**Fig. 6.** Comparison of image and event frame.

A discernible distinction emerges when we compare the regions encompassing the windows and doors within the frames. In the event frame, the windows and doors remain largely unaffected by the intense lighting, facilitating the retention of substantial detail. This enhanced performance is attributed to the inherent advantages of the event-based approach, which outperforms DeepVO and ESP-VO in this specific scenario. Given the complementary nature of events and video frames, DeepEVO, which combines both data sources, exhibits a competitive edge over DeepVO, ESP-VO, and Pure-Event. This amalgamation of modalities empowers DeepEVO to surpass alternative methods, capitalizing on the strengths of each data source to achieve enhanced performance in this context.

In the assessment of the indoor_45_9_davis test sequence, DeepEVO demonstrates superior performance when compared to DeepVO, ESP-VO, and Pure-Event. This particular test sequence involves a drone with high-speed motion, reaching velocities as rapid as 11.23 m per second. As evidenced in Fig. 6(b), the video frames exhibit significant motion blur due to the swift and dynamic movement of the drone. In stark contrast, the corresponding event frames remain largely impervious to the challenges of motion blur, owing to their exceptionally high temporal resolution.

The remarkable resistance of event frames to motion blur stems from their innate ability to capture events at a temporal granularity that greatly surpasses traditional video frames. Consequently, the event frames maintain clarity and preserve crucial visual information even when confronted with rapid motion, a distinct advantage in scenarios characterized by high-speed dynamics.

In the evaluation of the outdoor_forward_5_davis test sequence, DeepEVO achieves performance results that are in close proximity to those of DeepVO and ESP-VO. This specific test sequence primarily encompasses natural elements, such as trees, grass, and the sky, as illustrated in Fig. 6(c). Notably, the scene is characterized by its relative emptiness, with limited discernible texture information available for feature extraction. Consequently, the event camera records a rather sparse number of events in such an environment.

Furthermore, the irregular distribution of leaves and grass within the scene introduces a substantial amount of noise into the event data, which can have a detrimental effect on the quality of motion estimation. In this particular setting, the events tend to be less informative and less conducive to accurate motion estimation. As a result, the performance of the Pure-Event approach is notably suboptimal in this context, as it struggles to effectively harness the event data in the presence of a sparse and noise-laden visual landscape.

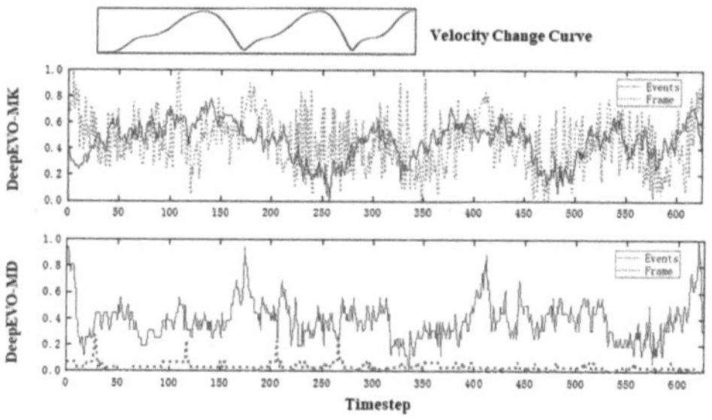


**Fig. 7.** DeepEVO-MK and DeepEVO-MD attention block weight visualization.

To investigate whether the attention modules designed for DeepEVO-MK and DeepEVO-MD can indeed achieve the fusion and complementation of multimodal data, we normalized the weights of the frame and event data in indoor_45_9_davis, resulting in Fig. 7. The horizontal axis represents the moments when each frame was generated, and the vertical axis represents the weights. The red line represents the weight of event data, while the green line represents the weight of frame data. First, it can be observed that the weight of event data is strongly correlated with the blue velocity change curve. This is because a higher speed leads to a higher number of events, contributing to a larger weight for the event modality. This also validates the sensitivity of our proposed module to speed. Secondly, the weights of the two modalities do not exhibit synchronized changes, indicating the effectiveness of the attention module.

## 5 Conclusion

In this research endeavor, we introduce DeepEVO, a novel end-to-end trainable system designed for ego-motion estimation. DeepEVO operates by effectively integrating information sourced from both event streams and video frames, thus enabling a comprehensive fusion of visual data modalities. A pivotal element of the DeepEVO architecture comprises two distinct mixed fusion modules, strategically devised to dynamically select and prioritize dominant features from the two distinct vision modalities, accommodating variations arising from diverse operational conditions.

The experimental findings, obtained through evaluations conducted on both simulated and real-world datasets, provide compelling evidence of DeepEVO's efficacy. DeepEVO is observed to deliver substantial improvements in terms of accuracy and robustness in the domain of visual odometry when juxtaposed with the conventional video-based approaches. This outcome underscores the value and potential of our approach, signifying its relevance and applicability in diverse practical scenarios.

## References

1. Bryner, S., Gallego, G., Rebecq, H., Scaramuzza, D.: Event-based, direct camera tracking from a photometric 3d map using nonlinear optimization. In: International Conference on Robotics & Automation (2019)
2. Censi, A., Scaramuzza, D.: Low-latency event-based visual odometry. In: IEEE International Conference on Robotics and Automation (ICRA), pp. 703–710. IEEE (2014)
3. Delmerico, J., Cieslewski, T., Rebecq, H., Faessler, M., Scaramuzza, D.: Are we ready for autonomous drone racing? The UZH-FPV drone racing dataset. In: IEEE Int. Conf. Robot. Autom. (ICRA) (2019)
4. Gehrig, D., Rebecq, H., Gallego, G., Scaramuzza, D.: EKLT: asynchronous photometric feature tracking using events and frames. Int. J. Comput. Vision **128**(3), 601–618 (2020)
5. Gehrig, D., Rüegg, M., Gehrig, M., Hidalgo-Carrió, J., Scaramuzza, D.: Combining events and frames using recurrent asynchronous multimodal networks for monocular depth prediction. IEEE Robot. Autom. Lett. **6**(2), 2822–2829 (2021)
6. Geiger, A., Lenz, P., Stiller, C., Urtasun, R.: Vision meets robotics: the kitti dataset. Int. J. Robot. Res. **32**(11), 1231–1237 (2013)
7. Hidalgo-Carrió, J., Gallego, G., Scaramuzza, D.: Event-aided direct sparse odometry. In: Proceedings of the IEEE/CVF Conference on Computer Vision and Pattern Recognition, pp. 5781–5790 (2022)
8. Hu, Y., Liu, S.C., Delbruck, T.: V2E: from video frames to realistic DVS events. In: Proceedings of the IEEE/CVF Conference on Computer Vision and Pattern Recognition, pp. 1312–1321 (2021)

9. Jiang, H., Sun, D., Jampani, V., Yang, M.H., Learned-Miller, E., Kautz, J.: Super SloMo: high quality estimation of multiple intermediate frames for video interpolation. In: Proceedings of the IEEE Conference on Computer Vision and Pattern Recognition, pp. 9000–9008 (2018)
10. Kim, H., Kim, H.J.: Real-time rotational motion estimation with contrast maximization over globally aligned events. IEEE Robot. Autom. Lett. **6**(3), 6016–6023 (2021)
11. Li, H., Stueckler, J.: Tracking 6-DoF object motion from events and frames. In: 2021 IEEE International Conference on Robotics and Automation (ICRA), pp. 14171–14177. IEEE (2021)
12. Nah, S., Hyun Kim, T., Mu Lee, K.: Deep multi-scale convolutional neural network for dynamic scene deblurring. In: Proceedings of the IEEE Conference on Computer Vision and Pattern Recognition, pp. 3883–3891 (2017)
13. Nguyen, A., Do, T.T., Caldwell, D.G., Tsagarakis, N.G.: Real-time 6dof pose relocalization for event cameras with stacked spatial LSTM networks. In: Proceedings of the IEEE/CVF Conference on Computer Vision and Pattern Recognition Workshops (2019)
14. Pan, L., Scheerlinck, C., Yu, X., Hartley, R., Liu, M., Dai, Y.: Bringing a blurry frame alive at high frame-rate with an event camera. In: Proceedings of the IEEE/CVF Conference on Computer Vision and Pattern Recognition, pp. 6820–6829 (2019)
15. Rebecq, H., Horstschäfer, T., Gallego, G., Scaramuzza, D.: EVO: a geometric approach to event-based 6-DoF parallel tracking and mapping in real time. IEEE Robot. Autom. Lett. **2**(2), 593–600 (2016)
16. Vidal, A.R., Rebecq, H., Horstschaefer, T., Scaramuzza, D.: Ultimate slam? Combining events, images, and IMU for robust visual slam in HDR and high speed scenarios. IEEE Robot. Autom. Lett., 994–1001 (2018)
17. Wang, S., Clark, R., Wen, H., Trigoni, N.: DeepVO: towards end-to-end visual odometry with deep recurrent convolutional neural networks. In: 2017 IEEE International Conference on Robotics and Automation (ICRA), pp. 2043–2050. IEEE (2017)
18. Wang, S., Clark, R., Wen, H., Trigoni, N.: End-to-end, sequence-to-sequence probabilistic visual odometry through deep neural networks. Int. J. Robot. Res. **37**(4–5), 513–542 (2018)
19. Wang, X., Girshick, R., Gupta, A., He, K.: Non-local neural networks. In: Proceedings of the IEEE Conference on Computer Vision and Pattern Recognition, pp. 7794–7803 (2018)
20. Wang, Y., et al.: Visual odometry with an event camera using continuous ray warping and volumetric contrast maximization. Sensors **22**(15), 5687 (2022)
21. Weikersdorfer, D., Adrian, D.B., Cremers, D., Conradt, J.: Event-based 3d slam with a depth-augmented dynamic vision sensor. In: IEEE International Conference on Robotics and Dutomation (ICRA), pp. 359–364. IEEE (2014)
22. Weikersdorfer, D., Conradt, J.: Event-based particle filtering for robot self-localization. In: 2012 IEEE International Conference on Robotics and Biomimetics (ROBIO), pp. 866–870. IEEE (2012)
23. Ye, C., Mitrokhin, A., Fermüller, C., Yorke, J.A., Aloimonos, Y.: Unsupervised learning of dense optical flow, depth and egomotion with event-based sensors. In: 2020 IEEE/RSJ International Conference on Intelligent Robots and Systems (IROS), pp. 5831–5838. IEEE (2020)

24. Zhu, A.Z., Atanasov, N., Daniilidis, K.: Event-based visual inertial odometry. In: Proceedings of the IEEE Conference on Computer Vision and Pattern Recognition, pp. 5391–5399 (2017)
25. Zhu, A.Z., Yuan, L., Chaney, K., Daniilidis, K.: EV-FlowNet: self-supervised optical flow estimation for event-based cameras, arXiv preprint arXiv:1802.06898 (2018)
26. Zuo, Y.F., Yang, J., Chen, J., Wang, X., Wang, Y., Kneip, L.: DEVO: depth-event camera visual odometry in challenging conditions. In: 2022 International Conference on Robotics and Automation (ICRA), pp. 2179–2185. IEEE (2022)

# MFR-LSTM: A Robust Rainfall Estimation Model Based on Multi-feature Extraction Using Commercial Microwave Links

Zixuan Qin[1], Minghao Liang[1], Yong Liu[2], Biling Zhang[1], Caili Guo[1](✉), and Congzheng Han[3]

[1] School of Information and Communication Engineering, Beijing University of Posts and Telecommunications, Beijing 100876, China
{qinzixuan0615,mhliang,bilingzhang,guocaili}@bupt.edu.cn
[2] School of College of Humanities, Beijing University of Posts and Telecommunications, Beijing 100876, China
liuyong001@bupt.edu.cn
[3] Institute of Atmospheric Physics, Chinese Academy of Sciences, Beijing 100029, China
c.han@mail.iap.ac.cn

**Abstract.** The microwaves signals are attenuated by the scattering and absorption of raindrops when they propagate through the rainfall, which makes commercial microwave links (CML) a unique opportunity for rainfall monitoring. However, traditional power law CML based methods for rainfall estimation encounter computational complexity and degraded accuracy under light rainfall conditions. To address these challenges, we propose Multi-Feature based and Robust LSTM (MFR-LSTM), a novel deep learning (DL) framework for rainfall estimation using CML. MFR-LSTM integrates an Inception module for spatial features extraction, a NoisyLinear layer for enhancing model robustness, and a LSTM module for capturing the temporal dependence of CML data. The experimental results show that compared to the baseline, MFR-LSTM are 8.25% higher in correlation coefficient and 1.82% higher in dry-wet classification accuracy. In addition, under the Gaussian noise, MFR-LSTM's degradation in correlation coefficient is 6.2% less than the baseline, demonstrating its reliable potential in rainfall estimation and meteorological monitoring.

**Keywords:** Rainfall Estimation · Commercial Microwave Links · Multi-Feature Extraction · Long Short-Term Memory

## 1 Introduction

Commercial Microwave Links (CML), designed primarily for wireless backhaul connectivity in cellular networks, transmit high-frequency microwave signals


Y. Liu et al. (Eds.): ChinaCom 2025, LNICST 711, pp. 511–525, 2027.
https://doi.org/10.1007/978-3-032-33662-0_37

(typically 15–40 GHz, extending to E-band 71–86 GHz) between base stations. As microwaves propagate through rainfall, raindrops attenuate the signal through scattering and absorption, which makes CMLs a unintentional rainfall sensors to correlate rain-induced attenuation directly with precipitation intensity.

The traditional approaches to estimate the average rainrate on the CML path are based on the power law (PL) relationship between rain induced attenuation and rainrate [1,2]. However, these approaches heavily depend on the accurate dry-wet classification as well as the estimation of wet antenna attenuation, which not only increases the estimation complexity but also introduces error accumulation. Moreover, PL-based rainfall estimation methods are only available when the rainfall is heavy.

Recently, machine learning (ML) based algorithms [3,4] are introduced. For example, in [5], the Xgboost algorithm was first utilized to classify the wet and dry periods, and then the SVM algorithm was used for regression rainfall prediction. Experiments evidenced that machine learning algorithms were able to improve the performance of rainfall estimation compared to PL. However, the structure of traditional machine learning models was too simple to fully capture the deep-seated features in the relationship between signal attenuation and rainrate.

The current research on rainfall estimation using deep learning models mainly utilizes recurrent neural network (RNN) and its variant models for modeling time series. For example, the authors of [6] presented a Gated Recurrent Unit (GRU)-based rainfall estimation model that leveraged dry-wet classification results to improve precipitation estimation accuracy. In [7], the authors proposed a two-layer LSTM model with a fully connected output layer that achieved significantly lower RMSE in rainfall estimation compared to traditional weighted average methods. The model in [8] employed LSTM architecture for simultaneous rainfall estimation and dry-wet classification, incorporating optimizations in both network design and data processing. Beyond LSTM approaches, recent work has employed genetic algorithm-optimized back propagation neural networks (GA-BP) for rainfall estimation, demonstrating enhanced model performance through improved weight initialization [9]. Although these approaches avoid the errors introduced in the dry-wet classification and wet antenna attenuation in the PL method, they neglect the relationships between different frequencies and features in CML. Moreover, these approaches only model the temporal relationship and do not make full use of the link information, which limits the potential for further improvement in estimation accuracy.

To solve the aforementioned problems, deep Learning (DL) models are introduced into rainfall estimation in two ways. One approach is to apply DL models as a step in PL method. For example in the literature [10], an auto-encoder model was constructed for dry-wet classification using neural networks. The other is a data-driven approach where predictions are derived directly from link data, such as [6–9,11]. DL has been validated as a more accurate and efficient method achieving lower mean square error performance in rainfall estimation. However, these studies primarily focus on modeling the temporal relationships of CML, neglecting the relationships between different features within the signals. Furthermore, weather variations cause fluctuations in signals, yet the robustness of these models has not been well investigated.

Therefore, in this paper, we propose a DL model to estimate the rainfall accurately and reliably by effectively capturing both temporal and spatial features of CMLs. The main contribution of this article includes:

(1) An Inception and LSTM based model, named MFR-LSTM, is proposed for more accurate rainfall estimation, where Inception is used for spatial feature extraction and LSTM is used for temporal feature extraction. To improve the robustness of the model, a noisy neural network, i.e., NoisyLinear, is also incorporated into the proposed model.
(2) To smooth the severe fluctuations of rainfall size in the CML dataset, we propose a sliding window technique where the window size is adaptively set by a genetic algorithm (GA). Moreover, a loss function is proposed to train the MFR-LSTM.
(3) Comparative and ablation experiments show that compared to the baseline, MFR-LSTM are 8.25% higher in correlation coefficient and 1.82% higher in dry-wet classification accuracy. In addition, under the Gaussian noise, MFR-LSTM's degradation in correlation coefficient is 6.2% less than the baseline, demonstrating its reliable potential in rainfall estimation and meteorological monitoring.

## 2 Related Works

The current research on rainfall estimation using deep learning models mainly utilizes recurrent neural network (RNN) and its variant models for modeling time series. For example, the authors of [6] presented a Gated Recurrent Unit (GRU)-based rainfall estimation model that leveraged dry-wet classification results to improve precipitation estimation accuracy. In [7], the authors proposed a two-layer LSTM model with a fully connected output layer that achieved significantly lower RMSE in rainfall estimation compared to traditional weighted average methods. The model in [8] employed LSTM architecture for simultaneous rainfall estimation and dry-wet classification, incorporating optimizations in both network design and data processing. Beyond LSTM approaches, recent work has employed genetic algorithm-optimized back propagation neural networks (GA-BP) for rainfall estimation, demonstrating enhanced model performance through improved weight initialization [9]. Although these approaches avoid the errors introduced in the dry-wet classification and wet antenna attenuation in the PL method, they neglect the relationships between different frequencies and features in CML. Moreover, these approaches only model the temporal relationship and do not make full use of the link information, which limits the potential for further improvement in estimation accuracy.

# 3 The Proposed Model

In this section, we first introduce the structure of MFR-LSTM, which is constructed by four parts, i.e., data process, CNN predictor for spatial feature extraction, NoisyLinear for model robustness improvement and LSTM predictor for temporal feature extraction, as shown in Fig. 1. Then we introduce the loss function used to train the MFR-LSTM.

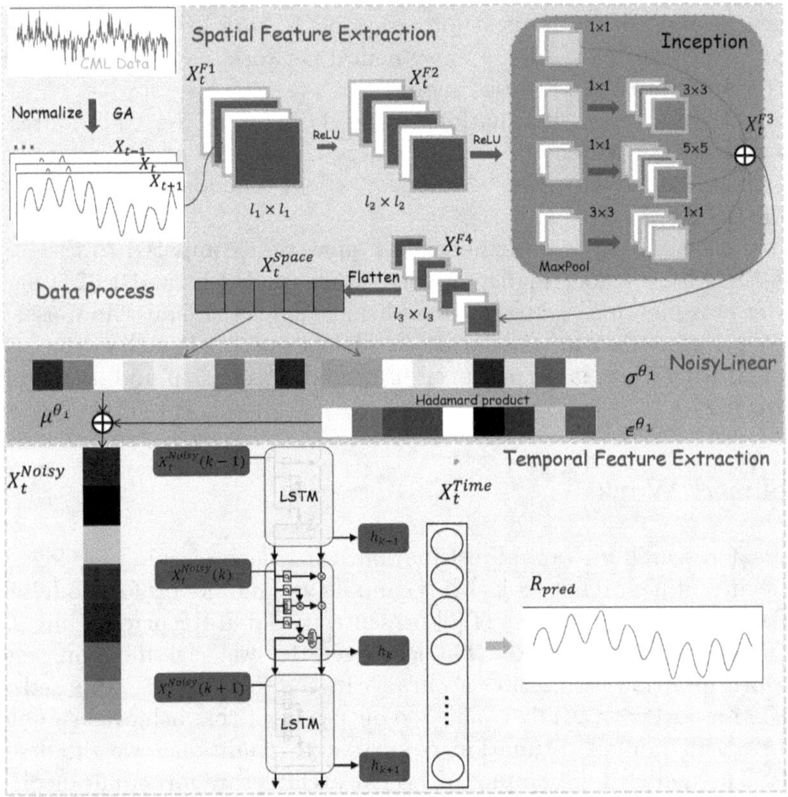


**Fig. 1.** Structure of MFR-LSTM.

## 3.1 Data Process

**Normalization.** Our experiment is based on a CML located in a city. Received Signal Strength Indication (RSSI) and Carrier Interference plus Noise Ratio (CINR) of microwave links operating at 71 GHz and 81 GHz are collected. At each moment $t$, the data of the link consists of four entries:

$$x_t = [\mathrm{CINR_{f_1,t}}, \mathrm{CINR_{f_2,t}}, \mathrm{RSSI_{f_1,t}}, \mathrm{RSSI_{f_2,t}}], \tag{1}$$

where $f_1$ and $f_2$ represent the two frequencies of the link, and $t$ represents the sampling moment. As the distribution of rainfall data in the dataset is highly unbalanced, we have censored the data for only a few extreme rainfall values to minimize the impact of these outliers, and then normalized the data.

**Sliding Window.** The raw rainfall data exhibits substantial fluctuations due to measurement errors and meteorological changes, which directly impacts model training effectiveness. Window size selection thus becomes a critical trade-off: oversized windows amplify noise interference while reducing temporal feature resolution, whereas undersized windows lead to insufficient smoothing that undermines extreme event prediction accuracy. This dual challenge requires balancing noise suppression with feature preservation to optimize model performance. We implemented sliding windows at two key stages. First, the sliding window is used to segment the CML data and construct the train set and test set, where the window size directly determines the temporal span of input data. The other sliding window is applied to smooth the observed rainfall values serving as training targets. Since both window size configurations involve trade-offs, we employed GA to optimize these parameters simultaneously.

GA is a heuristic optimization algorithm inspired by the process of biological evolution. In GA, the sizes of sliding windows are regarded as populations. Let the size of the sliding window for segmenting CML data be $W_{i1} \in [W_{i1min}, W_{i1max}]$, and the size of the sliding window for smoothing rainfall be $W_{i2} \in [W_{i2min}, W_{i2max}]$. Considering $W_{i1}$ and $W_{i2}$ as two genes on the individual in the GA algorithm, then each individual can be represented by $W_i = [W_{i1}, W_{i2}]$, which will be iteratively optimized through three steps, i.e., selection, crossover and mutation [12]. In the selection step, a random population is first initialized. Then the correlation coefficient of the rainfall estimation results from MFR-LSTM are used as the fitness function, i.e., $f_{\text{MFR-LSTM}}(W_i)$, to evaluate the individuals. With the fitness function, new window sizes are generated according to the probability $P(W_i)$ defined as follows:

$$P(W_i) = \frac{f_{\text{MFR-LSTM}}(W_i)}{\sum_{j=1}^{G} f_{\text{MFR-LSTM}}(W_j)}. \tag{2}$$

Next, in the crossover step, offspring samples $W_{pnew}$ and $W_{qnew}$ are computed by exchanging random segments and combining the parent pairs $W_{pi}$ and $W_{qi}$ (i = 1, 2):

$$W_{pnew} = \begin{bmatrix} W_{p1} \\ W_{q2} \end{bmatrix}, \qquad W_{qnew} = \begin{bmatrix} W_{q1} \\ W_{p2} \end{bmatrix}. \tag{3}$$

Finally, in the mutation step, flip genes with probability $p_m$. With the slide window, we are able to process the data and have the data at moment $t$, i.e., $X_t$.

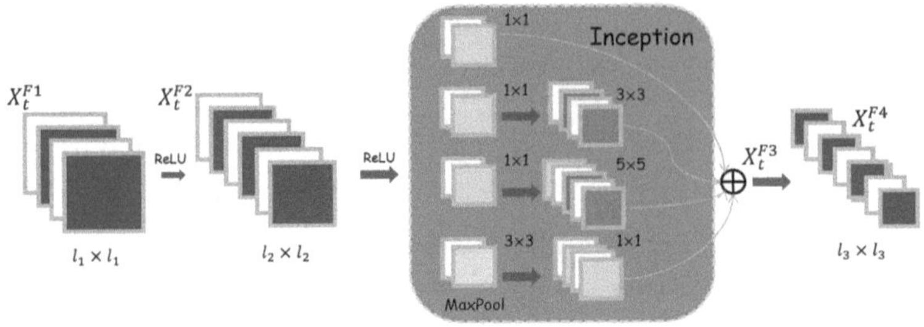


**Fig. 2.** Spatial Feature Extraction Module of MFR-LSTM.

### 3.2 Spatial Feature Extraction

The spatial feature extraction module of MFR-LSTM comprises four layers: three traditional CNN layers (first, second, and fourth) and an Inception layer (third), as illustrated in Fig. 2. The convolution kernel size of the first convolutional layer is $l_1 \times l_1$, and the value of the output feature map $X_t^{\text{conv1}}$ at position $(i, j)$ is:

$$X_t^{\text{conv1}} = \sum_{u=0}^{l_1-1} \sum_{v=0}^{l_1-1} X_t(i+u, j+v) \cdot K_{l_1 \times l_1}, \tag{4}$$

where $K_{l_2 \times l_2}$ represents the convolution kernel. The output feature map is processed by ReLU activation function and maxpool to obtain the first layer of spatial feature $X_t^{\text{F1}}$. Then $X_t^{\text{F2}}$ can be derived through the identical computational methodology.

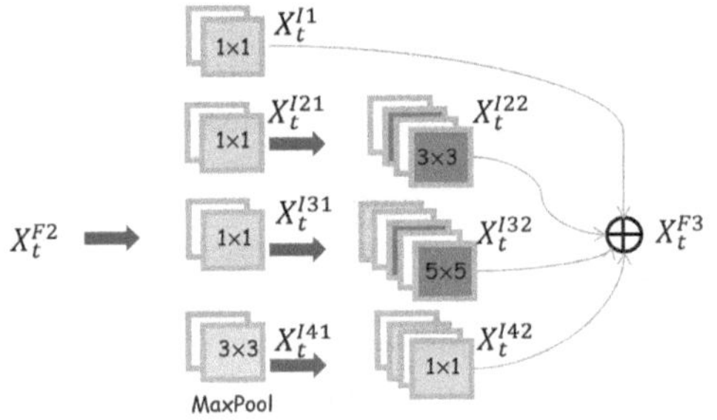


**Fig. 3.** Structure of Inception.

The third layer of the spatial feature extraction module is the Inception layer. Inception is a CNN architecture which use multiple convolutional kernels at different scales to extract features at different scales. As shown in Fig. 3, in Inception, convolutional kernels can be applied in parallel, and then their outputs are connected together to form a multi-channel feature map. The Inception layer contains four branches in parallel, and the first branch contains a $1 \times 1$ convolutional layer, then its output feature map $X_t^{\mathrm{I1}}$ is:

$$X_t^{\mathrm{I1}} = X_t^{\mathrm{F2}}(i,j) \cdot K_{1\times1}. \tag{5}$$

The second branch employs a $1 \times 1$ convolutional layer and a $3 \times 3$ convolutional layer, whose output feature maps $X_t^{\mathrm{I21}}$ and $X_t^{\mathrm{I22}}$ are respectively:

$$X_t^{\mathrm{I21}} = X_t^{\mathrm{F2}}(i,j) \cdot K_{1\times1}, \tag{6}$$

$$X_t^{\mathrm{I22}} = \sum_{u=0}^{2}\sum_{v=0}^{2} X_t^{\mathrm{I21}}(i+u, j+v) \cdot K_{3\times3}. \tag{7}$$

Following a similar procedure, $I_{32}$ and $I_{42}$ are obtained. The individual feature maps are then fused to obtain the third-layer spatial features $X_t^{\mathrm{F3}}$:

$$X_t^{\mathrm{F3}} = X_t^{\mathrm{I1}} + X_t^{\mathrm{I22}} + X_t^{\mathrm{I32}} + X_t^{\mathrm{I42}}. \tag{8}$$

Finally, our model applies a $l_3 \times l_3$ convolutional layer to the fused feature $X_t^{\mathrm{F3}}$ for additional high-dimensional feature extraction, obtaining the feature map $X_t^{\mathrm{F4}}$. The spatial feature extraction module then flattens $X_t^{\mathrm{F4}}$ to produce the final output $X_t^{\mathrm{Space}}$:

$$X_t^{\mathrm{F4}} = \sum_{u=0}^{l_3-1}\sum_{v=0}^{l_3-1} X_t^{\mathrm{F3}}(i+u, j+v) \cdot K_{l_3\times l_3}, \tag{9}$$

$$X_t^{\mathrm{Space}} = \mathrm{Flatten}(X_t^{\mathrm{F4}}). \tag{10}$$

### 3.3 NoisyLinear

As illustrated in Fig. 4, the NoisyLinear layer introduces learnable noise perturbations into the parameters of a conventional fully connected (FC) layer. This noise injection mechanism forces the model to dynamically adapt to parameter variations during training, thereby improving its robustness against input disturbances. When $X_t^{\mathrm{Space}}$ is input into the normal FC layer, the output is:

$$X_t^{\mathrm{FC}} = \theta_1 X_t^{\mathrm{Space}} + c_1, \tag{11}$$

where $\theta_1$ and $c_1$ are the weights and bias, respectively, which can be decomposed into the form of mean and variance combinations as:

$$\theta_1 = \mu^{\theta_1} + \sigma^{\theta_1}, \tag{12}$$

$$c_1 = \mu^{c_1} + \sigma^{c_1}, \tag{13}$$

where $\mu^{\theta_1}, \sigma^{\theta_1}, \mu^{c_1}$ and $\sigma^{c_1}$ are means and variances of $\theta_1$ and $c_1$ respectively. Two Gaussian distributions $\epsilon^{\theta_1}, \epsilon^{c_1}$ are sampled as noise in the parameter space, which are multiplied by $\sigma^{\theta_1}, \sigma^{c_1}$ respectively, and the amount of noise in the network is controlled by controlling the magnitude of the variance component.

Then the spatial feature $X_t^{\text{Space}}$ is fed into NoisyLinear, ultimately producing the output features $X_t^{\text{Noisy}}$:

$$X_t^{\text{Noisy}} = (\mu^{\theta_1} + \sigma^{\theta_1} \odot \epsilon^{\theta_1}) \times X_t^{\text{Space}} + \mu^{c_1} + \sigma^{c_1} \odot \epsilon^{c_1}, \tag{14}$$

where $\odot$ is the Hadamard product. NoisyLinear improves generalization ability and perturbation immunity by injecting controlled Gaussian noise into the model's input layer. This forces the model to learn robust feature representations that remain insensitive to noise during training. The theoretical basis of this approach is that noise injection is equivalent to imposing a smoothing constraint on the model parameters, forcing the optimization trajectory of the loss function to avoid sharp extreme value points and instead converge to a flatter region of very small values, and this flatness makes the model less sensitive to input perturbations by improving the generalization ability of the parameter space [13]. After incorporating NoisyLinear, the robustness of MFR-LSTM is improved to better cope with the variable CML data.

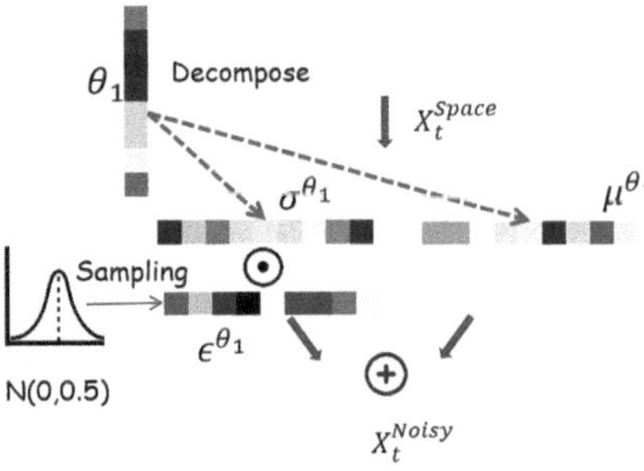


**Fig. 4.** Structure of NoisyLinear.

## 3.4 Temporal Feature Extraction

Temporal feature extraction is critical for rainfall estimation due to the highly time-dependent nature of precipitation patterns. We implement an LSTM-based network for this purpose.

LSTM is one of the most effective deep learning models for time series modeling [14]. The core of LSTM is the memory cell, which transmits information across time steps through the cell state to handle long-term dependencies, and regulates the flow and storage of information collectively by the forget gate, input gate, and output gate. The forget gate determines what information is discarded from the cell state and is calculated as:

$$f_k = \sigma\left(W_f \cdot X_t^{\text{Noisy}}(k) + W_f \cdot X_t^{\text{Noisy}}(k-1) + b_f\right), \tag{15}$$

where $\sigma$ is the sigmoid activation function, $W_f$ is the weight matrix for the forget gate, $X_t^{\text{Noisy}}(k)$ is the kth element in $X_t^{\text{Noisy}}$, and $b_f$ is the bias term for the forget gate.

The input gate consists of two parts, one that decides which values to update and the other that generates new candidate values to update the cell state, which is formulated as follows:

$$i_k = \sigma\left(W_i \cdot X_t^{\text{Noisy}}(k) + W_i \cdot X_t^{\text{Noisy}}(k-1) + b_i\right), \tag{16}$$

and

$$\tilde{C}_k = \tanh\left(W_C \cdot X_t^{\text{Noisy}}(k) + W_C \cdot X_t^{\text{Noisy}}(k-1) + b_C\right), \tag{17}$$

where $i_t$ is update value, $\tilde{C}_t$ is candidate value, $W_i$, $W_C$ are the corresponding weight matrices, $b_i$, $b_C$ are the corresponding bias terms. The cell state is then updated by combining the input and forgetting gates:

$$C_k = f_k \odot C_{k-1} + i_t \odot \tilde{C}_k, \tag{18}$$

The output gate determines the value of the next hidden state, which is calculated as:

$$o_k = \sigma\left(W_o \cdot X_t^{\text{Noisy}}(k) + W_o \cdot X_t^{\text{Noisy}}(k-1) + b_o\right), \tag{19}$$

$$h_k = o_k \odot \tanh\left(C_k\right), \tag{20}$$

where $W_o$ is the weight matrix of the output gate, $b_o$ is the bias term of the output gate, $h_k$ is the hidden state of the output at the current moment. MFR-LSTM is finally downscaled by two fully connected layers to derive the temporal features $X_t^{\text{Time}}$ of the CML and output the predicted values $R_{pred}$:

$$X_t^{\text{Time}} = \theta_2 h_k + c_2, \tag{21}$$

$$R_{pred} = \theta_3 X_t^{\text{Time}} + c_3. \tag{22}$$

### 3.5 Loss Functions for Rainfall Estimation

In order to cope with the effect of very uneven rainfall distribution in the dataset on the model and to improve the prediction performance of large rainfall with small sample size, the following loss functions $L_p$ specifically for rainfall estimation and $L_c$ for dry-wet classification were designed as:

$$L_p = \text{RDF} \times \text{MSE}, \tag{23}$$

$$L_c = \text{RDF} \times \text{CE}. \tag{24}$$

Here, RDF (Rainfall Distribution Factor) is proposed by the literature [6] to address the impact of the highly unbalanced distribution of rainfall in the dataset on the training effect. RDF is defined as follows:

$$\text{RDF} = 1 - \gamma_s \exp(-\gamma_r \cdot R_{pred}), \tag{25}$$

where $\gamma_s$ and $\gamma_r$ are hyperparameters. From (26) we can see that, RDF is a larger value when the rainfall is large. Multiplying RDF by the loss function results in a larger loss value, which can make the model pay more attention to these sparse data, and is conducive to improving the model's prediction accuracy for large rainfall. Moreover, we use Mean Square Error (MSE) for regression and Cross Entropy (CE) for classification.

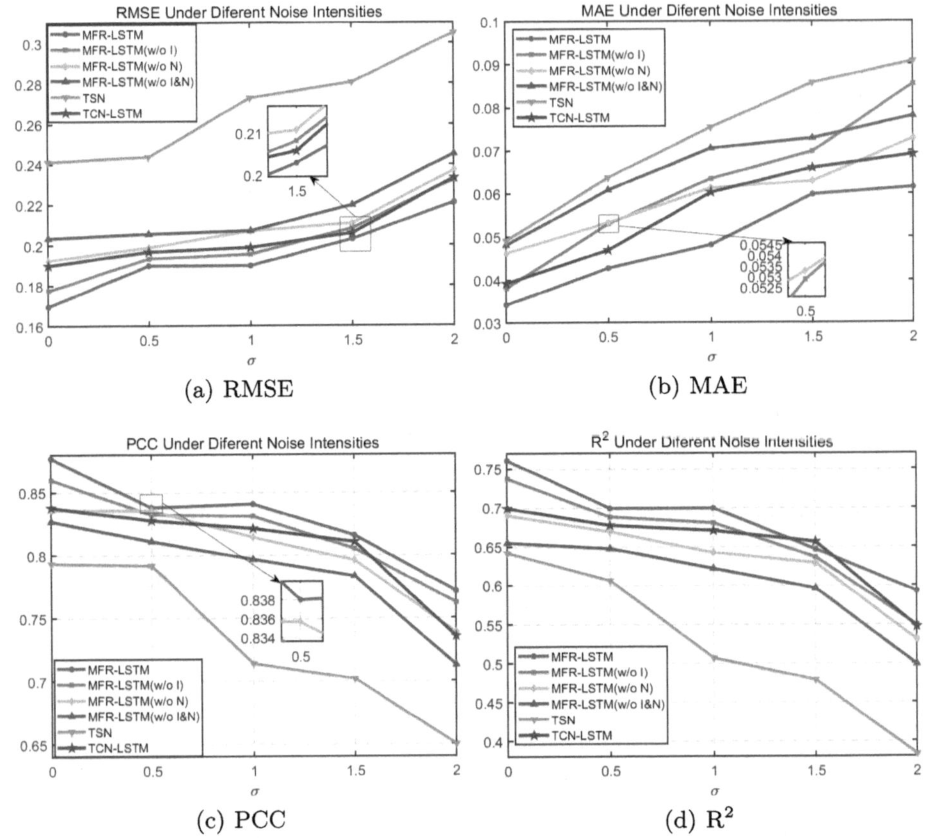


**Fig. 5.** Rainfall Estimation Robustness Under Gaussian Noise.

## 4 Experiment

This section evaluates the performance of the proposed MFR-LSTM using a total of 139,689 pieces data collected at 1-min intervals from December 17, 2019 to March 26, 2020 [15,16].

**Table 1.** Comparative Performance of Rainfall Estimation Models

| model | RMSE | MAE | PCC | $R^2$ |
|---|---|---|---|---|
| TSN | 0.2411 | 0.0491 | 0.7943 | 0.6148 |
| TCN-LSTM | 0.1899 | 0.0392 | 0.8378 | 0.6990 |
| MFR-LSTM(w/o I&N) | 0.2034 | 0.0754 | 0.8269 | 0.6549 |
| MFR-LSTM(w/o N) | 0.1911 | 0.0613 | 0.8363 | 0.6693 |
| MFR-LSTM(w/o I) | 0.1775 | 0.0381 | 0.8598 | 0.7372 |
| MFR-LSTM | **0.1695** | **0.0342** | **0.8768** | **0.7604** |

### 4.1 Experiment Setting

In the data preprocessing module, the CML data slicing window from the GA should be set to 93, and the rainfall smoothing window should be set to 11. The hiddensize of the LSTM is set to 64. The noise added in NoisyLinear is Gaussian noise with mean of 0 variance of 0.5.

We first verify the rainfall estimation performance of MFR-LSTM (in Sect. 4.2), then verify the dry-wet classification performance (in Sect. 4.3), and finally add Gaussian noise to dataset to verify the robustness (in Sect. 4.4).

### 4.2 Prediction Performance

For a comprehensive evaluation of MFR-LSTM, we choose four indicators to examine the performance of the model, i.e., root mean square error (RMSE), mean absolute error (MAE), correlation coefficient (PCC), and coefficient of determination ($R^2$).

To systematically evaluate the contributions of both the Inception and NoisyLinear in MFR-LSTM, we first performed ablation experiments. The results show that removing both modules leads to a 20.0% increase in RMSE and a 5.7% decrease in PCC, while removing only the NoisyLinear module leads to a 12.7% increase in RMSE and a 4.6% decrease in PCC. Removing only the Inception module results in a 4.7% increase in RMSE and an 1.9% decrease in PCC. This proves that both the NoisyLinear module and the Inception module are beneficial in improving the feature extraction capability of the model. We then compare our model with TSN [6], which uses GRU as the main structure, and TCN-LSTM [17], which combines TCN and LSTM. Both of them focus only on temporal feature extraction compared to our model. It is verified that our model reduces the RMSE and MAE by 29.7% and 30.3% compared to TSN and 10.7% and 12.8% compared to TCN-LSTM, while the PCC and $R^2$ are improved by 4.7–10.4% and 8.8–23.7%, respectively. As shown in Table 1, MFR-LSTM achieves the best results in all the indexes, which illustrates the advantage of multi-feature extraction over individual time-series features. In Tables 1, 2 and 3, MFR-LSTM(w/o I&N) denotes the variant replacing both the Inception layer with standard convolutional layers and the NoisyLinear layers with conventional fully-connected layers; MFR-LSTM(w/o N) utilizes regular FC layers in place of NoisyLinear exclusively; MFR-LSTM(w/o I) substitutes only the Inception layer with standard convolutional layers.

### 4.3 Dry-Wet Classification Performance

For the experimental results of the classification task, we chose accuracy and F1 score as the metrics to evaluate the performance. The classification performance of each model is given in Table 2. Bolded numbers represent the best results.

Ablation experiments on dry-wet classification validate the roles of the Inception and NoisyLinear modules in MFR-LSTM. Removing both reduces accuracy by 1.8% and F1-score by 13.2%. Removing only NoisyLinear decreases accuracy by 1.6% and F1-score by 8.1%. Removing Inception lowers accuracy by 1.2% and F1-score by 10.3%. In comparative experiments, MFR-LSTM outperforms TSN by 1.9% in accuracy and TCN-LSTM by 0.9%, with more significant F1-score improvements (15.2% and 5.7% respectively), achieving the best results across all metrics in Table 2. This superiority is attributed to the Inception module's multi-scale feature extraction capability, which enables it to better capture spatial patterns in microwave link data, and the NoisyLinear module's enhanced ability to handle complex fluctuations in CML data. These advantages are not present in TSN's GRU architecture or the TCN-LSTM model. For highly imbalanced CML data, the proposed multi-feature extraction model balances accuracy and F1-score, as reflected in its substantial F1-score improvement.

**Table 2.** Dry-Wet classification results of each model

| model | accuracy | F1 |
|---|---|---|
| TSN | 93.71% | 0.5909 |
| TCN-LSTM | 94.65% | 0.6444 |
| MFR-LSTM(w/o I&N) | 93.81% | 0.6043 |
| MFR-LSTM(w/o N) | 93.97% | 0.6255 |
| MFR-LSTM(w/o I) | 94.42% | 0.6110 |
| MFR-LSTM | **95.53%** | **0.6809** |

### 4.4 Robustness of Models

To test MFR-LSTM's robustness, we added Gaussian noise (variances: 0.5, 1, 1.5, and 2) to the dataset and compared results with TSN and TCN-LSTM models.

The performance of each model under the influence of Gaussian noise of different intensities is shown in Fig. 5. From Fig. 5, MFR-LSTM demonstrates strong robustness against Gaussian noise. Ablation experiments reveal a 4.4% PCC

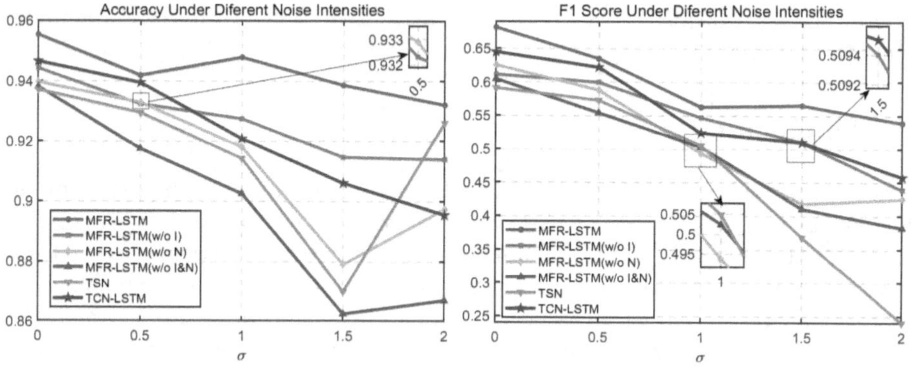


(a) accuracy (b) F1

**Fig. 6.** Dry-Wet classification Robustness Under Gaussian Noise.

**Table 3.** Model classification results for $\sigma = 1.5$ and $\sigma = 2$

| Model | $\sigma = 1.5$ | | $\sigma = 2$ | |
|---|---|---|---|---|
| | Precision | Recall | Precision | Recall |
| TSN | 0.2962 | 0.4859 | 0.6065 | 0.1499 |
| TCN-LSTM | 0.4295 | 0.6261 | 0.3843 | 0.5659 |
| MFR-LSTM (w/o I&N) | 0.3083 | 0.6143 | 0.2995 | 0.5276 |
| MFR-LSTM (w/o N) | 0.3348 | 0.5579 | 0.3779 | 0.4867 |
| MFR-LSTM (w/o I) | 0.4612 | 0.5688 | 0.4462 | 0.4316 |
| MFR-LSTM | 0.6307 | 0.5120 | 0.5724 | 0.5091 |

improvement from the NoisyLinear module at $\sigma = 2$, further enhanced by 3.8% through Inception module integration. Under maximum noise ($\sigma = 2$), MFR-LSTM maintains a PCC of *0.7722* (11.9% decline), outperforming TSN (18.1% decline) and TCN-LSTM (12.2% decline). The NoisyLinear module enables robust multi-feature extraction from noisy CML data, jointly improving prediction under noise interference.

The variation of the accuracy and F1 score of each model classification under the influence of Gaussian noise is shown in Fig. 6. From Fig. 6, MFR-LSTM demonstrates superior performance and robustness in dry-wet classification. Ablation experiments reveal a 26.7% F1-score improvement from the NoisyLinear module at $\sigma = 2$, further enhanced by 14.3% through integration with the Inception module. Under maximum noise intensity, MFR-LSTM maintains an F1-score of 0.5389 (22.4% degradation from noise-free conditions), outperforming TSN (59.3% decline) and TCN-LSTM (29% reduction). Notably, some models (e.g., TSN) exhibit increased accuracy with higher noise (e.g., from 86.99% at $\sigma = 1.5$ to 92.61% at $\sigma = 2$). Table 3 shows this anomaly stems from dataset imbalance: TSN's recall drops sharply as noise amplifies its bias toward dry-period samples (majority class). In contrast, MFR-LSTM preserves balanced precision and recall.

## 5 Conclusion

In this paper, we introduced MFR-LSTM, a robust rainfall estimation model that leverages multi-feature of CMLs. By incorporating Inception with LSTM, MFR-LSTM effectively captures both spatial and temporal features of CML data. To improve robustness, we introduce a NoisyLinear module, which significantly enhances the model's ability to adapt to noise and performs better under Gaussian noise disturbances compared to baseline models such as TSN and TCN-LSTM. The experimental results validate the effectiveness of our method, with the rainfall estimation PCC reaching 0.8768 and the dry-wet classification accuracy reaching 95.53%.

**Acknowledgments.** This work is supported by the National Key R&D Program of China (No. 2023YFC3010700).

## References

1. Zhang, P., Liu, X., Pu, K.: Precipitation monitoring using commercial microwave links: current status, challenges and prospectives. Remote Sens. **15**(19) (2023)
2. Pu, K., Liu, X., Liu, L., Zhao, Y.: A novel adaptive rain-induced attenuation model based on clustering algorithm for commercial microwave link-based rainfall inversion. IEEE Geosci. Remote Sens. Lett. **21**, 1–5 (2024)
3. Nallametti, N., Malarvizhi, C., Ahmed, S.J., Sathya, R., Vishnu, K.H., Naveen, J.N.: Intelligent rainfall prediction and flood alert system using ML. In: 2024 5th International Conference on Smart Electronics and Communication (ICOSEC), Trichy, India (2024)
4. Pandey, R., Upadhya, M., Singh, M.: Rainfall prediction using logistic regression and random forest algorithm. In: 2024 IEEE International Conference on Computing, Power and Communication Technologies (IC2PCT), Greater Noida, India (2024)
5. Zhang, C., et al.: Wireless microwave rainfall inversion study based on composite machine learning modeling. J. China Hydrol. **43**(06), 33–39 (2023)
6. Habi, H.V., Messer, H.: Recurrent neural network for rain estimation using commercial microwave links. IEEE Trans. Geosci. Remote Sens. **59**, 3672–3681 (2021)
7. Pudashine, J., et al.: Deep learning for an improved prediction of rainfall retrievals from commercial microwave links. Water Resour. Res. **56** (2020)
8. Habi, H.V., Messer, H.: RNN models for rain detection. In: 2019 IEEE International Workshop on Signal Processing Systems (SiPS), Nanjing, China (2019)
9. Minghao, X.: Study on the influencing factors and inversion methods of rainfall measurement by star-earth links. Ph.D. dissertation, University of Science and Technology for National Defense (USND) (2020)
10. Zhang, P., Liu, X., Pu, K.: Classification of dry and wet periods using commercial microwave links: a one-class classification machine learning approach based on autoencoders. IEEE Trans. Geosci. Remote Sens. **62**, 1–13 (2024)

11. Djenal, D.P., et al.: Rainfall prediction in central java based on comperatif analysis of LSTM and BiLSTM. In: 2024 Ninth International Conference on Informatics and Computing (ICIC), Medan, Indonesia (2024)
12. Lambora, A., Gupta, K., Chopra, K.: Genetic algorithm- a literature review. In: 2019 International Conference on Machine Learning, Big Data, Cloud and Parallel Computing (COMITCon), Faridabad, India (2019)
13. Zhang, Z., Jiang, J., Chen, M., Wang, Z., Peng, Y., Yu, Z.: A novel noise injection-based training scheme for better model robustness, *ArXiv*, vol. abs/2302.10802 (2023)
14. Miller, J.A., et al.: A survey of deep learning and foundation models for time series forecasting, *ArXiv*, vol. abs/2401.13912 (2024)
15. Han, C., Zhang, G., Ji, B., Huo, J., Messer, H.: On the potential of using emerging microwave links for city rainfall monitoring. IEEE Commun. Mag. **61**(11), 174–180 (2023)
16. Zheng, S., et al.: Research on rainfall monitoring based on e-band millimeter wave link in east China. Sensors **21**(5) (2021)
17. Dudukcu, H.V., Taskiran, M., Cam Taskiran, Z.G., Yildirim, T.: Temporal convolutional networks with RNN approach for chaotic time series prediction. Appl. Soft Comput. **133**, 109945 (2023)

# DPS-DETR: Lightweight Transformer-Based Object Detection for Industrial Safety Monitoring

YunTao Zhao and FengYi Wu(✉)

School of Artificial Intelligence and Automation, Wuhan University of Science and Technology Hubei, Wuhan, China
Wufengyi@wust.edu.cn

**Abstract.** To address the challenges of low small-target detection accuracy, limited robustness, and inadequate real-time performance in complex industrial environments, this study proposes DPS-DETR, an enhanced RT-DETR framework. The model integrates three key improvements: Deformable Attention to strengthen feature representation of irregularly distributed small and distant targets, Partial Convolution (PConv) for enhanced spatial detail retention during downsampling, and a Scale-aware Dynamic Loss (SD Loss) embedded in a PSConv module to adaptively reweight losses in favor of small-target localization. Experimental evaluations demonstrate that DPS-DETR achieves 63.04% mAP (+1.63% over RT-DETR) with 54.5 GFLOPs, effectively balancing accuracy and computational efficiency. Moreover, the model exhibits superior robustness and detection granularity under severe occlusion and dense small-target scenarios, underscoring its applicability to intelligent safety supervision in industrial contexts.

**Keywords:** Power plant safety monitoring; DPS-DETR; Deformable Attention(DAttention);Scale-aware Dynamic Loss

## 1 Introduction

With the rising demand for electricity, power supply enterprises have achieved higher operational efficiency, yet safety risks in complex on-site environments remain a major concern. In power plant operations, real-time monitoring of personal protective equipment (PPE) compliance is essential to safeguard workers. Traditional methods such as Histogram of Oriented Gradients (HOG) with Support Vector Machines (SVM) [1, 2] achieve a balance between speed and accuracy, but lack robustness under occlusion and multi-target interference.

Deep learning–based object detection offers stronger feature representation and generalization, making it more reliable in complex environments. The YOLO (You Only Look Once) series [3] has been widely applied in industrial monitoring. For example, Zhao et al. [4] detected improper helmet and mask usage with YOLOv5s, He et al. [5] improved YOLOv7-Tiny for occlusion scenarios in power operations, and Jadhav et al.


Y. Liu et al. (Eds.): ChinaCom 2025, LNICST 711, pp. 526–538, 2027.
https://doi.org/10.1007/978-3-032-33662-0_38

[6] developed a real-time helmet detection system with violation alerts. While efficient, YOLO models often struggle with small or dense targets and depend on Non-Maximum Suppression (NMS), which may erroneously discard true positives or retain redundant boxes, limiting accuracy in complex scenes.

To address these issues, Transformer-based detectors were introduced. Carion et al. [7] proposed DETR, which removes NMS via one-to-one matching for end-to-end detection. Zhu et al. [8] further enhanced DETR with deformable attention and multi-scale features, but the computational burden hinders real-time use. Zhao et al. [9] then proposed RT-DETR, the first real-time end-to-end detector, integrating a hybrid encoder with uncertainty-based query selection. Subsequent works extended RT-DETR: Li et al. [10] targeted UAV small-object detection with lightweight designs, Hu et al. [11] improved UAV imagery detection using attention and loss refinements, and Wu et al. [12] developed an Enhanced Pyramid RT-DETR for PCB defect detection. These approaches improve performance in specific domains, yet their generalization remains limited.

In this context, this study proposes an improved RT-DETR model for PPE compliance monitoring in power plant environments. Experiments on real surveillance data demonstrate its effectiveness, providing a practical solution for intelligent and reliable industrial safety supervision.

## 2 Improvements and Analysis Based on the RT-DETR Algorithm

RT-DETR is an end-to-end real-time detector that removes anchor box initialization and Non-Maximum Suppression (NMS), thereby reducing computational cost while preserving accuracy. Its architecture consists of three parts: a lightweight ResNet-18 backbone for multi-scale feature extraction; an efficient hybrid encoder with a Cross-scale Collaborative Fusion Module (CCFM) to enhance feature interaction across scales; and a Transformer decoder with an IoU-aware query selection strategy that aligns classification confidence with localization accuracy. This unified design enables direct prediction of bounding boxes and confidence scores in a fully end-to-end pipeline, as illustrated in Fig. 1

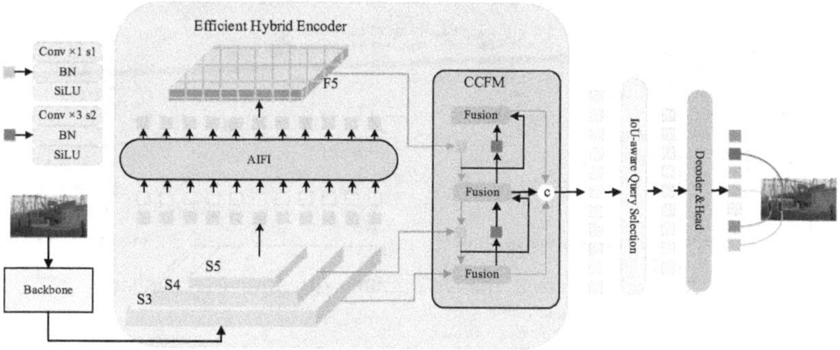


**Fig. 1.** The architecture of the RT-DETR network

### 2.1 The Deformable Attention Mechanism

In the dataset used for this study, the background often dominates the frame, with frequent occlusions such as poles and fences, and in some cases, building colors similar to workers' PPE. Many targets occupy only a small portion of the image, making detection more challenging. Conventional CNNs struggle with such distant small objects due to their limited ability to capture long-range dependencies, whereas Transformers excel at this through their large receptive field.

To address these challenges, we introduce the Deformable Attention (DAttention) mechanism [13], which adaptively adjusts the receptive field to better capture discriminative features in complex backgrounds. Unlike conventional attention that computes weights at fixed positions, DAttention learns positional offsets, enabling the model to focus on more informative regions. As shown in Fig. 2(a), reference points are first distributed on the feature map, and offsets are predicted from query features; the deformed positions are then used for feature sampling to obtain updated Key and Value representations. Fig. 2(b) details the offset generation network. By incorporating these learnable deformations, DAttention enhances the expressive power of multi-head attention and improves the detection of small objects. The single-scale deformable attention can be formulated as follows:

$$DeformAttention(z_q, p_q, x) = \sum_{m=1}^{M} W_m \left[ \sum_{k=1}^{K} A_{mqk} \cdot W_m^{'} \cdot x(p_q + \Delta p_{mqk}) \right] \tag{1}$$

where $p_q$ denotes the reference position of the input feature, represented as a 2D vector; $\Delta p_{mqk}$ denotes the positional offset of the $k$-th sampling point relative to the reference position of the $m$-th attention head; and $A_{mqk}$ denotes the learned attention weight, computed through a fully connected layer, thereby avoiding the traditional query–key dot product. This mechanism dynamically aggregates features from the sampled positions using the learned offsets and applies the attention coefficients $A_{mqk}$ to focus on the relevant regions of the input data.

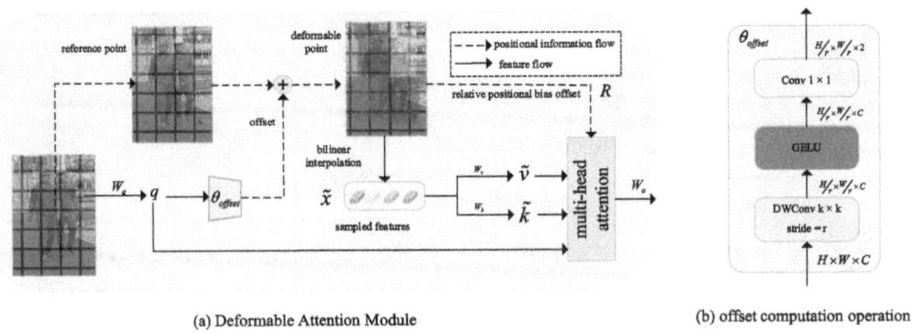


**Fig. 2.** Architecture of the Deformable Attention Mechanism

As shown in Fig. 3, the improved AIFI module can adaptively focus on key spatial features, effectively enhancing the detection performance for small objects.

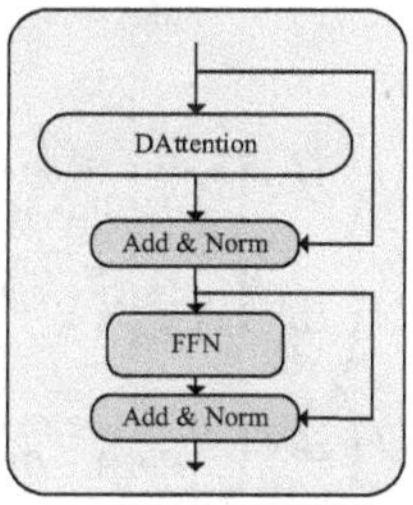


**Fig. 3.** Architecture of the AIFI_DAttention module

## 2.2 Fan-Shaped Convolution and Scale-Aware Dynamic Loss

In power plant surveillance, long monitoring distances often result in dim images with low signal-to-noise (SNR) and signal-to-clutter ratios (SCR), causing texture loss and increased background interference. Target size and shape also vary greatly with distance, further complicating detection. Conventional CNN-based methods, relying on standard convolutions, fail to exploit the spatial pixel distribution of small objects, while existing IoU-based loss functions insufficiently account for varying sensitivity to positional and scale errors across different target sizes.

To address these issues, this study introduces a fan-shaped convolution (PConv) module in the backbone downsampling stage and replaces the IoU-based loss with a scale-aware dynamic loss [14]. PConv employs grouped convolutions to expand the receptive field with minimal added parameters, thereby improving small-object feature extraction and overall detection performance. The structure of PConv is shown in Fig. 4.

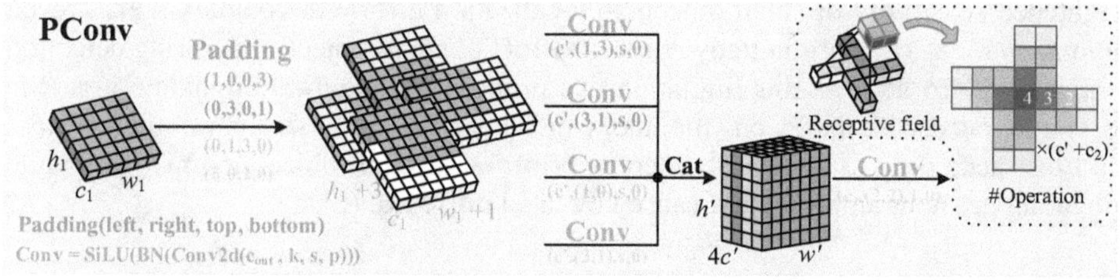


**Fig. 4.** Illustration of the PConv mechanism

The PConv module adopts an asymmetric padding strategy to construct convolutional kernels extended along horizontal and vertical directions, thereby better adapting to local feature distributions. After convolution, batch normalization (BN) and the SiLU activation function are applied to enhance training stability and convergence. The functional expression is given as:

$$\begin{aligned}
X_1^{(h',w',c')} &= SiLU\left(BN\left(X_{P(1,0,0,3)}^{(h_1,w_1,c_1)} \otimes W_1^{(1,3,c')}\right)\right)\\
X_2^{(h',w',c')} &= SiLU\left(BN\left(X_{P(0,3,0,1)}^{(h_1,w_1,c_1)} \otimes W_2^{(3,1,c')}\right)\right)\\
X_3^{(h',w',c')} &= SiLU\left(BN\left(X_{P(0,1,3,0)}^{(h_1,w_1,c_1)} \otimes W_3^{(1,3,c')}\right)\right)\\
X_4^{(h',w',c')} &= SiLU\left(BN\left(X_{P(3,0,1,0)}^{(h_1,w_1,c_1)} \otimes W_4^{(3,1,c')}\right)\right)
\end{aligned} \tag{2}$$

In Eq. (2), BN(·)and SiLU(·)denote batch normalization and the Sigmoid Linear Unit activation, respectively. The input feature map after asymmetric padding is $X_{P(a,b,c,d)}^{(h_1,w_1,c_1)}$, where (a,b,c,d) are the padding sizes. Each convolution group has weight matrix $W_i^{(k_n,k_w,c')}$ with kernel size $k_n \times k_w$ and output channels $c'$. The four groups of feature maps are concatenated along the channel dimension and fused through a 2 × 2 convolution, as formulated in Eq. (4).

$$X'^{(h',w',4c')} = Cat\left(X_1^{(h',w',c')}, \ldots, X_4^{(h',w',c')}\right) \tag{3}$$

$$Y^{(h_2,w_2,c_2)} = SiLU\left(BN\left(X'^{(h',w',4c')} \otimes W^{(2,2,c2)}\right)\right) \tag{4}$$

where $W^{(2,\,2,\,c2)}$ denotes the fusion convolutional kernel with a size of 2 × 2 and an output channel number of C2.Conventional object detection losses (e.g., GIoU, L1, CIoU) employ uniform error computation across object scales, failing to account for the heightened sensitivity of small objects to localization errors. In complex scenes, even minor deviations can substantially reduce the IoU of small objects, impairing detection performance. To address this limitation, we propose a scale-aware dynamic loss (SD Loss) integrated with the PConv module, which adaptively adjusts the weights of Sloss and Lloss according to target size, thereby prioritizing small-object optimization while mitigating gradient amplification caused by label noise Eq. (6).

$$\mathcal{L}_{SD} = \sum_{i=1}^{N} w_i \cdot \mathcal{L}_{\text{reg}}^{(i)} \tag{5}$$

$$w_i = \frac{1}{\sqrt{\text{area}_i} + \varepsilon} \tag{6}$$

where areai denotes the area of the i-th target, $\mathcal{L}_{\text{reg}}^{(i)}$ represents the regression loss for the i-th sample, and $\varepsilon$ is a small constant used to prevent division by zero.

## 2.3 The Improved Overall Model

To improve small-object detection while maintaining real-time performance and model compactness, we introduce a deformable attention mechanism into the AIFI module, forming the AIFI-DAttention module. This enhances spatial feature capture with reduced computational cost. Additionally, a fan-shaped convolution (PConv) is applied in the downsampling stage to better extract fine-grained structures of small objects. To further address scale-sensitive localization issues, a scale-aware dynamic loss (SD Loss) is employed. The overall improved model architecture is shown in Fig. 5.

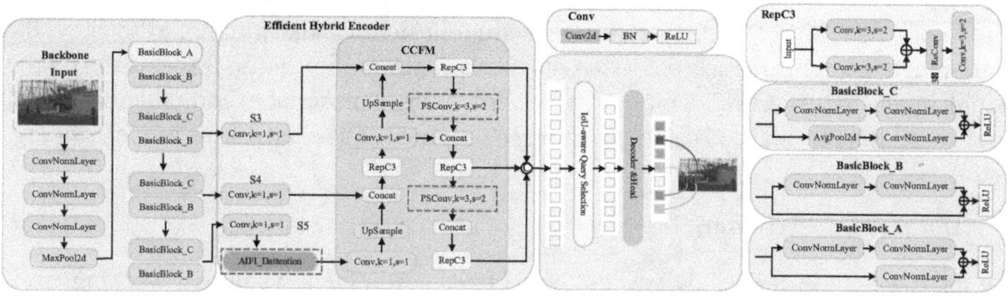


**Fig. 5.** The modified RT-DETR network architecture

# 3 Experiments and Results Analysis

## 3.1 Experimental Environment and Parameter Settings

The computing environment used for model training in this study is summarized in Table 1:

**Table 1.** Configuration of the experimental environment

| Configuration Name | Version |
|---|---|
| CPU | Intel(R) Xeon(R) Platinum 8269CY |
| GPU | NVIDIA GeFoce RTX3090 24G |
| Image processor acceleration library | CUDA 11.8 |
| Operating system | Ubuntu 20.04.6 LTS |
| Deep learning framework | PyTorch |
| Programming Language | Python 3.8 |

The experimental configuration is established as follows. The model is trained for 200 epochs to ensure adequate convergence and parameter stability. A batch size of 16 is adopted, which provides a trade-off between computational efficiency and gradient estimation stability. The AdamW optimizer is employed to update the network parameters due to its ability to decouple weight decay from the learning rate, thereby enhancing generalization and convergence behavior. The initial learning rate is set to 0.0001, and the momentum coefficient is initialized to 0.9 to achieve smooth and consistent gradient updates throughout training.To further stabilize the optimization process during the initial training phase, a warm-up strategy is applied for the first 2,000 iterations. During this stage, the learning rate is gradually increased from a small initial value, while the momentum starts at 0.8 and linearly rises to the target value of 0.9, effectively mitigating sudden gradient oscillations and facilitating a smoother transition into steady-state learning.

In consideration of both feature representation fidelity and training efficiency, the input image resolution is set to 640 × 640 pixels. This configuration preserves essential spatial details for object recognition while maintaining a reasonable computational load, thereby ensuring a balanced trade-off between accuracy and speed during model training.

### 3.2 Dataset Construction

The dataset used in this study was collected from seven cameras in real working environments within a power plant, comprising a total of 2,910 images. It includes four categories: safety helmets, insulating gloves, insulating boots, and workers, with both positive and negative samples for each category. The dataset is divided into training, testing, and evaluation sets in a ratio of 7:1.5:1.5. The overall dataset composition and distribution are illustrated in Fig. 6.

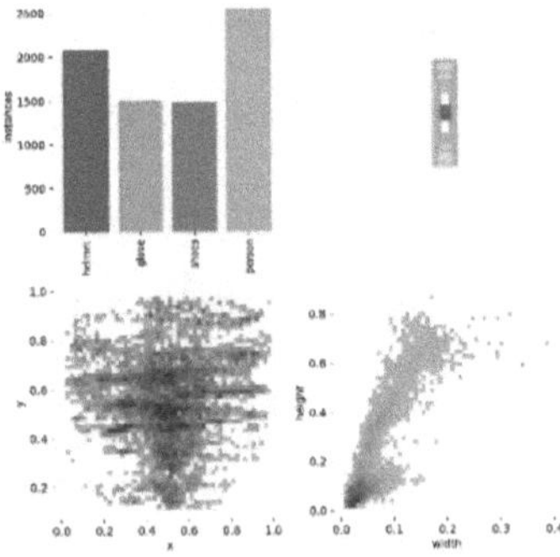

**Fig. 6.** Data distribution of the dataset

### 3.3 Evaluation Metrics

In this study, the algorithm performance is evaluated using the following metrics: mean Average Precision (mAP), frames per second (FPS), model parameter size (P/MB), and GFLOPs (billion floating-point operations per second).

Mean Average Precision (mAP) is a common metric for assessing object detection accuracy. In the experiments, mAP is calculated over IoU thresholds from 0.5 to 0.95. In the P–R curve, P (Precision) represents the proportion of correctly predicted positive samples among all predicted positives, while R(Recall) represents the proportion of correctly predicted positive samples among all actual positives. The relationships among precision P, recall R, and mean average precision mAP are expressed in Eq. (10):

$$P = \frac{TP}{TP + FP} \tag{7}$$

$$R = \frac{TP}{TP + FN} \tag{8}$$

$$AP = \int_0^1 P(R)dR \tag{9}$$

$$mAP = \frac{1}{n}\sum_{j=1}^{n} AP_j \tag{10}$$

TP (True Positives) are correctly predicted positives, FP (False Positives) are incorrect positives, FN (False Negatives) are missed positives, and TN (True Negatives) are correctly predicted negatives. Higher mAP indicates better detection performance. FPS (frames per second) evaluates real-time capability, computed here as the average over 500 inferences after 300 warm-up iterations. Model size, typically in MB, reflects parameters, memory usage, and storage requirements, impacting loading speed and inference efficiency. GFLOPs measure the model's computational cost, providing a reference for hardware deployment.

### 3.4 Experiments on the PSConv Module

The effectiveness of the PSConv module is highly dependent on its insertion point and quantity within the network, influencing detection accuracy, computational complexity (GFLOPs), and inference speed (FPS). Using RT-DETR as the baseline, PSConv modules were systematically incorporated at different positions within the B-scale fusion layers of the ResNet-18 backbone. As summarized in Table 2, deployment in deeper layers (third and fourth) maximizes semantic feature enhancement, achieving the highest mAP (62.46%) while simultaneously reducing GFLOPs and parameter count. In contrast, placement in lower layers improves inference speed but confers comparatively modest accuracy gains, indicating that optimal PSConv placement requires a trade-off between detection precision and computational efficiency tailored to the application scenario.

**Table 2.** Comparison of model performance with different numbers of PConv modules introduced

| Replace position | mAP/% | P/MB | GFLOPs | FPS |
|---|---|---|---|---|
| – | 61.41 | 38.6 | 56.9 | 180.12 |
| 1 | 61.88 | 38.4 | 56.4 | 187.56 |
| 1,2 | 61.13 | 37.9 | 55.8 | 185.15 |

(*continued*)

**Table 2.** (*continued*)

| Replace position | mAP/% | P/MB | GFLOPs | FPS |
|---|---|---|---|---|
| 1,2,3 | 62.14 | 39.9 | 56.4 | 178.35 |
| 2,3,4 | 61.93 | 38.7 | 56.4 | 176.8 |
| 3,4 | 62.46 | 38.6 | 54.3 | 173.21 |
| 1,2,3,4 | 62.33 | 39.5 | 56.8 | 178.6 |

### 3.5 Ablation Analysis

To evaluate the effectiveness of the DAttention and PSConv modules in small-object detection tasks, an ablation study was conducted. Each module was individually integrated into the baseline RT-DETR model, and the performance changes were compared, as summarized in Table 2. The original RT-DETR model achieved an mAP of 61.41% on the dataset used. With the addition of the DAttention module, the model could dynamically adjust its receptive field, enhancing its focus on key features in complex backgrounds, resulting in an mAP increase of 0.85% to 62.26%. Furthermore, replacing part of the backbone's convolutional layers with the PSConv module—which expands the receptive field via grouped convolutions while adding minimal parameters—improved the model's feature extraction capability for small objects. Combined with the scale-aware dynamic loss, the mAP increased to 62.19%. Experiments without the scale-aware dynamic loss showed that including this loss further improves accuracy. When both PSConv and DAttention modules were simultaneously integrated into RT-DETR, the model achieved a 1.63% mAP improvement, reaching 63.04%, while reducing both parameter count and computational complexity, demonstrating the effectiveness and practicality of the proposed architecture for small-object detection tasks.

**Table 3.** Ablation experiment

| Model | Dattention | PSConv | mAP/% | P/MB | GFLOPs | FPS |
|---|---|---|---|---|---|---|
| RT-DETR | – | – | 61.41 | 38.6 | 57.0 | 180.12 |
| + Dattention | √ | – | 62.08 | 36.7 | 54.5 | 183.21 |
| + PConv | – | √ | 62.26 | 38.6 | 57.2 | 162.96 |
| + SD Loss | – | √ | 62.46 | 37.7 | 54.3 | 173.21 |
| DPS-DETR(Ours) | √ | √ | 63.04 | 37.8 | 54.5 | 177.16 |

### 3.6 Comparison Experiments

To comprehensively evaluate the overall performance of the proposed model, this study compares the improved DPS-DETR with RT-DETR variants using mainstream backbone networks, RT-DETRv2, and representative single-stage detection models in the YOLO series, as shown in Table 3. The results indicate that the proposed model demonstrates superior performance across multiple key metrics. It achieves an mAP of 63.04%, surpassing RT-DETRv2 (60.70%) and the highest-performing YOLO model, YOLO11m (61.42%), reflecting strong detection accuracy. In terms of computational complexity, the model's GFLOPs is 54.5, lower than RT-DETRv2 (60.0) and all YOLO models, indicating higher computational efficiency. Regarding inference speed, the proposed model reaches 177.16 FPS, slightly lower than YOLO10m and YOLO11m but higher than the other models, maintaining good real-time performance while achieving high accuracy. Overall, the improved model achieves a favorable balance among accuracy, complexity, and inference speed, making it suitable for practical applications with stringent requirements for both real-time performance and detection precision (Table 4).

**Table 4.** Experimental comparison of different algorithms

| Model | mAP/% | P/MB | GFLOPs | FPS |
|---|---|---|---|---|
| Rdetr-EfficientViT | 60.53 | 21.7 | 27.2 | 205.12 |
| convnextv2 | 61.04 | 24.1 | 31.9 | 125.41 |
| fasternet | 61.58 | 32.7 | 49.5 | 171.92 |
| EfficientFormerv2 | 61.37 | 72.3 | 29.5 | 155.18 |
| CSwomTramsformer | 61.26 | 59 | 89.9 | 61.65 |
| YOLO8m | 60.66 | 49.6 | 78.7 | 164.70 |
| YOLO9m | 60.96 | 38.9 | 76.5 | 148.23 |
| YOLO10m | 60.47 | 31.9 | 63.4 | 187.16 |
| YOLO11m | 61.42 | 38.7 | 67.7 | 178.69 |
| YOLO12m | 61.00 | 38.9 | 67.1 | 153.01 |
| Deformable DETR | 60.33 | 37.9 | 192.2 | 46.6 |
| Efficient-DETR | 58.7 | 32.0 | 160.0 | 120.3 |
| DINO-DETR | 62.0 | 40.5 | 175.0 | 55.3 |
| RT-DETRr18 | 61.41 | 38.6 | 57.0 | 180.12 |
| RT-DETRr34 | 61.39 | 479.0 | 88.8 | 168.92 |
| Ours | **63.04** | 37.8 | **54.5** | 177.16 |

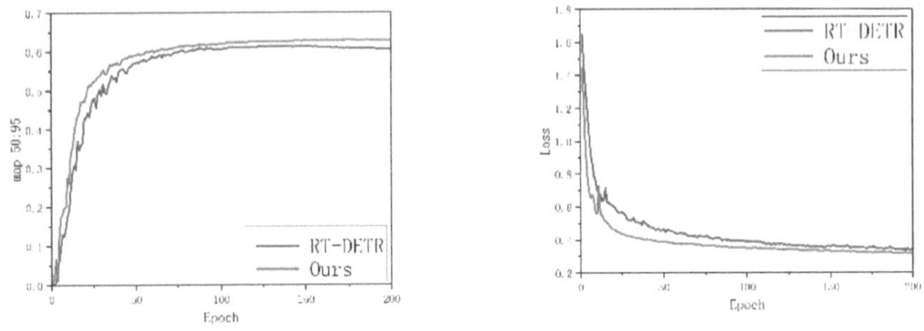


(a) Accuracy Curve (b) Loss Curve

**Fig. 7.** Training process curve

Figure 7 illustrates the training curves of the model before and after improvement. Fig. 7(a) shows the comparison of mAP (0.5–0.95) during training, indicating that the model converges after approximately 100 epochs, with the improved model demonstrating a clear increase in mAP and superior performance. Fig. 7(b) presents the comparison of loss functions during training. It can be observed that the improved model achieves a lower converged loss and faster convergence speed, with both models reaching stable convergence after 200 epochs.

(a) RT-DETR Recognition Results

(b) Recognition Results After Improvement

**Fig. 8.** Model detection results

The detection results of the RT-DETR model in practical scenarios are shown in Fig. 8(a). Due to significant background interference and small target sizes, the detection task is challenging. In the original model's results, misdetections occur, such as fences being incorrectly identified as workers, and missed detections include workers' boots and insulating gloves, with generally low confidence scores. In contrast, the improved model, incorporating the deformable attention mechanism and fan-shaped convolution, enhances small-object detection capability, effectively reducing both misdetections and missed detections, while also increasing confidence scores, as shown in Fig. 8(b).

## 4 Conclusion

This study addresses the challenge of detecting personal protective equipment (PPE) worn by workers in power plants under complex backgrounds, multi-object interference, and occlusion. We propose a structurally optimized RT-DETR model that incorporates deformable attention and a Scale-aware Dynamic Loss (SD Loss) integrated with PConv and PSConv modules to enhance feature perception and modeling of small objects, improving detection performance in complex scenarios. Experiments on a representative power plant dataset show that the model achieves an mAP of 63.04%, a 1.63% improvement over the original RT-DETR, while maintaining low computational complexity (54.5 GFLOPs) and high inference speed (177.16 FPS). Ablation studies validate the contribution of each module, and comparisons with mainstream YOLO models and RT-DETR variants demonstrate a favorable balance among accuracy, model compactness, and inference speed. These results provide a reliable foundation for intelligent safety supervision in industrial environments and offer insights for designing high-performance, lightweight real-time detection models.

Although the proposed model demonstrates competitive performance in PPE detection under complex industrial conditions, several limitations remain. First, the model's performance may degrade when facing extreme lighting variations, dense occlusions, or highly reflective surfaces, where fine-grained texture information becomes difficult to extract. Second, the training and evaluation are conducted on a dataset focused primarily on power plant environments, which may limit the generalization ability to other industrial scenarios. Future work will explore robustness under extreme conditions, such as multi-class, small-object, and heavily occluded scenarios, and investigate the integration of tracking algorithms to enhance continuous detection and generalization.

**Acknowledgment.** We would like to thank the anonymous reviewers for their valuable comments and suggestions to improve this paper.

## References

1. Zhengwei, C., Qian, P., Ying, C.: A safety supervision method for electric power operation sites based on machine learning and image recognition. China Electr. Power. **53**(04), 155–160 (2020)
2. Tingliang, Y.: Safety supervision of electric power operation sites based on machine learning and image recognition. Light Source Lighting. (06), 147–148 (2021)
3. Redmon, J., Divvala, S., Girshick, R., et al.: You only look once: unified, real-time object detection. In: Proceedings of the IEEE Conference on Computer Vision and Pattern Recognition, pp. 779–788. USA: IEEE Press, Las Vegas, NV (2016)
4. Enming, Z., Song, Y., Chuang, L., et al.: Research on safety protection equipment wearing detection for construction workers based on YOLOv5s. J. Dali Univ. **7**(12), 37–42 (2022)

5. Min, H., Liang, Q., Feng, Z., et al.: Intelligent detection algorithm for safety risk control in on-site operations of power systems. High Voltage Eng. **49**(06), 2442–2457 (2023)
6. Jadhav, C., Ansari, N.: Realtime safety helmet detection using deep learning. In: 2024 5th International Conference for Emerging Technology (INCET), pp. 1–5. IEEE (2024)
7. Carion, N., Massa, F., Synnaeve, G., et al.: End-to-end object detection with transformers. In: European Conference on Computer Vision, pp. 213–229. Springer International Publishing, Cham (2020)
8. Zhu X, Su W, Lu L, et al. Deformable detr: Deformable transformers for end-to-end object detection. arxiv preprint arxiv:2010.04159 2020
9. Zhao, Y., Lv, W., Xu, S., et al.: Detrs beat yolos on real-time object detection. In: Proceedings of the IEEE/CVF Conference on Computer Vision and Pattern Recognition, pp. 16965–16974 (2024)
10. Li Ning, Zhu Shuxian, Cao Jiangshan, et al. Target Detection Algorithm from UAV Perspective Based on RT-DETR . Microelectron. Comput. , pp. 1–12, [Online] Accessed 04 Jul 2025
11. Jiale, H., Min, Z., Fei, S.: An improved RTDETR detection algorithm for small targets of unmanned aerial vehicles. Comput. Eng. Appl. **60**(20), 198–206 (2024)
12. Binbin, W., Lihua, Z., Junwei, L., et al.: Small target PCB surface defect detection based on improved EP-RTDETR. Manuf. Technol. Mach. Tools. **03**, 139–148 (2025)
13. Xia, Z., Pan, X., Song, S., et al.: Vision transformer with deformable attention. In: Proceedings of the IEEE/CVF Conference on Computer Vision and Pattern Recognition, pp. 4794–4803 (2022)
14. Yang J, Liu S, Wu J, et al. Pinwheel-shaped convolution and scale-based dynamic loss for infrared small target detection, In: Proceedings of the AAAI Conference on Artificial Intelligence. 2025, 39(9): 9202–9210

# Internet of Things

# BLER Analysis of OOK Edge-Detection Receivers in Ambient IoT

Rang Su[1](✉), Tianle Xiong[1,2], and Hang Long[1]

[1] School of Information and Communication Engineering, Beijing University of Posts and Telecommunications, Beijing, China
{surang,lhrzrzlh}@bupt.edu.cn, xiongtianle@jx.chinamobile.com
[2] China Mobile (Jiangxi) Virtual Reality Technology Co., Ltd., Jiangxi, China

**Abstract.** Ambient Internet of Things (A-IoT) devices operate by harvesting energy from environmental sources such as radio waves, light, or heat. Their extremely low energy budget mandates the use of simple communication architectures, predominantly On-Off Keying (OOK) demodulated by ultra-low-power, edge-detection-based receivers. However, the performance limits of these receivers, particularly in terms of block error rate (BLER), remain poorly understood. To address this research gap, we develop a novel theoretical framework based on level crossing rate theory, derive a BLER expression for OOK edge-detection receivers, and extend the analysis to Rayleigh fading channels. Our results are validated through Monte Carlo simulations, showing excellent agreement with a performance gap of less than 0.3 dB. This work provides a foundational analytical tool for the design and optimization of A-IoT systems, offering insights into the impact of key system parameters on receiver performance.

**Keywords:** Ambient IoT · On-Off Keying · Edge detection

## 1 Introduction

The Internet of Things (IoT) has undergone rapid development in recent years, with the number of connected devices projected to exceed 41 billion by 2030 [1]. To address the connectivity demands of these massive-scale devices, Ambient Internet of Things (A-IoT), a new paradigm for low-power IoT, has attracted significant attention. A-IoT [2–5] devices leverage ambient energy harvesting, such as from radio frequency (RF) signals and solar power, to achieve battery-free operation [5]. This capability, often referred to as "zero-power", allows A-IoT networks based on backscatter communications to support ultra-low-power, maintenance-free network topologies. These features are essential for applications requiring long operational lifetimes and stable wireless connectivity [6], such as

This research is supported by Beijing University of Posts and Telecommunications-China Mobile Research Institute Joint Innovation Center.


Y. Liu et al. (Eds.): ChinaCom 2025, LNICST 711, pp. 541–555, 2027.
https://doi.org/10.1007/978-3-032-33662-0_39

in supply chain management and smart agriculture [7], thereby complementing the existing 5G IoT landscape. The 3rd Generation Partnership Project (3GPP) has identified A-IoT as a key technology direction for 5G-Advanced, with formal standardization work initiated in Release 19 [8].

The primary challenge in A-IoT downlink transmission lies in the "zero-power" constraint imposed on the receiver. A-IoT devices must operate with microwatt-level power consumption [5,9], limiting the use of power-intensive components like local oscillators and analog-to-digital converters. Consequently, the design of A-IoT signal transmissions relies on non-coherent modulation schemes, among which On-Off Keying (OOK) is widely adopted for its simplicity and robustness. To conserve power in A-IoT systems, Type 1 devices utilize edge detection [10], decoding information from the signal's rising and falling edges to lower computational overhead and energy consumption. This method significantly reduces the computational and power overhead. However, the theoretical performance limits of this simple edge-detection technique in noisy wireless environments remain a critical and unaddressed question in the A-IoT literature. Conventional performance analysis, often for more complex receivers, are not directly applicable. Therefore, a non-coherent demodulation technique suitable for A-IoT scenarios must be proposed, and its performance requires systematic modeling and theoretical analysis, which is currently lacking in the A-IoT literature.

To address the aforementioned problem, we propose a theoretical framework for analyzing the block error rate (BLER) of an edge-detection receiver in the downlink of an A-IoT system that employs OOK. We derive the BLER expression for the AWGN and Rayleigh fading channels. To validate the effectiveness of our theoretical analysis, we conduct link-level simulations and evaluate the BLER performance.

*Notations:* The ceiling function is denoted by $\lceil\cdot\rceil$, the modulo operation by mod, and the time derivative by the dot notation $(\dot{\cdot})$. The Hermitian transpose and the matrix inverse are denoted by $(\cdot)^{\mathrm{H}}$ and $(\cdot)^{-1}$, respectively. The sets of real and complex numbers are denoted by $\mathbb{R}$ and $\mathbb{C}$, respectively. For a scalar, $|\cdot|$ denotes the absolute value; for a complex number, it denotes the modulus. The expectation operator is denoted by $\mathbb{E}[\cdot]$.

## 2 System Model

This section outlines a basic model for the A-IoT downlink data transmission process. To ensure coexistence with existing New Radio (NR) systems, the A-IoT downlink signal is an OOK waveform generated using Orthogonal Frequency Division Multiplexing (OFDM) modulation [10].

### 2.1 Transmitter

The source data is a binary sequence $\mathbf{b} = (b_i)_{i=0}^{N_b-1}$, where $b_i \in \{0,1\}$. This sequence is encoded using Manchester line coding into a chip sequence $\mathbf{c} = (c_j)_{j=0}^{2N_b-1}$. The mapping is defined as:

$$\{c_{2i}, c_{2i+1}\} = \begin{cases} (0,1), & b_i = 0 \\ (1,0), & b_i = 1. \end{cases} \tag{1}$$

Consider an OFDM system with $N$ subcarriers. If $M$ chips, each representing an "ON" or "OFF" state, are transmitted within a single OFDM symbol duration $T_s$, then the number of samples per chip, $L$, is given by $L = N/M$. By upsampling the chip sequence $\mathbf{c}$, we obtain the time-domain discrete waveform $\mathbf{c}^L = \{c_k^L\}_{k=0}^{2N_bL-1}$, where the relationship with $\mathbf{c}$ is given by:

$$\mathbf{c}^L = (\underbrace{c_0, \cdots, c_0}_{L \text{ samples}}, \underbrace{c_1, \cdots, c_1}_{L \text{ samples}}, \cdots, \underbrace{c_{2N_b-1}, \cdots, c_{2N_b-1}}_{L \text{ samples}}). \tag{2}$$

To generate the waveform for a single OFDM symbol, this upsampled sequence $\mathbf{c}^L$ is partitioned into blocks of length $N$. Let $\mathbf{G}_m$ be the $m$-th block:

$$\begin{aligned} \mathbf{G}_m &= \{c_{mN}^L, c_{mN+1}^L, \cdots, c_{mN+N-1}^L\} \\ m &= 0, 1, \cdots, \left\lceil \frac{2N_b}{M} \right\rceil - 1. \end{aligned} \tag{3}$$

Here, $\mathbf{G}_m \in \mathbb{R}^N$ is the target time-domain waveform for the $m$-th OFDM symbol. Assuming a system sampling rate of $F_s$, the duration of a data packet containing $N_b$ bits is $T_{\text{block}} = 2(NN_b)/(MF_s)$. At this point, we have obtained the target waveform $\mathbf{G}_m$ for each OFDM symbol.

## 2.2 OOK Waveform Based on OFDM

This section details the method for synthesizing the OOK waveform within the OFDM system. We generate the OOK waveform using a least-squares method [11].

The OFDM modulator takes a frequency-domain input $\mathbf{x} \in \mathbb{C}^N$ and produces a time-domain output $\mathbf{y} \in \mathbb{R}^N$. The input vector $\mathbf{x}$ is partitioned into two segments: $\mathbf{x}^a \in \mathbb{C}^K$ and $\mathbf{x}^o \in \mathbb{C}^{N-K}$. The subcarriers allocated to $\mathbf{x}^a$ are used to transmit the A-IoT downlink data, while the subcarriers for $\mathbf{x}^o$ can be used for conventional NR data transmission. The relationship is described as:

$$\mathbf{y} = \mathbf{F}\mathbf{x} = \mathbf{F} \begin{bmatrix} \mathbf{x}^a \\ \mathbf{x}^o \end{bmatrix}, \tag{4}$$

where $\mathbf{F}$ is the Inverse Discrete Fourier Transform (IDFT) matrix, whose $(m, n)$-th entry is given by $\mathbf{F}_{m,n} = \frac{1}{N} e^{j\frac{2\pi mn}{N}}$. The A-IoT device's low-pass filter allows us to simplify the model by considering only the downlink transmission:

$$\mathbf{y}^a = \tilde{\mathbf{F}}\mathbf{x}^a. \tag{5}$$

Here, $\mathbf{y}^a \in \mathbb{R}^N$ represents the A-IoT time-domain signal. The submatrix $\tilde{\mathbf{F}} \in \mathbb{C}^{N \times K}$ is formed by extracting columns from $\mathbf{F}$ according to the index set $\mathcal{I}$. This set is to ensure that $\mathbf{y}^a$ is a real signal and is defined as:

$$\mathcal{I} = \{((m - K/2) \pmod N) + 1\}_{m=0}^{K-1}. \tag{6}$$

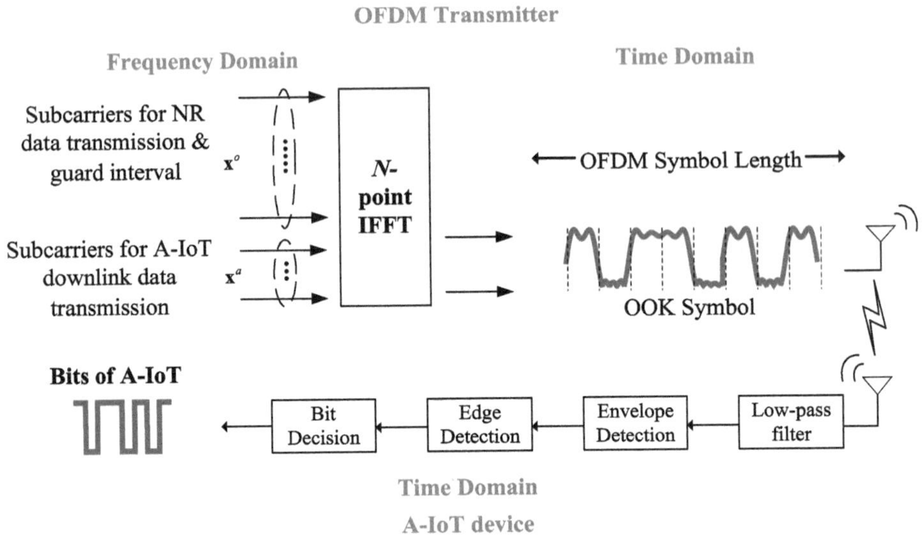


**Fig. 1.** System model of A-IoT downlink.

The optimal frequency-domain vector $\mathbf{x}_{\mathrm{ls}}$ [11] is found by solving the following least-squares problem:

$$\begin{aligned}\mathbf{x}_{\mathrm{ls}} &= \arg\min_{\mathbf{x}^a} ||\widetilde{\mathbf{F}}\mathbf{x}^a - \mathbf{G}_m||^2 \\ &= (\widetilde{\mathbf{F}}^{\mathrm{H}}\widetilde{\mathbf{F}})^{-1}\widetilde{\mathbf{F}}^{\mathrm{H}}\mathbf{G}_m.\end{aligned} \tag{7}$$

Thus, we obtain the input vector $\mathbf{x}_{ls}$ for the OFDM modulator that corresponds to the target waveform $\mathbf{G}_m$. To simplify our analysis, we employ an equivalent low-pass model and neglect the addition of a cyclic prefix to the OFDM symbols.

### 2.3 Receiver

As shown in Fig. 1, the simple receiver comprises a low-pass filter, an envelope detector, an edge detector, and a decoder. The signal at the receiver front-end passes through a low-pass filter and a non-coherent envelope detector to yield the baseband signal envelope. The complex baseband representation of the received signal is $r(t) = y(t) + n(t)$, where $y(t)$ is the desired real baseband signal and $n(t)$ is the band-limited noise, respectively. The noise term, $n(t)$, is a Gaussian process whose in-phase, $n_{\mathrm{i}}(t)$, and quadrature, $n_{\mathrm{q}}(t)$, components are independent, with zero mean and a variance of $\sigma_n^2$. Consequently, the baseband signal envelope $a(t)$ is given by:

$$a(t) = |y(t) + n(t)|, t \in [0, T_{\mathrm{block}}]. \tag{8}$$

The receiver is designed to make a decision at the expected transition instant of each chip, $t_k$ (for $k = 0, 1, \ldots, 2N_b - 1$). To do this, it takes two samples of the envelope in the vicinity of $t_k$: one at $t_k - \Delta t$ and another at $t_k + \Delta t$. These samples are then compared against a decision threshold $V_{\text{th}}$.

The edge detection is defined as follows:

- If $a(t_k - \Delta t) < V_{\text{th}}$ and $a(t_k + \Delta t) > V_{\text{th}}$, a rising edge is determined to be present at time $t_k$.
- If $a(t_k - \Delta t) > V_{\text{th}}$ and $a(t_k + \Delta t) < V_{\text{th}}$, a falling edge is determined to be present at time $t_k$.
- If neither of the above conditions is met, no edge is detected at $t_k$.

Based on the preceding receiver model, the receiver's performance is primarily constrained by two factors: noise power and signal bandwidth. First, noise introduces random fluctuations in the sampled voltage, which can cause the receiver to make erroneous edge decisions. Second, a finite signal bandwidth results in slower signal transitions, making these edges more susceptible to noise-induced errors.

Let $B_{\text{sig}}$ be the A-IoT signal bandwidth and $BW$ be the system bandwidth. To ensure a fair performance evaluation across configurations with different $B_{\text{sig}}$ and $BW$, the Carrier-to-Noise Ratio (CNR) is used as the primary metric. It relates to the Signal-to-Noise Ratio (SNR) as follows:

$$\text{CNR} = \frac{P_{\text{sig}}/B_{\text{sig}}}{N_0} = \text{SNR} \times \frac{BW}{B_{\text{sig}}}, \tag{9}$$

where $P_{\text{sig}}$ is the received signal power and $N_0$ is the single-sided noise power spectral density. This allows for a unified performance comparison regardless of the low-pass filter settings.

## 3 Block Error Rate Analysis

This section develops a rigorous theoretical model for the BLER of the A-IoT downlink. We use level crossing rate theory to analyze the random process of the signal envelope crossing the decision threshold, ultimately deriving an expression for the BLER.

### 3.1 Received Signal Model and Statistical Properties

The statistical properties of the envelope $a(t)$ are determined by the state of the $y(t)$. Within the duration of a single chip, $T_c$, the amplitude of the ideal signal $y(t)$ is approximately constant. For the OOK modulation scheme used in A-IoT, there are two possible states:

1. **"ON" State:** When the transmitted chip is a "1", the envelope $a(t)$ possesses a desired amplitude, denoted as $A_s$. In this case, the received envelope

amplitude, represented by the random variable $A$, follows a Rician distribution. Its probability density function (PDF), conditioned on the hypothesis $H_1$ (an "ON" chip was sent), is given by [12]:

$$p_{A|H_1}(A) = \frac{A}{\sigma_n^2} \exp\left(-\frac{A^2 + A_s^2}{2\sigma_n^2}\right) \cdot I_0\left(\frac{AA_s}{\sigma_n^2}\right), \quad A \geq 0, \tag{10}$$

where $I_0(\cdot)$ is the zeroth-order modified Bessel function of the first kind.

2. **"OFF" State:** When the transmitted chip is a "0", the desired amplitude of $a(t)$ is zero. In this scenario, the envelope amplitude $A$ follows a Rayleigh distribution. Its PDF, conditioned on the hypothesis $H_0$ (an "OFF" chip was sent), is [13]:

$$p_{A|H_0}(A) = \frac{A}{\sigma_n^2} \exp\left(-\frac{A^2}{2\sigma_n^2}\right), \quad A \geq 0. \tag{11}$$

### 3.2 Derivation of Level Crossing Rate for Edge Detection

The decoding process relies on the accurate detection of rising and falling edges. An information bit is composed of two chips (e.g., 01 or 10), and correct decoding is contingent upon detecting the expected level transition within a predefined time window. Error events primarily arise when the received signal envelope, $a(t)$, fails to cross the decision threshold, $V_{\text{th}}$, as anticipated.

To simplify the analysis, we assume that the primary source of error is false alarms. This is because a missed detection can only occur within the extremely brief interval of a decision edge, lacks a time-accumulation effect, and requires the instantaneous noise amplitude to approach the signal amplitude, which is a highly improbable event under high CNR conditions.

The foundation for this analysis is the general formula derived by S. O. Rice, which is used to calculate the expected number of times per unit time that a random process $a(t)$ crosses a given level $A$ with a positive slope. This value is known as the level crossing rate denoted by $N_A^+$ [14]. Its general formula is:

$$N_A^+ = \int_0^\infty \dot{a}\, p_{a,\dot{a}}(A, \dot{a})\, \mathrm{d}\dot{a}, \tag{12}$$

where $\dot{a}(t)$ is the time derivative of $a(t)$, and $p_{a,\dot{a}}(a, \dot{a})$ is the joint PDF of the process and its derivative.

We consider a scenario where the received signal consists solely of narrowband noise, which is typical for an "OFF" state in many communication systems. The noise can be represented by its in-phase and quadrature components, $n_{\text{i}}(t)$ and $n_{\text{q}}(t)$. Both are assumed to be independent, stationary, zero-mean Gaussian processes with variance $\sigma_n^2$. The received signal envelope, denoted by $a_0(t)$, is:

$$a_0(t) = \sqrt{n_{\text{i}}^2(t) + n_{\text{q}}^2(t)}. \tag{13}$$

This definition implies that the envelope $a_0(t)$ follows a Rayleigh distribution, with its PDF given by (11). The time derivative of the envelope, $\dot{a}_0(t)$, is found using the chain rule:

$$\dot{a}_0(t) = \frac{n_\mathrm{i}(t)\dot{n}_\mathrm{i}(t) + n_\mathrm{q}(t)\dot{n}_\mathrm{q}(t)}{a_0(t)}. \tag{14}$$

For a stationary Gaussian process, the process itself is independent of its time derivative at the same instant [15]. Thus, $n_\mathrm{i}(t)$ is independent of $\dot{n}_\mathrm{i}(t)$, and $n_\mathrm{q}(t)$ is independent of $\dot{n}_\mathrm{q}(t)$. The derivatives $\dot{n}_\mathrm{i}(t)$ and $\dot{n}_\mathrm{q}(t)$ are also zero-mean Gaussian processes with a variance $\sigma_{\dot{n}}^2$ determined by the second derivative of the autocorrelation function $R_n(\tau)$ of the noise processes:

$$\sigma_{\dot{a}_0}^2 = \frac{\mathbb{E}[{n_\mathrm{i}}^2] \cdot \mathbb{E}[\dot{n}_\mathrm{i}^2] + \mathbb{E}[{n_\mathrm{q}}^2] \cdot \mathbb{E}[\dot{n}_\mathrm{q}^2]}{\mathbb{E}[{a_0}^2]} = \sigma_{\dot{n}}^2 = -R_n''(0). \tag{15}$$

Assuming the low-pass filter is ideal with a bandwidth of $B_\mathrm{sig}$, the variance of the narrowband noise can be expressed as [16]:

$$\sigma_{\dot{n}}^2 = \frac{\pi^2}{3}\sigma_n^2 B_\mathrm{sig}^2. \tag{16}$$

The four random variables $n_\mathrm{i}, n_\mathrm{q}, \dot{n}_\mathrm{i}, \dot{n}_\mathrm{q}$ are mutually independent. Their joint PDF is the product of their individual Gaussian PDFs:

$$p(n_\mathrm{i}, n_\mathrm{q}, \dot{n}_\mathrm{i}, \dot{n}_\mathrm{q}) = \frac{1}{(2\pi)^2\sigma_n^2\sigma_{\dot{n}}^2} \exp\left(-\frac{n_\mathrm{i}^2 + n_\mathrm{q}^2}{2\sigma_n^2} - \frac{\dot{n}_\mathrm{i}^2 + \dot{n}_\mathrm{q}^2}{2\sigma_{\dot{n}}^2}\right). \tag{17}$$

To find the joint PDF $p_{a,\dot{a}}(a, \dot{a})$, we transform the variables in (17) from Cartesian coordinates $(n_\mathrm{i}, n_\mathrm{q}, \dot{n}_\mathrm{i}, \dot{n}_\mathrm{q})$ to a polar representation and then integrate out the phase. This procedure yields:

$$p_{a_0,\dot{a}_0}(a, \dot{a}_0) = \underbrace{\frac{a}{\sigma_n^2} \exp\left(-\frac{a^2}{2\sigma_n^2}\right)}_{p_{a_0}(a_0)\ \text{(Rayleigh)}} \underbrace{\frac{1}{\sqrt{2\pi\sigma_{\dot{n}}^2}} \exp\left(-\frac{\dot{a}_0^2}{2\sigma_{\dot{n}}^2}\right)}_{p_{\dot{a}_0}(\dot{a}_0)\ \text{(Gaussian)}}. \tag{18}$$

Equation (18) reveals a key result: for a narrowband Gaussian process, the envelope $a_0(t)$ and its derivative $\dot{a}_0(t)$ are statistically independent.

We can now derive the level crossing rate for a given threshold level, which we denote as $V_\mathrm{th}$. Substituting the joint PDF from (18) into the general level crossing rate formula (12) with $A = V_\mathrm{th}$, we get:

$$\begin{aligned}
N_{V_\mathrm{th}}^+ &= \int_0^\infty \dot{a}_0\, p_{a_0,\dot{a}_0}(V_\mathrm{th}, \dot{a}_0)\, \mathrm{d}\dot{a}_0 \\
&= \int_0^\infty \dot{a}_0 \left[\frac{V_\mathrm{th}}{\sigma_n^2} \exp\left(-\frac{V_\mathrm{th}^2}{2\sigma_n^2}\right) \frac{1}{\sqrt{2\pi\sigma_{\dot{n}}^2}} \exp\left(-\frac{\dot{a}_0^2}{2\sigma_{\dot{n}}^2}\right)\right] \mathrm{d}\dot{a}_0 \\
&= \frac{V_\mathrm{th}}{\sigma_n^2} \exp\left(-\frac{V_\mathrm{th}^2}{2\sigma_n^2}\right) \int_0^\infty \frac{\dot{a}_0}{\sqrt{2\pi\sigma_{\dot{n}}^2}} \exp\left(-\frac{\dot{a}_0^2}{2\sigma_{\dot{n}}^2}\right) \mathrm{d}\dot{a}_0.
\end{aligned} \tag{19}$$

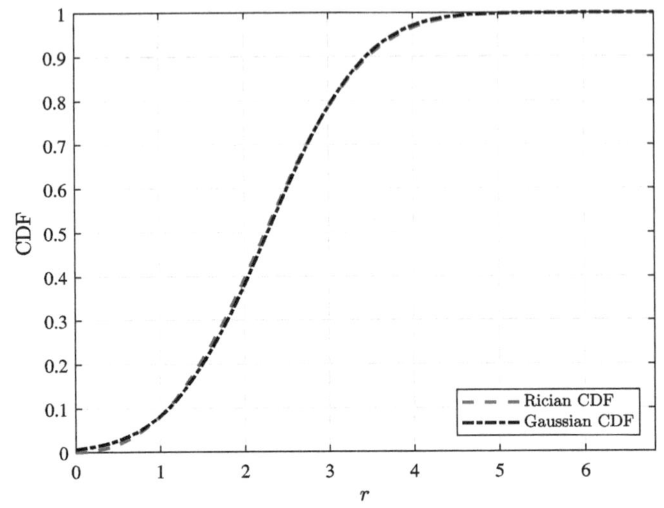


**Fig. 2.** Gaussian approximation of the Rician distribution CDF for CNR = 5, $A = 1$.

The final expression for the level crossing rate is:

$$N_{V_{\text{th}}}^{+} = \frac{V_{\text{th}}}{\sigma_n^2} \exp\left(-\frac{V_{\text{th}}^2}{2\sigma_n^2}\right) \frac{\sigma_{\dot{n}}}{\sqrt{2\pi}}. \tag{20}$$

By substituting the expression for $\sigma_{\dot{n}}$ from (15), we can write the level crossing rate in terms of the noise bandwidth $B_{\text{sig}}$:

$$N_{V_{\text{th}}}^{+} = \frac{V_{\text{th}} B_{\text{sig}}}{\sigma_n} \exp\left(-\frac{V_{\text{th}}^2}{2\sigma_n^2}\right) \sqrt{\frac{\pi}{6}}. \tag{21}$$

Now, consider the case where a non-zero signal is present. We assume the desired amplitude of the signal component at the receiver is $A_s$. The received signal envelope is then:

$$a_1(t) = \sqrt{(n_{\text{i}}(t) + A_s)^2 + n_{\text{q}}^2(t)}. \tag{22}$$

This envelope $a_1(t)$ follows a Rician distribution.

To simplify the analytical process, we employ a Gaussian process as an equivalent model for the Rician process, matching the mean and variance of the original distribution. The Rician PDF is thus approximated by:

$$p_{A|H_1}(A) \approx \frac{1}{\sqrt{2\pi\sigma_{\text{eq}}^2}} \exp\left(-\frac{(A - \mu_{\text{eq}})^2}{2\sigma_{\text{eq}}^2}\right), \tag{23}$$

where the equivalent mean $\mu_{\text{eq}}$ and variance $\sigma_{\text{eq}}^2$ are given by:

$$\begin{aligned}
\mu_{\text{eq}}(\sigma_n) &= \mathbb{E}[a_1(t)] = \sigma_n \sqrt{\frac{\pi}{2}} e^{-K/2} \left[ (1+K) I_0 \left( \frac{K}{2} \right) + K I_1 \left( \frac{K}{2} \right) \right], \\
\sigma_{\text{eq}}(\sigma_n) &= \mathbb{E}[a_1^2(t)] - \mu_{\text{eq}}^2 = 2\sigma_n^2 + A_s^2 - \mu_{\text{eq}}^2, \\
K(\sigma_n) &= \frac{A_s^2}{2\sigma_n^2},
\end{aligned} \tag{24}$$

$I_0(\cdot)$ and $I_1(\cdot)$ are the modified Bessel functions of the first kind.

As illustrated in Fig. 2, the cumulative distribution function (CDF) of the Gaussian approximation closely matches the Rician CDF for a CNR of 5 dB. This approximation holds particularly well for high CNR ($K \gg 1$), where the Rician distribution converges to a Gaussian distribution. While some deviation exists at low CNR, this method provides an analytically tractable framework for performance evaluation.

Assuming the signal is in the "ON" state, the down-crossing rate of the random process $a_1(t)$ for a level $A$ is denoted as $N_A^-$. Following a derivation method similar to that used for (14)–(19), we can obtain:

$$N_A^- = \frac{\sigma_{\dot{n}}}{2\pi\sigma_{\text{eq}}} \exp\left( -\frac{(A - \mu_{\text{eq}})^2}{2\sigma_{\text{eq}}^2} \right). \tag{25}$$

By substituting (16) into the expression above and setting the level $A = V_{\text{th}}$, we obtain the final down-crossing rate:

$$N_{V_{\text{th}}}^- = \frac{\sigma_n B_{\text{sig}}}{2\sqrt{3}\sigma_{\text{eq}}} \exp\left( -\frac{(V_{\text{th}} - \mu_{\text{eq}})^2}{2\sigma_{\text{eq}}^2} \right). \tag{26}$$

### 3.3 Derivation of Block Error Rate

We use the previously derived level crossing rate to analyze block errors caused by noise-induced false alarms. The analysis requires a defined decision threshold, $V_{\text{th}}$. We select a threshold that lies between the mean of the "ON" state envelope and the mean of the "OFF" state envelope. A logical choice is the average of these two means:

$$V_{\text{th}} \triangleq \frac{1}{2} \left( \mathbb{E}[a_1(t)] + \mathbb{E}[a_0(t)] \right) = \frac{1}{2} \left( \mu_{\text{eq}} + \sigma_n \sqrt{\frac{\pi}{2}} \right). \tag{27}$$

Assuming the level crossing events follow a Poisson process, the average number of false alarm events, $\lambda$, within a block of duration $T_{\text{block}}$ is the sum of the crossing rates in the "ON" and "OFF" states, scaled by their respective durations. Since Manchester encoding ensures each state occupies half the total time, $\lambda$ is given by:

$$\lambda = \frac{T_{\text{block}}}{2} \cdot (N_{V_{\text{th}}}^- + N_{V_{\text{th}}}^+). \tag{28}$$

Substituting (21) and (26) yields:

$$\lambda = \frac{T_{\text{block}} B_{\text{sig}}}{2} \left[ \frac{\sigma_n}{2\sqrt{3}\sigma_{\text{eq}}} \exp\left( -\frac{(V_{\text{th}} - \mu_{\text{eq}})^2}{2\sigma_{\text{eq}}^2} \right) + \frac{V_{\text{th}}}{\sigma_n} \exp\left( -\frac{V_{\text{th}}^2}{2\sigma_n^2} \right) \sqrt{\frac{\pi}{6}} \right]. \tag{29}$$

Here, $T_{\text{block}}$ and $B_{\text{sig}}$ are constants, while $V_{\text{th}}$, $\sigma_{\text{eq}}$, and $\mu_{\text{eq}}$ are functions of $\sigma_n$. We define $\gamma$ as the instantaneous CNR:

$$\gamma \triangleq \frac{A_s^2/2}{2\sigma_n^2} = \frac{A_s^2}{4\sigma_n^2}. \tag{30}$$

Based on this definition, we can express $\sigma_n$ in terms of $\gamma$:

$$\sigma_n = \frac{A_s}{2\sqrt{\gamma}}. \tag{31}$$

Let $Q$ be the number of false alarm events. Assuming $Q$ follows a Poisson distribution with parameter $\lambda$, its probability mass function is $P(Q = q) = \mathrm{e}^{-\lambda}\lambda^q/q!$. Block errors will occur if at least one false alarm event happens. Therefore, the BLER is the probability that $Q \geq 1$:

$$P_{\text{BLER}}(\gamma) = 1 - P(Q = 0) = 1 - \exp[-\lambda(\gamma)]. \tag{32}$$

The parameter $\lambda(\gamma)$ is obtained by substituting the expressions for $N_{V_{\text{th}}}^{+}$ and $N_{V_{\text{th}}}^{-}$ into (28), with all terms expressed as functions of $\gamma$. The key parameters $\mu_{\text{eq}}$, $\sigma_{\text{eq}}^2$, and $V_{\text{th}}$ can now be written as functions of the CNR, $\gamma$, by noting that the Rician K-factor is $K = A_s^2/(2\sigma_n^2) = 2\gamma$:

$$\begin{aligned} \mu_{\text{eq}}(\gamma) &= \frac{A_s\sqrt{\pi}}{2\sqrt{2\gamma}} e^{-\gamma} \left[ (1 + 2\gamma) I_0(\gamma) + 2\gamma I_1(\gamma) \right], \\ \sigma_{\text{eq}}^2(\gamma) &= A_s^2 \left( 1 + \frac{1}{2\gamma} \right) - \mu_{\text{eq}}^2(\gamma), \\ V_{\text{th}}(\gamma) &= \frac{\mu_{\text{eq}}(\gamma)}{2} + \frac{A_s}{4} \sqrt{\frac{\pi}{2\gamma}}. \end{aligned} \tag{33}$$

Substituting these expressions into the formulas for $N_{V_{\text{th}}}^{+}$ and $N_{V_{\text{th}}}^{-}$ provides the full expression for $\lambda(\gamma)$, yielding a complete, albeit complex, closed-form model for $P_{\text{BLER}}(\gamma)$ under AWGN.

The preceding analysis provides the BLER performance as a function of the CNR, $\gamma$, under AWGN channel. To evaluate the system's performance in a more realistic mobile environment, we now extend this framework to single-path Rayleigh fading channels, where the instantaneous CNR fluctuates randomly.

Our methodology is to average the CNR-dependent BLER, $P_{\text{BLER}}$, over the probability distribution of $\gamma$ in a Rayleigh fading environment. It is a well-established result that for a Rayleigh fading channel, the instantaneous CNR $\gamma$ follows an exponential distribution, with its PDF given by:

$$p_\gamma(\gamma) = \frac{1}{\bar{\gamma}} \exp\left( -\frac{\gamma}{\bar{\gamma}} \right), \quad \gamma \geq 0, \tag{34}$$

where $\bar{\gamma}$ is the average CNR. The average BLER, $P_{\text{BLER, Rayleigh}}$, is then obtained by taking the expectation of $P_{\text{BLER}}(\gamma)$ with respect to $\gamma$:

$$P_{\text{BLER, Rayleigh}} = \mathbb{E}_{\gamma}[P_{\text{BLER}}(\gamma)] = \int_0^{\infty} P_{\text{BLER}}(\gamma) \cdot p_{\gamma}(\gamma)\, \mathrm{d}\gamma. \tag{35}$$

Substituting the PDF, we get the integral expression for the average BLER in a Rayleigh fading channel:

$$P_{\text{BLER, Rayleigh}} = \int_0^{\infty} [1 - \exp(-\lambda(\gamma))] \cdot \frac{1}{\bar{\gamma}} \exp\left(-\frac{\gamma}{\bar{\gamma}}\right) \mathrm{d}\gamma. \tag{36}$$

The resulting integral does not have a known closed-form solution due to the complexity of $\lambda(\gamma)$ and must therefore be evaluated numerically.

## 4 Simulation Results

To validate the accuracy of the theoretical BLER analysis model proposed in this paper, and to evaluate the impact of key system parameters on performance, a simulation platform was developed. This section presents and analyzes the simulation results. The general parameters used in the simulations are summarized in Table 1. In the simulation setup, one Resource Block (RB) occupies a bandwidth of 180 kHz.

**Table 1.** Simulation Parameters

| Parameter | Value |
|---|---|
| Antenna Config | 1T 1R |
| Subcarrier Spacing | 15KHz |
| Block Size | 20 bits |
| System BW | 10MHz |
| Line Coding | Manchester code |
| BB Filter | 3rd order Butterworth |

To validate the effectiveness and accuracy of the theoretical BLER derivation proposed in Sect. 3, we present a comparison between the theoretical calculations and Monte Carlo simulation results in Figs. 3 and 4. It can be clearly observed that under all tested parameter combinations, both in the AWGN and Rayleigh fading channels, the theoretical analysis curves and the simulation results exhibit strong consistency. The overall trends of the curves are in close agreement in both the low and high CNR regions. This high degree of consistency strongly validates the correctness and precision of the proposed BLER model.

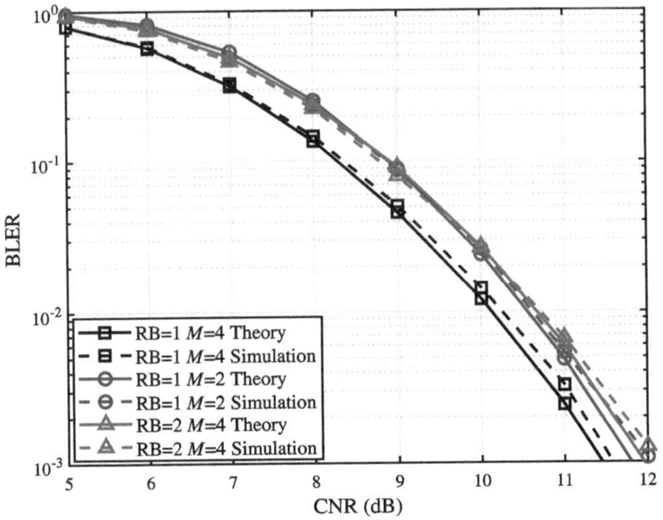


**Fig. 3.** Simulation Validation of the Theoretical BLER Model under AWGN Channel.

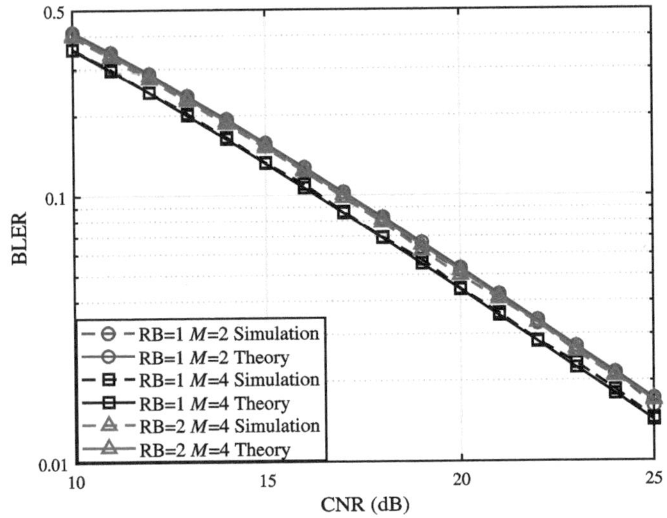


**Fig. 4.** Simulation Validation of the Theoretical BLER Model under a Single-Path Rayleigh Fading Channel.

We also observe that the simulation curve is consistently positioned to the right of the theoretical curve, indicating a small, persistent performance gap between the two. We have quantified this gap and found that, along the CNR axis, it is always less than 0.3 dB. This phenomenon can be attributed to the simplifying assumptions made during our analysis, namely the neglect of missed detection errors and the use of an ideal low-pass filter for the modeling process.

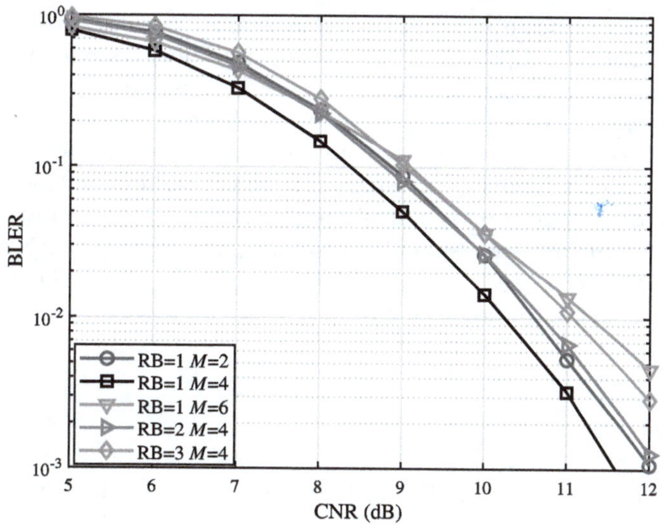


**Fig. 5.** BLER performance comparison for different RB and $M$ Configurations under AWGN Model.

From Fig. 5, we can make the following two observations:

- **Impact of Parameter $M$:** For a fixed allocation of one RB, comparing $M = 2$ and $M = 4$ reveals that a larger $M$ yields better BLER performance at the same CNR. This is because a larger $M$ shortens the block duration $T_{\text{block}}$. For a given level-crossing rate of the noise, this shorter duration reduces the expected number of total crossings, thus lowering the BLER. This trend does not continue indefinitely. For instance, when $M = 6$, the bandwidth of 1RB cannot support the generation of sufficiently steep signal edges, consequently degrading BLER performance.
- **Impact of the Number of RBs:** With a fixed $M = 4$, using fewer RBs (e.g., 2 RBs vs. 3 RBs) results in better BLER performance for a given CNR. This occurs because, for a given noise power spectral density, a wider bandwidth incorporates more high-frequency noise components. These components cause the noise envelope to exhibit more rapid fluctuations, thereby increasing the probability of false alarms. This observation is consistent with (16), which indicates that the variance of the noise derivative increases with the noise bandwidth.

## 5 Conclusion

In this paper, we presented a theoretical framework to analyze the BLER for A-IoT downlinks employing OOK with edge-detection receivers. We derived a BLER expression for AWGN and Rayleigh channels using level crossing rate theory. The model's accuracy was validated against Monte Carlo simulations, confirming its utility and providing key insights into how system parameters like signal bandwidth and packet structure impact performance.

Future research efforts should extend the analysis to more complex operational environments, including performance evaluation under alternative channel models such as Rician fading to accommodate line-of-sight deployment scenarios, and assessing the impact of co-channel interference in dense network configurations. Crucially, future work should investigate system sensitivity to practical hardware impairments (e.g., timing synchronization errors). These continuing endeavors are essential for advancing robust design and standardization of future AIoT systems.

## References

1. Guo, F., Yu, F.R., Zhang, H., Li, X., Ji, H., Leung, V.C.M.: Enabling massive IoT toward 6G: a comprehensive survey. IEEE Internet Things J. **8**(15), 11891–11915 (2021)
2. Xu, H.: 5G based passive internet of things: challenges and potential solutions. In: IEEE 2024 International Symposium on Broadband Multimedia Systems and Broadcasting (BMSB), pp. 1–6 (2024)
3. Marasinghe, D., et al.: Ambient iot devices in future cellular networks: a system level study. In: 2024 IEEE International Conference on Communications Workshops (ICC Workshops), pp. 129–134 (2024)
4. Jian,R., et al.: Ambient IoT: insight and challenge of enabling technologies for future study. In: 2024 6th International Conference on Electronics and Communication, Network and Computer Technology (ECNCT), pp. 451–458 (2024)
5. Butt, M.M., et al.: Ambient IoT: a missing link in 3GPP IoT devices landscape. IEEE Internet of Things magazine **7**(2), 85–92 (2024)
6. Zheng, K., Xu, R., Mei, J., Yang, H., Lei, L., Wang, X.: Ambient IoT towards 6G: standardization, potentials, and challenges. IEEE Access, 33 (2024)
7. Arun, A.N.: Ambient IoT: communications enabling precision agriculture. IEEE Commun. Mag. **63**(4), 137–143 (2025)
8. 3rd Generation Partnership Project (3GPP), "New Work Item: Solutions for Ambient IoT (Internet of Things) in NR," 3GPP, Tech. Rep. RP-243326 (Dec 2024). https://www.3gpp.org/ftp/Meetings_3GPP_Sync/RAN/Inbox/
9. Griffith, D.: toward zero: power consumption trends in low data rate wireless connectivity. IEEE Solid-State Circ. Mag. **14**(4), 51–60 (2022)
10. 3rd Generation Partnership Project (3GPP), "Study on solutions for Ambient IoT in NR," 3GPP, Technical Report (TR) 38.769, Jan 2025, version 19.0.0. https://www.3gpp.org/dynareport/38769.htm
11. Mazloum, N., Edfors, O.: Interference-free OFDM embedding of wake-up signals for low-power wake-up receivers. IEEE Trans. Green Commun. Netw. **4**(3), 669–677 (2020)
12. Rice, S.O.: Mathematical analysis of random noise. Bell Syst. Tech. J. **23**(3), 282–332 (1944)
13. Proakis, J.G.: Digital Communications, 4th ed. McGraw-Hill (2001)
14. Rice, S.O.: Mathematical analysis of random noise. Bell Syst. Tech. J. **24**(1), 46–156 (1945)

15. Yacoub, M., Bautista, J., Guerrade Rezen de Guedes, L.: On higher order statistics of the Nakagami-m distribution. IEEE Trans. Veh. Technol. **48**(3), 790–794 (1999)
16. Leon-Garcia, A.: Probability, Statistics, and Random Processes for Electrical Engineering, 3rd edn. Pearson Prentice Hall, Upper Saddle River, NJ (2008)

# Application of Improved ConvNext and Fused Images of Gramian Difference Field and Sum Field in Gearbox Health Assessment

YunTao Zhao[1], Zengyi Ma[1(✉)], and WeiGang Li[2]

[1] School of Artificial Intelligence and Automation, Wuhan University of Science and Technology Hubei, Wuhan, China
1724830028@wust.edu.cn

[2] Engineering Research Center for Metallurgical Automation and Measurement Technology of Ministry of Education Hubei, Wuhan, China

**Abstract.** To address the challenges of extracting gearbox fault features and ensuring stable fault identification accuracy, this paper presents a gear fault diagnosis method based on the fusion of Gram difference field (GADF) and Gram sum field (GASF) images, combined with an improved CCB-ConvNeXt convolutional neural network. First, the original one-dimensional vibration signals are transformed into GADF and GASF images, and their timing and amplitude information are fully integrated through weighted fusion. Then, the ConvNeXt network is enhanced by introducing ContMIX dynamic convolution, a CBAM attention mechanism, and a bidirectional attention gate (BAG) module, thereby improving context modeling and key feature extraction capabilities. Experimental results on the Southeast University (SEU) gear fault dataset demonstrate that the proposed method achieves a classification accuracy of 99.9%, outperforming mainstream convolutional neural network models. These results indicate that the method offers strong robustness, good generalization, and provides an efficient and stable reference for mechanical fault diagnosis.

**Keywords:** Attention Mechanism · Convolutional Networks · Fault Diagnosis · Gram Angle Field · Gears

## 1 Introduction

The gearbox is a critical component widely used in aviation, wind turbines, and precision machinery. Due to prolonged exposure to high-speed and heavy-load conditions, gearboxes are susceptible to faults such as broken teeth, wear, and cracks, which may lead to equipment failures and safety incidents [1]. Therefore, accurate gear fault diagnosis has long been a key research focus [2]. Traditional fault diagnosis methods-such as power spectrum analysis, Fourier transform, envelope analysis, and VMD are often combined with classical classifiers like logistic regression and K nearest neighbors [3], However, these approaches struggle with the non-stationary and noise-prone nature of


Y. Liu et al. (Eds.): ChinaCom 2025, LNICST 711, pp. 556–567, 2027.
https://doi.org/10.1007/978-3-032-33662-0_40

real-world vibration signals, making it difficult to extract discriminative features and build robust models. Additionally, the lack of adaptive mechanisms limits their effectiveness in complex scenarios. Consequently, the application and promotion of these technologies encounter substantial challenge.

Recent advances in deep learning have enabled more powerful fault diagnosis frameworks. CNNs, in particular, have shown strong performance in feature extraction for image-based tasks and have been successfully applied to mechanical fault diagnosis. For example, Senanayaka [4] leveraged multi-classifier fusion, while Fu utilized CWT based time-frequency images with CNNs. However, methods like CWT require manual basis function selection, which limits adaptability. Consequently, Pang [5] proposed a planetary gearbox fault diagnosis model using Gram angle field-convolutional neural networks (GADF-CNN), finding that the GADF-CNN model achieves higher recognition accuracy in planetary gearbox fault diagnosis. Gu [6] also combined Gram angle field image encoding technology with deep convolutional generative adversarial networks (GANs)for data augmentation, and achieved excellent diagnostic results by integrating convolutional neural networks for fault diagnosis. Despite these advances, few methods fuse both GADF and GASF images to fully utilize temporal and amplitude features. To address this, we propose a novel method combining GADF and GASF image fusion [7] with an improved ConvNeXt model [8]. A weighted fusion algorithm enhances feature richness, while the ConvNeXt backbone is optimized by integrating ContMIX dynamic convolution [9]. CBAM attention [10], and a Bidirectional Attention Gate (BAG) module [11]. These improvements strengthen context modeling and key feature extraction. Experiments on the SEU gearbox dataset demonstrate the methods superior accuracy and robustness.

## 2 GAF Image Fusion Processing

The Gramian angular field (GAF) is a method of transforming data dimensions based on Gram matrices in polar coordinates. Each data point in a one-dimensional time series is treated as a point in a vector space. The cosine values of the angles between these points are then calculated and mapped to pixels in a two-dimensional image. This generates an image that reflects the dynamic and periodic characteristics of the time series. GASF and GADF represent two complementary Gramian Angular Field encodings: GASF emphasizes the cumulative characteristics of time series, capturing global trends and intensity, whereas GADF highlights local variations, emphasizing dynamic fluctuations. Given their distinct distributions and complementary features, this study employs a weighted average fusion strategy to integrate the two representations.

GAF uses polar coordinate transformation to convert the signal into a two-dimensional coded image. The conversion formulas for GADF and GASF are as follows:

$$G_{gadf} = \begin{bmatrix} \sin(\phi_1 - \phi_1) & \sin(\phi_1 - \phi_2) & \cdots & \sin(\phi_1 - \phi_n) \\ \sin(\phi_2 - \phi_1) & \sin(\phi_2 - \phi_2) & \cdots & \sin(\phi_2 - \phi_n) \\ \vdots & \vdots & \ddots & \vdots \\ \sin(\phi_n - \phi_1) & \sin(\phi_n - \phi_2) & \cdots & \sin(\phi_n - \phi_n) \end{bmatrix} = \sqrt{I - X^2}^T X - \overline{X}^T \sqrt{I - X^2} \tag{1}$$

$$G_{gasf} = \begin{bmatrix} \cos(\phi_1 + \phi_1) & \cos(\phi_1 + \phi_2) & \cdots & \cos(\phi_1 + \phi_n) \\ \cos(\phi_2 + \phi_1) & \cos(\phi_2 + \phi_2) & \cdots & \cos(\phi_2 + \phi_n) \\ \vdots & \vdots & \ddots & \vdots \\ \cos(\phi_n + \phi_1) & \cos(\phi_n + \phi_2) & \cdots & \cos(\phi_n + \phi_n) \end{bmatrix} = X\overline{X}^T - \sqrt{I - X^2}^T \sqrt{I - X^2} \tag{2}$$

Where $X$ is the signal sequence matrix and $I = [1, 1, \cdots 1]$. The fusion formula is:

$$I(x, y) = \omega_1 I_1(x, y) + \omega_2 I_2(x, y)\ (x, y) \in (I_1 \cap I_2) \tag{3}$$

Among them, $I_1$ $(x, y)$ and $I_2$ $(x, y)$ are the images to be fused. $\omega_1$ and $\omega_2$ are the weights when the pixel values of images $I_1$ $(x, y)$ and $I_2$ $(x, y)$ are added together. To fully demonstrate the frequency information extracted by GASF and GADF, the selected weights are 0.5 and 0.5, respectively. Fig. 1 shows the process of merging GAF signals into images.

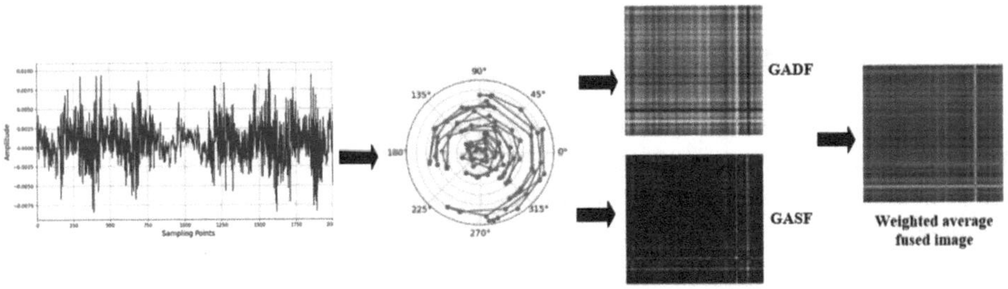


**Fig. 1.** The process of merging GAF signals into images

Due to the excessively long time series, the GAF transformation would generate a high-dimensional matrix, leading to an increase in computational workload. Therefore, we process the signal into a time series with 2048 samples and a step size of 1000, and then apply GAF to perform a two-dimensional graphical transformation on the processed signal.

## 3 ConvNext Neural Networke

ConvNeXt Neural Network as shown in Fig. 2, adopts a four-stage pyramid structure comprising Patchify Stem, ConvNeXt Blocks, Down sampling, and Classification Head modules. Each block integrates depthwise separable convolution, pointwise MLP, GELU activation, and Layer Normalization to balance computational efficiency and representational capacity. This structure is ideal for extracting multi-level semantic features from low to high levels in images.

Although ConvNeXt has certain advantages, it lacks adaptive mechanisms and performs fixed receptive field operations without attention modules, which limits its ability

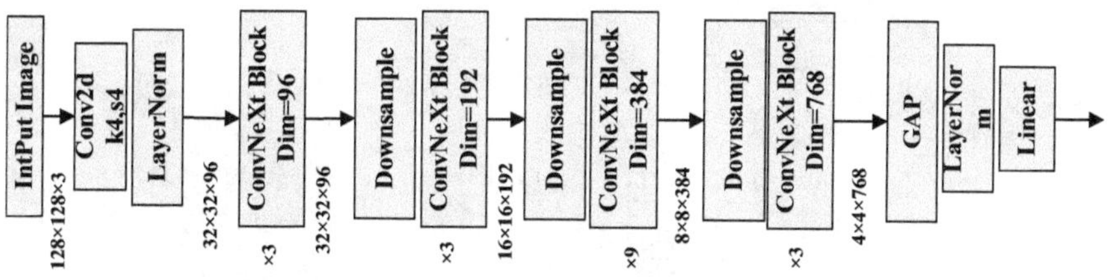


**Fig. 2.** ConvNeXt network structure

to capture key features in fault-related GAF images. In addition, deep convolutions operate independently on different channels, thereby weakening cross-channel correlation modelling [12].

In order to address these limitations, this study proposes CCB-ConvNeXt. which enhances the ConvNeXt architecture by integrating three key modules: (1) replacing the core component with ContMIX dynamic convolution, (2) using CBAM for spatial and channel-level attention mechanisms, and (3) employing BAG for deep semantic enhancement. These new modules enable the model to adaptively focus on discriminative features, enhance global-local dependency modelling capabilities, and improve feature discrimination ability, thereby significantly improving classification performance in fault diagnosis tasks.

## 4 Improved ConvNext Neural Networke

The proposed improved ConvNeXt is an enhanced convolutional neural network that has been tailored for the purpose of fault diagnosis in scenarios involving non-stationary and noisy time-series signals. The model builds upon the ConvNeXt backbone and incorporates three key improvements ContMIX, CBAM, and BAG to overcome limitations in global modelling, attention adaptability, and high-level semantic representation. This model is named CCB-ConvNeXt.

### 4.1 Context-Mixing Dynamic Convolution (ContMIX)

ContMIX replaces the standard depthwise convolution in ConvNeXt blocks with a dynamic context-mixing convolution. The method under discussion here involves the computation of an affinity map between each local token and central reference points across multiple spatial regions. This enables the adaptive aggregation of global contextual information. This mechanism serves to enhance the model's capacity to capture long-range dependencies and subtle feature variations. This is of particular importance in time-frequency images generated from non-stationary vibration signals. The structure diagram of the ContMIX convolution module is shown in Fig. 3. Additionally, the ContMix dynamic convolution module possesses strong generalisation and adaptability capabilities, enabling it to seamlessly integrate into the ConvNeXt neural network.

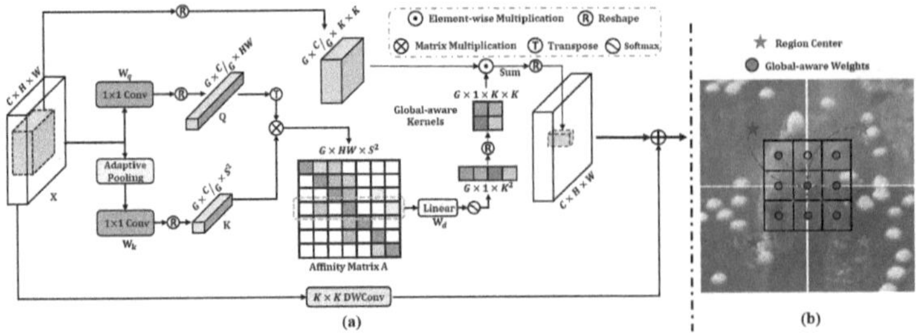


**Fig. 3.** The ContMIX convolution module structure diagram

### 4.2 Attention Mechanisms

In order to enhance the discriminative ability of neural networks in the recognition of fault images, this paper introduces the Convolutional Block Attention Module (CBAM) as an enhancement module for the main network. The CBAM is embedded after the critical ConvNeXt stage. The structural diagram of the CBAM module is shown in Fig. 4.

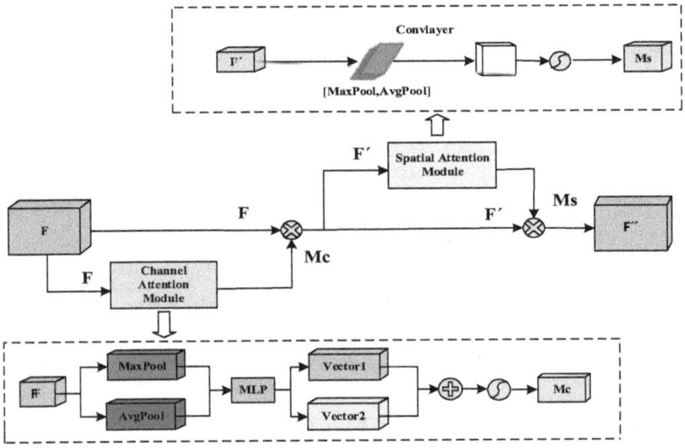


**Fig. 4.** CBAM principle structure diagram

In the CBAM module, the input feature map is first input, then the feature map is sent to the channel attention module, where the input feature map F undergoes global max pooling downsampling and global average downsampling, transforming the original H × W × C feature map into two 1 × 1 × C feature maps. These two feature maps are then fed into two fully connected layers, which output two 1 × 1 × C feature maps. These are summed and passed through a sigmoid activation function to restrict them to the range 0–1, yielding a channel attention map $M_c$ of size 1 × 1 × C. The feature map is multiplied by $M_c$ to obtain a feature map of size H × W × C. Spatial attention first performs global max pooling downsampling and global average pooling downsampling on the feature map, then applies a convolutional operation and sigmoid activation function to obtain an $M_s$ of size H × W × 1. Finally, $M_s$ is multiplied by the feature map. to obtain the final output, which has a size of H × W × C. The mathematical expressions for channel attention $M_c$ and spatial attention $M_s$ are as follows:

$$M_C(F) = \sigma(MLP(AvgPool(F)) + MLP(MaxPool(F))) \quad (4)$$

$$M_S(F) = \sigma\left(f^{(7\times7)}([AvgPool(F); MaxPool(F)])\right) \quad (5)$$

In the formula: *AvgPool*(*F*) is average pooling; *MaxPool*(*F*) is max pooling; *MLP*() is a multi-layer perceptron; $\sigma$ is the sigmoid activation function; $M_c(F)$ is the channel attention matrix, and $M_s(F)$ is the spatial attention matrix. Channel attention guides the model to focus on channels that are more strongly associated with faults during feature extraction by analysing the importance distribution of different channels in the feature map. Spatial attention identifies key areas in the image in the spatial dimension, further strengthening the model's local recognition ability of fault anomaly patterns. Furthermore, given the significance of deep features in semantic modelling, the Bidirectional Attention Gate (BAG) module is introduced in the deep layers (layers 3 and 4) of the ConvNeXt network to further enhance semantic modelling capabilities. The BAG module has the capacity to concurrently capture multi-dimensional correlation relationships along both the spatial and channel axes, thereby facilitating more precise identification of abstract and subtle fault patterns. This enhancement addresses the potential bottleneck issues CBAM may encounter when processing high-order features, thereby enhancing the network's generalisation capability in its entirety.

## 4.3 Improved ConvNeXt Network Structure

The overall architecture CCB-ConvNeXt four-stage hierarchical design. Initially, the Patchify Stem module employs a 4 × 4 convolution with stride 4 and Layer Norm, thereby performing preliminary feature extraction and spatial down sampling. Each subsequent stage of the model incorporates a modified ConvNeXt Block, wherein the original depthwise convolution is substituted by a 3 × 3 ContMIX dynamic convolution, enabling adaptive modelling of global-local contextual relationships. In order to enhance the localization of fault patterns, a CBAM (Convolutional Block Attention Module) is integrated following the final convolutional stage, with the application of sequential channel and spatial attention weighting. Additionally, Bidirectional Attention Gate (BAG) modules are embedded at the outputs of Stage 3 and Stage 4 with a view to enhancing deep semantic representation and mitigating the potential expressiveness bottleneck of CBAM at higher feature levels. In conclusion, the implementation of a global average pooling (GAP) layer is instrumental in the aggregation of spatial features. This is subsequently followed by the integration of a fully connected classifier, which functions to predict the designated fault category. The complete architecture is illustrated in Fig. 5.

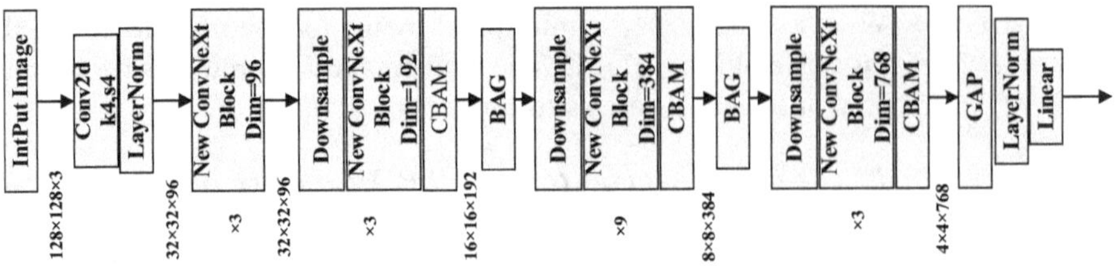


**Fig. 5.** CCB-ConvNeXt Network Structure

# 5 Experiments

## 5.1 Introduction to the Experiment

To validate the effectiveness of this method, this study used a gearbox dataset collected by Southeast University [13]. The SEU gearbox fault diagnosis dataset consists of a fault diagnosis platform consisting of a motor, motor controller, planetary gearbox, reducer, brake, and brake controller. Experiments were conducted under two operating conditions: 20 Hz speed, 0 V load; and 30 Hz speed, 2 V load, with a sampling frequency of 5120 Hz. The dataset contains five different fault categories under both operating conditions: chip fault, healthy fault, missing fault, root fault, and surface fault. For each category, 1047 samples were acquired using an overlapping sliding window method with a window length of 2048 and a step size of 1000, for a total of 5235 samples.Randomly divide the samples and ensure that the ratio of training set,validation set,and test set for each type of sample is 7:2:1. The Southeast University gearbox data acquisition experimental platform is shown in Fig. 6.

**Fig. 6.** Southeast University Data Collection Platform

This experiment uses the Pytorch framework based on the Python language to build a virtual environment. The computer configuration is as follows: AMD Ryzen 7 5800 Hz CPU @3.2 GHz, NVIDIA GeForce RTX 3060 graphics card, 16 GB memory, and Windows 11 operating system.

### 5.2 Experimental Evaluation Metrics and Analysis

To evaluate the effectiveness and generalization capability of the proposed CCB-ConvNeXt model, we conducted comparative experiments under two typical operating conditions: low-speed, no-load (20 Hz/0 V) and high-speed, loaded (30 Hz/2 V). The original 1D vibration signals were transformed into GAF (GASF + GADF) time–frequency images and input into both the baseline ConvNeXt and the Improved ConvNeXt networks.

When evaluating classification models, the confusion matrix and accuracy curve are two intuitive and complementary tools. The former provides a tabular representation of the detailed breakdown of model predictions, while the latter uses a curve to show how model performance changes with thresholds.

The following are the formulas for determining accuracy, precision.

$$Accuracy = \frac{TP + TN}{FP + FN + TP + TN} \tag{6}$$

$$Precision = \frac{TP}{TP + FP} \tag{7}$$

The term "TP" refers to the number of positive samples that were projected to be positive. The term "FP" refers to the number of samples that are truly negative but anticipated to be positive. FN refers to samples that were wrongly anticipated as negative. TN denotes samples that are appropriately predicted as negative.

The training and validation accuracy and loss curves for both conditions are presented collectively in Fig. 7. Across both operating conditions, CCB-ConvNeXt has been shown to superior performance in terms of convergence speed, training stability, and validation accuracy.

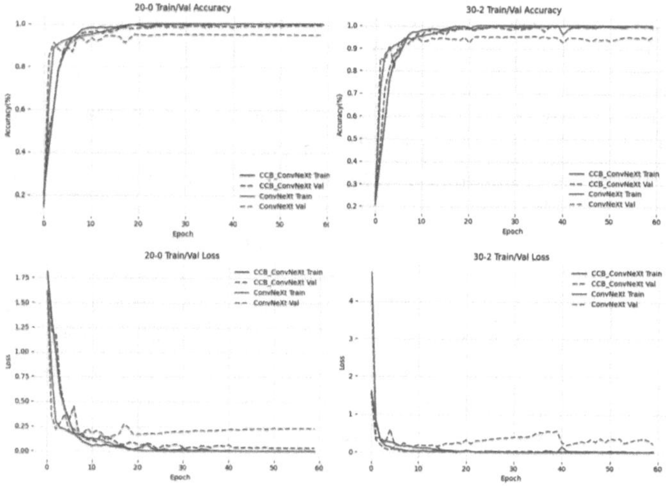


**Fig. 7.** Accuracy and loss curves of ConvNeXt and CCB- ConvNeXt under 20 Hz-0 V and 30 Hz-2 V conditions.

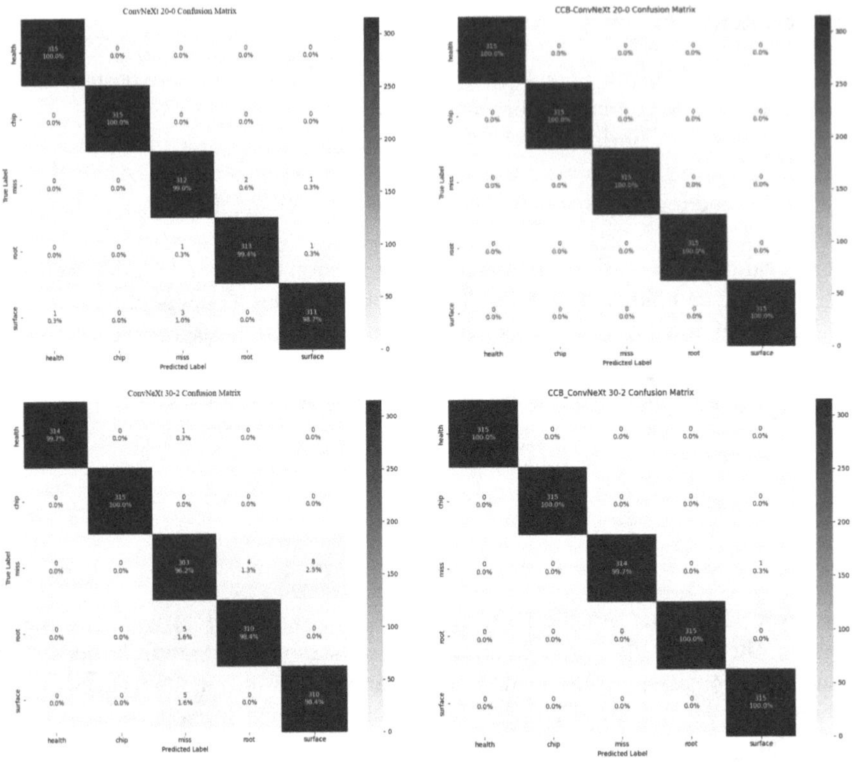


**Fig. 8.** Confusion matrices of ConvNeXt and CCB- ConvNeXt under 20 Hz-0 V and 30 Hz-2 V conditions.

Observations revealed that the training accuracy of the CCB-ConvNeXt increased rapidly under both workloads, demonstrating rapid convergence and effective early feature learning. As training progressed, the training accuracy of both models approached 1, but their performance on the validation set differed significantly. The ConvNeXt validation accuracy curves under both workloads fluctuated significantly, demonstrating significant overfitting. In contrast, the CCB-ConvNeXt maintained high validation accuracy, reaching 100% under low-load conditions and 99.9% under high-load conditions. The CCB-ConvNeXt validation curve not only had a higher peak but also a smoother curve, demonstrating stronger generalization and robustness. In terms of loss function behavior, the validation loss of CCB-ConvNeXt is lower and more stable than that of ConvNeXt under both conditions, further indicating that the improved model achieves a better balance between minimizing empirical risk and controlling generalization error.

Fig. 7 shows the combined confusion matrices for the two operating conditions. Under the 20 Hz/0 V condition, CCB-ConvNeXt achieved 100% classification accuracy for all five fault categories, with all test samples correctly classified. In contrast, ConvNeXt failed to accurately identify three different fault types, resulting in misclassifications in the "miss," "root," and "surface" categories. Under the 30 Hz/2 V condition, the signal complexity increased due to the presence of the load, which in turn made diagnosis more difficult. Despite this, CCB-ConvNeXt still achieved a validation accuracy of 99.9%, with only one intermittent fault misclassified as a surface fault. ConvNeXt performed poorly under these conditions, accurately classifying only one fault category and misclassifying the remaining four.

### 5.3 Experiments Comparing Different Algorithm

To demonstrate the effectiveness and superiority of the improved method in this study, we conducted an experimental comparison of the performance of each module in the improved ConvNeXt model and several popular CNN models, including ConvNeXt, ResNet-50, VGG, and ShuffleNet V2, on the SEU gear fault dataset. The experimental results are the average of the training and test sets under two different conditions. The performance of different models is shown Table 1.

**Table 1.** Fault identification accuracy of different models

| Model | Training set average accuracy rate (%) | Test set average accuracy rate (%) |
|---|---|---|
| ConvNeXt | 99.8 | 98.6 |
| RestNet-50 | 99.7 | 98.4 |
| VGG | 98.8 | 97.8 |
| ShuffleNet V2 | 98.9 | 97.5 |
| ConvNeXt+ContMIX | 98.4 | 98.0 |
| ConvNeXt+CBAM | 99.9 | 99.1 |
| ConvNeXt+BAG | 99.7 | 98.3 |
| CCB-ConvNeXt | 100 | 99.9 |

As shown in Table 1, the model proposed in this study demonstrates obvious performance advantages in fault diagnosis tasks. Compared with existing mainstream convolutional neural networks (such as ConvNeXt, ResNet-50, VGG, and ShuffleNet V2), the model proposed in this paper achieves the highest average classification accuracy on both the training set and the test set, reaching 100% and 99.9%, respectively, almost achieving full-precision identification of fault samples. The test results under two typical operating conditions are also outstanding. Compared to the current mainstream high-performance convolutional architectures ConvNeXt and ResNet-50, the test accuracy has improved by 1.3% and 1.5%, respectively. This indicates that the structure proposed in this paper is more targeted and effective for current fault diagnosis tasks, especially when dealing with minor differences in fault images, where the proposed method can more accurately distinguish between different fault types.

## 6 Conclusion

To address the high complexity of non-stationary signals and the difficulty in feature extraction in gearbox fault diagnosis, this paper proposes a novel diagnostic method that combines Gram Angular Difference Field (GASF) and Gram Angular Sum Field (GASF) images and uses a CCB-ConvNeXt convolutional neural network for diagnosis. This method helps enhance the model's ability to perceive weak fault modes and extract features from complex signals. The proposed method was experimentally verified on a gearbox fault dataset from Southeast University, and its advantages in diagnostic accuracy and other aspects were compared. The proposed image fusion mechanism and multi-scale attention-enhanced network design have significant advantages in fault feature modeling and identification, providing a more robust and efficient solution to the problem of fault identification under non-stationary and complex background conditions.

**Acknowledgments.** We would like to thank the anonymous reviewers for their valuable comments and suggestions to improve this paper. This work is supported by the Hubei Province's Central Leading Local Science and Technology Development Special Project [grant number 2023EGA005].

## References

1. Wu, Z., et al.: Intelligent fault diagnosis method for gearboxes based on deep transfer learning. Process. **11**(1), 68 (2022)
2. Fu, Y., Chen, X., Liu, Y., et al.: Gearbox fault diagnosis based on multi-sensor and multi-channel decision-level fusion based on SDP. Appl. Sci. **12**(15), 7535 (2022)
3. Yao, D., Liu, H., Yang, J., et al.: A lightweight neural network with strong robustness for bearing fault diagnosis. Measurement. **159**, 107756 (2020)
4. Senanayaka, J.S.L., Van Khang, H., Robbersmyr, K.G.: Multiple classifiers and data fusion for robust diagnosis of gearbox mixed faults. IEEE Trans. Ind. Inform. **15**(8), 4569–4579 (2018)
5. X, P.A.N.G., Y, T.O.N.G., Z., W.E.I.: A fault diagnosis method for planetary gearbox based on GAF-CNN. Trans. Beijing inst. Technol. **40**(11), 1161–1167 (2020)
6. Ying-Kui, G.U., Chang-Wu, S.H.I., Jia-Fang, C.: Fault diagnosis of planetary gear box based on Gramian angular Fieldsand deep convolutional generative adversarial network. Noise Vib. Control. **44**(1), 111 (2024)
7. Tong, A., Zhang, J., Xie, L.: Intelligent fault diagnosis of rolling bearing based on Gramian angular difference field and improved dual attention residual network. Sensors. **24**(7), 2156 (2024)
8. Liu, Z., Mao, H., Wu, C.Y., et al.: A convnet for the 2020s. In: Proceedings of the IEEE/CVF Conference on Computer Vision and Pattern Recognition, pp. 11976–11986 (2022)
9. Lou, M., Yu, Y.: OverLoCK: an overview-first-look-closely-next ConvNet with context-mixing dynamic kernels. In: Proceedings of the Computer Vision and Pattern Recognition Conference, pp. 128–138 (2025)
10. Woo, S., Park, J., Lee, J.Y., et al.: Cbam: convolutional block attention module. In: Proceedings of the European Conference on Computer Vision (ECCV), pp. 3–19 (2018)

11. Wang, J., Jiang, W., Ma, L., et al.: Bidirectional attentive fusion with context gating for dense video captioning. In: Proceedings of the IEEE Conference on Computer Vision and Pattern Recognition, pp. 7190–7198 (2018)
12. Wu, Q., Ma, X., Liu, H., et al.: A classification method for soybean leaf diseases based on an improved ConvNeXt model. Sci. Rep. **13**(1), 19141 (2023)
13. Shao, S., McAleer, S., Yan, R., et al.: Highly accurate machine fault diagnosis using deep transfer learning. IEEE Trans. Ind. Inform. **15**(4), 2446–2455 (2018)

# Research on Fault Diagnosis Technology of Bidirectional LLC Resonant Converter Based on CSA-DBN

Jianyu Liu[1(✉)], Chengzhao Shan[1], Zhuoming Li[1], Shuai Yuan[2], Xiaoying Zhang[2], and Yi Lou[3]

[1] School of Electronics and Information Engineering, Harbin Institute of Technology (HIT), Harbin, China
921547765@qq.com, {czshan,zhuoming}@hit.edu.cn
[2] China Academy of Space Technology, Beijing, China
[3] School of Information Science and Engineering, Harbin Institute of Technology (Weihai), Weihai, China

**Abstract.** Aiming at the bidirectional LLC resonant converter topology, and combining the advantages of the Deep Belief Network (DBN) in feature self-learning, this study proposes a structural fault diagnosis scheme based on the Crow Search Algorithm (CSA) optimized DBN. The scheme first undergoes hierarchical unsupervised pre-training, and then optimizes the network structure and parameters using CSA. The final experimental results demonstrate that compared with traditional machine learning fault diagnosis methods, the improved model with crow search algorithm significantly enhances the generalization ability and powerful representation ability of DBN for complex data by adaptively adjusting the number of hidden layer nodes and learning rate, thereby improving the learning and classification performance of the network and significantly improving the accuracy of fault diagnosis.

**Keywords:** Fault diagnosis · Machine learning · Deep belief networks · Crow search algorithm · Bidirectional LLC resonant converter

## 1 Introduction

In power systems, the power control loop plays a pivotal role. The Battery Charge and Discharge Governor module (BCDR), which manages the storage of bus energy in the battery or the release of battery energy to the bus, is a crucial component of this loop. However, research on fault diagnosis techniques specifically for BCDR is relatively scarce. Addressing issues like high switching losses in the power converter of BCDR, this article introduces a bidirectional LLC resonant converter as the main power topology for BCDR.

Currently, as a deep learning technique, the Deep Belief Network [1–3] stands out as a prevalent data-driven approach for fault diagnosis, can ingest raw signals directly and produce diagnosis results immediately, exhibiting superior data


Y. Liu et al. (Eds.): ChinaCom 2025, LNICST 711, pp. 568–577, 2027.
https://doi.org/10.1007/978-3-032-33662-0_41

analysis and processing capabilities for enhanced recognition. DBN is a multi-layer neural network adept at training high-dimensional data, learning and recognizing input data features through the training of multiple layers of Restricted Boltzmann Machines (RBMs). In fault diagnosis [4], DBN-based methods have demonstrated effectiveness in various domains, including analog circuits [5], mechanical bearings [6], and wind turbines [7]. However, research indicates that the performance of DBN-based fault diagnosis is heavily contingent on the initial model parameter settings, which often rely on experience and multiple trials to achieve the desired outcome, an inefficient process. To tackle this, scholars have employed intelligent optimization algorithms to optimize DBN's fault diagnosis model parameters, thereby enhancing DBN's diagnostic performance and accuracy.

The Crow Search Algorithm [8], an intelligent optimization algorithm emulating the food caching and theft behaviors of crows, has emerged in recent years. It is lauded for its straightforward computational process and remarkable optimization capabilities. Within the realm of DBN parameter optimization, CSA has garnered significant scholarly interest. Notably, Sun Q introduced a CSA-DBN-based approach for fault diagnosis in DC power transformers [9]. These applications have achieved improved results to varying degrees. Therefore, facing the issues with DBN and capitalizing on deep learning's prowess in pattern recognition and feature extraction, this article explores an enhanced fault diagnosis methodology for bidirectional LLC resonant converters, employing an improved DBN optimized by the CSA.

## 2 Fault Diagnosis Method Utilizing Deep Belief Network

The Deep Belief Network, introduced by Geoffrey Hinton in 2006 [10], has become a prominent deep learning technique with broad applications in diverse domains, including the condition assessment of power equipment and the fault diagnosis and health monitoring of power converters. The Restricted Boltzmann Machine (RBM) serves as the core component of a DBN, with a DBN being essentially an assembly of multiple RBMs layered on top of each other.

### 2.1 The Deep Belief Network

As depicted in Fig. 1, the RBM adopts a bipartite topology comprising visible units $\boldsymbol{v}$ and hidden units $\boldsymbol{h}$. This architecture enforces conditional independence through the absence of intralayer connections, while maintaining full undirected connectivity via symmetric weight matrix $\boldsymbol{w}$ between layers.

Operating under the energy-based modeling framework, RBMs characterize binary neural activation patterns where each neuron assumes a discrete state $s \in \{0, 1\}$ representing inactive and active firing modes, respectively. The system configuration energy is formulated as:

$$\begin{aligned} E(\boldsymbol{v}, \boldsymbol{h}; \boldsymbol{\theta}) &= -\boldsymbol{a}^T \boldsymbol{v} - \boldsymbol{b}^T \boldsymbol{h} - \boldsymbol{v}^T \boldsymbol{w} \boldsymbol{h} \\ &= -\sum_{i=1}^{n} a_i v_i - \sum_{j=1}^{m} b_j h_j - \sum_{i=1}^{n} \sum_{j=1}^{m} w_{ij} v_i h_j, \end{aligned} \tag{1}$$

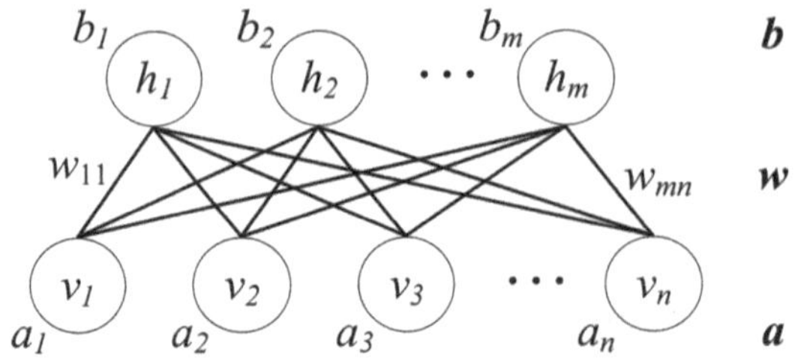


**Fig. 1.** Schematic diagram of RBM structure.

here, the model parameters $\boldsymbol{\theta} = \{\boldsymbol{w}, \boldsymbol{a}, \boldsymbol{b}\}$ comprise interlayer weights $w_{ij}$ connecting visible unit $v_i$ to hidden unit $h_j$, alongside bias terms $\boldsymbol{a}$ and $\boldsymbol{b}$ modulating activation propensities for the respective layers.

The DBN architecture emerges from hierarchical composition of RBMs, establishing a deep generative framework. Its parameter estimation follows a dual-phase paradigm: bottom-up greedy layer-wise pretraining succeeded by top-down global discriminative fine-tuning.

### 2.2 The Crow Search Algorithm

Coates et al. conducted experimental studies and analysis, highlighting that the selection of the number of neurons in the hidden layers is more critical than the model's depth in deep neural network models [11]. Consequently, this article proposes employing CSA to optimize and determine the optimal number of hidden layer nodes, thereby enhancing the fault diagnosis rate.

CSA introduced by Askarzadeh in 2016 [12], is a metaheuristic optimization algorithm. Crows are regarded as among the most intelligent avian species, and the algorithm emulates specific behavioral traits of crows: (1) Crows live in social groups, (2) Crows can recall the places where they have cached food, (3) Crows engage in following each other to pilfer food, (4) Crows have a certain probability of safeguarding their stored food from theft. Consequently, it is posited that in a d-dimensional space, there are numerous crows, with the population size denoted as $N_p$. The position of crow i in the search space at iteration It is $x^{i,It}$, where $(i = 1, 2, \cdots, N_p; It = 1, 2, \cdots, It_{\max})$, and $x^{i,It} = [x_1^{i,It}, x_2^{i,It}, \cdots, x^{i,It}d]$, with $It\max$ being the maximum number of iterations. At iteration $It$, crow $i$'s memory of the hidden food location is $m^{i,It}$, which is the best position that crow $i$ has found so far. Suppose crow $j$ wants to find its hidden location at iteration $It$. At this time, crow $i$ decides to follow crow $j$ to reach crow $j$'s hidden location. In this scenario, two situations may occur: (1) Crow $j$ i is oblivious to crow $i$'s pursuit, leading to crow $i$ arriving at crow $j$'s hidden location and obtaining a new position $x^{i,It}$. (2) Crow $j$ is aware of crow $i$'s pursuit and, to prevent its cached food from being stolen, flies to an alternative search location to mislead crow $i$. From these two scenarios, we can deduce:

$$x^{k+1} = \begin{cases} x^k + r_i \times fl^k \times (m^k - x^k) & r_j \geq AP^k \\ a\ random\ position & otherwise \end{cases}, \tag{2}$$

where $k = (i, It)$, $r_j$ is a uniformly distributed random number between $0 - 1$, and $AP^k$ represents the self-awareness probability of crow $j$ at iteration $It$. The convergence and diversity of the CSA algorithm are primarily adjusted by the parameter $AP$. When $AP$ has a smaller value, the CSA may converge to a local area search; when $AP$ has a larger value, it can increase the diversity of solutions.

## 3 Fault Data Extraction

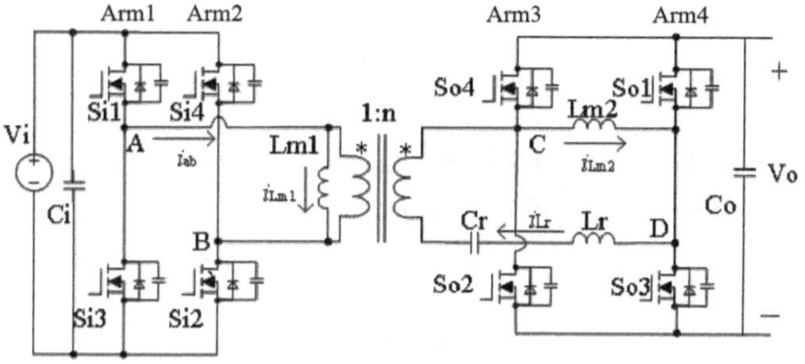


**Fig. 2.** Topology of bidirectional full bridge LLC resonant converter.

To achieve non-invasive fault diagnosis of power converters, facilitating signal acquisition in practical engineering, the input conditions of the model should be a collection of voltage matrices composed of key point input and output voltages in the power converter. Therefore, we choose voltage as the type of parameter for fault characteristic extraction. Taking Fig. 2 as an example, for convenience of marking, the selected voltage signals are named as: $U_i$, $U_a$, $U_b$, $U_c$, $U_d$, $U_e$, and $U_o$.

The corresponding collection locations are shown in Table 1.

**Table 1.** Key fault feature extraction points for circuits

| Name | Corresponding collection location |
|---|---|
| $U_i$ | Input voltage |
| $U_a$ | A to ground voltage |
| $U_b$ | Voltage between A and B($L_{m1}$) |
| $U_c$ | Output voltage of transformer's secondary |
| $U_d$ | Voltage across capacitor $C_r$ |
| $U_e$ | Voltage between C and D($L_{m2}$) |
| $U_o$ | Output voltage |

In summary, this article has obtained structural fault data of the MOS transistor through fault injection experiments based on simulation models, as shown in Table 2. The data was collected under operating conditions of the simulation model with an input voltage of $80V$-$100V$ and an output power of $2kW$. Except for the MOS transistor faults, all other components were functioning normally. Ultimately, 11 sets of fault data were acquired.

**Table 2.** Structural Fault Mode of Bidirectional Full Bridge LLC Resonant Converter

| Fault Number | Fault Mode |
|---|---|
| SF1 | L2 Open Circuit |
| SF2 | L2 Short Circuit |
| SF3 | Lr Open Circuit |
| SF4 | Lr Short Circuit |
| SF5 | Q1-d Open Circuit |
| SF6 | Q1-gd Short Circuit |
| SF7 | Q1-gs Short Circuit |
| SF8 | Resonant Capacitor Open Circuit |
| SF9 | Resonant Capacitor Short Circuit |
| SF10 | Input Capacitor Open Circuit |
| SF11 | Output Capacitor Open Circuit |

## 4 Algorithm Design of CSA-DBN

As shown in Fig. 3, the DBN we designed employs a three-layer RBM network structure, and in the last layer, a nonlinear classifier, the softmax function, is used in a BP neural network for classifying different fault patterns. Let the number of hidden layer nodes in the first and second layers be $n_{h1}$ and $n_{h2}$, respectively. The goal of optimizing the DBN network structure with CSA is to obtain the optimal number of hidden layer nodes $n_{h1}$, $n_{h2}$, and the learning rate $r$ to maximize the fault diagnosis accuracy. If the fault diagnosis accuracy rate is denoted as $Acc = f(n_{h1}, n_{h2})$, and since the maximum value of the diagnosis rate is 100%, this article considers $g(n_{h1}, n_{h2}) = 1 - Acc$ as the fitness function for the CSA optimization algorithm, which is a minimization problem.

The procedure for fault diagnosis of a bidirectional full-bridge LLC resonant converter using the CSA-DBN is depicted in Fig. 4 and includes the following steps:

(1) Collect voltage signals from the test points of the bidirectional full-bridge LLC resonant converter circuit;

(2) Employ the method of mean decrease impurity (typically Gini impurity or information gain) in the random forest to perform an importance analysis on all features, and then select the four features with the highest importance.

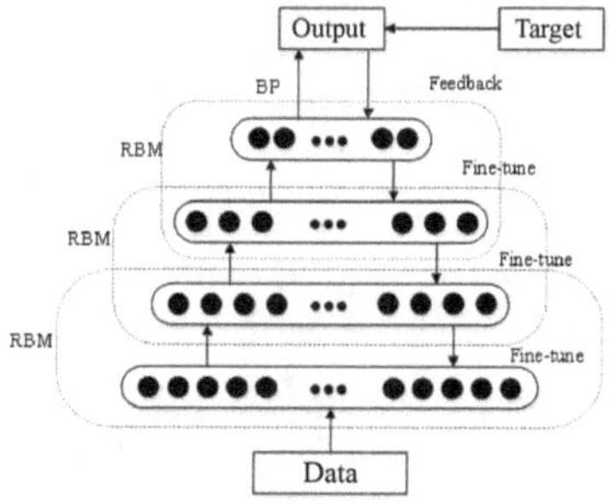


**Fig. 3.** DBN algorithm structure.

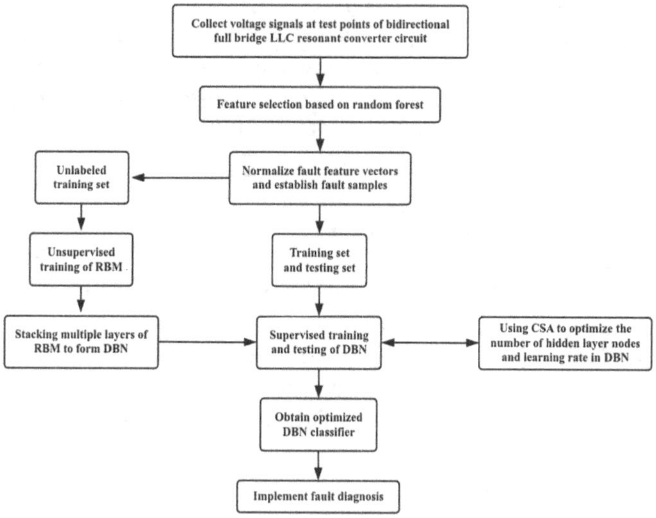


**Fig. 4.** The basic process of fault diagnosis for bidirectional full bridge LLC resonant converter based on CSA-DBN.

(3) Use wavelet packet decomposition to extract fault features from the voltage signals, that is, perform wavelet packet decomposition on the voltage signals, calculate the wavelet packet energy spectrum, construct fault feature vectors, and normalize them to obtain data samples for each fault mode. At the same time, set corresponding labels for each sample based on the fault type it corresponds to, resulting in a set of labeled data;

(4) Divide the fault samples into a training set, a test set, and a set of data with removed labels;

(5) Initialize the RBM training function and use the unlabeled training set to conduct unsupervised training of the RBM. Since our training samples are independently distributed, the maximum likelihood function for training the RBM can be formulated as:

$$L(\boldsymbol{\theta}) = \prod_{n=1}^{N} L(\boldsymbol{v}|\boldsymbol{\theta}) = \prod_{n=1}^{N} p(\boldsymbol{v}) \tag{3}$$

To obtain the optimal model parameters $\boldsymbol{\theta}$, the stochastic gradient descent method is commonly used.

(6) Stack multiple RBMs to form a DBN network and initialize the basic parameters of the DBN network (number of network layers, network training iterations, learning rate, type of activation function, etc.). The aforementioned training steps constitute the first phase of DBN network training, which is an unsupervised greedy layer-wise training process.

(7) After the pre-training of the DBN network is completed, use data with labeled information to perform supervised fine-tuning of the entire DBN network through backpropagation. This process involves adjusting the network parameters from the last layer to the previous layer, using known label information, until the set maximum number of iterations is reached. The global fine-tuning process of the DBN involves all layers of the network, adjusting network parameters from top to bottom to reduce the error between network output and actual labels, thereby improving classification accuracy and further optimizing the training results of the DBN network model.

(8) Input the results of the supervised training and testing of the DBN network model into the CSA algorithm for optimization and solution.

(9) Initialization. Define the objective function to be optimized, decision variables, constraints, etc. Set the parameters of the CSA algorithm, such as population size $N_p$, maximum number of iterations Itmax, flight length $fl$, and self-awareness probability AP.

(10) Initialize the positions and memories of the crows. Within the d-dimensional search space, randomly define the positions of $N_p$ crows, where each crow represents a feasible solution to the problem to be solved, and d represents the number of decision variables.

$$Crows = \begin{bmatrix} x_1^1 & x_2^1 & \dots & x_d^1 \\ x_1^2 & x_2^2 & \dots & x_d^2 \\ \vdots & \vdots & \vdots & \vdots \\ x_1^N & x_2^N & \dots & x_d^N \end{bmatrix} \tag{4}$$

Initialize the memory for each crow. Since the crows have no experience at the initial iteration, it is assumed that they have hidden their food at their initial positions.

$$Memory = \begin{bmatrix} m_1^1 & m_2^1 & \dots & m_d^1 \\ m_1^2 & m_2^2 & \dots & m_d^2 \\ \vdots & \vdots & \vdots & \vdots \\ m_1^N & m_2^N & \dots & m_d^N \end{bmatrix} \tag{5}$$

(11) Evaluate the fitness function by substituting the decision variables into the objective function to calculate the values.

(12) Generate the latest positions of the crows in the search space according to equation (2) and determine the feasibility of each crow's new position. If the new position of a crow is feasible, update its position; otherwise, it remains in the current position. Additionally, calculate the fitness function value for each crow's new position.

(13) Update the memories of the crows. When the fitness function value of a crow's new position is better than the fitness function value of its memory position, the crow updates its memory with the new position.

$$x^{i,iter+1} = \begin{cases} x^{i,iter} & f(x^{i,iter}) \ is\ better\ than\ f(m^{i,iter}) \\ m^{i,iter} & otherwise \end{cases} \tag{6}$$

Where $f(\cdot)$ represents the objective function value.

(14) Check whether the termination condition is met. Repeat steps (9)–(13) until the maximum number of iterations Itmax is reached. When the termination condition is met, the best position obtained from the memory based on the objective function value is the optimal solution to the problem to be solved.

(15) Solve the fitness function using the CSA algorithm to obtain the optimal number of hidden layer nodes $n_{h1}$, $n_{h2}$, and the learning rate $r$ that maximize the fault diagnosis rate, and return them to the DBN network for re-optimization training, thus achieving the optimal parameter structure;

(16) Input the test samples into the optimized DBN network for testing, determine the fault type of each sample, and ultimately achieve accurate identification and localization of each fault mode.

## 5 Experimental Results and Analysis

We compared the test results of two feature combinations using the CSA-DBN. We trained and tested all three feature combinations without making any changes to the model except for the features used. From Table 3, we can see that when all seven features were loaded into the model, the test accuracy was 95.39%. When loading the feature set $[U_i, U_o, U_a, U_d]$, the model's test accuracy was 98.07%. When loading the feature set $[U_i, U_o, U_d, U_e]$, the model's test accuracy was 99.51%. All three selections met the hardware requirement of greater than 95% accuracy, but the feature set $[U_i, U_o, U_d, U_e]$ achieved an extremely high accuracy rate, which is what we desired, significantly reducing the occurrence of errors. This also proves that this feature selection is more suitable for the model we designed. Therefore, we will continue to use these four features in subsequent model comparisons.

In our comparison of the CSA-DBN with other fault diagnosis algorithms such as SVM, DBN, ADAM-DBN, and DBN with cyclical learning rate warm-up strategies, the results are as shown in Table 4. When dealing with relatively large and complex data volumes, the DBN model structure is better equipped

**Table 3.** Comparison of fault classification results of different feature combinations in CSA-DBN

| Data Feature | Test Accuracy(%) |
|---|---|
| All features | 95.39 |
| $U_i, U_o, U_a, U_d$ | 98.07 |
| $U_i, U_o, U_d, U_e$ | 99.51 |

to handle such situations compared to traditional machine learning methods like SVM. We employed three improvement strategies based on DBN, each with its advantages. For instance, the ADAM-DBN and DBN with cyclical learning rate warm-up strategies both utilize an optimization method to fine-tune a parameter. The ADAM optimizer can achieve model convergence in a relatively short time (98.45%), and the cyclical learning rate warm-up strategy can achieve a relatively higher accuracy rate (98.78%), although it is also the most time-consuming.

The CSA-DBN we used not only optimizes multiple parameters and improves model results but also, compared to the cyclical learning rate warm-up strategy, this model can achieve better test results in fewer iterations, reducing training time. Moreover, the optimal model parameters obtained through CSA can be directly applied to models without CSA in the later period, further reducing training time. This demonstrates the effectiveness of the CSA-DBN approach in optimizing the model for fault diagnosis tasks.

Currently, the proposed scheme can be fully implemented for training and testing on a personal computer. However, considering the constraints of deploying it on low-computing-power hardware platforms in the future, we have designed to transfer the trained weight files to hardware devices for application. Model training can be performed on a server, so that the scheme can be normally applied under the limitations of hardware platforms.

**Table 4.** Fault diagnosis results of different algorithms

| Model Name | Test Accuracy(%) |
|---|---|
| CSA-DBN | 99.51 |
| SVM | 88.68 |
| DBN | 90.38 |
| ADAM-DBN | 98.45 |
| CLRPS-DBN | 98.78 |

## 6 Conclusion

power converters, traditional machine learning diagnostic methods struggle to effectively identify and locate faults in such scenarios. Therefore, leveraging the superior pattern recognition capabilities of DBN, this article proposes a CSA-DBN-based fault diagnosis method for bidirectional LLC resonant converters. By optimizing the number of hidden layer nodes, the classification performance of the DBN network is enhanced for situations with a multitude of fault modes, thereby accurately discriminating fault types and improving the accuracy and detection capability of fault diagnosis. Simulation and experimental studies have verified that the fault diagnosis accuracy of the method proposed in this article can reach 99.51%, which is superior to traditional machine learning and conventional DBN optimization diagnostic methods.

Through the development of an intelligent fault diagnosis platform for power converters and tests, intelligent fault diagnosis technology for satellite power converters is realized, which is of great significance for improving the stability of power control loops.

## References


1. W.Y.: Exhaust gas temperature baseline model of aeroengine based on kernel principal component analysis and deep belief network. Aeroengine **46**(1), 54–60 (2020)
2. Jiang L.C., Wang H.J., Zhang S.L.: Flow excitation fault diagnosis model of gas turbine based on deep belief network. J. Electr. Measurem. Instrument.
3. Y.L.: A gas path fault diagnostic method of gas turbine based on deep belief network. J. Eng. Thermophys. **41**(4), 840–844 (2020)
4. ge Q.: Research on data-driven fault diagnosis method based on deep belief network. Harbin Institute of Technology (2016)
5. Zhang C.: Analog circuit fault diagnosis method using DBN based feature extraction. IEEE Access **1**(1) (2018)
6. Jiang L.: Bearing fault diagnosis based on deep belief network and information fusion technology. J. Wuhan Univ. Sci. Technol. **42**(1), 40-44 (2019)
7. L.M.: Fault diagnosis method for wind turbines based on deep belief network. Electr. Mach. Control **23**(2), 114–122 (2019)
8. ASKARZADEH A.: A novel metaheuristic method for solving constrained engineering optimization problems: Crow search algorithm. Comput. Struct. **169**, 1-12 (2016)
9. Sun Q.: A novel fault diagnostic approach for DC-DC converters based on CSA-DBN. IEEE Access **6**, 1-13 (2018)
10. Hinton, G.: A fast learning algorithm for deep belief nets. Neural Comput. **18**(7), 1527–1554 (2006)
11. Coates, A.: An analysis of single-layer networks in unsupervised feature learning. J. Mach. Learn. Res. **15**, 215–223 (2011)
12. Askarzadeh, A.: A novel metaheuristic method for solving constrained engineering optimization problems: crow search algorithm. Comput. Struct. **169**, 1–12 (2016)

# Identification of IoT Devices Based on Probability Adaptive Boosting

Jian Du[1], Linjia He[1(✉)], Ming Dai[1], Jie Luo[2], Tao Yang[2], Hongwei Xing[1], and Qingqing Chu[1]

[1] Transport Information Security Center Co., Ltd., Beijing 100011, China
qqyutou@126.com
[2] School of Information and Communication Engineering, Xi'an Jiaotong University, Xi'an, Shaanxi 710049, China

**Abstract.** With the rapid development of the Internet of Things (IoT), device identification has become a critical research direction for IoT security. Traditional two-stage device identification methods based on Internet fingerprints suffer from low identification accuracy, high model redundancy, and significant time complexity. To address these issues, this paper proposes a method for IoT device identification based on probability adaptive boosting, aimed at improving identification accuracy and reducing time complexity. This method constructs new fingerprint features by analyzing network protocol fields and traffic behavior patterns, employing the adaptive boosting algorithm to learn traffic behavior patterns, and incorporating traffic perturbations to enhance performance. Experimental results demonstrate that the proposed method significantly improves the accuracy and efficiency of device identification, holding practical application value and better meeting the device detection demands in the current network environment.

**Keywords:** Internet of Things · Device Identification · Scanning Techniques · Machine Learning

## 1 Introduction

With the widespread adoption of 5G technology and the rapid development of the Internet of Things (IoT), IoT devices are increasingly integrated into daily life and are widely used in various fields, including smart transportation, industrial automation, and healthcare [1–4]. In smart transportation systems, IoT technology significantly enhances urban traffic efficiency and convenience by enabling real-time monitoring of traffic flow, optimizing routes, and improving safety. However, the extensive use of IoT devices in transportation also poses security risks [5], as evidenced by the 2016 Mirai attack, which exposed the vulnerabilities of IoT devices to cyber threats. Device identification, as a crucial component of IoT security, effectively identifies and classifies devices, helping


Y. Liu et al. (Eds.): ChinaCom 2025, LNICST 711, pp. 578–597, 2027.
https://doi.org/10.1007/978-3-032-33662-0_42

administrators respond promptly to potential security threats. Therefore, IoT device identification has become an important research direction for large-scale device management and protection [6].

As IoT devices rapidly proliferate, ordinary households and urban transportation systems are expected to host over 50 IoT devices, including smart traffic lights, in-vehicle sensors, and traffic surveillance cameras. The heterogeneity of these devices due to varying hardware and operating systems presents challenges for device identification [7]. To ensure the security and stability of the IoT environment, device identification must not only address authentication and privacy protection but also mitigate risks associated with cyberattacks. Given the limited computational capabilities of IoT devices, relying on complex security solutions like traditional internet devices is often impractical, thereby imposing higher demands on the accuracy and efficiency of device identification [8].

Traditional IoT device identification relies on a two-stage approach based on active traffic [9]. In the first stage, devices are broadly classified into IoT devices and Internet devices, while the second stage further subdivides IoT devices into various product types, achieving a classification macro accuracy of over 90%. However, the challenge with this method lies in the significant impact that the accuracy of the second stage has on the first stage, which severely affects the performance of the second stage. Vishwakarma et al. proposed a machine learning-based honeypot detection framework [10], which identifies device types to mitigate DDoS attacks from IoT botnets. In [11], a normative approach for wireless sensor networks is introduced, with expecting network operators to define rules. However, this approach is impractical as it increases the operators' workload, especially as the variety of device types grows. In [12], the authors propose using machine learning for intrusion detection systems (IDS) in mobile ad hoc networks, aiming to maximize the accuracy of device type detection. Currently, the accuracy and effectiveness of IoT device identification remain low [13]. Therefore, establishing a suitable fingerprint model for IoT device identification and addressing the challenges of accurately identifying IoT devices, while further integrating traffic behavior models to improve identification accuracy, are pressing issues to resolve.

IoT traffic, as a significant component of network traffic, possesses distinctive fingerprint characteristics [14]. To address the issue of low identification accuracy, this paper employs passive detection to reduce network congestion caused by additional traffic, redesigning the fingerprint features of IoT devices. We propose a method for IoT device identification based on probability adaptive boosting as a substitute for the underperforming two-stage identification algorithm, thereby enhancing overall identification performance and accuracy. By constructing an environment and collecting traffic, we integrate the dimensional features of IoT with network protocols to build a new fingerprint model, which is experimentally validated in a real-world environment using metrics such as macro recall, macro precision, and macro F1-score to evaluate model performance. Compared to other algorithms and traditional methods, the Real AdaBoost method employed in this paper demonstrates higher classification accuracy and superior model performance in identifying traffic IoT devices.

## 2 IoT Device Identification Method Based on Probabilistic Adaptive Boosting

In response to the challenges posed by existing methodologies, this paper aims to address the identified shortcomings. For traffic collection, we propose a passive collection approach through gateway monitoring, capturing the traffic of devices passing through the gateway. This ensures the normal operation of IoT devices while collecting authentic interaction data among devices. By drawing on the characteristic dimensions used in traditional Internet device identification and integrating the unique attributes of IoT devices, we introduce new feature dimensions that are more suitable for the classification of IoT devices. This paper compares the Real AdaBoost algorithm from probabilistic adaptive algorithms with the original AdaBoost algorithm, demonstrating that the proposed method achieves optimal performance in terms of accuracy.

The proposed method is divided into three parts: As illustrated in Fig. 1, the first part, the passive traffic collection and preprocessing phase, involves the passive collection of traffic to generate a raw dataset, providing the necessary data for subsequent algorithm model training and preprocessing to obtain numerical data. The second part, the feature analysis phase, involves deriving new feature dimensions based on the protocol fields in the transport layer, network layer, and application layer from the data obtained in the previous step. The third part entails classification based on the traffic fingerprint model, categorizing devices into their correct product categories to complete the classification process.

### 2.1 Passive Traffic Collection and Preprocessing

Conducting experiments on IoT devices necessitates the establishment of an intelligent environment, where devices are selected based on specific requirements. This paper utilizes the company's intelligent environment for experimentation, optimizing data collection methods according to actual conditions.

**Traffic Collection.** The devices employed in this paper consist of a range of demonstration equipment, encompassing over 10,000 devices, including smart cameras, lights, plugs, motion sensors, and health monitors, thereby providing instruments for the intelligent environment. To ensure accuracy and effectiveness in identification, devices from the same manufacturer, similar devices from different manufacturers, IoT devices from various application scenarios, and some internet devices such as Android smartphones, Windows PCs, and Mac computers were selected.

As illustrated in Fig. 2, a schematic representation of the company's experimental environment shows that IoT and internet devices are connected to the

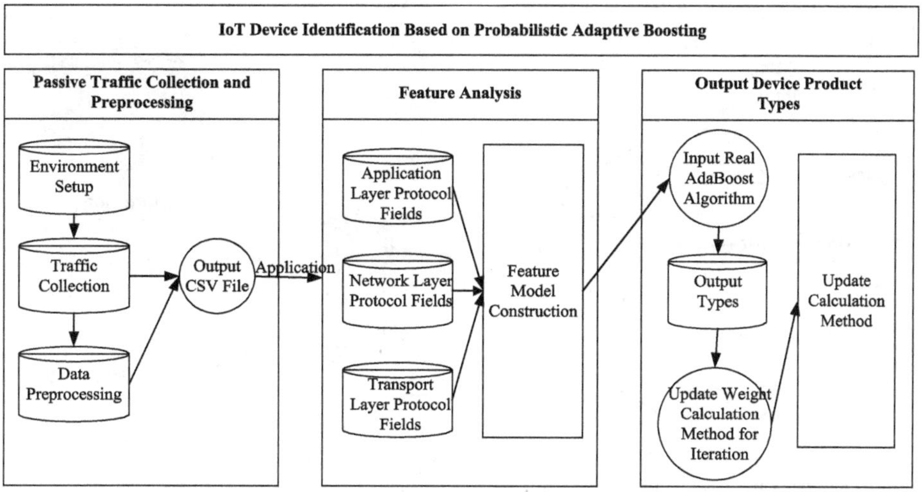


**Fig. 1.** Device Identification Flowchart.

current network node via both wired and wireless methods. Traffic from the current network node is collected using third-party devices. During traffic collection, packet sniffing techniques are employed to observe and gather network traffic without requiring communication with the target devices. This non-intrusive approach ensures that no artificial traffic is introduced into the network, thereby preserving the integrity of device identification results [15].

During traffic collection, data packets flowing through the gateway device in the intelligent environment were monitored, capturing daily traffic and using the resulting dataset from three days for model training and validation. The devices employed for data collection had the MAC address spoofing prevention feature enabled to mitigate the risk of network attacks that could spoof the MAC addresses of target devices, thereby capturing noise traffic packets.

During the traffic capture process, it was observed that the captured packets contained hostname information, which could potentially facilitate device identification. However, hostname information was filtered out due to the limited number of devices designed with specific hostnames and the subjective nature of hostname configuration, which allows for arbitrary changes. Therefore, device identification should not be influenced by variable factors.

Figure 3 illustrates the data traffic collection process, where Wireshark was utilized to analyze the captured traffic. Fields were compared and filtered, categorizing similar types of devices to select features with greater discriminative power. The data was arranged according to collection time, with the order of packets based on timestamps. It is important to note that these timestamps do not represent the actual time of packet generation and transmission, but rather relative time; thus, the packet transmission time has negligible relevance to device identification and was consequently excluded from analysis.

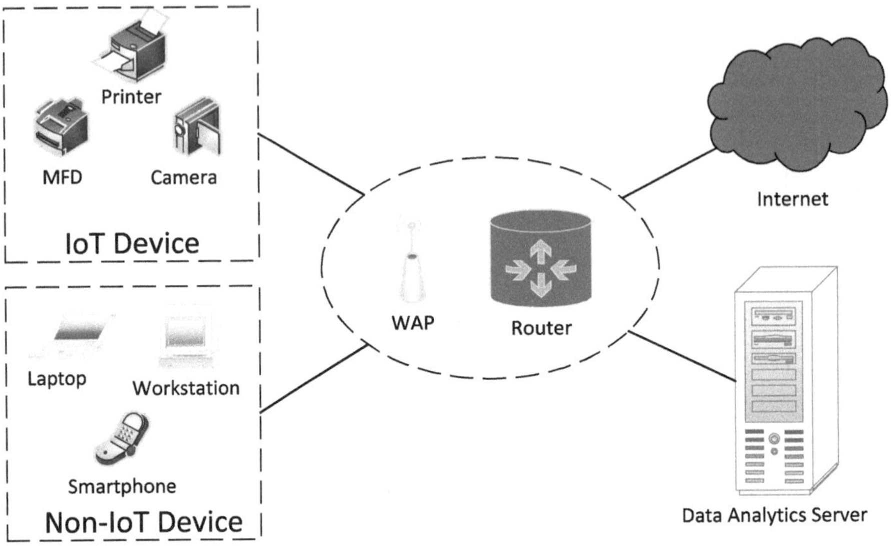


**Fig. 2.** Experimental Scenario Diagram.

From the figure, basic information can be discerned, including the originating device of the packets, the receiving and forwarding device, the final destination host, the type of network protocol used, the size of the packets, and the remaining time-to-live (TTL) of the packets. By subtracting the remaining TTL from the original value, the number of hops traversed by the packets in the network can be determined. Each field can be displayed in the Wireshark interface for further analysis.

In the original traffic packets, hostname information was deemed insecure and thus not suitable for labeling. During the parsing of traffic packets, the MAC address was used to identify which device generated a given traffic flow. A data dictionary containing MAC addresses and device types was referenced to label each traffic instance according to the current device type, which would be used for subsequent experimental datasets. The evaluation metrics were computed based on the classification results of the current test set traffic.

**Data Preprocessing.** In the data preprocessing stage, common attribute values and extraneous features, such as timestamps, were excluded, along with other captured information like sequence (seq) and acknowledgment (ack) numbers at each layer. These fields could not serve as features due to their random configuration based on the current device's sequence number queue, which lacked effective information for device identification. Unique behavioral patterns and flow-based features were extracted from the packet headers and payloads of IP, TCP, and UDP protocols, eliminating redundant traffic. A single extracted fingerprint was used to identify a device, establishing a one-to-many relationship

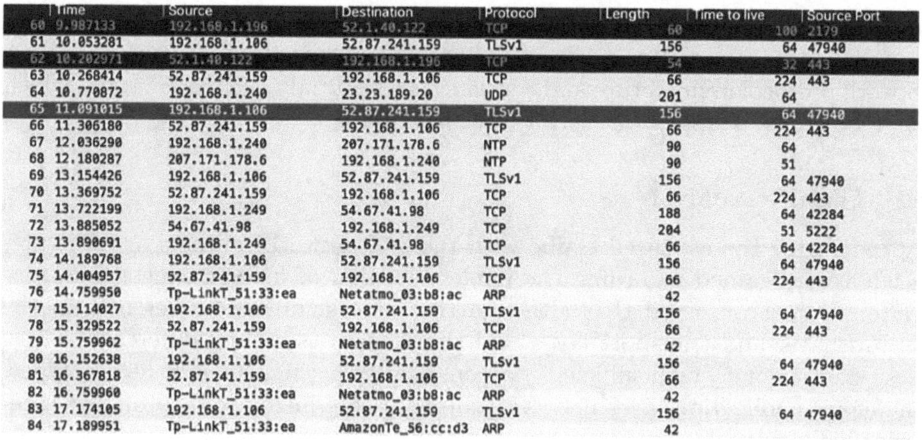

| | Time | Source | Destination | Protocol | Length | Time to live | Source Port |
|---|---|---|---|---|---|---|---|
| 60 | 9.987133 | 192.168.1.196 | 52.1.40.122 | TCP | 60 | 100 | 2179 |
| 61 | 10.053281 | 192.168.1.106 | 52.87.241.159 | TLSv1 | 156 | 64 | 47940 |
| 62 | 10.202971 | 52.1.40.122 | 192.168.1.196 | TCP | 54 | 32 | 443 |
| 63 | 10.268414 | 52.87.241.159 | 192.168.1.106 | TCP | 66 | 224 | 443 |
| 64 | 10.770872 | 192.168.1.240 | 23.23.189.20 | UDP | 201 | 64 | |
| 65 | 11.091015 | 192.168.1.106 | 52.87.241.159 | TLSv1 | 156 | 64 | 47940 |
| 66 | 11.306180 | 52.87.241.159 | 192.168.1.106 | TCP | 66 | 224 | 443 |
| 67 | 12.036290 | 192.168.1.240 | 207.171.178.6 | NTP | 90 | 64 | |
| 68 | 12.180287 | 207.171.178.6 | 192.168.1.240 | NTP | 90 | 51 | |
| 69 | 13.154426 | 192.168.1.106 | 52.87.241.159 | TLSv1 | 156 | 64 | 47940 |
| 70 | 13.369752 | 52.87.241.159 | 192.168.1.106 | TCP | 66 | 224 | 443 |
| 71 | 13.722199 | 192.168.1.249 | 54.67.41.98 | TCP | 188 | 64 | 42284 |
| 72 | 13.885052 | 54.67.41.98 | 192.168.1.249 | TCP | 204 | 51 | 5222 |
| 73 | 13.890691 | 192.168.1.249 | 54.67.41.98 | TCP | 66 | 64 | 42284 |
| 74 | 14.189768 | 192.168.1.106 | 52.87.241.159 | TLSv1 | 156 | 64 | 47940 |
| 75 | 14.404957 | 52.87.241.159 | 192.168.1.106 | TCP | 66 | 224 | 443 |
| 76 | 14.759950 | Tp-LinkT_51:33:ea | Netatmo_03:b8:ac | ARP | 42 | | |
| 77 | 15.114027 | 192.168.1.106 | 52.87.241.159 | TLSv1 | 156 | 64 | 47940 |
| 78 | 15.329522 | 52.87.241.159 | 192.168.1.106 | TCP | 66 | 224 | 443 |
| 79 | 15.759962 | Tp-LinkT_51:33:ea | Netatmo_03:b8:ac | ARP | 42 | | |
| 80 | 16.152638 | 192.168.1.106 | 52.87.241.159 | TLSv1 | 156 | 64 | 47940 |
| 81 | 16.367818 | 52.87.241.159 | 192.168.1.106 | TCP | 66 | 224 | 443 |
| 82 | 16.759960 | Tp-LinkT_51:33:ea | Netatmo_03:b8:ac | ARP | 42 | | |
| 83 | 17.174105 | 192.168.1.106 | 52.87.241.159 | TLSv1 | 156 | 64 | 47940 |
| 84 | 17.189951 | Tp-LinkT_51:33:ea | AmazonTe_56:cc:d3 | ARP | 42 | | |

**Fig. 3.** Data Traffic Collection Diagram.

between devices and traffic, as IP addresses may change while MAC addresses serve as identifying information.

During data preprocessing, scripts were developed to extract fields from the transport layer, network layer, and application layer of network protocols. For any missing attributes or protocols, numerical zero was used to fill in the gaps. Binary features were employed to identify protocol information in the traffic; if a specific protocol was present in the device's traffic packet header, the feature value was set to 1; otherwise, it was 0. These binary features represented the types of protocols utilized by IoT devices, encompassing common network protocols used in the network and application layers, suitable for the current intelligent environment.

In the payload of the network protocol headers, the valid data offset was extracted, which primarily provides initial information to the upper network layers. Normalization was applied based on the maximum and minimum values of the valid offsets to quantify the data offsets. The valid data offset indicates the degree of offset when the device processes the traffic packets, which is often closely related to the device's computational capacity and performance. Different types of devices may configure valid offsets differently; thus, valid offsets were also considered as a feature dimension in internet device identification.

When processing PCAP packets, the traffic packets were displayed as arrays. The *haslayer*() function was used to determine the presence of specific protocols. Upon detection, the relevant protocol fields were accessed, and fields of character type were quantified into numerical form, with normalization applied based on the size of the value space as needed. Different versions of protocols were handled by distinguishing necessary feature dimensions. Some captured traffic packets lacked any valid features, often comprising only one or two protocol layers used for addressing or liveliness checks, and such packets were discarded. Only packets with significant features were retained, as normal traffic packets are typically used for data transmission or for sending information requests to target devices for collaborative operations. These packets generally adhered to the four-layer network protocol architecture and contained substantial valid information, which was retained as a single fingerprint after processing.

## 2.2 Feature Analysis

By comparing the captured traffic with the IoT network protocol architecture, insights were gained regarding the implementation of fields during traffic generation. It was observed that although there are significant differences in the network layer and transport layer field characteristics among different devices, these fields alone are insufficient to completely distinguish IoT device types. Therefore, application layer network protocols were introduced to further categorize IoT devices.

Different device types exhibit variations in the implementation of transport layer, network layer, and application layer protocols. Analysis will proceed based on the distinctions across these three protocol layers. Initially, a comprehensive analysis of the dataset revealed that IoT devices predominantly utilize TCP/UDP/IP protocols at the transport and network layers, with field selection from these protocols serving as a primary direction for feature selection.

Analyzing from the perspective of different layer protocols, variations in the fields used within IP packets can be attributed to version differences. Devices design their implementation of the IP protocol and field settings according to their specific requirements. The IP protocol is divided into multiple versions, each with different architectural designs, which warrants further analysis based on these differences. Most transport layer protocols employ UDP/TCP, with variations in the fields carried. To ensure reliable data transmission, additional fields are often incorporated into the network layer protocols for security, such as adding the TLS protocol to enhance transmission safety, tailored to the needs of the devices. Common application layer protocols include HTTP; however, IoT devices, due to performance constraints, often implement various lightweight application layer protocols tailored to their requirements, which serve as distinguishing features.

TCP/IP is the most common and frequently used network transport protocol, and analyzing the fields of TCP/IP protocol traffic packets is critical. Both the IP and TCP protocols contain optional extension fields, which are crucial for ensuring TCP functionality, describing the current device's processing capabilities and network conditions.

Most of the collected data includes these extension fields, which exhibit variability in their attributes. By analyzing the scaling factor field and segmentation attributes, insights into the processing capability of the device regarding data packets can be derived. The default values for scaling factors and segmentation attributes are set based on device requirements.

The Maximum Segment Size (MSS) attribute in the packet header ensures the TCP protocol's integrity by checking for anomalous packets during data reception, filtering out oversized packets; the MSS field can enhance device security.

MSS values are typically set according to varying requirements from different manufacturers. The field values in both internet and IoT contexts are generally initialized based on the computational capabilities of the devices, resulting in different initial values across IoT devices. Internet devices, with superior computational capabilities, often have larger MSS values, effectively differentiating between IoT and internet devices.

Given the diversity of field types, feature selection and elimination are conducted based on the variation of information entropy values across fields. Scatter plots were created using the values of certain fields categorized by device types, vividly illustrating the relationship between device types and current features, thereby providing compelling evidence for feature selection. A total of 31 device types were selected for display. Figure 4 (a) presents a scatter plot of device types against traffic packet sizes from the dataset. The plot demonstrates the variability in packet sizes generated by different device types, with the Length field representing the size of traffic packets constructed under the TCP/IP protocol. Notable differences in packet sizes can be observed across device types, reflecting their specific requirements; for instance, a baby monitor may generate 0.7MB of traffic daily, while a single photograph from a smart camera can yield up to 10MB. Consequently, the Length field can serve as a valuable selection criterion.

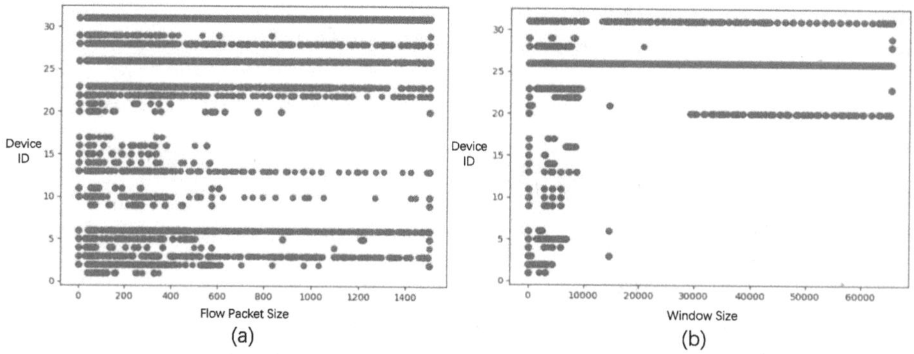


**Fig. 4.** (a) Scatter Plot of Device Types and Packet Size Distribution. (b) The distribution scatter plot of device types and window sizes.

Figure 4 (b) shows the distribution scatter plot of device types and window sizes. It can be observed from the figure that the window sizes vary among different device types. The window size is determined based on the conditions under which traffic packets are transmitted. Since the sizes of the traffic packets generated by different device types differ, the window sizes also change accordingly. Variations in window size are typically associated with the Wsize and Scale fields. From the collected traffic information, it is evident that the Scale field is configured according to the device's ability to adjust the window size. This field's value remains constant and acts as a loading factor that alters the current window information, with its magnitude indicating the performance level of the device.

Field settings within network protocols are generally established according to different device types, and certain field values are standardized and do not vary across manufacturers, as specified by the Manufacturer Usage Description (MUD). The Time to Live (TTL) value describes the lifespan of a packet. Its configuration differs based on the broad category of devices; in internet devices, TTL values are typically set to 16, 32, or 64 depending on the operating system version. In contrast, for IoT devices, the TTL value is primarily determined by the underlying requirements of the IoT device, varying between [1, 255]. Furthermore, the implementation of the TTL value in IoT devices can be influenced by the IP protocol version; in IPv6, the TTL value is consistently set to 1, which lacks reference and theoretical significance. Thus, this value is treated as an exception and not considered a feature.

The type of application layer protocol is included as a feature, as the application layer protocol represents the format of the data packets. Typically, it contains few fields and does not provide high discrimination. Therefore, only the application layer protocol type is utilized as a feature.

### 2.3 Algorithm Model

Table 1 presents the fingerprint fields parsed from a data packet emitted by a smart baby monitor, with a MAC address of 00:24:e4:11:18. The table indicates that the extracted fields are related to the protocol type and protocol version, highlighting the variability in extracted fields across different protocols.

**Table 1.** Selected Fingerprint Fields.

| Feature | Value | Feature | Value |
|---|---|---|---|
| IPv4_ttl | 64 | Eap_Len | 0 |
| Tcp_wsize | 5816 | IPv4 | 1 |
| Tcp_srcPort | 58387 | IPv6 | 0 |
| IP_length | 52 | Eapol | 0 |
| Tcp_Mss | −1 | Tcp | 1 |
| Tcp_Scale | −1 | Udp | 0 |
| Udp_len | 0 | Tls | 0 |
| Udp_srcPort | 0 | Dhcp | 0 |

Experiments are conducted on the improved Adaptive Boosting (AdaBoost) algorithm and the probabilistic adaptive boosting algorithm. Based on accuracy and time complexity, the probabilistic adaptive boosting algorithm was selected as the core algorithm for system implementation.

AdaBoost adjusts weights according to the classification performance of the current learners, increasing the weights for types with higher error rates while slightly decreasing the weights for those with lower error rates. The original AdaBoost algorithm is relatively slow in establishing base learners, and the rapid increase in weights may lead to overfitting. Figure 5 illustrates the flowchart of the original algorithm.

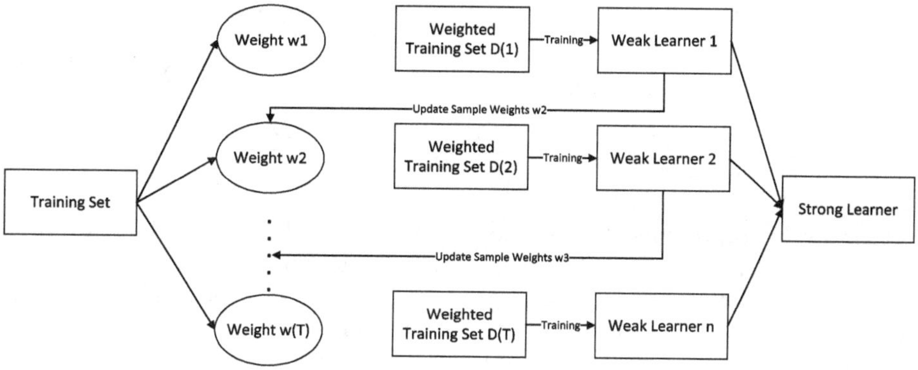


**Fig. 5.** Algorithm Schematic Diagram.

By improving the computation method of base learners, the generation speed of these learners can be accelerated, thereby enhancing the overall algorithm performance.

**Improvement of the Base Learner Computation Method.** By employing Taylor series expansion and mathematical derivations, the complex logarithmic functions can be transformed into simpler arithmetic operations, significantly increasing computational efficiency. The derivation process is as follows:

$$\mathrm{f}(x) = f(0)+f'(0)x+\frac{f''(0)}{2!}x^2+\ldots+\frac{\mathrm{f}^{(n)}(0)}{n!}x^n+\frac{f^{(n+1)}(\theta x)}{(n+1)!}x^{n+1} \quad (0<\theta<1). \tag{1}$$

Let $f(x)$ be defined as $lnx$, it is noted that $lnx$ is undefined at $x$=0, so $ln(x+1)$ is used instead.

$$\ln(x+1) \approx x-\frac{1}{2}x^2+\frac{1}{3}x^3+\ldots\ldots+(-1)x^{n-1}\frac{1}{n}x^n. \tag{2}$$

Setting $x = x-1$,

$$\ln(x) \approx (x-1)-\frac{1}{2}(x-1)^2+\frac{1}{3}(x-1)^3+\ldots+(-1)\frac{1}{n}(x-1)^n. \tag{3}$$

$$\ln(x) \approx (x-1)-\frac{1}{2}(x-1)^2+\frac{1}{3}(x-1)^3, x\in[0,1] \tag{4}$$

we can substitute this expression into the formula for the information gain ratio.

$$Info(D) = -\sum_{i=1}^{m} P_i \log_2(P_i) = -\sum_{i=1}^{m} \frac{D_i}{D} \log_2\left(\frac{D_i}{D}\right) \tag{5a}$$

$$= -\sum_{i=1}^{m} \frac{D_i \ln \frac{D_i}{D}}{D \ln 2} = -\frac{1}{D \ln 2} \sum_{i=1}^{m} D_i \ln \frac{D_i}{D} \tag{5b}$$

$$= -\frac{1}{D \ln 2} \sum_{i=1}^{m} D_i \left[\left(\frac{D_i}{D} - 1\right) - \frac{1}{2}\left(\frac{D_i}{D} - 1\right)^2 + \frac{1}{3}\left(\frac{D_i}{D} - 1\right)^3\right] \tag{5c}$$

$$= -\frac{1}{D \ln 2} \sum_{i=1}^{m} \frac{D_i(D_i - D)(11D^2 + 2D_i^2 - 7D_iD)}{6D^2} \tag{5d}$$

Euation (5) represents the method for calculating the information gain ratio used at each split. From this formula, it is evident that the computation of the information gain ratio has been improved by converting the original logarithmic calculations into simpler arithmetic operations. This enhancement can expedite the construction of decision trees, consequently accelerating the training speed of the entire model.

**Introduction of a Penalty Term to Reduce Weight Increase Rate.** Traditional IoT device identification experiences high misclassification rates when identifying device types. The original AdaBoost algorithm increases the weight of the current class, which can lead to continuous weight escalation if the current device is frequently misclassified, potentially resulting in overfitting. To address this issue, a penalty term is introduced to slow down the weight increase for devices with high misclassification rates, while not affecting the weights of correctly classified devices.

When updating the weight distribution, the weight formula for correctly classified devices is as follows:

$$w_{k+1,i} = \frac{w_{ki}}{Z_k} \exp(-a_k), y_i G_k(x_i) = 1 \tag{6}$$

For incorrectly classified devices, the weights are adjusted by reducing the increase rate based on the false positive rate (FPR) and false negative rate (FNR).

$$w_{k+1,i} = \frac{w_{ki}}{Z_k} \exp(a(1 - FNR)), \quad y_i G_k(x_i) = -1 \tag{7a}$$

$$w_{k+1,i} = \frac{w_{ki}}{Z_k} \exp(a(1 - FPR)), \quad y_i G_k(x_i) = -1 \tag{7b}$$

The method for calculating weights has been modified so that in the event of misclassification, the weights are dynamically altered based on the magnitude of the error rate. A higher error rate results in a reduced weight increase for the

**Algorithm 1.** The proposed Real AdaBoost algorithm.

**Initialize:** Set $t = 0$, and initialize Dataset: $S$, Number of classifiers: $w_1$, Number of classifiers: $T$

**Repeat:**

1. Partition dataset (9), calculate the normalization factor $Z_t$ for weak classifiers (12)

2. Select the weak classifier with the minimum normalization factor and add it to the strong classifier list: $h(x)$.
3. Update sample weights for the next iteration based on previous weights (10a) (10b) and weak classifiers (13).
4. $t := t + 1$.

**Until:** When $t = T$, select $T$ weak classifiers and combine them to form the final classifier (14)

next iteration due to the subtraction effect. When the error rate is substantial, the weights for the next iteration change minimally.

The output of the Real AdaBoost algorithm is a confidence score, which is a floating-point number representing a probability adaptive boosting algorithm. The classic AdaBoost algorithm has limitations in that each weak classifier outputs only {0,1} or {−1,+1}, making its classification capability relatively weaker compared to the Real AdaBoost algorithm. The Real AdaBoost algorithm demonstrates superior classification capabilities over the original AdaBoost algorithm. The algorithmic workflow will be described next, with Fig. 6 illustrating the Real AdaBoost algorithm.

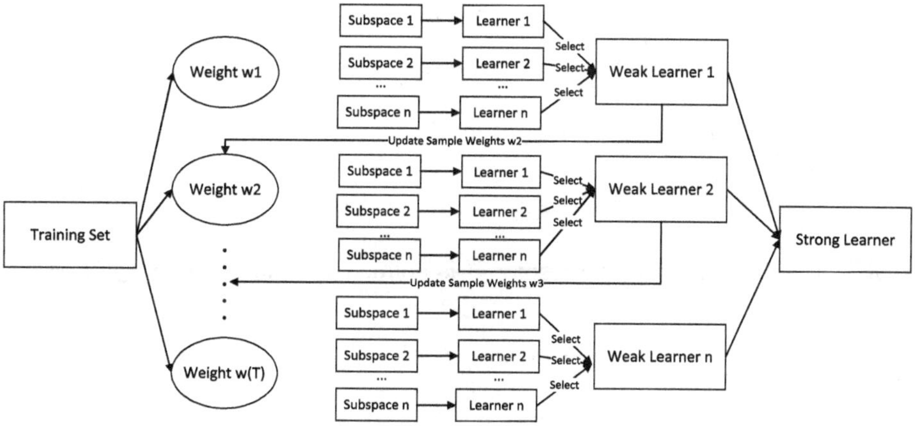


**Fig. 6.** Real AdaBoost Algorithm Schematic Diagram.

**Step 1**:Given the training set $(x_1, y_1)$, $(x_2, y_2)$,... $(x_N, y_N)$, where $x_i$ is a feature vector of length $m$ and $y_i$ denotes the correct class label for $x_i$,for $i = 1, ..., N$.

**Step 2**: The initial distribution of samples in the training set is defined as follows:

$$w_i^1 = \frac{1}{N}, i = 1......N \tag{8}$$

**Step 3**: Determine the number of weak classifiers $T$, for=1,...,T.

**Step 4**: Partition the value space S of each feature dimension into several disjoint subspaces $S1, ...Sn$.

$$S = S1 \cup S2 \cup \ldots\ldots \cup S_n, i \neq j, S_i \cup S_j = \emptyset \tag{9}$$

**Step 5**: Calculate the cumulative sample weights for positive and negative classes within each subspace.

$$w_+^{jt} = \sum_{x:(x_i \in S_j, y_i = 1)} w_i^t \tag{10a}$$

$$w_-^{jt} = \sum_{x:(x_i \in S_j, y_i = -1)} w_i^t \tag{10b}$$

Compute the output of each weak classifier. Let $\sigma$ be the smoothing factor, a small positive constant used for output smoothing.

Calculate the normalization factor.

$$h(x) = \frac{1}{2} \ln(\frac{w_+^{jt} + \sigma}{w_-^{jt} - \sigma}), j = 1, 2 \ldots\ldots, n; \forall x \in S_j \tag{11}$$

$$Z_t = 2 \sum_{j=1}^{n} \sqrt{w_+^{jt} w_-^{jt}} \tag{12}$$

Select the classifier $h(x)$ such that the value of $Z$ is minimized, which will be the weak classifier chosen for this iteration.

Adjust the weights for the next round.

$$w_i^{t+1} = \frac{w_i^t}{Z_t} \exp(-y_i h_t(x_i)) \tag{13}$$

**Step 6**: The final strong classifier H is defined as follows: Where $f(x)$ is

$$H(x) = sign f(x), f(x) = \sum_{t=1}^{T} h_t(x) \tag{14}$$

The above outlines the complete process of Real AdaBoost, and the following is the pseudocode for the aforementioned algorithm.

The Real AdaBoost algorithm selects weak classifiers based on the value space of the dataset's features, with the output of each weak classifier being a real-valued number, typically interpreted as a confidence score for classification. Compared to other AdaBoost algorithms, the advantage of Real AdaBoost lies in achieving higher accuracy with fewer iterations.

# 3 Experimental and Simulation Results

## 3.1 Description of Experimental Data

The data collected in this paper comprises a real dataset obtained from the experimental environment of the company, totaling 1,114,393 entries. This dataset encompasses various types of devices, with each traffic flow quantified as a fingerprint record. Some device traffic is generated automatically through applications on smart devices, while other devices produce minimal traffic. This is primarily because each device sends data packets at scheduled intervals during the application phase or only transmits "heartbeat" packets periodically, resulting in limited traffic capture. Certain IoT devices, however, can generate substantial traffic due to more frequent activity or the necessity to transmit collected data back to the server at short intervals, leading to higher traffic volumes. In contrast, internet-connected devices typically generate less traffic than IoT devices, as the demand for data transmission differs; without human intervention, internet devices do not produce a large number of data packets. Consequently, significant disparities arise in data generation. When partitioning the data, it is divided based on device type, ensuring that each category is proportionally allocated to the test and training sets, thereby ensuring the validity of the experiments.

## 3.2 Experimental Evaluation Metrics

This paper employs four metrics—recall, precision, accuracy, and F1 score—to evaluate the algorithm's performance from various perspectives. Additionally, macro metrics are introduced to describe the mean testing indicators of product types after classification across all devices.

Precision is defined as the proportion of true positive samples among all samples classified as positive during the classification process. It provides insight into the true correctness ratio of fingerprint records classified as positive for a particular device within a smart environment.

$$P = TP/(TP + FP). \tag{15}$$

Recall describes the proportion of true positive samples among all samples classified as positive. It is used to assess how many of the fingerprints of a specific device in the current smart environment have been correctly classified.

$$R = TP/(TP + FN). \tag{16}$$

The F1 score refers to the harmonic mean of recall and precision in the algorithm's training model, with a typical range of [0, 1]. Generally, recall and precision are the most commonly used evaluation metrics; however, they may not be applicable in certain scenarios. For instance, if Device A has a higher precision than Device B, but Device B has a higher recall than Device A, technicians may find it challenging to determine performance superiority by directly comparing parameter values. Therefore, this paper introduces the F1 score to address this issue.

$$F1 = 2PR/(P + R). \quad (17)$$

In the context of multi-class classification, macro metrics are introduced to evaluate the algorithm's recognition performance. Macro precision is calculated as the average precision across all classes, providing an overall assessment of precision performance, while macro recall is the average recall across all classes.

### 3.3 Analysis of Experimental Results

This paper employs internet fingerprints for experimentation, utilizing the original AdaBoost algorithm, a traditional two-stage method, and the proposed algorithm. A macro metric calculation is conducted for each experimental result to compare and demonstrate that the proposed algorithm is optimal for the current dataset. Given the numerous subcategories of classification, a macro approach is adopted to compute metrics across all classes as a validation result.

Bootstrap sampling is utilized, where 66.6% of the samples are designated for the training set of the base learners, while the remaining 33.4% serve as a validation set for out-of-bag validation. A classification result is deemed successful if it matches the identification information; otherwise, it is considered a classification misrecognition, allowing for the determination of device recognition accuracy.

Table 2 presents the macro metrics for device type classification validation obtained using the original AdaBoost applied to the internet fingerprint model. The classification accuracy for device types is 87.31%, with macro precision and macro recall values of 89.15% and 88.90%, respectively. All values fall below 90%, indicating that the original AdaBoost demonstrates a moderate identification capability for device type validation within the current dataset when using the internet fingerprint model.

**Table 2.** Macro Metrics for Feature Comparison Validation Results

| Method comparison | Internet Fingerprint Features | Features of This Study |
|---|---|---|
| Accuracy | 87.31% | 96.27% |
| Macro Recall | 88.90% | 97.07% |
| Macro Precision | 89.15% | 95.88% |
| Macro F1 Score | 88.99% | 93.61% |
| Number of Misclassified Samples | 141417 | 52711 |

The original AdaBoost algorithm was tested using the feature model proposed in this paper, demonstrating the macro metrics for IoT device type classification validation. Utilizing out-of-bag estimation, the device type identification accuracy was 96.27%, with a macro F1 score of 93.61%. The results indicate that the original AdaBoost exhibits strong recognition capability for the current device types, with 52,711 out of 1,114,393 data points being misclassified.

The experimental results show that when employing both the internet fingerprint model and the proposed feature dimensions with the original AdaBoost algorithm, the latter achieves higher accuracy with the proposed features, yielding a 4.62% improvement in the macro F1 score. This suggests that the internet fingerprint model is not suitable for IoT device identification; however, incorporating IoT device protocol features significantly enhances accuracy within the same algorithm framework.

As shown in Table 3, following experiments using the Real AdaBoost algorithm on the current fingerprint dataset and employing out-of-bag estimation, the device type verification accuracy reached 99.02%, with a macro F1 score of 98.02%. Only 10,921 data points out of 1,114,393 were misclassified. In contrast, the traditional two-stage recognition achieved an accuracy of 93.87%, but its macro F1 score was only 86.25%, resulting in 68,313 misclassified data points. The original algorithm's accuracy was 96.27%, with a macro F1 score of 93.61%, leading to 52,711 misclassifications. This evidence confirms that the method employed in this paper yields the highest accuracy and optimal performance.

**Table 3.** Macro Metrics for Method Comparison Validation Results

| Method comparison | Real AdaBoost | Original AdaBoost |
|---|---|---|
| Accuracy | 99.02% | 96.27% |
| Macro Recall | 99.26% | 97.07% |
| Macro Precision | 96.82% | 95.88% |
| Macro F1 Score | 98.02% | 93.61% |
| Number of Misclassified Samples | 10921 | 52711 |

By comparing the data in the previous table, it is evident that the Real AdaBoost algorithm employed in this paper achieves improved identification accuracy over the original AdaBoost algorithm. Additionally, the macro precision and macro recall values are significantly higher than those of the original version, with the F1 score increasing by 4.4%. This demonstrates that the algorithm proposed in this paper yields optimal results for the current dataset.

To further substantiate that the method used in this paper can distinguish between IoT devices, internet devices, and gateway devices, we will next analyze the device product types in the experimental results.

As observed in Table 4, the F1 score for IoT devices is 98.98%, while the classification accuracy for internet and gateway devices is 99.87% and 97.90%, respectively. The fingerprint model selected in this paper effectively categorizes device traffic according to device type. This is primarily due to the superior performance of internet devices, which possess a larger number of distinguishable feature values. In contrast, gateway devices achieve better classification results owing to the broader range of supported protocol types.

**Table 4.** Presentation of Product Type Results

| Product Type | IoT Device | Internet Device | Gateway Device |
|---|---|---|---|
| Recall | 98.32% | 99.97% | 98.49% |
| Precision | 99.65% | 99.74% | 97.32% |
| F1 Score | 98.98% | 99.87% | 97.90% |
| Sample Size | 958673 | 100295 | 55425 |
| Prediction Error Quantity | 9428 | 764 | 729 |

Table 5 presents the results of applying various machine learning algorithms to the dataset collected in this paper, utilizing the proposed feature dimensions. From the results, it is evident that the Real AdaBoost employed in this paper achieves the highest macro F1 score, while the F1 scores of the other algorithms are approximately 90%. Notably, Gentle AdaBoost and XGBoost also demonstrate high evaluation metrics, with macro F1 scores of 96.33% and 93.43%, respectively, indicating strong classification capabilities; both algorithms are branches of the Boosting model. The SVM algorithm is more suited for binary classification scenarios, whereas the focus of this paper is on classifying IoT devices by device type, making it a multi-class problem. The classic SVM algorithm has limitations in addressing multi-class classification challenges. The KNN algorithm is significantly affected by the dataset's characteristics; given the large size of the dataset used in this paper, KNN exhibits slower performance. Random Forest, which employs a Bagging method by constructing multiple uncorrelated decision trees for classification, does not outperform the AdaBoost algorithm. Comparatively, the Real AdaBoost utilized in this paper demonstrates the highest recognition accuracy and F1 score within the current dataset.

**Table 5.** Comparison with Other Algorithms

| Algorithm | Accuracy | Macro Recall | Macro Precision | Macro F1 Score |
|---|---|---|---|---|
| Real AdaBoost | 99.02% | 99.26% | 96.82% | 98.02% |
| Gentle AdaBoost | 96.54% | 96.92% | 95.93% | 96.33% |
| XGBoost | 94.57% | 94.43% | 92.40% | 93.43% |
| SVM | 92.20% | 81.75% | 81.65% | 81.69% |
| KNN | 90.31% | 88.93% | 89.15% | 88.99% |
| GBDT | 92.20% | 81.80% | 81.59% | 81.69% |
| Bagging | 94.82% | 86.72% | 85.80% | 86.25% |
| NB | 89.71% | 90.62% | 97.33% | 93.86% |
| Two-Stage | 93.87% | 86.72% | 85.80% | 86.25% |
| LSIF | 96.76% | 97.37% | 94.11% | 95.69% |

The algorithm proposed in this paper, along with traditional two-stage recognition methods used in other literature, was applied to the current dataset. From the results presented in the table, it is evident that the F1 score of the model proposed in this paper surpasses that of the current two-stage method, with a macro F1 score improvement of 11.77%. This enhancement is primarily attributed to the fact that the traditional two-stage recognition method's classification of device types is influenced by the first stage of classification, resulting in poorer experimental outcomes.

In comparison to the method published in 2021, which employed the LSIF approach utilizing locality-sensitive hashing and signature features for device identification, the LSIF algorithm was tested alongside the Real AdaBoost algorithm on the dataset used in this paper. The LSIF algorithm achieved an accuracy of 96.76% and a macro F1 score of 95.69%. The method employed in this paper exhibits the highest evaluation metrics on the current dataset, with a macro F1 score improvement of 2.33% over the LSIF algorithm.

As illustrated in Table 6, the time taken for current device identification is within 50 milliseconds, with the fastest identification occurring at 25 milliseconds. This demonstrates that the algorithm model used in this paper possesses rapid recognition efficiency, enabling quick identification of devices in intelligent environments, thereby making it suitable for the task of scanning IoT device traffic.

**Table 6.** Time Taken for Recognition of Selected Devices

| Device Type | Time (ms) | Device Type | Time (ms) |
|---|---|---|---|
| Smart Camera | 34 | Alarm | 37 |
| Intelligent Camera | 27 | Baby Monitor | 25 |
| Mobile Detector | 43 | Smart Temperature Controller | 39 |

The device identification method was not compared with deep learning approaches, primarily due to the need for high-performance and real-time algorithms in IoT device traffic scanning platforms. Although deep learning models achieve high accuracy, they tend to have significant performance overhead, making them unsuitable for integration into IoT device traffic scanning platforms. In the context of IoT device identification, the complexity of feature vectors is considerably lower than that found in fields such as image processing or natural language processing. Consequently, it is generally unnecessary to employ overly complex machine learning or deep learning algorithms to achieve satisfactory results.

## 4 Conclusion

This paper focuses on identification of IoT devices as a means of ensuring IoT security, examining both traffic scanning and device identification. By considering the strengths and weaknesses of different methods, a probability adaptive boost-based IoT device identification method was designed. This method compares the real AdaBoost algorithm with the original AdaBoost algorithm, demonstrating that the proposed method achieves optimal results while maintaining accuracy.

## References


1. Alharbi, S., Rodriguez, P., Maharaja, R., Iyer, P., Subaschandrabose, N., Ye, Z.: Secure the internet of things with challenge response authentication in fog computing. In: 2017 IEEE 36th International Performance Computing and Communications Conference (IPCCC), pp. 1–2 (2017)
2. Awan, K.A., Din, I.U., Almogren, A., Kim, B.-S., Guizani, M.: Enhancing IoT security with trust management using ensemble xgboost and adaboost techniques. IEEE Access **12**, 116609–116621 (2024)
3. Wu, Y., Liu, L., Yu, Y., Chen, G., Hu, J.: Online ensemble learning-based anomaly detection for IoT systems. Appl. Soft Comput. **173**, 112931 (2025)
4. Hameed, M., et al.: IOTA-based mobile crowd sensing: detection of fake sensing using logit-boosted machine learning algorithms. Wirel. Commun. Mob. Comput. **2022**, 6274114 (2022)
5. Yan, Z., Zhang, P., Vasilakos, A.V.: A survey on trust management for internet of things. J. Netw. Comput. Appl. **42**, 120–134 (2014)
6. Dash, P.B., Nayak, J., Naik, B., Oram, E., Islam, S.H.: Model based IoT security framework using multiclass adaptive boosting with SMOTE. Sec. Priv. **3**, e112 (2020)
7. Hamza, A., Gharakheili, H.H., Sivaraman,V.: Combining mud policies with sdn for iot intrusion detection. In: Proceedings of the 2018 Workshop on IoT Security and Privacy, pp. 1–7 (2018)
8. Iqbal, W., Abbas, H., Daneshmand, M., Rauf, B., Bangash, Y.A.: An in-depth analysis of iot security requirements, challenges, and their countermeasures via software-defined security. IEEE Internet Things J. **7**(10), 10250–10276 (2020)
9. Sivanathan, A., et al.: Classifying iot devices in smart environments using network traffic characteristics. IEEE Trans. Mob. Comput. **18**(8), 1745–1759 (2019)
10. Vishwakarma, R., Jain, A.K.: A honeypot with machine learning based detection framework for defending iot based botnet ddos attacks. In: 2019 3rd International Conference on Trends in Electronics and Informatics (ICOEI), pp. 1019–1024 (2019)
11. Beshah, Y.K., Abebe, S.L., Melaku, H.M.: Drift adaptive online ddos attack detection framework for iot system. Electronics **13**(6) (2024)
12. Ngo, M.V., Luo, T., Quek, T.Q.S.: Adaptive anomaly detection for internet of things in hierarchical edge computing: a contextual-bandit approach. ACM Trans. Internet Things **3**(1) (2021)
13. Mishra, D., Naik, B., Nayak, J., Souri, A., Dash, P.B., Vimal, S.: Light gradient boosting machine with optimized hyperparameters for identification of malicious access in iot network. Digital Commun. Netw. **9**(1), 125–137 (2023)

14. Chen, Q., Song, Y., Jennings, B., Zhang, F., Xiao, B., Gao, S.: Iot-id: robust iot device identification based on feature drift adaptation. In: 2021 IEEE Global Communications Conference (GLOBECOM), pp. 1–6 (2021)
15. Pajouh, H.H., Javidan, R., Khayami, R., Dehghantanha, A., Choo, K.-K.R.: A two-layer dimension reduction and two-tier classification model for anomaly-based intrusion detection in iot backbone networks. IEEE Trans. Emerg. Top. Comput. **7**(2), 314–323 (2019)

# Author Index





Y. Liu et al. (Eds.): ChinaCom 2025, LNICST 711, pp. 599–601, 2027.
https://doi.org/10.1007/978-3-032-33662-0

Kolibri 360 GmbH
Ferdinand-Jühlke-Straße 7
99095 Erfurt, Deutschland
produktsicherheit@kolibri360.de